1993

Man & Music

THE
RENAISSANCE

Man & Music

THE
RENAISSANCE

From the 1470s to the end of the 16th century

EDITED BY IAIN FENLON

PRENTICE HALL
ENGLEWOOD CLIFFS, NEW JERSEY 07632

First North American edition published 1989 by Prentice Hall Inc.,
a division of Simon & Schuster, Englewood Cliffs, New Jersey 07632

First published in the United Kingdom 1989 by
The Macmillan Press Limited
Houndmills, Basingstoke, Hampshire RG21 2XS and London

Companies and representations throughout the world

ISBN 0-13-773409-3

ISBN 0-13-773417-4

Typeset by Glyn Davies, Cambridge
Printed in Hong Kong

Contents

Illustration
Acknowledgments

The publishers would like to thank the following institutions and individuals who have kindly provided photographic material for use in this book.

2, Musée du Louvre, Paris/photo Lauros-Giraudon; 3, Österreichisches National-bibliothek, Vienna (Sign.Ink.5.G.9, f.D2a); 4, Mansell Collection, London; 7, 9, Scala, Florence; 8, 32, Musée du Louvre, Paris/photo Réunion des Musées Nationaux; 10, Civica Raccolta Stampe A. Bertarelli, Castello Sforzesco, Milan; 11, 13, 29, 61, courtesy of the Trustees of the National Gallery, London; 12, Royal Commission on the Historical Monuments of England; 16, Istituto Centrale per il Catalogo e la Documentazione, Rome; 17, courtesy of the Board and Trustees of the Victoria and Albert Museum, London; 18, Monumenti Musei e Gallerie Pontificie, Vatican City, Rome; 19, 20 (Cappella Sistina MS 611, f.lv), 50 (Chigi.C.VIII.234, ff.3v–4), Biblioteca Apostolica Vaticana, Rome; 21 (left, centre), 36, Alinari, Florence; 21 (right), 23, 25, 28, Mansell Collection, London/Alinari, Florence; 24, Kunsthalle, Hamburg/photo Elke Walford; 26, photo Paolo Marton, Treviso; 31, Biblioteca Casanatense, Rome/photo Nadia Murgioni; 33, Azienda di Promozione Turistica, Mantua; 34, Museo di S Martino, Naples/photo Scala, Florence; 35, National Gallery of Art, Washington, DC (Samuel H. Kress Collection); 37, Beinecke Rare Book and Manuscript Library, Yale University (Mellon Chansonnier, ff.lv–2); 38 (Fonds.it.973, f.23v), 47, Bibliothèque Nationale, Paris; 39, Musée Condé, Chantilly/photo Giraudon, Paris; 40, Musée des Gobelins, Paris/photo Lauron-Giraudon; 41, Library of the Boston Athenaeum; 42, Hôtel de Ville, Paris/photo Giraudon; 43, Governing Body, Christ Church, Oxford/photo Bodleian Library; 44 (Roy.20.A.XVI, ff.lv–2), 46 (Harley 4325, fold-out), 65 (Add.25716, f.l), 70, 74 (Add.35324, ff.31v, 31), Trustees of the British Library, London; 49 (MS 9092, f.9), 81, 82, Bibliothèque Royale Albert ler, Brussels; 51, City Archives, Mechelen (HH.Melanges.1, f.lv); 52, Kunsthistorisches Museum, Vienna (PS 5073, f.4); 55 (Mus.Ms.A-1, f.204), 56 (Mus.Ms.A-2, f.187), 57, 58 (Mus.Ms.A-2, f.188), Bayerisches Staatsbibliothek, Munich; 59, Staatliche Museen Preussischer Kulturbesitz, Kupferstichkabinett, Berlin/photo Jörg Anders; 60, Herzog-Anton-Ulrich Museum, Brunswick/photo Mansell Collection, London; 62, Lutherhalle, Reformationsgeschichtliches Museum, Wittenberg; 63, British Museum, London; 64, Staatsbibliothek Preussischer Kulturbesitz (Germ.fol.442, ff.9lv–92); 66, 68, Germanisches Nationalmuseum, Nuremberg; 67, Kunstsammlungen Veste Coburg; 69, Guildhall Library, City of London; 71, Governing Body, Christ Church, Oxford (MS 988, no.58); 72, Society of Antiquaries, London; 73, Photographic Archives of the National Gallery of Art, Washington, DC, from a negative made by Taylor and Dull for Parke-Bernet Galleries Inc.; 75, Private Collection/photo Courtauld Institute of Art, London; 76, National Portrait Gallery, London; 77, 78, 80, Museo del Prado, Madrid; 79, Biblioteca de Palacio, Madrid (MS 1335, ff.64v–65)/Patrimonio Nacional; 83, Gruuthusemuseum, Bruges/photo A.C.L., Brussels; 84, Musées Royaux des Beaux-Arts, Brussels/photo A.C.L.

The maps were prepared by Oxford Illustrators Ltd.

Abbreviations

AcM	*Acta musicologica*
AnM	*Anuario musical*
AnMc	*Analecta musicologica*
AnnM	*Annales musicologiques*
BWQ	*Brass and Woodwind Quarterly*
CEKM	Corpus of Early Keyboard Music
CHM	*Collectanea historiae musicae*
CMc	*Current Musicology*
CMM	Corpus mensurabilis musicae
CMP	*Cancionero musical de Placio*
CSM	Corpus scriptorum de musica
DTB	Denkmäler der Tonkunst in Bayern
DTÖ	Denkmäler der Tonkunst Österreich
EDM	Das Erbe deutscher Musik
EM	*Early Music*
EMH	*Early Music History*
FAM	*Fontes artis musicae*
GfMKB	*Gesellschaft für Musikforschung Kongressbericht*
Grove 6	*The New Grove Dictionary of Music and Musicians*
GSJ	*The Galpin Society Journal*
HMT	*Handwörterbuch der musikalischen Terminologie*
IMSCR	*International Musicological Society Congress Report*
JAMS	*Journal of the American Musicological Society*
JM	*Journal of Musicology*
JMT	*Journal of Music Theory*
JRBM	*Journal of Renaissance and Baroque Music*
JRMA	*Journal of the Royal Musical Association*
JWCI	*Journal of the Warburg and Courtauld Institutes*
LSJ	*The Lute Society Journal*
MGG	*Die Musik in Geschichte und Gegenwart*
ML	*Music and Letters*
MMA	*Miscellanea musicologica*
MME	Monumentos de la música española
MMq	*Monatshefte für Musikgeschichte*
MQ	*The Musical Quarterly*
MRM	Monuments of Renaissance Music
MSD	Musicological Studies and Documents, ed. A. Carapetyan (Rome 1951–)

MT	*The Musical Times*
MVGN	*Mitteilungen des Vereins für Geschichte der Stadt Nürnberg*
PMLA	*Publications of the Modern Languages Association of America*
PRMA	*Proceedings of the Royal Musical Association*
RBM	*Revue belge de musicologie*
RdM	*Revue de musicologie*
RIM	*Rivista italiana di musicologia*
RISM	*Répertoire international des sources musicales*
RMARC	*R[oyal] M[usical] A[ssociation] Research Chronicle*
RMI	*Rivista musicale italiana*
RRMR	Recent Researches in Music of the Renaissance
TVNM	*Tijdschrift van de Vereniging voor Nederlandse muziekgeschiedenis*

Preface

The *Man and Music* series of books – eight in number, chronologically organized – were originally conceived in conjunction with the television programmes of the same name, of which the first was shown by Granada Television International and Channel 4 in 1986. These programmes were designed to examine the development of music in particular places during particular periods in the history of Western civilization.

The books have the same objective. Each is designed to cover a segment of Western musical history; the breaks between them are planned to correspond with significant historical junctures. Since historical junctures, or indeed junctures in stylistic change, rarely happen with the neat simultaneity that the historian's or the editor's orderly mind might wish for, most volumes have 'ragged' ends and beginnings: for example, this Renaissance volume terminates, in Italy, in the 1570s and 80s, but continues well into the 17th century in parts of northern Europe.

These books do not, however, make up a history of music in the traditional sense. The reader will not find technical, stylistic discussion in them; anyone wanting to trace the detailed development of the texture of the madrigal or the rise and fall of sonata form should look elsewhere. Rather, it is the intention in these volumes to show in what context, and as a result of what forces – social, cultural, intellectual – the madrigal or sonata form came into being and took its particular shape. The intention is to view musical history not a series of developments in some hermetic world of its own but rather as a series of responses to social, economic and political circumstances and to religious and intellectual stimuli. We want to explain not simply *what* happened, but *why* it happened, and why it happened when and where it did.

We have chosen to follow what might be called a geographical, or perhaps a topographical, approach: to focus, in each chapter, on a particular place and to examine its music in the light of its particular situation. Thus, in most of these volumes, the chapters – once past the introductory one, contributed by the volume editor – are each devoted to a city or a region. This system has inevitably needed some modification when dealing with very early or very recent times, for reasons (opposite ones, of course) to do with communication and cultural spread.

These books do not attempt to treat musical history comprehensively. Their editors have chosen for discussion the musical centres that they see as the most significant and the most interesting; many lesser ones inevitably escape individual discussion, though the patterns of their musical life may be discernible by analogy with others or may be separately referred to in the opening, editorial chapter. We hope, however, that a new kind of picture of musical history may begin to emerge from these volumes, and that this picture may be more accessible to the general reader, responsive to music but untrained in its techniques, than others arising from more traditional approaches. In spite of the large number of lovers of music, musical histories have never enjoyed the appeal to a broad, intelligent general readership in the way that histories of art, architecture or literature have done: these books represent an attempt to reach such a readership and explain music in terms that may quicken their interest.

The television programmes and books were initially planned in close collaboration with Sir Denis Forman, the Chairman of Granada Television International. The approach was worked out in more detail with several of the volume editors, among whom I am particularly grateful to Iain Fenlon for the time he has generously given to discussion of the problems raised by this approach to musical history, and also to Alexander Ringer and James McKinnon for their valuable advice and support. Discussion with Bamber Gascoigne and Tony Cash, in the course of the making of the initial television programmes, also proved of value. I am grateful to Celia Thomson for drafting the chronologies that appear in each volume and to Elisabeth Agate for her invaluable work as picture editor in bringing the volumes to visual life.

London, 1989   STANLEY SADIE

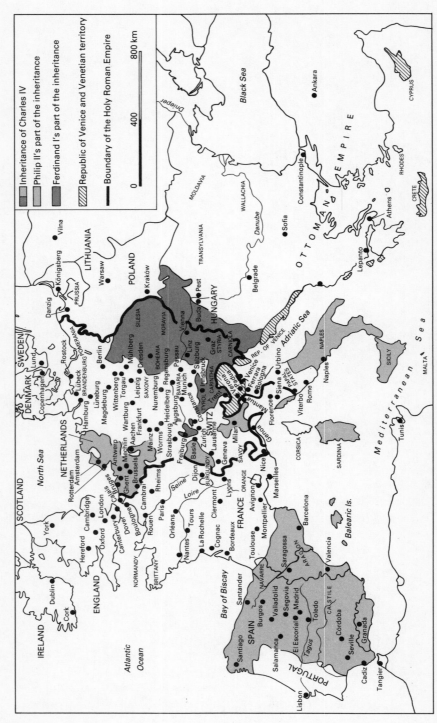

1. Map of Europe in the mid-sixteenth century showing the Habsburg dominions.

Chapter I

Music and Society

IAIN FENLON

As one scholar has put it, 'Renaissance music is not a set of compositional techniques but a complex of social conditions, intellectual states of mind, attitudes, aspirations, habits of performers, artistic support systems, intra-cultural communication, and many other ingredients which add up to a thriving matrix of musical energy'. It is the purpose of the present book to explore some of these features as they can be observed in different places and at different times in Europe during the Renaissance. As a glance at the table of contents makes clear, it is not our intention to do this in an encyclopedic way, but rather to proceed by contrast and analogy in order to tease out the common structural elements that were at work, while at the same time characterizing in quite a detailed way some of the more important differences between the musical life of various urban centres – Nuremberg and Venice, London and Naples – at various important moments in their histories. At the same time, while this book is emphatically not about Renaissance music seen merely as a set of compositional techniques, nor seen as a sequence of masterpieces, nor even as the aggregation of the biographies of great composers, that does not mean that we are not concerned with the activities of individuals or with details of musical styles and forms. On the contrary, three of the major phenomena of social significance in the period – the spread of humanism, the growth of bourgeois culture and the religious crises of the sixteenth century – all made a dramatic impact on the contemporary musical world in terms of the environment in which composers worked, and hence on the pieces that they wrote. To take one example, it is a commonplace of discussions about musical style in the Renaissance that the principal motor of change was humanism, which has a long and distinguished historiography as the main force for renewal in all the arts during this period. But it is equally true that those changes in style also reflect changes in the function of music itself, which are in turn responses to changes in the structures and needs of society. Beginning with humanism, and then moving on to other important developments such as religious change, the impact of printing and the growth in influence of the bourgeoisie, all of which are intimately and inextricably related, this introduction attempts to explore some of these broad themes, sometimes by reference to some of the essays which follow, and sometimes by introducing different illustrative material.

THE IMPACT OF HUMANISM

The various strands which make up the picture of musical humanism in the fifteenth and sixteenth centuries are not easy to isolate. For one thing, models derived from the experience of the other arts are not particularly helpful since in this, as in other features of the Renaissance, music is something of a special case. In the history of literature, painting and architecture, humanistic influences were at their most potent in the fifteenth and early sixteenth centuries. But in the case of music, where humanism is to be equated to a large extent with the study and emulation of the musical theory of antiquity, those influences started from fragile beginnings in the second half of the fifteenth century, reached their full force by the middle of the sixteenth, and then continued to exercise their intellectual power until the early decades of the seventeenth century. Despite some of their antiquarian characteristics, the importance of those influences must not be underestimated. To take the most significant example, it was largely because of the impact of humanism that music came to be thought of not as a mathematical science, which is how it had been considered during the Middle Ages, but rather as an art, moreover an art which had at its core an intimate relationship to the classical ideal – which had never been entirely lost sight of during the medieval period – of the power and authority of rhetorical eloquence. In this process music came to be valued for what was actually written rather than for its symbolic significance as number in sound. This one central aspect of musical humanism was the connection between words and music, and it is in this sense that it came to have a considerable practical effect upon the art of composition. This also meant that much humanist theory was in turn related to changes in style and form of the major musical repertories of the period, both sacred and secular, as they were shaped by religious, economic and social forces.

In its early stages, humanistic interest in music was not so much concerned with practical matters as with intellectual and philosophical ones. To return briefly to the roots of the tradition, the *studia humanitatis* were originally thought of as grammar, poetry, rhetoric, moral philosophy and history, and it was only later that the humanistic study of these subjects influenced other fields, including music. For writers and scholars such as Petrarch, Boccaccio and Guarino Veronese, major figures in the history of humanism, music had not been considered an appropriate subject for classically inspired renewal, though an early interest in the subject had been shown by Petrus de Abano (1250–

1315), whose commentaries on the pseudo-Aristotelian *Problems,* including a section dealing with music, are known from fourteenth-century manuscripts and their reprintings during the fifteenth and sixteenth centuries. Yet although the case of Abano is interesting, it is both marginal and untypical, and it was not until the early fifteenth century that music impinged to any great extent upon humanist thought.

When it did, the effect was not felt so much within university circles (Abano, for example, had taught at Padua) as within courtly ones. Here the first event of any real consequence was the appointment of Vittorino da Feltre (*d* 1446) as ducal librarian at the court of Gianfrancesco Gonzaga in Mantua. Vittorino's work at Mantua was principally directed towards establishing a court school, known as the Casa Giocosa, initially set up to educate the Marchese's children. Unlike many early humanist teachers, Vittorino's own interests were not exclusively literary, and it appears that the syllabus at the Casa Giocosa included both theoretical and practical music; one pupil, Francesco Prendilacqua, gives a list of the specialized teachers employed by Vittorino which includes, together with painters and grammarians, musicians, dancers, singers and instrumentalists. One teacher at the Mantuan court school, Johannes Gallicus de Namur, acknowledged that under Vittorino he 'diligently heard the music of Boethius' and as a result 'attained the true practice of this art'. Elsewhere in Italy music also occupied the attentions of serious scholars, most notably at Bologna where Pope Nicholas V established a chair in 1450 (a post eagerly sought by Bartolomeo Ramos de Pareia when he settled in the city in 1472) and at Pavia where Franchinus Gaffurius is recorded to have held a post between 1494 and 1499. Outside such institutionalized arrangements there is the example of the theorist and composer Johannes Tinctoris, who acted as a music tutor to the court of Ferrante of Aragon in Naples.

It is a distinct aspect of this early phase of musical humanism that interest was concentrated at the Italian courts. With few exceptions such as Henricus Glareanus, a Swiss monk who was an acquaintance of Erasmus and author of the *Dodecachordon* (1547), it was Italians who led the way in the late fifteenth and early sixteenth centuries in writing theoretical texts about music that show an interest in humanistic concerns. Central to this development was the rediscovery of ancient sources. There were few examples of Greek notation known during the Renaissance and they proved impossible to decipher; this situation is yet another important feature which marks off developments in music from those in the other arts during the period. If anything, the humanists would have stood a better chance of hearing echoes of ancient Greek musical practices by writing down and studying the performances of living musicians in the Greek islands rather than attempting to make sense of the surviving fragments, but this anthropological method was foreign to their approach. In the absence of manuscripts of ancient music, humanist commentators directed their attention to sources which contained classical writings about music. The process was gradual, and in its initial stages tentative. In the first instance the rediscovery of texts of musical interest was merely a by-product of the general activities of manuscript hunters; this is true, for example, of Abano's interest in the pseudo-Aristotelian *Problems*, a work on physics containing a section on music which reveals a great deal about Greek musical practice and theory. It was not until Ambrogio Traversari wrote his memorandum of 1433 describing his visit to Vittorino da Feltre in Mantua that we have any real evidence of humanistic interest in ancient musical theory *per se*. There, on Vittorino's shelves, Traversari noticed the *De musica* of Aristides Quintilianus and that of Bacchius Senior, the *Musica* of Claudius Ptolemy and the *De musica* of St Augustine. Elsewhere other collectors also showed an interest in acquiring theoretical treatises, so that by the end of the fifteenth century all the important ancient texts known today, with the notable exception of Aristoxenus's *Harmonics*, were known to Italian scholars. Thus in these early stages humanistic concern with music was essentially antiquarian and accidental, being for the most part a peripheral result of the broader preoccupation with the recovery of the classical past.

At this stage, the discovery and interpretation of classical texts was still a largely Italian concern, a by-product of the more central issues of humanist scholarship, while in geographical terms the phenomenon was quite widespread throughout northern and central Italy. The collections of Francesco Barbaro (who acquired some of Traversari's manuscripts) and Cardinal Bessarion (who donated his to the Biblioteca Marciana where they remain to this day) made Venice an important centre, though it was not until the middle of the sixteenth century that his books were finally made available for general study, installed in the new library designed by Jacopo Sansovino and built opposite the Basilica of St Mark in the symbolic and physical heart of Renaissance Venice. In Rome, the Vatican Library had assembled an important collection of classical texts by the 1470s, and there were also smaller collections in Florence, Urbino and Ferrara. So it is clear that by the early years of the sixteenth century a sizeable corpus of ancient theory was in Italian hands awaiting codification, commentary and discussion. In this enterprise the printing press was crucial from the start, as is demonstrated by the history of Giorgio Valla's single-handed resurrection of Greek musical science in the five books about music in his encyclopedic *De expetendis et fugiendis rebus opus*. This work began as an anthology of translations from the Greek, but grew to 49 books; published in 1501, it was the largest volume ever printed by the Venetian printer Aldus Manutius. More popular and influential was Carlo Valgulio's translation into Latin of Plutarch's *De musica*, first published in Brescia in 1507 and reprinted numerous times throughout the sixteenth century, at Basle in 1530, at Venice in 1532, in Paris in 1555, 1557 and 1566 among others.

In addition to the role of the press, the work of the translator was also vital. The notion that the Italian theorists of the sixteenth century were all sufficiently expert in Greek and Latin to be able to read ancient treatises in their original languages is misconceived. Only Lodovico Fogliano, Francisco de Salinas and Ercole Bottrigari possessed these abilities; others, for the most part, were dependent upon translations. The most striking case is that of Franchinus Gaffurius, who relied on a number of translators, including Giovanni Francesco Burana who completed for him three or four translations from the Greek including Aristides Quintilianus's *De musica* and Manuel Bryennius's *Harmonics*, of which Gaffurius's manuscript copy still survives. It was also for Gaffurius that Nicolo Leoniceno prepared his translation of the *Harmonics* of Ptolemy in 1499, another text which survives in Gaffurius's autograph. Yet although Gaffurius was assiduous in seeking out classical sources and arranging for translations of them, there is little evidence in his own writings that he penetrated far into them. His earliest work, the *Theorica musice* of 1480 (revised and expanded in 1492), is strongly reliant on Boethius's *De institutione musica,* which at times is repeated verbatim; and of the authors whose works he is known to have translated by this time, only Bacchius seems to be quoted directly. A similar picture is presented by the long gestation and publication history of Gaffurius's widely read treatise the *Practica musicae* of 1496; quotation from Greek writings is here more frequent but nevertheless still superficial. It would seem that although he was moderately well-versed in the ancient sources, Gaffurius remained committed to Boethian–Pythagorean orthodoxy. The case of Gaffurius is not untypical of the extent to which theorists possessed the necessary philological skills.

One of the most impenetrable difficulties for those few writers who were able to come to grips with ancient theory was the central question of the octave species and the tonoi of Greek theory. Beginning with Johannes Gallicus in the mid-fifteenth century, the question was discussed by a succession of commentators including Erasmus of Höritz, who taught at the University of Vienna, Gioseffo Zarlino, *maestro di cappella* at St Mark's in Venice, Francisco de Salinas, and finally Girolamo Mei and two Florentines under Mei's influence, Vincenzo Galilei and Giovanni de'Bardi. Only gradually did it become apparent that the modal system upon which plainchant was based was entirely different from the modes of ancient Greek theory. The source of the confusion was the *De institutione musica* by Boethius, the most widely read of all medieval treatises on music but one that was hardly ever placed in its proper context. It was only with Mei that the tonal system of the Greeks was treated to systematic critical and historical exposition;

although not even Mei properly understood the relationship of the octave species to the tonoi, his work finally made it plain that contemporary music could not have any tonal affinities with the music of the ancients, and so could not be expected to recuperate the ethos associated with the various species of Greek song. Although Mei did not publish his findings, the contents of the fourth and last book of his *De modis musicis antiquorum* was circulated to others interested in the problem in Florence in 1573; among those who took up Mei's evidence in condemnations of the orthodox view (which provided the plainchant modes with all the authority and status of a classical pedigree) was Vincenzo Galilei, whose *Dialogo* of 1581 contains a scathing attack on the fusion of modal and tonal categories in contemporary music.

Another was Giovanni de'Bardi, the prime mover of the Camerata, a group of prominent Florentines who met to discuss and listen to music under Galilei's guidance. A major concern of the Camerata was the letters about ancient music which Mei, a native Florentine who lived in Rome, sent to Bardi and Galilei. Bardi himself was a true Renaissance man who wrote plays, music and verse, and kept abreast of current scientific thinking; although he was influenced by Mei and Galilei he also studied the ancient sources independently. The question of the ancient modes as described by Ptolemy was for Bardi not only a matter of antiquarian and theoretical interest, but also a model for a modern system in which the choice of tonality for a vocal composition is made according to the sentiments of the words, and in his own music Bardi attempted to put this precept into practice. It is at this juncture that an interest in ancient music which had originally been directed towards research into the antique past now became engaged with the art of composition.

A significant point of difference between contemporary and ancient music, and one which struck sixteenth-century writers with particular force, was the idea that in the classical period poet and musician were inseparable. This belief runs like a thread through the writings of all the humanists, be they men like Gaffurius who were primarily interested in ancient music in a purely antiquarian way, or men like Galilei and Mei who believed ancient music to be superior to the compositions of their own times. Certainly it is symptomatic that the musicians of Bardi's Camerata confined themselves to setting dramatic and lyric poetry, precisely the kind of verse that Aristotle had considered to be indissolubly wedded to music. The same is true of the composers associated with Jean-Antoine de Baïf's Académie de Poésie et de Musique, founded in Paris in 1570. The pieces composed for Baïf by Le Jeune, Mauduit and Caurroy, whose severely homophonic settings (*musique mesurée à l'antique*) of French verse written in classical, quantitative metres matched those metres exactly, represent a particularly uncompromising attempt to imitate ancient music. In addition to its aesthetic objectives, Baïf's

Académie aimed at contributing to a *rapprochement* between Catholics and Huguenots at a moment of religious tensions and violence; sacred music was cultivated as well as psalms in *vers mesurée*, and both Protestant and Catholics participated. In terms of ruthlessness there is nothing comparable to the *musique mesurée à l'antique* of the Académie except perhaps for German metrical settings of Latin verse, spare pieces of obvious didactic purpose based on much the same rhythmic principles.

Works of this sort are certainly on the periphery of sixteenth-century musical experience. Yet behind these admittedly untypical products of humanistic thinking lay the common notion that the union between dramatic or lyric poetry and music should be intimate. In the course of the century there is a discernible and growing tendency, whose roots can be traced to the previous century, towards a closer bonding of word and note. The insistence on textual intelligibility in both Catholic and Protestant thinking, the vivid vocabulary of representational language deployed by madrigalists such as Wert and Marenzio, the attempts of the Pléiade to bring music and lyric verse together, the concerns of Bardi's Camerata – all these are in part manifestations of a shared set of aesthetic attitudes based on (or at least influenced by) humanistic theorizing about the equality of verse and music. A later stage, characterized in Italian writings by the term 'seconda prattica', was the subjugation of music to poetry, this being in effect a perversion of the union believed to have existed in antiquity. Indeed the lack of classical authority for this new arrangement of priorities was perceived as being less important than its benefits in attempts to resuscitate the ethical qualities of ancient music – its ability, testified to by innumerable classical authors, to move the hearts and minds of men. More than any other, it was this central difficulty of explaining and re-creating these effects that occupied musical humanists.

Even the most sceptical theorists expressed a firm belief in the historical validity of the effects of ancient music. Attempts to revive ancient music were primarily aimed at producing those effects, or at least at increasing the ethical and emotional power of music, whether by reintroducing the chromatic and enharmonic genera, reviving the modes or, more practically, by composing in the style of the *seconda prattica*. The great majority of musical humanists proposed that the resuscitation of the genera, in what was generally regarded to be their original form, would lead to a rediscovery of the miraculous effects of ancient music, but evidence of their practical application is slight. It is true that the growing popularity of chromatic writing evident in much music of the second half of the sixteenth century was due in part to the general humanistic concern with the ability of musical language to represent textual details. But the more extreme instances of chromaticism in pieces such as Rore's *Calami sonum ferentes* or Lassus's *Prophetiae*

Sibyllarum cannot be explained in terms of the strict level of the genera, and no contemporary theorist would have attempted to do so. In other words, as far as the Greek genera are concerned there is not much evidence of direct contact between humanistically inspired experiment and the activities of professional composers. As with the question of the modes, practice and theory did not find any common ground.

This brings us back to the most important way of explaining the effects of ancient music which also provided the key to contemporary attempts to reproduce those effects – the domination of text over music. Unfortunately, as the humanists were aware, classical authority for this conception was frail, since well-known passages in Aristotle attribute ethical and mimetic power to Greek instrumental music. In effect, explanations such as that offered by Zarlino were almost entirely *a priori* and only slightly dependent upon ancient justifications. In practice, three ambitions were striven for in setting texts – audibility, the preservation of rhythmic qualities and, above all, the vivid representation of sense. The influence of humanistic thinking about accent and stress is difficult to assess, since in practice it often coincided with a natural aesthetic inclination. Theorists such as Finck and Zacconi, who display little interest in the revival of ancient music, nevertheless insisted that the natural quantities and accents of a text should not be perverted in musical settings. Similarly, a composer such as Lassus, whose interest in humanistically inspired musical experiment was negligible, was praised for his 'right placing of the sillabelles upon the notes, and observing the accent in French and quantitie in Latin'. Concern for textual audibility produced more quantifiable results since, in the hands of writers such as Galilei, it amounted to an attack on contrapuntal music allied to the proposal that it be replaced either with monody or with homophony, and through this strain of humanistic argument the belief became established that the music of the ancients was monodic.

Behind these questions of fidelity to ancient practice in matters of rhythm, accentuation and audibility, lay an overriding concern with the dramatic portrayal of the sense of a text; what Monteverdi was later to call the 'natural way of imitation' ('via naturale all'immitatione'). Vincenzo Giustiniani's recollections of the north Italian virtuoso song styles of the 1570s and 80s capture perfectly the concomitant requirement placed upon performers that they should be able – through gesture, facial expression and body movements – to bring music to life through histrionic performance:

> The ladies of Mantua and Ferrara were highly competent, and vied with each other not only in regard to the timbre and training of their voices but also in the design of exquisite passages [*passaggi*] delivered at opportune points, but not in excess . . . Furthermore, they moder-

ated or increased their voices, loud or soft, heavy or light, according to the demands of the piece they were singing; now slow, breaking off sometimes with a gentle sigh, now singing long passages legato or detached, now groups, now leaps, now with long trills, now with short, or again with sweet running passages sung softly, to which one sometimes heard an echo answer unexpectedly. They accompanied the music and the sentiment with appropriate facial expressions, glances and gestures, with no awkward movements of the mouth or hands or body which might not express the feeling of the song.

It was this kind of relationship between words and music, a type of writing that came close to emotional speech, which for the most part found favour with humanist commentators. Beyond the familiar Platonic and Aristotelian references to music as a representational, mimetic art, there was little to guide them in the reinforcement of this opinion. Nevertheless, a number of authors, of whom Galilei was the most strident, explicitly rejected a style of writing in which individual ideas or images in the text were represented either literally (as with the imitations of birdsong in Janequin's chanson *Le chant des oiseaux*) or metaphorically, as in many madrigals. As might be expected, it was the composers of *musique mesurée* and the Florentine Camerata that came closest to the type of expression advocated by Galilei; both in Le Jeune's chansons and in Caccini's songs (some of which were in circulation as early as the 1580s), there is an almost complete absence of those responses to individual words and sentiments which are commonplace in the mid-century chanson and madrigal. Thus different theoretical positions are reflected in different styles of composition ranging from monody on one hand to conventional madrigals and chansons on the other. Yet despite these differences in outcome, composers and theorists of both persuasions working in the last third of the sixteenth century were united in a single aesthetic belief, namely that a musical setting must be expressive of its text in the fullest and most vivid manner. In this form the influence of humanistic theorizing can be detected in a wide range of music composed in many different parts of Europe, and also becomes inextricably involved with the views of those concerned, from a purely doctrinal point of view, with the inappropriateness of complicated polyphony for the celebration of church liturgy.

Through the exploration of these various practical and theoretical concerns music was perceived in the fifteenth and sixteenth centuries as part of the broader phenomenon of humanism, the major intellectual experience of the period and one whose roots lay in the activities of the Italian city states. Despite its emphasis on 'the humanities', with which music was finally able to take its place, humanism embraced the complete spectrum of human knowledge, from classical Roman and Greek literature to natural science and geography. From its very beginnings the humanist emphasis had been upon civic consciousness, the position and function of man in society. And although some humanists came from ordinary backgrounds, the educational ideals of humanist society could only be realized in a society which included privileged élites. In other words, humanism was directed at those who were destined to occupy leading positions in society – noblemen, rich bourgeois, princes, prelates, curial officials, administrators and professional men. A complete humanistic education of the kind specified by Vittorino at Mantua was a lengthy process, so much so that it could not be contemplated even in rich merchant families where boys entered the family business at thirteen or fourteen years of age. In the hands of the ruling classes, humanism became a tool that was used to refine and strengthen the values through which power was exercised; as such it became a necessary part of a politically and socially expedient educational code.

At this more private, educational level, what might be thought of as the syllabus of humanism was ideally suited for appropriation. Humanism emphasized the social values of subjects such as rhetoric, history and ethics by concentrating on their utility, their political and social purposes. And while the technical foundations of humanism lay in grammar, the ultimate objective was the perfection of rhetoric, the art of eloquence and persuasion or, to put it more prosaically, simply the ability to write and speak effectively. The models were classical and of the highest ideals; in humanistic theory, derived from Cicero and Quintilian, the perfect orator possessed that knowledge of ethics and philosophy which led to goodness and wisdom. In the political context of late fifteenth- and early sixteenth-century cities, whether oligarchic or not, the humanist appeal to rhetoric and eloquence was not merely a matter of manners but was a direct injunction to the ruling classes. The incorporation of music into this complex of humanist interests conferred upon it a new authority and status; alongside other skills, both practical and theoretical, music now formed part of an aristocratic ideal the spirit of which was taken up by Baldassare Castiglione and others and evolved into an educational ideal for the emulation of courtiers and gentlemen throughout Europe.

There is perhaps no more vivid picture of court life anywhere during the early decades of the sixteenth century than that provided in the pages of Castiglione's classic text *Il libro del cortegiano*. Usually described as a courtesy book, a manual of behaviour and practice for the Renaissance courtier, the *Cortegiano* is an attempt, as Castiglione himself put it, 'di formar con parole un perfetto Cortegiano' – to make the perfect courtier through words. Yet while Castiglione clearly intended to improve the manners of contemporary Italy (if not of Europe) by writing the *Cortegiano*, he also had other complex objectives in mind far beyond the codified instructions of traditional etiquette. The book is

2. Baldassare Castiglione: portrait (c1515) by Raphael

not laid out as a series of compact rules, like Erasmus's *De civilitate* or Giovanni Della Casa's *Galateo*. Rather it is a sequence of conversations, cast in the form of the classical dialogue, which reveal the author to be interested in social and moral questions. And while the major concern of the *Cortegiano* is to present a human and social ideal for imitation through analysis and example, it is also intended as a memorial to Duke Guidobaldo de Montefeltro, the court of Urbino and its inhabitants. To achieve this Castiglione casts himself in the role of court historian, and early in the first book gives the *Cortegiano* a very precise sense of time and place. Urbino is described, and its recent history recounted. The achievements of Duke Federico, who built the elegant palace in which the discussions take place, and of his successors, are catalogued. Finally, Castiglione carefully establishes a time in the autumn and winter of 1506–7 for the conversations at Urbino by relating them to real histori-cal events. Here and elsewhere the presence of verifiable fact makes it clear that the *Cortegiano* aims both to present an illusion of historical reality and to idealize it. It must be read partly as a social document which presents accurate details and impressions of court life.

In this context the part that music plays in the conversations of Castiglione's courtiers is an interesting reflection of progressive thinking about its function in contemporary courtly society, based not merely upon an idealized conception, but also upon experience. Scattered throughout the *Cortegiano* are a few allusions to music and occasional comments on contemporary performers and composers, including Bidon, a French-born singer from Ferrara who later joined the court of Leo X, and Marchetto Cara, best known as a frottolist and then employed by the Gonzaga at Mantua. Of rather greater significance is the fact that the topos of music is raised twice by Castiglione's courtiers in the course of their four days of conversation, and that on both occasions the acquisition of practical musical skills is strongly advocated. In a passage towards the end of Book 1 dealing with the courtier's accomplishments, Count Lodovico di Canossa establishes music together with letters as worthy objects of serious study by enlisting the support of passages from classical literature. Later, in the course of a passage in the second book, it is recommended that courtiers should be able to sing at sight, from notation, 'con bella maniera'. In addition to sight-singing, Castiglione continued, the courtier should also be adept at what he calls 'il cantare alla viola per recitare', a clear reference to the widespread tradition at the north Italian courts of improvised declamatory song performed to a simple instrumental accompaniment such as that provided by the lira da braccio. It is an interesting

3. *Recitation with lira da braccio accompaniment: woodcut from the epic 'Morgante maggiore' by Luigi Pulci (Florence, c1500)*

reflection not only upon the increasingly ceremonial and formal character of court life during the course of the sixteenth century, but also upon purely technical developments, that by the time Vincenzo Giustiniani came to admire the virtuosos of Ferrara and Mantua, much court entertainment was moving in the direction of new levels of accomplishment which partly displaced the courtly domesticity of Castiglione's world. Certainly the former entertainers had by then become the entertained, audience rather than participants, but the seeds of that change were already sown by Castiglione's day.

Musical literacy was probably not yet a generally accepted part of humanistic education when the *Cortegiano* was begun, but it was evidently increasing in importance. On one level Castiglione's remarks reflect a recent attitude in north Italian courtly society, in which the emphasis was now upon music as a social accomplishment, as a form of entertainment, to be performed with a certain professionalism. The practice of music had become an aspect of manners, and Castiglione's courtier is one of the earliest instances in the literature of the period of the cultivated amateur. At the same time there was also a new emphasis on the status of performed music (and particularly vocal and instrumental music), a status acquired through association with humanist values, and particularly with Platonic and Pythagorean ideas. As has been mentioned already, in the absence of classical models for contemporary music Renaissance musicians appealed to the reported miraculous effects of ancient music as a justification for their art; this is precisely the point of Canossa's *laus musicae*, with its frequent appeals to ancient authority, and in turn explains the perennial attraction of the figure of Orpheus in Renaissance tales about music, including the earliest operas. In his depiction of these twin components of a new configuration of attitudes towards both the theory and practice of music, Castiglione was reporting humanistically inspired trends in courtly behaviour.

However influential it may have been in practice, the popularity of Castiglione's book in sixteenth-century Europe was immense. It went through more than twenty Italian editions in the course of the century and was translated into a number of European languages. In Castiglione's hands the humanist pursuit of eloquence was turned into an ideal for Renaissance gentlemen who, in addition to being prepared in classical letters, were meant to be men of the world – versatile, accomplished, socially at ease and, one might add, musically skilled. Allied to the wider dissemination of music made possible by music printing, the educational message of Castiglione and his many imitators was a powerful force for the cultivation of music by the bourgeoisie throughout sixteenth-century Europe.

The early spread of such ideas to a notably conservative section of society is powerfully revealed in Paolo Cortese's book *De cardinalatu*. Published in 1510, and one of the few treatises written as a handbook for

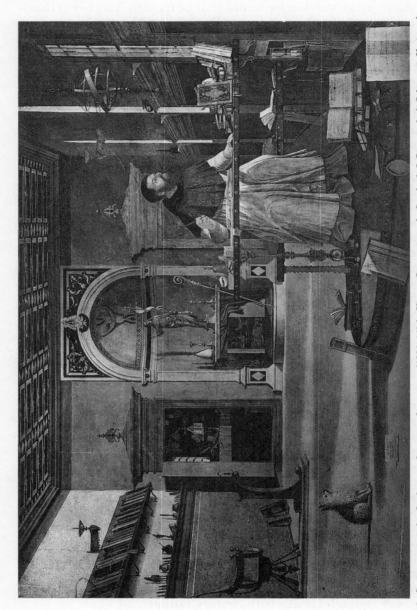

4. *St Augustine in his Study, one of a series of paintings (1501–11) by Vittore Carpaccio in the Scuola di S Giorgio degli Schiavoni, Venice; the saint is shown surrounded by symbols of Christian humanist learning, including two pieces of polyphonic music, one a Petrucci print (right foreground)*

clerics by a humanist and from a humanistic perspective, it reveals the full integration of Renaissance humanist values into the world of the Roman curia. From its pages emerges a picture of the ideal cardinal as a composite figure, with different powers and responsibilities towards different interest-groups. His ability to operate as both a temporal and spiritual leader is now partly based on the adoption of humanist ideals; the curia's successful appropriation of humanist culture along the lines that Cortese advocated allowed it to press the new learning into the service of the church. As in the secular world, the authority of the humanist image was regarded as a powerful ally.

Cortese was a member of the curia, and his treatise reflects actual Roman practices. For our purposes this becomes of particular interest in the second book of *De cardinalatu*, the *Liber oeconomicus*, where Cortese discussed the cardinal in his public role as an ecclesiastical prince. Except for some small details there are few differences between the kind of household advocated by Cortese and that which would have been expected of a secular ruler. Beginning with an outline of the finances necessary for maintaining a proper *famiglia*, Cortese argued that it should correspond to contemporary expectations, and that since display was admired, a modestly extravagant way of life was considered appropriate. The cardinal's *famiglia* should consist of about 140 members and would need about 12,000 ducats a year for its upkeep. In accordance with princely status, this *famiglia* should be housed in a large *palazzo*, built according to recent architectural theories. It should be decorated with modern paintings and sculpture and should include a library, a chapel and an auditorium for discussions and lectures.

It is in this domestic setting that Cortese introduced his remarks about music. Interestingly, his specification of the cardinal's palace includes what he called a 'cubiculum musicae', one of the earliest references on record to a music room. Later in the *Liber oeconomicus* Cortese turned to a more detailed discussion of music. Josquin is praised as a composer of masses, though more because of the genre than the composer's skill. Motets receive less acclaim, because their texts are less concerned with the central ritual of the liturgy. Finally, Serafino Aquilano is held up as the master of secular music. The precise extent to which Cortese's manual is a reflection of actual Roman practice is unclear, but the extent of humanist influence is very striking despite the occasional echoes of traditional reservations about polyphony. In its emphases upon practical music, its elevation of practitioners in a variety of genres, and its appeal to ancient authority albeit Christian (St Gregory) rather than classical, the *De cardinalatu* is analogous in its concerns, if decidedly less elegant in argument and style, to Castiglione's *Cortegiano*. In details such as the cultivation of the madrigal, the foundation of academies with strong musical interests, and the growing fashion for instrumental music, the pattern of Italian musical developments in the early decades of the sixteenth century is a powerful testimony to the potency of the new attitudes towards music exemplified in the work of both Castiglione and Cortese as well as to other factors such as the impact of music printing. These new emphases are first evident in the attitudes of such patrons as Isabella d'Este, Lucrezia Borgia and Ippolito d'Este, as well as in the activities of such humanist theorists and composers as Gaffurius in Milan and Tinctoris in Naples. And it is against this background that our attention now naturally shifts to the question of the importance of courtly society for the cultural and musical life of Renaissance Europe.

COURTLY SOCIETY

In 1860 Jacob Burckhardt's book *Die Kultur der Renaissance in Italien* was published in Basle. After a substantial introductory essay, 'The state as a work of art', Burckhardt devotes himself to a detailed exploration of his main argument that the Renaissance witnessed 'the discovery of the world and of man', that it inaugurated the attitudes and preoccupations of modern European civilization. Although more than a century later Burckhardt's view of the period remains remarkably powerful despite attempts to undermine it, the impact of his magisterial work has not always been positive. In writing his famous account of Burgundian culture, *The Waning of the Middle Ages*, the Dutch historian Johan Huizinga effectively reinforced this vision of fifteenth-century Italy as the cradle of modern culture with an autumnal characterization of northern France and the Lowlands as 'medieval society in its last age, like a tree with overripe fruit'. Huizinga's picture of the fifteenth century in the north as 'an epoch of fading and decay' has so dominated the historiography of the subject that the notion that Burgundian culture had a real influence not only in England and Spain but even in Italy may seem startling. The history of music provides a clear, if in general cultural terms untypical, instance of the extent of this northern influence; even Burckhardt was forced to admit that 'musical composition down to the year 1500 was chiefly in the hands of the Flemish school', though he rapidly added the qualification that 'side by side with this there nevertheless existed an Italian tradition which probably stood nearer to our present taste'. Certainly there is no need to apologize for beginning discussion of the role of courtly society in the musical culture of Renaissance Europe not in Naples or Ferrara but north of the Alps.

By the middle of the fifteenth century, the economic power of the Lowlands combined with the position of the Burgundian territories, strategically located between the Empire and France, had made Burgundy the dominant power in Europe. As the result of a carefully contrived sequence of dynastic marriages and land acquisitions, the Duchy of Burgundy had grown to become larger than France in both extent and power, a vast swathe of territory beginning with Burgundy and Franche-Comté in the south, extending northwards through Luxembourg, Hainault, Picardy, Artois and Boulogne, and including almost the whole of modern Belgium and the Netherlands. Among the Burgundian possessions were some of the wealthiest northern cities – Bruges, Ghent, Lille, Brussels and The Hague – all of which were used as stopping places for a peripatetic court. In this period, at the height of its power, Burgundian supremacy was not only political and economic but also cultural. As early as the 1420s the court of Burgundy had surpassed in magnificence not only neighbouring courts such as Blois and Foix, but even the royal courts of England and France, to present a picture of a wealthy and chivalrous society that had not been seen in Europe since the fall of the Hohenstaufen Empire. Opulent, ostentatious and self-confident, the Burgundian court presented a behavioural model in literature, the arts and chivalry which other European rulers sought to imitate.

5. Map of the acquisitions of the dukes of Burgundy up to the death of Charles the Bold in 1477

This exceptional political and cultural vitality was partly due to a continuous tradition which deliberately associated court society with artistic skill in accordance with cherished chivalric ideals. From generation to generation the dukes of Burgundy were bibliophiles, patrons of the arts and sovereigns of the Order of the Golden Fleece – a quasi-Arthurian society of knights drawn from the European monarchy and the higher reaches of the aristocracy, for whose elaborate ceremonies a number of composers, including Guillaume Dufay and Josquin Desprez, wrote pieces. The stable conditions which permitted such activities to flourish were partly ensured by a skilfully organized system of court officials who controlled inherited institutions. At the core of this bureaucracy was the ducal household (what Cortese, in a curial context, called the *famiglia*), ranging from court secretaries and treasurers to cobblers and grooms. It was a mutually advantageous system. On the one hand the dukes needed an army of servants to look after their affairs: aristocrats, diplomats, lawyers and accountants to manage their business and to protect their interests, tutors to instruct their children, physicians to oversee their health in this world and ecclesiastics to supervise it in the next; and on the other, well-placed members of this élite exerted considerable pressure for rewards (enhanced salaries, titles, benefices and land) in return for their services in ensuring the continued stability and prosperity of the system. The court itself was larger than the household; it might include for example foreign princes and other visitors such as Edward IV of England who spent a period of exile in 1470–71 in Bruges, or Italians such as Francesco d'Este or Rodolfo Gonzaga who arrived to represent the interests of the dukes of Ferrara and Mantua. Through such contacts at home, and those of its ambassadors and representatives abroad, the Burgundian court maintained an important position on the international circuit. Famed for its magnificence, wealth and liberality, princely virtues which humanism was eventually deployed to support, the Burgundian system became a potent model for courts elsewhere.

This extraordinary cosmopolitan concentration of power and skills created an atmosphere in which artists, musicians and men of letters and science were able to practise their talents to an extent that was unusual in the highly stratified societies of fifteenth-century Europe. From early in the century the Burgundian court maintained a chapel that included musicians, and a number of the most important northern composers of the time, including Baude Cordier and Jean de Noyers dit Tapissier, served the Burgundian princes. Under Philip the Good and his successor Charles the Bold these musical interests continued and, among others, the important song composers Robert Morton and Hayne van Ghizeghem were employed. Nevertheless, while the court of Burgundy was undoubtedly an important centre for the cultivation of music, both secular and sacred, it was not there so much as at the large churches and choir schools of the north, such as Cambrai (strictly speaking not a Burgundian city at all but part of the Holy Roman Empire), that the great composers of the age received their training. Similarly, while Gilles Binchois was a court musician from about 1467 when he joined the household of Charles the Bold, many other composers who are credited with the formulation of the 'Burgundian style', including Dufay (another Cambrai product) were not, as far as it is known, formally connected with the court at all.

In this sense the traditional notion of a uniform Burgundian musical culture is somewhat suspect, since in practice a great deal of music was written for cities and collegiate churches throughout northern Europe which maintained their own traditions. In fifteenth-century Bruges for example, then the artistic and commercial centre of Flanders, musical life was concentrated on the collegiate church of St Donatian, which had both Dufay and Binchois among its canons as well as Jacob Obrecht for its choirmaster. Elsewhere in the city the performance of polyphony during Mass was well established at the collegiate church of Our Lady by the middle of the fifteenth century, and there was also active musical involvement at some of the smaller parish churches and hospitals. Music was performed in convents and confraternities, during processions and pageants, to accompany jousting and dancing, and as part of civic and political occasions. Bruges was an important place for the Burgundian court, one of the major sources of its wealth and the site of one of the ducal palaces that were scattered throughout the Burgundian territories. Yet it is clear that the rich musical life of the city (and of other major centres in the area such as Brussels and Lille) existed independently of the court and that, if anything, the court itself merely used local musical resources when it was in residence. A similar pattern of urban and corporate patronage operated in many of the commercially and politically important centres in the north.

Yet whatever the realities of the situation, the reputation of the Burgundian court was inextricably bound up with the considerable prestige which 'Burgundian' culture enjoyed elsewhere in Europe. In Tudor England, for example, the reign of Henry VII was a transitional period during which forms of poetry, drama, chivalry, architecture, painting and scholarship were directly copied from Burgundy. The situation is symbolized by Henry's construction of the new royal palace of Richmond, begun in 1497 and heavily indebted to Flemish models. Filled with sumptuous Flemish tapestries and paintings, illuminated manuscripts of the renowned Bruges–Ghent school for the palace library, and windows of Flemish stained glass, Richmond was a magnificent architectural symbol of the new dynasty, a visible sign that Henry's court was the equal of any in Christendom. Continuing the work begun in a rather hesitant and random way by Edward IV (who had been deeply affected by what he had seen in Bruges during his exile there), Henry established a royal household at Richmond clearly patterned after that of the Burgundian court. Similarly, he also founded there an artistic and literary establishment largely staffed by poets, printers, artists and illuminators who had been trained in Flemish-Burgundian styles. In imitation of Philip the Good, one of the first European rulers to appoint an official court chronicler, Henry put at the head of this establishment Bernard André, a blind poet from Toulouse whose first official commission, the *Vita Henrici VII*, strikes an uneasy balance between history and encomium. A Flemish bibliophile, Quentin Poulet, entered royal service as the first royal librarian; as a result of his efforts both Henry VII and his successor were to read romances, chronicles and histories in Burgundian prose.

Similarly, by the beginning of the sixteenth century the first of a whole succession of Flemish painters and artisans arrived in London, the precursors of a tradition that included Gheeraerts and the De Heeres and endured well into the seventeenth century when Rubens and Van Dyck were appointed to the service of Charles I. In other areas the cultural affects of northern influence were equally long lived. Cornysh's adaptation of Burgundian pageants into Tudor disguisings lived on in Elizabethan entries and the Accession Day tilts, and behind the seventeenth-century English masque (Italian in name and, in the hands of Inigo Jones, Italian also in its technology and visual appearance) lay a conception which in its structural outlines was still recognizably indebted to northern example. This thoroughgoing transformation of English court culture in the first decades of the sixteenth century, which inevitably affected in turn the tastes of bureaucrats, courtiers and aristocrats, is mirrored elsewhere in Europe, for example at the courts of Spain and Maximilian I, and even as we shall see to some extent in Italy.

The first major occasion when these talents were on open display was the two-week celebration that accompanied the marriage of Arthur, Prince of Wales (an appropriate name for this heir to a Camelot by the Thames), to Catherine, Infanta of Spain. Some of the details of this occasion reflect its comprehensively Burgundian character and invite direct comparison with the marriage ceremonies in Brussels in 1496–7 for Joanna of Castile and Philip the Fair. Catherine was welcomed to London by a spectacular triumphal procession based upon a Burgundian model, and among the other entertainments a tournament, fought beneath the Tree of Chivalry, was devised along specifically Burgundian lines. Henry's own court painter, probably a Walloon, frescoed the walls of the chapel and great hall at Richmond with a sequence of portraits (later to influence Holbein in his great Privy Chamber painting at Whitehall) following a Burgundian scheme. And in the earliest of his court entertainments, the composer William Cornysh introduced pageant cars of Burgundian type, most familiar from Hans Burgkmair's later woodcuts of *The Triumph of Maximilian* of 1526 (see fig.54 below). As Henry's Spanish guests departed to the increasingly Burgundian atmosphere of their home environments, they may well have been convinced that the Tudor court was equal in magnificence to any in Europe.

Quite clearly, the decisive moment for the reception of humanist ideals in northern Europe also occurred at this time, when the urban origins of Italian humanism had become sufficiently submerged in a dynastic way of life which more closely matched the aristocratic nature of northern patronage than it had a century before. Further encouraged by the mood of neo-Platonism, which produced an attitude more consonant with northern ideals than the earlier civic principles had been, the north now became fertile ground for the new ideas. In terms of music, the continental repertory assumes a new importance during the early years of Henry VIII; through the activities of foreign musicians and composers in England, the experiences of English visitors to Europe and the circulation of continental music in manuscripts and printed books, contact with continental traditions was greater than it had been before. For the most part 'continental' means Franco-Flemish; although Henry VIII was presented with a manuscript of madrigals and motets including works by composers working in Italy, most of the manuscripts that found their way to England contain northern repertory, much of it from French court circles. As for the manuscripts themselves, most of them are richly illuminated presentation copies, and may say more about the ascendancy of the English court to a position of European significance than about its musical tastes.

The Burgundian tradition of learned chivalry firmly established by Henry VII and his successor runs through later English sixteenth-century culture alongside a more thoroughbred humanist tradition. One line of descent leads to Spenser and Sidney (above all to the *Arcadia*), the other to Erasmus and More. In the tapestries, paintings and manuscripts prepared for the Tudor court either by or under the influence of Flemings during the early decades of the century can be seen the first stages of that invasion of foreign influences that transformed native traditions into the more cosmopolitan style of Elizabeth's reign. Similarly, it was from the initial example of the court itself under Henry VIII that the seeds of interest in foreign music and musicians began. The discontinuity in English musical life which is usually associated with the Edwardine and Marian periods is in fact a more gradual process than often described, and some of the social changes which took place may actually have had a beneficial effect upon the employment as household musicians of many of those released from church service. Certainly it was during these middle decades of the century that a greater interest in both the viol and the lute in English society arose – tangible reflections of a growing musical involvement

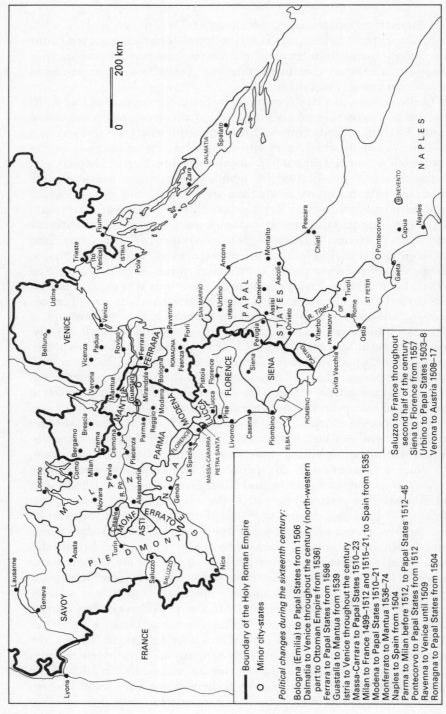

6. *Map of northern and central Italy in the sixteenth century*

Boundary of the Holy Roman Empire
○ Minor city-states

Political changes during the sixteenth century:

Bologna (Emilia) to Papal States from 1506
Dalmatia to Venice throughout the century (north-western part to Ottoman Empire from 1536)
Ferrara to Papal States from 1598
Guastalla to Mantua from 1539
Istria to Venice throughout the century
Massa-Carrara to Papal States 1510–23
Milan to France 1499–1512 and 1515–21, to Spain from 1535
Modena to Papal States 1510–21
Monferrato to Mantua 1536–74
Naples to Spain from 1504
Parma to Milan before 1512, to Papal States 1512–45
Pontecorvo to Papal States from 1512
Ravenna to Venice until 1509
Romagna to Papal States from 1504

Saluzzo to France throughout the second half of the century
Siena to Florence from 1557
Urbino to Papal States 1503–8
Verona to Austria 1508–17

that was itself merely an aspect of a general increase in literacy.

It was with the 1560s that the new pattern of musical life in England achieved a sense of definition and permanency, and again the example of the court played a crucial role. Elizabeth I continued and expanded the cosmopolitan musical establishment at court which, being frequently in London as well as travelling on progresses, acted as both example and inspiration for aristocrats such as Henry Fitzalan, Earl of Arundel (*d* 1580). From about 1553 Arundel lived at Nonesuch Castle in Surrey, originally built for Henry VIII in 1538 and, during the early decades of Elizabeth's reign, an important centre of musical activity in England and an echo of the royal court. Among the surviving books and manuscripts from the Nonesuch library, a number contain Italian music acquired by Arundel on his visit to Italy in 1565–6, but the majority are devoted to Franco-Flemish repertory, much of which was copied by the Flemish composer Derick Gerarde whom Arundel employed. Gerarde often took his Italian pieces from northern sources, and this pattern of transmission is typical of many manuscripts of Elizabeth's reign; contrary to the impression created by historians keen to identify the progressive with the Italianate, not all foreign influences during the Elizabethan 'golden age' came from south of the Alps.

In Italy itself, the emergence of courtly society took a different but by no means totally separate path. It had been in medieval Italy that the previous governmental system, the commune (a city republic ruled by a mercantile patriciate), had reached its most developed form. But between approximately 1280 and the middle of the fourteenth century, the Italian communes had been faced with such serious difficulties, both internal and external, that there was no choice other than constitutional change. There were two options: either one-man rule under a single family in hereditary succession, or a republican system in which political power was concentrated in the hands of a narrower group of citizens. During the Renaissance, Venice, Florence, Siena and Lucca all took the republican route, while three other important cities, Bologna, Genoa and Perugia, oscillated between signorial and republican systems. In Florence, perhaps the most familiar example, the republican councils and magistracies remained in force almost until the middle of the fifteenth century. Then, after a short period of thinly disguised signorial government (*c*1470–94), the city revitalized its republican institutions for a time (1494–1512) before the Medici regime was restored. Finally, in 1530, after three years of ardent republican agitation, the city, besieged by foreign soldiers, settled under the rule of the Medici who, by the end of that decade, had established themselves as dukes (by the 1570s grand-dukes) of Tuscany, a position they were to maintain until the end of the eighteenth century.

This pattern, though more complicated than most examples, is characteristic of the general process in which, at the end of the Middle

Ages, the crisis of the cities led to the extinction of their liberties. In Italy (and then later in Flanders), the new monarchies replaced the old city republics. From about 1440, for at least a hundred years and in some cases more, the wealth, energy and extravagance of the Italian courts combined to give a distinct direction to the élite culture of the peninsula. By 1500 the major Italian courts, which in turn acted as cultural models for scores of satellites, were those of Milan, Naples, Ferrara, Savoy and Mantua. To these must be added papal Rome, a centre of both spiritual and temporal power and resonant with international standing as the capital of Western Christendom even though it had less political influence than Milan and not even half that city's fiscal income. Those few city republics which survived ceased to assert their independence. Genoa became dependent upon the King of Spain, and Venice retreated into comparative neutrality from which it emerged only to join crusades against the Turks; outside Italy, Geneva survived, to become an important centre of Calvinist thought, only through French protection, while the free cities of Germany were guaranteed their liberty by the Empire on one hand and by the fragmentation of Germany itself on the other. This shift from republican to monarchical systems marks a profound social change throughout Europe, but nowhere more so than in Italy. There the new rulers founded their states on a different social base by relying on wider support to counteract the urban patriciate, whose attachment to older ideas of liberty and republicanism remained strong, and justified it with a new political philosophy which depended heavily upon humanism. In some ways many writers such as Machiavelli, whose books both advised and justified princely rule, continued to endorse the values and concepts that had been promoted by the earlier humanists; but in others the changing character of their audience encouraged them to introduce new and often severely pragmatic elements into their moral and political thought.

In turn these features coloured the character of the Italian courts, whose cultural style was more indebted to Burgundian example than is often recognized; this is particularly true, though not exclusively so, of the courts of northern Italy, whose libraries were filled with French romances and where French itself was still thought of as the most suitable vernacular for the transaction of official diplomatic business. The support of Italian humanists for courtly style can be found as early as the end of the fourteenth century, and Buonaccorso's influential treatise on chivalry was an Italian production. But by the middle of the fifteenth century Burgundy had become the example of courtly magnificence *par excellence*; it is indicative that Buonaccorso's book had become best known, even in Italy, in Jean Mielot's translation which, in turn, provided the starting-point for other versions such as the English translation of John Tiptoft, Earl of Warwick. At the north

Italian courts, and above all at Ferrara, poetry on chivalric themes was much in vogue, and the deeds of Orlando (i.e. the French Roland) and his fellow knights were to be seen in tapestries and paintings. Writing in the first half of the fifteenth century, Sabadini degli Arienti described a fresco on chivalric themes at the Estense villa of Belfiore, and in the 1440s Pisanello was commissioned by Ludovico Gonzaga to paint an ambitious cycle based on an episode from *Lancelot*, a thirteenth-century French romance on Arthurian themes, for the ducal palace at Mantua (fig.7). But perhaps nowhere is the influence of northern European culture upon Italian courtly style more evident than in the realms of literature and, to an even greater extent, music.

First, a literary example. Boiardo's *Orlando innamorato*, first published while still incomplete in 1484, is usually regarded as the first great epic poem in the Renaissance revival of the chivalric mode. And it was this poem, still left unfinished by Boiardo at his death, that Ariosto decided to continue in the *Orlando furioso*; as he put it in a letter of 1512, 'un mio libro al quale gia molti di (continuando la inventione del conte Matteo Maria Boiardo) io diedi principo' ('a book which I began many days ago, continuing the invention of Count Matteo Maria Boiardo'). And indeed Ariosto takes over Boiardo's characters and the main action of his poem: the war, the love of Orlando and the story of Ruggiero, just as Boiardo had outlined them at the beginning of his

7. *Detail of the fresco cycle on Arthurian themes (1440s), by Pisanello, in the ducal palace at Mantua*

Third Book. Yet while Ariosto plundered Boiardo for his main characters and action, he also drew upon numerous other sources, including northern ones. From the Estense library he was able to become acquainted with chivalrous romances; he makes especially frequent use of the *Aspramonte*, the *Spagna in Rima*, *Ancroia*, the *Storia di Merlino* and *Guerrin Meschino* as well as of contemporary writings. In terms of character and action, Ariosto's epic is merely the most recent stage in a long historical process. Boiardo's poem carries on the adventures of Orlando, whose birth is described in the last book of Andrea da Barberino's *Reali di Francia* of *c*1400. And in its turn, the *Reali di Francia* is a recasting and reordering of a vast body of narrative prose and verse which had accumulated around the legends of Charlemagne, the origins of which are to be found in the French *chansons de geste*, and particularly in the late eleventh-century *Chanson de Roland*. This same Roland, whose tragic death at Roncevaux is described in the French poem, is the protagonist of Ariosto's poem 400 years later.

A rehearsal of these well-established continuities is not meant to obscure the fact that the tone of this sequence of narratives had been constantly shifting in that intervening period. For example, when the French *chansons de geste* had first made their way over the Alps in the twelfth century, they were copied down in the northern cities, notably Ferrara and Venice. And as these versions, often in Franco-Venetian dialect, multiplied, the material was modified to suit Italian tastes. In their new environment, the serious, religious and patriotic note of the early French *chansons de geste* became fainter. Later still, in the fifteenth century, the romance evolved from its medieval origins to the society and culture of the Renaissance; Andrea da Barberino's most popular work, the *Reali di Francia*, is a serious attempt to rationalize and clarify the confusions of the tradition and to relate it more effectively to a fifteenth-century audience.

In terms of musical developments, connections with centres north of the Alps also had a long pedigree, but they became of crucial significance in the second half of the fifteenth century as the prominent Italian courts embarked upon a more sustained and consistent interest in practical music than hitherto. Contemporary recognition of the importance of this development is made explicit in the preface to Johannes Tinctoris's *Proportionale*, written about 1476, when the author was in the service of his Neapolitan patron, King Ferrante I of Aragon. Tinctoris divided the history of music into three periods beginning, inevitably, with classical antiquity, passing to the Christian Middle Ages and finishing with the music of his own period. Discussing the latter, Tinctoris wrote:

> the most Christian princes . . . desiring to augment the divine service, founded chapels after the manner of David, in which at extraordinary

expense they appointed singers to sing . . . praise to our God with diverse (but not adverse) voices . . . . And since, if their masters are endowed with the liberality which makes men illustrious, the singers of princes are rewarded with honour, glory and wealth, many are kindled with a most fervent zeal for this study.

These remarks constitute a remarkably perceptive account of the burgeoning interest in music at the more prominent Italian courts that occurred in the 1460s and 1470s. During the early fifteenth century courtly interest in the art had been principally concentrated on the employment of the singers and instrumentalists needed for entertainment and ceremonial; the numbers involved were often small and many of the musicians were recruited from northern Europe. Much of the music played by these ensembles of trumpeters, *piffari* (bands of trombones and shawms) and singers and string players (these groupings of performers are found, for example, at Ferrara, Milan and Naples during this period), was orally transmitted. Unwritten traditions, which are largely lost except for occasional polyphonic reworkings, reached their most sophisticated expression not in the hands of foreigners, but in the art of Italian poet-improvisers, about whom a little information has survived thinly scattered through letters and archival documents. Famous as many of these men were in their own times (Antonio di Guido was probably the best-known musician in Florence in the fifteenth century), details of their careers have largely disappeared leaving little trace of their existence. So too have the details of their musical performances and the repertories of melodies which they drew on in their recitations of epic verse. Their songs belong to the substantial corpus of unwritten music of the Renaissance, a largely vanished tradition which represented an important and common aspect of musical experience.

Among the poet-improvisers who made their careers in the courts a small number achieved the status of masters, becoming legends in their own lifetimes. Most famed of all was the Ferrarese singer and lute player Pietrobono; praised by a long line of humanist writers including Tinctoris, Pietrobono was a member of Borso d'Este's court and his services were also eagerly sought at the courts of Naples, Mantua and Milan. From descriptions of his playing in Cornazzano's long poem *La Sfortiade*, it is clear that he was particularly admired for his performances of narrative verse in which he accompanied himself on a string instrument. At Ferrara he was so esteemed that a number of portrait medals were struck in his honour; it is both ironic and characteristic of our knowledge of these *maestri* of the improvised tradition that more is known about Pietrobono's appearance than about the sound of his art. Yet despite the fact that his music cannot be recovered, Pietrobono enters our history as one of the most celebrated and influential Italian musicians of the fifteenth century, the practitioner of a song style that continued to exist alongside the Franco-Flemish chanson which became fashionable at the Italian courts in the last third of the century.

The notion, strongly familiar from later literary works such as Castiglione's *Cortegiano*, that music was a necessary part of courtly manners, had become increasingly widespread during those last decades of the century, partly as a natural consequence of the growth of humanistic culture with its emphasis on individuality and personal refinement. Even so, the musical interests of Ercole I d'Este, Duke of Ferrara, were quite exceptional for the time. Many of his efforts were directed towards the operation of his *cappella di cantori*; as early as 1472, the first full year of Ercole's rule, it had included fifteen singers, and by the end of the century it had been expanded to a size that placed it on a par with any similar body in Europe, including the papal chapel. This side of Ercole's interest in music was partly promoted by his religiosity and the desire to present himself to the world and to posterity as the model Christian prince. At the same time, all the evidence suggests that Ercole had a quite genuine interest in music as an art, and that this interest was expressed in the pleasure he took in performance. It is reported that on his deathbed he called for the keyboard player Vincenzo de Modena and instructed him to play for an hour and that even during the war with Venice he sang and played every day. At times Ercole sang with his sons, at times with the professional singers of his chapel.

By making extensive use of Ferrarese diplomatic agents at the major centres both in Italy and abroad, as well as occasional forays through special representatives, the new *cappella* was continually increased in both size and quality throughout the 1470s. While there were purely local considerations and temperamental reasons for this phenomenon, including Ercole's serious religious devotion, his efforts were also motivated by a desire to compete with Galeazzo Maria Sforza at Milan. Using similar methods of recruitment, by 1474 Galaezzo had assembled the largest establishment of its kind. Further impetus to Ercole's initiative may have been provided by the example of Rome, where Sixtus IV had begun the construction of what was to become the Sistine Chapel and had established a new *cappella* of singers for St Peter's by 1473. Given the strength of the Burgundian influence upon the literary and musical culture of the Italian courts, it seems highly likely that all these foundations were modelled upon northern examples, fuelled by the direct or indirect experiences brought south by the many northern musicians who were recruited to fill these expanded or newly created institutions. The idea was not new. As early as the fourteenth century, the papal chapel in Rome had included a large number of Netherlanders, thus inaugurating a tradition which was to be maintained until well into the sixteenth century. And at Ferrara in the 1440s,

Leonello d'Este established a chapel of ten singers which was entirely made up of singers from the north. The continuing strength of this Netherlands influence in Italian chapels and courts is symbolized by the careers of the major composers Ciconia, Dufay, Josquin and Willaert; each represents a different generation, and all spent substantial portions of their careers south of the Alps.

Quite apart from their consequences for sacred repertories, the formation of new princely chapels also had an impact on the dissemination of the French chanson in Italy, since so many of the musicians sought out for service in the *cappelle* were foreigners. At Ferrara during the 1470s, Ercole's *cappella di cantori* contained a significant number of Flemings and a large number of French musicians together with occasional members of other nationalities; indeed, for most of his period of rule these two groups of northerners together made up the majority of the chapel. In Naples, where ties with Aragon had given the royal chapel under Alfonso I a markedly Spanish and consequently somewhat provincial character, the accession of Ferrante I coupled with the serving of those ties inaugurated a period in which new recruits were often Franco-Netherlanders. The enthusiasm for the Italian courts for chansons written by the post-Dufay generation is in part a reflection of this influx and the taste, once established, was only further strengthened, at least in the north, by the French invasion of 1494. Throughout the late fifteenth century and well into the sixteenth, the chanson repertory was widely cultivated at the Italian courts and provided an alternative to the Italian traditions of popular and improvised song which continued to be performed. In general, music at court was substantially reliant upon Franco-Netherlands polyphony, whether in chapel or chamber, and upon *oltramontani* to perform it.

It was presumably these developments, as well as the activities of his own patron, that Tinctoris had in mind. In this way rulers discovered a new way of both competing for status with one another and with asserting their own *virtus* by projecting an image of themselves as model Christian princes, and in this they were supported and encouraged by contemporary political thought. Giovanni Pontano, for example, devoted two treatises to the qualities of liberality and magnificence, and *De splendore*, which specifies how princes should demonstrate their status and virtue according to well-defined rules, insists that a reputation for creating 'noble buildings, splendid churches and theatres' is a necessary demonstration of princely fame. This is not merely an endorsement of the values and concepts articulated by the earlier humanists, who had been concerned to analyse the *virtus* of the citizen body as a whole, but an adaptation of the traditional mirror-for-princes style to suit the changing situation in the Italian courts at the end of the fifteenth century. What would have been previously regarded as inappropriate ostentation, was now incorporated within a theory of decorum.

The Renaissance

Further changes of emphasis are discernible in the musical interests of the following generation of Italian princely patrons, nowhere more clearly than in the activities of Ercole d'Este's first child, Isabella, who grew up in Ferrara where many of her later attitudes and aspirations, including an interest in music, were formed. Other aspects of her artistic concerns can also be traced to her Ferrarese education, most notably a lifelong interest in painting. Both of her parents were enthusiastic and discriminating patrons of the arts, and Isabella had been raised in an atmosphere where humanistic discussion of such matters was commonplace and where the somewhat eclectic work of Cosimo Tura and Francesco Cossa was highly prized. Later in life Isabella took pride in her image as 'una decima Musa'; she took her role as patron of poetry, music and art with great seriousness and was, on her own admission, *appetitosa*, hungry for art. Through agents in all the major Italian cities she assiduously assembled an impressive collection of classical antiquities, acquired sculptures and bronzes including works by Antico and Michelangelo and commissioned paintings from some of the finest artists of the age including Giovanni Bellini, Andrea Mantegna and Leonardo da Vinci.

Music also played a significant part in Isabella's upbringing. At Ferarra she received a good musical education under the guidance of

8. *Parnassus (c1496) by Andrea Mantegna; the painting has been interpreted as an allegory of the arts at the Mantuan court under the patronage of Isabella d'Este and Francesco Gonzaga*

the central figure of Ercole's chapel, the singer and composer Johannes Martini, and it is known from Isabella's later letters that she became an accomplished musician. At Mantua she was to make dramatic changes to musical life at a court which had, until then, been slow to emulate the examples of Milan, Naples and Rome. Her initial efforts were directed not towards the formation of a *cappella di cantori* for the performance of liturgical polyphony, a task which was undertaken by her husband Francesco, but rather towards the provision for the composition and performance of secular music, particularly frottolas (vernacular songs composed by Italian composers), a form that Isabella encouraged at Mantua and that later spread to other centres through musical intermediaries. In essence an Italian courtly art, the frottola marks an important juncture in the re-emergence of native Italian composers after a long period in the fifteenth century when musical life in the peninsula had been dominated, at all levels except for improvisation, by musicians from France, Burgundy, the Low Countries and England.

Isabella's interests in music and the way in which she pursued them were exceptional; in this respect, as in other aspects of her cultural patronage, her activities do not represent the norm. But the philosophy which lies behind those interests, different in character and emphasis from that of patrons of her father's generation, became increasingly influential during the early decades of the sixteenth century. For Isabella music was, above all, a secular, social activity in which she was able to participate, an art to be practised as entertainment rather than merely listened to or promoted as an elaboration of the liturgy. What had been regarded by the mid-fifteenth century as a mere frivolity was now prized as an essential part of a courtier's education. Thus aristocratic practical involvement in music was elevated to the status of a serious enterprise through its association with idealized music, the power of music to influence human emotions, that lies behind the practical art. In this way music was not only entertainment, but also a means towards that balance and harmony of spirit that was one of the highest objectives of the Renaissance courtier.

In the politically uncertain world of sixteenth-century Italy, the fundamental cultural changes, mirroring political shifts, came after 1500 when papal Rome began to assume the leadership of the Italian courts both in terms of ambition and resources. Under Leo X, a musically informed holder of the triple crown, a court-like atmosphere encouraged the cultivation of new rather than eclectic forms of secular music, including settings of Petrarch's poetry. Despite the disruptions caused by the horrors of the sack of Rome, when many artists, writers and musicians fled the city never to return, the musical life of Rome had become firmly re-established by mid-century. Typically portrayed as a bastion of musical conservatism through its association with the music of Palestrina and his contemporaries, sixteenth-century Rome was in fact a cosmopolitan centre where cardinals from all over Italy and beyond built palaces and imported their own cultural tastes. Elsewhere there were also changes. As Naples and Milan came under foreign control, first French and then Spanish, they lost their cultural vitality. At Mantua and Ferrara, on the other hand, political stability ensured continuation of existing musical traditions, which can be observed undergoing processes of adaptation in the changed circum-stances of late sixteenth-century Italy, particularly at Mantua where the ultra-pious duke, Guglielmo Gonzaga, established the private family chapel of S Barbara with a separate rite and extensive provision for music. Apart from the distinctive case of republican Florence, Venice was the only major centre outside papal Rome and the princely courts where musical life flourished. Beyond the confines of the Italian states, the model of the Italian court provided a potent stimulus to the refashioning of musical life and institutions in the sixteenth century, as the examples of the French court during the reign of François I and of the Bavarian court during the time that Orlande de Lassus served as Kapellmeister so clearly demonstrate.

Throughout sixteenth-century Europe the courts appropriated not only power itself but also the propagandistic means through which it could be consolidated and perpetuated. This change of emphasis is evident everywhere. In the Middle Ages universities had been princi-pally founded to supply theologians for the church; the new colleges founded at Oxford and Cambridge in the sixteenth century were primarily intended to raise middle-class gentlemen (courtiers, diplomats and administrators), as well as divines, to staff what was now the state church. Similarly, most of the art produced during the medieval period was a form of propaganda for the church, even though through identifi-cation with local saints such images might also contain political resonances; now art was most often propaganda for the prince. Among court artists (or, more correctly, their patrons), the triumphs, victories and apotheoses of monarchs were now a fashionable theme. In Vasari's famous depiction of Cosimo I, Duke of Tuscany, painted on the ceiling of the Sala del Cinquecento of the Palazzo Vecchio (seat of the former republican government), the insignia of Florentine cities encircle the central image, with its unnerving echoes of the traditional iconography of the coronation of the Virgin (fig.9).

In terms of music, the example of Medicean Florence is particularly pertinent. Unlike papal Rome, Venice or the northern courts of Mantua and Ferrara, the Medici were not notable patrons of musicians in a consistent and systematic way. This was partly due to historical precedent; instead of maintaining a court chapel, the central organism of court music, the Medici continued their sponsorship of music at the cathedral, much as their forebears had done during the late fifteenth century. And although there were some resident musicians at court, the

9. *Apotheosis of Duke Cosimo I, by Giorgio Vasari (1511–74), painted on the ceiling of the Sala del Cinquecento of the Palazzo Vecchio, Florence*

major musical events in sixteenth-century Florence occurred when the family celebrated important dynastic occasions. These were done on a scale remarkable even by the standards of an age in which increasingly sophisticated technology and great financial resources combined to inspire elaborate private and public spectacles, as sanctioned by contemporary theories of princely magnificence. Typically such celebrations included processions and games to entertain the ordinary people, while banquets and plays were reserved for the élite of the city and visiting dignitaries. But customarily most effort and money was allocated to the production of a comedy supported, and later in the century often overshadowed, by spectacular *intermedi* involving music, elaborate lighting and decorative effects and complicated stage machinery. The 1589 *intermedi* to accompany the comedy *La Pellegrina*, devised to celebrate the marriage of Duke Ferdinando de' Medici to Christine of Lorraine, mark a highpoint in Medici cultivation of this particular form of the politics of spectacle and provide a striking example of the appropriation of the power of music itself in the interests of statecraft.

The subject of *intermedi* is music, or rather classical myths about neo-Platonic concepts of music, illustrated in allegories and through symbolic figures. Three of the *intermedi* deal with the supreme harmony of the cosmos, while the remaining three represent the power of human harmony. Giovanni de' Bardi was responsible for their *invenzioni*, or content, the complicated and detailed series of classical allusions upon which this vast edifice of musical and theatrical effects was constructed,

10. *The Descent of Rhythm and Harmony, the sixth intermedio in the 1589 performance of 'La Pellegrina': engraving by F. Succhielli*

while both the music and the choreography were directed by a Roman aristocrat, Emilio de' Cavalieri. Giulio Caccini and Luca Marenzio were among the many composers and performers employed to realize this elaborate conception.

There are many instances in sixteenth-century art where music functions as a symbol of a political system, as an image of consonance, perfect harmony. The general implications of this common idea for a reading of the 1589 *intermedi* are obvious, taking as they do the idea of the power of music as the basic material for the celebration of a dynastic marriage. There is also another set of contemporary ideas, derived from theories of princely magnificence, which are exploited in these *intermedi*. Magnificence, liberality and erudition were all thought of as regal virtues, and that belief is well expressed in a spectacle of great elaboration, based on classical myths. Also important is the Renaissance admiration of 'wonder' as an experience, and this was catered for in costumes, lighting and scenic effects. 'Wonder' was also a necessary ingredient of the music, which had to amaze the listeners through the virtuosity of the performers or the sheer size of the forces required.

These various threads come together in the final *ballo* of the 1589 *intermedi*. The scene, impeccable in its humanist credentials, is modelled on a passage in the second book of Plato's *Laws* which deals with the gods' gift of music and dance to the mortals. In the size of its conception

34

and the intricacy of its choreography, Cavalieri's dance is certainly full of 'wonder': the elaborate machines bring the gods from their clouds to the stage, and the brilliance of the costumes proclaims the magnificence of the provider of this particular feast for the eyes and the ears. In the final stanzas the allusions accumulate. The dance is already a symbol of authority and order. Now Plato's gods descending merge with the couple through whose union that authority and order will be extended and consolidated. In the final couplet the mere mortals in the audience are exhorted to join the gods in songs of praise celebrating the future of Medici power:

> Cantiam lieti lodando
> Christina e Ferdinando.

Thus, through the agency of music, celestial and terrestrial deities are conveniently fused and confused. There could hardly be a clearer demonstration of the appropriation by a ruler of the humanist notion of the power of music as part of the rhetoric of the politics of prestige, a vital ingredient in the business of ruling.

THE RISE OF THE BOURGEOISIE

Throughout the fifteenth and sixteenth centuries, courtly society acted as a behavioural model, not only for the diplomats, ecclesiastics and administrators who served it, but also for the upper reaches of the wider world. The rise of the middle classes was already a feature of life in the fifteenth century, and by the sixteenth it had become a phenomenon. In general, the new bourgeoisie were thought to occupy the terrain that lay between the two other classes: those who had to work for their living, on the one hand, and those at the top of the social and political system who lived off unearned income. Writing in 1613, the French jurist Loyseau refers to 'the Third Estate' when discussing this middle layer of society, and in 1560 the Parlement of Paris defined the bourgeoisie as being 'good citizens living in the cities, whether royal officials, merchants, people who live off rents, or others'. These two elements, the possession of substantial property and residence in towns or cities, define the bourgeoisie as the urban élite. Throughout the length and breadth of Europe this group became increasingly important in political and economic terms in the course of the sixteenth century, often to the distaste of the aristocracy. As a member of the Norman nobility writing about 1650 put it, 'Another kind of person has risen among us, born to bring about the ruin of others. It is they who have chased the two pillars of the state, the gentry and the peasantry, from their ancient holdings'.

How large was the bourgeoisie? Figures are hard to come by, and problems of definition make them difficult to interpret even where they exist; but nevertheless, there is a consistency in the pattern that emerges. In Norwich in the early sixteenth century the upper middle classes accounted for about six per cent of the population and owned about 60 per cent of the land and goods upon which the city raised taxes. In late sixteenth-century Venice the *cittadini* also comprised about six per cent of the total population. These are, of course, extremely crude definitions which tend to disguise the different types and status levels among the bourgeoisie. Beneath the 'good citizens' there was a lower level which consisted of minor officials, small traders and craftsmen, all of whom were of independent means; in early sixteenth-century Norwich this accounted for a further fourteen per cent of the population. The tax records of late seventeenth-century Beauvais show that of the 3250 families who paid taxes, some 300 constituted a middle stratum of society, and of these 100 formed an élite group. So while there was certainly regional variation, it would seem that the urban élite constituted a significant and growing percentage of the total population in European towns and cities in the sixteenth century. In as much as the data can be interpreted, it would seem that the expansion of musical literacy and practice, of which the growing market for music and books about music is a symptom, occurred for the most part within this stratum of society.

The members of this group had achieved their status through trade, finance and office holding. Perhaps the most familiar figure is that of the bourgeois merchant, a type already common in the medieval period, a man to be found in all the major industrial centres, seaports and market towns of Europe from Antwerp to Seville. Unlike those whose financial activities were firmly centred upon one place, the merchant trader had international horizons. By the end of the fifteenth century great trading communities had established themselves throughout Europe; the Florentines were to be found in Lyons and Antwerp, the Spanish in Nantes, the Genoese in Seville, the Netherlanders in the Baltic. The trade routes, the main arteries of communication, bore not only the main traffic in goods and diplomacy, but were also the principal channels of cultural exchange. In these places and elsewhere, the figure of the wealthy foreign merchant, with contacts throughout Europe, had become familiar.

A likeness of one of them has come down to us in one of the best-known of all fifteenth-century portraits, the so-called 'Arnolfini Marriage Group' in the National Gallery in London, painted by Jan van Eyck in 1434 (fig.11). In the foreground Giovanni Arnolfini (*d* 1472), a merchant from Lucca, raises his right hand as he prepares to take his solemn marriage vows; beside him stands his bride Giovanna Cenami. Above their heads the lighted candle symbolizes the presence of God, while a small dog (emblematic of marital fidelity) stands at Giovanna's feet; to one side stands the conjugal bed. Reflected in the

11. *The Arnolfini Marriage Group (1434) by Jan van Eyck*

mirror behind is the solid bourgeois interior of Arnolfini's house in Bruges, and the figures of the artist (who dated and signed the picture 'Johannes de Eyck fuit hic' above the mirror) and a business partner of Giovanna's father, both witnesses to the ceremony. From documents we know that Arnolfini lived in the parish of St James, one of the wealthiest parts of the city and a favourite district with many foreign merchants who lived in Bruges at the height of its commercial prosperity; there he was a prominent figure in church affairs and a member of a number of confraternities. From fairly humble origins as societies of ordinary citizens who met for prayer and undertook to provide for the spiritual and temporal needs of their members, these had grown to become clubs with a large membership which included members of the professions, the nobility and the court. Among Arnolfini's fellow members in the Franciscan confraternity of the 'Dry Tree' were Philip the Good and Isabella of Portugal, aristocrats, clerics and members of the Spanish, English and Italian communities. Here, in an arrangement remarkably free by fifteenth-century standards, members of different social classes worked and prayed together.

The confraternity of the 'Dry Tree' also included among its members a number of singers from the ducal chapel, and it may have been through contacts with them that Arnolfini made arrangements, towards the end of his life, to commission the large choirbook, copied and illuminated in the Bruges–Ghent manner, containing masses and motets by a wide range of northern composers including Dufay and the Englishman Walter Frye, whose music was popular on the Continent. Under the terms of his will, Arnolfini made provision for the newly founded chapel in the cathedral of his native city, where Lucca's most venerated relic, the *Volto Santo*, was kept, and the codex was evidently another gift to the chapel. With its repertory of English music from the period *c*1440–70 and Franco-Flemish compositions of a slightly later date, the history of the Lucca manuscript, of which only fragments now survive, is a good example of the way in which music or musicians might travel from northern to southern Europe as the result of commercial contacts; we may think of it as a musical equivalent of the famous Portinari altarpiece, painted by Hugo van der Goes on the instructions of the Medici agent Tommaso Portinari, and sent to Florence in about 1475.

Clearly it is no accident that many fifteenth-century music manuscripts are to be found today in towns and cities along the old trade routes, at Aosta, Milan, Basle, Regensburg, Kraków and, above all, at Trent. There the largest group of all has survived, some of them testimony to the musical interests, social status and contacts of Johannes Wiser, 'rector scolarum' at the cathedral school and later chaplain to Johannes Hinderbach, Cardinal-Archbishop of Trent. For beyond the rich merchant classes typified by Arnolfini and Portinari, music was increasingly becoming the concern of diplomats, ecclesiastics, aristocrats and intellectuals, influenced by the high status accorded to the art by humanist thought and the behavioural models provided by the princely courts. The ownership of music books is not necessarily a guide to genuine interest let alone practical skills (the motivations for Arnolfini's codex may have been no more than piety and commemoration), but it is indicative of an important social change that many late fifteenth-century sources both sacred and secular were copied for, and sometimes by, middle-class patrons. One important manuscript of early fifteenth-century polyphony now in Munich (the St Emmeram Codex) was copied by Hermann Potzlinger, a university-educated priest and bibliophile with a similar social profile to Johannes Wiser. The most lavish of all late fifteenth-century Italian chansonniers was first owned by a court official, Alessandro Braccesi, though it is unlikely that it was originally prepared for him. Of course, richly illuminated library copies of this kind may well have been valued and collected for non-musical reasons, but there are also examples of more everyday music books written for or by members of this growing middle-class élite audience.

By the early years of the sixteenth century, members of the bourgeoisie who had made their way in trade, land and office were interested in consolidating their gains both in terms of social status and political power, and it was this aspect of their influence which had the most profound effects upon cultural life throughout Europe. The history of that most characteristic of all sixteenth-century musical genres, the madrigal, is indicative of the extent to which a growing body of music could be shaped and adapted by these forces. In terms of its origins, the early Italian madrigal came out of Roman, and to a much greater extent Florentine, literary and musical circles in the 1520s; the principal composer at this stage was Philippe Verdelot, a northerner who had worked briefly in Rome before moving to Florence at the beginning of the decade. Before the adoption of the single-impression method by the Venetian printers at the end of the 1530s, this new and initially very local repertory circulated in manuscripts, just as fifteenth-century song repertories had done, though the earlier choirbook format had now been replaced by partbooks, one for each voice. The broad appeal of the early madrigal, stretching in social terms from princes to merchants, is reflected in the character and appearance of the sources, which range from the fine-quality illuminations and elaborate bindings of one set of partbooks, probably prepared as a diplomatic gift for Henry VIII from the last Florentine republic, to the fortuitous survival of the single sheets of paper which transmitted new pieces from one place to another, usually enclosed in letters.

One prominent Florentine merchant family, the Strozzi, exchanged the latest pieces as part of an extended family and commercial network which connected Florence, Rome, Venice and Lyons, very much a Florentine outpost in this period and itself a musical centre of some significance. Other families of similar status such as the Capponi, the Biffoli and the Sostegni were the original owners of surviving manuscripts. The impact of music printing was gradual rather than immediate, but from the 1540s onwards the Italian market for music of all kinds expanded greatly, and the madrigal and its various offshoots became the basis of amateur, bourgeois domestic music. This was true not only within Italy but also beyond, as printers in Paris and Antwerp made their own selections from Italian publications for their anthologies, designed for local middle-class tastes. Last to follow the pattern was London, where the composer and skilled entrepreneur Thomas Morley adapted the lighter Italian pieces of the 1580s and 90s to English words and thus laid the foundations of the brief but conspicuous popularity of the English madrigal. From London to Lisbon, Copenhagen to Coimbra, books of madrigals found their way into the libraries of the bourgeoisie.

Indeed, the example of expanding musical literacy in England during the period is a particularly striking one; it presents a pattern unlike any other in Europe. Our knowledge of English musical culture in the fifteenth century is severely limited by the poor survival of sources; it is significant that no major polyphonic manuscript dating from the period between the compilation of the Old Hall Manuscript early in the fifteenth century and the end of the century, when the Eton Choirbook was written, has survived. We are in consequence largely dependent upon fragmentary music manuscripts and scattered references to musical life in pay-registers, letters and literary descriptions. The picture that emerges from this admittedly uneven evidence is of a society in which, for the most part, polyphony was commissioned by institutions. The contrast with the situation in the later sixteenth century, a period which witnessed the effects of 'the educational revolution' in England, is dramatic. In the early decades of that century English musical culture continued to be centred on church and court, but information about aristocratic households, the universities and the Inns of Court suggests that from the early years of Elizabeth's reign there was a significant growth in English musical literacy and patronage.

The most important model for these developments was the Tudor court, the gateway to success and preferment. And, since the court was often in residence in London, the capital acted as a focal point for the nobility and ambitious bourgeoisie alike. It has been estimated that by 1560 half the peerage owned a London town house (a figure that grew considerably in the second half of the century) in addition to a country seat. As the century progressed, the network which connected the court to the grander country houses became an increasingly important channel for the expansion of musical life in the houses of wealthy families, such as the Cavendishes of Chatsworth and Hardwick, the Talbots of Welbeck and the Pastons of Norfolk. These developments were encouraged by education (the influence of courtesy books such as Sir Thomas Elyot's *The Boke named The Governor* and Castiglione's *Cortegiano*, published in an English translation by Sir Thomas Hoby in 1561, was considerable), by travel (particularly after 1588 when the psychological effect of the defeat of the Spanish Armada seems to have had a liberating effect upon English minds) and by the printing of instructional manuals and music books.

From about 1540, when a viol consort ('The Brethren Venetian') had been established at the court of Henry VIII, chests of viols begin to appear in the accounts of aristocratic households, as do payments to music tutors. Similarly, the earliest English printed book of lute instruction, translated from the French, appeared in 1568, and from about the same time there is a gradual increase in the number of surviving lute tablatures. This level of amateur interest in music, quite new in England, was also stimulated by the Reformation crisis, since the

12. *The long gallery at Hardwick Hall, built by Robert Smythson, 1591–7*

unfavourable attitude towards elaborate polyphony taken by the church forced many musicians to find employment in private houses. Among recusants – such as Edward Paston, whose extensive music collection included works for liturgical performance, or the Petres of Ingatestone in Essex, who had contacts with William Byrd – the employment of household musicians became part of the preservation of the old religion. And, for quite different reasons, the newly arrived members of the gentry and nobility were keen to cultivate music as part of establishing their status. By the 1570s there are firm indications of both a wider constituency for music (and of a more cosmopolitan taste) in the sudden increase in manuscript sources and by the revival, after a 40-year interlude, of English music printing. But, as this late flowering of music printing suggests (late that is by comparison with developments in Italy, France and the Low Countries), it was not until Elizabeth was well established on the throne that the growth of a musical élite outside court circles is really detectable.

Throughout the length and breadth of England, many visible symbols of this expansion of courtly style have survived, in the buildings of the ancient universities, the London Inns of Court and, above all, in the great country houses of Elizabeth's reign. Built by ministers and courtiers, administrators and political servants, the great houses are part of a cult of sovereignty, tangible expressions of loyalty. Many of them were built or specifically enlarged as places where the queen herself might be received during one of her royal progresses, to be palaces fit for Oriana and her retinue. Some music publications of the period were also overtly related to this cult, most noticeably the anthology *The Triumphs of Oriana*, put together by Morley and issued in 1601. But on a more general level the cultivation of the practice of music at court was now widely emulated in the upper echelons of society – at Longleat, Hardwick Hall, Burghley House – and in many lesser establishments, reaching down the social scale as far as the merchant and professional classes. In these environments music was written and performed, and it was for this audience that much of the madrigal and lute-song repertory was intended. Some of the more enlightened patrons employed musicians on a permanent basis; in the early seventeenth century the composer John Wilbye spent his entire career working for the Kytson family at Hengrave Hall, just outside Bury St Edmunds. The new importance of this domestic market for music is reflected in the character of many of the surviving manuscript sources, many of which were compiled as commonplace books filled with a mixture of music – sacred and secular, English and continental, vocal and instrumental.

The same is true of other collections of books and manuscripts from elsewhere in Europe. Many of the sixteenth-century music manuscripts now in the University Library in Basle were originally copied in the city for the private use and enjoyment of a fairly close-knit circle of local middle-class citizens, members of the Amerbach, Iselin and Hagenbach families. As might be expected, many of the books are substantially devoted to Tenorlieder, a corpus of songs by composers such as Hofhaimer, Senfl and Lassus, that made up the principal repertory of domestic music in German-speaking countries. But in addition to this kind of music, the Basle manuscripts also contain Italian madrigals and motets and French chansons – 'central' repertories of amateur song which had become popular, if only in untexted versions for instrumental performance, outside their areas of origin. A similar range of interests is revealed by the enormous music library, containing more than 450 printed books and many manuscripts, assembled by the Augsburg patrician Hans Heinrich Herwart (1520–83) and now in Munich. Herwart, a member of a prosperous commercial family with business interests all over Europe, gathered his collection from different sources in a number of countries. At a less grand social level, a small collection of manuscripts now in Heilbronn shows that similar tastes were cultivated by a local poet and teacher, Johannes Lauterbach (1531–93), who lived there. Such examples could be multiplied.

One phenomenon of bourgeois society with considerable importance for the expansion of musical life was the proliferation of the academies. The earliest groups of this kind were founded in Italy as a direct outgrowth of humanism; the first of any real significance was the so-called Accademia Romana which, having been established by Pomponio Leto in the 1460s, resumed its gatherings during the pontificate of Julius II in the gardens surrounding the villa of the poet Angelo Colucci. Here the major concerns were the discussion and promotion of the literature of classical antiquity and the presentation of Latin compositions, on antique models, by its members. Music was sometimes among the interests of the early academies; it played a major part, for example, in the life and thinking of Marsilio Ficino, founder of the Accademia Fiorentina. We know that he performed music both for his own relaxation and before the Medici, that he was concerned with aspects of ancient musical theory and that he composed a short treatise on the subject. Certainly by the early decades of the sixteenth century musical performances appear among the miscellaneous activities, literary and dramatic, of what were slowly becoming middle-class cultural clubs. Versification, orations and learned disputations formed the staple fare, but the more ambitious academies promoted theatrical productions which sometimes involved musical *intermedi*. One of the early and most famous of all Italian academies, the Intronati of Siena, founded about 1527, included all disciplines and the liberal arts among its exercises.

From the 1540s comes the first instance, in any country, of the foundation of an academy with specifically musical aims, the Accademia Filarmonica of Verona. The institution of the Accademia Filarmonica was a consequence of the rising social and cultural claims of a number of the arts, including painting, sculpture and architecture, to share in the prestige which had traditionally been allocated to literature, and to separate themselves from the crafts with which they had previously been associated. Analogous to the foundation of the Filarmonica, and symptomatic of the same socio-cultural pressures, was the formation by painters, sculptors and architects under the leadership of Giorgio Vasari of the Accademia del Disegno in Florence in 1563. An important aspect of both was that they offered instruction; the Filarmonica maintained a library and a large collection of instruments, both of which survive, and the activities of the members were directed and supervised by the composer Giovanni Nasco who was appointed for the purpose.

By the middle of the sixteenth century there were more than 200 academies in the towns and cities of Italy and many of them were engaged in some sort of musical enterprise from time to time. It was an academy, the Accademia Olimpica, which built the famous theatre on Greek models in Vicenza; the opening performance consisted of a translation of Sophocles' *Oedipus rex* with musical choruses by Andrea Gabrieli, from nearby Venice. It was often through membership of an academy that poets and composers might meet, and it is indicative that a number of madrigal publications are dedicated to academies.

Specialized academies continued to be founded in the second half of the century (Bardi's Florentine Camerata was an academy of a fairly informal kind); it was from within such circles that the interests were generated that led to the composition of Peri's *Euridice* (1600) and Monteverdi's *Orfeo* (1607).

Outside Italy the idea of the academy was imitated, though hardly on the scale of its country of origin. In Paris, Baïf, who was born in Venice, founded the Académie de Poésie et de Musique in 1570 together with Courville; its interests were encyclopedic (Baïf was a mathematician as well as a poet-musician), but one of its main concerns was the establishment of new musical styles through the study of ancient poetry. Its interests were therefore strongly humanist and broadly analogous to Bardi's Camerata, but in the case of the Académie, court support seems to have been stronger. For the marriage of his favourite, the Duc de Joyeuse, in 1581, Henri III of France organized a series of entertainments culminating in the *Balet comique de la Royne*, whose thematic material reflects the themes and images of the French monarchy during one of its most troubled periods. Known as the *Joyeuse magnificences*, these celebrations have roots in the *Magnificences* of the Valois court, but a major novelty was the widespread involvement of Baïf and other members of the Académie, notably the composer Le Jeune whose music for the occasion has survived. In England the functions of the academy were largely taken over by bodies such as the Inns of Court, who sponsored drama, literature and music as part of the 'new learning'. In the German-speaking world the Collegium musicum was similar in function to those Italian academies which were more concerned with performance than with aesthetic or philosophical matters. Historically, though, the Collegium was more akin to earlier associations of enthusiasts such as the Meistersinger, whose influence was still strong, as can be seen in the celebrated case of Nuremberg.

More numerous were the confraternities. These associations of the laity, who, placing themselves under the patronage of the Virgin, the Trinity, Corpus Christi or one of the saints, cared for the spiritual and temporal needs of their members, have a long history in the religious life of pre-Reformation Europe. Within this broad categorization various different types can be observed, from the humblest fraternity which might be able to do no more than arrange for a decent funeral for one of its deceased, to the wealthier institutions which were able to run schools and almshouses and to provide a good deal of practical help for poverty-stricken colleagues. Yet despite different emphases on penitential discipline, charitable works and liturgical observance, and considerable variety in income, the basic pattern of a pious society administered by laymen and open to both rich and poor was followed throughout Europe. Wealthy or not, the fraternities appointed their own clergy, sometimes in some numbers. At one extreme was Holy Trinity Coventry, which had a large membership including people from all over the country as well as foreign dignitaries, employed thirteen priests and owned the church of St John Bablake; but even the most modest confraternity would appoint a priest to guide them in the spiritual affairs which were their *raison d'être*. It is impossible to estimate how many confraternities there were in pre-Reformation Europe, but the numbers were large; London, for example, had 40 in the early decades of the century. North and south, in town and country, they played a conspicuous part in the religious, social and cultural lives of the communities they served.

The larger confraternities were usually in the major centres of population, and typically were dominated by local luminaries so that they effectively constituted the town government at prayer. Their social and economic functions were considerable, as were their resources. At Boston, Lincolnshire, the guild of St Mary had an annual income of over £900 in the mid-1520s, derived from lands and rents as well as members' subscriptions. In fifteenth-century Venice, the corporate funds of some of the *scuole grandi* such as S Marco and S Giovanni Evangelista, both of which had originated as flagellant societies in the thirteenth century, had grown so large that enormous sums were expended on the building and interior decoration of new meeting-houses. Giovanni Arnolfini was a member of two confraternities where he rubbed shoulders with other merchants, clerics and members of the aristocracy.

Although many members of confraternities might not be sufficiently wealthy to commission works of art or to endow charitable institutions individually, they were prepared to do so collectively. During the early sixteenth century, as urban confraternities increasingly turned into more élite groups with a higher concentration of wealthy members, this tendency became more marked. It was a confraternity in Milan which commissioned the *Virgin of the Rocks* from Leonardo da Vinci and the De Predis brothers; Corpus Christi in Urbino ordered the *Institution of the Eucharist* from Justus Ghent and the *Profanation of the Host* from Paolo Uccello. The growing wealth and influence of such fraternities is also reflected in their heightened interest in music, which developed beyond the performance of liturgical chants, and in Italy of the *laude* (vernacular religious songs), which had always been part of their traditions. From many different parts of Europe both statutes and archival documents, and in some cases the surviving music itself, testify to this development. One or two examples will have to suffice to represent a widespread phenomenon. A late fifteenth-century cantional from Jiřidrichuv Hradec, mostly given over to monophonic music in Bohemian chant notation, also contains a small number of polyphonic pieces; so too does a similar compilation from Hradec Králové. From 30 or 40 years later come three finely illuminated

13. The Feast Day of San Rocco (c1735) by Antonio Canaletto

manuscripts containing mass compositions; they were originally assembled for the confraternity of Our Lady at 's-Hertogenbosch whose continuing interest in elaborate music is revealed by three more manuscripts from a decade or so later.

The importance of the confraternities for the development of cultural and musical life of the towns and cities of Europe can be seen to spectacular effect in Venice, where the sumptuous building for the long-established Scuola di S Rocco, begun in 1515 and finally completed in 1549, was then decorated with an enormous cycle of canvases by Jacopo Tintoretto, a member of the *scuola*. In this magical if extravagant setting, musical events of increasing elaboration took place in the second half of the sixteenth century, particularly on major feast-days when the *scuola*'s own musicians were often supplemented by musicians from St Mark's; such traditions, firmly embedded into the civic and ritual life of Venice, the European city of processions and ceremonies *par excellence*, continued until the fall of the Republic. The history of the Scuola di S Rocco provides an untypically lavish example of the musical consequences of a generally observable social phenomenon: the urban confraternities throughout Catholic Europe came to be dominated by members of the bourgeoisie who, with resources to hand and in emulation of secular models both princely and corporate, cultivated more formal and sophisticated types of public ceremonial. By the early seventeenth century, when the English traveller Thomas Coryat heard music 'so good, so delectable, so rare, so admirable, so super excellent' at the Scuola di S Rocco, the buildings of these bodies, which had been founded as charitable organizations for the poor, had been transformed to become one of the visual wonders of the Republic.

THE GROWTH OF MUSIC PRINTING

Undoubtedly the most important structural element in that broadening of musical culture which is so characteristic of the sixteenth century was the much greater availability of music of all kinds made possible by the press. In the early decades of the century the reproduction of music began to move from the copyist's desk to the printer's workshop. As with all such revolutions, the rate of motion in the wake of Ottaviano Petrucci's 'invention' of music printing in 1501 was somewhat slower than is often assumed. Indeed the novelty of his technological achievement is in some respects more apparent than real, since the technique of producing different elements (staves, notes, text) by multiple impression had long been used by printers for the black and red layers of liturgical incunabula. Petrucci's books were evidently expensive to produce by comparison with most other kinds of printing, and a number of the surviving copies have retained original bindings of considerable beauty and elaboration, suggesting that they were regarded more as library copies than practical books. In terms of creating a market for printed music, it was not until the widespread adoption of single-impression printing, first used by the Parisian printer Pierre Attaingnant in 1528

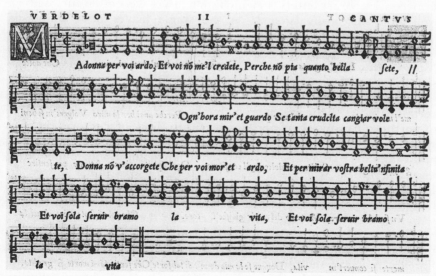

14. *Philippe Verdelot, 'Primo et secondo libro di madrigali' (Venice: Scotto, 1540); an example of single-impression printing (the divisions between the individual pieces of type are clearly visible)*

and then taken up (at first rather tentatively) by Italian printers some ten years later, that any sizeable constituency for printed music began to be formed. Attaingnant's process involved the reduction of music printing to a simple, one-stage operation; each symbol, whether clef, note, rest or accidental, was cast in a single piece of type that included a small section of staff, so that the compositor made up each line of musical text on a composing stick much as a literary text was set. In contrast to Petrucci's system, which required the sheets to be put through the press two or three times, this new method, enthusiastically and successfully exploited particularly by the Venetian firms of Scotto and Gardane, was much less expensive in terms of labour and time, though not of paper – still the most costly element in book production.

Yet even within Italy, some of the characteristic fifteenth-century patterns of transmission continued to operate until about the middle of the sixteenth century. The early madrigal repertories of Arcadelt and Verdelot, for example, largely circulated in manuscript during the 1520s and 30s, principally within Florentine aristocratic circles; it was only later that they were printed, and only after the success of Arcadelt's *Primo libro di madrigali a quattro voci* of 1538–9 (which is partly to be explained in terms of the adoption of single-impression printing and partly by the popularity of a single madrigal, *Il bianco e dolce cigno*), that the shift from script to print really begins to make an impact on the distribution patterns of much of this repertory. Until well into the sixteenth century, pieces continued to circulate if not in fascicle manuscripts, at least as single pieces often in part form; this is clear from contemporary letters (in which such pieces were often enclosed) as well as from survivals such as the single leaves now bound as 'partbooks' from the Herwart collection. Special cases excepted (such as the Sistine Chapel where manuscript choirbooks continued to be copied), the displacement of script by print was almost total by the second half of the century.

This is true for Italy, the larger urban centres of France and, certainly by 1600, the areas served by the presses of Susato and Phalèse in northern Europe. It is perhaps useful to think of a centre, roughly speaking an area bounded by Paris and Lyons to the west, Nuremberg and Frankfurt to the east, Antwerp to the north and Rome to the south, and a periphery where the impact of printing was much slower. In London, for example, printing made little difference to established traditions of transmission until the 1590s, and even then it co-existed with manuscript forms rather than replacing them.

The greater availability of music as a result of print culture now made it possible for individuals to acquire a great deal of 'new' or 'foreign' music on their travels. A spectacular example from early in the sixteenth century is that of Ferdinand Columbus, an obsessive bibliophile who bought books of all kinds as he travelled throughout Europe and kept meticulous records of his library. If it were not for Columbus, much of whose vast collection still survives in Seville despite the depradations of later centuries, our knowledge of the published musical repertories of the first two decades would be immeasurably poorer and our historical view radically different. After a somewhat tentative start, the commercial possibilities of the new technology were vigorously pursued within the central area, and by the second half of the century the buying and selling of music and theoretical works had become a considerable enterprise conducted on a European basis, as the catalogues of the Frankfurt book fairs, then as now the major showcase for publishers' wares, reveal.

At the centre of the trade stood Venice, a cosmopolitan city with a long-established tradition of printing. With a control of both a large overseas empire and important towns in the *terraferma* such as Vicenza, Verona and the old university city of Padua, the Republic also commanded extensive markets. The preservation of copies of Italian printed music in places along the Istrian and Dalmatian coasts (then part of the Venetian Terra da Mar) and the important collection of books and manuscripts bequeathed to the town library in Gdańsk (then Danzig, one of the Hanseatic ports) by Georg Knophius are just two examples which show how music could travel along established trade routes in some quantity. Indeed, traditional commercial patterns could profoundly affect musical taste. The case of the English enthusiasm for the Italian madrigal provides a good example. Many of the versions copied into English manuscripts from the 1560s onwards, after Elizabeth I's accession had secured both greater stability in the country and a more cosmopolitan cultural outlook encouraged by the example of the court, were taken from northern printed sources (particularly the anthologies produced by Phalèse in Antwerp) rather than from Venetian editions. Thus in music as in architecture, the English taste for the Italianate was acquired at one remove, already carefully filtered to accommodate the enthusiasms of Antwerp merchants. In this way, the long-established cultural links between England and the Low Countries, which extended back to the fifteenth century, were a conditioning factor upon English fashions.

Thus some of the old patterns of cultural contact and exchange continued. After the religious upheavals of the mid-century, the church and its administrative network no longer played such a dominant role in the supra-national dissemination of music, though it clearly continued to be of considerable importance. On the other hand, the bureaucracy of the Empire continued to function on this sort of scale, as the distribution pattern of manuscripts produced in the workshop of the singer, scribe and composer Pierre Alamire reveals. For much of the first half of the century presentation manuscripts continued to be copied for wealthy clients much as they had been previously, and a number of admittedly less elaborate examples have also survived from the second half of the century. Under Charles V, whose court still maintained a late medieval peripatetic existence, contacts between the imperial Flemish and Spanish chapels were clearly important for the north–south exchange of repertories. At the level of more occasional contacts, the diplomatic system continued to provide important channels for the exchange of music and musicians throughout the sixteenth century, much as it had done in the fifteenth. In terms of personnel, competition between states for the most talented performers and composers was often conducted through diplomatic agents; one consequence of this international trade was that musicians were themselves sometimes employed as spies. Alamire spent the years from 1515 to 1518 working at Mechlin in this capacity for Henry VIII, while at Henry's own court the Venetian organist Dionisio Memmo was busily engaged in espionage on behalf of the Republic. Many examples of this phenomenon could be cited and they are indicative of the increasing extent to which the musical profession was conducted across national boundaries. Again the pattern had been established much earlier, but in the sixteenth century it gathered strength.

At a more ceremonial level, political and dynastic alliances often continued to open up important lines of cultural communication, much as they had done in the fifteenth century. This may have occurred for example at the Field of Cloth of Gold in 1520, when it is recorded that the movements of a mass *De Trinitate* were sung by the French and English royal chapels alternately. In a world where ceremony and display were becoming a more important part of statecraft, these encounters often involved large forces of professional musicians rather than just the *alta cappella* more commonly found in the previous century. For example, it is known from documents in the Casa Real at Simancas that Philip II of Spain took a great number of musicians (including Antonio de Cabezón and Philippe de Monte) with him to England for his marriage to Mary Tudor in 1554. Although performances (whether of polyphony or plainchant is not clear) took place, the effect on English musicians was probably slight on this occasion. The same could not be said however in the case of another English royal marriage, that of James I to Anne of Denmark, the sister of Christian IV. In 1611 Jacob Ørn was sent to England together with Mogens Pedersøn, Hans Brachrogge and Martinus Otto to serve the queen. This fact is reflected in the appearance of Danish repertory in a number of contemporary English manuscripts as well as in the preservation of a complete set of the two volumes of Melchior Borchgrevinck's *Giardino novo* (Copenhagen, 1605/6) in the Royal Library (this is incidentally a good example of the spread of the Italian madrigal culture to the peripheries of its orbit). Perhaps the most spectacular example of all is that of the Scottish court, where the introduction of two French queens by James V (in

1537 and then 1538) inaugurated a period of French cultural dominance. In the case of music, this is exemplified by a repertory of
partsongs clearly indebted in style to the chansons of the Claudin
generation.

Important changes in government or political affiliation could have
profound cultural effects. The sack of Rome in 1527 created a diaspora
of artists at least within Italy, and many sought a haven in Venice, a
city comparatively undisturbed by internal and external strife. The fact
that Adrian Willaert mysteriously appeared in Venice in that year (as
did Francesco Sansovino and Pietro Aretino) to take up the appointment as *maestro di cappella* at St Mark's may be due to this as much as the
evident determination of the doge, Andrea Gritti, to seize the moment
and make of Venice a second Rome. Again within Italy, the persecution
of the Jewish communities in the papal states by the Inquisition only
served to consolidate the communities in more liberal places such as
Mantua or Ferrara, a fact which helps to explain the artistic richness
and diversity of these states in the late sixteenth century. It may also
explain the sudden influx of Italian musicians into Tudor England, for
many of them are now known to have been of Jewish extraction.
Persecutions elsewhere in Europe (whether religious or political)
produced similar movements of musicians who took with them their
own music and performance styles; one of considerable influence upon
the emergent music publishing business in Lyons was the group of anti-
Medici sympathizers grouped around Francesco de Layolle at the
Chapel of Notre-Dame de Confort, the church of the Florentine
community in the city. The defeat of the Spanish Armada by the
English in 1588 seems to have had a liberating effect on English
attitudes towards the Catholic countries on the Continent, just at the
very moment when enthusiasm for the Italian light madrigal was being
generated, partly by that entrepreneurial spirit Thomas Morley
(Nicholas Yonge's anthology of Italian madrigals 'Englished', *Musica
transalpina*, appeared in the same year). The growing fashion for
making what the eighteenth century was to call the 'Grand Tour' thus
reinforced and amplified an existing, imported style.

RELIGIOUS CHANGE

On 31 October 1517, an Augustinian monk nailed his '95 Theses' to the
door of the Schlosskirche in Wittenberg, thus proclaiming his wish to
debate the long-established and highly lucrative practice of selling
indulgences. That monk was Martin Luther, a professor of theology at
the local university, and his distaste for the commercialism and world-
liness of the church (which had been quickened by what he had seen
during a two-year stay in Rome) was no provincial matter. These theses
were quickly distributed throughout Germany and despite all attempts

to silence him Luther continued to oppose the ecclesiastical authorities. Then in 1520 he published three pamphlets which embody some of the fundamental ideas of the church that was eventually to bear his name; one is a powerful statement against the sacramentalism of the Roman Church, another argues against the power of the papacy and a third states that Christians are not bound by church law but are free to follow the teachings of the Gospel. Following Luther's excommunication by the Diet of Worms in 1521, he returned to Wittenberg the next year and there began to reorganize the church. Although this involved changing the form of worship, that was a minor consequence; in essence the Lutheran Reformation was involved with questions of doctrine and only incidentally with the content of ritual acts. Nevertheless, Luther's concern for the role of music in worship, which reflects not only his experiences in Rome (where he had encountered the music of Senfl and Josquin Desprez) but also his own skills as a singer and instrumentalist, is evident from his first liturgy, the *Formula missae* of 1523, designed for use in cathedrals and collegiate churches; a modified version of the Latin Mass, this retained the five parts of the Ordinary sung to plainchant. The introduction of German hymns, allowed for in the *Formula missae*, was rapid, and the early popularity of simple congregational music to vernacular texts is also evident from the publication of the *Deutsche Messe* in 1526, intended for ordinary church use.

Both these liturgies found favour, and both were flexible, as can be seen from the large number of *Kirchenordnungen* with both German and Latin elements that were issued in the course of the sixteenth century. While the composition of German hymns was a prominent feature of the Lutheran Reformation, and a great number of *Gesangbücher* were published from the 1520s onwards, it should not be forgotten that the plainsong element in Lutheran worship continued to remain strong in some places, particularly in the larger cities and university towns, as late as the eighteenth century. The interest in polyphonic music for Lutheran worship, such as Walter's popular *Geystliches gesangk Buchleyn* which was intended for use in both home and school, is not only a consequence of the new religious ideas which Luther and his followers promoted, but also indicative of the growing degree of musical literacy which the powerful alliance of Lutheranism and the printing press now encouraged. On a more popular level, the emphasis on congregational singing takes us into a world where written and unwritten traditions, popular and élite cultures meet; in this broad sense the experience of German-speaking countries in its reaction to reform was similar, both theologically and musically, to aspects of popular reform elsewhere in Europe, notably in England and Italy.

There are some obvious analogies with the consequences of the slightly later constitutional and religious crisis in England. There, during the period of the Henrician Reformation, the daily services continued to be said and sung in Latin, though some steps were taken to make them more comprehensible to the congregation. It was in other areas that changes took on a distinctly Lutheran tinge; relics and images were destroyed, pilgrimages discouraged and, most important of all, the 'Bishop of Rome's pretended power' denounced. In the main the effects were slight; the king's first objective was to enhance the power of the crown at the expense of the church, principally through the suppression of the monasteries and the appropriation of lands and goods, and it was not until after Henry's death in January 1547 that there was any serious attempt at a radical and thoroughgoing policy of liturgical reform. Within six months of Edward's coronation a Royal Visitation was instituted to secure the end of 'popish' practices, and restrictions were placed on the more extravagant forms of Latin service music; in their place, simple settings of English texts were encouraged. Music was a minor issue in the process of reform, but it did attract a good deal of criticism on the grounds of its expense and irrelevancy. An early, and in England influential, critic was Erasmus, and in his famous commentary on the New Testament he wrote about music in words strongly reminiscent of one of the sermons of the fifteenth-century Italian reformer and visionary, Girolamo Savonarola:

> St Paul says he would rather speak five words with a reasonable meaning in them than ten thousand in an unknown tongue. They chant nowadays in our churches in what is an unknown tongue and nothing else, while you will not hear a sermon once in six months telling people to amend their lives. Modern church music is so constructed that the congregation cannot hear one distinct word. The choristers themselves do not understand what they are singing, yet according to priests and monks it constitutes the whole of religion. Why will they not listen to St Paul? In college or monastery it is still the same: music, nothing but music.

By the time the first *Book of Common Prayer* came into use in England, in the summer of 1549, the major programme of liturgical reform had been completed, and with it many of the large choral foundations had been dissolved and their musicians dispersed. Nevertheless, some choirs survived through the brief period of the Marian reaction and into the Elizabethan period. At the queen's coronation in Westminster Abbey in 1559, the service followed its traditional course, and it seems that Elizabeth herself was at first prepared to allow considerable freedom of practice and belief within the framework of earlier legislation. In her own chapels, and above all in the Chapel Royal, the services were so far from the tastes of some of her more Protestant subjects that the Spanish ambassador wrote to Madrid confidently predicting another Catholic Reformation. The remarkable fact that the first book of printed music to appear under the terms of the royal monopoly, the

Cantiones sacrae of 1575 by Thomas Tallis and William Byrd, consisted of a collection of Latin motets with an elaborate dedication to the queen, can only be a reflection of the considerable latitude that existed in the Chapel Royal which both composers served. But outside the court, and particularly in the administrative circles of the English church, the spirit of Geneva was at large.

The effects of the Reformation upon English musical life may have been gradual, but they were undoubtedly decisive. In terms of institutions, the widespread disbanding of choirs and removal of church organs, allied to the economic inflation of the second half of the century, combined to impoverish the musical traditions of the cathedrals and larger churches. There is some evidence that, at least during the experimental period of the 1540s, Latin motets continued to be performed adapted to English words (a number of Tallis's pieces have survived in this form), but the general picture is of an accommodation to the new liturgical requirements through new composition in simplified polyphonic styles. The roots of this musical trend certainly lie partly in the past, but the Reformation now firmly focussed attention on the need for a comprehensive style which would allow the Scriptures to be presented in the simplest possible terms. By the middle of the century, at least a dozen composers, most of them working in London and at the Chapel Royal, were writing for the new English services.

The insistence on greater clarity of the Word, with everything that might imply for musical style, was not the exclusive property of the Lutheran and Anglican Churches. On the contrary, the Roman Church, influenced by past debates and humanist philosophy, turned its attention to musical issues as part of a more general movement of Catholic reform and resistance to Protestantism. In what can be seen as a series of reflex defensive actions, such phenomena as the foundation of the Jesuits, the Council of Trent and the crusading activities of the later sixteenth-century popes, were all related to this central concern. At the same time, rather than being merely a direct consequence of Protestantism, the Catholic Reformation had deep historical roots which went back to the *Devotio moderna* and the reforming spirit evident in some fifteenth-century monastic circles if not earlier.

In the history of Renaissance music, the question of the Council of Trent and its effect on the composition of polyphonic sacred music has long occupied a central position. The traditional starting-point, though not a particularly instructive one, is the Council's own *Canon on Music to be used in the Mass*, approved in September 1562, which then formed the basis for the abbreviated and imprecisely worded statement on the subject that subsequently became an official part of the Council's decrees. Its main conclusion was that music must serve to uplift the faithful, that the words should be intelligible and that secular elements should be excluded. In this rather general way the decree attempted to respond to a body of complaint about the complex and inappropriate character of much elaborate liturgical polyphony that had been growing among churchmen during the previous decades. Yet on the subject of what an appropriate sacred musical style should actually sound like, the Council was silent. This has been interpreted as an essentially negative approach, more concerned with reiterating common abuses than with recommending alternatives, but this is to misunderstand the relationship of the Council to the reformed institutions of diocesan church government who were envisaged as the instruments of many aspects of its policies. In common with some of its other pronouncements, such as the decree relating to painting and images, the Council's statement about music, which was in any case a rather peripheral aspect of the question of church reform, was never intended to be anything more than a series of general guidelines to be entrusted to local diocesan synods for clarification.

In this, as in other matters, it has become increasingly apparent that the reformation and revitalization of the Italian church was not wholly dependent upon papal initiatives. It is true that after 1560 the papacy willingly assumed the responsibilities of leadership that it had shirked before the pontificate of Paul III. A seemingly unending stream of special instructions were issued, nuncios and apostolic visitors were appointed to see that those instructions were carried out, reports were required from bishops during their visits, and a certain degree of uniformity was achieved by demanding compliance with the Tridentine decrees. The papal visitors in the decades after Trent did their utmost to enforce the decrees to the letter, even when they encountered tough-minded and powerful opposition. Nevertheless, the striving for uniformity did not preclude diversity in practice, owing to differences in the backgrounds and inclinations of the leading reformers. Certainly it cannot be assumed that the most famous *exemplum* of ecclesiastical reorganization, that of Carlo Borromeo in Milan, was a model that was widely adopted. This is as true of individual reactions to the decree on music as it is of other aspects of institutionalized reform, though it is also true that outside Rome the diocese of Milan provides the best-documented example of a local interpretation of the decree on music, largely because the matter was so actively pursued by Borromeo himself.

It was as part of his reorganization of the liturgy that Borromeo promoted the revision of the Ambrosian rite, despite some opposition from Rome where the general trend was towards the abolition of local liturgies. As for polyphonic music, the first Provincial Council, convened in Milan in the autumn of 1565, issued guidelines covering four main points. First, no secular melodies were to be used in the Divine Office, a reference to the common practice among composers of using *soggetti* from madrigals or chansons as cantus firmi in sacred pieces.

Next, music was to be used in church 'so that simultaneously the words shall be understood and the listeners aroused to piety'. Both these concerns are commonplace in the literature of complaint against contemporary church polyphony and appear in the Council of Trent's decree from which the Milan statement is clearly derived. Following these two major resolutions the Council went on to stipulate that where possible singers should be clerics, and that instruments other than the organ were to be banned in church. These more specific requirements typify Borromeo's strict views about the suppression of secular elements in worship. Nevertheless, in practical terms these resolutions took matters little beyond what Trent had stipulated, and Borromeo's real innovation was to promote composition of the type of polyphony which he believed to be in conformity with Trent's intentions, principally through the work of Vincenzo Ruffo, who had been in Milan as *maestro di cappella* at the cathedral since 1563. Ruffo's four-voice masses, published in Milan in 1570, in their adoption of a syllabic chordal style designed to make the words intelligible, are a clear response to Tridentine thinking. As Ruffo himself put it in his preface to the collection:

> in accordance with the decrees of the Most Holy Council of Trent I was to compose some masses that should avoid everything of a profane and idle manner in worship . . . Accordingly . . . I composed one mass in this way so that the numbers of the syllables and the voices and tones together should be clearly and distinctly understood by the pious listeners . . . later, imitating that example, I more readily and easily composed other masses of the same type.

Churchmen were not, of course, the only people in a position actively to encourage and experiment with styles of composition. Among princely patrons, the most startling example of interest in the question of a suitable polyphonic style for the liturgy is provided by the works commissioned for Duke Guglielmo Gonzaga's specially constituted ducal basilica of S Barbara at Mantua (fig.15). Here there is the added consideration that Gonzaga clearly conceived the project as a way of presenting and extending a particularly distinctive image of himself as the embodiment of the 'True Christian Prince'. The new church was planned as a dynastic temple, a theatre for Gonzaga politico-dynastic ceremonies, as well as a highly individual interpretation of Catholic reformist attitudes towards sacred art. Its special character, expressed through extraordinary papal privileges including a separate rite and prestigious positions for its clergy, unprecedented outside Rome, automatically conferred a status upon the institution which made it the envy of other Italian princes. And since the building, begun in 1562–3 when the last session of the Council was finally drawing to a close, was the particular brainchild of Gonzaga (who was also an amateur composer), it is not surprising that the recruitment of musi-

15. View of the high altar of S Barbara, Mantua, during the obsequies of Carlo II Gonzaga (1666): engraving Frans Geffels

cians and the composition of polyphony to conform with the special requirements of the S Barbara rite played an important part in the initial conception and were a major preoccupation during the early stages of planning, construction and operation. More than that, it is clear from Guglielmo's correspondence with composers both in Mantua and elsewhere, from his own compositions and from works (such as Palestrina's 'Mantuan' masses) commissioned for S Barbara from others, that these pieces are consistent in their restraint, their use of cantus firmi taken from plainsong, their concern for clarity of text, their emphasis upon old-fashioned contrapuntal skills and their avoidance of extravagant representational devices and adventurous effects. This is the best-documented example outside Milan of reformist ideas about music and liturgy being put into practice, for all that Gonzaga's motives were undoubtedly complex and embraced secular as well as spiritual concerns.

16. Interior of the Oratory of S Filippo Neri, Rome, built by Borromini, 1637–50

The example of Duke Guglielmo Gonzaga in Mantua is an extreme version of the musical consequences of the appropriation of reformist ideas whether for reasons of genuine piety or in the interests of state-craft. This general idea was clearly attractive to rulers both inside and outside Italy (the case of the Munich court comes to mind), but again the practical effects are limited to a handful of compositions. To these should be added the taste for publishing contrafacta of secular pieces, a practice which was largely associated with reformist centres, but the instances are again few. In general, artistic traditions seem to have remained comparatively undisturbed by local interpretations of the spirit of Trent. It is true that Trent itself was the culmination of a body of complaint about sacred polyphony that dates back at least as far as the late fifteenth century (with precedents going back to the twelfth), but these earlier pronouncements, which are usually of the most vague and unspecific kind, occur almost as a rhetorical gesture and seem to have had little practical effect. Except for a handful of special cases, the Council of Trent had as little practical effect on the various styles of liturgical polyphony that continued to be composed and performed throughout Europe as it did on other arts.

In addition to the tradition of conciliar concern with the character of sacred music, there was another reformist tendency at work; its roots lie in late medieval monasticism, but its effects in the second half of the sixteenth century were potent. That is not to suggest that this development, which found an effective and coherent voice for the first time during the Savonarolian interlude in Florence between 1494 and 1498, did not interact with the polyphonic tradition which, initially at least, it set out to counterbalance. On the contrary, it was the combination, in the fertile soil of mid-century Rome, of a Savonarolian aesthetic and the skills of professional musicians attuned to that philosophy, that produced a more characteristic and influential body of 'reformist' music than either Ruffo's masses for Borromeo or Palestrina's for Guglielmo Gonzaga. A consideration of these two differently motivated and constituted attitudes, the one conciliar, the other monastic in origin, emphasizes that there were different reactions, at different times and in different places, to the question of musical reform; it underlines the unhelpfulness of some cherished distinctions between sacred and secular music and written and unwritten traditions and also reveals the extent to which the importance of the musical aspects of more popular forms of devotion have been underestimated. This is clearly true in the case of Rome, where the emphasis has traditionally been on the contributions of Palestrina and his contemporaries, working in the major churches of the city and composing in the central polyphonic tradition. Against this must be placed the music cultivated in the oratories, whether simple monophonic *laude* or more elaborate pieces, judged not simply as the precursors of the early oratorio but rather as the direct descendants of late fifteenth-century Florentine traditions. These powerful connections between Savonarola's philosophical attitudes and the emergence of early Oratorian ideas towards music in the circles around Filippo Neri in mid-century Rome have been underestimated. Appreciation of their importance underlines not only the continuing influence of Savonarolian thought on music and the arts in sixteenth-century Italy, but also, at a more practical level, the strong repertorial bonds between the Florentine and Roman *lauda*. In this sense Florence and Rome, Neri and Savonarola, represent the twin poles of an axis along which music and composers travelled united by a common set of ideas about the position of the art in a reformed church.

The *lauda* was usually a simple vernacular sacred song performed congregationally. Originally it had been associated with the Franciscans and particularly with the many confraternities that had been founded in Umbria and Tuscany during a wave of penetential fervour in the second half of the trecento. Most of the early *laude* are monophonic, but polyphonic examples survive from as early as the end of the fourteenth century and are scattered extensively throughout fifteenth-century sources, both monophonic and polyphonic. It seems likely that the more elaborate examples of the type were performed by the professional or semi-professional performers, the *laudesi*, that have been documented for various parts of Tuscany and were particularly strong in Florence during the quattrocento, while the simpler, monophonic *laude* were sung congregationally. There was no sequential development from monophonic to polyphonic varieties; they co-existed, and the overwhelming presence of the more elaborate versions from the fifteenth- and sixteenth-century sources has more to do with the difference between written and unwritten traditions and with the patterns of survival than with the evolution of a genre. Similarly, the two species are intimately related in their musical material, the melodies from the monophonic traditions often providing the starting-point for more elaborate polyphonic elaborations. Nor can it be assumed, in a period of growing musical literacy and sophistication, that the two categories necessarily represent 'amateur', 'congregational' or 'popular' music on the one hand and professionally produced decoration for communal worship on the other. Although *laude* were often sung in church, they have no liturgical function but were sung in monasteries and convents in the course of daily devotions in public religious processions; sometimes they were incorporated into the *sacre rappresentazione* that were such a feature of Florentine life during the fifteenth and sixteenth centuries. To a greater extent than any other kind of music that has come down to us, the *lauda* was closely woven into the fabric of Florentine social, religious and civic life.

By incorporating the *lauda* into his daily 'spiritual exercises', Neri was clearly drawing upon his own experience of Florentine traditions, but from the early days of the Oratory the music that was performed there began to depart from the roots of those traditions in a number of significant ways. While simple monophonic *laude* continued to be sung congregationally, much as they had been in Florence during the Savonarolian period, more complex polyphony (of the kind that Savonarola so vehemently criticized) was also performed. And in addition to elaborations of traditional *lauda* melodies, specially composed pieces were also now written. These developments, which took the *lauda* away from its late fifteenth-century social functions and monophonic simplicity, are largely to be explained on the evidence of contemporary observers of the Oratory by two important social factors: the involvement of professional musicians in the affairs of the congregation and the changing character of the crowds who flocked to the Oratory in ever-increasing numbers during the 1560s and 70s. In effect, that process which was ultimately to take every aspect of the Oratory's activities away from the emphasis on simplicity, which is such an essential feature of Neri's philosophy, had already begun in response to the tastes of the bourgeois and aristocratic congregations which now began to attend the Chiesa Nuova. In this sense some of the social forces which contributed to the emergence of such characteristically 'Baroque' forms as the oratorio and, above all, to the opera, were present here as elsewhere.

★

In a famous passage in his *Liber de arte contrapuncti* (1477), Tinctoris wrote:

> At this present time . . . there flourish, whether by the force of some celestial influence or by the force of assiduous practice, countless composers, among them Jean Ockeghem, Jean Regis, Antoine Busnoys, Firmin Caron, and Guillaume Fauges, who glory in having studied this divine art under John Dunstable, Gilles Binchoys, and Guillaume Dufay, recently deceased . . . As Virgil took Homer for his model and that divine work the Aeneid, so I, by Hercules, have used these composers as models for may modest works.

One interesting feature of this list is the absence of Italian names. For while in many fields such as philosophy, science, architecture, painting and sculpture, the early Renaissance is conceived as a primarily Italian phenomenon, in music it was principally a northern development. It is true that the papal chapel, the Aragonese court and the Este and Gonzaga families in Ferrara and Mantua all sponsored music, sometimes on an elaborate scale, as the essays in this book reveal, but the musicians they employed were often *oltramontani*, men from beyond the Alps. Dufay, born in Cambrai, worked for the Malatesta in Rimini in the 1420s, later in Rome, and was commissioned to write by the Medici. Josquin was employed in Milan in the 1460s and subsequently held appointments in Rome and Ferrara before returning to his homeland. At the less exalted level of ordinary singers and instrumentalists these examples could be multiplied many times, and this pattern continued well into the sixteenth century. Of the major composers of the early Italian madrigal (Verdelot, Arcadelt and Costanzo Festa), only one was a native Italian, and as late as the 1560s some of the major positions in the Italian musical world were still filled by northerners such as Willaert in Venice and Giaches de Wert in Mantua. The domination of northern composers and performers in Italian musical life is in turn reflected by the predominance of their music in Italian sources. In this sense one centre of the early Renaissance musical landscape was in the north, for it was in that environment that much of their music was written. At the same time, many made the trip south, no doubt attracted by the wealth of the Italian courts and the centrality of Rome in European cultural and religious life.

During the second half of the sixteenth century, for reasons that have been touched upon elsewhere in this introduction, this historical pattern altered. By 1600 Italian composers, trained on home territory, were prominent, while Venice and Rome (though not the Este court, which had now entered a period of terminal decline, an example shortly to be followed at Mantua) retained their positions as important centres of musical culture to which foreigners now gravitated. In Venice Schütz studied with Monteverdi.

This example is characteristic of a general phenomenon of shifting relationships not only between north and south, but also between other urban centres which lay outside this orbit, sustained, conditioned and encouraged by the supra-national system of musical contacts which is typical of the period as a whole. In these circumstances to speak of a distinction between 'centre' and 'periphery' is not as relevant as it may be for earlier periods. The English madrigal in its earliest phases is modelled, even in a plagiaristic way, upon actual Italian examples, but it is not true that all English composers were in the thrall of Italian music (William Byrd, for one, was not), nor that English traditions, for all that they had been disturbed by the religious and constitutional crises of the mid-century, did not possess a currency of their own. For despite the tendency towards greater stylistic uniformity that greater communication and the power of the printing press might be thought to have encouraged, local and national traditions continued to be just as distinct and vibrant as they had been during the era of manuscript transmission. The greater availability of music by the end of the period, and the increased exchange of repertories that the press made possible, does not fundamentally alter the fact that the composition, dissemination and performance of music should be regarded primarily as processes conditioned at every level by political and social factors. It is the examination of those factors, to which essays in this book make a contribution, that will lead historians towards a richer and more convincing explanation of some of the more important characteristics of the music of the Renaissance.

Chapter II

Rome: a City of Rich Contrast

CHRISTOPHER REYNOLDS

There are two popular images of musical life in Renaissance Rome. The Rome of Leo X looms as a vibrant, international arena in which Italian and northern musicians composed and performed in a variety of sacred and secular styles; this contrasts easily – too easily, perhaps – with the image of Rome during the Counter-Reformation as an austere, conservative city, best represented by the uncomplicated devotional music of the *lauda* and by the controlled polyphony of Palestrina. While the earlier period contributed to the birth of the Italian madrigal, the legacy of the latter was the Baroque oratorio and the stylized ecclesiastical counterpoint of the *prima prattica*. However, these opposing images are too sharply drawn, the contrast between them oversimplified. As a city Renaissance Rome was too large, its sources of musical patronage too diverse for any one style to dominate. Josquin, the Greek organist Isaaco Argyropulo and the Florentine humanist Aurelio Brandolini were contemporaries in late fifteenth-century Rome, as were Marenzio, Palestrina, Girolamo Mei and S Filippo Neri a century later. Each possessed distinct musical convictions. All of them contributed substantially to the musical life of the city.

Many aspects of Roman culture were inherently conservative. Erasmus attacked Rome in 1528 for glorifying its pagan heritage, and in so doing he linked the traditional papal concern for religious orthodoxy to a more recent emphasis on linguistic orthodoxy among Roman humanists. Whatever their regional backgrounds, scholars in Rome valued uniformity to an extent uncharacteristic of Florentine humanism. They gave classical models an absolute authority in matters of style, turning to Cicero for prose and to Virgil for poetry. Likewise, theological treatises and sermons emanating from the papal court already showed a consciously conservative intent by the end of the quattrocento.[1] In architecture the remnant edifices of Rome's pagan past shaped contemporary styles, despite the abundance of Tuscan architects, and the writings of Vitruvius guided architects long before Roman humanists formed the Accademia dell Virtù to initiate a complete edition in the 1540s.[2]

Conservatism in each case depended on the existence of an older

Roman model. Because musicians could not turn to ancient models for inspiration in the same way as poets, theologians, architects and artists, musicians in Renaissance Rome initially enjoyed an exceptional freedom to embrace foreign styles. The latest French and Flemish polyphonic compositions resounded in Roman churches, while Florentine and northern Italian poet-musicians entertained Rome's humanistic circles. These secular improvisers at least had ancient texts to emulate, as well as verbal descriptions of how and when certain types of music should be performed. Although Rome now has a reputation for being musically conservative during the Renaissance, this reputation is in many respects unwarranted. In order to determine which aspects of Roman musical life were conservative, we must first establish when distinctively Roman styles and practices developed.

The difficulties of identifying an emergent Roman style are twofold. On the one hand, it is hard to discuss generalized Roman features in isolation from local institutional practices. The traditions of the Cappella Sistina are the most visible to us today, but they are unique to that institution. Rome possessed an extraordinary number of music patrons, both individual and corporate, private and public, each with distinct stylistic and performance traditions. On the other hand, a Roman style must be viewed in the wider context of the regional and national styles that took shape throughout Europe during the sixteenth century. Music in this instance differs sharply from the visual and plastic arts. With each passing decade in the sixteenth century, Italian painting 'became less regionally differentiated',[3] due in large measure to the proliferation of engravings and drawings. Yet despite the impact of printing on the circulation of Renaissance music, Italian and European compositional styles assumed ever more distinct regional identities. Palestrina was only one of several Roman composers to publish substantial numbers of works in Venice after 1550, precisely the period when a Venetian style asserted itself.

MUSICAL INSTITUTIONS AND PATRONAGE

The uncommon breadth of musical opportunities in Rome stems from the unique structure of Roman society. At other Italian courts the line of power often flowed directly from the dynastic ruler, whether a king (Naples) or a duke (Milan, Ferrara and elsewhere). However, in Rome the pope presided over his own extensive *famiglia*, and also the large, compartmentalized bureaucratic court, the Roman curia, that included between twenty and 50 resident cardinals, each with his own household. During the century between the papacies of Pius II (1458–64) and Paul IV (1555–9), the number of courtiers and servants in the papal family grew more or less steadily from about 150 to more than 1000; and by 1520, under Leo X, the officials in the curia numbered well in excess of 2000. Social interaction was as a consequence rigidly hierarchical. Genius could quickly be recognized and rewarded in smaller Italian courts, but in Rome personal stature often depended less on individual talent than on having reliable and highly placed friends within the curial hierarchy.[4] Palestrina acquired an unusually influential connection at the very beginning of his career. He was probably not yet 25 when the Bishop of Palestrina, Cardinal Giovanni del Monte, became Pope Julius III in 1550. By the end of the next year Palestrina was chosen to lead the Cappella Giulia, the prestigious music chapel of St Peter's. The source of his patronage is plainly stated in a disapproving report of his appointment to the papal choir in 1555: he became a member 'on the orders of his Holiness Pope Julius, without any examination . . . and without the consent of the singers', and despite his being married. Surely Palestrina merited these posts, but Julius is also the pope who rewarded the fifteen-year-old keeper of his pet monkey by making him a cardinal.

Rome owed its international musical connections to the curial bureaucracy. Cardinals and other church dignitaries, diplomats to the Holy See, wealthy pilgrims, bankers – all contributed to the comings and goings of musicians, music and even instruments. Examples of musical exchanges and interaction abound. Some encounters resulted in new compositions. The Flemish Jacquet de Berchem wrote his madrigal *Glorioso pastore* (1555) for a Spanish prelate in Rome, probably the Inquisitor-General, Juan Alvarez de Toledo. Lassus is thought to have met the British cardinal Reginald Pole during his Roman stay, leading to his motet *Te spectant Reginalde Poli* (1556). The very transience of many musicians and patrons assured a steady flow of the latest compositional styles, turning Rome into a clearing-house for music and performers. In the 1480s musicians from Siena journeyed to Rome, rather than nearby Florence, to search for sacred music. Ferdinand Columbus purchased a Neapolitan chansonnier while he visited Rome in 1515. From Lyons the banker Luigi Sostegni in 1538 delivered several works of Francesco de Layolle to Rome, where they were received by the poet Annibale Caro, and Palestrina sent a group of masses to Munich with Cardinal Otto, Lord High Steward of Waldburg. Foreign musicians also knew that in Rome they could not only find Roman patrons, but patrons from courts throughout the Italian peninsula. The papal court had its share of agents from Ferrara, Mantua and elsewhere, reporting the arrival of talented performers and composers, relaying evaluations – their own and hearsay – about everything from the size of a singer's voice to the likely terms of employment.

For musicians seeking patronage in Rome the most desirable posts were those closest to the pope: a position either in the papal choir or in the pope's group of private musicians. After Martin V returned a unified papacy to Rome in 1420, he maintained a choir of nine to four-

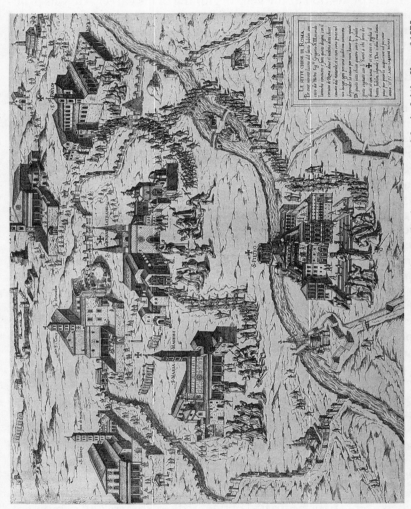

17. *The Seven Churches of Rome, a pilgrims' guide, showing this devotion, engraved for the Jubilee Year of 1575: engraving from Antoine Lafrey, 'Speculum romanae magnificentiae' (1575–83)*

teen northern musicians, many of them, including Dufay, from the diocese of Cambrai. The subsequent growth of the choir mirrored that of the court as a whole, step by step. Once papal coffers had been enriched by pilgrims attending the jubilee celebrations of 1450, Nicholas V (1447–55) expanded the choir to eighteen; Sixtus IV (1471–84) rebuilt the *cappella grande*, known since as the Cappella Sistina, and staffed it with up to 25 singers; no pope exceeded this total until the music-loving Leo X (1513–21) employed 31, making it one of the largest choirs in Italy. In the decades that followed the golden years of Leo's papacy, the size of the papal choir normally oscillated between 22 and 24 voices. In addition to his chapel choir, Leo also maintained a separate group of up to sixteen *musici segreti* – that is, singers and instrumentalists for his personal amusement at banquets, theatrical events, hunting expeditions and the like. Although he gave these private musicians an unaccustomed prominence, his predecessors and successors also seem to have supported organists, singers and instrumentalists for many of the same purposes.

Perhaps because the papal financial records are relatively accessible and well organized, too much emphasis has been placed on the influence individual popes exerted over music in Rome. Other than Sixtus IV and Leo X, whose contributions to music were unrivalled, there were also popes with notorious disinterest in music and the other arts, chiefly Calixtus III (1455–8), Adrian VI (1522–3) and Paul IV (1555–9). Most popes, however, fell between these extremes. Dufay served under two popes who had little time for artistic pursuits; Josquin surfaced during the pontificate of Innocent VIII, a weak pope politically and physically; and Palestrina had a distinguished career at three Roman basilicas, despite being ejected from the Cappella Sistina by Paul IV because of his marriage. It was not the popes alone, but the diversified network of curial patronage that attracted generations of musicians, for while popes generally retained two or three dozen musicians, other Roman patrons attracted scores, if not hundreds, more.

The social life of Rome revolved round the households of the curial cardinals. As 'senators' of the Roman court, cardinals were expected to maintain a conspicuously lavish way of life, the better to promote the *magnificentia* of their high station. In his treatise *De cardinalatu* (1510), the humanist Paolo Cortese advised cardinals to maintain households of about 150 servants, cooks, artists, silversmiths, musicians and others, and, to house them all, a private palace that should include a well-stocked library and a music room furnished with hollow vases to enhance the resonance of performances. By Cortese's time the nationality of cardinals living in Rome was overwhelmingly Italian, with each of the major ruling families represented by at least one member. From Milan came Ascanio Sforza, patron of Josquin and Serafino dall' Aquila; from Ferrara, Willaert's patron Ippolito I d'Este; and from

Florence the future pope, Giovanni de' Medici, appointed cardinal at the age of fourteen. Letters and archival evidence suggest that French and Flemish singers often came to Rome in the company of a northern cardinal; once there, they appear just as often to have attached themselves to an Italian patron. The reverse situation, an Italian musician in the family of a French cardinal in Rome, seems to have been comparatively rare. Alfonso Ferrabosco's service with Cardinal Charles de Guise in 1559 is perhaps the earliest-known example and it is just one indication of the declining availability of French musicians in Rome.

As sponsors of the arts, cardinals provided an element of continuity in an otherwise transient city. Papal interests and policies could change drastically with the death of one pope and the election of another, as when Adrian VI replaced Leo X or Paul IV followed Julius III. When Paul II (1464–71) showed little patience for the humanists that Pius II had encouraged, cardinals sustained them; and even in the strictest days of Counter-Reformation Rome, there were always a few cardinals bent on preserving customary levels of artistic display. Cardinal Ippolito II d'Este began the construction of the opulent Villa d'Este at Tivoli in 1560, including in his famous gardens a water organ. By the late 1560s, just as reforms and cutbacks in the papal *famiglia* had limited the scope of many cultural events in Rome, Palestrina was among those who found respite with Cardinal d'Este in nearby Tivoli. According to the French humanist Marc-Antoine Muret, the cardinal kept 'a house crammed by learned men from whose society and conversation one was always learning something'.[5]

Aside from the Cappella Sistina, several Roman churches and basilicas had important music chapels. Chief among these, and chronologically the first, was a chapel at the Vatican basilica, St Peter's. Founded by Julius II in 1513, the Cappella Giulia was initially much the same in size and national diversity as the choir St Peter's had employed since the mid-1400s. Its charter called for twelve adult singers and as many boys, together with a *maestro di cappella* and a *magister puerorum*. While the number of boys never came close to this goal (see below), the Cappella Giulia provided a model for the chapels subsequently founded at the basilicas of S Giovanni (1535) and S Maria Maggiore (by 1537). Additionally, there were choirs at many Roman churches – notably at the so-called French 'national' church, S Luigi dei Francesi (from 1515) – and at other religious institutions such as the Ospedale di S Spirito, the Seminario Romano and the English and German colleges.

Many Italian singers and composers, Palestrina among them, received their childhood training in these choirs. In the first half of the sixteenth century the instructor was most often a French or Flemish *maestro di cappella*. But after 1550 Italians were increasingly chosen to lead the major Roman chapels. Table II.1 lists the *maestri di cappella* of

Table II.1 MAESTRI DI CAPPELLA OF ROMAN CHAPELS TO *c*1580

Maestri di cappella	Period of office
Cappella Giulia	
Silvestro	*c*1519 – ? Feb 1526
Silvestro de Angelis	Nov 1534 – 1537–9
*Jacobus Flandrus (Arcadelt?)	1 April 1539 – 30 Nov 1539
*Rubino Mallapert	1 Dec 1539 – 31 Jan 1545
Johannes Baptista	1 Feb 1545 – 31 March 1546
Domenico Ferrabosco	Feb 1546 – Dec 1547
*François Roussel	12 Feb 1548 – 26 Feb 1550
*Rubino Mallapert	26 Feb 1550 – Sept 1551
Giovanni Pierluigi da Palestrina	1 Sept 1551 – 13 Jan 1555
Giovanni Animuccia	Jan 1555 – 20 March 1571
Giovanni Pierluigi da Palestrina	April 1571 – 2 Feb 1594
S Giovanni in Laterano	
*Rubino (Mallapert)	*c*1535 – June 1538
	1 Oct 1548–30 Nov 1549
Paolo Animuccia	Jan 1550 – 1552
*Orlande de Lassus	spring 1553 –
Bernardino Lupacchino	1553 – 1555
Giovanni Pierluigi da Palestrina	1 Oct 1555 – July 1560
Annibale Zoilo	16 Jan 1568 – 30 June 1570
*Bartolomeo (Le) Roy	July 1570 – 31 Dec 1571
*François Roussel	11 Oct 1572 – 10 May 1575
Annibale Stabile	Sept 1575 – May 1576
Giovanni Andrea Dragoni	June 1576 – Dec 1598
S Maria Maggiore	
*Rubino Mallapert	13 June 1538 – 24 April 1539
Robert	1540 –?
*Firmin Lebel	1540 –?
*Adrien Valent	?1553 – 1561
Giovanni Pierluigi da Palestrina	March 1561 – 1564 or 1566
Giovanni Maria Nanino	prob.1567 – 24 April 1575
Ippolito Tartaglini	10 Oct 1575 –?
Orazio Caccini	1577 –?
S Luigi dei Francesi	
*Desiderius Babel	Nov 1515 – 31 Aug 1519
*Jacques Level	1 Oct 1519 – 31 March 1521
*Johannes Lhéritier	28 July 1521 – 31 Aug 1522
*Jacques Du Pont	1536 – 31 Jan 1538
*Rubino Mallapert	25 April 1539 – 30 Nov 1539
*Henri Ouldin	1 Dec 1539 –? 1543
*Firmin Lebel	25 Oct 1545 – 30 Sept 1561
Annibale Zoilo	5 Oct 1561 – 11 Aug 1566
*François Roussel	1 Dec 1566 – 26 March 1571

*Stephanus Toustain	27 March 1571 – 17 Dec 1571
*Bartholomeus Le Roy	3 Jan 1572 – 20 April 1575
Giovanni Maria Nanino	26 April 1575 – 30 Oct 1577
Giovanni Pellio	2 Dec 1577 – 30 April 1578
Francesco Soriano	4 May 1578 – 31 Jan 1581

Collegio Germanico

Tomás Luis de Victoria	24 Oct 1571 – 1577
Francesco Martini	20 Sept 1577 – 31 May 1578
Annibale Stabile	*c* July 1578 – *c* Feb 1590

Collegio Inglese

Monte (Cola Nardo de ?)	? – Sept 1579
*Bartolomeo Le Roy	Sept 1579 – 9 Aug 1581

Seminario Romano

Giovanni Pierluigi da Palestrina	1566 – 1571
Tomás Luis de Victoria	1571 – *c* June 1573
Pietro Paolo Lanza	1573 – 1576
Paolo Vicuaro	1577 – ?
Pietro Amico Jacobetti	1579 – 1583

* denotes a northerner

Table II.2 SINGERS WHO SERVED AS MASTERS OF MORE THAN ONE ROMAN CHAPEL

Singer	Roman chapel	Period of office
Firmin Lebel	SMM	1540 – ?
	SLF	25 Oct 1545 – 30 Sept 1561
Bartolomeo Le Roy	SGL	July 1570 – 31 Dec 1571
	SLF	3 Jan 1572 – 20 April 1575
	Col I	Sept 1579 – 9 Aug 1581
Rubino Mallapert	SGL	*c* 1535 – June 1538
	SMM	13 June 1538 – 24 April 1539
	SLF	25 April 1539 – 30 Nov 1539
	SP	1 Dec 1539 – 31 Jan 1545
	SGL	1 Oct 1548 – 30 Nov 1549
	SP	26 Feb 1550 – Sept 1551
Giovanni Maria Nanino	SMM	prob. 1567 – 24 April 1575
	SLF	26 April 1575 – 30 Oct 1577
Giovanni Pierluigi da Palestrina	SP	1 Sept 1551 – 13 Jan 1555
	SGL	1 Oct 1555 – July 1560
	SMM	March 1561 – 1564 or 1566

	Sem R	1566–1571
	SP	April 1571–2 Feb 1594
François Roussel	SP	12 Feb 1548–26 Feb 1550
	SLD	c1562–30 Nov 1566
	SLF	1 Dec 1566–26 March 1571
	SGL	11 Oct 1572–10 May 1575
Annibale Stabile	SGL	Sept 1575–May 1576
	Col G	c July 1578–c Feb 1590
Tomás Luis de Victoria	Sem R	1571–c June 1573
	Col G	24 Oct 1571–1577
Annibale Zoilo	SLF	5 Oct 1561–11 Aug 1566
	SGL	16 Jan 1568–30 June 1570

Col G – Collegio Germanico; Col I – Collegio Inglese; SGL – S Giovanni in Laterano; SLD – S Lorenzo in Damaso; SLF – S Luigi dei Francesi; SMM – S Maria Maggiore; SP – St Peter's; Sem R – Seminario Romano

---

these institutions. Excluding the English and German colleges and the Seminario Romano (which were founded towards the end of our period), just over half the 41 names are northern. And of those musicians who led a succession of Roman choirs (listed in table II.2), there were as many northerners as Italians. The influence and presence of northern musicians waned more rapidly still after 1550. French and Flemish *maestri di cappella* disappeared from St Peter's in 1551, S Maria Maggiore in 1561, and from S Giovanni in Laterano and S Luigi dei Francesi in 1575. By 1561 the French national church had already engaged its first Italian *maestro di cappella*, Annibale Zoilo. One generation experienced a complete reversal in the national identity of musical leaders. Nor was the Cappella Sistina immune. By the end of the century there were twenty singers from Italy, five from Spain, one from Flanders (Christian Ameyden, who retired in 1596) and none at all from France.

Some of the events that most affected Roman music were – to parody Napoleon on the Holy Roman Empire – neither Roman nor musical. Political changes in France and ecclesiastical reforms in Trent so altered the traditional opportunities for patronage that French and Flemish singers had little incentive to make the long journey to Rome. Musical reforms had comparatively little to do with this reversal. Northern musicians had travelled to Rome from 1420 until the 1550s, enduring pestilent summers, winter flooding of the Tiber and periodic outbursts of anti-French sentiment. Not even the extreme horrors of the 1527 sack of Rome, when imperial troops burnt and terrorized the city, stemmed the flow. Historians of art and politics consider this event to have sounded the death knell of the Renaissance in Rome. Yet within a few years of the sack, the migration of musicians from the north had resumed, fuelled – as before – by hopes of acquiring an ecclesiastical benefice. The old patterns that the sack had left undisturbed were irreparably broken in the four years between the Treaty of Cateau-Cambrésis (1559) and the conclusion of the Council of Trent (1563). Signed in north-eastern France, the treaty effectively ended the French presence in Italy and consolidated Spanish control over much of the peninsula, from Milan to Sicily. Spanish singers and composers became more prominent than ever in Rome, to the exclusion of the French.

Curial patronage had relied heavily on benefices at least since the period of the papal residency in Avignon during the fourteenth century. Popes vied perpetually with French kings, with Burgundian dukes and others for the right to award the benefices located in their territories. The powers of conferral provided rulers with the means to support those singers, writers and other individuals who were also clerics. Thus since the pope had access to benefices in the diocese of Cambrai (among many others), Dufay and generations of later musicians from Cambrai journeyed to Rome to seek his patronage. For musicians and other clerics, minor benefices such as prebends and canonries offered a relatively secure lifelong income, usually without any responsibility to live at the church, abbey or cathedral that paid the benefice. Indeed, 'non-residency' was one of the chief abuses addressed in the final session of the Council of Trent (1562–3).[7]

The decision to enforce residency requirements had an immediate impact on papal patronage of all kinds. Musicians, bureaucrats and even bishops and cardinals were forced to decide between remaining in Rome and forfeiting a benefice, or keeping it but leaving Rome. The singer Marino Lupi tried unsuccessfully in 1567 to keep both his benefice and his position in the Cappella Sistina. After a year of procrastination, he gave up the benefice. Similarly the prominent patron of musicians, Cardinal Cristoforo Madruzzo, elected to resign his bishopric at Trent and returned in the 1570s to Rome, where Marenzio then joined his household. Because of financial constraints after the Council of Trent, Cardinal Otto, the Lord High Steward of Waldburg and Bishop of Augsburg, dismissed Jacobus de Kerle and the other nine singers in his private chapel in 1565. For similar reasons, but on a much grander scale, Pope Pius IV immediately enforced a dramatic reduction in the size of his own household; he fired 400 members in July and August 1564 and fourteen papal singers a year later. According to Cardinal Commendone (1564), 'the Curia . . . no longer had the free disposal of benefices'; northern musicians therefore turned increasingly to leaders who did, primarily Maximilian II in Vienna and Philip II in Spain.

The extent to which the pope used benefices as a form of patronage was anomalous in Italy. No other Italian ruler had access to benefices in northern lands, and even when the Este dukes in Ferrara or the Aragonese kings in Naples wanted to confer a local benefice, they often had to get papal permission first. This power gave the pope an upper hand in his ability to attract certain Flemish composers; paradoxically, however, this advantage may explain why Rome attracted many of the most prominent non-Italian composers but could not hold them. Dufay set a precedent by serving in the papal chapel just long enough to acquire the benefice in Cambrai he desired, about eight years in all. Josquin's arrival and departure dates are conjectural, but his tenure was probably only a little longer than that of Dufay. Still later, Arcadelt retired from Rome in 1551, presumably with his benefices in hand, after a dozen years or so. Martini, Willaert, Verdelot, Lassus and others came to visit or to secure a position elsewhere. The names of those who settled in Rome for two, three and four decades have a decidedly less familiar ring: Johannes Monstreuil, Ivo Barry, François Roussel and Christian Ameyden are representative. The most notable exception is Gaspar van Weerbeke, with between twenty and 25 years in the Cappella Sistina spread over two tours of duty. In the second half of the century, when Spaniards had largely supplanted French and Flemish singers, Victoria was one of several musicians to prosper during lengthy stays in Counter-Reformation Rome. Arriving as a youth in 1563, he had left by 1587, still in his prime.

Few northern composers were in Rome long enough to influence compositional styles significantly, as Willaert did in his 35 years in Venice. And none was able to dominate the musical life of a city in the way Johannes Martini and Maistre Jhan did in Ferrara, or Jacques Colebault (known for 33 years as Jacquet of Mantua) and Giaches de Wert did at the Gonzaga court. Before the Counter-Reformation the musical styles of composers in the papal chapel were shaped by a mixture of papal tastes, liturgical considerations and performance traditions. No single composer – northern or Italian – determined the musical practices of the Cappella Sistina as significantly as the singers of the chapel did themselves. In the bureaucratic world of the curia, the institutional workings of the group took precedence over the talents of an individual.

PERFORMANCE TRADITIONS

The choir of the Cappella Sistina had several long-standing performance traditions. Like other choirs of the period, they improvised some polyphony, presumably according to rules described by the papal singer Vicente Lusitano in his treatise *Introdutione facilissima* (1553). His many examples of contrapuntal improvisations above and below a cantus firmus – at times quite intricate – document a practice for which the Cappella Sistina was particularly renowned. The theorist Nicola

18. A choir of eight singers depicted in a fresco (late 1480s) by Bernardino Pinturicchio in a lunette of the Loggetta at the Villa Belvedere, the Vatican

Vicentino, having previously 'indulged in slanderous remarks' about the abilities of the papal choir,[8] criticized many of the same rules Lusitano had formulated, calling them old-fashioned. Yet while Vicentino valued novelty, the papal singers revered tradition; so much so that in the 1640s they still practised an improvisatory technique described by Lusitano, that of repeating one contrapuntal figure for as long as possible above the chant in the bass. This we know from G. B. Doni's complaint about its over-use.

In addition to contrapuntal improvisations, the choir also sang easier chordal types of improvisation such as three-voice fauxbourdon and four-voice *falsobordone*. The latter style, particularly apt for reciting psalms, seems to have originated in the last decade of the quattrocento, under the influence of Spanish singers drawn to Rome by Alexander VI.[9] Yet several decades later *falsobordone* performances were evidently still something of a novelty. After a Maundy Thursday service in 1518, the papal master of ceremonies Paride de Grassis voiced his official disfavour in his diaries: 'At the end of the Office, I was not pleased because the singers sang the psalm *Miserere mei* in *falsobordone*, and the pope [Leo X] wanted it that way'.[10] However slowly the tradition took hold, by the end of the century it was firmly ensconsed.

Recently it has been suggested that the choir of the Cappella Sistina regularly performed much of its polyphony with just one singer to a part, regardless of how large the choir was as a whole.[11] Theorists writing about performance traditions in other Italian cities generally make a distinction between secular music, sung one voice to a part and softly, and church music, performed by a large choir singing loudly. 'Large' is a relative concept. The 'large' choir at St Mark's in Venice usually consisted of two singers to a part, in Rome the choir at S Luigi dei Francesi functioned with two adults and two boys until 1552, when Fermin Lebel enlarged the choir to nine or ten singers. Thus even if the Cappella

Sistina choir sang some polyphonic works with soloists, the difference between the solo and 'choral' ensembles may not have been so great as we might otherwise imagine. In any case there is also evidence that the papal choir sang with several voices to a part. At the Vatican a fresco painted in the late 1480s for Innocent VIII's new villa, Belvedere, depicts a choir of eight singers performing together in a balcony, presumably two to a part (fig.18).[12] Paride de Grassis was struck by a performance in 1507 with a full sixteen voices. Then there is the report of Gregory Martin, a British priest who lived in Rome from 1576 to 1578; according to his account of music in the Cappella Sistina:

> The quyer standeth a loft at one side, with voices like so many belles tuneable one to an other. *No organes bycause the quyer is so ful for al partes* [my italics]. No descant [improvised counterpoint] but such pricke song [written polyphony] as every syllable may be heard in thy eares like a Preachers voice.[13]

A full choir 'for al partes' could conceivably mean either 'for all voices' or 'for all parts of the service', that is without an alternation between organ and choir. Quite possibly both interpretations apply.

Whatever the ambiguities in his account, this British priest plainly acknowledged the tradition of unaccompanied polyphony. No musical practice of the Cappella Sistina has attracted more attention. The origins of the *a cappella* tradition are unknown, but it dates at least from the fifteenth century, since the Cappella Sistina (completed in 1483) has never had an organ. Contemporaries occasionally noted the lack of accompaniment, as when Leo X travelled to Florence.[14] However, on the many instances when the pope celebrated Mass in a church that had an organ, the singers at least had the option of performing with it. Organs certainly participated at some services. When Pius II built a church for himself in his home town of Pienza, a papal singer oversaw the construction of an organ, and there are payments from other Roman churches for tuning or moving an organ just before a papal visit.[15] Leo X in particular was known for his love of organs and received several as gifts. Popes also contributed organs to Roman churches, most importantly to St Peter's, where the pope and his choir regularly celebrated many high feast-days. The choir at St Peter's frequently sang with the organ in *alternatim* performances, but Palestrina, perhaps influenced by papal tradition, reportedly considered alternations of polyphony and chant more appropriate for 'occasions of high solemnity' than those that alternated polyphony with organ.[16]

Performances with instruments other than organs became commonplace in churches throughout Europe in the sixteenth century, and Rome was no exception. The following account of church music is again supplied by Gregory Martin, based on his residence there during the pontificate of Gregory XIII. Only the musical practices mentioned in the last lines are essentially different from those of pre-Tridentine Rome:

> It is the most blessed varietie in the world, where a man may goe to so many Churches in one day, chose where he wil, so heavenly served, with such musike, such voices, such instrumentes, al ful of gravitie and majestie, al moving to devotion and ravishing a mans hart to the meditation of melodie of Angels and Saintes in heaven. With the Organs a childes voice shriller and louder then the instrument, tuneable with every pipe: Among the quyre, Cornet or Sagbut, or such like above al other voices. Wherein this is singular and much to be noted, that they deliver every word and everie syllable so distinctly, so cleane, so commodiously, so fully, that the hearers may perceave al that is sung. And that Verse which the Organs doth playe, one of the quyre in the meane time with a base voice very leasurely, rather sayth then singeth which there is common, in other places I have not seene it.[17]

Organ with boy soprano, organ with full choir, and choir with instruments – this description is remarkable because it dates from the heyday of Roman reforms, and yet the richness of the performance options is comparable to that found in the opulent churches of Venice and Paris, or even of Rome during the first half of the century. Only the emphasis on clarity of diction is unusual. At the beginning of the century it was already possible to hear a boy singing with the organ in St Peter's and instruments were commonplace in European churches by the 1520s. At the time of Martin's report, the combination of voices and instruments was a daily occurrence at the Collegio Germanico, where Victoria directed the musical activities. The express purpose of these performances was to attract 'worldly men, or not too devout ecclesiastics', who would grow tired of services sung only in chant.[18]

Papal celebrations also included instruments, probably more frequently than we suppose. Popes kept their own cadre of brass and wind players in the Castel Sant' Angelo. These instrumentalists routinely contributed fanfares for processions and entertainment for banquets, along with more prosaic duties such as accompanying the cannons that sounded a volley whenever a cardinal crossed the Tiber on his way to the Vatican. Most of the official collaborations between papal singers and the pipers and trumpet players (*piffari* and *tibicines de castello*) apparently took place at processions. Here Gregory Martin's description of a Corpus Christi procession is typical (and note once again the implication of a full choir singing polyphony).[19] As soon as the pope appeared at the gates of the papal palace, riding in his sedan chair, 'the Trompeters play their part with melodious blastes, and the gonnes ar heard thicke and thundering from the Castel of Sainct Angelo. The peale being finished, the Popes quyer continewe all the way [to St Peter's] with most excellent music'.

Most reports mention instruments out of doors, but they did not always stop at the church door. The famous account of the papal dedication of Brunelleschi's dome at Florence Cathedral specifically places instruments inside the church. Similarly at St Peter's in Rome, instruments added a festive lustre to at least one of the services Pius II presided over, the reception of the head of St Andrew in 1462.[20] Easter festivities even required a cacophonous collaboration between singers inside St Peter's or the Cappella Sistina and a battery of brass and artillery outside. That is when a German pilgrim in 1554 heard 'trumpets, guns [cannons] and bells' (*trumeetten, büchsen und gloggen*) compete with the Gloria of a Mass on Holy Saturday, and also Easter Sunday.[21]

One further tradition in the Cappella Sistina, that of the castratos, developed only at the end of the Renaissance. The earliest castratos came from Spain, entering the chapel about 1565, just as the Spanish presence in Italy increased following the Treaty of Cateau-Cambrésis. Within a few years they had spread northwards as far as Munich. Generally castratos are thought to have replaced male falsettists in the papal chapel. However, even the papal chapel, it now seems, permitted boys to sing with them more often than previously suspected. That at any rate is the implication of an engraving of a service in the Cappella Sistina, made by Etienne Dupérac in 1578, where three boys stand at the front of the choir immediately before the lectern (see figs.19*a* and *b*).[22]

It is noteworthy that this is exactly the number of boys mentioned in two earlier reports. At the election of Leo X, the King of France, Louis XII, sent three French boys, including Jean Conseil and Hilaire Penet, to the new pope as musical 'gifts'. They arrived under the care of Leo's *maestro di cappella*, Carpentras. When one of them needed replacing, Pietro Bembo, functioning as Leo's secretary, asked the Cardinal of Siena, Alfonso Petrucci, to yield one of 'his' boys to the pope.[23] The puzzling 'secundus puer' designation found in a copy of Isaac's *Missa Paschale* prepared for Leo X may have been intended for a member of this trio.[24] After the sack of Rome, Clement VII recruited an entirely new trio, again of French boys. Jean Conseil succeeded in finding one, and the Archbishop of Sens supplied the others. By the first months of 1529 they were with Conseil in Rome, apparently performing with the papal chapel.[25] Still earlier, in 1427 the chapel recorded six boys in the choir. Although none of these boys was in any official sense a chapel member, an unknown number of singers joined Roman choirs while still adolescents. Hilaire Penet joined the Cappella Sistina at fifteen or sixteen, and the Cappella Giulia engaged Felice Anerio as a soprano when he was about fifteen.

Boys were apparently always prominent as musical performers in Rome. It is true that after abandoning Rome for Avignon in 1309 the papal chapel did not support a *schola cantorum*. Moreover, the famous deathbed attempt of Julius II to found a chapel at St Peter's that would educate local (i.e. Italian) youths met with only partial success. Julius

19a. *Interior of the Cappella Sistina during a celebration of Mass: engraving (1578) by Etienne Dupérac (for a detail of the choir in the singing gallery on the right, see fig.19b)*

19b. Choir in the singing gallery of the Cappella Sistina (detail of fig.19a)

intended that the Cappella Giulia should train twelve Italian boys in order to lessen papal dependence on French and Spanish musicians; however, until much later in the century the number of *pueri* seldom rose above two or three. Palestrina presided over the largest group, numbering seven, after 1571. In comparison with the opportunities available to boys in French and Flemish cathedrals and in British collegiate chapels, those offered at the papal court were poor indeed. In large measure it was the patronage of curial cardinals and other Roman churches which helped musically trained boys to fare well in Rome throughout the Renaissance.

Many northern singers may have come to Rome while still boys. Some arrived with French cardinals, some as the wards of adult musicians who were themselves travelling with a cardinal. The household of Cardinal Jean du Bellay was probably typical of those supported by other wealthy French ecclesiastics. When he travelled to Rome in 1548, it included two boys and two lute players.[26] According to the 1516 report of a Ferrarese informer, the composer Jean de la Fage came in the entourage of a French cardinal, bringing with him some 'boys who sing very well . . . But he tells me that if he goes to stay with anyone he wants the boys to go with him'.[27]

Greater numbers of boys are implied by the existence of an entire choir of *garzoni tedeschi* at S Agostino during the last decades of the fifteenth century, founded by the influential Archbishop of Rouen, Cardinal Guillaume d'Estouteville. Aside from the meagre efforts at the Cappella Giulia, there appears to have been no similar organization for Italian boys until after the sack. In the 1530s there were schools at S Giovanni in Laterano and S Maria Maggiore, the latter numbering Palestrina among its students. Nevertheless, young Italian singers participated, and occasionally starred, in papal and Roman ceremonies as early as the papacy of Pius II. For the Corpus Christi festivities of 1462, Pius and the curial cardinals took their households to nearby Viterbo for extravagant celebrations. Pius described the procession in his diaries, noting the decorations and theatrical displays sponsored by individual cardinals, as well as music. Singing boys were heard at every turn: 'boys [from Pistoia] . . . sang sweetly'; 'eighteen boys [from Viterbo] like angels . . . sweetly sang responsive verses'; while a group of boys from Rome 'winged like angels . . . sang epic verses or elegiacs by learned scholars'.[28] At banquets in Rome the musical entertainments included boys singing in a variety of musical styles. Angelo Poliziano wrote back to Florence about the eleven-year-old son of his Orsini host, describing in rapturous terms the child's performance of polyphonic songs, and also a 'heroic song which he had himself recently composed in praise of our own Piero dei Medici'.[29]

MUSIC THEORY

Rome stands curiously alone among Italian cities in its failure to produce or attract a major theorist until Nicola Vicentino and then Girolamo Mei arrived in the latter half of the sixteenth century. Even then, the ideas of these two theorists were better received elsewhere than in Rome. Every other important musical centre (and some lesser ones) supported at least one theorist, and often many more. To name only the most illustrious, Johannes Tinctoris wrote his twelve treatises during the twenty years he resided in Aragonese Naples; Franchinus Gaffurius studied briefly with Tinctoris and then returned to a lengthy career in Milan; in Florence there was Pietro Aaron at the beginning of the sixteenth century and the circle around Vincenzo Galilei at the end; between Giovanni del Lago and Ludovico Zacconi in Venice, Zarlino dominated musical life for the better part of three decades; and Nicolaus Burtius, the Spaniard Bartolomeo Ramos de Pareia, and his student Giovanni Spataro kept Bologna at the centre of theoretical controversy for over half a century, a polemical tradition later emulated by Ercole Bottrigari and the contentious Artusi. Even Lucca, Brescia and Parma belong in this list, because of John Hothby, Giovanni Maria Lanfranco and Pietro Pontio respectively. In contrast only a handful of treatises survive from Rome, mostly the work of little-known practical musicians who lived in the city briefly or not at all. Stephano Vanneo (*Recanetum de musica aurea*, 1533) and Diego Ortiz (*Trattado de glosas sobre clausulas*, 1553) both published their treatises in Rome, but Vanneo, an Augustinian monk, lived in Ascoli Piceno on the other side of the peninsula, and Ortiz, a Spanish composer, worked in Naples.

Apart from these, there are just four treatises with stronger Roman associations, and three of them are clustered together between 1551 and 1555. Most notorious, yet in many ways unrepresentative of Roman thought or practices, is the *L'antica musica ridotta alla moderna prattica* (Rome, 1555) of Nicola Vicentino. By the time he came to Rome in 1549, Vicentino's ideas about the mixture of diatonic, chromatic and enharmonic genera had grown through fifteen years of theoretical study and practical experimentation in Vicenza, Venice and Ferrara. During his early years he quite probably studied with the Vicentine humanist Giangiorgio Trissino, who also believed the music of ancient Greece to be superior to that of his own day. In 1541 Trissino wrote to Pope Paul III, dismayed about 'how much is lacking in the music of our time';[30] among other things he named the chromatic and enharmonic genera. Vicentino did not come to Rome because of the intellectual climate or the opportunity to consult classical treatises in the papal library (he seems to have possessed little appetite for classical scholarship), but because the ecclesiastical duties of his Ferrarese patron, Cardinal Ippolito II d'Este, demanded extended periods of residence there.[31] When Ippolito left Rome for Siena or Ferrara, Vicentino went with him. By the time Vicentino ended his service with Ippolito in 1563, he had built for the cardinal one of three microtonal archiorgans, on which to play music composed in any of the three genera. Bottrigari reported it still in Rome in 1594, though seldom used.

Vicentino's principal contribution to musical life in Rome was the debate about his theories which precipitated not only his own treatise, but also those of the papal singers Vicente Lusitano and Ghiselin Danckerts. Held in 1551, the debate pitted Vicentino against the Portuguese Lusitano, then among the newest members of the papal chapel. Since the event was judged by two of Lusitano's colleagues from the Cappella Sistina, one of them Danckerts, the outcome could never have been in serious doubt, notwithstanding Vicentino's protestations of surprise and disbelief. Lusitano advocated a pragmatic point of view – that contemporary polyphony could be adequately explained with reference to the diatonic genus alone – and emerged victorious to publish his arguments in a short treatise, *Introdutione facilissima et novissima de canto fermo* (Rome, 1553). Lusitano devotes considerable attention in this treatise and its two revisions (Venice, 1558 and 1561), and in a longer manuscript treatise on 'practical music', to improvised counterpoint – a sign of his practical training and interests.

The practical bias is espoused with even more fervour by Danckerts, the third participant in the debate. He was the first to write a treatise, the *Trattato sopra una differentia musicale* (c1551), which, though never published, circulated in manuscript.[32] After recounting the debate from his perspective and defending the judges' decision, he launches into a reactionary attack on the faults of modern music. With a churchman's vigilance for modal purity, he derides the 'novice composers' (*compositori novelli*) who destroy the modal system by their indiscriminate use of accidentals. Young composers write in a chromatic style, 'since they see that also others do it, and thus . . . they all tumble down into the ditch'.[33] In addition to his opposition to modern styles, Danckerts also discounts ancient tales of physical wonders caused by music composed in the enharmonic and chromatic genera. Diatonic music is best simply because it is 'easier, more practical, more natural, and more gratifying for the ears'.

Danckerts's musical tastes were certainly conservative, but his opinions were not so much conservative or progressive as antitheoretical. His predisposition towards music which is 'piu naturale, e piu grato all'orecche' has nothing to do with an Aristoxenian trust in the senses over the intellect. Nor can his impatience with ancient claims about the wondrous powers of music be construed as conservative – such claims had been commonplace since the 1480s. Written at a time when the numbers and the influence of Franco-Flemish musicians in the papal court were in decline, his treatise has a defensive ring to it. Simply to rebut the speculative aspects of Vicentino's theory was not sufficient; he also tried to disavow any music written in accordance with humanist ideals. But earlier members of the Cappella Sistina were not known for their theoretical interests. A generation before Danckerts, the singers of Leo X had dismissed the chromatic composition of Willaert, *Quidnam ebrietas*, because they 'found it too difficult to sing'. Danckerts may be unusual only in having put his views into writing.

Before Girolamo Mei began writing down his theories in the 1560s, the only theorist in Rome with a solid humanist background was Carlo Valgulio. Secretary to a papal treasurer (1481–5) and then to Cardinal Cesare Borgia (cardinal 1493–8, and son of Pope Alexander VI), Valgulio was not a musician at all. Nevertheless he combined 'an incredible love for music and musicians'[34] with a broad scholarly knowledge of Greek treatises. His most significant endeavour was a translation of Plutarch's *De musica* (Brescia, 1507), a work which greatly influenced Galilei and supported Valgulio's own interest in music as a moral and ethical force. This translation of Plutarch is the probable source of cinquecento interest in the enharmonic genus, hailing it as 'the most beautiful genus of all and the most fitting, which the ancients cherished for its majesty and severity'.[35] Trissino, Vicentino, Bottrigari and others followed his lead. In comparison, Valgulio found contemporary music lifeless and devoid of power: 'I would lament here the music of our time, if it had not already been mourned as dead . . . Their [i.e. modern musicians'] whole art and science consists in certain few syllables and they sing almost nothing without reading from a book'.[36] Valgulio's disapproval of northern polyphony – common among humanists – was probably also encouraged by another member of Cesare Borgia's household, the frottolist Filippo da Lurano.

The earliest treatise associated with Rome, unpublished but beautifully copied and illuminated, is the *Liber musices* written by Florentius de

Faxolis for his patron Cardinal Ascanio Sforza some time between 1484 and 1492.[37] It is an idiosyncratic work, without obvious debts to the work of Tinctoris, Gaffurius or other contemporaries or mention of illustrious musicians (the latter is particularly odd since Josquin and Serafino dall'Aquila were also members of the Ascanio household). Although he made copious citations from ancient Greek and Roman writers and described some modern compositional methods, Florentius aimed his discussion neither at other theorists nor at performers. Instead, the uncommonly perfunctory definitions, the total avoidance of more arcane mathematical issues and the lavish illuminations, leave the impression that the treatise was commissioned by Ascanio specifically for himself, as a kind of primer for a patron with humanistic inclinations. It is essentially utilitarian, not for performers or scholars, but for a specific patron.

Rather than comparing it to other music treatises, one may do better to consider it as a specialized forerunner to handbook-treatises like the humanist Paolo Cortese's manual on the proper demeanour for cardinals, *De cardinalatu* (1510), or its secular counterpart, Castiglione's *Il cortegiano* (1528). Ascanio Sforza's part in commissioning this treatise from Florentius is especially noteworthy in the light of his subsequent role in convincing Cortese not to write a treatise on princes, as Cortese had originally intended, but on cardinals.[38] Both Cortese and Florentius wrote for a new breed of Italian patron, the wealthy cardinal; from politically prominent families, schooled in classical texts and the most recent interpretations of them, such men were often more concerned about the social duties of their office than the spiritual. Florentius, like Cortese, essentially describes the status quo in humanistic terms, but without idealizing the classical past; thus, for example, both regard modern polyphony favourably, rather than reviling it as other humanists were wont to do. In this sense Florentius's treatise is a peculiarly Roman document, even if unrelated to subsequent music treatises of the period.

Cortese occupies an important place in Roman intellectual life by his efforts to bridge the gap between scholastic theologians and humanists. His conciliatory approach allowed him to identify merits and faults on both sides of the intellectual divide. Humanists, he argued, needed to concern themselves with theological issues, and theologians and scholastic philosophers had to overcome their distrust of eloquence. Eloquence was neither opposed to wisdom, as Pico della Mirandola had claimed, nor inappropriate for Christian teachings because it was essentially pagan, founded in classical rhetoric. These beliefs lie behind his advice to cardinals to be versed in both classical texts and theology, to be aware of canon law and of literature.[39] When it comes to music he is no less eclectic. Cortese praised the sacred polyphony of Flemish composers – Josquin for his masses, Isaac and

Obrecht for their motets – and the secular music of Italian poet-musicians: Serafino dall'Aquila for his poems and melodies, Baccio Ugolini, Jacopo Corso and Bernardo Accolti for their extemporaneous performances of poetry accompanied by the lira da braccio.[40]

The glowing words for Serafino have been interpreted as a sign 'of the humanists' mixed feelings toward polyphony';[41] but the alternation of praise for sacred (northern) and secular (Italian) styles is in keeping with the evenhandedness with which Cortese balances the opposing concerns of the rival camps. His encouragement of a humanism open to scholastic thought, and a receptivity among churchmen and theologians to humanistic expression, came at a propitious time. In the coming decades Rome witnessed a practical expression of his ideas: the confluence of northern musical styles and Italian poetry in the polyphonic madrigal. In the light of Cortese's open-minded appreciation of Italian and Flemish musicians, Ascanio Sforza may have done more than influence Cortese's choice of topic. Cardinal Sforza's simultaneous patronage of Josquin and Serafino provided Cortese with an exemplary model of enlightened patronage.

The views of Valgulio (an Italian humanist and non-musician) are diametrically opposed to those of Danckerts (a Flemish musician), and both of them in turn differ from Florentius de Faxolis. Respectively they had found patronage from a Spanish cardinal, the Cappella Sistina and a Milanese cardinal. Of the others, Cortese had a position in the papal bureaucracy, Vicentino worked in the entourage of a Ferrarese cardinal, Mei in a Tuscan's, and the Portuguese Lusitano with the Cappella Sistina and a Roman noble. No one of these theorists alone represents the Roman musical scene as they do together, as manifestations of the competing musical styles supported by non-Roman patrons employed in the curia. Overall, their treatises are essentially practical in their various ways; in addition to those of Florentius and Cortese, and Danckerts and Lusitano, this is also seen in those treatises published in Rome by Ortiz and Vanneo.

No doubt the coming and going of patrons in Rome goes far to explain the absence of an identifiably Roman school or tradition of theory. But other factors contributed. Unlike Bologna or Padua, for example, Rome was not a city with a strong medieval university. The University of Rome (known as the Sapienza) was not a major source of employment for humanists during the Renaissance, nor was the *Studium* of the Roman curia. Music theorists in Bologna often held a chair at the university, Gaffurius lectured in Milan, and Stoquerus and Salinas taught in Spain at the University of Salamanca; theorists in Rome, however, had no such outlet. Moreover, the practical tendencies of Roman music theory should be understood in the larger context of Roman humanism, which tended to favour literary, historical and archaeological studies over philosophical speculation.[42] In music this bias was perhaps aggravated by the sustained prominence of Franco-Flemish musicians in Rome and their evident lack of enthusiasm for theoretical matters.[43]

Finally, the demands placed on papal singers, with a continuous round of liturgical, devotional and secular duties, would have left little time for study and contemplation, particularly when singers were also composers or served more than one patron. Humanists employed in the curia also encountered difficulties finding adequate time for scholarly work. Cortese left Rome in 1503 precisely because he wanted a less hectic environment for writing *De cardinalatu*. He found it in Montepulciano. A few humanists 'became intellectually barren' (and wealthy) under the weight of their curial responsibilities.[44] This aptly describes the charge against Ghiselin Danckerts when he was removed from the Cappella Sistina in the purge of 1565: 'he has no voice, is exceedingly rich, given to women, [and] useless'. Artists and composers at the papal court may have faced similar temptations and pressures. As soon as Sebastiano del Piombo became Keeper of the Seal for the curia in 1531, his artistic activities virtually ceased, and after Arcadelt received his first benefice, he published no madrigals for four years. With the exception of the composers who worked for Leo X (Festa, Carpentras and de Silva) and Paul III (Morales and Arcadelt), papal singers were in general not prolific composers. Very few approached the productivity of Palestrina and Victoria, who spent their careers with other institutions.

COMPOSITION AND THE QUESTION OF A ROMAN STYLE

Compositional styles in Rome reflect the disparate backgrounds of patrons and musicians in the city. It is not simply that the number of non-Italians was exceptionally high. Until well into the sixteenth century the percentage of native Romans was quite small among Italians at the curia. After Martin V (1417–31) no pope came from a Roman family until Paul III (1534–49). Under Leo X some 90 per cent of curial humanists were Italian, but of those only eleven per cent were native Romans.[45] Local musicians and artists of any stature probably did not match even this small percentage for several decades. The artist Giulio (Pippi) Romano was born at the end of the fifteenth century, but in music his contemporary, the frottolist and instrumental composer Eustachio Romano, is only a minor figure. Roman composers first constituted a significant presence in the latter half of the sixteenth century, led by Palestrina (*b c*1525). He and the likes of Alessandro Merlo (della Viola, *c*1530), Annibale Zoilo (*c*1537), Giovanni Dragoni (*c*1540) and Giovanni Maria Nanino (*c*1543), were among the generation which benefited from the foundation of Roman choir schools during the pontificate of the Roman pope, Paul III. Previously, the prominent

Italian musicians in Rome came from Florence, Mantua, Verona and other northern cities.

Since music, as noted already, lacked an indigenous Roman heritage, the musical life of Rome was remarkably cosmopolitan by 1500. From north of the Alps came French chansons and Franco-Flemish masses and motets; from Tuscany and the Po valley came the frottola, *lauda* and vocal improvisations with the lira da braccio; from Spain came a new way of performing the Passion, exotic string instruments such as the vihuela and large viols, and perhaps also the technique of *falsobordone* recitations. During the reigns (1513–31) of the two Medici popes, Leo X and Clement VII, the madrigal was developed by Bernardo Pisano, Costanzo Festa and other Tuscan musicians working in Florence and Rome. Other styles to take hold in Rome's international market were the three-voice chanson (1520s and 1530s), and from the 1540s on, the Neapolitan villanella (although Tomaso Cimello in Naples claimed that Roman singers performed *villanesche* incorrectly). Composers in mid-century Rome favoured the *madrigale arioso*, a descendant of the black-note style of the 1540s.[46] Roman publishers achieved a series of printing firsts, all involving secular music: the first publication to include music for a play, coincidentally the first printed frottola (1493); the first book of Italian keyboard music, a collection of frottole (1517); the first known book of instrumental music (1521); and the first print with the word 'madrigali' in its title (1530).

In the absence of a pronounced regional style, the liturgical traditions of Roman churches and chapels fostered polyphony with distinct institutional traits. For example, when Ockeghem's setting of the *L'homme armé* mass was copied for the Cappella Sistina, the scribe recomposed a portion of the Credo, adding a cadence just before the phrase 'Et incarnatus est'. This provided time for the pope and other celebrants to kneel, as the papal liturgy required.[47] *Magnificat* settings copied for St Peter's in the 1460s had to be rearranged and even at times recomposed to suit the basilica's *alternatim* tradition; instead of singing polyphony on even-numbered verses as at most Italian churches, the choir at St Peter's sang odd verses of the *Magnificat* and of hymns polyphonically. The Cappella Sistina, in contrast, required polyphony for all verses. Thus Costanzo Festa composed all of the *Magnificat* verses for the papal chapel, but when four of them were copied at S Maria Maggiore, the odd-numbered verses were omitted, to satisfy their preference for even-verse polyphony. These traditions survived the Counter-Reformation. Palestrina's hymn cycle (1589) adheres to the St Peter's practice, while Victoria, writing neither for St Peter's nor the Cappella Sistina, set the even verses in his cycle (1581).

More consistent stylistic features begin to appear around the beginning of the sixteenth century: a penchant for thoroughly imitative counterpoint, for canonic writing and for an increased number of voices in both the Agnus Dei of the Mass and the concluding doxology of the *Magnificat*. Canons emerge not only in masses and *Magnificat* settings, but also in hymns copied at St Peter's just before the jubilee of 1500, and slightly earlier in the hymns composed and arranged for the Cappella Sistina, apparently by Josquin and Marbrianus de Orto. Through the works of Costanzo Festa, Palestrina, Antonio Cifra and others, canons remained a characteristic device into the seventeenth century. Leo X brought together three composers with individual styles: Festa, Elzéar Genet (Carpentras) and Andreas de Silva. These were the great contemporaries of Raphael in art and Bramante in architecture. The papal chapel continued to sing works of each composer until the latter half of the century; the Carpentras Lamentations, which include *falsobordone* passages, were an annual tradition until 1587, and a *Te Deum* and antiphon of Festa endured as late as 1616. With the exception of *falsobordone*, there is nothing blatantly Roman about techniques such as canon and pervasive imitation. In many cases individual works seem to have become Roman by custom rather than by technique.

Composers did write works in honour of individual popes, but not as often as artists designed paintings and frescoes in the Vatican Palace with a 'programmatic' content, and less obviously than in the elaborate parodies of ancient Roman poems that humanists penned in honour of popes, cardinals and lesser officials. Certainly musicians in Rome were aware of practices in the other arts. From the years that Dufay and

Alberti spent together at the papal court, one characteristic of curial life was the regular opportunity for exchanges between musicians, writers and artists. The goldsmith and sculptor Benvenuto Cellini played the shawm with musicians of Clement VII, the composer and papal singer Bertrandus Vaqueras wrote humanist poetry, Arcadelt set madrigal verses of Michelangelo, and musicians were always important participants at retreats Roman patrons made to their villas on the outskirts of Rome. Few composers or artists were humanists, but artistic expressions of humanistic ideas could not be avoided.

In Roman humanism the classicizing impulse was pronounced, affecting scholars, theologians and artists equally. Popes and cardinals identified themselves with historical leaders from Christian and pagan antiquity. Julius II encouraged his image as a second Julius Caesar, and also as a new Moses, the law giver; others likened him (less kindly) to Tiberius or to Mars. The ancient heritage provided an irresistible source of models to curial humanists who saw in the Roman Church a rebirth of the Roman Empire. This urge penetrated to the deepest levels of Christian doctrine. Pàolo Pompilio (*d* 1491) concocted an elaborate classical paraphrase of the Nicene Creed, and in a tract from the 1460s the Church Fathers received classical identities: Jove, Phoebus and Mars were equated with SS Peter, Paul and Jerome.[48] Even after the sack, when such allusions were tempered, Paul III (Alessandro Farnese) planned to move two colossal statues of Alexander the Great to the Piazza di Campidoglio, thereby linking his own rule to the empire headed by the Macedonian leader.[49] Rodrigo Borgia, as Pope Alexander VI, had previously enjoyed the same association. Tinctoris was among the first to evoke the image of Alexander's illustrious namesake, composing the motet *Gaude Roma*, of which the text survives but not the music.

The motet by Tinctoris is an isolated instance. Papal musicians wrote few overtly political motets of any kind,[50] but those which refer to figures from ancient Greece and Rome are virtually unknown. Further musical examples of allusions to pagan emperors and gods certainly existed within the unwritten practices of humanist poet-musicians, such as Aurelio Brandolini, who reputedly sang the praises of Sixtus IV on a daily basis. This is the sort of text he eventually collected together under the title *De laudibus ac rebus gestis Sixti IV*.[51] However, in the polyphony sung in the papal chapel there are no musical counterparts to Raphael's *School of Athens, Expulsion of Heliodorus* and the *Repulse of Attila*. While the pagan themes developed by curial humanists provided a rich source of themes and images for artists, papal musicians turned instead to figures from Christian antiquity. It would be wrong to attribute this discrepancy solely to a disaffection with humanist ideals on the part of the predominantly northern musicians in the papal choir. Rather, the lack of pagan symbolism in compositions in Cappella

Sistina manuscripts is the result of the Renaissance concern for *decorum*: the notion that actions, dress, language and artistic expression should be appropriate to the occasion.

This is the most probable explanation for Alexander VI's decision not to hear the Tinctoris motet after the offertory, *inter missarum solemnia*, but after the Mass in his private chambers. For the same reason sermons preached before the papal court during Mass invariably discussed theological topics, 'divine things'. Political sermons, such as the oration Giles of Viterbo delivered on the alliance between Julius II and Emperor Maximilian I in 1512, had to wait until the liturgy was completed.[52] The visual arts also observed this distinction. Raphael painted his frescoes with characters from pre-Christian Greece in the Vatican *stanze*, matching the subject of the painting to the functional purpose of the room.[53] Meanwhile, the tapestries he designed for the Cappella Sistina illustrated biblical stories, among them *Paul Preaching at Athens* and *The Martyrdom of Stephen*.

Commemorative motets and polyphonic masses more frequently mention the pope by name, or they favour comparisons with religious figures. Dufay honoured the newly elected Eugenius IV (Gabriele Condulmer) in the motet *Ecclesie militantis*, drawing on two cantus firmi pertaining to the archangel Gabriel – *Gabriel* and *Ecce nomen domini*. In the middle of the fifteenth century the choir at St Peter's sang the (anonymous) *Missa 'Thomas'*, based on a chant for St Thomas Becket of Canterbury. The Thomas in question is probably not Pope Nicholas V (Tommaso Parentucelli) but the Byzantine refugee Thomas Paleologus, much honoured by Pius II.[54] Marbrianus de Orto is the likely composer of the *Salve regis mater*, which hails Alexander VI in the cantus firmus simply by adding his name to the Alleluia verse for the Common of Confessor Popes: 'Hic est sacerdos Alexander, quem coronavit Dominus'. Cristóbal de Morales lauded Paul III, Emperor Charles V and King François I by name in his motet: *Jubilate Deo omnis terra*, composed for treaty-signing ceremonies in Nice (1548). Finally, while Paul III was linked with Alexander the Great outside the church, the obvious allusion inside was to St Paul the Apostle. Morales honoured both Pauls with his *Missa 'Tu es vas electionis'*; the versicle was appropriate both for the Feast of SS Peter and Paul (29 June) and for the Conversion of St Paul (25 January), and Paul III had chosen 'Tu es vas electionis' as his motto.[55]

References to popes or cardinals could employ other forms of musical symbolism. The two Medici popes, Leo X and Clement VII, elicited more musical tributes than other popes, not just from papal singers but also from composers at courts throughout Europe. For the creation of Giovanni de' Medici as Leo X there are congratulatory motets from Jean Mouton (court of Louis XII), Heinrich Isaac (court of Maximilian I) and also from the new papal singer Andreas de Silva.

When Leo had taken possession of the papacy, the procession to the Lateran had followed a route decorated with the six balls (or *palle*) of the Medici coat-of-arms, as well as triumphal arches bedecked with lions (*leone*) suggested by his papal name Leo.[56] These same images appear in the motets of de Silva and Isaac. In his *Gaude felix Florentia* de Silva contrived a cantus firmus that represents melodically the configuration of the six *palle*, including even the crowning fleurs de lys.[57]

Isaac, intimately acquainted with Medici symbolism from earlier years of service in Florence, composed his six-voice motet *Optime pastor* for the ceremony at which Maximilian declared his 'obedience' to Leo through his emissary Cardinal Lang. The imagery of the newly written motet text and the double cantus firmus were all carefully designed to portray Leo in as many guises as possible. Thus the cantus firmus antiphons, *Da pacem Domine* ('Give us peace Lord') and *Sacerdos et pontifex* ('Priest and Pontiff . . . the Good Shepherd of his people'), have an emblematic significance. They identify his office and the widespread perception of Leo as a peacemaker, as opposed to his predecessor, the warrior-pope Julius II. The Latin poem dwells on hopes for peace, asking Leo to restore a *pax alma* and *pax aurea*, and with an allusion to Leo's musical proclivities, it directs him to lead his flock 'to a league of concord' with his reed-pipe. Familiar plays on his name are not overlooked: from his family name comes the reference to him as doctor (*medicus*), and from his papal name, that to the 'true lion' (*leone*).[58]

Occasionally clusters of certain references suggest a probable association. For example, the three motets in the Medici Codex (by Boyleau, La Fage and Willaert) that praise John the Baptist and St John the Apostle, probably refer to Leo X by alluding to his Christian name, Giovanni; so too the anonymous *Credo de Sancto Johanne Evangelista* and *Missa de S Johanne Baptiste*, both contained in de luxe manuscripts Alamire copied for Leo. From the entire repertory of music at the papal chapel, there appear to be just three settings of the sequence *Verbum bonum et suave*, all with links to Rome during the papacy of Leo: the six-voice version by Willaert (which the papal singers mistakenly attributed to Josquin), the four-voice setting by Pierrequin de Therache and the mass based on it by Jean Mouton (both in Roman manuscripts). Surely the localization of this particular text in Leonine Rome relates to the *impresa* Leo had formulated for himself; namely, a yoke with the motto 'SUAVE', standing for the Gospel verse, *Iugum meum suave est* ('For my yoke is easy'). When Leo made his inaugural procession from the Vatican to S Giovanni in Laterano to take 'possession' of the papal cathedral, bands of his musicians were resplendently dressed in white, green and red velvet, with the word 'suave' emblazoned on their backs.[59]

As Medici devices proliferated during the reign of Leo X, so also did images of the Della Rovere oak (*rovere* or *quercia* in Italian) under

Sixtus IV and Julius II, at least in art and architecture. To cite only one of countless artistic examples, the portrayal of music on the tomb of Sixtus features a female Musica playing an organ signed with the Della Rovere coat-of-arms. Sermons and writings of Giles of Viterbo, Marco Vigerio and Pietro Bembo during the papacy of Julius included plays on the Latin *robur*.[60] In contrast to the practices in Leo's papacy, sacred polyphony in Rome under Sixtus, Julius and other popes seemingly avoided or minimized the self-aggrandizing tendencies of the other arts. The only known musical reference to the Della Rovere name occurs in a peripheral piece that Filippo da Lurano – significantly, not a church musician – wrote for the wedding of Julius's niece to Marcantonio Colonna in 1506. The Della Rovere oak, the Colonna column and the church Julius had held as a cardinal (S Pietro in Vincoli) are all addressed in the first verse: 'The oak is joined to the column; chains bind the oak' ('Quercus iuncta columna est, nectunt vincula quercum'). And the sole mention of Julius himself is anything but flattering. *Sola caret monstris* by Loyset Compère, seditiously copied into a Sistine manuscript, excoriates Julius as 'a wild animal' for his anti-French policies.

There is no questioning Leo's pre-eminence among popes as a patron of music and musicians; still, it is difficult to evaluate the apparent discrepancy between the number of works associated with Leo and the paucity of compositions for other popes or papal celebrations. It would, for instance, be extraordinary for an event so portentous as Julius's decision to rebuild St Peter's not to have been commemorated in music. Even for an occasion we know to have been celebrated with music, such as the triumphant return of Julius to Rome in 1507, there is no known connection with any surviving polyphony.

In music, as in art and poetry, popes were probably represented not by biblical characters related to their papal or family names, but by any Old or New Testament figure, including Christ, who possessed some quality a pope desired to emulate. In his papacy Julius strongly invoked the images of King Solomon and Moses. The authority of Solomon, builder of the temple in Jerusalem, fitted well with his own architectural plans for St Peter's and for Rome as the 'new Jerusalem'. His identification with Moses, a leader equally admired for his *terribiltà*, was well known to his contemporaries. The statue of Moses that Michelangelo sculpted for Julius's tomb has often been held to bear 'an idealized likeness' to Julius.[61] The two genealogy motets by Josquin and Prioris copied into a Cappella Sistina manuscript between 1507 and 1512 refer in passing to Solomon. And Josquin's motet *Rubum, quem viderat Moyses*, copied slightly later, quickly mentions Moses and the burning bush. There is no basis for associating any of these pieces with specific papal events, however, particularly since neither of the composers resided in Rome at the time.

It is one thing to associate a motet such as Dufay's *Ecclesie militantis* with Eugenius or de Silva's *Gaude felix Florentia* with Leo; one has an emblematic cantus firmus, the other a newly composed text with sophisticated musical symbolism. But it is much harder to associate a particular event or person with the most common types of sacred composition in Rome – motets with a liturgical or para-liturgical text and masses with a sacred cantus firmus or polyphonic model. Among motet texts from Josquin's period of service in the Cappella Sistina until that of Arcadelt, the Tract for Ash Wednesday, *Domine, non secundum*, is especially prominent. Its popularity can be judged from the nine settings in Cappella Sistina manuscripts, yet one cannot say what broader significance this penetential text had within the papal chapel. Most popular of all and suitable for a variety of occasions are the *Missae de beata virgine*. The Cappella Sistina collection contains thirteen in manuscript sources, mostly by composers from the papal chapel and all written before the Counter-Reformation.

Once the Roman reformation had began, musical allusions to popes apparently became more straightforward, and at the same time less symbolic. Palestrina's *Missa Papae Marcelli* carries no known secret reference to Pope Marcellus II in the music itself, certainly nothing to compare with Josquin's *soggetto cavatto* in the *Missa 'Hercules Dux Ferrariae'*. Previously he had honoured Julius III with a *Missa 'Ecce sacerdos magnus'*, based appropriately enough on the antiphon for a pope-confessor. It was published in his first book of masses (1554), each entrance of the antiphon motif marked by the coat-of-arms of Julius III. At the end of the century Curzio Mancini followed with a *Missa Papa Clemens VIII*, neutrally built on the hexachord syllables 'ut, re, mi, fa sol, la'. The office rather than the individual personality of the pope becomes the focus of attention in such compositions by Palestrina as *Ecce sacerdos magnus, Tu es pastor ovium* (two settings) and the *Missa Dum esset summus pontifex*. The change of focus is clearly visible in the transformation of de Silva's *Gaude felix florentia* into *Gaude felix ecclesia* when the motet was copied into a papal manuscript in 1563. References to the Virgin Mary replaced those to Leo.[62] Composers of *laude* relied on the same formula. In 1563 Razzi and Giovanni Animuccia compiled the first two books of *laude* printed during the Counter-Reformation, in Venice and Rome respectively. Both included contrafacta of 80-year-old Florentine Carnival songs.

REFORMS AND THE QUESTION OF CONSERVATISM

When the presence of northern musicians declined in Rome after the Treaty of Cateau-Cambrésis (1559), there were qualified Italians waiting to assume positions of leadership, among them the first Romans educated under Franco-Flemish choirmasters in the schools of S

Giovanni in Laterano and S Maria Maggiore. Palestrina and his generation were also children of the sack of Rome (1527), raised in a more cautious atmosphere than Romans had known before the sack. The earliest record of Palestrina as a boy at S Maria Maggiore is from 1537, the year the Reform Council was first summoned to Mantua (though it did not convene until 1545, and then in Trent). His first important patron, Pope Julius III, desired a tranquil papacy, an understandable wish for one who as a cardinal-hostage during the sack had been tortured and hung by his hair. As Palestrina and Annibale Zoilo reached maturity, the prospects of ecclesiastical and musical reforms were inescapable. At the age of 30 Palestrina designed the *Missa Papae Marcelli* in accordance with Marcellus's admonition for textual clarity. Zoilo was 25 in 1562 when the Council of Trent enjoined musicians to sing words intelligibly and to 'banish from church all music that contains, whether in the singing or in the organ playing, things that are lascivious or impure'.[63]

From this point on, reform guidelines for music shaped the careers of many Roman composers. They had a visible impact on composers and printers eager to provide singers with acceptable material. One year after the call to purify church music, Razzi and Animuccia issued their books of *laude* and a scribe at the Cappella Sistina copied the newly texted motet of de Silva. Subsequently the Council appointed the ascetic Cardinal Carlo Borromeo, one of the key forces in the Counter-Reformation, as part of a Commission of Cardinals to study the particular problems of church polyphony. While the Council had heard sentiments against secular influences on church polyphony, such as a mass based on a madrigal or chanson, the commission did not expressly forbid these influences. After conducting tests of actual mass cycles at Rome in 1565, the commission formulated its vague recommendations to observe proper Latin accentuation and avoid melismas. St Peter's quickly requisitioned Animuccia to write five masses 'according to the requirements of the Council' (1566), and in the ensuing years Palestrina, Vincenzo Ruffo and Costanzo Porta were among those who published their own.

Post-Tridentine efforts to reform the liturgy soon prompted new compositions, especially in Italy and Spain, but also in Catholic Germany. The attempts to unify Mass and Office texts resulted first in a reformed Roman breviary (1568) and a Roman missal (1570). Pope Gregory XIII then enlisted Palestrina and Zoilo to adapt existing chant melodies of the Roman *Graduale* to the revised liturgical texts (1577). This ill-fated project lasted only a year. However the reformed breviary spawned a flurry of extensive new hymn cycles from major composers. As soon as the new breviary appeared, Animuccia composed fourteen hymns for St Peter's; then came those by Lassus (manuscript 1580–81), Victoria (Rome, 1581), Palestrina (in manuscript by

1582; Rome, 1589), Guerrero (Rome, 1584) as well as others.[64] Palestrina did not stop with hymns. His encyclopedic efforts encompassed a cycle of Lamentations (begun by 1574; Rome, 1588), *Magnificat* settings (two complete sets; Rome, 1591) and his greatest, the cycle of 68 offertories (Rome, 1593).

New religious institutions arose, providing new sources of patronage and opportunities for different types of musical expression. S Filippo Neri founded what became known as the Congregazione dell'Oratorio for his popular devotional services. His work began in 1554 with simple religious gatherings of laymen at S Girolamo, moving ten years later to S Giovanni dei Fiorentini, and finally in 1575 to their own quarters in the Chiesa Nuova. For music to supplement his sermons and prayers, Neri turned to the Latin and Italian *laude spirituale* of his fellow Florentine, Giovanni Animuccia. Their simple homophonic style made them suitable 'for the consolation and needs of many spiritual and devout persons, religious and secular alike'. The more worldly and musically sophisticated Jesuits encouraged the German and English colleges to become important patrons for musicians of all nationalities, starting in the 1560s and 1570s respectively. For the edification of the common man, they permitted vernacular songs and music for Jesuit plays in addition to liturgical music. Jesuit ideals doubtless also permeated the Seminario Romano, formed in the mid-1560s in response to the Council of Trent. Palestrina became their first director of music from 1566 to 1571.[65]

Palestrina clearly identified more with the positive aspects of reform – as represented by the Jesuits and Roman liturgical reforms – than he did with repressive manifestations of the age. In dedicating his setting of the Song of Songs (1584) to Gregory XIII, Palestrina made his famous, seemingly pro forma, apology for having published his first book of madrigals (1555) as a youth. Doubts about the sincerity of his professed embarrassment stem from the publication of his second book of madrigals in 1586, one year after Pope Gregory died. Yet Einstein is too harsh in calling it 'pure hypocrisy'. Such apologies were part of the dedicatory rhetoric of the age. The poet and musician Tomaso Cimello had repudiated his early love poems in 1579, and the sculptor Bartolomeo Ammannati repented, with genuine fervour, the public nudity of his own sculptures in 1582. Much earlier, Carpentras in Rome had renounced his settings of secular texts and turned exclusively to sacred works, because motets and masses 'would always bring tears of piety' to the eyes of Leo X. Given the few surviving secular works by Carpentras, the veracity of his claim is beyond reproach; but his report that Leo 'seemed to experience a sort of repulsion for the music on which other princes doted' is difficult to reconcile with what we know about Leo's support of *musici segreti*.[66]

Apologies, retractions and conversions came as church authorities tried to eliminate impurities in all art forms. Women were prohibited from Roman dramatic productions in 1568, while during the year of Palestrina's apology, 1584, Pope Gregory XIII forbade performances of comedies in private homes.[67] The Senate of Milan gave official sanction to censorship in 1538 with the first Index of Prohibited Books. Other cities followed suit, including Rome (1554), until Paul IV outdid them all with the 1559 Index. The Council of Trent took a more temperate stance, publishing an *Index expurgationis* (1564) that banned some books simply 'until they are corrected'. This approach applied no less to art and music than to poetry and drama. Artistic 'correctors' painted loincloths on the nudes in Michelangelo's *Last Judgment*. Musical 'correctors' purged from Cappella Sistina manuscripts the texts of Mass tropes which the Council had banned. Even Vasari appended a 'corrected' assessment of Michelangelo's fresco in the revised edition of his *Lives* (1550, rev. 1568), expressing cautious new doubts about the propriety of nudes in church. As with Palestrina's apology, the sincerity of his statement has been questioned. Another critic, Gilio da Fabriano, objected to the pagan presence of Charon in the *Last Judgment*, echoing those reformers who sought to remove secular intrusions into church polyphony. Palestrina bowed to decorum by publishing his mass on the Domenico Ferrabosco madrigal *Io mi son giovinetta* under the title *Missa Primi toni* (1570). As he and other composers turned to *madrigale spirituale*, writers turned to *rime spirituale* and *dramme spirituale*.

Humanists and musicians involved with monody and the *seconda prattica*. and churchmen seeking musical reforms valued the intelligibility of text.[68] The aesthetic foundation for each is a relationship between music and the text that is perceived as new, and the reverse of existing practice. In fact Monteverdi's image of harmony being the 'servant' rather than the 'mistress' of the words was explicitly anticipated some 40 years earlier in Counter-Reformation Rome by Gilio da Fabriano. Writing about Michelangelo's *Last Judgment* (1564), Gilio condemned Michelangelo for essentially the same reason that Giulio Cesare Monteverdi later criticized *prima prattica* composers: the relationship between art and subject is the opposite of what it should be. Gilio first acknowledged that Michelangelo possessed an incomparable command of art, but then concluded that the 'artist who fits his art to the truth of the subject [is] far wiser than one who adapts the purity of the subject to the beauty of art'.[69] Ecclesiastical reformers judged music, literature and art according to a uniform standard: art was to be the servant rather than the mistress of the message.

As the supreme composer of the Roman Counter-Reformation, Palestrina understood this standard well. But it is mistaken to view him as a conservative. Neither his contemporaries, nor musicians of the following generation, perceived him as such. Agostino Aggazzari went so far as to name Palestrina and the Council of Trent as sources of the

95

seconda prattica (1607), a claim endorsed by Michael Praetorius (1619).[70] This is a view of Palestrina we have yet to appreciate fully. Too much attention is paid to how few of his 104 masses are based on secular sources (as compared to Lassus and others) and to personal traits such as his lifelong employment in his native city and region (a trait of many Italians, including the Gabrielis). We have learnt much about his counterpoint, but there is still a great deal to investigate about the chordal nature of Palestrina's style (which Aggazzari specifically mentioned), about his harmonic rhythm and about how both of these relate to sixteenth- and seventeenth-century ornamentation practices. For the same reason that intabulators preferred straightforward and diatonic works like Palestrina's *Vestiva i colli*, Cipriano de Rore's *Anchor che col partire* and Lassus's *Del freddo Rheno*, the prolonged popularity of madrigals by Arcadelt and Palestrina among music publishers – as opposed to those of Wert, Luzzaschi and Gesualdo – may derive in part from the comparative ease successive generations of performers would have had in applying to them the latest embellishments. Indeed, much Baroque ornamentation is dependent upon a regularized harmonic structure.

Palestrina's works achieved an unsurpassed authority only in the seventeenth century. His style became the epitome of Roman style, or rather of the conservative Roman style, at least for composers in the Cappella Sistina. The papal singers had begun to show a tendency towards an inbred glorification of their own composers by the 1530s and 1540s, the decades following the sack; but at that time no individual had dominated all other composers so completely. Josquin, Carpentras, de Silva, Festa, Morales and Arcadelt all shared the stage. After the Council of Trent the repertory copied into papal manuscripts narrowed still further. The chapel admitted no works by the Gabrielis, and pointedly few by Animuccia, their colleague at St Peter's.

The focal point of musical conservatism in Rome was the Cappella Sistina. Much of the conservatism was institutional, some of it the influence of its reflexively conservative Spanish contingent, men like Fernando de las Infantas (in Rome 1571–97), who objected to Palestrina's revisions of the gradual. But even for the papal singers, one must distinguish between their corporate service within the chapel and the individual careers they pursued outside. Alessandro Merlo, for example, wrote very little sacred music during his three decades in the Cappella Sistina (1561–94) and was better known for his three-octave vocal range and his performances of secular music; his serious madrigals were influenced by Rore and his lighter ones by villanellas. In the next century Gregorio Allegri maintained this tradition of separate compositional styles: unaccompanied polyphony for the Cappella Sistina and concertato church music for other choirs.

Ecclesiastical reforms and the rapid decline of northern musicians, occurring simultaneously in the 1560s, affected all of Italy, but few centres so drastically as Rome. Yet few cities weathered the changes so successfully, accommodating both those composers intent on reform and those interested in exploring the latest musical developments. Throughout the Renaissance there were always periods when a private or institutional patron elsewhere in Italy could claim a greater, larger or more modern musical establishment than any to be found in Rome. Naples, Ferrara and Milan each had superior groups of musicians for a time during the latter half of the fifteenth century; Venice built a first-rate ecclesiastical choir under the leadership of Willaert and then Zarlino; and Wert, Luzzaschi and others put Ferrara and Mantua in the avant garde of secular styles.

The crowning advantages of music in Rome were the consistency of quality and the catholicity of styles. Rome maintained its greatness throughout the Renaissance by virtue of its system of ecclesiastical patronage. This insured a steady supply of clerical musicians and, equally important, of wealthy ecclesiastical patrons anxious to display the talents of their own musicians. Those musicians with the greatest security, the papal singers, were also those most susceptible to the constraints of tradition. As long as northern musicians came and went with reasonable frequency, these constraints were tempered. But once northerners stopped coming, cardinals and churches, colleges and confraternities all provided musicians in Rome with vital and progressive musical alternatives. The variety of employment and performance opportunities not only survived the strictest years of the Counter-Reformation, it actually increased.

NOTES

[1] C. Stinger, *The Renaissance in Rome* (Bloomington, 1985), 146–7 and 289; and J. D'Amico, *Renaissance Humanism in Papal Rome* (Baltimore, 1983), pp.xvi and 7.

[2] P. Portoghesi, *Rome of the Renaissance*, trans. P. Sanders (London, 1972), 16.

[3] J. Hale, *Italian Renaissance Painting from Massacio to Titian* (Oxford, 1977), 36.

[4] P. Partner, *Renaissance Rome 1500–1559: a Portrait of a Society* (Berkeley, 1976), 117–18; and for a more detailed description of the curia, see D'Amico, *Renaissance Humanism*, 19–28.

[5] This translation is from D. Coffin, *The Villa in the Life of Renaissance Rome* (Princeton, 1979), 336. He discusses the Villa d'Este on pp.311–38; see also his *The Villa d'Este at Tivoli* (Princeton, 1960).

[6] This table is based on lists compiled by P. A. Myers in *An Analytical Study of the Italian Cyclic Madrigals Published by Composers Working in Rome ca. 1540–1614* (diss., U. of Illinois, Urbana, 1971), 34–46. I have made additions and corrections to her lists where appropriate.

[7] See C. Reynolds, 'Musical Careers, Ecclesiastical Benefices, and the Example of Johannes Brunet', *JAMS*, xxxvii (1984), 49–97.

[8] The quotation is from the papal singer Ghiselin Danckerts; in H. Kaufmann, *The Life and Works of Nicola Vicentino (1511 – c.1576)*, MSD, xi (1966), 22.

[9] On this style see M. Bradshaw, *The Falsobordone* (Neuhausen-Stuttgart, 1978); and Bradshaw, *Giovanni Luca Conforti: 'Salmi Passaggiati' (1601–1603)*, Miscellanea, v (1985).

[10] R. Sherr, *The Papal Chapel ca. 1492–1513 and its Polyphonic Sources* (diss., Princeton U., 1975), 95.

[11] J. Lionnet, 'Performance Practice in the Papal Chapel during the 17th Century', *EM*, xv (1987), 4–15; and R. Sherr, 'Performance Practice in the Papal Chapel during the Sixteenth Century', *EM*, xv (1987), 453–62. I am grateful to Prof. Sherr for providing me with a copy of his article before it was published.

[12] David Coffin includes a photograph of the fresco in *The Villa in the Life of Renaissance Rome*, 80, fig.48.

[13] G. Martin, *Roma sancta (1581)*, ed. G. B. Parks (Rome, 1969), 101. It is difficult to interpret his report of 'no descant', because *falsobordone* and other types of improvised polyphony are securely documented practices in the papal chapel.

[14] J. Shearman, 'The Florentine *Entrata* of Leo X, 1515', *JWCI*, xxxviii (1975), 153, n.60.

[15] See, for example, J. M. Llorens, 'Juan Escribano, cantor pontificio y compositor (d. 1557)', *AnM*, xii (1957), 108.

[16] Iain Fenlon quotes this passage of a letter from 1578 in his *Music and Patronage in Sixteenth-Century Mantua* (Cambridge, 1980), i, 91

[17] G. Martin, *Roma sancta (1581)*, 96.

[18] T. Culley, *Jesuits and Music* (Rome, 1970), 76.

[19] *Roma sancta (1581)*, 88; for another example, see Llorens, 'Juan Escribano', 108.

[20] See C. Reynolds, 'Early Renaissance Organs at San Pietro in Vaticano', *Studi musicali*, xv (1986), 42, n.10.

[21] Gmelin, 'Die Romreise des Salemer Conventuals and späteren Abtes, Matthäus Rot, 1554', *Zeitschrift für die Geschichte des Oberrheins*, xxxii (1880), 234–73. The relevant passage (p.252) reads, '24 Mar., quod erat sabbatum Pasce, fui mane in sacello pontificis, ubi officio post nonas completo et cantanto (!) in missa Gloria in excelsis deo incipiebatur Et in terra simul mit der music, trumeetten, büchsen und glogge'. The next day 'intonerunt campane, bombarde, et buccine'.

[22] Neils Krogh Rasmussen discusses this engraving at length, in '*Maiestas Pontificia*: Liturgical Reading of Etienne Dupérac's Engraving of the *Capella Sixtina* from 1578', *Analecta Romana Instituti Danici*, xii (1983), 109–48. I would like to thank Professor Sherr for calling my attention to this study.

[23] A. Pirro, 'Leo X and Music', *MQ*, xxi (1935), 8.

[24] David Fallows examines this and several other instances of 'secundus puer' in 'The Performing Ensembles in Josquin's Sacred Music', *TVNM*, xxxv (1985), 44–6.

[25] Anne-Marie Braggard finds no evidence of a private papal chapel in these years; 'Détails nouveaux sur les musiciens de la cour du Pape Clément VII', *RBM*, xii (1958), 12–18. After several payments for boys' clothes, there are no further references to them in the account books. This does not necessarily indicate that they left Rome or even papal service (as Braggard presumes; p.15), since they would have been under the care of a singer in any case. As a rule there were also no payments to the boys during Leo's papacy.

[26] G. Dickinson, *Du Bellay in Rome* (Leiden, 1960), 90.

[27] L. Lockwood, 'Jean Mouton and Jean Michel: New Evidence on French Music and Musicians in Italy, 1505–1520', *JAMS*, xxxii (1979), 222.

[28] Florence Gabel translated this section from Book VIII of the *Commentaries* (Northampton, Mass., 1951), 551–5. Regarding a similar scene in Rome during the time of Julius II, see L. Partridge and R. Starn, *A Renaissance Likeness: Art and Culture in Raphael's 'Julius II'* (Berkeley, 1980), 57.

[29] There is an extended translation in N. Pirrotta and E. Povoledo, *Music and Theatre from Poliziano to Monteverdi*, trans. K. Eales (Cambridge, 1982), 36.

[30] Claude Palisca quotes the letter in *Humanism in Italian Renaissance Musical Thought* (New Haven, 1985), 119–20.

[31] Kaufmann, *The Life and Works of Nicola Vicentino*, 11.

[32] Karol Berger discusses the disputation between Danckerts and Vicentino in Chapter 1 of *Theories of Chromatic and Enharmonic Music in late 16th Century Italy* (Ann Arbor, 1980).

[33] Quoted from Berger, *Theories of Chromatic and Enharmonic Music*, 34.

[34] Quoted in Palisca, *Humanism in Italian Renaissance Thought*, 88. Palisca treats Valgulio's work in detail on pp.88–110.

[35] ibid, 109.

[36] ibid, 16.

[37] Regarding the date of Florentius's treatise, Edward Lowinsky argues for a probable completion by about 1487; see his 'Ascanio Sforza's Life: a Key to Josquin's Bibliography and an Aid to the Chronology of his Works', in *Josquin des Prez: New York 1971*, 47–50. The treatise is more fully discussed by Albert Seay, in 'The *Liber Musices* of Florentius de Faxolis', in *Musik und Geschichte: Leo Schrade zum sechzigsten Geburtstag* (Cologne, 1963), 71–95.

[38] K. Weil-Garris and J. D'Amico, 'The Renaissance Cardinal's Ideal Palace: a Chapter from Cortese's *De cardinalatu*', in *Studies in Italian Art and Architecture 15th through 18th Centuries*, ed. H. Millon (Rome, 1980), 49. D'Amico further evaluates Cortese's treatise in *Renaissance Humanism*, especially 227–37.

[39] My discussion is indebted to D'Amico, *Renaissance Humanism*, 148–54 and 227–37.

[40] Pirrotta provides a facsimile and commentary for the relevant pages of *De cardinalatu* in 'Music and Cultural Tendencies', 96–112.

[41] ibid, 91–2.

[42] D'Amico, *Renaissance Humanism*, 90.

[43] Palisca, *Humanism in Italian Renaissance Musical Thought*, 10.

[44] *Renaissance Humanism*, 111.

[45] Stinger, *The Renaissance in Rome*, 133; on the variety of nationalities present in Rome, see Partner, *Renaissance Rome*, 76–111.

[46] J. Haar, 'The *Madrigale Arioso:* a Mid-Century Development in the Cinquecento Madrigal', *Studi musicali*, xii (1983), 203–19.

[47] G. Reese, *Music in the Renaissance* (New York, 1954, rev. 2/1959), 125, n.154.

[48] Stinger, *The Renaissance in Rome*, 235–54; D'Amico, *Renaissance Humanism*, 122–3 and 144–168.

[49] Stinger, *The Renaissance in Rome*, 260.

[50] Albert Dunning notes the scarcity of political motets from Rome, especially after the papacy of Leo X, in *Die Staatsmotette, 1480–1555* (Utrecht, 1970), 234–5. For the early fifteenth century Reinhard Strohm notes that 'very little Mass music of the period can be related definitely to the chapel of Eugene IV, or to the papacy at all', in 'European Politics and the Distribution of Music in the Early Fifteenth Century', *EMH*, i (1981), 319.

[51] For further details and bibliography, see L.D. Ettlinger, 'Pollaiuolo's Tomb of Pope Sixtus IV', *JWCI*, xvi (1953), 266.

[52] J. O'Malley, *Praise and Blame in Renaissance Rome* (Durham, North Carolina, 1979), 33–5.

[53] S. J. Freedberg, *Painting of the High Renaissance* (New York, 1972), i, 114–15.

[54] C. Reynolds, 'The Origins of San Pietro B 80 and the Development of a Roman Sacred Repertory', *EMH*, i (1981), 284–5.

[55] J.-A. Reif, 'Music and Grammar: Imitation and Analogy in Morales', *EMH*, vi (1986), 240–41.

[56] Stinger, *The Renaissance in Rome*, 56.

[57] Richard Sherr makes a persuasive case for this musical stemma and also additional number symbolism in 'The Medici Coat of Arms in a Motet for Leo X', *EM*, xv (1987), 31–5.

[58] Dunning, *Die Staatsmotette*, 46–53; Stinger, *The Renaissance in Rome*, 300.

[59] Stinger, *The Renaissance in Rome*, 55–6; and M. Perry, '"Candor Illaesus": the "Impressa" of Clement VII and other Medici Devices in the Vatican Stanze', *Burlington Magazine*, cxix (Oct 1977), 676–86, especially 683.

[60] Partridge and Starn, *A Renaissance Likeness*, 56–7; and J. O'Malley, 'Man's Dignity, God's Love, and the Destiny of Rome: a Text of Giles of Viterbo', *Viator*, iii (1972), 389–416, especially 411–13.

[61] Stinger, *The Renaissance in Rome*, 218.

[62] E. Lowinsky, 'A Newly Discovered Sixteenth-Century Motet Manuscript at the Biblioteca Vallicelliana in Rome', *JAMS*, iii (1950), 174–6 and 201–2.

[63] A full text of the 'Canon on Music to be used in the Mass' is printed, among other places, in Lewis Lockwood's edition of the *Pope Marcellus Mass* (New York, 1975), 19.

[64] These have been reviewed by D. Zager, *The Polyphonic Latin Hymns of Orlando di Lasso: a Liturgical and Repertorial Study* (diss., U. of Minnesota, 1985).

[65] Regarding music at the two Jesuit colleges, see T. Culley, *Jesuits and Music* (Rome, 1970); and his 'Musical Activity in Some Sixteenth Century Jesuit Colleges, with Special Reference to the Venerable English College in Rome from 1579 to 1589', *AnMc*, no.19 (1979), 1–29. See also the first chapter of J. Roche, *North Italian Church Music in the Age of Monteverdi* (Oxford, 1984).

[66] Albert Seay has translated the preface to Carpentras's book of hymns in his Introduction to *Elziarii Geneti (Carpentras): Opera omnia*, CMM, lviii/3 (1972), p.xiii.

[67] B. Ferraro, 'Form, Reform and the Counter-Reformation in G.M. Cecchi's *Commedie osservate*', *Bibliothèque d'humanisme et Renaissance*, xlvii (1985), 321–42.

[68] Lewis Lockwood comments on the 'close connection' between the concerns of humanists and church reformers in this regard in *The Counter-Reformation and the Masses of Vincenzo Ruffo* (Venice, [1970]), 129–31.

[69] *Due dialogi* (Camerino, 1564); quoted from A. Blunt, *Artistic Theory in Italy 1450–1600* (Oxford, 2/1962), 121–2.

[70] Helmut Hucke cites these theorists and others in 'Palestrina als Autorität und Vorbild im 17. Jahrhundert', *Congresso internazionale sul tema Claudio Monteverdi e il suo tempo: Venezia, Mantova e Cremona 1968*, 253–61.

BIBLIOGRAPHICAL NOTE

History

Studies of Renaissance Rome have flourished in the past decade. Among the many recent works on historical and cultural aspects of life in Renaissance Rome, see especially J. D'Amico, *Renaissance Humanism in Papal Rome* (Baltimore, 1983); C. Stinger, *The Renaissance in Rome* (Bloomington, 1985); and J. O'Malley, *Praise and Blame in Renaissance Rome: Rhetoric, Doctrine, and Reform in the Sacred Orators of the Papal Court, ca. 1450–1521* (Durham, North Carolina, 1979). For an overview of the last half of the period covered in this essay, there is P. Partner's *Renaissance Rome 1500–1559: Portrait of a Society* (Berkeley, 1976); on economic questions see F. Gilbert's study of Julius II's papacy, *The Pope, his Banker, and Venice* (Cambridge, Mass., 1980), and J. Delumeau's, *Vie économique et sociale de Rome dans la seconde moitié du XVIe siècle* (Paris, 1957–9). Regarding the papacy as an institution and the careers of individual popes, L. Pastor's nineteenth-century narrative survey, for all its obvious biasses, is still essential: *The History of the Popes*, ed. and trans. P. Antrobus and others (St Louis, 1891–1953). An excellent historical account of the papacy, with a particular concern for efforts to mount a crusade, is K. Setton, *The Papacy and the Levant (1204–1571)* (Philadelphia, 1976–8).

The arts

As an introduction to artistic styles, but not for any sense of artworks as cultural-historical documents, two works of S. J. Freedberg are still standard, his *Painting in Italy, 1500 to 1600* (London, 1971) and *Painting of the High Renaissance in Rome and Florence* (New York, 1972). By contrast there is the interpretative collaboration of L. Partridge and R. Starn, *A Renaissance Likeness: Art and Culture in Raphael's 'Julius II'* (Berkeley, 1980). Of the many thorough architectural studies, see J. Ackermann, *The Architecture of Michelangelo* (Harmondsworth, 1970), and C. Frommel, *Der römische Palastbau der Hochrenaissance* (Tübingen, 1973). Two very useful studies of urban history are D. Coffin's *The Villa in the Life of Renaissance Rome* (Princeton, 1979) and P. Portoghesi's *Rome of the Renaissance*, trans. P. Sanders (London, 1972). For theatre and literature see, respectively, F. Cruciani's anthology (with Italian translations from Latin), *Teatro nel Rinascimento Roma 1450–1550* (Rome, 1983), and N. Borsellino and M. Aurigemma, *Il cinquecento dal Rinascimento alla Controriforma* (Rome, 1973).

Music history

On various questions of ecclesiastical patronage of music and musicians, see for the fifteenth century J. Noble, 'New Light on Josquin's Benefices', in *Josquin des Prez: New York 1971*, 76–102; C. Reynolds, 'The Origins of San Pietro B 80 and the Development of a Roman Sacred Repertory', *EMH*, i (1981), 257–304; and his 'Musical Careers,

Ecclesiastical Benefices, and the Example of Johannes Brunet', *JAMS*, xxxvii (1984), 49–97; and also A. Roth, ' "Primus in Petri aede Sixtus perpetuae harmoniae cantores introduxit": alcune osservazioni sul patronato musicale di Sisto IV', in *Un pontificato ed una città Sisto IV (1471–1484): Rome 1984*, 217–4. For the sixteenth century, of the many and diverse studies of R. Sherr, see his 'Performance Practice in the Papal Chapel during the Sixteenth Century', *EM*, xv (1987), 453–62; 'The Medici Coat of Arms in a Motet for Leo X', *EM*, xv (1987), 31–5; 'From the Diary of a 16th-Century Papal Singer', *CMC*, xxv (1978), 83–98; and *'Illibata Dei virgo nutrix* and Josquin's Roman Style', *JAMS*, xli (1988), 434–64. In addition see L. Lockwood, 'Adrian Willaert and Cardinal Ippolito I d'Este: New Light on Willaert's Early Career in Italy, 1515–21', *EMH*, v (1985), 85–113; A. Pirro, 'Leo X and Music', *MQ*, ii (1935), 1–16; and J. J. Dean, 'The Repertory of the Cappella Giulia in the 1560s', *JAMS*, xli (1988), 465–90. Finally, Albert Dunning discusses the political contexts of many motets written in Rome in his *Die Staatsmotette* (Utrecht, 1970), which is now being translated into English.

For a discussion of the madrigal in Rome, much of A. Einstein's *The Italian Madrigal* (Princeton, 1949) is still pertinent. Among those revising his ideas, see J. Haar, 'The *Madrigale arioso*: a Mid-Century Development in the Cinquecento Madrigal', *Studi musicali*, xii (1983), 203–19, as well as his 'The Early Madrigal: a Re-Appraisal of its Sources and its Character', in *Music in Medieval and Early Modern Europe*, ed. I. Fenlon (Cambridge, 1981), 163–92; and also N. Pirrotta, ' "Dolci Affetti" i musici di Roma e il madrigale', *Studi musicali*, xiv (1985), 59–104.

Developments in Counter-Reformation Rome are discussed in H. Smither's *A History of the Oratorio*, i (Chapel Hill, 1977); Lewis Lockwood's *The Counter Reformation and the Masses of Vincenzo Ruffo* (Venice, [1970]), as well as his comments in the Norton Critical Score of Palestrina's *Pope Marcellus Mass* (New York, 1975); and T. Culley's 'Musical Activity in Some Sixteenth Century Jesuit Colleges, with Special Reference to the Venerable English College in Rome from 1579 to 1589', *AnMc*, no.19 (1979), 1–29.

Music

There are complete editions of varying quality and ages for many of the composers active in Rome from the time of Dufay to that of Palestrina, including (roughly in chronological order) Pullois, Vaqueras, Josquin, Carpentras, de Silva, Lhéritier, Festa Morales, Arcadelt, Roussel and Victoria. In addition there are works of lesser composers in *Early Sixteenth-Century Sacred Music from the Papal Chapel*, ed. N. Josephson, CMM, xcv (1982). And despite E. E. Lowinsky's lengthy argument to the contrary, the manuscript copied in Rome for Leo X, preserved in Florence, and popularly known as the Medici Codex, is available in Lowinsky's exemplary edition published as volumes iii–v of MRM (1968).

Chapter III

Venice: Theatre of the World

IAIN FENLON

In 1608, the English traveller and eccentric Thomas Coryat visited Venice, an experience which he described in some detail in his *Crudities* published in London three years later. Among the wonders of the city 'hastily gobled up' (as the title-page puts it) were a number of musical events, principally the celebration of the feast-day of S Roch which Coryat had attended in the main hall of the Scuola di S Rocco. There, surrounded by the vast glowing canvases of Jacopo Tintoretto, he had listened for some three hours to what seems to have been a concert (rather than a strictly liturgical occasion), which:

> consisted principally of musicke, which was both vocall and instru-
> mental, so good, so delectable, so rare, so admirable, so super excel-
> lent, that it did even ravish and stupifie all those strangers that never
> heard the like . . . For mine own part I can say this, that I was for the
> time even rapt up with Saint Paul into the third heaven.

His lyrical description continues by praising the choir of 20 voices and the instrumental ensemble of 24 performers (ten trombones, four cornetts, two violas da gamba, one violin and seven organs), precisely the kind of forces which we normally associate with Venetian polyphony of the High Renaissance. Coryat's strongest memory was of one singer who had so impressed him that:

> I thinke the country where he was borne may be as proude for breed-
> ing so singular a person as Smyrna was of her Homer, Verona of her
> Catullus, or Mantua of Virgil: But exceeding happy may that Citie, or
> towne, or person bee that possessth this miracle of nature.[1]

This is remarkably fulsome, even by the standards of Coryat's hyperbolic prose.

By the early seventeenth century, reports of the sumptuous musical life of Venice had become commonplace. During the previous hundred years the richness of musical activity in the city had, for a complex of reasons, surpassed the somewhat modest achievements of the fifteenth century. At the *scuole grandi* such as S Rocco, where music was particularly encouraged, professional musicians had been employed since the second half of the quattrocento, and instrumentalists had now been

added to the vocal forces available. In the field of music publishing,
Ottaviano de' Petrucci's production in 1501 of the first collection of
polyphonic music had established Venice as an important centre; by
the second half of the sixteenth century the city had become the capital
of music printing not only in Italy but in Europe, a position that it was
to retain until the second half of the seventeenth century. In this development the crucial moment was not so much Petrucci's 'invention' of
music printing (in reality an adaptation of an existing technology), but
rather the importation from Paris in the 1530s of Attaingnant's system
of single-impression printing. It was this method, which greatly
simplified the printing process and so made it cheaper, that effectively
launched the bourgeois European market for music printing, a market
which was largely fostered by the Venetian workshops, particularly the
firms of Gardane and Scotto. The increased availability of music for
domestic performance must have made a considerable impact upon the
musical and social life of the city; in the *palazzi* along the Grand Canal,
and in the houses of the aristocracy, banquets and entertainments were
held 'con bufoni e tutta la musicha . . . si poté trovar'.[2] At a more
public level, the great occasions of church and state were celebrated
with increasingly elaborate music and ceremony as the sixteenth
century unfolded, a development which had at its centre the musicians
of the basilica of St Mark, the principal church of the city (though not
its cathedral).

The number of singers employed at St Mark's increased dramatically during the century; by 1616 the *cappella* comprised a *maestro* (by
then Claudio Monteverdi), a *vice-maestro*, 24 singers, two organists, two
maestri dei concerti (who were responsible for directing the instrumental
music) and sixteen instrumentalists. The position of *maestro di cappella*,
instituted only in 1491 when Pietro de Ca' Fossis had been appointed,
was held during the sixteenth century by an impressive succession of
distinguished musicians of international repute, beginning with
Adrian Willaert who held the post from 1527 until his death in 1563.
Among the others, a number of whom were Willaert's pupils, were the
Flemings Jacques Buus (first organist 1541–50) and Cipriano de Rore
(*maestro di cappella* 1563–4); these were succeeded, as in other important
centres of musical activity in northern Italy, by native composers
(among whom were a number of Venetians) including Girolamo
Parabosco (first organist 1551–7), Annibale Padovano (second
organist 1552–65), Gioseffo Zarlino (*maestro di cappella* 1565–90),
Claudio Merulo (first organist 1557–84) and Andrea Gabrieli (second
organist 1566–84, first organist 1584–5). Their successors included in
turn Giovanni Gabrieli, Claudio Monteverdi and Francesco Cavalli.
From modest beginnings in the fifteenth century the *cappella* of St
Mark's developed in the course of the sixteenth to become what was
arguably the finest music establishment of any church in Europe.

That it did so was not due to historical accident, nor to the influence of any single patron, but rather to an evolving official policy which saw the music and ceremonial of the Venetian church and state as intimately related and vital components of the elaboration, through artistic means, of the 'myth of Venice', a myth which upheld the reputation and unique qualities of Venice and deployed them as a powerful weapon of propaganda.[3] There were various aspects to this potent political idea, but its essentials had been neatly embodied as early as 1364, when Petrarch wrote his famous description of the Venetian celebration of a victory in Crete:

> The august city of Venice rejoices, the one home today of liberty, peace and justice, the one refuge of honourable men, the one port to which can repair the storm-tossed, tyrant-hounded craft of men who seek the good life. Venice – city rich in gold but richer in renown, mighty in works but mightier in virtue, founded on solid marble but established on the more solid foundations of civic concord, surrounded by the salty waves but secure through her saltier councils.[4]

As Petrarch's words make clear, at the centre of the myth was the notion of the uniqueness and perfection of Venice, qualities epitomized in the official epithet 'La Serenissima'. On one level Venice inspired admiration for its physical beauty, and for its geography and topography.

Venice was never like other cities. Foreigners expressed envy and awe at the richness of the city churches, the mosaics of St Mark's and the ceremonies surrounding the doge. Along the Rialto, with its mixture of traders and merchants from every part of Europe and the Orient, sights were to be seen that could be seen nowhere else in Europe. Praise of Venice during the Renaissance invariably began with applause for its unparalleled beauty and urban charm as a city quite literally (and, as legend emphasized, miraculously) founded upon the seas. The sentiments of Petrarch's words were endlessly repeated throughout the fifteenth and sixteenth centuries, particularly in the wake of major victories which usually prompted a flood of poetic offerings based on the most traditional and conservative themes. A central figure in Venetian political rhetoric was Venetia herself; since at least the end of the fourteenth century she had been represented as a modified figure of Justice, holding scales and sword and seated upon a Solomonic throne of lions. And since, according to official legend, the city had been founded on the feast of the Annunciation, the *Origo Venetiarum*, Venetia also assumed the attributes of the Virgin, in particular her purity and immortality. Venice was not the only Italian state dedicated to the Madonna, but Venetian devotion was distinguished by a particularly complex and distinctive mixture of sacred and civic conceptions.

On all the major feast-days of the Virgin the doge attended Mass at St Mark's and the Venetians celebrated two major feasts of the Madonna, the Annunciation and the Assumption, as great civic celebrations of the Republic. In all, a third of the major Marian feasts in the Venetian calendar had civic connotations. In addition to being constantly reminded of the local resonances of the cult of the Madonna through the annual liturgical cycle, the inhabitants of the city were everywhere confronted by Marian images. On the façade of St Mark's itself, that most politically charged of all Venetian churches, reliefs of the Virgin and the Archangel Gabriel are accompanied by other protectors of the city, SS George and Demetrius, and Hercules, the mythical tribal hero of the Venetii, who is represented twice (see fig.21). The Annunciation is again shown on the Rialto bridge, this time flanked by St Theodore, the first patron saint of the Republic, and by his successor St Mark. At a more general level, the figure of the Virgin as protectress occurs on dozens of canvases executed for Venetian churches and other buildings in the course of the sixteenth century; for the citizens of the Republic her comforting image carried a quite precise political and civic message that was intimately connected to the origins and evolution of La Serenissima. In these circumstances, it is hardly surprising that so many Marian texts, either of a liturgical or para-liturgical character, were set by composers associated with St Mark's.

These twin associations of the Madonna and Justice with Venice appear, among other places, in a sequence of three poems by the Venetian Domenico Venier set as madrigals by Baldassare Donato and published in 1550. In the first, *Quattro Dee che'l mondo honora et ama*, the attributes of Victory, Peace, Wisdom and Fame are personified as goddesses. There follows a second piece which opens with an invocation to 'Gloriosa felice alma Vineggia/Di Giustizia, d'amore di pace albergo' and ends with a celebration of 'Vergine gia mill'anni intatte pura'. The final madrigal, cast in triple mensuration, is frankly celebratory:

> Viva sempre in ogni etade
> Con la gratia d'ogni stella,
> Questa pura verginella
> Gran regina in libertate . . .[5]

These three pieces, placed together at the end of Donato's book, appear to have been specially composed for some festive occasion. With their recourse to an iconography in which Olympian deities and pagan heroes join the traditional figures of the Madonna and Justice, Venier's texts evoke the spirit of the Venetian world after the Peace of Bologna (1530) in which state rhetoric took up the theme of the Republic as a haven of political virtues. Through the publication of such music in a volume of light-hearted *canzon villanesche alla Napolitana*, the myth of Venice entered the world of bourgeois domestic entertainment.

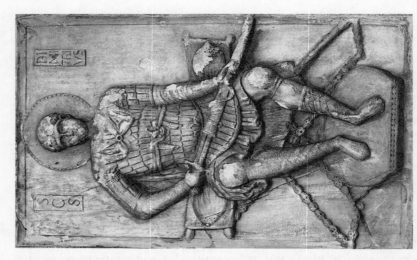

21. St George (left), the Virgin and St Demetrius: reliefs (Venetian–Byzantine school, thirteenth century) on the west façade of St Mark's

Petrarch's words also introduce one of the most common political aspects of the myth of Venice: the twin themes of liberty and domestic peace. The notion of Venetian political stability, its freedom from internal division and strife, was enlarged in the fifteenth century by humanists who began to identify Venice with classical models of republicanism. It was during this period that the central idea of the Venetian constitution as a modern realization of the classical model of mixed government was elaborated. The doge represented the monarchical element, the senate the aristocratic element, and the Great Council the democratic element. In this way the Venetian constitution came to be seen as a modern embodiment of ancient political wisdom, and in turn this was held by the Venetians to be the reason why Venice, almost alone among the Italian states, had remained unconquered, though unwalled, for more than a millennium. The unique aspects of the Venetian constitution were a powerful element in the myth of Venice and exerted a considerable influence on the development of European republicanism well into the eighteenth century. At home this political myth was a precious political asset which served to unify the citizens and to foster a civic spirit.

Underlying the myth was the economic strength of the Venetian empire. Throughout the late Middle Ages Venice and its territories had dominated the European economy, and already by the end of the fourteenth century the primacy of the city was unquestioned. In 1383 she occupied Corfu, the gateway to the Adriatic, and then between 1405 and 1427 the towns of the *terraferma* (Padua, Verona, Vicenza, Brescia and Bergamo). Among Venetians, the expansion of the empire was not seen as a policy of territorial expansion for its own sake, but rather as the basis for rising capital investment in trade. The expansion of markets lay at the root of Venetian power, and by the fifteenth century her merchants firmly controlled all the major commodity trades in the Mediterranean: pepper, spices, Syrian cotton, grain, wine and salt. Signs of the city's wealth could be seen in the enormous concentration of might in the Arsenal, and in the sheer number of galleys and cargo vessels to be seen in what was probably the largest industrial complex of medieval Europe. Equally telling was the constant embellishment of the city which gradually took on a new appearance; the streets of beaten earth were paved and the old wooden bridges and piers of the canals were replaced by stone bridges and *fondamenta*. This new emphasis on building is symbolized by the construction of the Ca' d'Oro on the Grand Canal where many new palaces were springing up between 1421 and 1440. A spate of new construction also occurred in other Italian cities during this period, but in Venice it was a particularly expensive enterprise; thousands of oak piles were sunk into the sand and mud of the lagoon, and stone had to be brought from Istria. In addition to private individuals, the state also embarked on projects including the restoration of the ducal palace and the building of the new Loggia on the Rialto (which functioned as a stock exchange for merchants) which was constructed in 1459. These are the beginnings of a tradition of state patronage of architecture which culminated in the remodelling of the central civic space of the city, St Mark's Square, in the early decades of the sixteenth century.[6]

All this can be ascribed to the politics of prestige, an enterprise in which art was a powerful ally. In the course of the century the image of Venice as a holy and apostolic city was presented and enhanced in innumerable altarpieces, while state commissions to artists produced direct memorials to empire in new civic buildings and in historical allegorical paintings such as Veronese's *Apotheosis of Venice* in the Ducal Palace. Likewise, the improvements to St Mark's Square placed a relentless emphasis on imperial themes. Similar motivations were responsible for the noticeable increase in civic and religious ceremonial in Renaissance Venice, and it was as part of this phenomenon that the state also embarked upon a more extensive patronage of music, perhaps encouraged by the examples of both the papacy and the north Italian courts of Mantua and Ferrara. In other words, the importance of music in Venetian society during the Renaissance was not due to some mysterious evolutionary process, or merely to patrician demands for social entertainment or to the church's desire to ornament its services, though both these motivations played some part in the phenomenon. On the contrary, music was consciously cultivated by the Republic as part of its development of civic and religious ritual.

One way in which the Venetians may have consolidated their constitutional stability was through a pious adherence to a strong tradition of inherited legend and ritual. Throughout Renaissance Europe public ceremonies and processions were, in the broadest sense, an expression of the political order. In Venice the hierarchic conception of the Republic was most powerfully displayed in the ducal procession (*andata*) which was, in effect, a visual demonstration of the Venetian constitution and of its mixed character. The importance of the procession is clear from the number of officials who were employed to record and oversee this and other civic ceremonies. Its actual form has survived in a number of contemporary descriptions and pictorial sources, the most informative of which is Matteo Pagan's famous woodcut showing the procession of the doge on Palm Sunday (fig.22). The participants in this procession were organized according to their rank and status. At the centre was the doge, accompanied by the two most prestigious foreign ambassadors resident in the city; in front came squires holding symbols of authority and behind further ambassadors and the sword-bearer. Behind the doge a patrician held an elaborate gold-cloth umbrella over the doge's head. It is possible to account for every person shown in this woodcut. In other words, the ducal procession was not merely a piece of

22. Procession of the Doge on Palm Sunday: detail of the woodcut (c1550) by Matteo Pagan

public display and entertainment; it portrayed and enforced the essential characteristics of the Venetian constitution. It suggested a broad social participation in the government and a general acceptance of it, both features which mark off Venice from the other major Italian states.[7]

By the end of the sixteenth century, the doge and the *signoria* participated in about sixteen annual processions. Since the 1540s the number of such occasions had increased dramatically; solemn processions and rituals were becoming, if anything, a more popular and important characteristic of Venetian life. Most of the important ones coincided with major Christian feasts, and in general outline the Venetians adopted the liturgical calendar of Christianity. At the same time, the Republic had its own particular liturgy, called the *patriarchino*, which was derived from the use of Aquileia. The Offices of the *patriarchino* were normally longer than in other rites, and all changes in it could only be made by the doge. Until the fifteenth century the rite was practised throughout Venice, but in 1456 a papal brief abolished it everywhere except in St Mark's. As the exclusive property of the doge and the *signoria*, the liturgy became, in effect, a liturgy of state, and as such was particularly susceptible to political influence.[8]

In these circumstances it is hardly surprising that by the later sixteenth century the major annual feast-days in Venice might correspond to saints' days in the Roman calendar, but equally might commemorate important events in Venetian history. In this way what was characteristically Venetian was associated with what was universally Christian; patriotism and faith were thus conveniently and inextricably fused. The most obvious case is that of St Mark, whose cult lay at the centre of Venetian mythology. As the possessors of the Evangelist's body, supposedly transferred to the city in 827, the Venetians modelled their relationship to Mark on that of the popes to St Peter. In Venetian eyes Venice was as autonomous as Rome, and the doge's authority, inherited from Mark, as absolute and independent as that of the occupant of the Chair of St Peter. It is not surprising that the rituals which took place on St Mark's feast-day (25 April) emphasized this bond between St Mark and the doge and the idea of descending authority. Through such acts of popular piety and civic patriotism St Mark had come to personify far more than merely the privileges of the doge, but rather the Republic itself. As a fifteenth-century canon of St Mark's, Gabriele Fiamma, put it: 'I was born a Venetian and live in this happy homeland, protected by the prayers and guardianship of St Mark, from whom that Most Serene Republic acknowledges its greatness, its victories, and all its good fortune'.[9] The churches of the city bristled with paintings showing events from the life of the Evangelist. No fewer than four festivals were dedicated to St Mark, and his symbol was extensively used as an image of Venetian authority.

Together with the ducal palace, the basilica of St Mark and the square constitute a distinctive civic and ceremonial space symbolic of the unity of the religious and political features of the Venetian constitution. In view of the strong identification of the Venetian Republic with St Mark, it is not surprising that liturgical or para-liturgical texts in praise of Venice's principal patron saint are so common in the repertories of music written by musicians working in the city, especially those associated with the basilica itself. The words of Claudio Merulo's five-voice motet *Cumque beatissimus Marcus*, for example, are exclusive to the *patriarchino*. On the other hand, texts such as the so-called 'oration de S. Marco', *Deus, qui beatum Marcum*, which was set twice by Andrea Gabrieli and once by Giovanni Gabrieli and Giovanni Bassano, all as large-scale motets, were not part of the liturgy that was enacted on any of the four feasts in the Venetian calendar that were devoted to St Mark and were presumably written for performance at major state and religious occasions. The same is true of obvious derivations from this text, such as Giovanni Bassano's five-voice motet *O rex gloriae, qui beatum Marcum Evangelistam*. Through such means the constitution and government of Venice was both celebrated and sanctified:

Deus qui beatum Marcum Evangelistam tuum, Evangelicae praedicationis gratia sublimasti; tribue quaesumus, eius nos semper & eruditione proficere & oratione defendi. Alleluia.[10]

Clearly, music was a prominent aspect of the major civic and religious rituals in Renaissance Venice. In addition to its symbolic values as the emblem of a harmonious state, it was essential to the propagation of the Venetian myth on a more practical level, through performance. At the centre of institutional musical life in the city was the musical chapel of the basilica of St Mark.[11] The dramatic expansion of the *cappella* and its activities during the sixteenth century reflect the increasingly important part that ceremonial had come to play in the civic and religious life of Venice. It also indicates the determination with which music was now pressed into the service of the state.[12] Little is known about the musicians of the chapel during the fourteenth and fifteenth centuries, but from the early years of the sixteenth century the government took a more active interest in the musicians of St Mark's, and it is during this same period that descriptions of civic and religious ceremonies increase. As with every other aspect of the organization of St Mark's, the music was under the direct control of the procurators, and their records reveal the growing importance of music to the state and a concern to attract musicians of quality to the basilica.[13]

The year 1527 represents a watershed in the early history of the chapel of St Mark's for it saw the appointment of the Flemish composer Adrian Willaert as *maestro di cappella,* largely it seems at the instigation

23. *Interior of St Mark's, built 1063–73*

of Doge Andrea Gritti. Willaert held his appointment for some 35 years, until his death in 1562. During his tenure the musical *cappella* at St Mark's was transformed from a somewhat provincial body into an institution of central importance in the Italian musical scene, eventually rivalling the reputation of the papal choir. The extent of Willaert's achievement can be gauged by the increasingly elaborate music that was performed at St Mark's as well as by the variety of his own numerous publications. As a teacher he was one of the most influential figures of the century, and after his death the succession at St Mark's passed to his pupils, first to Cipriano de Rore (who remained in the post for just over a year), and then to the composer and theorist Gioseffo Zarlino. It is a token of the importance the Procurators attached to the post that the brief requires the successful candidate to be superior to all other musicians, 'che sia non solamente dotto e pratico della musica, ma come quello che he da essere superiore agli altri musici'. During the second half of the sixteenth century, and well into the seventeenth, the names of Willaert, Rore and Zarlino were rhetorically invoked as the founders of music at St Mark's, and indeed of the entire Venetian tradition. In 1603, for example, when the post of *maestro* fell vacant, the Procurators cited the achievements of this illustrious triumvirate as a justification for searching outside Venice for a suitable replacement, despite the opposition of Doge Marino Grimani who preferred a local candidate. Ten years later, when the post fell vacant again, it was filled by Claudio Monteverdi, summarily dismissed from the service of the Gonzaga in Mantua the previous year.

During Zarlino's time as *maestro di cappella* the organists of St Mark's began to assume an important role as composers. This was partly due to Zarlino's preferences; his chief interest lay in his work as a theorist, and his own compositions are neither as numerous nor as varied in style as those of Willaert. At the same time, the increasingly heavy burdens of state and religious ceremonial brought with them extra duties. New music was required for such occasions, and the day-to-day organization of the chapel was now more complex; in response to the taste for large-scale pieces the chapel had expanded to include some 30 singers and six instrumentalists by the turn of the century, to which further musicians were added on special occasions. This expansion is also reflected in the Procurators' decisions to create new posts for a third organist in 1588, and (towards the end of the century) for an assistant *maestro di cappella*.[14]

The first notable organist-composer at St Mark's was Claudio Merulo, appointed in 1557, but it was with the employment of Andrea Gabrieli that the musical activities of St Mark's entered a new phase. During his youth Andrea had been organist at one of the Venetian parish churches, but in his 30s he spent some time at the Bavarian court at Munich. There he came under the influence of Orlande de Lassus, arguably the most famous composer of the time, who directed a large *cappella* of singers and instrumentalists. When he returned to Venice, Gabrieli brought with him ideas that had been refined by his experience of music written for *cori spezzati*, with the choir separated into two or more groups and the singers supported by instruments. It is a feature of such pieces that the groups engage in a dialogue, passing themes and harmonic ideas from one to another to create a kaleidoscopic effect; generally, the forces are united from time to time to emphasize the sense of the text, and this always happened at the end, which often involved a lively interpolation cast in a dance-like triple measure. Although Andrea Gabrieli also wrote more modest church music suitable for smaller establishments, it was the large-scale works for two or more choirs that earned him his reputation, and it was this style that was widely imitated, particularly by his own pupils. Of these the most important was Giovanni Gabrieli, Andrea's nephew, who followed in his uncle's footsteps by working under Lassus at Munich for a time and then returning to become organist at St Mark's.[15]

The major musical monument to the polychoral style in the period immediately after Willaert is the *Concerti* of 1587, in which most of the motets are by Andrea Gabrieli; published within two years of his death, the collection has the character of a commemorative volume. With their texts taken from the liturgy for the major feast-days in the Venetian calendar (Christmas, Easter, St Mark's Day and Corpus Christi) the *Concerti* preserve the musical elements of some annual ceremonial occasions, of both civic and religious importance, when the ducal *trionfi* were carried in procession and all the ritual apparatus of the state was on display. Similarly, Venetian mass publications are often scored for such large forces that they too were probably written for special occasions; Andrea's own sixteen-voice Gloria, for example, published in the *Concerti*, may have been written for a state visit of some Japanese princes in 1585. Publications for smaller forces, on the other hand, such as Andrea's collection of four-voice motets published in 1546, reflect what was done on saints' days of lesser importance.

St Mark's maintained a sense of tradition; in consequence, the new concertato manner of the early seventeenth century did not displace the older *cori spezzati* style, but rather co-existed with it. Throughout the 1600s composers working at St Mark's, including Monteverdi, continued to write in the traditional manner of Willaert and the Gabrielis. Settings of Vespers psalms for two four-part choirs or, in collections published after 1597, for two four-part choirs with basso continuo, are obvious examples. There is a specifically Venetian series of such works beginning with Willaert's famous collection of 1550 and extending well into the seventeenth century. All of them are characterized by the texts that are set and by their relatively simple style, excluding elaborate solo writing. By the seventeenth century, a large variety of musical styles had come to be used for Vespers psalms by composers working in north Italy: large-scale settings involving choirs, instruments and soloists, small-scale *concerti* and virtuoso settings for solo voice and basso continuo. Against this background, the continuing tradition of double-choir settings written by composers associated with St Mark's appears extremely conservative. It is almost as though this retrospective style was officially sanctioned and consciously cultivated.

It used to be thought that the origins and strength of this tradition lay in the architecture of St Mark's and in the arrangement of its ritual spaces, the large number of works for two or more choirs written by musicians employed by the basilica being a compositional response to the architectural arrangement of two organ-lofts placed on either side of the choir. Indeed, it used to be believed that the whole practice of double-choir psalms was evolved by Willaert in response to the building in which he worked and that his collection of 1550 contains the earliest examples of the style. This is no longer accepted. In the first place, the practice of *cori spezzati* was already well established in the Veneto by the time of Willaert's publication, and there are also some examples written for Ferrara and dating from the end of the fifteenth century.[16] Moreover, from the surviving documents it seems that double-choir psalms were usually performed not from the choir-lofts, as might be supposed, but from the octagonal structure placed to the right of the iconostasis.[17] Correctly known as the *pulpitum magnum cantorum*, and more familiarly as the *bigonzo* (or 'tub'), this is precisely the place that the singers of St Mark's occupy in Canaletto's famous sketch (fig.24). In other words, it seems that for double-choir psalms at least, the choirs were not separated but sang from the same place, the differentiation arising from the fact that one choir consisted only of soloists. (The organ-lofts may have been used on the rare occasions when large-scale ceremonial pieces for three or four choirs were performed.)

The performance of double-choir psalms was not an everyday occurrence; it was reserved for special occasions when the *pala d'oro*, the large gold altarpiece which is the major treasure of the basilica, was opened. Built in Constantinople in 976, the *pala* was enlarged with gold panels in the twelfth century, decorated with jewels after the sack of Constantinople in the thirteenth, and placed in its present frame in the fourteenth. On weekdays and minor feasts it was hidden behind a special wooden altarpiece, painted by Paolo Veneziano and his sons in 1345. But on the major feasts of the church year an elaborate mechanism was used to remove Paolo's altarpiece and to unfold the *pala d'oro* for the population to see. On these occasions, when the *pala d'oro* was displayed, the singers of St Mark's used to perform the psalms in plainchant, but from some time about the middle of the sixteenth century it became established that psalms should be sung in eight parts arranged in two choirs. By the end of the sixteenth century there were

24. The pulpits to left and right of the iconostasis in St Mark's; ink and wash drawing (1766) by Antonio Canaletto

over 50 days in the church year when the *pala d'oro* was opened and double-choir psalms performed from the *bigonzo*.

The large number of double-choir Vespers settings in the publications of musicians employed by St Mark's is a reflection of this fact. It seems that on the most important feasts a traditional liturgy was required for Vespers with music in a traditional style. Here, as elsewhere in the relationship between music and ceremonial in the state church of St Mark's, there seems to have been a set of broader principles at work. The musical style which the St Mark's composers might choose for their works was not necessarily the result of free artistic design, but could be very closely constrained by liturgical function and by acute awareness of tradition. For the Venetians of the seicento, a period of decline and uncertainty, the service of Vespers on a major feast-day was surely a powerful evocation of the past glories of La Serenissima. Then, in a liturgical framework peculiar to the basilica itself, before an altar captured from Byzantium, the singers of St Mark's performed music in an idiom which recalled the origins of the Venetian musical tradition, the great days of Willaert, Rore and Zarlino.[18]

Identification with the Republic through participation in civic and religious ceremonial was only one kind of allegiance which structured the lives of sixteenth-century Venetians; at a local level there was the

25. Corpus Christi Procession in St Mark's Square (1496) by Gentile Bellini; detail showing the five cantadori nuovi of the Scuola di S Giovanni Evangelista, accompanied by lute, rebec and harp

parish and the *scuola*. Most citizens would have belonged to one of the 200 *scuole piccole*, whose membership was often restricted according to criteria of occupation or national origin and which were sometimes patronized by wealthy patrician families who acted as benefactors. Such pious fraternities were to be found in all Italian cities during this period, but nowhere else was there anything quite like the principal Venetian institutions of this sort, the *scuole grandi*. The four oldest (S Maria della Carità, S Maria Valverde della Misericordia, S Marco and S Giovanni Evangelista) had begun in the thirteenth century as communities of flagellants; in 1481 the fraternity of S Rocco was added to their number, and the ancient Scuola di S Teodoro in 1552. Their main function, like that of the *scuole piccole*, was to promote virtuous living and to distribute benefits, both material and spiritual, among both their members and impoverished outsiders; in addition they provided manpower for the Venetian galleys. Membership was open to both rich and poor, but priests and nobles were excluded from positions of responsibility in the *scuole* (though not from membership itself). By the sixteenth century their financial resources had become very great, and much was spent on the erection and decoration of their meeting-houses. At the time there were some who believed that such ostentatious behaviour was not becoming conduct for bodies which were essentially charitable foundations, but the results were much admired and by the second half of the century *scuole* established themselves as one of the sights of Venice. The first court of the Scuola di S Giovanni Evangelista is ornamented with a delicate marble screen and portal by Pietro Lombardo, while the familiar façade of the Scuola di S Marco is the work of Mauro Coducci and the Lombardi. Most sumptuous of all is S Rocco (fig.13 above); behind its splendid main façade by Scarpagnino is a rich interior decorated with over 50 paintings by Jacopo Tintoretto, a Brother of the Confraternity, who took almost a quarter of a century to complete this remarkable cycle.[19]

Before the middle of the fifteenth century the music performed in the *scuole* during their frequent religious services and processions was provided either by musically talented members or by clerics. This music was monophonic, comprising either liturgical chant or *laude*. Beginning in the 1440s, however, the officers of the *scuole grandi* began to request the Council of Ten for permission to employ professional musicians from outside. An early example is provided by the Scuola di S Giovanni Evangelista which:

> has the greatest need for singers, who accompany [the *scuola*] and sing in processions for the dead and other solemnities . . . owing to the small number of singers at the *scuola* as well as to the great age of those that are here at present. Therefore, if singers are not permitted to be received [into the *scuola* to be apprenticed] under those here at present, to learn from them their customs and manner of singing, in a brief time the said *scuola* will have no singers . . .

Continuity was evidently difficult to achieve; a request for outside singers from an officer at the Scuola di S Marco writing in the 1460s reported that:

> because the singers are worn out like old men, it is with great difficulty that they are able to bury the dead and go to processions and to devotions in the city. These men are weakened and unsuitable, and in such a condition [they] go through the city silently as if dead.

From the 1470s or so, music began to play a much greater role in the activities of the *scuole*. As a result, the burden placed on the groups of four to six singers which the *scuole* maintained was too great, and in order to meet increased demands on their resources a second group of singers was established. The original group (*cantadori vecchi* or *cantadori di corpi*) were now required to sing mainly at funerals, while the second body (*cantadori nuovi* or *cantadori de laude*) was mainly expected to sing on Sundays and in processions. On important occasions both groups would combine. By the early decades of the sixteenth century most of the *scuole grandi* employed about ten singers; four to six *cantadori vecchi* who were employed on an occasional basis and four *cantadori nuovi* who were paid annual salaries.[20]

Although the *scuole grandi* were independent foundations, they were regulated by the state and were expected to participate in processions on public occasions. It is in this role that the group of five *cantadori nuovi* of the Scuola di S Giovanni Evangelista are shown in a detail from Gentile Bellini's famous painting, dated 1496, of the Corpus Christi procession in St Mark's Square (fig.25).[21] Here the singers are also accompanied by an instrumental group comprising lute, rebec and harp. Instrumentalists, who like the singers were employed on a part-time basis, began to take part in the activities of the *scuole* from about this date, and by 1540 or so a combination of four to six viole or lironi (occasionally supplemented by trumpets and shawms) had come to be standard, replacing the older grouping shown in Bellini's painting. As the ceremonial life of Venice became more elaborate in the course of the sixteenth century, so the demands upon this public and civic aspect of the activities of the *scuole* increased. The procession which celebrated the conclusion of a peace treaty between France and Spain in 1598 included, among other entertainments, a *carro* (literally a cart) mounted by the Scuola Grande di S Maria della Misericordia from which could be heard 'un maraviglioso, & nobilissimo concerto di liuti'. Later in the procession the Scuola di S Teodoro contributed another *carro* on which could be seen 'cinque valenti musici, che cantavano con somma melodia', while the representatives of the Scuola Piccola del Ss Rosario brought up the rear with a display which included 'tre giovani, che suonavano . . . uno con spinetta, l'altro con viola da gamba, e l'ultimo con violino i quali facevano una musica eccellentissima'.[22]

At the *scuole* of S Marco and S Rocco music was taken with particular seriousness. At S Marco the number of singers and instrumentalists was steadily increased during the first half of the sixteenth century; it was also the practice there to supplement the *cantadori vecchi* and the *cantadori nuovi* with yet a third group, the *cantadori solenni*, who were employed on the first Sunday of each month and on major festivals. In the early sixteenth century the *cantadori solenni* were often among the best known and trained in Venice, and in 1517 all twelve adult singers of the *cappella* of St Mark's were engaged. By contrast, the Scuola di S Rocco seems to have specialized in employing a small number of gifted singers, and in the 1520s it held auditions for new *cantadori* rather than relying on the normal practice of accepting the first men who offered their services. In 1550 the *scuola* passed the somewhat laconic resolution that 'those players who cannot play *canzoni* in processions shall be deprived of their employment', and a further stage in the expansion (and concomitant professionalization) of the musical provisions occurred later in the century when the doge and *signoria* instituted an annual *andata* to S Rocco. An account book which gives details of the festival of S Roch in 1595 reveals that a large body of singers and instrumentalists were involved, including the musicians of St Mark's and Giovanni Gabrieli, all under the direction of Giovanni Croce.[23] It was precisely an occasion of this sort that sent Thomas Coryat into raptures a few years later.

According to the surviving documents, the music performed in processions by the musicians of the *scuole* consisted mostly of polyphonic *laude*, but beyond this there is no more precise information. Nothing is known about the music (evidently quite elaborate by Coryat's day) that was performed at Mass, Vespers and on the great feast-days. Clearly there was collaboration between the *scuole* and the *cappella* of St Mark's, and by the end of the sixteenth century it seems to have become the practice for musicians from the basilica to be imported by the *scuole* on important occasions to perform pieces from their repertory. Yet while it is difficult to know how important the *scuole grandi* were to the development of Venetian music, it is clear that each *scuola* contributed a good deal to the musical life of its immediate area, acting as a focal point for local enactments of civic and religious ritual. Singers and instrumentalists were involved in the Solemn Mass which was celebrated in each of the *scuole* on the first Sunday of every month. Following this, the musicians formed a vital part of the procession which wound its way from the *scuola* to the church with which the foundation was particularly associated; after a further Mass celebrated there the procession returned to the meeting-house of the *scuola*. On all the other Sundays of the month the musicians of the *scuole* participated in a Mass celebrated in one of the religious houses in the vicinity. Without doubt the most spectacular event of the year was the celebration of the feast-day of the patron saint of the *scuola*; usually the musicians of all the *scuole* would join forces – singers, organists, instrumentalists and even the *maestro di cappella* of St Mark's itself. It was an event of this kind that Coryat witnessed in 1608; the elaborate nature of the musical arrangements on feast-days is confirmed by the words of Jean Baptiste du Val, secretary to the French ambassador to Venice, who on the feast-day of S Teodoro in 1607 was present at Vespers celebrated by the *scuola* in the church of S Salvatore: 'Il s'y fit un concert des meilleurs musiciens qu'ils eussent, tant de voix que d'instruments, principalement de six petits jeux d'orgues, oultre celuy de l'eglise qui est fort bon, et de trombones ou sacqueboutes, haultbois, violles, viollons, luths, cornets a bouquins, fleustes douces et flageolets'.[24]

Outside the *scuole grandi* there was a considerable amount of musical activity in the other churches of the city. This is especially true of the larger institutions, particularly the major monastic foundations. At the Frari, for example, Du Val was present at the celebration of Mass in 1608 when music was provided by 'trombones, espinettes, basses de voilles, dessus de viollons, luths et haults bois', and the following year, during Compline, he recorded the participation of 'deux jeux d'orgues portatifs . . . trombones, luths, theorbes, cornets a bouquins et basses de violon'. Although these recollections come from the early seventeenth century, Sanudo's diary reveals quite vigorous musical life in parish churches in the early part of the cinquecento. This is not surprising; many members of the *cappella* of St Mark's held ecclesiastical status (sometimes in defiance of propriety), and this enabled the Procurators to provide them with additional income from *mansionarie* and other benefices. Thus many Venetian churches had a formalized connection with at least one musician from St Mark's. The Procurators were well placed to distribute such sinecures, for in addition to administering the church treasury they were also executors for a large number of estates which had been entrusted to their care. Through this system of additional payments and benefits, analogous to the method by which members of the papal chapel in Rome were rewarded, the Procurators attempted to maintain a high quality of musical life in St Mark's; at the same time the practice may occasionally have benefited musical activity at a parish level.[25]

The musical life of basilica, church and square during the sixteenth century is much easier to reconstruct than that of the more private world of bourgeois social activity. Yet the performance of music was clearly a popular activity in the houses and *palazzi* of the Venetian nobility, and in the embassies of the various foreign nations that contributed to the cosmopolitan atmosphere of La Serenissima. Similarly, the Palladian villas which the Venetian aristocracy built in the countryside of the *terraferma* must have resounded to madrigals and other kinds of domestic music-making, or so we must infer from the iconography of Paolo Veronese's fresco cycle in the Villa Barbaro at Maser, or the scenes by Giovanni Antonio Fasolo on the walls of the Villa Caldogno, near Vicenza (fig.26). Unlike the *avvisi* and occasional accounts of visitors which provide glimpses of daily life inside the Villa d'Este at Tivoli, for example, there are no descriptions of social activities inside any of the villas in the Veneto. At Maser, however, Veronese painted every room of the upper level with scenes from poetic allegories, ancient mythology and the contemporary country life of the aristocracy. Some walls are frescoed with landscapes, as if the viewer were able to look through the internal walls of the villa to distant prospects, some with romantic ruins; others are painted with doors that seem to open to reveal members of the Barbaro family and their servants entering the real space of the rooms. It is surely indicative of actual practice that in the midst of this triumph of illusionism, in which the worlds of the gentleman and the farmer are combined (a fair reflection of Daniele Barbaro's own interests), musicians, both mythological and contemporary, have a place.

Occasional snippets of information provide some sense of the rich texture of Venetian domestic music-making in the city proper during the first half of the sixteenth century. When the printer Antonio Gardane dedicated a volume of six-voice motets by Willaert to the future doge, Marcantonio Trevisano, in 1542, Gardane himself noted that Trevisano was the owner of a large collection of musical instruments and an active patron of the musical profession. From a number of sources it is known that the house of Neri Capponi, a Florentine resi-

26. Domestic music-making depicted in a fresco (c1570) by Giovanni Antonio Fasolo in the main salon of the Villa Caldogno, near Vicenza

dent in the city, was a meeting-place for those with musical interests. And Girolamo Parabosco, Annibale Padovano, Baldassare Donato, Claudio Merulo and Giulio Abondante dal Prestino and the singers and instrumentalists of the Compagnia de' Fabbretti et Fruttaruoli were all frequent visitors to the home of Antonio Zantani, who also had a keen interest in the science of acoustics.[26] These examples, taken from different areas of the Venetian social hierarchy, are presumably typical of the society as a whole. From inventories prepared for the Venetian magistrates it is clear that a large number of middle-class households owned musical instruments, usually of the plucked and keyboard variety. These preferences are confirmed by what little is known of the instrument-making trade; two separate inventories made in 1581 of the possessions of the lute maker Moise Tieffenbrucker list hundreds of finished and unfinished pieces in his house and workshop.[27]

Some impression of the widespread popularity of music among the aristocracy and bourgoisie of Renaissance Venice is vividly conveyed by the large number of Venetian paintings, whether religious, mythological or narrative, which incorporate musicians, instruments or musical inscriptions. The extent to which music was cultivated as a social *divertissement* is powerfully illustrated in Giacomo Franco's print

27. *Musical divertissements on the Grand Canal: engraving from Giacomo Franco's 'Habiti d'huomini' (1609)*

of the Grand Canal, which shows precisely the sort of scene that the English visitor Richard Lassells described some decades later; 'they steere for two miles upon the laguna, while the musick plays, and sings epithalamiums all the way along, and makes Neptune jealous to heare Hymen called upon his Dominions'.[28] Apart from the music-making that was arranged by Venetian residents, the visits of foreign dignitaries to this most cosmopolitan of all cities often brought with them a fresh influx of musicians. In 1562, for example, 30 musicians from the court of Ferrara (eighteen singers, seven cornett players and trombonists, three organists and two viol players) accompanied Duke Alfonso II d'Este on a journey to Venice. In this way the visits of foreign princes clearly offered opportunities for contact between musicians and sometimes for the exchange of personnel and perhaps of new compositions that had not yet found their way into print.[29]

For many visitors it was not only the physical beauty of Venice that was attractive, but also the endless spectacle and ceremony in this city of processions. Throughout the sixteenth century, the traditional incorporation of significant events in Venetian history into the city's civic and religious ceremonial was a continuing process, actively promoted by a government only too aware of its political benefits. Among the fourteen occasions listed by the Venetian historian Sansovino in 1581 as involving the full ducal *andata*, three had been instituted within the century. The earliest of these was the feast-day of S Marina who was given the credit for the recovery of Padua from the troops of the League of Cambrai. On this day, 17 July, the elaborate procession of ecclesiastical and civic dignitaries accompanied by members of the *scuole grandi* made their way to the parish church that bore her name. The second newly established feast, of Christ the Redeemer, had a more supplicatory character and was intimately related to contemporary events. In 1577 the foundation stone of Andrea Palladio's church of the Redentore, his major work of the 1570s, was laid; it was built on the orders of the senate and placed in the hands of the Capuchins in fulfilment of a vow made when the city was finally delivered from the devastating plague of 1575–6. The doge and senate pledged that the church would be visited annually on the third Sunday in July. Some 30 per cent of the Venetian population perished in this plague; the procession to the Redentore was a popular event and its penitential character was in keeping with the pious preoccupations of the Catholic Reformation. The senate's instructions had imposed on Palladio three almost autonomous types of ecclesiastical architecture related to the function they were to perform: monastic in the choir, votive in the tribune and congregational in the nave and chapels. These areas also seem to have been designed with the musical implications of the *andata* clearly in mind. At the church itself the ceremony consisted of a Low Mass accompanied by motets sung by the choir of St Mark's at the Offertory and Elevation; this public ceremony before a large congregation explains the distinct separation of the long nave from the choir and tribune which lies beyond it.[30] Although no polyphony has survived that seems to have been specially composed for the feast of the Redentore, the text of Andrea Gabrieli's eight-voice motet *O crux splendidior* seems particularly suited to the foundation ceremony itself and may well have been written for that occasion.

Important political events were often recognized with public processions: the birth of a son to François I of France in 1518, a new league in 1537, the peace of Cateau-Cambrésis in 1559, the victory of Catholic forces over the Huguenots in 1563, the elections of new popes, and the conclusion of peace between France and Spain in 1598. For the visit of Henri III to Venice in 1574 elaborate celebrations were devised and a number of Venetian composers were commissioned to produce music: Andrea Gabrieli wrote two large-scale madrigals, *Hor che nel suo bel seno* and *Ecco Vinegia bella,* and a play by Cornelio Frangipane was given with music by Claudio Merulo; the French king also heard a Mass with 'soave concerto di musica' at the Frari and was present at another liturgical function at St Mark's at which Gabrieli and Merulo directed the *cappella.*[31] But the most popular celebration of all came to be the feast of S Giustina on 7 October, when Venetians recalled their famous victory over the Turks at the Battle of Lepanto in 1571. The progress of the various celebrations that took place in the city from the moment that the news was announced can be recovered in some detail; the picture that emerges provides the most complete example we have of the extent to which music, poetry, painting, architecture and civic and religious ritual were intimately connected in a rhetoric of state whose prime purpose was to project the myth of Venice. Nowhere else can the very particular Venetian conception of music as something more than either social distraction or devotional ornament be followed with so much clarity.

In Italy in general, and in Venice in particular, the Turkish question was one of abiding interest throughout the sixteenth century. Both culturally and politically the outcome of the War of Cyprus and the Battle of Lepanto affected the whole of the peninsula, but it was above all in Venice and the *terraferma* that Lepanto was celebrated.[32] News of the victory arrived in the city twelve days after the engagement. Almost immediately a great concourse of people gathered in St Mark's Square. Mass was said and the *Te Deum* was sung. The following Sunday a Solemn Mass was celebrated in St Mark's punctuated by 'concerti divinissimi' which were clearly, according to a contemporary account, motets for double choir (*cori spezzati*). The victory was thus immediately confirmed as Christ's victory secured by the Venetians through the agency of Divine Protection, a ubiquitous motif in the flood of literature produced in the aftermath of Lepanto. The precise pieces performed on this occasion cannot be identified, though any number of motets from the Venetian repertory would have been appropriate. For example, Andrea Gabrieli's eight-voice setting of the benediction text *O salutaris hostia* seems particularly appropriate for the events of summer 1571:

> O salutaris hostia
> Quae coelis pandis ostium;
> Bella praemunt hostilia,
> Da robur, fer auxilium.[33]

A population which had been kept in touch with the progress of the war through pamphlets and broadsheets, and who strongly identified with this Christian crusade against the infidel, now lauded the news in print. A torrent of ephemera poured from the presses of Venice; short anthologies of poetry, paraphrases of the psalms, cheap woodcuts showing the disposition of the galleys at the battle and blow-by-blow accounts of Lepanto itself. Some of this crude and chauvinistic verse did find its way into settings written by composers working in the Veneto. Ippolito Baccusi, for example, a Mantuan working in Verona, published a *Canzon nelle gran vittoria* in his second book of six-voice madrigals of 1572; the text is taken from Celio Magno's long poem *Fuor, fuori o Muse*, a firm favourite in the poetic collections. In a further burst of patriotic fervour the same composer also published that year a seven-section cycle in praise of Lepanto. Once again the text, *Ai piu soavi accenti* (by Vincenzo Giusto of Udine), was one that had been widely circulated in popular anthologies.

The motifs and themes which run through much of this popular verse recur in many of the stock images which were either issued as woodcuts or formed part of the many independent celebrations organized in Venice in the weeks after the victory. The first of these seems to have come from the German merchants who decorated the Fondaco dei Tedeschi with tapestries and then celebrated for three successive nights. The latter included not only the rumbustious clamour of *piffari* and drums and the 'trombe squarciate' that traditionally formed part of such popular celebrations, but also 'diversi bei concerti' performed in covered arbours. Following this spirited example different parts of the community competed to produce the most impressive celebrations. Another three-day affair, organized by the *Drappieri*, was concentrated in the area around the Rialto bridge, then a rather squalid quarter of the city. With the help of tapestries, canopies and lanterns the streets were transformed. Again there was not only the usual impromptu music, but also what seems to have been more decorous polyphony performed both during the religious ceremonies and in various places around the Rialto: 'una Messa solenne con musiche rari' sung under a canopy in front of the church of S Giacomo, Vespers with elaborate music a few days later, and throughout the day and night 'divini concerti' from various spots nearby.[34]

The theme of the Venetians as the Chosen People, through whose timely action the Infidel had been punished, reappears in the next celebration which seems to have had some official status, the *Trionfo di Christo contra Turchi*. This was given, as its opening lines make clear, before doge and senate on St Stephen's Day 1571. A short and simple drama cast in the mould of the traditional *Sacra rappresentatione*, the *Trionfo* was again specially composed for the occasion by Celio Magno. Unfortunately nothing is known of the music, described as 'straordinarie' by the Ferrarese ambassador, which was presumably written for the three choruses. Magno's drama proceeds in an entirely emblematic fashion by first introducing David, then the patron saints of the three Christian states involved in the conflict, and finally S Giustina and the Angel Gabriel.[35] Issues of history were thus neatly intertwined with the theme of Venetian sovereignty (by association with David) and the familiar topic of the Venetians as a Chosen Race. Nor was the choice of St Stephen's Day for the performance of the *Trionfo* accidental; Stephen's name also carried a local resonance since his body had been brought to Venice in 1109 and was reputedly buried in S Giorgio Maggiore. The *Trionfo di Christo* is an early example of a series of plays, usually involving music, which were given before the doge on important Venetian feast-days, notably St Stephen's Day and the Feast of the Ascension; although the texts of these plays clearly indicate the involvement of music, none has survived.

The intervention of S Giustina towards the end of Magno's *Trionfo* leads us from the realm of ephemeral celebration to that of permanent celebration. Fortuitously, the victory at Lepanto occurred on the feast-day of S Giustina, one of the patron saints of Padua, a city then under Venetian control. There in particular her association with the victory not only strengthened local belief in the idea of the Venetians as divinely favoured, but also encouraged an already strong tradition of veneration. Inevitably, the figure of S Giustina often appears in Vene-tian triumphal art associated with Lepanto. It was equally inevitable, perhaps, that the day of S Giustina should enter the Venetian calendar of annual celebrations. A decree from the senate ordered that an annual procession, taking the form of the traditional *andata*, be held from St Mark's Square to the church of S Giustina, and this took place for the first time in 1572. Even in a century which witnessed a dramatic increase in civic and religious rituals, the S Giustina procession rapidly assumed an important position in the Venetian calendar, soon becoming second in popularity only to the commemoration of the legendary defeat of Emperor Frederick Barbarossa. This new-found popularity is also reflected in musical compositions such as Giovanni Bassano's five-voice motet *Beata virgo et martyr Iustina*, published in his *Motetti per concerti ecclesiastici* of 1598 and presumably written for the annual celebration.

As in other victory celebrations, the *andata* to S Giustina provided the government of the Republic not only with the opportunity to honour a saint and commemorate the dead, but also to strengthen social cohesion through displays of piety and patriotism. In the case of the Turks, who remained uneasily lodged in the Venetian collective consciousness despite Lepanto, there was the added attraction of annu-ally re-identifying a common enemy. Similar motives are apparent in the *mascherata* devised for the Carnival of 1572, a highpoint in the celeb-rations of the victory. It took the form of a procession which began in the north of the city and gradually wound its way through the narrow streets to St Mark's Square; 340 people took part, including a large number of musicians and 100 costumed as Turkish slaves.[36] The appearance of the latter in groups between the various *carri* may have lent the procession some superficial semblance of unity, but it does not disguise the fact that the *mascherata* fell into two distinct segments. The first part presented in striking terms a simple political allegory. At the head was Faith trampling on the Turkish serpent, preceded by Hope and Charity and followed by the four Cardinal Virtues who had reputedly inspired the leaders of the victorious armies. The next three *carri* displayed personifications of Rome, Spain and Venice. Finally came Victory, a woman dressed in red velvet carrying a palm branch and laurel wreaths; under her feet was a Turkish slave, and the chariot itself provided the symbolic image of the serpent cut into two.

It is with this initial allegorical part of the *mascherata* that Andrea Gabrieli's music is associated. Following immediately there were three groups of four singers, each representing a different continent. The first was dressed 'alla Turchesca' to represent Asia, the second 'alla Moresca' to suggest Africa, and the last in silk 'all' Italiana' to personify Europe. Finally, all twelve joined together in an exuberant demonstration of universal joy. Here the familiar motif of the victory as Christ's victory makes a reappearance:

> Cantiam dunque cantiamo; e in ogni parte
> Gratie si renda al sommo Re del Cielo
> Et sol a lui si dia con puro zelo
> Lode, e Gloria de ben che a noi comparte.

The music for the three continents (but not for the final peroration) survives in Gabrieli's *Madrigali et ricercari a quattro* of 1589 where it occurs in a miscellaneous selection of madrigals, instrumental pieces and simple choruses from plays all composed over a number of years. Andrea was perhaps the obvious choice to provide the music for this official victory parade since he had the experience of composing a sonorous eight-voice dialogue *Felice d'Adria* for the visit of Archduke Karl of Carinthia to Venice in 1569. The four-part *trionfi* for the Lepanto celebrations are quite different in conception and it must be assumed that their simple harmonies and largely homophonic textures were designed with the practical difficulties of open-air performance in mind.

Following Gabrieli's musicians, the *mascherata* proper began. The remaining *carri* were both more miscellaneous and more traditional in character. Most were connected with annual Venetian feasts and customs, and a number involved groups of musicians. The feast of the First of August was represented by Bacchus accompanied by five Germans, with flasks of Malvasia and glasses in hand, singing 'Viva, viva, Bacco, Bacco'. In some cases the music which accompanied these tableaux belonged to specifically Venetian popular traditions; a number of the sung texts are in dialect and accompanied stock figures from Venetian life. None of this music seems to have survived, but it was presumably similar in style to Andrea Gabrieli's *mascherate*.

In common with the other public processions and the celebrations organized by the merchant communities, the Lepanto *mascherata* was propaganda. Much of its effect was achieved by drawing on a simple and traditional series of images accompanied by rousing and unsophisticated music. At the same time some of the more dignified elements operated on a different level; this is true for example of the initial group of five allegorical *carri trionfali* with which Andrea Gabrieli's music was associated. In fact, with its rather obvious division into two parts, the

28. Jacopo Sansovino's Loggetta (1537–49) at the base of the campanile in St Mark's Square

Carnival *mascherata* of 1572 is a perfect demonstration of differentiated modes of celebration. What is of interest here is not only the strong involvement of music and the way that it was used to support some of the main iconographical themes of the pageant, but also the hierarchical ordering of musical genres and styles. The *mascherata*, like the other Venetian processions which filled the calendar, was not only a form of public entertainment, but also an instrument of social order. In this, music had an important and carefully calculated role.

In this context it is worth recalling Jacopo Sansovino's explanation of the iconography of the new Loggetta at the base of the campanile of St Mark's which he designed in 1537 (fig.28). The old structure had been used by the nobility as a meeting-place when they came to the square on government business. Sansovino's replacement, decorated with precious materials and rich sculptural decoration based on classical allegory and mythology, imposed a different dimension. In the first place it is a remarkable symbol of the 'renovatio urbis' inaugurated by Andrea Gritti towards the end of his dogeship, a policy which brought both Adrian Willaert and Jacopo Sansovino to the city. In architectural terms its forms and colours complement those of the nearby ducal palace, while the façade, with its obvious overtones of a triumphal arch, is an essay in a classicizing style which is specifically associated with state buildings of the period. Indeed, the Loggetta has been described as the 'most complete surviving visual representation of the myth of Venice', the specifically Venetian view of their own state as the perfect republic.[37] It served not only to impress the supremacy of the Venetian state on foreign visitors, but also to remind the Venetian population of its own myth. It was presumably in accordance with this purpose that its old function as a casual meeting-place gradually declined, and the Procurators started to hold meetings there themselves. During the sessions of the Grand Council it was occupied by three Procurators attended by 50 guards supplied by the Arsenal, and Coryat described the Loggetta as 'a place where some of the Procurators of Saint Markes doe sit in iudgement, and discuss matters of controversies'.[38] A plate from Franco's *Habiti* shows the building being used in this way.

At the centre of the decorative scheme are four bronze statues representing Minerva, Apollo, Mercury and Peace, which occupy niches in the façade. Recalling his father's explanation of the significance of Apollo, Francesco Sansovino wrote:

> the statue of Apollo is the sun, which is singular and unique, just as this Republic, for its constituted laws, its unity, and uncorrupted liberty, is a sun in the world, regulated with justice and wisdom; furthermore, it is known how this nation takes a more than ordinary delight in music, and Apollo signifies music. Moreover, from the union of the magistracies, combined with the equable temperament, there arises an unusual harmony, which perpetuates this admirable government: for these reasons was Apollo represented.[39]

This evocation of the richness of the city's musical life is not a mere rhetorical flourish; behind the conceit lay a musical reality in which state patronage of music occupied a central place in Venetian civic and religious ceremonial. This is evident in the steady growth in size and importance of the musical establishment of St Mark's in the decades after the appointment of Willaert as *maestro di cappella*, a process in which the state was actively involved through the Procurators. The increased vitality of Venetian musical life by the mid-century is reflected in the city's importance as the European capital of music printing and instrument making, both areas in which government support and intervention was critical, as well as in the expanded musical activities of the *scuole*. Parallel to these developments was an increased emphasis on state ceremonial and pageantry, particularly on specially designated *feste* which served to promote the myth of Venice among the city's cosmopolitan population. In all these developments the government of the Republic played a conscious and deliberate role, fully recognizing the propaganda value of an art which was available in printed form and had become immensely popular, particularly among the middle strata of society. It was partly on the basis of these developments that Venice, city of carnival and of processions, became one of the most important centres of musical life in late sixteenth- and early seventeenth-century Europe.

NOTES

1 T. Coryat, *Coryat's Crudities Hastily Gobled up in Five Moneths Travells in France, Savoy, Italy, Rhetia* (London, 1611), 251–3.
2 From the diary of Marino Sanudo describing an entertainment given on 20 April 1517 in the house of one 'conte Mercurio'; cited in D. Bryant, 'La musica nelle istituzioni religiose e profane di Venetia', in *Storia della cultura veneta dalla controriforma alla fine della repubblica, 4/1: Il seicento* (1983), 433–47.
3 The literature on the myth of Venice is large and continues to grow; see in particular F. Gilbert, 'The Venetian Constitution in Florentine Political Thought', in *Florentine Studies, Politics and Society in Renaissance Florence*, ed. N. Rubenstein (London, 1968), 463–500; L. J. Libby, jr, 'Venetian History and Political Thought after 1509', *Studies in the Renaissance*, xx (1973), 7–45; W. J. Bouwsma, 'Venice and the Political Education of Europe', in *Renaissance Venice*, ed. J. R. Hale (London, 1973); and E. Muir, *Civic Ritual in Renaissance Venice* (Princeton, 1981), 13–61. The question of the involvement of music in the propagation of the myth was first approached in E. Rosand, 'Music in the Myth of Venice', *Renaissance Quarterly*, xxx (1977), 511–37; see also D. Bryant, 'Liturgia e musica liturgica nella fenomenologia del "mito di Venezia"', in *Mitologie*, ed. G. Morelli (Venice, 1979), 205–14.
4 Petrarch, *Epistolae seniles*, iv, 3.
5 Donato, *Il primo libro di canzon villanesche alla Napolitana* (Venice, 1550).
6 For a general survey see D.S. Chambers, *The Imperial Age of Venice 1380–1580* (London, 1970), especially 33ff and 122ff.
7 Muir, *Civic Ritual*, 189–211; see also the same author's 'Images of Power: Art and Pageantry in Renaissance Venice', *American Historical Review*, lxxxiv (1979), 16–52.
8 G. Fasoli, 'Liturgia e ceremoniale ducale', in *Venezia e il Levante fino al secolo XV*, ed. A. Pertusi (Florence, 1973–4), i, 261–95.
9 For St Mark see Muir, *Civic Ritual*, 78–92, with Fiamma's remarks quoted on p.91.
10 G. Bassano: *Motetti per concerti ecclesiastia* (Venice, 1598).
11 For the importance of the basilica see O. Demus, *The Church of San Marco in Venice* (Washington, 1960), 1–60; S. Sinding-Larsen, *Christ in the Council Hall: Studies in the Religious Iconography of the Venetian Republic* (Rome, 1974), 179–217.
12 The history of the *cappella* can be approached through F. Caffi, *Storia della musica sacra nella gia cappella ducale di San Marco in Venezia dal 1318 al 1797* (Venice, 1854), with some useful supplementary information in G. Benvenuti, *Andrea e Giovanni Gabrieli e la musica strumentale in San Marco* [Milan, 1931–2] and, for the sixteenth century, R.B.M. Lenaerts, 'La chapelle de Saint-Marc à Venise sous Adrien Willaert', *Bulletin de l'Institut historique belge de Rome*, xix (1938), 205–55.
13 For the Procurators see R. C. Meuller, 'The Procurators of San Marco in the Thirteenth and Fourteenth Centuries: a Study of the Office as a Financial Trust', *Studi veneziani*, xiii (1971), 105–220; D. Howard, *Jacopo Sansovino: Architecture and Patronage in Renaissance Venice* (New Haven and London), 8–37.
14 For a summary of the main changes in the organization and size of the chapel see Rosand, 'Musc in the Myth of Venice', 519–22.
15 The present essay concentrates on the period up to the death of Andrea Gabrieli in 1585; for the career and music of his nephew Giovanni see D. Arnold, *Giovanni Gabrieli and the Music of the Italian High Renaissance* (London, 1979).
16 For the *terraferma* see G. D'Alessi, 'Precursors of Adriano Willaert in the Practice of *Coro spezzato*', *JAMS*, v (1950), 187–210; A. T. Carver, 'The Psalms of Willaert and his North Italian Contemporaries', *AcM*, xlvii (1975), 27–83.
17 D. Bryant, 'The *Cori spezzati* of St Mark's: Myth and Reality', *EMH*, i (1981), 165–86; J. H. Moore, 'The *Vespero delli cinque laudate* and the Role of *salmi spezzati* at St Mark's', *JAMS*, xxxiv (1981), 249–78.
18 For the seventeenth-century tradition see J. H. Moore, *Vespers at St. Mark's 1625–1675: Music of Alessandro Grandi, Giovanni Rovetta and Francesco Cavalli* (diss., U. of California, Los Angeles, 1979).
19 For a general survey of the *scuole* and their role in Venetian society see B. Pullan, *Rich and Poor in Renaissance Venice: the Social Institutions of a Catholic State, to 1620* (Oxford, 1971), especially Pt 1.
20 J. Glixon, 'Music at the Venetian Scuole Grandi, 1440–1540', in *Music in Medieval and Early Modern Europe: Patronage, Sources and Texts*, ed. I. Fenlon (Cambridge, 1981), 193–208.

21 H. M. Brown, 'On Gentile Bellini's Processione in San Marco (1496)', *IMSCR*, xii *Berkeley 1977*, 649–58.

22 G. L. Collini, *Esplicatione dei carri trionfali fatti nella processione per la pace tra Franza e Spagna della Scola di S. Teodoro il 26. Luglio 1598* (Venice, 1598).

23 D. Arnold, 'Music at the Scuola di San Rocco', *ML*, xl (1959), 229–41.

24 J. B. du Val, *Les remarques triennales*, F-Pn fr.13977, f.45*v* (see A. Pirro, 'La musique des italiens d'après les remarques triennales de Jean-Baptiste Duval (1607–1609)', in *Mélanges offerts à M. Henry Lemonnier* (Paris, 1913), 175–85.

25 G. Ongaro, 'Sixteenth-Century Patronage at St Mark's, Venice', *EMH*, viii (1988), 81–115.

26 This celebrated and much-discussed dedication is from A. Willaert, *Musicorum sex vocum, que vulgo motecta dicuntur . . . liber primus* (Venice, 1542); see now M. S. Lewis, 'Antonio Gardane's Early Connections with the Willaert Circle', in *Music in Medieval and Early Modern Europe*, ed. I. Fenlon, 219–20. For the Zantani house see E. Selfridge-Field, *Venetian Instrumental Music from Gabrieli to Vivaldi* (Oxford, 1975), 50.

27 D. Bryant and M. Morell, 'La vita musicale a Venezia all'epoca di Andrea Gabrieli', *Edizione nazionale delle opere di Andrea Gabrieli [1533]–1585* (Milan, 1988), 42.

28 R. Lassells, *The Voyage of Italy* (Paris, 1670), 413.

29 *La solenissima entrata dell'illustrissimo et eccellentissimo signor duca di Ferrara ne la citta di Venetia cominciando dalla partita di sua eccellenza da Ferrare per insino al suo ritorno* (Bologna, 1962); *La entrate che fece in Vinegia L'Illustissimo et Eccellentissimo S. Duca Alfonso II Estense, Duca V di Ferrara* (Venice, 1562).

30 J. S. Ackerman, *Palladio* (Harmondsworth, 1966), 129–35; P. Murray, 'Palladio's Churches', in *Arte in Europa: scritti di storia dell' arte in onore di Edoardo Arslan* (Milan, 1966), i, 597–608.

31 R. Benedetti, *Le feste et trionfi fatti della . . . Signoria di Venezia nelle felice venuta di Henrico III* (Venice, 1574), ff.5–6*v*, and T. Porcacchi, *Le attioni d'Arrigo terzo re di Francia . . . le feste, con i quali e stato ricevuto in Venetia* (Venice, 1574), ff.34 and 28*v*. P. di Nolhac and A. Solerti, *Il viaggio in Italia di Enrico III re di Francia e le feste a Venezia, Ferrara, Mantova, e Torino* (Turin, 1890).

32 E. H. Gombrich, 'Celebrations in Venice of the Holy League and of the Victory of Lepanto', in *Studies in Renaissance and Baroque Art Presented to Anthony Blunt on his Sixtieth Birthday* (London, n.d.), 62–8; I. Fenlon, '*In Destructione Turcharum:* the Victory of Lepanto in Sixteenth-Century Music and Letters', in *Andrea Gabrieli e il suo tempo: Venice 1985*, 293–317.

33 R. Benedetti, *Ragguaglio delle allegrezze, solennita, e feste fatte in Venetia per la felice Vittoria* (Venice, 1571), f.[A4]; the suggestion about Gabrieli's motet was first made in D. Bryant, *Liturgy, Ceremonial and Sacred Music in Venice at the Time of the Counter-Reformation* (diss., U. of London, 1982), 49ff.

34 R. Benedetti; *Ragguaglio delle allegrezze*, ff.B3–[B3]*v*.

35 L. Groto, *Trofeo della Vittoria sacra, ottenuta della Christianiss. Lega contre Turchi nell'anno MDLXXI* (Venice, 1572), ff.13–16; for further discussion see A. L. Bellina and T. Walker, 'Il melodramma: poesia e musica nel'esperienza teatrale', in *Storia della culture veneta*, 409–10.

36 *Ordine, et dechiaratione di tutta la mascherata, fatta nella citta di Venetia la domenica di carnevale, 1571, per la gloriosa vittoria contra Turchi* (Venice, 1572).

37 Howard, op cit,34.

38 Coryat, *Coryat's Crudities*, 185.

39 F. Sansovino, *Venetia vitta nobilissima . . . con aggiunta da D. Giustiniano Martioni* (Venice, 1663), 307ff.

BIBLIOGRAPHICAL NOTE

There is a large literature on sixteenth-century Venice. Although I have in the main restricted myself here to works published in English, the relevant volumes of the *Storia della cultura veneta* are fundamental. Among general studies the following are particularly useful: W. J. Bouwsma, *Venice and the Defense of Republican Liberty: Renaissance Values in the Age of the Counter-Reformation* (Berkeley, 1968); D. S. Chambers, *The Imperial Age of Venice 1380–1580* (London, 1970); O. Logan, *Culture and Society in Venice 1470–1790: the Renaissance and its Heritage* (London, 1972); and F. C. Lane, *Venice, a Maritime Republic* (Baltimore, 1973). There is also a number of helpful essays in *Renaissance Venice,* ed. J. R. Hale (London, 1973). On the myth of Venice and related topics see F. Gilbert, 'The Venetian Constitution in Florentine Political Thought', in *Florentine Studies,* ed. N. Rubinstein (London, 1968), 463–500, and, for musical ramifications, E. Rosand, 'Music in the Myth of Venice', *Renaissance Quarterly,* xxx (1977), 511–37. A still valuable introduction to the debates over the Venetian economy in the period is *Crisis and Change in the Venetian Economy in the Sixteenth and Seventeenth Centuries,* ed. B. Pullan (London, 1968). A short account of the workings of Venetian government is given in C. T. Davis's, *The Decline of the Venetian Nobility as a Ruling Class* (Baltimore, 1962). For a helpful and very readable account of what is both symptom and part cause of Venetian decline in an adjacent period see A. Tenenti's *Piracy and the Decline of Venice 1585–1615* (London, 1966). The old study of the development of the printing press by H. F. Brown, *The Venetian Printing Press, 1469–1800* (London, 1891), is still useful, and to it should be added P. F. Grendler's *The Roman Inquisition and the Ventetian Press, 1540–1605* (Princeton, 1977).

The central position of St Mark's basilica in Venetian life is emphasized by a reading of O. Demus, *The Church of San Marco in Venice: History, Architecture, Sculpture* (Washington, 1960). Some of the most important public buildings erected during the period are discussed in D. Howard's *Jacopo Sansovino: Architecture and Patronage in Renaissance Venice* (New Haven and London, 1975), and some of the public decorative schemes of the time are interpreted, in an admittedly controversial way but with analogies in Venetian music (for which see D. Bryant in *Storia della cultura veneta,* iv/1, 433–48), in S. Sinding-Larsen's *Christ in the Council Hall: Studies in the Religious Iconography of the Venetian Republic* (Rome, 1974). The importance of music theory for Venetian architecture, and above all the work of Palladio, is elegantly demonstrated in R. Wittkower's *Architectural Principles in the Age of Humanism* (New York, 3/1971). On public processions and other aspects of civic ritual in the city see E. Muir's *Civic Ritual in Renaissance Venice* (Princeton, 1981) and for the importance of the *scuole grandi* B. Pullan's *Rich and Poor in Renaissance Venice: the Social Institutions of a Catholic State to 1620* (Venice, 1971).

The principal study of music in sixteenth-century Venice remains that of F. Caffi, *Storia della musica sacra gia cappella ducale di San Marco in Venezia* (Venice, 1854–5). For further details of the *cappella* of St Mark's, the main body of musicians in the service of church and state in the period, see also R. B. M. Lenaerts, 'La chapelle de Saint-Marc à Venise sous Adrien Willaert', *Bulletin de l'Institut historique belge de Rome,* xix (1938), 205–55, and G. Ongaro, 'Sixteenth Century Patronage at St Mark's, Venice', *EMH,* viii (1988), 81–115. Some of the implications of the *patriarchino* for polyphonic composition are explored in J. H. Moore, 'The "Vespero delli cinque laudate" and the Role of *salmi spezzati* at St Mark's', *JAMS,* xxxiv (1981), 249–78; the same author's '*Venezia favorita da Maria*: Music for the Madonna Nicopeia and Santa Maria della Salute', *JAMS,* xxxvii (1984), 299–355, largely deals with seventeenth-century material but has implications for the earlier period. On the musical activities of the *scuole* see J. Glixon's, 'Music at the Venetian Scuole Grandi 1440–1540', in *Music in Medieval and Early Modern Europe,* ed. I. Fenlon (Cambridge, 1981), 193–208, and the same author's 'A Musicians' Union in Sixteenth Century Venice', *JAMS,* xxxvi (1983), 392–441. On music printing see M. Lewis, 'Antonio Gardane's Early Connections with the Willaert Circle', in *Music in Medieval and Early Modern Europe,* ed. I. Fenlon, 209–26. The role of music in Venetian festivals is examined in A. Solerti's 'Le rappresentazioni musicali Venezia dal 1571 al 1605, per la prima volta descritte', *RMI,* ix (1902), 554–8; for a more detailed discussion of the most elaborate celebrations in the period see I. Fenlon's 'Lepanto: the Arts of Celebration in Renaissance Venice', *Proceedings of the British Academy,* lxxiii (1987), 201–36.

Chapter IV

North Italian Courts, 1460–1540

WILLIAM F. PRIZER

On 28 November 1373, less than a year before his death, the poet and humanist Petrarch wrote a letter to Francesco di Carrara, Lord of Padua, detailing the qualities of the ideal prince. The *signore*, wrote Petrarch, should regulate every facet of the life of the state including the construction and restoration of public buildings, churches, streets and city walls, and should also give his patronage and friendship to 'viros egregios', particularly men of letters.[1] Since Petrarch himself was a connoisseur and collector of art, and since he had actually completed his *De viris illustribus* because of Francesco's desire for a room in his palace dedicated to the portraits of famous men, Petrarch might well have placed the welfare of artists also in the prince's charge.[2] This letter is of primary importance because it is the earliest-known humanist call to individual patronage of the arts, although in this instance Petrarch seems to have been a harbinger of future trends rather than a spokesman for contemporary ideas; patronage on a wide scale remained essentially corporate rather than individual throughout the fourteenth and early fifteenth centuries.[3]

It is significant that Petrarch does not mention music as the object of the prince's patronage. True, the distinguished trecento composers Maestro Piero, Jacopo da Bologna and Giovanni da Firenze seem to have worked for the Scaligeri in Verona and Padua, and for the Visconti in Milan,[4] but systematic patronage of music by the noble families of northern Italy did not begin until the early quattrocento, and even then the records speak only of one or two musicians in residence, the rest being employed on a casual basis from among travelling performers. Of the three courts that will be the centre of our attention – Ferrara, Mantua and to a lesser extent Milan – notices of musicians during the trecento are sparse indeed. In Ferrara only a single shawm player is listed at court in the late trecento; in Mantua there are isolated references to persons with the surname 'Viola', but no certain notices of resident musicians until the time of Gianfrancesco Gonzaga (ruled 1407–44); in Milan, apart from Luchino Visconti's early (and apparently isolated) patronage of Jacopo da Bologna, we must await the rise of the Sforza in the second half of the quattrocento for systematic patronage of music.

The courts of Ferrara, Mantua and Milan were the principal centres of musical patronage in northern Italy in their day and were also the only courts to keep the same dynasty of rulers intact for a sufficiently long period to allow one to observe the historical trends developing. (The court of Urbino could make a claim for our attention, but much of its relevant documentation has been destroyed; from what remains it seems that Urbino was of minor importance, relying heavily for musicians upon its larger relatives – particularly Mantua, to which it was tied through marriage.)

Ferrara, situated near the Po in Reggio-Emilia, was ruled by the Este family from the trecento. The rulers during the period under discussion here were Leonello (ruled 1429–50) and his brothers Borso (ruled 1450–71) and Ercole I (ruled 1471–1505). Ercole was followed by his son Alfonso I (ruled 1505–34). From the time of Borso the Este enjoyed the titles of Duke of Ferrara and Duke of Modena. Ferrara was

29. The Concert (c1480) by Lorenzo Costa, an artist who trained in Ferrara and became court painter at Mantua in 1506

tied to Milan and Mantua through a series of political marriages designed to ensure the safety of its borders and strong alliances with its neighbours. The Duchy of Ferrara was linked to Milan through the marriage of Alfonso I to Anna Sforza, and through the marriage of Ercole d'Este's daughter Beatrice to Ludovico Sforza. Under Ercole, Ferrara was perhaps the most important musical centre of northern Italy.

Mantua, on the banks of the river Mincio (which runs from the Lago di Garda in Verona to the Po in the south), is situated in southern Lombardy. Since the trecento it had been ruled by the Gonzaga family, who came originally from the village of Gonzaga in the Mantuan *contado*. The ruling members of the family, who reigned as marchesi until 1530 when Federico II was raised to duke by the Emperor Charles V, were Gian Francesco (ruled 1407–44, made marchese in 1433), Ludovico (ruled 1444–78), Federico I (ruled 1478–84), Francesco II (ruled 1484–1519) and Federico II (ruled 1519–40). The Gonzaga were allied both to Milan and to Ferrara through politics and marriage. Ludovico, Federico I and Francesco II were all generals of the Milanese army; Margherita, daughter of Gianfrancesco Gonzaga, married Leonello d'Este in 1435, and Francesco II married Isabella d'Este, daughter of Ercole I, in 1490.

Milan, in north-western Lombardy, was ruled by the Visconti family until 1450. They were overthrown by the Sforza, who ruled until 1499, when they in turn were overthrown by Louis XII of France. During the period that concerns us the dukes were Francesco (ruled 1450–66), Galeazzo Maria (ruled 1466–76), Gian Galeazzo Maria (*d* 1494), Ludovico il Moro (*d* 1508) and Massimiliano (*d* 1530). The dynastic situation in Milan was complicated; after the death of Galeazzo Maria in 1476, Ludovico seized power and became the virtual ruler of Milan with the official title of Duke of Bari until Gian Galeazzo Maria's death in 1494, when he assumed the title of Duke of Milan. Massimiliano, the son of Ludovico, ruled Milan only from 1512 to 1515, spending the rest of his life in exile. The Sforza were allied to Ferrara through the marriage of Ercole's daughter, Beatrice, to Ludovico in 1491, and therefore to Mantua, where Beatrice's sister Isabella was the reigning marchesa.

By the later 1470s, there were four groups of musicians resident at north Italian courts: the corps of trumpeters, the wind band of shawms and trombones (known collectively as the *piffari*), the string and keyboard players who were also the singers of secular music, and the chapel of singers responsible for the performance of chant and polyphony for church services (this group might also include a keyboard player for the organ). Although there was some overlap in their duties, these bodies were essentially separate, even though (loosely speaking) all were part of the ruler's household and were employed on a continuing basis.

At its fullest, this household might number approximately 44 musicians among its members, although the number was generally smaller than this. In Ferrara in 1476, for example, the chronicler Ugo Caleffini listed 37 musicians in Ercole d'Este's services: four trumpeters, four *piffari*, eight secular singers and players, twenty singers in the chapel and a chapel organist.[5]

Maintaining so many musicians on the court payroll was an expensive business. In Milan in 1469 Galeazzo Maria Sforza spent 5758 lire on his musical household before he instituted his chapel.[6] In Ferrara, Borso d'Este, who also did not maintain a chapel, spent the much smaller sum of 1824 lire on musicians' salaries in 1456. In 1476 Borso's successor Ercole was spending 2678 lire on the same kinds of musicians,[7] that is, the amount he paid for wind and string players and singers of secular music had increased by 32 per cent, although it was still far short of the expenses in Milan. Lucrezia Borgia, who as a woman did not maintain a chapel or players of loud instruments (trumpeters and *piffari*), spent only 998 lire on singers, string players and a pipe-and-tabour player and dancing-master in 1508. This figure represents, however, almost 5.4 per cent of Lucrezia's entire annual revenues as Duchess of Ferrara.[8]

The true expense of supporting a complete musical staff at court becomes apparent when we add the salaries of the members of the chapel to these totals. In 1473 Galeazzo Maria Sforza spent almost 4000 ducats (12,127 lire) on his chapels alone, although this may well have been exceptional.[9] Ercole d'Este paid the singers of his *cappella dei cantori* 4068 lire in 1476; thus his total expenditure for musicians' salaries was 6746 lire per year, an increase of almost 370 per cent over Borso's outlay.[10] This figure represents 5.8 per cent of Ercole's expenditure for his entire household, including the members of his own family, and if we exclude them, then the costs for music climb to almost ten per cent of the duke's annual payments.[11] Indeed, in the climate of fierce competition the courts created for the best musicians, individuals could become rich almost overnight. At Milan in the early 1470s one tenor, a certain Jean Cordier, earned 100 ducats a month.[12] This is a phenomenal sum; in theory he could have retired on an investment of six months' salary.[13]

Before about 1470, courtly patronage of music was mostly lavished on the forces for instrumental and secular vocal music, for with the single exception of Leonello d'Este in Ferrara, the *signori* do not seem to have identified the maintenance of a chapel of singers with an expression of their power. Nevertheless, from the early quattrocento the rulers did begin to support the forces necessary for secular festivities and entertainments. There remains little trace of this music at the three north Italian courts, however, since the art of wind players and secular singers was basically an oral one. In this practice, which has been called 'the unwritten tradition',[14] musicians would memorize tunes with melodic and perhaps harmonic formulae over which they would improvise settings of lyric and narrative verse, dances and the like.

In terms of the size of the musical establishments the three courts maintained before about 1470, the order of importance is Milan, then Ferrara and finally Mantua. From the beginning of his reign, Galeazzo Maria Sforza generally employed twenty trumpeters as well as four or five *piffari* and several string players and singers. The number of trumpeters alone equals the total number of musicians salaried by Borso d'Este in 1462, and this number in turn is probably greater than the number of musicians employed in Mantua around the same time. It is impossible to assess the size of the musical household in Mantua because the payment registers do not survive, but Ludovico Gonzaga seems to have supported no more that four trumpeters, four *piffari* and three or four string players or singers.

Numbers, of course, are by no means the only indicator of importance. It was in Ferrara, for example, and not in Milan that Pietrobono – arguably the greatest Italian lutenist of the fifteenth century – worked, almost without a hiatus from 1445 until his death in 1497. Pietrobono performed in purely instrumental ensembles and sang to his own accompaniment both narrative and lyric verse in a basically unwritten tradition. He also taught students from Milan, Venice and Mantua, as well as Ferrara.[15]

From Ferrara too comes one of the few extant north Italian sources of polyphony from the courts before the 1470s: the manuscript Oporto 714. This manuscript, from the 1450s,[16] contains a number of chansons by the northern musician Guillaume Dufay (c1397–1474), who had already visited Ferrara in 1437, as well as several works by English masters, including John Bedingham, Robertus de Anglia and Galfridus de Anglia. Some of these latter works bear Italian texts and may stem from English students at the University of Ferrara.

For the most part during this early period, the north Italian lords left the sponsorship of sacred music to the church, and although they occasionally nominated members for the clerical choirs, they did not maintain chapels of singers of their own. The exception is Leonello d'Este in Ferrara, who shortly after his installation as marchese in 1441 founded, 'in the royal manner', his own *cappella di corte* and sent to northern Europe for singers to join it. This initiative, the earliest in northern Italy, resulted in a chapel of up to ten singers from France, Burgundy, the Low Countries and England, and in the production of an important series of manuscripts of sacred polyphony that included works by major continental composers such as Dufay and Binchois, and those of important English composers like Dunstable, Power and Plummer. The *cappella* seems to have been established in imitation of the royal chapel of Alfonso I of Naples, and perhaps the chapel of Duke Philip the Good of Burgundy. In all this Leonello was ahead of his time, at least in northern Italy, and after his death in 1450 his successor Borso allowed the northern singers to depart without replacing them, leaving the area without a princely chapel.

This situation changed in the early 1470s with the institution of princely chapels far grander than anything Leonello had imagined. Ferrara and Milan competed for primacy; Mantua was to remain a spectator at the competition until as late as 1510. In 1471 both Galeazzo Maria Sforza and Ercole d'Este had announced the founding of *cappelle dei cantori*, and by 1473 Ercole had established two choirs, one of four-teen men and another of fourteen German boys. By the same year Galeazzo Maria had also established two choirs, a *cappella* consisting of twenty adults and a *cappella da camera* with thirteen adult members. In subsequent years the number of singers fluctuated within narrow limits. Ercole's chapel consisted of 27 singers in 1476, although a more typical number of singers was closer to twenty; Galeazzo Maria's com-bined chapels numbered 40 in 1474, but were reduced to 26 members by the end of 1475.

The documents from both courts are fairly detailed in the record they provide of the development of these chapels and of the rivalry between Ercole and Galeazzo Maria. One, a letter from the Mantuan ambassador at the Milanese court to his master Ludovico Gonzaga, is especially piquant in its description of the frequent auditions being held and the enormous salaries being paid; reading between the lines we sense the competition with Ercole for the recruitment of singers:

> His most illustrious Lordship [Galeazzo Maria] thanks your Lordship greatly for the effort you have made concerning the tenor [Andrea da Mantova, previously in the services of Ercole d'Este]. He wishes very much to have him and says that he pays tenors twelve ducats a month in salary and that he shall do the same for him and that he can come assured that he will be accepted. His Excellency has certainly made a fine beginning with these singers and is spending fabulously for them. He has given to one alone [Heinrich Knoep][17] the equivalent of 4000 ducats in a house, land, money, clothing and so forth and has made him his personal chamberlain. He is a young man of 24 from Liège in Germany [*recte* the Low Countries], which was destroyed by the Duke of Burgundy. He is a tenor and is married. His Lordship has also given others houses in Milan worth 700 or 800 ducats each and has written to Rome to request the pope to agree that every bishop of his principal cities – Milan, Pavia, Novara, Cremona, Piacenza and Parma – can confer benefices up to the sum of 300 ducats for each city specifically for singers in order to have in every city a *cappella* in the cathedral. And he says that, in addition to the 300 ducats in benefices, he will give the rest necessary for the said singers from his income from those cities. For this he has written most insis-

tently to the [papal] court and says that he wants to sustain music in Italy. And then his Excellency will be able to choose from these *cappelle* the best singers and in this way will have the best chapel of all, and then when he wants to hear a great noise, he will send for all [the singers] and have them shout at once in such a way that their voices will go up to heaven. I, my lord, as an accomplished musician, have often been a judge of these singers and have been in the chapel every day.[18]

Such spending and ostentation was soon to be severely curtailed at the Milanese court. With Galeazzo Maria's assassination on the day after Christmas in 1476, the *cappella* was cut to half its former size, many of the singers transferring to Ferrara, to the papal chapel in Rome or returning to their homelands. Ercole, on the other hand, continued his interest in his chapel. He was forced to disband the group during his war with Venice in the early 1480s and never again had a separate choir of boys, but he persevered in maintaining one of the largest and best chapels in Europe throughout the latter years of his reign. In 1485 there were fourteen adult members of the *cappella* on his payrolls and this figure grew to 26 in 1493; in 1504, the last full year of his life, there were 35 members of the chapel including two organists.

Although a significant number of the singers in these chapels were Italian, the majority were from northern Europe. These northerners were indispensable, since no native Italians from this period are known to have been composers of liturgical polyphony, and these composers were necessary for the development of local repertories and styles. Each chapel accordingly had at least one or two members who could be counted on to provide music for the chapel's use.

At Milan the leading early composers were Josquin Desprez, Gaspar van Weerbeke, Alexander Agricola and Loyset Compère. Josquin (*c*1440–1521) had been in Milan since at least 1459, when he is first recorded as an adult singer in the cathedral choir; in 1473, however, he moved to the ducal chapel.[19] After Galeazzo Maria's death, Josquin passed eventually into the service of his brother, Cardinal Ascanio Sforza.[20] Weerbeke (*c*1440 – after 1518), from Flanders, was one of the longest serving of the ducal musicians. He was already in Milan in 1472 and served as the master of the *cappella da camera* during its first years. Weerbeke eventually left Milan in 1481 to join the papal chapel, although he returned to court under Ludovico il Moro. Agricola (*c*1446–1506), from the Low Countries, was in Milan by 1471 and served as a member of the *cappella* until June 1474, when he was released from Sforza service. Compère was in Milan much more briefly, during 1474 and 1475, but he nevertheless contributed important works to the local repertory.

These composers combined to create a new, indigenous style at court. This style was based on the syntax of the text; for the first time,

30. *Josquin Desprez: woodcut from 'Opus chronographicum' (1611) by Petrus Opmeer*

composers were minutely attentive to the meaning and rhetoric of the text and adapted the rhythms and textures of their music to it. In their more complex works, they adopted imitation, sometimes called accordingly 'syntactic imitation', as a primary structural element. Although earlier composers had been moving towards a more imitative technique, it was Josquin above all who brought the style to its zenith. In other works the 'Milanese school' developed a much simpler, often almost purely homorhythmic style that may have derived its inspiration from the local Italian *lauda*; but whatever its precise roots, the style clearly evolved from Italian rather than northern techniques. At the same time, and under the influence of the local Ambrosian liturgy, these composers began to compose cycles of motets, called 'motetti missales', which were substituted for parts of the Ordinary and Proper of the Mass.[21] So similar to the *lauda* were many of these homorhythmic works that Petrucci could include Josquin's substitution motet *Tu solus qui facis mirabilia* in his second book of *laude* with the text 'O Mater Dei et hominis', and could publish a version of Weerbeke's motet *Verbum caro* with the text 'O inextimabilis', in the same source. The typical texture of the music of Josquin's generation, then, became one of alternating points, sections featuring syntactic imitation contasting with those in a more nearly homorhythmic style.

It is generally accepted that this novel style arose in Italy (and at the north Italian courts) as a result of the new, humanistic interest in the structure and meaning of the text. This is undoubtedly true, though it is also possible that another influence was felt at the same time: the new and relatively grandiose size of the chapels themselves. The kinds of music most appropriate for these new, larger forces differed sharply from those of earlier masters like Dufay and Ockeghem, who had been writing, in general, for much smaller ensembles. The new style at Milan (and, although slightly different, at Ferrara) may therefore have been the dual result of an intellectual interest in humanistic concerns and a practical interest in felicitous music for greater forces.

At Ferrara, too, resident composers were necessary. Here the major figures were Johannes Martini, Johannes Brebis, Jacob Obrecht and Josquin. Martini seems to have been brought to Ferrara from Constance by Ercole in 1471 and to have remained there, with the exception of a brief period in 1474 in Milan, until his death in 1498. Brebis was one of the original members of Ercole's chapel in 1471; he was listed as the chapel's *maestro di cappella* in 1472 and died in late 1478 or early 1479. Obrecht (*c*1450–1505) was in Ferrara on two different occasions: he was there briefly in 1487 and was later engaged in 1504 as *maestro di cappella*. Josquin was Obrecht's immediate predecessor as *maestro di cappella*, from 1503 to 1504.

These composers also created a newly simple and idiosyncratic local style. In Ferrara, though, there is less trace of *lauda*-based textures, but rather another development based on practical considerations: the birth of polychoral polyphony. Composers such as Martini and Brebis invented a manner of treating the Vespers psalms by dividing the verses between the two choirs, that is, between Ercole's choir of boys and his choir of adults.

Josquin's *Missa 'Hercules Dux Ferrariae'* is another influential musical monument from Ferrara. Its date is not certain, but it was most probably written during the period 1480–81 when Josquin's patron Ascanio Sforza was in exile in Ferrara. The mass makes an eloquent statement concerning the personal identification of the patron with the work of art, for Josquin took the syllables of Ercole's name and title and used them as a tenor cantus firmus. It even seems likely that the ducal tenors sang the syllables of Ercole's name rather than the text of the Ordinary of the Mass. This being the case, we are confronted with a work which explicitly glorifies its patron, a secular lord, within the most sacred context of the Mass, and one which in a certain sense equates the greatness of Ercole with the true religion. This work, which was to be imitated by other composers in the following century, is a revealing instance of the ability of a patron's music and musicians to contribute directly to his self-glorification and magnificence.

During the period of Ercole d'Este and his contemporaries Italian secular music remained an essentially oral art although, just at the end of their floriate, more and more examples of this unwritten practice began to be included in manuscripts dedicated to the other major secular repertory of the courts: the French chanson. Indeed, there are more surviving chansonniers of Italian provenance than there are of French or Burgundian origin. The earliest of these manuscripts were apparently compiled in Naples in the 1460s, but from the 1490s there are several that must have originated at the north Italian courts. These manuscripts contain the elegant, polished examples of the French *rhétoriqueurs*' art and the musical settings of their poetry.

These chansons formed an integral part of the repertory of secular music at court. They must have been sung for the court's pleasure by the northern, French-speaking musicians of the chapel, and there is even evidence that members of the court sang them themselves. Galeazzo Maria Sforza, for example, learnt French chansons as a youth.[22] Furthermore, on the evidence of the sole surviving Ferrarese chansonnier from Ercole's reign (now in the Biblioteca Casanatense, Rome, no.2856; see fig.31), intended for the court *piffari*, it is clear that chansons were also performed instrumentally.

Works like these must have found their way into the repertory included in the dramatic representations featured at north Italian courts during the Carnival season. Beginning in 1486, Ercole d'Este presented classical comedies at court – principally those of Plautus and Terence – and these typically included *intermedi* between the acts that featured instrumental and vocal music. The court *piffari* participated in

31. The chansonnier of Isabella d'Este (copied in Ferrara, 1480–90) showing the opening folio, with part of the chanson 'Tant fort me tarde' by Philippon

these *intermedi*, as did the singers of secular music. At one particularly festive occasion in 1509, for example, the court at Ferrara saw a performance of Plautus's *Phormicone* that included five *intermedi*. In the first, 'six people with various instruments played and sang on a balcony'; the second was 'a music with four dolzaine ('sordine'), [the musicians] in the guise of shepherds'; the third was 'five "Ethiopians" who with five lutes played a long song'; the fourth was performed by 'eight people who with various instruments and with a fine melody played a dance tune'; finally, at the close of the comedy there was a *moresca* (a vigorous, costumed dance-mime) by a band of armed dancers.[23]

The next generation of important music patrons in northern Italy is made up almost exclusively of the children of Ercole d'Este and their respective spouses: Alfonso d'Este and his wife Lucrezia Borgia, Beatrice d'Este and her husband Ludovico il Moro, and Isabella d'Este and her husband Francesco Gonzaga.[24] Although they continued the traditions of Ercole, they also established new ones, notably of written secular vocal music in the Italian tongue.

At Mantua, where Isabella went as the bride of Francesco Gonzaga in 1490, these events were particularly important. Although the Gonzaga had maintained a small group of musicians throughout the quattrocento, it was only with the arrival of Isabella and her determined and sometimes demanding patronage that Mantua became a musical centre of the first rank.[25] Indeed, Isabella's preoccupation with music permeates virtually every area of her patronage. Her continual search for verse from the major poets of her time was caused, at least in part, by her desire for new texts for her musicians to set; her artistic patronage, too, include a strong musical component, since she often specified musical subjects and themes for the paintings she commissioned. Following her lead, Francesco also became an influential patron of music, on a much broader scale than his wife.

Any study of Isabella d'Este's musical patronage must begin with her own abilities as a musician, since her view of these abilities fundamentally conditioned the kinds of music she sponsored. Isabella began to study singing and keyboard instruments as a girl in Ferrara; she continued taking singing lessons from Martini and from Charles de Lannoy in Mantua during the year after her marriage in 1490. Shortly after this she asked Girolamo Sestola to come from Ferrara to continue her study of keyboard instruments and she began learning string instruments with her own musician, Giovanni Angelo Testagrossa. By the very end of the quattrocento she was an accomplished singer and player of keyboard instruments, lute, viol and lira da braccio. The refined climate of the courts, with their constant flattery of the ruling family, makes it difficult to determine the exact level of Isabella's abilities as a musician; nevertheless, her skill is routinely mentioned in the humanist treatises describing her virtues and in the letters of visiting magnates.

32. Isabella d'Este: portrait (1499) by Leonardo da Vinci

She was confident enough of her prowess to perform for the visiting French ambassador at the wedding of her brother Alfonso in Ferrara in 1502, to play and sing for Pietro Bembo when he visited Mantua in 1505, and for Giovanni Aquaviva, Marchese of Bitonto, during her visit to the Kingdom of Naples in 1514.

No matter what her strengths and weaknesses as a performer, the central issue is that she viewed herself as an outstanding musician. This self-image is clear in her letters regarding music and, again, in the dedications of poetry to her and in the flattering humanist descriptions of her general demeanour and abilities. Almost without fail these dedications and descriptions mention her musical proficiency. In Giangiorgio Trissino's *I ritratti*,[26] for example, she is compared to the beauties of classical antiquity; she has 'lovely wrists that join her soft arms to her delicate hands, which have long fingers'. Trissino has the great humanist and poet Pietro Bembo praise her spiritual beauties. He said that she had several small rooms 'full of the rarest books, of most beautiful paintings, and of marvellous antique and modern sculpture [all of which] she keeps with cameos, intaglios, medals and wonderful gems' (see fig.8 above).[27] She also 'delights in poetry, and is very adept at it'. She did not patronize 'buffoons, clowns or trumpeters', but rather 'good, virtuous and learned persons' whom she rewarded with great liberality. The longest description in the work, however, has to do with Bembo's depiction of Isabella's musical abilities:

> When she sings, especially to the lute, I believe that Orpheus and Amphion, who knew how to bring inanimate objects to life with their song, would be stupefied with wonder on hearing her, and I do not doubt that neither of them would have known how to do as well as she does in keeping the harmony most diligently so that the rhythm never falters, but rather measures the song, now rising, now falling, and keeps the harmony on the lute and at once according her tongue and both hands with the inflections of the song. Thus if you were to hear her sing even a single time, I am certain that you would be like those who heard the Sirens and forgot their native lands and their own homes.

The fulsomeness of this praise is evident; indeed Isabella wrote to Trissino in 1514 thanking him for the treatise and quoting the Italian proverb 'so che tu non dici il vero, pur mi piace' ('I know that you are not telling the truth, but still it pleases me'). Nevertheless, Isabella herself put her 'delicate hand' on the crucial point: no matter how exaggerated such statements might be, they were acceptable to her because they were echoes of her own view of herself as a virtuoso musician. This strongly colours Isabella's musical patronage, for she seems to have supported only that kind of music which she herself could perform. Undoubtedly her selection of secular vocal music as the object of her patronage was also directly influenced by the social convention whereby Italian noblewomen were not expected to maintain their own chapels or to support players of loud instruments. Isabella's patronage was therefore narrowly focussed, concentrating on secular music in Italian, namely the frottola. Francesco's patronage, on the other hand, was much broader in scope; he too was a patron of the frottola, but he also supported the loud instruments of the court, music in the secular theatre and, from 1510, a chapel of singers responsible for sacred music.

The frottola is the first music written by native Italians of the Renaissance, and Isabella had an integral and indispensable role in its origins and development.[28] The genre, most often a solo song accompanied by string or keyboard instruments in one of the fixed Italian poetic forms such as the strambotto or the barzelletta, was based on older, unwritten traditions, in which improvisers like Pietrobono would perform from memory lyric verse for the enjoyment of courtly society. Beginning in the 1490s, however, their products began to be copied down more and more frequently and they are represented in several north Italian manuscripts that date from the middle of the decade.

Perhaps the earliest extant frottola manuscript was the one copied in Padua in 1495 now in the Biblioteca Estense, Modena (α F.9.9). Included in this collection is a setting of the strambotto *Arboro son*, a

33. Marquetry panels showing contemporary musical instruments, in the Grotta of Isabella d'Este at the Palazzo Ducale, Mantua

poem by Isabella herself that she had apparently sent to Ferrara in 1490 for a composer there to set.[29] The work is therefore arguably one of the earliest-known representatives of the frottola and sheds light on the musical situation surrounding the very beginnings of the genre and Isabella's involvement in its inception. First, that Isabella had a professional musician set her poem indicated that she herself did not compose; indeed, with one exception, there is no evidence that any Italian nobleman or noblewoman of her time was a composer.[30] Second, since Isabella did not compose, she would have been unable to perform in the earlier, unwritten tradition, in which every improviser was to a certain extent a *faiseur*, that is, a composer. It could be argued in fact that the appearance of manuscripts and then, after 1504, of printed books of frottole was the direct result of Isabella's and other amateurs' desire to perform music in the style of the unwritten tradition. If this were the case then the presence of these manuscripts represents a new trend intended to allow the noble amateur an important role in music.

A further conclusion can be drawn from Isabella's actions concerning *Arboro son*: although her decision to turn to Ferrara may simply have been a result of her familiarity with the musical scene there, it may also have been caused by a lack of suitable talent in Mantua. If the latter was the case, then Isabella was soon to change the situation. She began quickly to employ musicians of her own, to buy instruments for her own and her retainers' use, and to send away for music paper on which her musicians' compositions could be copied. By the end of the fifteenth century her personal household included singers, lutenists and viol players, as well as players of the lira da braccio and keyboard instruments.

The most important of these musicians was Bartolomeo Tromboncino (*c*1470 – after 1535). Tromboncino, who had earlier been a trombonist in the service of Isabella's husband Francesco, was a singer, lutenist and, most important, the most prolific frottolist of his time. Tromboncino remained with Isabella until about 1505, when he transferred to Ferrara, working for Isabella's arch-rival Lucrezia Borgia. Tromboncino's duties for Isabella must have included playing and singing for her pleasure as well as, perhaps, instructing her in music. Surely, however, one of his chief responsibilities was to compose music for Isabella herself to sing.

It is with Tromboncino that we gain a vital glimpse of another way in which Isabella was important to the new genre of the frottola. In 1504, apparently dissatisfied with the trivial nature of much frottola poetry, she wrote to the poet Niccolò da Correggio, asking him to recommend a canzone by Petrarch which he thought might be particularly suitable for musical setting. Niccolò selected *Si è debile il filo*, and a setting by Tromboncino of this poem survives. It is hard to overestimate the importance of this event, for Isabella took a major and crucial step in requesting a setting of a poem by Petrarch. Her action raised both the level of poetry that was to be set in the genre and the subtlety of the musical form of the frottola; with its varied line-lengths, the poetry of Petrarch was not amenable to the kind of schematic setting that frottolists had been giving the barzelletta and the strambotto. In the years following, both Tromboncino and other frottolists set the poetry of Petrarch and the verse of his imitators with increasing frequency.

Francesco Gonzaga was also a patron of the frottola, supporting in his household the second great figure of the genre, Marchetto Cara (*c*1465–1525), who came to Mantua from Verona by 1494 and who remained there for the rest of his life. Francesco also maintained his own string and keyboard players, although he does not seem to have been as historically important to the development of the frottola as his wife. Until the departure of Tromboncino, when Isabella and Francesco began to share the services of Cara, there is little evidence to suggest that Cara set Petrarchan verse. Although Cara is clearly the most important composer of the new text forms in his later years, more typical of his early works are such pieces as *Forsì che sì, forsì che no*, setting a Gonzago motto, or *Sonno che gli animali*, a simple lullaby in black notation, or *Quis furor tanti rabiesque morti*, a Latin ode to syphilis, from which Francesco suffered from about 1510 until his death. Many of these works, like *A la absentia* or *S'io sedo a l'ombra*, are miniature masterpieces, but they do not have the historical importance of Tromboncino's frottole for Isabella. Nevertheless, Francesco maintained a complete group of the musicians responsible for the composition and performance of frottole, and he must be viewed as one of the genre's leading patrons.

Francesco was the primary Mantuan patron of instrumental music.

It was he who supported the court *piffari* and who established a court school for the training of young instrumentalists. The court wind players, numbering about five in Francesco's time, namely three shawm players and two trombonists, were a versatile group who could play not only the shawm and the trombone but other wind and string instruments as well. They could read music and were capable of playing arrangements of motets and secular songs as well as purely instrumental pieces.

Francesco and his uncle Bishop Ludovico Gonzaga were both important patrons of classical comedies, which they presented in series on the last days of Carnival. Most of our information concerning the *intermedi* of these comedies, although in the Mantuan archives, refers to the court of Ferrara. Nevertheless, there is sufficient Mantuan documentation to show that musical *intermedi* were a part of these presentations and a Mantuan manuscript of 1502 provides music intended for these occasions.[31]. These pieces, mostly representational works depicting fishing, hunting and so forth, would have been performed by the court singers and instrumentalists while they or others mimed the actions on the stage, perhaps in a *moresca*. *A la pesca* depicts a fishing party whose members exhort each other to take their catch to 'monsignore' and to the 'vescovo', a clear reference to Ludovico Gonzaga, who was a passionate patron of classical comedy.[32] *Anguilles, anguilles, anguillons* is a macaronic song concerning eels which probably refers to the peculiarly Mantuan 'Procession of the Eels' on Ascension Day.

Francesco Gonzaga was also the major Mantuan patron of sacred music, since noblewomen did not maintain their own chapels. Although there are some traces of simple liturgical polyphony in Mantua in the late fifteenth and early sixteenth centuries, such as Tromboncino's Lamentations and his *Benedictus Dominus Deus Israel* for Holy Week, the real beginnings of sacred polyphony in Mantua occur only in 1510: that year Francesco founded his own court chapel with singers from the *cappella* of Alfonso d'Este from Ferrara and with his own singer and former cleric Marchetto Cara as *maestro di cappella*. At its height numbering slightly under twenty members, this chapel performed the most important masses and motets of the day to a high standard. Immediately after founding his choir, Francesco began a determined search for new repertory for the group, which eventually included Petrucci's printed versions of the masses and motets of Josquin, Obrecht, Brumel, Agricola and others.[33] Although Mantua was remarkably late in supporting a court chapel, it was early in its support of the polyphonic *lauda* – the devotional music intended for spiritual recreation and for the many liturgical processions during Holy Week and on other feast-days. Late fifteenth-century Mantuan documents already show the use of *laude* in these processions.

At Ferrara Alfonso d'Este and his wife Lucrezia Borgia continued previous Ferrarese traditions and established new ones much like those in Mantua. New composers continued to be engaged and new local repertories created. With his assumption of the rule of the duchy in 1505, Alfonso continued his father's *cappella dei cantori*, employing Antoine Brumel as *maestro di cappella* in 1506 to replace Jacob Obrecht who had died of plague the previous year. In 1509, for example, the Ferrarese *cappella* numbered nineteen members including Brumel himself, presumably the resident composer as well as *maestro di cappella*. The chapel was active until 1510 when Alfonso, under the papal interdict and at war with the members of League of Cambrai, was forced to disband the group to divert resources towards the military defence of Ferrara. From about 1513 the activities of the chapel were gradually resumed, although it was several years before it reached anything like its former strength. By 1520 it numbered only nine members, including, however, Adrian Willaert.

Alfonso seems to have been particularly fond of French music and musicians for his chapel. There is strong evidence of his recruiting in France and Savoy early in his reign and he himself travelled to the two courts in 1502 engaging musicians for himself and his father. This continued into the later years of his reign; during the second decade of the sixteenth century his musical retainers, other than Antonio da l'Organo and Agostino della Viola, seem almost uniformly to have come from France or Savoy. During this same decade Alfonso and others of the Estensi were in close contact with the French composer Jean Mouton, and important letters survive that reveal attempts to obtain repertory from the French royal chapel.[34]

Alfonso himself was an informed amateur musician. He played the viol and employed both Agostino and Alfonso della Viola as members of his household. His patronage of secular music in the Italian language, at least early in his reign, was not strong, and here too he seems to have preferred French musicians and their compositions, relying on the musicians of his brother, Cardinal Ippolito, and on those of his wife Lucrezia for native works. Lucrezia, on the other hand, was a leading patron of the frottola, having in her employ Tromboncino, Niccolò da Padova and Dionisio da Mantova, all composers of the genre. She was accordingly the patron of many of Tromboncino's later works, including some of his settings of Petrarch and his works with Spanish texts, such as *Muchos son che van perdidos*, published in 1519 but surely written for the Spanish-speaking and Spanish-customed Lucrezia. She also had in her services at various times both men and women singers and a dancing-master. Other musicians, like the trumpeters, *piffari* and bagpipe players she used at Carnival and at other festivals, she borrowed from her husband Alfonso or her brother-in-law Ippolito.

In addition to Alfonso and Isabella, two other children of Ercole d'Este were important patrons of music. Sigismondo, crippled with syphilis, was, like his brother Alfonso, particularly interested in French music and musicians. He too had contacts with Mouton, from whom he received motets and chansons, and he too maintained a music copyist on his payrolls; in 1516 this copyist was apparently Jacques Colebault, later the major musician of Cardinal Ercole Gonzaga at Mantua, where he was known simply as 'Jacquet of Mantua'.[35]

Cardinal Ippolito, on the other hand, was principally interested in Italian music and in instrumental music.[36] He played the viol and, although he had two French singers on his payrolls early in the sixteenth century and although he employed Willaert, from 1510 his musical household consisted mainly of Italians. Among this body of musicians were several players of string and keyboard instruments as well as three frottolists: Alessandro Demophonte of Bologna, Michele Pesenti of Verona and Tromboncino, whom he employed in 1511 and 1512. It must have been while serving as a member of Ippolito's court that Tromboncino composed his famous setting of *Queste non son più lagrime*, an ottava from Ludovico Ariosto's *Orlando furioso*; Ariosto was a member of Ippolito's court at just this time.[37]

The next generation of major patrons in northern Italy consists of the grandchildren of Ercole I d'Este, Federico II Gonzaga and Cardinal Ercole I Gonzaga at Mantua and Alfonso II d'Este at Ferrara. Because they were in some ways extending patterns of patronage already established by Ercole and his children, they may be dealt with briefly here.

Federico II Gonzaga took control of the Marquisate of Mantua on the death of his father Francesco in 1519. His patronage, in one sense, represents simply the continuation of trends already evident under Francesco and Isabella. He continued to support the court *piffari*, the players of string instruments and secular singers.[38] Nevertheless, Federico established new patterns as well, the decisively novel element in his patronage being a turn away from Ferrara as the quintessential model and towards Rome, where Federico had spent an important and fondly remembered part of his youth at the court of Pope Julius II. In 1523 Federico returned to Rome to consult Pope Adrian VI on military matters. While there, however, he seems to have combined his political meetings with a certain amount of artistic recruiting. He took time to examine a unique alabaster organ, made for the late Pope Leo X, which he eventually purchased, and he also seems to have convinced three musicians to forsake Rome and its austere new pope for Mantua. One of these was the same Michele Pesenti who had been in Ferrara earlier in the century, but the other two were of major importance for music in Mantua.

Shortly after Federico's visit, the Spanish or Netherlandish composer Andreas de Silva, who had been in the chapel of Leo X, appeared in Mantua and was paid by Federico; de Silva may well have remained in Mantua until about 1530. Just after Federico's Roman visit the leading ultramontane composer Jean Lhéritier also left his post at the church of S Luigi dei Francesi in Rome: by 1525 he was a member of Federico's chapel, and it is likely that he travelled directly from Rome to Mantua in 1523.[39]

Cardinal Ercole Gonzaga, too, was an important patron of music.[40] Made Bishop of Mantua at fifteen and cardinal in 1526, Ercole began to take over the administration of the clerical choir of S Pietro shortly after acquiring the red hat. He maintained both a clerical choir and a group of mostly northern boy sopranos throughout his reign. Even though he was often not in residence in Mantua, he maintained a close control over the choir and its repertory through detailed correspondence with his factor there.

The most important musician resident in Mantua, however, was Jacquet of Mantua (1483–1559), who had earlier been in Ferrara and Rome. Under Ercole, Jacquet became both *maestro di cappella* and singing teacher to the young clerics at the cathedral, and he produced a large series of masses, motets, hymns, polychoral psalms and music for Holy Week, including a *St Matthew* and a *St John Passion*. Jacquet's importance lies not only in his prolific output, but also in the fine quality of his works. He has been described as 'the leading master of sacred polyphony between Josquin and Palestrina',[41] and an examination of his motets and other sacred works supports this view. His style moves from one with alternating points of imitation and homophony within a four-voice framework in the style of the Josquin generation to a relatively seamless style of pervasive imitation within a five-voice framework. He is, at the very least, the equal of his great contemporary Willaert in Venice in terms of the artistic level of his compositions.

Although Ercole's patronage was focussed to a large extent on sacred music for the cathedral of S Pietro, we should not forget that, as a cardinal, he was also a secular prince. In this capacity he purchased strings and bows for string instruments, masks for use during Carnival and sponsored elaborate theatrical presentations in Mantua. Thus in 1542 he mounted two banquets, three comedies and a *moresca*. The costumes for these presentations were designed by the court artist Giulio Romano, and the *moresca* was performed with singing and instruments – a viol, two lutes and a recorder. Among the musicians was Abramin de Louin dall'Arpa, a Jewish harp player recently arrived in Mantua.[42]

★

In retrospect, the musical patronage of Ercole I d'Este seems crucial to the course of the promotion of music at north Italian courts throughout the late fifteenth century and the first half of the sixteenth. This statement is supportable on several grounds. First, his children and their consorts continued to support music with the same enthusiasm that Ercole had. These patterns were in turn continued by his grandchildren Federico II and Ercole I Gonzaga at Mantua and Ercole II d'Este at Ferrara. Second, the types of musical forces at court were clearly set by Ercole and his contemporary and rival, Galeazzo Maria Sforza; the Italian princely chapel was essentially a creation of these men, and the secular singers and string players and the *piffari*, although at courts before their time, were clearly strengthened by their patronage and marked as necessities for a cultured court life. Third, Ercole to a certain extent set the patterns for the kinds of music patronized. Before Alfonso I, he had already established French music and musicians as principal sources of repertory and composers; before Ippolito I and Francesco II Gonzaga, he had bolstered the *piffari* and string ensembles and had sponsored music for them to perform; even in the newest genre of music, the frottola, he had in a certain sense set the trend through his patronage of Pietrobono and other *cantori al liuto*.

Certainly, crucial details of patronage were the result of his descendants' personal tastes and the necessities of contemporary society, but Ercole had laid out the basic lines of musical patronage, and the education of his children, both formal and informal, must have shown them the techniques and benefits of musical patronage on a large scale. Indeed, Ercole set patterns for yet later generations of patrons in Ferrara and Mantua. At the former court, the Estensi were enthusiastic supporters of the works of Cipriano de Rore, Luca Marenzio and Luzzasco Luzzaschi. At Mantua the descendants of Federico II were the patrons of Giaches de Wert, Benedetto Pallavicino and Claudio Monteverdi.

NOTES

[1] *Epistolae seniles*, xiv, 1; published, among other places, in *Epistole di Francesco Petrarca*, ed. U. Dotti (Turin, 1978), 760–837. See also C. H. Clough, 'Federigo da Montefeltro's Patronage of the Arts, 1468–1482', *JWCI*, xxxvi (1973), 129; reprinted in Clough, *The Duchy of Urbino in the Renaissance* (London, 1981).

[2] T. E. Mommsen, 'Petrarch and the Decoration of the Sala Virorum Illustrium in Padua', *Art Bulletin*, xxxiv (1952), 95–116; reprinted in Mommsen, *Medieval and Renaissance Studies* (Ithaca, NY, 1959), 130–74.

[3] On the corporate nature of patronage during this time, see J. Larner, *Culture and Society in Italy, 1290–1420* (London, 1971), 63–96.

[4] For the Scaligeri and Visconti as patrons of trecento composers see conveniently R. Hoppin, *Medieval Music* (New York, 1978), 438–9 and 448–9.

[5] L. Lockwood, *Music in Renaissance Ferrara, 1400–1505* (Oxford, 1984), 180.

[6] This figure derives from two separate orders to the treasurer, one for the seventeen ducal trumpeters and the other for the remaining musicians, five *piffari*, a lutenist, a viola player and a pipe-and-tabour player ('tamborino'); see G. Barblan, 'Vita musicale alla corte sforzesca', in *Storia di Milan*, ix (Milan, 1961), 794–5 and 806.

[7] See Lockwood, *Music in Renaissance Ferrara*, 180, for these figures.

[8] Lucrezia's income was 6000 ducats or 18,600 lire per year; see W. F. Prizer, 'Isabella d'Este and Lucrezia Borgia as Patrons of Music: the Frottola at Mantua and Ferrara', *JAMS*, xxxviii (1985), 11.

[9] Barblan, 'Vita musicale', 826, reproduces a payment list of *c*1473 in which the monthly total for the chapel is 326 ducats, or 3912 ducats per year (throughout this section, I use an exchange rate of 3.1 lire to the ducat, the rate given in several Ferrarese registers). Using other figures, L. Lockwood, 'Strategies of Music Patronage in the Fifteenth Century: the *Cappella* of Ercole I d'Este', in *Music in Medieval and Early Modern Europe: Patronage, Sources and Texts*, ed. I. Fenlon (Cambridge, 1981), 233, estimates that Galeazzo Maria was spending 5000 ducats annually for his chapel.

[10] For these figures see Lockwood, *Music in Renaissance Ferrara*, 177–80, and my review of Lockwood's book in *JAMS*, xl (1987), 95–105.

[11] These figures are taken from W. Gundersheimer, *Ferrara: the Style of a Renaissance Despotism* (Princeton, 1973), 285–96. They do not include Ercole's expense for his wife Eleanora d'Aragona, who received 8400 lire a year, less than half the income of her successor Lucrezia Borgia.

[12] B. Corio, *Storia di Milano* (Venice, 1554); cited from E. Motta, 'Musici alla corte degli Sforza', *Archivio storico lombardo*, xiv (1887), 31.

[13] L. Martines, *Power and Imagination: City-States in Renaissance Italy* (New York, 1979), 227.

[14] N. Pirrotta used this expression in a series of seminal articles, now conveniently collected in his *Music and Culture in Italy from the Middle Ages to the Baroque* (Cambridge, Mass., 1984). See also W. F. Prizer, 'The Frottola and the Unwritten Tradition', *Studi musicali*, xv (1986), 3–37, and the additional bibliography cited there.

[15] On Pietrobono, see L. Lockwood, 'Pietrobono and the Instrumental Tradition at Ferrara in the Fifteenth Century', *RIM*, x (1975), 115–33; Lockwood, *Music in Renaissance Ferrara*, 95–108; and Prizer, 'The Frottola and the Unwritten Tradition', especially 23–7.

[16] On Oporto 714, see Lockwood, *Music in Renaissance Ferrara*, 109–18; a slightly later date is proposed by D. Fallows, 'Robertus de Anglia and the Oporto Song Collection', in *Source Materials and the Interpretation of Music: a Memorial Volume to Thurston Dart* (London, 1982), 99–128; Fallows, in his review of Lockwood's book (*EMH*, vi (1986), 293), still proposes the 1460s as the most likely dating of the manuscript.

[17] The only singer known to be from Liège is Knoep, who, however, is listed as a priest and accumulated many benefices. See Motta, 'Musici alla corte degli Sforza', 330–31. On the other hand, if this singer was Knoep, it would help to explain the wording of a 1482 document which states that Knoep was helpful 'in music as well as in a number of other fields . . .'. See Lowinsky, 'Ascanio Sforza's Life: a Key to Josquin's Biography and an Aid to the Chronology of his Works', in *Josquin des Prez: New York 1971*, 39. If Knoep were a chamberlain of the duke, then these other fields would be explained.

[18] Letter of 5 Feb 1473, partially published in Canal, 'Della musica in Mantova', *Memorie del R. Istituto di scienze, lettere ed arti*, xxi (1897), 660–61. For further on the competition between Milan and Ferrara, see Lockwood, 'Strategies of Music Patronage'.

[19] See C. Sartori, 'Josquin des Prés, cantore del Duomo di Milano', *AnnM*, iv (1956), 55–83. On the choirs of Italian churches, as opposed to those attached directly to courts, the basic study is that of F. A. D'Accone, 'The Performance of Sacred Music in Italy during Josquin's Time', in *Josquin des Prez: New York 1971*, 602–18. The most recent and up-to-date treatment of Josquin's biography is that by J. Noble and G. Reese in *The New Grove High Renaissance Masters* (London and New York, 1984), 1–90.

[20] On Josquin and Ascanio, see E. E. Lowinsky, 'Josquin des Prez and Ascanio Sforza', in *Il duomo di Milano: Milan 1968*, 17–22; and Lowinsky, 'Ascanio Sforza's Life', 31–75.

[21] The question of the *motetti missales* is complex and the literature on them is extensive. For a recent contribution see L. H. Ward, 'The *Motetti Missales* Repertory Reconsidered', *JAMS*, xxxix (1986), 491–523, where the previous writings on the subject are listed.

[22] A letter from Guiniforte Barizza, Galeazzo's humanist tutor, reports in 1452 that the young prince 'is studying singing diligently and has learnt eight French chansons and every day he learns others with the greatest pleasure'. See A. Cappelli, 'Guiniforte Barzizza, maestro di Galeazzo Maria Sforza', *Archivio storico lombardo*, xxi (1894), 405.

[23] Letter from Bernardino de' Prosperi in Ferrara to Isabella d'Este, 18 Feb 1509, published in W. F. Prizer, 'Bernardino Piffaro e i pifferi e tromboni a Mantova: strumenti a fiato in una corte italiana', *RIM*, xvi (1981), 183–4. For similar though less detailed descriptions of three

comedies presented at Ferrara in 1499, see L. Luzio and R. Renier, 'Commedie classiche in Ferrara nel 1499', *Giornale storico della letteratura italiana*, xi (1888), 177–89. The standard sources on music in Renaissance theatre are N. Pirrotta and E. Povoledo, *Music and Theatre from Poliziano to Monteverdi*, trans. K. Eales (Cambridge, 1982), and W. Osthoff, *Theatergesang und darstellende Musik in der Italienischen Renaissance* (Tutzing, 1969).

24 For what can be said at present concerning Ludovico Sforza and Beatrice d'Este, see W. F. Prizer, 'Music at the Court of the Sforza: the Birth and Death of a Musical Center', *MD*, xliii (1989).

25 On Isabella and music, see, in addition to the works already cited, W. F. Prizer, *Courtly Pastimes: the Frottole of Marchetto Cara* (Ann Arbor, 1980), 1–33 and passim, I. Fenlon, *Music and Patronage in Sixteenth-Century Mantua* (Cambridge, 1980), 15–22; and Fenlon, 'Isabella d'Este e i suoi contemporanei: musica e mecanitismo presso le corti dell'Italia settentrionale', in *Bernardo Clesio e suo tempo*, ed. P. Prodi (Rome, 1987), 607–36.

26 Published in Rome in 1524, although the work was written about 1513 or 1514. In the physical description of Isabella, however, she is said to be 'not much [older] than twenty-three'. She is therefore being described as she was at the end of the fifteenth century. There is now a modern edition of Trissino's work in W. Hirdt, *Gian Giorgio Trissinos Porträt der Isabella d'Este: ein Beitrag zur Lukian-Rezeption in Italien* (Heidelberg, 1981). For a penetrating view of *I ritratti* and Trissino's relations with Isabella, see S. Kolsky, 'Images of Isabella d'Este', *Italian Studies*, xxxix (1984), 47–62, especially 49–51.

27 On Isabella's *camerini*, which included the famous *studiolo* and *grotta*, on the piano nobile of the Castello di S Giorgio, see, in addition to the works of Fenlon already cited, E. Verheyen, *The Paintings in the Studiolo of Isabella d'Este at Mantua* (New York, 1971), and C. M. Brown, 'The Grotta of Isabella d'Este', *Gazette des beaux-arts*, 6th ser., lxxxix (1977), 155–71, and xci (1978), 72–82; on her collection of antiquities, kept in the *camerini*, see Brown, ' "Lo insaciabile desiderio nostro de cose antique": New Documents on Isabella d'Este's Collection of Antiquities', in *Cultural Aspects of the Italian Renaissance: Essays in Honour of Paul Oskar Kristeller* (Manchester, 1976), 324–53 and 497.

28 On the musical nature of the frottola, see Prizer, *Courtly Pastimes*, and J. Haar, *Essays on Italian Poetry and Music in the Renaissance: 1350–1600* (Berkeley and Los Angeles, 1987), chaps.2–4. Older and still valuable treatments include W. Rubsamen, *Literary Sources of Secular Music in Italy (ca. 1500)* (Berkeley and Los Angeles, 1943), and A. Einstein, *The Italian Madrigal* (Princeton, 1949).

29 This poem and its setting are discussed in C. Gallico, 'Poesie musicali di Isabella d'Este', *CHM*, iii (1963), 109–19.

30 The single Italian exception is Giovanni de' Medici, later Pope Leo X, who composed a chanson based on Colinet de Launoy's *Cela sans plus*. See A. Pirro, 'Leo X and Music', *MQ*, xxi (1935), 3–5.

31 *F–Pn* Vm.⁷ 676. On this manuscript see N. Bridgman, 'Un manuscrit italien du début du XVIᵉ siècle à la Bibliothèque Nationale . . .', *AnnM*, i (1953), 177–267, and iv (1956), 259–60; Bridgman, 'La vie de cour au quattrocento à Ferrare et à Mantoue à travers la musique', *Quadrivium*, xiv/1 (1974), 137–45; and, on its Mantuan provenance, W. F. Prizer, 'Paris 676 and the Courtly Reception of the Frottola', *IMSCR*, xiv *Bologna 1987*.

32 On Bishop Ludovico Gonzaga as a patron of the theatre, see U. Rossi, 'Commedie classiche in Gazzuolo nel 1501–1507', *Giornale storico della letterature italiana*, xiii (1890), 305–15.

33 On Francesco's chapel and its repertory, see Prizer, *Courtly Pastimes*, 14–27.

34 L. Lockwood, 'Jean Mouton and Jean Michel: New Evidence on French Music and Musicians in Italy, 1505–1520', *JAMS*, xxxii (1979), 191–246.

35 L. Lockwood, 'Jean Mouton and Jean Michel', 232–4.

36 On Ippolito I as a patron of music, see L. Lockwood, 'Adrian Willaert and Cardinal Ippolito I d'Este: New Light on Willaert's Early Career in Italy', *EMH*, v (1985), 85–112.

37 Trombonchino's ottava is discussed in Haar, *Essays on Italian Poetry and Music in the Renaissance*, 94–6. A modern edition of the work is included on p.189.

38 This is essentially the view of Fenlon, *Music and Patronage in Sixteenth-Century Mantua*, 47–53.

39 On Lhéritier in Mantua, see W. F. Prizer, 'A Mantuan Collection of Music for Holy Week, 1537', in *Renaissance Studies in Honor of Craig Hugh Smyth* (Florence, 1986), i, 613–25.

40 On Ercole and music, see G. Nugent, *The Jacquet Motets and their Authors* (diss., Princeton U., 1973), and Fenlon, *Music and Patronage in Sixteenth-Century Mantua*, 47–78.

41 G. Nugent, 'Jacquet of Mantua', *Grove 6*.

[42] The letter describing these events, from the Mantuan poet and humanist Ippolito Capilupi to Ferrante Gonzaga, is published, among other places, in *Mantova, le lettere*, ed. E. Faccioli, ii (Mantua, 1962), 564–5.

BIBLIOGRAPHICAL NOTE

Ferrara

The chief source is L. Lockwood's *Music in Renaissance Ferrara, 1400–1505* (Oxford, 1984). The notes to the present essay and the bibliography of Lockwood's book both give further references to articles by Lockwood on specific patrons and aspects of music in Ferrara.

Milan

There is little on music in Milan in English, the standard writings being E. Motta, 'Musici alla corte degli Sforza', *Archivio storico lombardo*, xiv (1887), 29–64, 278–340 and 514–61 (reprinted Geneva, 1977); G. Barblan, 'Vita musicale alla corte sforzesca', in *Storia di Milano*, ix (Milan, 1961), 787–852; and F. Degrada, 'Musica e musicisti nell' età di Ludovico il Moro', in *Milano nell'età di Ludovico il Moro* (Milan, 1983), ii, 409–15. General information is included in both the following studies: E. Lowinsky, 'Ascanio Sforza's Life: a Key to Josquin's Biography and an Aid to the Chronology of his Works', in *Josquin des Prez: New York 1971*, 31–75; W. F. Prizer, 'Music at the Court of the Sforza: the Birth and Death of a Musical Center', *MD*, xliii (1989).

Mantua

Music in Mantua before 1500 is covered only by works in Italian: P. Canal, 'Della musica in Mantova', *Memorie del R. Istituto di scienze, lettere ed arti*, xxi (1897), 655–774, and A. Bertolotti, *Musici alla corte dei Gonzaga in Mantova dal secolo XV al XVIII* (Milan, 1891); both are reprinted in *La musique à Mantoue aux XVᵉ et XVIIIᵉ siècles* (Geneva, 1978). The following works are concerned with music in Mantua in the sixteenth century: I. Fenlon, *Music and Patronage in Sixteenth-Century Mantua* (Cambridge, 1980), and W. F. Prizer, *Courtly Pastimes: the Frottole of Marchetto Cara* (Ann Arbor, 1980). There are also a number of articles on specific aspects of music in Mantua. Two by W. F. Prizer, not referred to in the course of this essay, are 'Lutenists and the Court of Mantua in the Late Fifteenth and Early Sixteenth Centuries', *Journal of the Lute Society of America*, xiii (1980), 4–34, and, 'Isabella d'Este and Lorenzo da Pavia, "Master Instrument Maker"', *EMH*, ii (1982), 87–127.

Chapter V

Aragonese Naples

ALLAN W. ATLAS

In June 1442 Alfonso V of Aragon (Alfonso I of Naples, *b* 1396, called 'the Magnanimous') emerged victorious from seven years of warfare against René of Anjou and thereby added the Kingdom of Naples to his already vast Aragonese realm.[1] In at least one respect, though, the victory was hollow, for the intellectual and cultural life of Naples had been nearly moribund since the heady days of Robert 'the Wise', a century and more earlier, when Naples was host to the likes of Giotto, Boccaccio and the leading music theorist of the day, Marchetto of Padua. It is therefore to Alfonso's credit that, having chosen to establish Naples as his capital (to the dismay of Barcelona), he quickly turned both city and court into one of the leading artistic-cultural centres in Italy. And amid the comings and goings of the humanist writers, Spanish poets and international cast of painters, sculptors and architects, there was no shortage of musicians.

Of the various ensembles that made up the musical establishment at court, it was probably the royal chapel – the ecclesiastical, musical and educational organization that saw to the everyday spiritual needs of the court – upon which the sincerely devout Alfonso lavished greatest attention. Indeed, one senses that Alfonso bestowed an almost paternalistic care on the chapel, and throughout his reign (1442–58) it constituted a strong link with his deeply felt Spanish heritage.

The importance Alfonso attached to the chapel is reflected in its rapid growth. From a small group of no more than six or seven singers who accompanied the king from one encampment to another during the years of war against the Angevins, the chapel grew to include fifteen adult chaplains and singers by October 1444, 21 by February 1451 and 22 by November 1455 – to which should be added, in each instance, two organists and an unspecified number of boys. Thus by the middle of the century, Naples could boast one of the largest chapels in Christendom and by far the biggest in Italy. Among its personnel were the theorist and rhetorician Jaume Borbó and the composers Pere Oriola and Juan de Cornago, the latter receiving the phenomenal salary of 300 ducats, exemption from the *elagio* (payroll tax) and, possibly, a cut from the state-controlled salt monopoly. To be sure, though, Cornago's hand-

34. View of the Bay of Naples (the 'Tavola Strozzi', left-hand side) by ?Francesco Pagano showing the Castel dell'Ovo, Torre di San Vicenzo, Castelnuovo (centre) and the Molo

some compensation must have derived as much from his high position in the ecclesiastical hierarchy of the court – he was Alfonso's chief almoner – as from his musical talents (some 50 years later, Josquin Desprez, the greatest composer of the age, would ask for no more than 200 ducats from Ercole I d'Este at Ferrara, though his income would have been augmented by various clerical benefices).

Nor was the chapel distinguished only by its size; the quality of both its performances and some of its repertory must also have been high, to judge by the esteem in which both were apparently held. In June 1451 the chapel was welcomed and lauded in Florence, where it sang at the Duomo and the SS Annunziata as part of a goodwill mission through which Alfonso hoped to improve his poor relationship with the Medici. (In the event, music was not the panacea he sought, for a true rapprochement between Aragonese Naples and Medicean Florence was not achieved until 1479.) In 1454 Leonello d'Este founded his own chapel according to the 'more regio', which may well mean that he modelled his chapel after that of Naples (though a reference to the French royal chapel cannot be ruled out). Two decades later, in January 1473, Galeazzo Maria Sforza, Duke of Milan, who had by then become accustomed to raiding the Neapolitan chapel in his effort to recruit singers, instructed his ambassador at Naples to obtain copies of the psalms that the chapel had sung to commemorate Alfonso's military victories. The royal chapel, then, was a musical institution of some note.

As for its duties and manner of performance, the chapel was required to sing – presumably polyphony – with the accompaniment of organs at both Mass and Vespers of major feast-days, while on certain occasions the singers may have been joined by wind instruments, as witness an order that Alfonso issued in August 1420 for an organ to be built for his chapel at Barcelona that would be in tune with such instru-

157

ments. Since Alfonso maintained many of the Spanish traditions of the
chapel when he transplanted it to Naples – he had new copies made of
fourteenth-century Aragonese household ordinances – the court may
well have known the occasional use of wind instruments during the performance of the liturgy, a practice not unheard of at the time, but one
that would not become customary until the sixteenth century.

Finally, praise for Alfonso's chapel must be tempered in at least one
respect: there was an air of 'provincialism' about it. Throughout
Alfonso's reign, the personnel of the chapel was overwhelmingly
Spanish, many of the singers having already been associated with the
court before its transfer to Naples. Thus Alfonso's strategy of recruitment stands in contrast to that followed at, say, Florence and Ferrara,
where in the 1450s singers and composers were already being sought in
the domains of France and Burgundy (as they were even earlier in the
century at many cathedrals and courts of northern Italy). It is difficult
to say whether Alfonso was unaware of the new directions being
explored by the skilled Franco-Burgundians (he certainly appreciated
and collected northern paintings, tapestries and other *objets d'art*),
whether he felt more comfortable with a chapel made up of his Spanish
compatriots, or whether he was simply unable to attract the ultramon-
tanes for cultural and political reasons (the French, of course, always
considered him a usurper). But, as was true of the court as a whole,
where the main poetic language was Castilian, with Catalan being used
in the chancery and treasury, the Spanish tinge of the chapel never
paled.

Secular music at the court was also heavily Spanish in flavour, as
befitted a centre that served as a meeting-place for poets from various
regions of a yet uncentralized Spain. The leading composer of secular
song was Juan de Cornago, who had arrived at Naples no later than

April 1453. Typical of the poetry he set – with a musical style often just as dark and sombre – is the following *canción*, attributed in different poetry sources to Juan de Mena or (probably more accurately) to Pere Torroella, a Catalan poet who resided at Naples from about 1456 to 1458:

Yerra con poco saber	He errs from little knowledge
quien toviere tal creencia,	who holds to such a belief,
que firmeza de mujer	that the steadfastness of a woman
a los peligros d'ausencia	in the perils of an absence
se pueda mucho tener.	can be held to be of much worth.
Con fe de presta tornada,	With faith of a prompt return,
non cessando el escrivir,	and never ceasing to write,
Bien podra alguna guardada	Perhaps a well kept one [woman]
dos o tres dias bevir.	will survive two or three days.
Mas a la mas detener	But for the rest, it is not enough
no les abasta la ciencia,	to give them freedom,
por qu'es se natural ser	for it is their natural being
tienen aquesta dolencia,	that they have this defect,
qu'es olvidança sin ver.	that is, to forget what they don't see.[2]

Thus Naples was home to a flourishing tradition of music and lyric poetry that formed a Spanish counterpart (musically more modest, of course) to the brilliant chanson tradition that the generation of Ockeghem and Busnois was beginning to cultivate in the French and Burgundian realms. And Alfonso's court at Naples, more so than any single centre in Spain, was the birthplace of this Spanish courtly polyphonic song.

Just as important to the musical life of the court as those who sang either the liturgy or secular song were the many instrumentalists, or *ministres* – lutenists, harpists, keyboard players and players of wind instruments – who figure in the account books from as early as the 1430s, when they, like the chapel singers, followed Alfonso from one battle camp to another. Especially valued were the wind players who formed the *alta cappella*, a group made up of two discant or tenor shawms (a double-reed instrument that was the forerunner of the oboe), a bombard (low shawm) and, eventually, a trombone. As Johannes Tinctoris pointed out in his *De inventione et usu musicae* (published *c*1481–3), the *alta cappella* performed at weddings, banquets, public and civic ceremonies, and even on the battlefield and in church. But perhaps their most important function was to provide music for social dancing, a courtly diversion enjoyed as much at Naples as anywhere else. Here, too, the influence was Spanish; preference was given to 'li balli maravigliusi/tratti di catalani', as one anonymous mid-century poet put it before going on to offer a short list of dances that were popular at the court: the *cascarda*, the *palonella*, the *moresca*, the costumed *momos* and the *basce e l'alta* (the Spanish name for the paired basse danse and saltarello).

As at all the great courts of Europe, music also played a major role at the grand occasions of state where it could serve as an artistic expression of dynastic splendour. By far the best documented of these occasions, as far as music is concerned, was Alfonso's spectacular triumphal entry into the city of Naples on 23 February 1443, an event commemorated on the frieze of the Triumphal Arch which Alfonso had erected as a gatehouse to Castelnuovo (fig.36). In addition to the customary pennant-draped royal trumpeters – at least twelve of them on this day – who were set on a 'carro trionfale', there were numerous other music-filled floats that wended their way through the streets. Among them, according to the court chronicler Panormita (Antonio Beccadelli), was a tower with four singers who, dressed as the allegorical figures Magnanimity, Constancy, Clemency and Liberality (certainly a reference to Alfonso's attributes), went 'cantantes suam quaeque compositus versibus cantionem'. Elsewhere, in the Largo del Mercato, six young boys dressed as angels sat upon a gilded wooden arch and sang, while in each of the *seggi* (quarters) of the city, costumed women danced in the streets to the music of the *ministres*.

Not quite so grand, perhaps, was the music the court heard during one of the state dinners in honour of Emperor Frederick III's visit to Naples during Holy Week of 1452. This time the scene was Castelnuovo

36. *Alfonso I's entry into Naples on 23 February 1443, commemorated in the frieze by Francesco Laurana on the Triumphal Arch into the Castelnuovo*

where, according to the diary of one of Alfonso's chaplains, dinner was followed by 'moltes maneres de sons, menistres, xantres e moltes maneres de festes que no se escrivir ni dir'. (Alfonso was a lavish host, reportedly spending 100,000 ducats during the ten-day visit.)

Finally, a few words are necessary about Castelnuovo itself, for Alfonso had taken music very much into account when he began to renovate the royal residence at the beginning of his reign. To begin with, one room was officially designated as the 'cambre della musica' and was fitted with organs and other instruments (see below). In addition, the great hall of the castle, the heavily tapestried Sala dei Baroni, had on its east wall two balconies, one above the other, where musicians and entertainers could be situated (and at the same time be kept out of the way). Also containing an organ of its own was the 'camera delle reggiole', which served as the royal dining room. Lastly there was the Cappella Palatina, situated off the central courtyard, where the royal chapel sang music for Mass and Vespers. The Castel Capuano, which served as the official residence of the Duke of Calabria, the title held by the king's eldest son and heir to the throne, also had a special music room.

With Alfonso's death on 27 June 1458, the political situation at Naples changed dramatically; so too did cultural activities in general and music in particular. When Alfonso died, the Aragonese realm was split: the Spanish territories and the islands (see note 1) went to Alfonso's younger brother, Juan, while the Kingdom of Naples on the Italian mainland went to his illegitimate son, Ferrante I (*b* 1423). Though no small possession itself – the kingdom extended over approximately the southern third of present-day Italy and thus constituted its single largest political entity – it meant that Naples and Ferrante were isolated. No longer was Naples part of the Crown of Aragon, and the Spanish influence at the court, though it never disappeared entirely, began to wane. Under Ferrante, Naples became Italianized and, in its musical outlook, internationalized.

In terms of the royal chapel, Ferrante's style of patronage differed from that of his father. In part, it was a difference in personality, and in part, a difference in the political-symbolic status that court chapels came to have throughout Italy as the century progressed. Though Alfonso was as hard-headed a politician as any, he was something of a dreamer when it came to the arts. And particularly with music, he never abandoned his Spanish-Gothic heritage, being seemingly unimpressed with (or possibly unaware of) new developments elsewhere. With Ferrante, on the other hand, one senses that musical patronage, like everything else, was measured in terms of its political advantages. His was a strategy that fitted happily with a new attitude towards music and musical institutions that developed throughout Italy during the last third of the century: one in which the court chapel became an ever more important symbol of the cultural status of the state and one that led such courts as Naples, Milan, Ferrara, Florence and the papacy to compete intensely with one another for the services of the most renowned Franco-Netherlandish composers and singers, who had by now come to dominate the field of polyphonic music. At the same time, the chapel, though it never lost its ecclesiastical-religious function, began to grow in importance as a purely musical organization; by the end of the century, at least at some courts, the position of *maestro di cappella* was assigned to the leading musician in the chapel and not necessarily to a high-ranking cleric. Finally, there was a third ingredient that led the chapel in new directions: Ferrante's spectacular (at least initially) political success. After turning back the renewed Angevin claims on Naples of Jean II and allied, pro-French Neapolitan barons (1458–65), Ferrante forged strong political and cultural links, sometimes through dynastic marriages, with Milan, Ferrara, Budapest and Burgundy. And in 1479 Naples even reached an accommodation with Medicean Florence. Thus not only was Ferrante willing to enter the competition for the best musicians, but he also had the prestige to do so.

Signs of change in the chapel are already evident by the late 1460s, when its members included the composer Vincenet (by 1469, at the latest) and the singer Filippet Dortenche, who in 1470–71 was dispatched to France to recruit new singers. However, at the same time as Ferrante was collecting singers, he was losing them, often to Milan where the voracious musical appetite of Duke Galeazzo Maria Sforza seemed never to be satisfied. Indeed, the Neapolitan chapel became a favourite musical hunting-ground for the duke, with the raids sometimes taking a nasty turn, as in late 1473 or early 1474, when Naples and Milan nearly severed diplomatic relations over the services of the peripatetic singer Johannes Cordier, whom Galeazzo Maria had lured to Milan on the sly. Eventually Charles the Bold of Burgundy was called in to mediate in the dispute, and Naples was the loser, as it often was in this courtly game of musical chess.

The most auspicious moment in the development of the chapel – and for music at the Aragonese court of Naples in general – was the arrival in the early 1470s (the precise date is unknown) of Johannes Tinctoris, singer, composer, jurist, humanist and one of the seminal figures in Renaissance music theory. Simply put, Tinctoris put Naples in the centre of the musical mainstream. It was there that he presumably wrote all twelve of his extant treatises, five of which have dedications either to Ferrante or to the Princess Beatrice, whom Tinctoris may have tutored in music. In addition, the same two members of the royal family are the dedicatees of two of the most distinctive works in Tinctoris's known compositional output: Ferrante was honoured with a large-scale setting of the Ordinary of the Mass in which the basses must descend to the low contra *C* (thus raising questions about performing practice in terms of pitch and the use of instruments in music for the liturgy), while Beatrice was addressed in the short motet *O virgo, miserere mei*, in which there is a dazzling display of compositional number symbolism. Finally, there can be no doubt that Tinctoris played an important role in disseminating the sacred and secular Franco-Netherlandish repertory of the Ockeghem–Busnois generation at the court of Naples, and that he played a role in the compilation of some of the Neapolitan music manuscripts that contain this repertory seems beyond question.

Tinctoris was not the only theorist of note to make Naples his home during the 1470s and 1480s, though the others admittedly enjoyed a much more transient relationship with the city. Foremost among these was Franchinus Gaffurius, who spent about two extremely productive years at Naples, from late 1478 to late 1480. While there, he completed and saw through the press (in October 1480) his first major work, the *Theoricum opus musicae disciplinae*; he added glosses to two earlier treatises and began work on what would eventually become Book IV of his *Practica musicae*. He also composed a small amount of music and generally enlivened Neapolitan intellectual and musical life by taking part in discussions about music with Tinctoris (with whom he exchanged pedagogical motets) and other theoretically minded musicians resident in the city. Although Gaffurius does not seem to have had any official connection with the court, he did, according to the sixteenth-century Neapolitan musician Giovan Tomaso Cimelo, hold the position of *maestro di cappella* at the nearby church of SS Annunziata.

Three other theorist-teachers who were at Naples in the late 1470s or early 1480s deserve mention. First there is the Spanish singer and composer Bernardus Ycart, who served in Ferrante's chapel from *c*1476 until at least October 1480. No treatises by Ycart survive, but a contemporary biography of Gaffurius tells us that he and Ycart engaged in dialogues on music (as Ycart did with the English theorist John Hothby, who was active at Florence and Lucca). Another musician with whom Gaffurius discussed matters of music theory at Naples was the well-known pedagogue Guillelmus Guarnerius, who resided in the city during the period 1476–9. And while there is no known documentation of an official position at the court, Guarnerius's presence there is attested to by his having taught music to the young Serafino dall'Aquila, who, as we shall see, played an important role in the development of secular music at the court. Finally, the years 1481–2 saw Florentius de Faxolis at Naples, where he was part of the retinue (possibly with Josquin Desprez) of the exiled Ascanio Sforza. It was no doubt during this Neapolitan sojourn that Florentius came across the work of the rather obscure 'Abbas populeti sive Magister Blasius' (later cited in his *Liber musices*, a book on musical 'manners' for Ascanio) who is probably to be identified with both the Blasius Romero who was abbot of the Neapolitan monastery of S Maria del Popolo and the Blas Romero who was a singer in Alfonso's chapel in 1451. Thus while one cannot speak of a Neapolitan 'school' of theorists or musical thought, the late 1470s and early 1480s saw both city and court buzzing with discussions covering the gamut of music theory.

The royal chapel continued to grow and develop along international lines throughout the 1470s and into the 1480s. Indeed, the middle ten years or so of these two decades may well mark the highpoint of music at Aragonese Naples, the years in which the court enjoyed its greatest flourish of musical creativity, influence and prestige. On 1 September 1479, Sixtus IV issued a *motu proprio* in which he set aside benefices for each of 44 (unnamed) members of the chapel. From October 1480 there is a payment record for the fabrics needed to clothe twenty singers, among whom were Tinctoris, Ycart, the composer Jacobus Villette, the singer Dortenche (now at Naples for at least a decade, after having been unsuccessful in his attempts to move to Florence) and the highly acclaimed soprano Johannes de Lotinis Dinantinus, to whom Tinctoris dedicated one of his treatises. And at the very end of the decade – 1489 – the records again speak of 44 members in the chapel.

Despite the impressive numbers of 1489, the chapel may already have entered a period of artistic decline by the late 1480s. In October 1487 Tinctoris was sent across the Alps on a recruiting mission, his charge being to find singers of a type that could not be found locally. However, since the chapel was in fact admitting an ever growing number of local personnel from the south of Italy, it could be that Ferrante sought more than just a singer; he may have been trying to get a major figure from the ranks of the Franco-Netherlandish composers, a group that, so far as we know, was then represented only by Tinctoris. The results of the search are unknown. And Tinctoris himself would leave Naples by the end of 1490 or the beginning of 1491 at the latest, thus leaving the court without a composer of real international stature.

Tinctoris left a sinking ship, for by the early 1490s it was more than just the royal chapel that was in a state of decline. Naples was in political trouble. Two of Ferrante's staunchest allies, Matthias Corvinus and Lorenzo de' Medici, were either dead or soon to die (Matthias in April 1490, with his heirs refusing to recognize the rights of his wife, Beatrice, and Lorenzo in April 1492). In France, Charles VIII was preparing to renew French–Angevin claims to Naples, while in Italy the signing of the Pact of S Marco in April 1493 (by the pope, Milan, Venice, Ferrara, Mantua and Siena) left Naples politically isolated and ripe for French picking. It is therefore sad to read Ferrante's correspondence of 1493 to his French ambassador concerning the composer Alexander Agricola, who had visited Naples in May–June 1492, and whom Ferrante was hoping to lure – quite secretly – to his court. The letters begin optimistically enough in February 1493, as Ferrante offers Agricola 300 ducats a year. But by June–September, Ferrante is conveying a very different message: tell Agricola to forget about everything – we have no need of him at Naples – war with France is imminent. (Agricola would, however, return to Naples in February–March 1494, and in the company of the composer Johannes Ghiselin, alias Verbonnet.)

Four months later Ferrante was dead (25 January 1494). His successor, Alfonso II (*b* 1448), abdicated one year after that, turning the kingdom over to his own son, Ferrandino (Ferrante II, *b* 1467). However, within a month, in February 1495, Naples was host to a new group of musicians, the French royal trumpeters, as the forces of Charles VIII occupied the city. Though the occupation was short-lived – the Aragonese were in full control again by the end of the year – and though the chapel continued to function as a musical organization until the reign of the last Aragonese king, Federico (Alfonso II's younger brother, *b* 1451) – it sang at the funeral of Joanne Vasallo, Bishop of Aversa, on 6 June 1500 – it was probably little more than a shadow of its old self.

The stature of the chapel thanks to Ferrante's strategy of internationalization is perhaps best described in contemporary terms by the humanist Raffaele Brandolini, in his *Opusculum de musica et poetica*, written *c*1513 for Pope Leo X:

> Ferdinand [Ferrante] pursued musical science with such affection that not only did he cultivate it himself most frequently in his private leisure but also attracted from all over Europe by means of most excellent rewards men most learned in this discipline . . . He had in fact . . . a most flourishing throng of singers selected from the French, British, Spanish, and German territories and charged only with the regular appointed praises and ceremonies of the church. In his chapel in Naples there are . . . two organs.[3]

While the portrait of Ferrante as a musically sensitive patron might be somewhat overdrawn, the description of the chapel rings true. It was one of the leading musical organizations of its time.

If the cultivation of sacred music became international in scope during the period of Ferrante, secular music – or at least the local product (thus qualified because the Franco-Netherlandish chanson was imported in large quantities) – became more Italianized. This came about as a corollary of the development in the 1460s and 1470s of a well-defined tradition of Italian lyric poetry. If some of the poets at the court took Petrarch – newly imported from Tuscany – as their model, others sought a more 'popular' tone, drawing on such forms as the barzelletta and the strambotto siciliano, and often spicing their verses with heavy doses of Neapolitan dialect. In all, such poets as Pietro Jacopo de Jennaro, Francesco Galeota and the transplanted Catalan Benedetto

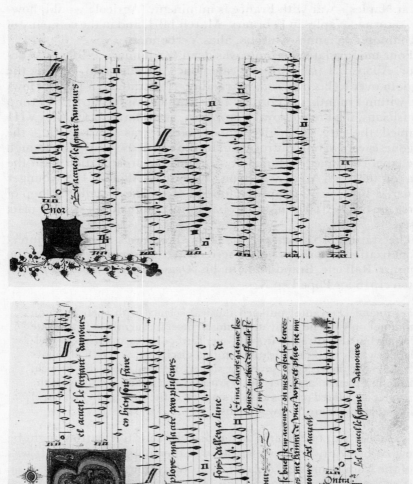

37. *The three-voice rondeau 'Bel acueil' by Antoine Busnois from the 'Mellon Chansonnier', copied in Naples, c1476*

Gareth (called 'il Chariteo') – to say nothing of Jacobo Sannazaro and Giovanni Pontano, who surely transcend the purely local – carried Naples into the mainstream of the Italian lyric tradition.

An example of the popular side of this development can be seen and heard in the barzelletta *Ora mai che fora suno*, a lively homophonic, declamatory setting which gained popularity throughout Italy, as shown by the many moralizing *laude* (including one by Savonarola) that parodied its text while retaining its melody. The ripresa and first two stanzas, taken here from a source which retains some of the dialectal touches, read as follows:

Ora mai che fora suno	Now that I'm out,
non voglio esere chiù monicha,	I no longer want to be a nun,
Arssa gli sia la tonicha	Let the tunic be burned
a chi se la veste chiuno.	by whoever wants to wear it.
Istavo allo munisterio	I was in that monastery
chom'una chosa perduta,	like a lost thing,
senza nullo refrigerio,	without any refreshment,
né mmai non ero veduta:	never was I seen:
Ora mai che ne son sciuta,	Now that I'm out,
non voglio essere chiù monicha.	I no longer want to be a nun.
Arssa gli sia la tonicha	Let the tunic be burned
a chi sse la veste chiuno.	by whoever wants to wear it.
Sora mia, tu ài ragione	Sister, you're right
a ben dici la veritati,	and really do tell the truth,
che nonn è piggior prigione	that there's no worse prison
che perder la libertati:	than to lose one's liberty:
in poter di questi frati	in the power of those friars,
s'io vi stevo, io ero morta;	if I'd stayed there, I'd have died;
che venivono alla porta:	they come to the door:
'Aprite a me, fra Petro suno'.[4]	'Open up, it's brother Peter'.

Just as popular as the barzelletta was the strambotto siciliano, whose eight-line, four-couplet structure followed the rhyme scheme *abababab* (in contrast to the 'Tuscan' variety, which rhymed *abababcc*). The extant Neapolitan music manuscripts of the 1470s and 1480s transmit settings of such strambotti by the dozen. And while some of the poems attain a measure of literary worthiness, the majority are the product of 'Sunday' poets who gathered about such patrons as Prince Federico and Giovanni Cantelmo, Count of Popoli. The following lament is typical:

Un tempo che facea lo sacrificio,	During a time when I performed Mass,
era tenuto prevete sacrato.	I was thought to be a holy priest.
Fortuna me avea dato un beneficio;	Fortune had given me a benefice;
tenealo senza bolla accomandato.	I held it without official sanction.

Un jorno che mancai a lo servizio,	One day when I missed the service,
perdendo le fatiche, fui cassato:	and my efforts came to naught,
Cossi che piu non fazzo tale officio,	I was sacked:
guastordene da tutti so' chiamato.	Since I no longer officiate,
	everybody calls me a ne'er-do-well.[5]

Although both *Ora mai* and *Un tempo* survive in Neapolitan music manuscripts as fully notated compositions, their utter simplicity and occasional polyphonic rough edges betray their relationship to the so-called 'unwritten' tradition, in which versatile poet-improvisers recited verses extempore, singing them to simple melodic formulae and accompanying themelves on bowed or plucked string instruments. In this tradition, Naples was a leading centre. It was at Naples, as a page in the service of Antonio de Guevare, Count of Potenza, that the teen-age Serafino de' Ciminelli dall'Aquila learnt to sing and play the lute, and though Serafino came to be more closely associated with Ascanio Sforza and other patrons of northern Italy, his two three-year sojourns at Naples (1478–81 and 1491–4) and his active role in Pontano's famed academy left a deep impression upon him. Other well-known poet-performers at Ferrante's court were Aurelio Brandolini (known as the 'Christian Orpheus') and Benedetto Gareth, who entertained the royal family and its guests by singing the verses of Virgil.

Ferrante's court was both well staffed and well equipped for a wide range of entertainments in the area of secular music. To cite Raffaele Brandolini again: '[Ferrante] had not far from his own chambers a certain hall most elegantly furnished with paintings and sculptures to which he could quickly come and in which no instruments that might be sounded with hand, plectrum, or mouth was wanting'.[6] Complementing the 'music chamber' was the royal 'chamber music' – Brandolini's 'cubicularios musices' – an ensemble of singers and instrumentalists that performed at everything from intimate evenings of secular song and chamber music at Poggioreale, the country retreat of the Duke of Calabria, to the large-scale celebrations in the Sala dei Baroni of Castelnuovo.

Some of the chamber musicians enjoyed more widespread fame: Messer Laurenzo de Cordova, rewarded with the post of Abbot of S Cruce at Venafro, was cited in Paolo Cortese's *De cardinalatu* of 1510 as the most renowned player of the 'gravecordium' (clavichord); the singer Anna 'Inglese' had performed at the courts of Monferrato and Milan; and Giovanni da Gaeta, one of the 'governors' of the music chamber, was one of the better-known organ builders of the late fifteenth century. The 'chamber music' was still intact as an ensemble in 1499, just two years before the demise of the dynasty, when a roster of its personnel shows that it consisted of eleven musicians, not including the unnamed wind players.

Two final aspects of secular entertainment remain to be discussed:

38. *Three dancers accompanied by a harp: miniature from the 15th-century dance manual 'De practica seu arte tripudii' by Guglielmo Ebreo da Pesaro*

dance and theatrical productions. In the former activity, Naples was distinguished by two sojourns at the court (in 1465–8 and 1474) by Giovanni Ambrosio da Pesaro (known also as Guglielmo Ebreo), author of *De practica seu arte tripudii,* one of the most valuable dance manuals of the period. Having arrived at Naples in 1465 in the company of Ippolita Sforza (who became Duchess of Calabria that year), he taught the Princesses Beatrice and Eleonora how to dance in the 'Lombard' manner. It was undoubtedly at Naples that he composed his well-known arrangement of the famous basse-danse melody known as *La spagna,* a whimsical enough piece to be sure, but one that is important for the light it sheds on the improvisatory style of fifteenth-century dance bands.[7] One can appreciate the roles that social dancing and the *alta cappella* played in the festive life of the court from a letter of 18 August 1488 from Ferrante to Francesco Gonzaga, in which the king implores the Marquis of Mantua to order two wind players to return to Naples immediately; for not only had Ferrante advanced them 148 ducats, but they were sorely needed for 'le feste che se fanno in Napoli, in le quale multo spesso è necessario che danze la serenissima Regina . . . insieme con la Illustrissima Infanta'.

As for the place of music in theatrical productions, it suffices to cite two works that were staged in March 1492 to celebrate the Spanish victory over the Moors at Granada (Ferrante and Ferdinand 'the Catholic' were cousins). The first, a *farsa* entitled *La presa di Granata* and attributed to Sannazaro, concluded with Gaiety singing to the accompaniment of three nymphs who played the cornamusa, flute and violetta, after which Prince Federico, dressed as the King of Castile, took to the stage with others in the audience and danced the *bassa e l'alta.* Two days later it was Apollo, in Sannazaro's *Il triunfo de la Fama,* who with viola in hand sang verses in praise of the victory.

169

In all, Naples experienced a wide range of secular music activities, and especially in its cultivation of Italian song, both written and unwritten, it helped pave the way for the development of the mature frottola that came to be associated with the likes of Marchetto Cara and Bartolomeo Tromboncino. And though the frottola would attain its definitive style at such northern Italian courts as Mantua and Ferrara, one cannot help but wonder to what extent the course of Italian music in the early sixteenth century might have differed had Aragonese Naples not had its very life snuffed out and its status relegated to that of a political-cultural vice-royalty of an uncaring and even oppressive Spain.

To view the course of music at the Aragonese court of Naples from the beginning of the dynasty to its end, a period of about 60 years, is to see a development laden with contradictions. First there are the obvious differences in the styles and goals of musical patronage fostered by Alfonso and Ferrante. Though Alfonso abandoned Barcelona as his capital, immersed himself in the adventures of Italian politics and showed a deep appreciation of Franco-Burgundian achievements in the visual arts, his patronage of music was almost 'sentimental' in its adherence to his Spanish heritage. Apparently, music was something with which Alfonso had to feel culturally comfortable, and thus both sacred and secular music during his reign were Spanish to the core. With Ferrante, on the other hand, one suspects that the patronage of music took on a somewhat less personal tone. Both musical personnel and repertory became thoroughly international, and the star-studded cast of musicians and their wide-ranging repertory were probably less a reflection of Ferrante's own tastes and preferences than an expression of the pomp and power of the state.

No less apparent is the discrepancy between what the court accomplished in its cultivation of and influence on sacred and secular music. Naples had produced, in Cornago's *Missa 'Mapamundi'*, one of the earliest examples of a cyclic cantus-firmus mass based on a 'popular' melody; it knew the large-scale sacred works of the Ockeghem–Busnois generation of Franco-Netherlanders (possibly introduced in quantity by Tinctoris); and it had access to the polyphonically 'crude' style of native Italian composers active at nearby monasteries and cathedrals. Yet neither city nor court played a vital role in the development of new stylistic trends. In the field of secular music, on the other hand, Naples stood among the leaders. From Cornago's nurturing of courtly polyphonic Spanish song during the period of Alfonso to the production of barzellete, strambotti and formulaic improvisation in that of Ferrante, the Neapolitan contribution was consistent, brilliant and influential.

Finally, this dichotomy between achievement in sacred and secular music calls attention to a third contradiction, which brings us back to sacred music at the court and, more specifically, to what might be seen as a gap between potential on the one hand and achievement on the other. Why, with such a stellar group of personnel and, in the 1470s and 1480s, such composers as Tinctoris, Vincenet, Ycart and Villette, did Naples not become a centre of stylistic innovation? The answer would seem to lie in the absence at the court of a leading composer of the maturing Josquin generation – during the very years in which other Italian musical centres – Milan, Ferrara, Florence and Rome – were busy engaging such composers. Naples, then, fell stylistically behind just as the other courts were reaching out in new directions? Why? Could it have been Ferrante's brand of patronage, which does not seem to have been marked by any great sensitivity? Is it possible that Ferrante was simply complacent, so impressed with the presence of Tinctoris that he felt little need for the services of a composer of the younger generation? Or was Tinctoris himself the stumbling-block? Does the lack of citations from composers of the Josquin generation – and they had produced at least their early works while the treatises were in progress – mean that he was unsympathetic to the new stylistic trends? Obviously we can only speculate. But by the time Ferrante turned his attention to Alexander Agricola, Naples was in dire political trouble and music had to surrender to more urgent concerns. In the end, after more than half a century, in part as leader, in part as a brilliant reflection of developments that arose elsewhere, music at the Aragonese court of Naples withered with the kingdom itself and was little remembered, if at all, by the century that followed.

NOTES

[1] The Crown of Aragon, as it was called, included the Spanish regions of Aragon, Catalonia and Valencia, as well as the Balearics, Mallorca, Minorca, Corsica, Sardinia and Sicily.

[2] Text and translation from *Johannes Cornago: Complete Works*, ed. R. L. Gerber, Recent Researches in the Music of the Middle Ages and Early Renaissance, xv (1984), pp.xxvi–xxvii, and pp.56–7 for a modern edition of the music.

[3] Translation from *The Mellon Chansonnier*, ed. L. L. Perkins and H. Garey, i (New Haven, 1979), 30; the Latin text appears on p.34.

[4] Four different versions of the poem in its entirety appear in G. B. Bronzini, 'Poesia popolare del periodo aragonese', *Archivio storico per le province napoletane*, 3rd ser., xi (1973), 260–66. The various versions range from the heavily Neapolitan to what is virtually a 'Tuscan translation'. A modern edition of the music is in A. Atlas, *Music at the Aragonese Court of Naples* (Cambridge, 1985), 220–21; the present essay is based on this monograph.

[5] Text and translation from *The Musical Manuscript Montecassino 871: a Neapolitan Repertory of Sacred and Secular Music of the Late Fifteenth Century*, ed. I. Pope and M. Kanazawa (Oxford, 1978), 646; a modern edition of the music appears on pp.477–8.

[6] Translation from *The Mellon Chansonnier*, ed. Perkins and Garey, i, 30.

[7] A modern edition appears in Atlas, *Music at the Aragonese Court of Naples*, 230–31.

BIBLIOGRAPHICAL NOTE

Historical-political background

The most informative account in English of Alfonso's reign (to 1458) is A. F. C. Ryder's, *The Kingdom of Naples under Alfonso the Magnanimous: the Making of a Modern State* (Oxford, 1976); there is nothing comparable in English for the period of Ferrante, with E. Pontieri's *Per la storia del regno di Ferrante I d'Aragona, re di Napoli* (Naples, 2/1969), being less a biography than a series of essays on various aspects of Ferrante's life. An overview of the 60 years of Aragonese rule at Naples can be had from the articles in the two massive volumes on Aragonese Naples in *Storia di Napoli*, iv/1–2, ed. E. Pontieri (Naples, 1974); finally, there are the always interesting but highly subjective interpretations of B. Croce, *History of the Kingdom of Naples*, trans. F. Frenaye, ed. H. S. Hughes (Chicago, 1970; originally published, Bari, 1925).

Literature and the visual arts

There is a fine survey of literary developments at the court (with generous excerpts and extensive bibliography) in F. Tateo's *L'Umanesimo meridionale* (Bari, 1976); painting is best treated in F. Bologna's *Napoli e le rotte mediteranee della pittura da Alfonso il Magnanimo a Ferdinando il Cattolico* (Naples, 1977); sculpture and architecture are dealt with in two studies by G. L. Hersey, *Alfonso II and the Artistic Renewal of Naples, 1485–1495* (New Haven, 1969), and *The Aragonese Arch at Naples, 1443–1475* (New Haven, 1973). One of the most beautifully illustrated books on Naples is R. Pane's *Il Rinascimento nell'Italia meridionale* (Milan, 1975 and 1977), which deals with both art and literature; T. De Marinis's *La biblioteca dei re d'Aragona* (Milan, 1947–51, supplement 1959), is a monumental study on all aspects of the royal library from the beginning to the end of the dynasty (the transcription of the archival documents – more than 800 – are especially valuable owing to the destruction of almost all the documents during World War II); a good, concise article on the patronage of Alfonso I in particular is E. R. Driscoll, 'Alfonso of Aragon as a Patron of Art', in *Essays in Memory of Karl Lehmann* (New York, 1964), 87–96. Finally, see also J. H. Bentley, *Politics and Culture in Renaissance Naples* (Princeton, 1987).

Music

The most comprehensive account of the subject is my own study, *Music at the Aragonese Court of Naples* (Cambridge, 1985), which contains extensive documentation and bibliography as well as modern editions of eighteen pieces that can be associated with the court. Also valuable are two integral editions of music manuscripts that were compiled either at or near the court: *The Mellon Chansonnier*, ed. L. L. Perkins and H. Garey (New Haven, 1979), and *The Musical Manuscript Montecassino 871: a Neapolitan Repertory of Sacred and Secular Music of the Late Fifteenth Century*, ed. I. Pope and M. Kanazawa (Oxford, 1978); three composers associated with the court have had their works appear in reliable editions: the works of both Vincenet (ed. B. E. Davis) and Cornago (ed. R. L. Gerber) appear in the series Recent Researches in the Music of the Middle Ages and Early Renaissance, ix–x (1978) and xv (1984), respectively. The musical works of Tinctoris (but without the recently discovered *Missa 'Nos amis'*) appear in *Johanni Tinctoris: Opera omnia*, ed. W. Melin, CMM, xviii (1976), while the theoretical works can be found in *Johannis Tinctoris: Opera theoretica*, ed. A. Seay, CSM, xxii (1975–6); four of Tinctoris's treatises have appeared in English translation, either in whole or in part: *Johannes Tinctoris (c. 1435–1511): the Art of Counterpoint*, ed. A. Seay, MSD, v (1961); Seay, 'The *Proportionale musices* of Johannes Tinctoris', *JMT*, i (1957), 22–75; *J. Tinctoris: Concerning the Nature and Propriety of Tones*, ed. Seay (Colorado Springs, 1967, rev. 2/1976); A. Baines, 'Fifteenth-Century Instruments in Tinctoris's *De inventione et usu musicae*', *GSJ*, iii (1950), 19–26; and C. Parrish, *Dictionary of Musical*

Terms by Johannes Tinctoris (London, 1963); this last work, the *Terminorum musicae diffinitorium*, one of the earliest music dictionaries, has recently been made available in a facsimile edition, *Documenta musicologica*, ed. P. Gülke (Leipzig, 1983). On Alfonso's activities as a patron of music before his period at Naples and on music at Naples in the early sixteenth century (i.e. on the periods that surround the present essay) see H. Anglés, 'La música en la corte real de Aragón y de Nápoles durante el reinado de Alfonso V el Magnánimo', *Cuadernos de trabajos de la escuela española de historia y arqueología en Roma*, xi (1961), 81–142, and D. G. Cardamone, 'The Debut of the "*Canzona villanesca alla napolitana*"', *Studi musicali,* iv (1975), 65–130. Finally, for an updated account of Alexander Agricola's relations with Naples, see A. Atlas and A. Cummings, 'Agricola, Ghiselin, and Alfonso II of Naples', *Journal of Musicology,* vii (1989).

Chapter VI

Paris and the French Court under François I

RICHARD FREEDMAN

THE ROYAL COURT

'The French recognize only the nobility of arms', wrote Baldassare Castiglione in his famous *Il cortegiano* of the early sixteenth century, 'and esteem all else as naught. Thus they not only fail to prize but they abhor letters, and hold all men of letters most base'. With such an opinion of the artistic tastes of French noblemen one would hardly expect Castiglione to hold any northern prince in high regard. Yet he was not always so pessimistic, for he saw great promise in a certain 'Monseigneur d'Angoulême' who might soon accede to the French throne. In him Castiglione saw 'such loftiness, joined however with a certain gracious humanity that the realm of France must always seem small for him'.[1] Indeed, the subsequent reign of this man as King François I, between 1515 and 1547, brought with it renewed interest in the value of letters and of the other arts, thus combining in a single regime the seemingly contradictory values of military valour and patronly liberality.

> The reign of François I is the most radiant, the most creative in French history, a reign in which two brilliant cultures came together, those of Gothic France and Renaissance Italy. Everywhere there was splendour, King François riding, dancing, or promenading in an unending pageant, escorted by glittering nobles, by famous poets, painters, and savants.[2]

The pervasive influence of François I upon learning and the plastic arts is legendary. Sponsor of great scholars such as Guillaume Budé, Etienne Dolet and Jaques Le Febvre d'Etaples, the king and his interest in classical learning helped to found both the Collège de France and the Bibliothèque Royale, later to become the Bibliothèque Nationale. Under François's protection the Ecole de Fontainebleau flourished, and thanks to him Italian artists – from Leonardo da Vinci to Benvenuto Cellini – were brought to France. French literature also prospered during the reign of François I, when Mellin de Saint-Gelais, Clément Marot and Pierre de Ronsard wrote with expressive freedom and

39. François I with his three sons and members of the church and French court: miniature (c1530)

renewed interest in classical models. Even the king himself seems to have composed a fair number of such verses.

Thanks to the sponsorship of this prodigious royal patron, musical life, too, flourished in Renaissance France, and nowhere so splendidly as in the capital, Paris. As we shall see, François I offered the weight of royal authority to many musical institutions there, from the printing presses of the Latin quarter to the musical guilds of the surrounding *ville*. But surely the most important privileges were those meted out to the musicians of the royal household itself, an itinerant institution that travelled almost continually between its various residences in Paris and the provinces in an unending pageant celebrating power and political might.

Such travels are certain to have been the occasion for musical performances of special splendour. Indeed, performances that marked state occasions – official entries, coronations, weddings, funerals and treaties – were often spectacles in themselves. During the summer of 1520, for instance, when the courts of France and England gathered near Calais for the meetings at the Field of Cloth of Gold, the musicians of two royal households collectively celebrated a festive Mass in honour of the event. The singers of one realm were accompanied by the organist of the other, and together the two teams, periodically joined by a band

40. Detail of a mille-fleurs tapestry (Loire workshop, c1510) showing musicians playing lute and organ

of wind players, performed the various sections of the Mass in alternation.[3] Musical collaboration, in short, may well have been a metaphor
for the spirit of princely cooperation that brought the two monarchs
together. Much the same air of political and musical goodwill may have
obtained some twelve years later, when King François I again met
King Henry VIII, this time at Boulogne-sur-Mer. One French witness
to the meetings saw fit to note the musical activities heard by the assembled nobles:

> Two oratories for the kings were fitted up near the high altar of the
> church of Our Lady. The King of England went into that on the right,
> and heard a Low Mass, and then as he was waiting for the king,
> another was begun. Francis came in at the beginning of the Gospel,
> accompanied by princes, cardinals and noblemen. The King of
> England came out of his oratory and embraced him, and then
> returned with the cardinal of Lorraine to his oratory, to hear the end
> of the Mass, and the French king went to his oratory to hear his Mass,
> while the singers sang *motez*. After Mass the kings returned to the
> abbey and dined separately, while music was made by trumpets,
> *hautboys*, cornetts and singers.[4]

The report is characteristically vague with respect to the music heard or
even the size and constituency of the various ensembles present. Yet
there is good reason to suppose that the music performed during this
meeting – like that heard near Calais in 1520 – was of several specific
types, each of which was the special province of a particular group of
musicians maintained in the royal household. A musician in the direct
employ of the French monarch would find himself in one of three
groups, each with duties and privileges defined largely by the three
chief social and administrative divisions of the *maison du Roi*: the
Chapelle, the Chambre and the Ecurie or stable.

The music played by each of the king's ensembles depended
primarily upon the social circumstances during which they normally
served. Thus the trumpeters of the royal Ecurie played chiefly during
large public gatherings, and in doing so probably drew on a number of
stock signals or calls with clear melodic and rhythmic profiles. If the
aim of such figures was to command attention and action, the trumpeter's repertory must have been terse and formulaic indeed. The
trompettes du roi, sometimes as many as a dozen strong during the early
years of François's reign, seem to have enjoyed privileges otherwise
reserved for members of the military guard; in addition to their ordinary wages they sometimes received patents of nobility, appointments
as officers in royal domains, exemptions from taxation and even grants
of immunity from legal prosecution.

The shawm players of the Ecurie (in the 1532 report they are also
named as the king's *hautboys*) also received preferential treatment from
their patron. Most of the eight players in this wind band seem to have

been Italians by birth, yet François I apparently saw fit to grant some of them special rights under the *droit d'aubaine*, provisions of which pertained to foreigners living permanently in the French kingdom. But if the *hautboys* resembled the trumpeters in the types of royal sponsorship they received, they nevertheless differed considerably when it came to musical duties, for among their main tasks was the accompaniment of courtly dances. The domination of this ensemble by Italian players was probably a direct reflection of the increasing vogue for Italian dance steps, including the pavan and galliard, in France.[5] The musicians of the Ecurie, therefore, accompanied the ceremonials of Renaissance statecraft, with its stylized entries, dances and spectacles.

Members of King François's private chamber ensemble, which at times consisted of an organist, a lutenist, some singers and even a consort of viols, will also have accompanied him to Boulogne-sur-Mer. Shortly before the trip, for example, the French monarch bought each of his four chamber singers a new black velour coat, no doubt in anticipation of their forthcoming performances before Henry VIII. The precise duties of these singers are not documented, but we may suppose that they were often called upon to perform the four-voice chansons much admired at court during the 1530s and 1540s. The king's chamber singers, in short, may well have entertained their patron with the latest offerings of French musical fashion.

Just as important as the cultivation of vocal performance, however, was the sponsorship of instrumental music in the royal Chambre. An organist, a lutenist and perhaps a rebec (or fiddle) player had occasionally figured in the private royal households of François's predecessors, particularly Queen Anne de Bretagne. Such men probably performed both individually and in combination with vocalists during the early years of the sixteenth century. But during the reign of François I solo instrumental performance was cultivated with particular intensity. By far the most famous of the king's chamber players was the lutenist Alberto da Ripa of Mantua. Praised by literati both north and south of the Alps, Alberto travelled widely even while in royal service, and several years before the meetings of 1532 he had journeyed to the court of England. At the French court, da Ripa's position in the musical Chambre was without peer. Like the king's personal physicians and advisers, musicians of the royal chamber were styled *valets de chambre* in recognition of the respect in which they were held, but all sorts of additional privileges and rewards were lavished upon Alberto da Ripa: he received about twice the salary of previous lutenists at court, and when it came to garnering the seigneurial grants of title and income that traditionally fell to officers of the king's Chambre, he again received more than an ordinary share of the spoils of royal patronage. His novel fantasias and other improvisatory compositions were so admired in France that his foremost pupil and successor at court, Guillaume

Morlaye, supervised the posthumous publication of Alberto's works in six volumes.[6]

Of all the musicians at the French court, however, the most regular and perhaps the most important duties fell to the singers of the king's chapel. It was this ensemble that saw to the daily celebration of Mass and the observance of the many other requirements of divine worship. During the early 1530s the chapel employed some three dozen singers, and according to one surviving register they were divided into two principal groups. About a third of them, called simply *chantres*, were responsible for plainchant during the various regular services. The remaining two dozen singers, in contrast, were listed according to their vocal ranges – contratenors, tenors and basses – suggesting that they, together with the choirboys for the soprano lines, specialized in the performance of polyphonic compositions, including masses, motets and perhaps even chansons. So it was in October 1532, as we have seen, when a chronicler's account reported how François I first heard a mass (doubtless celebrated to the accompaniment of plainchant melodies) and then heard certain *motez* (polyphonic motets). Indeed, another account of the same ceremony, contained in a dispatch obtained by the Venetian historian and diarist Marino Sanudo, is even more exact than the first in its description of this part of the music heard at Boulogne-sur-Mer:

41. The French Court at Mass: woodcut by Oronce Finés from 'Primus liber tres missas' (Paris: Attaignant, 1532)

> This morning, the 22d, the most Christian king sent the English king
> the gift of a rich and beautiful gown, coat, and doublet, and the king
> clad himself in like manner. Entering into a church, one went to one
> chapel, the other to another, both of which were very richly furnished;
> and the Mass being ended, they joined company, and a motet was
> sung in [the king's] chapel, namely, *Da pacem, Domine, in diebus nostris*.[7]

The motet in question was almost certainly the one with that incipit
printed some three years later and ascribed to Claudin de Sermisy, then
leader of the musical chapel of François I. As we shall see, Latin works
such as this, which combines the opening phrase of a well-known
antiphon for peace with verses of Psalm 122, were often written to mark
important political occasions. The chapel, in short, was as much an
implement of statecraft as it was of worship.

These seemingly contradictory purposes are reflected in what we
know of the careers of chapel singers. During the early 1530s, for
example, musical direction of the royal chapel fell to the composer and
singer Claudin, who also saw to the musical supervision of the choirboys and the maintenance of the choirbooks used by his ensemble. For
all of this he received a handsome annual wage. Yet such earnings were
only one of several sources of income available to Claudin and his
colleagues, for as clerics or priests they might also hold ecclesiastical
offices at any of a number of churches and cathedrals scattered
throughout the French provinces, even though they might rarely set
foot in those institutions. During the late fifteenth and early sixteenth
centuries, for instance, royal composers and singers – including Johannes
Ockeghem, Loyset Compère and Jean Mouton – held canonical posts
at the church of St Martin of Tours in the Loire valley and in the parish
church of St Quentin in northern France.

Yet by far the most important ecclesiastical institution to have supported royal musicians was the Sainte-Chapelle, parish church of the
Parisian royal palace on the Île de la Cité. The Sainte-Chapelle, which
had its own endowments and special liturgical observances, was quite
separate in administrative terms from the royal household it served, but
the lines of distinction between the musical components of this elegantly decorated church and those of the king's *maison* were not always so
clear. Claudin de Sermisy had been a minor cleric at the parish church
long before his appointment in the king's chapel, and at the height of his
career he was nominated by his patron to receive one of its prized
canonical posts. Conversely, Pierre Certon, *maître des enfants* and ranking musical member of the parish church from 1532 onwards, was
called *chantre de la chapelle du Roy* in 1567 and was still later styled as
compositeur de musique de la chapelle du Roy. Either or both of these titles
may have been purely honorary, but the distinction suggests that the
Sainte-Chapelle and royal chapel might simultaneously offer employment and honour to musicians. Indeed, the pursuit of such ecclesiasti-

cal offices prompted François I, like other monarchs before him, to intercede with papal authorities on behalf of his singers in order to obtain for them benefices or other canonical appointments throughout the kingdom. And by virtue of their superior opportunity to exploit this vast network of financial support, French and Netherlandish singers continued to dominate the royal choirs, even as the personnel of the Chambre and Ecurie, the other principal musical institutions at court, became increasingly international.

The sponsorship of musicians at the royal court of France, therefore, was shaped in part by the various kinds of support the king could provide. Monetary affairs and royal offices directly within his control cannot have posed a very real barrier to the subjects of his favour. 'In an age of personal monarchy the court was both the royal household and the center of government. It was at court that decisions were taken, careers advanced, and patronage distributed.'[8] But the monarch himself, doubtless wishing to maintain the very finest group of singers and players available, was under considerable obligation both to cultivate various networks of influence among his peers and to compete with other rulers who might otherwise outshine him as a beacon of princely liberality.

> The urban elite of each major city – consisting of the dynastic house and its collateral lines, the court, and a small group of aristocratic families – is by virtue of its dominant local role forced to raise its political and intellectual sights and to measure its achievement against that of similarly placed elites in other cities. Such local elites know that their own clients will judge them in comparison with their peers elsewhere. This is no less true for republics controlled by oligarchical factions and clans than for signorial regimes. A subtle rivalry of Big Men is thus set in motion.[9]

François I is not likely to have considered his own predicament in precisely these terms. Yet in practice his patronage of music had much the same effect. The royal chapel, for instance, was under the musical direction of Claudin de Sermisy, but its chief officer was no musician at all, as the ranking member of the choir was the king's close friend and ally, the Cardinal François de Tournon. And François I also enlisted Cardinal Jean de Lorraine, 'France's most prodigal patron of art',[10] in the sponsorship of royal musicians and musical institutions. The lutenist da Ripa apparently travelled to and from Italy in the cardinal's retinue, and Jean, from his Parisian residence in the Hôtel (now Musée) de Cluny, seems to have offered his protection to the king's official music printer, Pierre Attaingnant. Even within the French royal family King François I was not the only sponsor of music: queen and princes alike maintained their own modest private musical ensembles. And the division of François's musical household into chapel, chamber and Ecurie was anticipated during the reigns of his Valois predecessors, Charles VIII, Louis XII and their consort, Anne de Bretagne. Even the trend towards the import of Italian music and musicians had actually begun before the reign of François I, when French armies repeatedly invaded the Italian peninsula.

PARIS

Music-making in the French capital was in part dictated by the structure and ceremony of life with the itinerant court, but it also depended on agencies and establishments whose connections with the monarchy took a variety of forms. At the nearby cathedral of Notre Dame de Paris,

42. Paris, c1540: gouache copy of a tapestry plan of the city

for instance, the prerogative of nominating two high-ranking musical canons fell to the ruling monarch, a principle that obtained additional income and prestige for esteemed singers of the royal household. Yet the many other musical posts at Notre Dame – over three dozen including the choirboys – were assigned not by the king, but instead by an assembly of clerics. Here statute and custom rather than the caprice of princely pleasure governed the making of musical appointments, and so, too, the needs of liturgy and of scholastic tradition determined the structure of services and of the music that accompanied them.[11]

Other churches scattered throughout the *ville de Paris* reflected musical heritages quite different from either of those just described. The parish church of St Merry on the right bank of the Seine, for instance, was the site of the Confraternity of St Julien, the religious organization of the minstrels of Paris. Founded during the fourteenth century, the corporation and its confraternity periodically chose from among their ranks a leader, the *roi* or *maître des ménéstriers*, whose title was summarily approved by the King of France. This chief minstrel, by authority of his guild and the throne, oversaw the rules of conduct and contract by which all members of this popular band of Parisian players were obliged to abide. Musical standards, too, were enforced by the organization, and no doubt the special patterns and formulae of variation and improvisation later promoted in printed manuals on instrumental performance as essential to any musical education had long been part of the rich oral tradition passed between masters and apprentices of the Parisian minstrels.[12]

Across the river on the left bank of the Seine, music took yet other forms, quite different from the popular dances and improvisations of the *joueurs d'instruments* ensconsed at St Merry. At the University of Paris, for example, music figured prominently in the curriculum of the quadrivium, together with astronomy, geometry and mathematics. Thus it is not so surprising that musical treatises by members of its faculty often stressed the speculative and mathematical elements of sound over any practical advice for players or singers. Some of the most learned men of the French Renaissance echoed a largely medieval theoretical heritage when they presented geometric and proportional justifications for elemental intervals of sound. Jaques Le Febvre d'Etaples, professor in the Collège de Cardinal Lemoine (he was also teacher of the famous Swiss music theorist Heinrich Glarean), published just such a speculative treatise, *Musica libris quatuor demonstrata*, at Paris in 1496, and Oronce Finés, first professor of mathematics at the Collège de France, wrote a similarly abstract consideration of sound and proportions, the *Protomathesis*, that appeared in 1532.[13] Like the celestial music of the spheres, however, it is unlikely that such speculation was ever imagined as bearing directly on the art of composition or performance.

Still other tendencies, at once practical and esoteric in their application, were also cultivated at the University of Paris, particularly during the 1540s, when Jean Dorat was professor of Greek there. Dorat's musical philosophies are known only in scant detail, yet the influence of his programme of musical and literary renovation along ancient models was no doubt great. It was from his lectures that the group known as the Pléiade was formed, including such great poets as Jean-Antoine de Baïf, Joachim du Bellay and Pierre de Ronsard. These were poets and literary critics of considerable acumen, and the theories they advocated eventually held sway over a number of musical experiments with classical poetic metres that were conducted by French musicians during the late sixteenth century.

There is nevertheless still good reason to suspect that musical thought in the university community was not always so abstract as these intellectual pursuits might suggest. The mathematician Oronce Finés, for instance, apparently took a keen interest in instrumental music, compiling an instruction manual for lutenists that was printed in both French and Latin not long before his appointment to the Collège. In 1512 the schoolmaster Nicolas Volcyr, lecturer at the University of Paris during the first two decades of the sixteenth century, enlarged and reprinted his manual of notation, plainchant and counterpoint, the *Enchiridion musices*. It is not certain whether Volcyr's treatise or others of its kind were ever intended as textbooks in the modern sense of the term, yet there were probably many students for whom the information it contained was an appropriate subject for earnest study. The choir schools of northern France maintained scholarships in various colleges of the University of Paris expressly for the academic training of choirboys during the years that their voices were maturing. Perhaps these young singers relied on texts like Volcyr's to refresh their musical learning. On the other hand, by no means all the students in Paris were musical novices, for in 1549 the composer Clément Janequin, then in his seventh decade, was inscribed as a student there.

THE DISTRIBUTION OF MUSIC

Perhaps the most powerful force in musical life in the Latin Quarter, however, was the printing press, and no printer was so closely identified with the rise of music publishing in the French capital as Pierre Attaingnant. His firm, in the rue de la Harpe not far from the Pont St Michel, published over 150 music books containing several thousand compositions in the years between 1528 and 1558. For Attaingnant, not surprisingly, success depended on good political and musical relations with the royal court, and he wasted no time in cementing his bonds with that influential establishment. An early volume offered by the firm spared nothing in its dedicatory praise for the 'most worthy Cardinal of

Tournon', master of the royal chapel:

> Since therefore I see that you are the ornament of our century and a most successful student of the art of music, I have considered this collection of Masses notated with type should be dedicated to Your Eminence. I beg that you take it in good part in the meantime until better things are produced. I shall be able to supply bigger and better works if I meet with the favour of your kindness. I know how great your authority and influence are with this Prince, since he has never yet denied you aught.[14]

Attaingnant's esteem for Tournon's musical expertise may have been somewhat inflated, but his belief in the cardinal's standing with the king surely was not. Quite to the contrary, for at the head of the same set of masses Attaingnant printed the text of a royal patent that he had first received in 1529, giving 'our well beloved Pierre Attaingnant, printer and bookseller dwelling at the University of Paris' exclusive rights to publish and sell music in the French capital. Attaingnant's press, in short, operated at the pleasure of the king and the ranking member of his musical household. Yet the wording of the royal patent acknowledged that the firm had a musical audience that extended well beyond the court, for in recognition of the labour he invested in the perfection of his printing process, it gave Attaingnant the right to print:

> the said notes and characters both of the said music and *choses faictes* as of the said tablatures for the playing of lutes, flutes, and organs, of which he has printed, has had printed and hopes in the future to print, many books and quires of masses, motets, hymns, chansons, as well as for the said playing of lutes, flutes, and organs, in large volumes and small, in order to serve the churches, their ministers, and generally all people, and for the very great good, utility, and recreation of the general public.[15]

Royal protection might have given Attaingnant the official monopoly he sought, but he had still to reckon with the breadth and scope of the market for his work. In fact the firm balanced these two competing demands rather successfully. Several of Attaingnant's early collections of chansons and of sacred music showed his almost overwhelming interest in the music of the royal court, and especially in the music of its leading composer, Claudin de Sermisy. But in other prints Attaingnant's musical attentions were directed to broader horizons. He once executed certain commissions for liturgical books destined for the diocese of Noyon (of which he may have been a native); and many of the prints offered by the shop during the 1530s and 1540s show an increasing awareness, not just of composers active in Paris itself, but also of those who served the neighbouring courts of Lorraine and of the Habsburg Netherlands, as well as the many important cathedral choirs of the French provinces.

Novelty and versatility above all else seem to have been the requirements of Attaingnant's music-buying public. Secular vocal anthologies – collections of chansons for either three or four voices were the norm – were frequently advertised as 'chansons nouvelles' or 'nouvellement et correctement imprimées', even if some of the works in question were plainly of a retrospective character. Anthologies of music for keyboard – decorated chansons or modest liturgical compositions – similarly advertised that their tablature notations were suited for performance on 'organs, spinets, manichordons and all similar musical instruments'. The lute, too, was evidently an instrument of growing popularity among the printer's public, and consequently Attaingnant offered his customers anthologies that mixed preludes and dances for solo lute with arrangements of polyphonic chansons for lute or for voice with lute accompaniment. So popular were these means of performance that one such print included Oronce Finés's *Très brève et familière introduction*, a manual giving practical advice on how musicians might make such arrangements on their own. And it was thanks to Attaingnant's efforts that Clément Marot's French translations of the psalms, together with some of the musical settings they received at the hands of royal musicians, were brought to public attention.

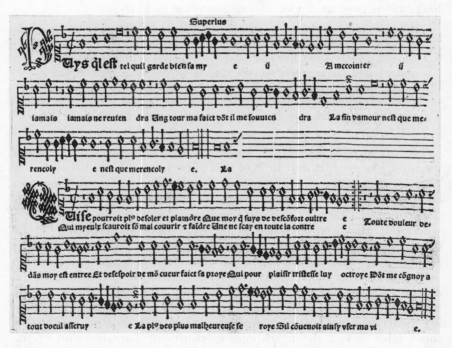

43. *Page from the 'Second livre contenant XXVII chansons nouvelles' (Paris: Attaingnant and Jullet, 1538), showing the superius part of two pieces by Claudin de Sermisy*

186

The Attaingnant shop must have provided a common meeting-ground not only for the stellar trio of Claudin, Certon, and Janequin, but also for countless other musicians and music lovers from all parts. For this reason, if for no other, Francis I's music printer may be said to have established a new institution in the cultural life of the nation. The role of the music press as a clearinghouse for ideas and as an arbiter of taste was something to be reckoned with henceforth in French music.[16]

By the middle of the sixteenth century Attaingnant's prints had travelled far and wide. Indeed, collectors not just in France but also in England, Portugal and the German-speaking territories to the east had either acquired his carefully printed partbooks or had copied compositions from them in impressive numbers. And perhaps in testimony to the success and influence of Attaingnant's venture, various competitors emulated his techniques and even borrowed his repertory. During the 1530s a rivalry had already developed between the royal music printer and the firm run by Jacques Moderne in Lyons, and after Pierre Attaingnant's death in 1551 or 1552, his heirs had to compete with two Parisian rivals: Nicolas Du Chemin and the partnership of Adrian Le Roy and Robert Ballard. During this entire period other elements of the book trade helped to promote this vibrant musical culture, for there survive a number of poetic anthologies issued by Attaingnant's Parisian colleagues that offer the texts of the French chanson repertory independently of their music.

The printed page, however, had not always been the preferred means by which French music was disseminated. During the years before the start of Attaingnant's activity, for instance, musicians of the realm relied almost exclusively on manuscript anthologies to preserve and to distribute their works, even while Italian firms like Petrucci, Dorico and Antico were hard at work producing music books – many of which drew heavily on French repertories – by machine. Unfortunately, very few French manuscripts have survived, but those that have reveal that while the production of music books by hand was often a laborious process, it was nevertheless undertaken by, and for, musicians of all callings, and moreover that these varied occupations helped to bring the music of Paris and the royal court to the attention of their colleagues in the provinces and abroad. Johannes Heer, for instance, a student at the University of Paris about 1510, subsequently carried the music of the French capital back to his native Switzerland; and when the royal composer Jean Mouton and the music scribe Jean Michel stayed in Italy during the second decade of the sixteenth century they were sought out by members of the Este family of Ferrara specifically for the music they carried with them to the Italian peninsula.[17]

In the kingdom of France itself, however, it was in aristocratic circles that the most impressive music manuscripts were produced.

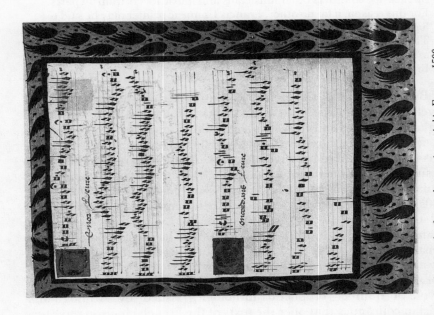

44. *Opening folios, showing the music of 'L'heure est venue' by Alexander Agricola, from a chansonnier copied in France, c1500*

Like the music books assembled at the Burgundian court some 25 years before, manuscripts produced for the princes and peers of France during years around 1500 were refined in both their appearance and their repertory. Ornately decorated with calligraphic borders and painted heraldic emblems, such books were often presented to their owners – among whom were dukes, kings, queens and a royal mistress – as lavish gifts, and may well reflect the musical and literary fashions of their courtly contexts. While no music manuscripts survive from the court of François I, those associated with courtly circles during the years immediately preceding his reign suggest that aristocratic tastes changed profoundly during his *jeunesse*.

Unfortunately none of these manuscripts gives clear evidence of the precise circumstances, audience or performing medium for which they were intended, as these must have seemed self-evident to their owners and to the musicians who might have performed or copied from them. Nevertheless, intriguing evidence of both musical practice and style is offered by what the scribes chose to include and to omit from their collections. A number of these manuscripts were organized according to musical genres – sacred separated from secular or works for three voices distinguished from those in four parts. Within such subsections, moreover, the compilers of these chansonniers might group together works on a common poetic theme or compositions of a particular musical type, and pride of place might be given to a work with particular relevance to the dedicatee of the manuscript. Indeed, the organization of a book of monophonic melodies compiled about 1500 was such that the first letters of the first sixteen poems in the collection spelt out the name of its owner in acrostic: Charles de Bourbon, an intimate of the royal court.

Musicians, too, were left to deduce or to infer some of the information they might need in order to perform the music of these collections, particularly when it came to the problem of fitting poetic texts to the notes they accompanied. Not all musical parts were texted, even in the most carefully produced of these sources, a practice that would seem to leave open the possibility of playing such works with voices and instruments alike. Even the parts clearly intended for vocal performance, moreover, might have additional strophes inscribed at the foot of a page, thus requiring refined sensibility to the relation of rhymed lines and musical phrases of the often complex poetic forms at hand. It seems unlikely, therefore, that such music manuscripts – in contrast to the later offerings of Attaingnant and his colleagues – were ever intended for any but the most skilled musicians. And nowhere was the concentration of such experts so great as in aristocratic households.[18]

MUSIC AND SOCIETY

It is a paradox that the relationships between social circumstance and musical works can be both obvious and elusive. The ordered rituals and ceremonies of everyday life in Renaissance France would naturally have helped to determine the form and general character of the music that habitually accompanied them, from liturgical chant to formulaic dance music. But special events had their own music, too. The Anglo-French meeting of 1532, as we have seen, was the occasion for the performance of at least one such topical motet, *Da pacem, Domine, in diebus nostris*, and celebrations at court were often commemorated by settings of Latin texts that alluded to the events in question and the worthiness of the princes whom they concerned. Mathieu Gascongne's *Christus vincit, Christus regnat*, for instance, was evidently composed in 1515 for the coronation of François I, 'pro rege nostro', as Attaingnant's typesetter was later to designate it. Jean Richafort's *O praesul egregie*, another of the motets printed by Attaingnant, was apparently intended as a generic encomium for a bishop – 'de uno episcopo' reads the printed heading – of the Catholic Church, whose name was evidently to be inserted by the singers during performance. Works with French texts, too, might commemorate historical events, as when Clément Janequin's four-voice setting of *Chantons, sonnons, trompettes* welcomed 'les enfans du noble roy Françoys' on their return to France in 1530. Indeed, the *chanson historique* seems to have been a poetic genre in its own right, and there survive many such texts concerning the heated battles – both military and religious – of the sixteenth century.[19]

Other works, however, were hardly so exuberant in their countenance or purpose as any of the celebrations just mentioned. When Queen Anne de Bretagne died in 1514, for example, the royal composer Jean Mouton lamented her passing with his *Quis dabit oculi*, as did Pierre Moulu in his *Fiere atropos mauldicte*. Musicians, too, were the subject of such poetic and musical epitaphs. When the royal singer Jean Braconnier died in 1510 the court poet Guillaume Crétin penned a versified lament recalling how Jean's colleagues there had affectionately called him 'Lourdault' or clod, and *Nymphes de bois*, Crétin's poignant deploration on the death of the royal composer Johannes Ockeghem in 1497, implored 'Josquin, Brumel, Pirchon and Compère' – all celebrated composers associated with leading aristocratic households in France, the Netherlands and Italy – to mourn their loss. Indeed, the setting of this text by Josquin Desprez pays eloquent homage to the departed composer, juxtaposing a first section of antique counterpoint in the style of Ockeghem with a second part in Josquin's own modern idiom, all over a slowly intoned cantus firmus from the Requiem Mass.

By far the majority of extant works, however, give only indirect testimony to the circumstances from which they might have arisen. But such pieces, especially some chansons, may nevertheless offer important clues about the place of music and poetry in French society during the early sixteenth century. This genre, by virtue of its cultivation in a broad range of social and geographical settings, is an apt image of French Renaissance culture, above all in its humanistic responses to the legacy of Gothic forms and ideas. The chanson 'reflected humanist dreams, to be sure, because it was a mirror reflecting life in all its infinite variety, not excluding the crudest'.[20]

By the start of the sixteenth century the French chanson already embraced a surprising range of traditions at once aristocratic and popular, Gothic and Renaissance in their derivation. The poems chosen by Alexander Agricola, Loyset Compère and other composers active at the French court during the last years of the fifteenth century, for instance, couple fixed formal schemes (especially the rondeau and virelai) and complex syntax with the pessimistic literary themes commonly associated with Jean Molinet, Jean Lemaire de Belges and other of the *grands rhétoriqueurs*. The artificial language of much of this literature, moreover, often enjoys only a loose formal relationship to the accompanying music: poetic sections are distinguished by clear cadences, and the syntactic intertwining of successive lines is reflected in overlapping points of imitation and other sophisticated musical techniques. Rarely, however, do these works attend closely to prosody, declamation or word-painting to heighten their effect. Refined in both conceit and construction, such pieces seem to have been known during the early sixteenth century as *chansons musicales*.

Other genres cultivated by courtly connoisseurs of the early sixteenth century, however, look for their literary and musical inspiration to a set of ideals very different from those just described. Avoiding both the obscure language and the fixed formal schemes of the courtly pieces, these *chansons rustiques* instead rely on simple strophic designs and, at times, even nonsensical refrains. Many of the songs concern a *gaulois* world inhabited by shepherds, fools and cuckolds who tease and converse in frank, formulaic locutions utterly foreign to the often pessimistic rhetoric of the aristocratic love lyrics. Furthermore, the polyphonic *chansons rustiques* composed by such royal musicians as Jean Mouton and Antoine de Févin were frequently based upon the tunes of popular songs, many of which were heard in the farces and political satires of the French secular theatre thriving in the public squares.[21]

The *chansons rustiques* range in subject matter from frank love lyrics to obscene *grivoise* dialogues, and from stories of the unhappily married (and ill-mannered) to narrations of historical events. Some of the melodies draw heavily upon a common stock of poetic locutions and musical phrases – often with the dependency typical of an improvisatory tradition – yet here, too, are elements of a more literate courtly heritage, for some of the texts echo the dour sentiments of the *rhétoriqueurs*, and many are cast in the *formes fixes*.

During the early years of the sixteenth century, therefore, the chanson was a meeting-ground for radically different cultures and musical traditions. The heritage of a Gothic past, at once aristocratic and subtle, met the comparatively free and bold offerings of a popular art. This mingling of traditions allowed minstrels and improvisers to mimic the conventions of courtly chansons. But it also invigorated aristocratic music-making with new tunes and fresh techniques borrowed from the urban populace.

The advent of music printing in France, as we have seen, did much to promote the continued interchange of musical and poetic thought among the various levels of French society. Indeed, the printed chansonniers of the 1530s and 1540s embraced a wide variety of works, the diversity arising not only from the kinds of lyric found there but also from the regional affiliations or social circumstances of the composers who set them. Here we find narrative chansons about frustrated lovers and pastoral landscapes, poems whose alternating sections of dialogue and description elicited lively rhythms and mercurial polyphonic textures from the musicians who set them. Clément Janequin seems to have specialized in compositions of this sort, and his long programmatic compositions like *Les cris des Paris* and *L'alouette* justly won him lasting fame.

Alongside such compositions, however, Attaingnant's prints also offer examples of serious love poetry at once more refined and lofty than any of the common jests encountered before. The lyrical outpourings of court poets, including Mellin de Saint-Gelais, Clément Marot and even the king himself, aspired to this ideal with special fervour. It is among settings of these poems, moreover, that the relations between place and musical style are clearest. The works of Claudin de Sermisy and of Nicolas Gombert, composers associated respectively with the courtly household of France and the Habsburg court of the Netherlands, for instance, are typical of the so-called Parisian and Franco-Flemish schools of chanson composition. Gombert's pieces, with their long melodic lines and contrapuntal textures, are exercises in a thoroughly polyphonic art, and therefore quite different from the concise and chordal approach to text and music taken by the royal composer Claudin. The same concern for coordinated polyphonic motion and text declamation can be heard in the works of Pierre Certon, who, as we have seen, was also closely associated with the court of France. The simple chordal style of the popular *voix de ville* and the symmetrical phrases of bourgeois dances also seem to have attracted the attention of composers associated with the royal household, and by mid-century these, too, were enlisted as vehicles for some of the musical and poetic experiments of the French humanists under Pierre de Ronsard and other members of the Pléiade.

Composers from the cathedral choirs of Paris and the French provinces at first only occasionally acknowledged the principal stylistic types fostered at the imperial court under Gombert and at the French royal court under Claudin. The efforts of Parisian music printers like Attaingnant and his colleagues, however, brought the competing styles of a host of provincial masters to mingle with the more lyrical and succinct ideal pioneered at the French court. Perhaps in testimony to the popularity won by this expressive and immediate style, there developed in Paris and in other musical centres a thriving commerce in the reworking of certain songs in both reduced and expanded musical textures, as well as an important trade in the distribution of similar melodies as timbres for religious *chansons spirituelles* and French psalms. Through this exchange of ideas – drawn from courtly fashions, popular traditions and the literary musings of intellectual circles in Paris, Lyons and elsewhere – the music of the French Renaissance was once again transformed.[22]

The sponsorship of musicians by patrons like François I seems to have been a necessary obligation of Renaissance princes. The appointments, privileges and international opportunities he afforded musicians like Claudin, da Ripa and Attaingnant, moreover, stemmed directly from the organization and aims of the social fabric in which they all found themselves involved. But the pressures exerted upon musicians at the royal court, and in a city as rich in musical history as Paris, can hardly have determined the character of their creative efforts with quite the same success with which it shaped their material and administrative surroundings. Despite the obvious obligations to royal authority due from chapel singers, virtuoso *valets*, university scholars, aspiring pressmen and guild officials alike, there was nevertheless a certain abstract freedom that remained the exclusive province of musicians. Patronage, in all its varied forms, may well have shaped the conditions of musical life in Renaissance France, but the musical products of that age often transcended those circumstances in subtle ways that we have only begun to understand.

The Renaissance

NOTES

1. B. Castiglione, *The Book of the Courtier*, trans L. E. Opdycke (New York, 1903), 56–7.
2. D. Seward, *Prince of the Renaissance: the Life of François I* (London, 1974), 13. Seward's informative and wonderfully illustrated study of the French monarch is among the best of its kind.
3. Concerning the political and musical circumstances of the meeting between the French and English courts, see J. G. Russell, *The Field of Cloth of Gold: Men and Manners in 1520* (New York, 1969); and P. Kast, 'Remarques sur la musique et les musiciens de la chapelle de François Ier au camp du drap d'or', in *Fêtes et cérémonies au temps de Charles Quint, [Fêtes de la Renaissance II]: CNRS Bruxelles, Anvers, Gand, Liège 1957*, 135–46.
4. I have adapted the English translation from J. Gairdner, *Letters and Papers Foreign and Domestic, of the Reign of Henry VIII* (London, 1880), v, 624–5.
5. The character and history of dance music in the Renaissance are briefly explored in A. Rooley, 'Dance and Dance Music of the Sixteenth Century', *EM*, ii (1974), 79–82.
6. For more on Alberto's life and works, see L. Nordstrom, 'Albert de Rippe, joueur de luth du Roy', *EM*, vii (1979), 378–85.
7. I have based my translation on the one from Gairdner, *Letters and Papers, Foreign and Domestic*, iv 336.
8. K. Thomas, review of *The Courts of Europe: Politics, Patronage and Royalty 1400–1800*, ed. A. G. Dickens (London, 1977), in *New York Review of Books*, xxiv/21–2 (26 Jan 1978), 18.
9. W. L. Gundersheimer, 'Patronage in the Renaissance: an Exploratory Approach', in *Patronage in the Renaissance*, ed. G. F. Lytle and S. Orgel (Princeton, 1981), 17.
10. D. Heartz, *Pierre Attaingnant, Royal Printer of Music: a Historical Study and Bibliographical Catalogue* (Berkeley and Los Angeles, 1969), 83.
11. For a model study of music at a French cathedral, see C. Wright, 'Antoine Brumel and Patronage at Paris', in *Music in Medieval and Early Modern Europe: Patronage, Sources and Texts*, ed. I. Fenlon (Cambridge, 1981), 37–60.
12. Concerning the social and musical history of popular players in France and especially in Paris, see F. Lesure, 'La communauté des joueurs d'instruments au XVIe siècle', *Revue historique de droit français et étranger*, i (1953), 79–109.
13. Additional information on music in the scholastic community at Paris appears in N. C. Carpenter, *Music in the Medieval and Renaissance Universities* (Norman, Oklahoma, 1958).
14. From Attaingnant's first volume of polyphonic masses, issued in 1532. For the complete text and a translation of the dedication, see Heartz, *Pierre Attaingnant*, 177.
15. The privilege of 1529 was renewed by François I and his successor Henri II until Attaingnant's death in 1551 or 1552. For text and a translation, see D. Heartz, 'A New Attaingnant Book and the Beginnings of French Music Printing', *JAMS*, xiv (1961), 22.
16. Heartz, *Pierre Attaingnant*, 104.
17. Two recent studies trace in eloquent detail the paths by which French music of the early sixteenth century came to be known and cultivated in the Italian peninsula: *La couronne et fleur des chansons a troys*, ed. L. F. Bernstein, Masters and Monuments of the Renaissance, iii (New York, 1984); and L. Lockwood, 'Jean Mouton and Jean Michel: New Evidence on French Music and Musicians in Italy, 1505–1520', *JAMS*, xxxii (1979), 191–246.
18. Concerning manuscripts from Renaissance France and their implications for musical performance, see L. Litterick, 'Performing Franco-Netherlandish Secular Music of the Late 15th Century: Texted and Untexted Parts in the Sources', *EM*, viii (1980), 474–85.
19. The rich cultural context of political motets and chansons is treated in A. Dunning, *Die Staatsmotette, 1480–1555* (Utrecht, 1970); and E. Picot, *Chants historiques français du seizième siècle* (Paris, 1903).
20. D. Heartz, 'The Chanson in the Humanist Era', in *Current Thought in Musicology*, ed. J. W. Grubbs (Austin, 1976), 219.
21. On the vibrant musical and literary milieu that surrounded the *rapprochement* of the *chansons musicales* and *chansons rustiques*, see H. M. Brown, *Music in the French Secular Theater* (Cambridge, Mass., 1963).
22. Further to the diverse stylistic and literary context of the chanson during the second quarter of the sixteenth century, see L. F. Bernstein, 'The "Parisian Chanson": Problems of Style and Terminology', *JAMS*, xxxi (1978), 193–240.

BIBLIOGRAPHICAL NOTE
General
The cultural life of Renaissance France is the subject of a number of excellent studies. D. Thomson's *Renaissance Paris: Architecture and Growth 1475–1600* (London, 1984), for instance, suggests the diversity of contexts – royal, ecclesiastical and civic – in which the arts were cultivated in the French capital, while F. Lot and R. Fawtier, *Histoire des institutions françaises au moyen âge* (Paris, 1957–62), helps to show the rich range of local institutions and activities elsewhere in the kingdom. Artistic patronage at the royal court of France is considered in D. Seward's *Prince of the Renaissance: the Life of François I* (London, 1974), and in *Literature and the Arts in the Reign of Francis I: Essays Presented to C. A. Mayer* (Lexington, Kentucky, 1985). W. S. Gundersheimer, 'Patronage in the Renaissance: an Exploratory Approach', in *Patronage in the Renaissance*, ed. G. F. Lytle and S. Orgel (Princeton, 1981), 3–23, offers some penetrating observations on liberality and competition among Renaissance princes, including François I. This comparative approach to the study of artistic patronage may be pursued in R. C. Strong, *Splendor at Court: Renaissance Spectacle and the Theater of Power* (Boston, 1973), and in *The Courts of Europe: Politics, Patronage and Royalty 1400–1800*, ed. A. G. Dickens (London, 1977).

Music
Studies of the French musical Renaissance embrace a wide range of perspectives and audiences. Perhaps the single best introduction to the institutions, performers and genres of this period is I. Cazeaux, *French Music in the Fifteenth and Sixteenth Centuries* (Oxford, 1975). S. Bonime, 'The Musicians of the Royal Stable under Charles VIII and Louis XII (1484–1514)', *CMc*, xxv (1978), 7–21, and H. Prunières, 'La musique de la chambre et de l'écurie sous le règne de François 1ᵉʳ, 1516–1547', *L'année musicale*, i (1911), 215–51, document the material circumstances of musicians in the French royal household. And L. Nordstrom, 'Albert de Rippe, joueur de luth du Roy', *EM*, vii (1979), 378–85, provides specific details on the career of one particularly important player at the French court. L. Lockwood, 'Jean Mouton and Jean Michel: New Evidence on French Music and Musicians in Italy, 1505–1520', *JAMS*, xxxii (1979), 191–246, sheds much-needed light on the means by which French music – especially that of the royal court – was brought to Italy. Musical journeys to the north are examined in J. G. Russell, *The Field of Cloth of Gold: Men and Manners in 1520* (New York, 1969), and P. Kast, 'Remarques sur la musique et les musiciens de la chapelle de François 1ᵉʳ au camp du drap d'or', in *Fêtes et cérémonies au temps de Charles Quint [Fêtes de la Renaissance II]: CNRS Bruxelles, Anvers, Gand, Liège 1957*, 135–46.

The social history of music in civic, ecclesiastical and academic circles has also been the subject of a number of studies. D. Heartz's *Pierre Attaingnant, Royal Printer of Music: a Historical Study and Bibliographical Catalogue* (Berkeley and Los Angeles, 1969) traces the history of the Parisian musical press in eloquent detail, while C. Wright, 'Antoine Brumel and Patronage at Paris', in *Music in Medieval and Early Modern Europe: Patronage, Sources and Texts*, ed. I. Fenlon (Cambridge, 1981), 37–60, is an exemplary study of the musical requirements of the Cathedral of Notre Dame during the early sixteenth century. N. C. Carpenter's *Music in the Medieval and Renaissance Universities* (Norman, Oklahoma, 1958) includes sections on musical life at the University of Paris. And the Parisian schools of minstrelsy and stage music are documented by H. M. Brown, *Music in the French Secular Theater* (Cambridge, Mass., 1963), and F. Lesure, 'Communauté des joueurs d'instruments au XVIᵉ siècle', *Revue historique de droit français et étranger*, i (1953), 79–109.

Still other studies have focussed on the history of specific musical genres and techniques. D. Heartz's 'The Chanson in the Humanist Era', in *Current Thought in Musicology*, ed. J. W. Grubbs (Austin, 1976), 193–230, for instance, provides a broad overview of the French chanson against the principal literary and intellectual developments of the sixteenth century. In consort, L. F. Bernstein, 'The "Parisian Chanson": Problems of Style and Terminology', *JAMS*, xxxi (1978), 193–240, and H. M. Brown, 'The Genesis of a Style: the Parisian Chanson, 1500–1530', in *Chanson and Madrigal, 1480–1530*, ed. J. Haar (Cambridge, 1964), 1–50, gauge the growth and dissemination of the musical vogue that this genre enjoyed. *La couronne et fleur des chansons a troys*, ed. L. F. Bernstein, Masters and Monuments of the Renaissance, iii (New York, 1984), provides a detailed study and modern edition of an important printed collection of three-voice chansons from the early sixteenth century.

The textual types embraced by the chanson during the period in question are the subject of B. Jeffery, 'Thématique de la chanson entre 1480 et 1525', in *La chanson à la renaissance: Tours 1977*, 51–60. *Chanson Verse of the Early Renaissance*, ed. B. Jeffery (London, 1971–6), provides modern editions of many of the texts set to music by French composers. E. Picot's *Chants historiques français du seizième siècle* (Paris, 1903) draws together chanson texts that commemorate political and religious affairs of the sixteenth century, while A. Dunning's *Die Staatsmotette, 1480–1555* (Utrecht, 1970) provides textual and musical analyses of the political allusions – many to do with France – found in Renaissance sacred music.

The study of performing practice has also held the attention of writers on French Renaissance music. A. Rooley, 'Dance and Dance Music of the Sixteenth Century', *EM*, ii (1974), 79–82, for instance, traces the types and instrumentation of dance music, while L. Litterick, 'Performing Franco-Netherlandish Secular Music of the Late 15th Century: Texted and Untexted Parts in the Sources', *EM*, viii (1980), 474–85, examines the vexing vocal problems presented by the French manuscript tradition.

Chapter VII

Lyons: Commercial and Cultural Metropolis

FRANK DOBBINS

Geography and history conspired to make Lyons one of the largest and wealthiest cities in Europe during the Renaissance. The city's favourable situation at the meeting-point of important trade routes between the navigable rivers of the Rhône and Saône, and its proximity to Italy and Switzerland, ensured its international mercantile prosperity. The strategic significance of Lyons was recognized by the French crown, which in 1271 offered its protection to a commune of leading citizens opposed to the ecclesiastical authorities that had governed the seat of the primate of France since 843. Royal privileges reinforced the city's considerable administrative fiscal independence and encouraged expansion in commerce, industry and banking.[1] In the fifteenth century toll- and tax-exemptions, safe-conduct guarantees for foreigners, legalized interest charges and credit facilities gave a great boost to its market and particularly to the international trade fairs.[2] These fairs, held during four fortnights each year after 1463, attracted a large émigré community that included many Florentine republicans and wealthy bankers and merchants from Genoa, Lucca and Milan. They helped to make Lyons the financial centre which organized funding for the military campaigns in pursuit of the French royal claims to Milan and Naples between 1494 and 1525 and intermittently thereafter until 1559.[3]

During this period the frequent presence of the opulent Valois court and the aspirations of affluent bankers and merchants combined to create an environment in which music and the arts flourished. The enterprise of wealthy citizens encouraged the new printing industry to expand, and the fairs enabled its products to reach a wide international market. Supported by the large cosmopolitan community, a new generation of humanist philosophers and poets were thus able to propagate the ideas of the Renaissance.[4] The traditional anti-clerical and liberal proclivities of the local council and the enlightened attitudes of some of the royal governors made Lyons a safer haven than Paris for evangelical humanists and neo-Platonists like Aneau, Dolet, Des Périers and

45. *View of Lyons in the mid-sixteenth century: engraving by B. Salomon from 'Épitome de la Corographie d'Europe', ed. G. Guéroult (Lyons: Arnoullet, 1552)*

Rabelais. During the second half of the sixteenth century the active support of nearby Calvinist Geneva and Lausanne helped the advance of the Reformation. This was reflected in the widespread publication of psalms and *chansons spirituelles* until the ensuing persecutions and religious wars impoverished the city culturally as well as materially.

MUSIC IN THE LITERATURE OF LYONS

The eminent writers who made Lyons the literary capital of sixteenth-century France accorded a major role to music as a sign of nobility, the sister of poetry and the food of love. Symphorien Champier, Jean Lemaire de Belges and others[5] discussed music theory in their neo-Platonist academies, but also listened to the lute, the flute and the singing of birds. The poet-musician Eustorg de Beaulieu[6] also enjoyed the sounds of nature and the company of other musicians in the garden of his friend and fellow composer, the Florentine organist Francesco de Layolle.[7] Beaulieu related that he played 'little motets' on the spinet, that he taught Hélène, daughter of the wealthy banker Antoine de Gondi, and that he enjoyed the patronage of other prominent citizens. Beaulieu moreover reflects the prevailing religious and musical trends in Lyons in that he abandoned the priesthood and the composition of 'carnal' polyphonic chansons to embrace Calvinism, metrical psalms and *chansons spirituelles*.

Other free spirits of the time include the writer Rabelais[8] and his publisher, the philologist, poet and agnostic martyr, Etienne Dolet.[9] Dolet expressed his enthusiasm for music in his *Commentarii lingue latinae* (1536–8). The atheist Bonaventure Des Périers provides some delightful portraits of musicians and musical instruments in his short stories *Les nouvelles récréations et joyeux devis* (1558)[10] and describes in verse a boat journey down the Saône to a monastery on the Île-Barbe celebrating St Martin's Day in 1539, with the singing of recent chansons and the playing of the spinets, rebecs and the lute of Alberto da Ripa. Two strophes of this poem were set for four voices by Gabriel Coste, quoting snatches of chansons mentioned by the poet.[11]

Recent art songs were also cited, along with more popular tunes, as *timbres* in plays performed and published in Lyons, like those of Barthélemy Aneau, a teacher at the Collège de la Trinité, a free grammar school established by the municipality in 1527,[12] where the pupils were required to sing *Salve regina* and *De profundis* daily and to perform music as well as games every Thursday. In *Lyon marchant* (1541), Aneau's topical satire on the supremacy of Lyons, *Doulce mémoire*, a recent *épigramme* by François I, known in settings by Sandrin, Layolle and others, was sung by Arion (representing its royal author) sitting astride a dolphin. Aneau's nativity play *Chant natal* begins with seven noëls and a pastoral dialogue which are contrafacta of verses by Clément Marot,

François I and others known in polyphonic settings by Sermisy, Sandrin, Villiers and others recently printed in Paris or Lyons; the ensuing *Mystère de la Nativité* is also based on 'the tunes of various chansons' while the concluding *Chant royal* ends with a 'Noel mustic sur le chant *Le dueil yssu*', known in a four-part setting by Villiers.[13] A second Christmas sequence by Aneau, *Genethliac: noel musical et historial de la conception de la Nativité . . . par vers et chants divers* (1559), is the first surviving example of a French play to be published with newly composed or arranged polyphony – in this case by Didier Lupi, Claude Goudimel and an anonymous composer who, according to a pun on the title-page, may be Etienne du Tertre.[14]

The change from adapting existing music to composing new pieces for dramas, seen in the two Nativity sequences of Aneau, is reinforced by the author of the *Quintil Horatien* (1556), who rejected the Pléiade's strophic *timbre* and contrafactum principle when he wrote:

> For it is not usual, as you [Du Bellay] say elsewhere, that poets should be subservient and follow the music when they write chansons: on the contrary musicians follow the words and subject, as they call it, suggested to them by the poets. For testimony I refer you Claudin [de Sermisy], Certon, Sandrin, Villiers and other famous musicians.

This anonymous author might have been Aneau or another teacher at the Collège de la Trinité, Charles Fontaine, whose *épigrammes* were set to music in Lyonnais publications.[15]

Music must also have played some role in the plays presented in the first permanent theatre at Lyons, built in 1538. Ten years later the city witnessed the new fashion for classical Italian theatre with elaborate machines and musical *intermedi* (by Piero Mannucci) when Bibbiena's *Calandra* was presented by the Gelosi troupe as part of the festivities in honour of Henri II and Catherine de' Medici.[16] The publication by Jean Saugrin of the anonymous *Musique de David* in 1566, with music for one, two or four voices by Goudimel (and possibly others), suggests that the biblical dramas of Joachim de Coignac and Louis des Masures may have been performed in Lyons during the years of Protestant ascendancy (the 1560s).[17] A manuscript copy of a *Pastorale* by Loys Papon, celebrating a Catholic victory in 1587, includes two pieces of notated music in four parts sung by young actors and played by the band of shawms and trumpets, indicating the kind of music presented in French provincial plays of the late sixteenth century.

Musical skill was considered a most desirable attribute for society ladies. Thus Pernette du Guillet, whose *épigrammes* were set to music in anthologies published locally in 1540–41, was one of a number of refined ladies skilled in writing verse, singing and playing the lute, spinet and other instruments, who opened their houses to artists, writers and musicians. Another was Louise Labé, the wife of a wealthy

46. Scene from the 'Pastorale' by Loys Papon celebrating the Catholic victory at Monbrison in 1587: from a manuscript dedicated to the Duke of Mayne

rope merchant, whose Petrarchan poetry, published in 1555, describes music as the invention of love and the way to a lady's heart. Her preface explains how a knowledge of music, foreign languages and literature can be of benefit to women.

The symbolic aspects of music, particularly neo-Platonist and Pythagorean ideas of harmony and proportion, imbued the writings of the leading poet of Lyons, Maurice Scève,[18] some of whose *épigrammes*, set by Villiers and Phinot, were published locally. Scève's disciple Pontus de Tyard[19] devoted an entire book, *Solitaire second, ou Prose de la musique* (1555), to the philosophy of music, relating it to ethics, physics and astrology. Music also figured prominently in the writings of later Lyonnais poets like Guillaume de la Taissonière, [20] who sang and played the lute, which he often extols in his verse.

COURT MUSIC, CEREMONIAL ENTRIES AND CHURCH MUSIC

While this rich treasury of literature provides valuable insights into amateur music-making, it is sometimes coloured by Platonist idealism or symbolism. More factual information is available in contemporary chronicles and correspondence, supported by local and foreign archival records. From this it is evident that the most notable and elaborate musical events were arranged during the frequent visits of the French and other courts, while a more modest patronage was sustained by the local aristocracy and the immigrant plutocracy.

King Louis XII and Anne de Bretagne brought their musicians with them when they set up court at Lyons between 1499 and 1503. As well as the band of six shawms and sackbuts brought back from Milan in 1502, their musicians included members of the royal chapel, like Ghiselin and Josquin Desprez. The Habsburg Archduke Philip the Fair and his chapel (which included Agricola, La Rue and de Orto) visited Lyons in 1503 for the betrothal of his son Charles to Louis's two-year-old daughter Claude. The day after his arrival on 22 March, Philip heard Mass at the cathedral of St Jean, sung by his choir;[21] on 26 March he was invited to a banquet at the residence of the Arch-bishop of Lyons, Charles II de Bourbon, along with his singers and instrumentalists, to be entertained by local instrumentalists.[22] On 2 April the choirs of Louis and Philip combined to sing Mass at the cathedral. On 12 April the Mantuan ambassador to the French court at Lyons reported that Ghiselin and Josquin had arrived from Paris in a splendid carriage and had spent the night in his house before proceeding to Ferrara.[23] Philip's retinue probably passed through Lyons again on its way from the Netherlands to Spain early in 1506.[24] Margaret of Austria also visited the town between 1501 and 1504, when she resided nearby at Pont d'Ain with her husband Philibert II le Beau, Duke of

Savoy. After Philibert died in 1504 at least one of his singers, the composer Antoine Brumel, moved to Lyons, where he lived between July and December 1505 before becoming *maestro di cappella* to Duke Alfonso I at Ferrara.[25]

When François de Rohan was installed as Archbishop of Lyons at the cathedral on 14 August 1506, a place of honour in the procession was accorded to the singer Rolin de Semur, and the clergy chanted 'Inter natos mulierum',[26] however, nothing is known of the music that accompanied the two allegorical *histoires* performed at the Porte de Bourgneuf or on the cathedral steps, nor of those that were presented during the ceremonial entry of the new king, François I, in July 1515. François and his court made Lyons their base during the Marignano campaign, returning in 1522 and again in 1524 for a new Italian expedition. After François's defeat at Pavia and his subsequent imprisonment in Spain, his mother, Louise de Savoye, acting as regent, remained in Lyons. The release of François I from prison was celebrated on 8 July 1530 with more *histoires*, the singing of a *Te Deum* at the cathedral and a procession, led by a band of trumpets and shawms that very melodiously played 'chansons faictes et musicalles'. Although one chanson, 'newly composed' for the occasion was sung simply to the tune of an old song, an anonymous four-voice motet celebrating the release, *Letare et exultare*, was unusual in its virtuoso, melismatic word-painting.[27] The entry of the new Queen Eleanor in May 1533 was greeted by a procession led by trumpets and clarions followed by shawms, sackbuts and other instruments, with theatrical entertainments, including an aquatic spectacle with masquers and 'marvellous' singers, a mermaid playing a shawm astride a dolphin and nymphs dancing to the playing of *ménestriers*.[28]

Dramatic and musical entertainments were also organized by the *Basochiens* (law clerks) for their Ascension Day festivities on the Île-Barbe. A Latin eclogue by the priest Philibert Girinet[29] describes the blare of 'loud' instruments – trumpets, sackbuts and shawms – that accompanied a firework display as well as 'soft' ones – recorder and lyre (possibly a lute or guitar) – that performed a concert together with unaccompanied voices. For the ceremonial entry of the new archbishop, Ippolito d'Este, on 17 May 1540, Maurice Scève, with the Florentine painter Benedetto dal Bene, organized moralities, mysteries and other dramatic entertainments. However, these hardly matched the elaborate programme that celebrated the entry of Henry II and his new Queen Catherine de' Medici in September 1548. Trumpets, fifes and drums from the surrounding areas were brought in to supplement the royal band and the town waits for the processions and aquatic spectacles, while 'diverse instruments like shawms, dulcians, sorduns and cornetts' were played by Charles Cordeilles and his colleagues, with lyres and flutes by others, for allegorical *tableaux* at different points along the route. But the most varied music was composed by Piero

Mannucci, organist of the Florentine community at Notre-Dame-[de-Confort], for Bibbiena's *Calandra*, with *intermedi* representing the Seven Ages and Apollo, 'singing and reciting to the accompaniment of his Lyre . . . employing a new mode not used before in reciting plays'.[30]

The Chronicle of Jean Guérard mentions the music that was included in minor festivities like weddings, banquets and a *Momerie* presented in 1552 for the Luccan community with flutes, violins and strange Moorish instruments, including cymbals and 'inverted cornetts'. It also records the celebrations for the peace of Cateau-Cambrésis in April 1559, with trumpets, shawms and violins playing for processions, pageants and fireworks. During the visit of Charles IX and Henri de Navarre in June 1564 the aldermen, now equally divided between Catholics and Protestants, organized much more modest festivities with music, arranged by Philibert Jambe de Fer, at a cost of only 26 *écus d'or* (crowns). The highpoint was an allegory with the nine Muses playing various instruments, and a choir, situated higher in the theatre, replying with a harmonized canticle, before a 'delightful' instrumental finale.[31] The municipal archives record that the Catholic victory at Jarnac in 1569 was celebrated by a procession with a band of violins 'avec musique organicque et instrumentale de hautbois et cornetz à bouquin'.

Carnivals and burlesque cavalcades, like the *Chevauchée de l'âne*, the *Fête du cheval fol* and the *Dimanche gras*, used instrumental music in a manner similar to the Florentine *feste*. Instrumentalists also played for civic or guild festivities and for private commissions like weddings, banquets, serenades or aubades. Although not organized into guilds with restrictive practices like their Parisian colleagues, the professional musicians of Lyons must have served similar apprenticeships, largely concerned with mastering technique and with imbibing an aural improvisatory tradition. However, the specific references to their playing 'chansons faictes et musicalles' – the four polyphonic, if crude, compositions by the shawm bandsman Charles Cordeilles printed in Moderne's *Parangon des chansons* in 1540 – and the mention of the composer Guillaume de La Moeulle as an instrumentalist suggest that some waits were musically literate.

The surviving archival documents include mainly municipal accounts and notarized contracts recording tax payments, receipts and official commissions concerning professional instrumentalists of the kind usually spurned by the philosophers and poets. It is hardly surprising that there is abundant information about the official drummers who led the town guard and the trumpeters who were employed on a regular basis to signal the opening and closing of the city gates and to support the town criers' proclamations. Thus the names of some 30 drummers and twenty trumpeters appear during the century; at least one trumpeter, Jean Dupré, described also as a watchman who sounded the alarm from the tower on Fourvière Hill, was wealthy enough to own two houses, a garden and a vineyard in 1509. But another, Claude Cheval, lived in a house provided by the municipality and could not afford to replace his livery and a broken trumpet in 1531. A third, Simon Pojoud, was referred to also as a 'brigandier' (sergeant) and in 1516 was nicknamed 'Simon of thirteen trades'.

The high proportion of flute makers to players reflects the popularity of the flute and recorder among amateurs, as does contemporary Lyonnais literature, iconography and publications like Simon Gorlier's lost *Tablature de flûte d'Allemand* (1558) and Philibert Jambe de Fer's treatise, *Epitome musicale* (1556).[32] Similarly, the sixteen luthiers who made viols, guitars and lutes, and seven string makers and dealers compared to only eleven professional lutenists and one professional viol player, reflects the largely amateur status of these instruments. At least two of the lutenists and three of the eleven violinists mentioned between 1566 and 1600 were Italians. The high proportion of Italian (and to a lesser extent German and Jewish) players parallels that found at the

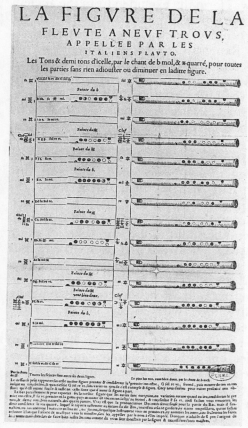

47. Fingering chart for the recorder from Jambe de Fer's 'Epitome musicale' (Lyons, 1556)

Valois court and in the publications of Lyons, Paris and Antwerp, reflecting the important role they played in French instrumental music.

The names of six rebec players (including one Italian and one Scot) all date from the first half of the century. These, like the later violinists, seem to have been professionals; but an attempt in 1518 to organize professional recognition and engagements with the Parisian system of corporation and associations under a 'Roy des violons' seems to have failed,[33] though the exact significance of 'maître' and 'compagnon' for certain organists and cornett or shawm players later in the century is unclear. At all events in this city where free trade was important, players were not restricted and were paid individually rather than collectively. The fact that many instrumentalists ended their days in poverty is supported by Robert de Balsac's morality play *Le droict chemin de l'hôpital*, which mentions 'vieux tabourins et ménétriers' who needed charitable aid. On the other hand the records of the Charitable Hospital suggest that blind orphans were taught the violin, but they also show that vagabonds included instrumentalists and dancing-masters.[34]

Although vocal polyphony was formally excluded from the ancient liturgy of Lyons and although there was no permanent organ at the cathedral before the nineteenth century, many churches and convents employed organists during the Renaissance. About 30 organists are listed in the archives. A 'fine and magnificent organ' installed at St Paul before 1501 was sold (and presumably replaced) in 1539. In the church of the Cordeliers, where the Luccan community had its chapel, the organ installed before 1553 was destroyed when the Huguenots siezed control of Lyons in 1562 and not replaced until 1592. An inventory of damages caused by the Protestants in 1562 also mentions a large and small organ at the church of the Carmelites, while at Notre-Dame-de-Confort Matthieu de Fleurs was pensioned off and the 'devastated' instrument, which had been installed before 1514, was eventually replaced by Francisque des Oliviers in 1570.[35]

Even if only plainchant was statutorily permitted, the cathedral had a clerical organization resembling that of the royal chapel and a choir school (*manécanterie*) with twelve boarders and twelve day pupils who learnt grammar and music from two separate masters. At Trinity College, the charity schools and the schools of St Paul, Ainay and the Abbey of the Île-Barbe, singing, grammar, arithmetic and religious studies were taught at primary level with music theory, poetry, mathematics, painting, architecture and scripture in the secondary curriculum. The names of some twenty singers survive, including four at the cathedral, five at St Nizier, one at St Paul and one at Fourvière. Few of their names recur in the city's numerous musical publications, although those of some composers like Loys Bourgeois, Philibert Jambe de Fer and Alamanne de Layolle are mentioned in records as 'musiciens' or 'joueurs'.[36]

MUSIC COPYING AND PRINTING

In the absence of sustained patronage from a resident court or cathedral, the great production that made Lyons one of the leading centres of music publication in the sixteenth century must not only have supplied the needs of the local aristocracy and bourgeoisie (as described in the literature) but also those of a wider national and even international trade through the fairs. Some insight into consumption is provided by letters between émigré banking and trading families like the Capponi, Manelli and Strozzi which mention motets and songs (*canzoni* or *canti*) by Layolle, Arcadelt, Festa and others sent between Lyons, Florence, Rome and Venice and performed at home by amateurs and professionals together.[37]

Four-part songs referring to Lyons, like the anonymous *Il estoit ung bon homme qui venoit de Lyon* and Mouton's *Resjuisses vous bourgeses, belles filles de Lion* and *En venant de Lyon*, appear in widely dispersed French and Italian manuscripts and publications of the late fifteenth and sixteenth centuries; but it has only recently been suggested that two manuscript chansonniers now in Scandinavian libraries may have originated in Lyons in the early sixteenth century.[38] The first of these, now in the Royal Library, Copenhagen, is an enormous collection of 255 polyphonic pieces, 52 motets, eleven *Magnificat* settings, three masses and 172 chansons of the late fifteenth and early sixteenth centuries copied about 1520. The second manuscript, in the Uppsala University Library, contains mainly three-voice chansons.

The case for Lyons being an important centre of music copying in the early sixteenth century awaits further illumination; but there can be no doubt that the city played a vital role in the history of music printing. A few important examples may be mentioned here. While liturgical incunabula with chant notation printed in woodblock already appear in the 1480s, the process of wood engraving used by Antico in Venice may have been introduced by Antoine du Ry for a collection of motets by Layolle and others, printed in Lyons about 1523.[39] Wood engraving was combined with movable type (double impression) for a book of thirteen Mass Propers and three motets printed in 1528.[40] The first book of polyphonic Mass Ordinaries printed in single impression by Jacques Moderne in 1532 was dedicated to Charles d'Estaing, count-canon of the cathedral.[41] Moderne, who like Antico came from Istria (then part of the Venetian republic), lived in Lyons between 1523 and 1562 and monopolized music printing there between 1532 and 1547, producing at least 56 musical editions, with an important repertory that is eclectic but often unique.[42]

The eight books of Moderne's *Motteti del fiore* series for four, five or six voices (1532–42) were probably mostly selected and edited by Francesco de Layolle, who was acknowledged as musical editor of the

48. *Bassus and secunda pars part of Layolle's 'Inter natos mulierum', from the 'del fiore' (Lyons: Moderne, 1532) Motteti*

ten masses printed in 1532. In all, Moderne published sixteen of Layolle's motets, as well as a number by leading contemporaries (some represented in earlier Italian manuscripts), with many new or unique pieces by important young composers and others unknown outside Lyons. While the majority of these motets have liturgical texts (mostly psalms, responsories and antiphons), some have political significance. Thus the first book includes pieces referring to recent events like the Siege of Florence, the marriage of François I to Eleanor of Austria and the release of the ransomed princes from their Spanish captivity. The third book for five and six voices is almost totally concerned with war and peace, including many motets composed for the peace conference between François I, Charles V and Pope Paul III in June 1538.

Moderne's chanson anthologies, which may have been edited by P. de Villiers, present a repertory similar to Attaingnant's, with many pieces by Sermisy, Gombert, Sandrin, Janequin, Certon, Gombert, Mornable, Maille, Maillard and P. de Villiers himself; but they include many unica and novelties by these and by a wider group of composers like Arcadelt, Bourgeois, Carpentras, Coste, Fresneau, Gardane and Layolle, as well as by minor figures like Abel, Cavillon, Cordeilles, P. de La Farge and F. de Lys, unknown outside Lyons.[43] The international flavour and destination of Moderne's publications is also reflected in the Italian *canzoni* of Layolle, a Spanish setting by Flecha, the masses, motets and *Magnificat* settings of Morales, Narváez, Eckel and Paminger, a few Italian and Provençal dialect pieces by P. de Villiers, the instrumental ricercars reprinted from *Musica nova* (1540) with French dances (some found later in Attaingnant's *Danceries* and elsewhere) as *Musique de joye* (*c*1544),[44] the lute books of the Hungarian Bakfark and the Italians Bianchini and Paladin. If the use of Italian lute tablature with numbers (rather than the French system with letters) suggests a primarily transalpine destination (as do the titles of some of the pavans and galliards), the number of transcriptions of chansons and psalms by La Moeulle, Mornable, Certon, Janequin and others reflects a French orientation. Moderne encountered local competition during his later years from the brothers Godefroy and Marcellin Beringen, Protestants of German origin who ran their printing and publishing business from a shop in the rue Mercière between 1544 and 1559. Thirteen of their 62 signed editions were musical, including monophonic French psalms and polyphonic settings by Loys Bourgeois and Simon Joly; they also issued Latin psalms and motets as well as French chansons and noëls by Dominique Phinot and Didier Lupi.

Protestants came to dominate music printing in Lyons, especially during the 1560s when they either controlled (1562) or shared the city's government (1563–7); they were heavily committed to publishing the popular Calvinist psalter translated by Marot and Bèze, with the melodies approved by the Genevan authorities, under the terms of the royal privilege granted in 1561 to the Lyonnais Antoine Vincent. Even earlier, in 1555, Michel du Bois, one of the many printers whose activity was divided between Geneva and Lyons, issued a complete psalter translated by Clément Marot, Jean Poitevin, Maurice Scève, Claude de Maistre and others, with melodies by Philibert Jambe de Fer, a Burgundian musician and professional gambler who lived in Lyons between 1553 and 1564. While the melodies for the psalms translated by Marot were the same as those published in Geneva in 1551, the others were presumably Jambe de Fer's own. In 1559 du Bois printed Jambe de Fer's *Psalmodie* with two-, three-, four- and five-voice settings of 41 psalms translated by Théodore de Bèze, using the common melodies found in the 83 psalms printed in Geneva in 1551. Du Bois also printed Jambe de Fer's practical treatise, *Epitome musical* (1556), which not only gives the usual rudiments, but includes original information on the flute, recorder, viol and violin and on differences between French and Italian musical practice.[45]

Between 1562 and 1566 at least thirteen editions of the 150 psalms with the approved melodies, probably composed by Bourgeois, Davantes and others in Geneva, were printed at Lyons;[46] this was fewer than the 33 editions issued at Geneva but surely more than was required to satisfy local demand, even during this period of cohabitation in the government of Lyons. In 1564–5 two complete psalters appeared in four-part harmonizations by Philibert Jambe de Fer and Richard Crassot. Both sets of harmonizations are simple and homophonic, retaining the Genevan melody in the Tenor or Superius (occasionally transposed by Crassot). As Jambe de Fer explains, in his dedication to Charles IX, harmonizations were normally reserved for domestic (rather than congregational) use; but some local reports suggest they had the same propaganda value as unison singing: thus Claude de Rubys wrote that the Protestants lured the lower classes with 'the melody of their songs of Marot and Bèze' and added, 'Satan always used the voices of men and women, singing together melodiously and in musical harmony, as bait to attract women and ignorant people to his cause'.[47] There was clearly also a continuing demand for four-part settings of *chansons spirituelles* and canticles; thus Didier Lupi Second's successful collection of Guéroult's verse, printed by the Beringen brothers in 1548, was supplemented with pieces by Maillard, Janequin, Certon, Arcadelt and Jambe de Fer in later editions (1561 and 1568).

Other publishers printed music sporadically, sometimes for the Italian community or for export (despite a decline in commerce during the religious wars). An example is provided by the Protestant Antoine Cercia who, in 1567, printed a book of four-voice madrigals by the Neapolitan, Giovanni Antonio di Mayo. A book of *Canzonelle* [sic] *alla napolitana* by Gasparo Fiorino of Rossano, published by the author at Lyons in 1577, with a dedication to Lucretia Buonvisi, includes only poems addressed to various ladies of important families in Lyons.[48]

The dismantling of Protestant presses began in September 1567 with forced loans and the imprisonment of the printer Jean II de Tournes. Antoine Cercia had moved to Geneva by 1568, when Antoine I Vincent died in prison in Lyons. Although three books of chansons and one of Latin psalms by George Buchanan set by Jean Servin were assigned to Charles Pesnot at Lyons in 1578–9, they were in fact reprinted in Geneva by Jean Le Royer and published by Simon Goulart. Similarly the *Quatrains du Sieur de Pibrac*, the *150 pseaumes de David*, the *Sacrae cantiones* and two books of *Octonaires de la vanité du monde* set by Pascal de l'Estocart, with title-pages attributing publication to Barthélemy Vincent at Lyons in 1582–3, were probably all printed in Geneva by Jean II de Laon. The fact that Lyons was given on these title-pages was probably intended to help distribution in France and Catholic countries during the religious wars. In reality, apart from the last book of Maillard and the reprints of Goudimel's contrafacta of Arcadelt's chansons (1586) and of Blockland's *Instruction* by the de Tournes press, there seems to have been no music published in Lyons during the 1580s. But some evidence of composers' activities there is provided in the dedications of Parisian publications like Jean de

Castro's trios, which explains that after leaving the Low Countries during troubled times, Castro had been in Germany, before going to Lyons where he enjoyed councillor La Porte's patronage. Nevertheless the religious upheavals, which hastened the decline of the fairs and commerce in general, affected the city's musical life. The flight of the Protestant printers was hardly compensated by the meagre efforts of Jesuits like Michel Coyssard who tried to imitate the didactic and popularizing intentions of the earlier Huguenot music.

★

During the Italian campaigns of Louis XII and François I, which brought Josquin, Mouton and other leading composers and singers from the French and Flemish courts to Lyons, the city enjoyed flourishing musical activity, continued with the support of the wealthy Italian banking and merchant community during the second third of the sixteenth century – a golden age in the city's literary history. After the rich international repertory of polyphonic masses, motets and chansons, selected for the prolific publications of Moderne by important musicians like Layolle and P. de Villiers to satisfy the intellectual élite and the international market, the Protestant printers of the next generation offered a simpler, more parochial fare of metrical psalms, canticles and *chansons spirituelles*, reflecting the upsurge of Protestantism among the bourgeoisie and urban proletariat. The instrumental music printed by Moderne and Gorlier usually followed Italian fashions. Distinguished foreign musicians also came to Lyons to publish vocal music, like Bourgeois from Geneva, Goudimel from Metz, Phinot and Roussel from Italy; others came from the French provinces, Italy or Germany to seek their fortune. Apart from widespread publication via the international fairs, the city offered a number of generous patrons, more from its wealthy banking and trading families (including many expatriate Italians) than from its ecclesiastical hierarchy and local aristocracy. Economic recession and the concomitant reduction in influence of the foreign communities later diminished the city's attractions, as much as the religious persecution and bigotry that succeeded the earlier toleration and liberalism which had encouraged the spread of the arts and humanities.

While the repertory of polyphonic masses, motets, chansons and lute tablatures published by Moderne has for the most part a cosmopolitan flavour typical of its geographical situation, many of the texts were by local poets, with music often by local composers. If the styles are essentially similar to those found in the publications of Attaingnant, Moderne did introduce some novelties – including monophonic noëls and the first polyphonic setting of one of the newly translated Huguenot psalms.[49] His successors, beginning with the Beringen brothers in 1547, were more innovatory in launching a series of vernacular metrical psalms and *chansons spirituelles* in more or less simple four-part settings by Bourgeois, Didier Lupi, Jambe de Fer and others, reflecting a compromise between the rigidity of nearby Calvinist Geneva, which permitted only monophonic psalm singing, and distant Catholic Paris, which generally disapproved of what was essentially a Protestant form.

NOTES

[1] C. de Rubys, *Les privilèges, franchises et immunitez octroyées par les roys trechrestiens aux consuls eschevins manans et habitants de Lyon* (Lyons, 1574).

[2] M. Brésard, *Les foires de Lyon aux XVe et XVIe siècles* (Paris, 1914).

[3] M. Vigne, *La banque à Lyon du et XVe au XVIIIe siècles* (Lyons, 1903).

[4] L. Romier, 'Lyon et le cosmopolitisme au début de la Renaissance française', *Bibliothèque d'humanisme et renaissance*, xi (1949), 37.

[5] E. Vial, 'La légende de l'Académie de Fourvière', *Bibliothèque d'humanisme et renaissance*, viii (1946), 253–66; F. Dobbins, *The Chanson at Lyons in the Sixteenth Century* (diss., U. of Oxford, 1972), 27–38.

[6] E. de Beaulieu, *Les divers rapportz* (Lyons, 1537/repr.1544, ed. M. A. Pegg, Geneva, 1964); see also F. Dobbins, 'Beaulieu, Eustorg de', *Grove 6*, and *The Chanson at Lyons*, 39–53.

[7] Layolle was also extolled by his fellow émigré in Lyons, the Florentine republican poet, Luigi Alamanni, and returned the compliment by setting two poems from his *Opera toscane*. D. Sutherland, *Francesco de Layolle (1492–1540): Life and Secular Works* (diss., U. of Michigan, 1968); F. de Layolle, *Music of the Florentine Renaissance*, ed. F. D'Accone, CMM, xxxii/3–6 (1969–73).

[8] N. C. Carpenter, *Rabelais and Music* (Chapel Hill, 1954); F. Dobbins, 'Rabelais, François', *Grove 6*.

[9] Dobbins, *The Chanson at Lyons*, 37; See also R. C. Christie, *Etienne Dolet, Martyr of the Renaissance* (London, 1880).

[10] For an English translation by R. and V. La Charité see B. Des Périers, *Novel Pastimes and Merry Tales* (Lexington, Kentucky, 1972).

[11] For a fuller discussion of Des Périers's musical references and settings of his verse and a transcription of his discourse on tuning lutes and guitars see Dobbins, *The Chanson at Lyons*, 54–60 and 241–250.

[12] Cf L. Gerig, 'Le Collège de la Trinité à Lyon avant 1540', *Revue de la renaissance*, ix (1908), 73; x (1909), 137, 204; Gerig, 'B. Aneau: a Study in Humanism', *Romantic Review*, i (1910), 181, 279 and 395ff; ii (1911), 163ff; and Dobbins, *The Chanson at Lyons*, 61–73

[13] F. Dobbins, 'Villiers, P. de', *Grove 6*. Other teachers at the Collège refer to Villiers, notably Charles de Sainte-Marthe who called him 'musicien tresparfaict', praising his 'science fantastique', and Charles Fontaine who exchanged verses with 'Hubert-Philippe de Villiers', composer of a three-voice *Aer funèbre* for the Protestant prince, Louis de Bourbon, who died at the Battle of Jarnac in 1569.

[14] Cf L. Guillo, *Recherches sur les éditions musicales lyonnaises de la renaissance* (diss., Ecole Pratique des Hautes-études, Paris, 1986), ii, no.36.

[15] Dobbins, *The Chanson at Lyons*, 61–73 and 80–82.

[16] ibid, 68–70 and 106–111.

[17] F. Dobbins, 'Music in French 16th Century Drama' (paper read to the Renaissance Society, London, 1982).

[18] V. L. Saulnier, 'M. Scève et la musique', *Musique et poésie au XVIe siècle*, ed. J. Jacquot (Paris, 1954), 89–103.

[19] P. de Tyard, *Solitaire second*, ed. C. Yandell (Geneva, 1980). See also Dobbins, *The Chanson at Lyons*, 85–93, and 'Tyard, P. de', *Grove 6*. J. McClelland, 'Structure and Proportionality in P. de Tyard's *Solitaire second*', *Bibliothèque d'humanisme et renaissance*, xl (1978), 561–70.

[20] Dobbins, *The Chanson at Lyons*, 81–5.

[21] G. van Doorslaer, 'La chapelle musicale de Philippe le Beau', *Revue belge d'archéologie*, iv (1934), 21–58 and 139–66.

[22] 'Aux instrumens . . . Jehan de la Senaz tabourin, Guillemin joueur de rebec, Jehan Barete joueur de lut et Poncet joueur des orgues qui jouererent audit banquet . . . £3.10s', Archives communales de Lyon, CC556, f.11*v*.

[23] C. Gottwald, 'Ghiselin [Verbonnet]', *Grove 6*.

[24] This renewal of contacts between the musicians of the French and Netherlandish chapels made at Blois in 1501 no doubt affected the repertory of masses and motets copied in certain contemporary manuscripts; cf H. Kellman, 'Josquin and the Courts of the Netherlands and France: the Evidence of the Sources', in *Josquin Desprez: New York 1971*, 181–218.

[25] E. van der Straeten, *La musique aux Pays-Bas* (Brussels, 1967–88), vi, 96–102.

[26] M. C. Guigue, 'L'entrée de F. de Rohan', *Bibl. Ecole des Chartes*, lxii (1902), 339.

[27] The text of the chanson is printed in Anon, *Les nouvelles venues de Lyon de la réception de nos seigneurs les Dauphins et duc d'Orléans en France* (Lyons, 1530); the music of the motet was printed in Moderne's first book of *Motteti del fiore* (*RISM* 1532[10]).

[28] Anon, *L'entrée de la royne faicte en l'antique et noble cité de Lyon* (Lyons, 1533).

[29] P. Girinet, *Idyllion* (Basle, 1541), French trans. in C. Breghot du Lut, *Le roi de la Basoche* (Lyons, 1838), 25; Dobbins, *The Chanson at Lyons*, 102–3.

[30] *La Magnifica & triumphale entrata* (Lyons, 1549, ed. G. Guigue, Lyons, 1927); Dobbins, *The Chanson at Lyons*, 103–111.

[31] A. Giraud, *Discours de l'entrée du . . . prince Charles de Valois . . . en sa renommée et fameuse ville de Lyon* (Paris, 1564, ed. V. de Valous and A. Steyert, Lyons, 1889). The Archives Communales (CC1112) of Lyons record payment to 'musitiens, chantres & joueurs d'instruments' including 'sept trompettes estrangiers'.

[32] 'L'*Epitome musicale* de Philibert Jambe de Fer (1556)', ed. F. Lesure, *AnnM*, vi (1963), 341–418.

[33] G. Tricou, 'Les musiciens lyonnais et le Roy des Violons', *Revue musicale de Lyon*, i (13 Jan 1904), 13–25.

[34] J.-P. Gutton, *La société et les pauvres: l'exemple de la généralité de Lyon, 1534–1789* (Paris, 1971), 187.

[35] G. Tricou, 'Les deux Layolle et les organistes Lyonnais du XVIᵉ siècle', *Documents sur la musique à Lyon* (Lyons, 1899); J. -M. Baffert, 'Les orgues à Lyon du XVIᵉ au XVIIIᵉ siècle', *Cahiers et mémoires de l'orgue* (special number of *L'orgue*).

[36] Dobbins, *The Chanson at Lyons*, 135–42; and L. Guillo, *Recherches*, document 33.

[37] R. J. Agee, 'Ruberto Strozzi and the Early Madrigal', *JAMS*, xxxvi (1983), 1–7, and 'Filippo Strozzi and the Early Madrigal', *JAMS*, xxxviii (1985), 227–37.

[38] *Dk-Kk* 1848 and *S-Uu* 76a; see H. Glahn, 'Et fransk musikhandskrift fra begyndelsen af det 16 arhundrede', *Fund og Forskningi Det Kgl. Biblioteks samlinger*, v–vi (1958–9), 90–109; P. Woetmann Christoffersen, *Musikhandskriftet Ny. kgl. Samling 1848 2°, Det Kgl. Bibliotek, København* (diss., U. of Copenhagen, 1978). Christoffersen's studies on the manuscripts *S-Uu* 76a and *F-LYm* 6632 are in progress. H. M. Brown, 'A "New" Chansonnier of the Early Sixteenth Century in the University Library of Uppsala: a Preliminary Report', *MD*, xxxvii (1983), 171–233, suggests that *S-Uu* 76a originated in the south-west of France. I am grateful to Dr Christoffersen for providing information on these manuscripts.

[39] L. Guillo, 'Les motets de Layolle et les psaumes de Piéton: deux nouvelles éditions lyonnaises du seizième siecle', *FAM*, xxxii (1985), 186–91.

[40] *The Lyons Contrapunctus (1528)*, ed. D. A. Sutherland, RRMR, xxi–xxii (1976).

[41] D. Crawford, 'Reflections on Some Masses from the Press of Moderne', *MQ*, lviii (1972), 82; F. de Layolle, *Music of the Florentine Renaissance*, ed. D'Accone.

[42] S. F. Pogue, *Jacques Moderne: Lyons Music Printer of the Sixteenth Century* (Geneva, 1969).

[43] F. Dobbins, 'A Bibliography of Chansons Published by Jacques Moderne (1538–44)', *RMARC*, xii (1974), 1–90.

[44] *Musica nova*, ed. H. C. Slim, MRM, i (1964); *Fröhliche Musik*, ed. F. J. Giesbert (Kassel, 1934); *J. Moderne: 29 Dances*, ed. B. Thomas (London, 1985).

[45] 'L'*Epitome Musical*', ed. Lesure, 341; Dobbins, *The Chanson at Lyons*, 156–7, 183–5 and 193–4.

[46] Guillo, *Recherches*, passim; P. Pidoux, *Le psautier Huguenot* (Basle, 1962).

[47] C. de Rubys, *Histoire véritable de Lyon* (Lyons, 1604), 390.

[48] Dobbins, *The Chanson at Lyons*, 197; Guillo, *Recherches*, ii, no.90.

[49] *Estant assis* in *RISM* 1540[16].

BIBLIOGRAPHICAL NOTE

Historical-political background

There is no comprehensive modern history of Lyons to replace A. Steyert's *Nouvelle histoire de Lyon* (Lyons, 1899), but a succinct survey is provided in J. Déniau's *Histoire de Lyon et du Lyonnais* (Paris, 1951). An interesting contemporary view is presented in S. Champier, *Cy commence ung petit livre de l'antiquité, origine et noblesse . . . de Lyon* (Lyons, 1529, repr.1884). A probing examination of the spread of the Reformation and its social effect is offered in N. Z. Davis's *Protestantism and the Printing Workers of Lyons* (diss., U. of Michigan, 1959). The only other substantial contribution in English is J. B. Wadsworth's *Lyons 1478–1503: the Beginnings of Cosmopolitanism* (Cambridge, Mass., 1964).

Literature

An indispensable aid to any study of books printed in Lyons is H.-L. and J. Baudrier, *Bibliographie lyonnaise* (Lyons, 1895–1921). Modern editions exist for many of the Lyonnais writers, including Champier, Lemaire, Alamanni, Beaulieu, Rabelais, Des Périers, Fontaine, C. de Sainte-Marthe, Du Guillet, Labé, Scève, Tyard and Bugnyon. Separate studies are also devoted to many of them – most notably V. L. Saulnier's *Maurice Scève* (Paris, 1948) – and for English readers, R. C. Christie, *Etienne Dolet, the Martyr of the Renaissance* (London, 1880); H. Harvitt, *E. de Beaulieu, a Disciple of Marot* (Lancaster, Pennsylvania, 1918); B. Des Périers, *Novel Pastimes and Merry Tales* ed. R. and V. La Charité (Lexington, Kentucky, 1972); and N. C. Carpenter, *Rabelais and Music* (Chapel Hill, 1954).

Archives: ceremonial entries, instruments and churches

There are contemporary printed accounts of the celebrations for many of the *entrées* (see notes 30–32), the most notable one of 1548 being reprinted with supporting documents by G. Guige at Lyons in 1927. A citizen's view of important events is found in *La chronique lyonnaise de Jean Guérard 1536–62*, ed. J. Tricou (Lyons, 1929). The surviving municipal archives are summarized in F. Rolle and A. Steyert, *Inventaire sommaire des archives communales anterieurs à 1790, ville de Lyon* (Paris, 1865–87). No systematic study of the departmental notarial archives (Rhône) has been made, but local archivists with special musical interests, notably Henri Coutagne and Georges Tricou, have published extracts and selections in local monographs and journals (e.g. *Mémoires de la Société littéraire, historique et archéologique de Lyon* (1888), 222–72; *Revue musicale de Lyon* (Dec 1903), 89; (Jan 1904), 13) and have left manuscript notes at the Bibliothèque Municipale in Lyons.

   An excellent study of Moderne's typography and bibliography is given in S. F. Pogue's *Jacques Moderne* (Geneva, 1969) and a thorough investigation of the other Lyonnais music publishers has recently been completed by L. Guillo, *Recherches sur les éditions musicales lyonnaises de la renaissance* (diss., Ecole Pratique des Hautes-études, Paris, 1986).

Music

The most comprehensive account of the music is in F. Dobbins, *The Chanson at Lyons in the Sixteenth Century* (diss., U. of Oxford, 1972), which includes a detailed study of the literature, archives and printed music, with a bibliography of the chansons (reprinted in *RMARC*, xii (1974), 1–90), and a second volume containing transcriptions of 86 chansons. Some of the chansons have since been published in *Thirty-Six Chansons by Provincial Composers*, ed. L. F. Miller, RRMR, xxxviii (1981) and F. Dobbins, *The Oxford Book of French Chansons* (Oxford, 1987). The American Institute of Musicology's Corpus

Mensurabilis Musicae series has issued the complete works of Layolle (ed. F. D'Accone, xxxii/3–6), Phinot (ed. J. Hofler and R. Jacob, lix/1–3) and Roussel (ed. G. Garden, lxxxiii). *The Lyons Contrapunctus*, ed. D. A. Sutherland, has also appeared in RRMR, xxi–xxii (1976). The two 1547 Lyons editions of psalms by Bourgeois are mostly available in modern editions by K. P. B. Kempers (Delft, 1937) and in Monuments de la Musique Suisse, iii (Basle, 1960), while the complete works of Goudimel, edited by P. Pidoux, M. Egan and others are published by the Institute of Medieval Music (Brooklyn, 1967–74).

Also useful are the *Grove 6* articles on E. de Beaulieu, Beringen, Blockland, Bourgeois, Colin, Cordeilles, Coste, Crassot, Goudimel, Granjon, Jambe de Fer, La Moeulle, Didier Lupi, Lyons, Moderne, Paladino, Phinot, F. Roussel, Tyard and P. de Villiers.

Chapter VIII

The Habsburg Courts in the Netherlands and Austria, 1477–1530

MARTIN PICKER

THE BURGUNDIAN-NETHERLANDS COURT UNDER MAXIMILIAN OF AUSTRIA AND PHILIP THE FAIR

Throughout the fifteenth and sixteenth centuries music played a major role in the religious and social life of the Burgundian-Netherlands court. Sacred music was closely bound to the daily activities of the court chapel – celebration of Mass, Vespers and special rituals such as memorial services, solemnization of treaties, marriages and so on. Chapel music was in the hands of the clergy and chaplains, two groups not easily distinguished. In the course of their duties members of the chapel combined the work of priest, singer, composer, administrator, organist, teacher and scribe. The high social standing of the clerics and singers is reflected in the court accounts where the chapel always precedes other household departments. The names of chaplains are usually prefixed by a respectful 'sire' or 'messire'. Whether or not they were priests, the chaplains belonged to the privileged clerical estate. The composers of the court were members of the chapel, wrote their sacred music for its services and performed it as chaplains or clerics.

Instrumental musicians of the court (excluding the chapel organist, who was generally proficient on all keyboard instruments and other instruments as well) were attached to the household as 'varlets' and were of a lower social rank than the chaplains. 'Trompettes' were generally divided into players of 'trompettes de guerre', straight or coiled trumpets, designed for military and ceremonial use, that could not play full scales and hence were limited to fanfares and signals, and 'trompettes des menestrels', chromatic slide trumpets and other wind instruments such as cornetts and shawms, used for dancing and court entertainment. A small ensemble of *bas* (soft) instruments, mainly string instruments such as lute, harp and various types of viol, but sometimes including wind instruments like the crumhorn and flute, was reserved for chamber music. When pomp and ceremony were called for, the minstrels joined with the chapel in performing music for the divine service. In turn, the chapel participated in the secular musical

49. Philip the Good attends Mass: miniature by ? Jean le Tavernier from a fifteenth-century Burgundian manuscript

life of the court, providing instruction in music to the nobility and even to the instrumentalists and performing for the court's entertainment. The chaplains also placed their talents at the service of their patrons by composing secular songs.

The participation of aristocratic amateurs in secular musical life is rarely recorded in the archives, but its extent can be deduced in many ways. Members of the highest nobility received an extensive musical education from a skilled chapel musician, often the organist: such was the case with Mary of Burgundy, Margaret of Austria and the children of Philip the Fair. Artistic representations of the period frequently show courtiers singing and playing. Luxurious books of songs and dances, notably those owned by Margaret of Austria, were perhaps prepared

217

for their use, but more likely to be displayed as prized objects to demonstrate their owners' refined taste. The manuscripts used in performance were ephemera that have failed to survive the centuries.

The chief musical institution of the Burgundian court was the chapel, founded in 1384 by Philip the Bold, enlarged by his successors John the Fearless and Philip the Good, and raised to new heights by Charles the Bold, who was deeply devoted to both religion and music. Charles was an able instrumentalist and composer and even joined in the singing of his chapel at Mass. In 1469, two years after becoming duke, he reorganized the court with regulations that were to remain the basis of its organization for more than half a century. The *Odonnances de l'hostel de monseigneur le duc de Bourgoine*, dated 1 January 1469, prescribe the duties of the chapel and household musicians as follows:

> The chapel shall consist of 25 persons: 13 chaplains, including a First Chaplain; 6 clerics; 5 *sommeliers* (assistants); and 1 *fourrier* (attendant), who shall perform the divine service daily. All but the *fourrier* shall be singers.
>
> The household shall have 5 battle trumpets, 6 minstrel trumpets and 3 players of soft instruments.
>
> High Mass will be celebrated daily in the chapel 'in chant and discant', according to the use of Paris, as is the custom.
>
> Vespers and Compline of the day, or First and Second Vespers of feasts, will be celebrated daily.
>
> The Lesser Hours will be celebrated on feast-days.
>
> The Office and Mass for the Dead will be performed as required by the Duke.
>
> There will be at least 6 trebles, 3 tenors, 3 basses and 2 contratenors in the choir, excluding the 4 chaplains occupied for High Mass and the 4 *sommeliers*, who must join with the others if they are not occupied at the altar.
>
> Only 2 members of the chapel may be absent at a time, and there must always be present at least 2 tenors and 2 basses.[1]

Thus the basic performing ensemble of chaplains and clerics consisted of twenty singers, of whom fourteen were specifically required for the performance of polyphony. The primary music of the liturgy was still Gregorian chant; polyphonic masses, motets, antiphons, hymns and canticles were used as amplifications or insertions. The enumeration of the four vocal types (treble, tenor, contratenor and bass) shows that four-voice polyphony was the norm as early as 1469, and the naming of tenor and contratenor separately – although they usually fall within the same range – shows that these parts imposed different demands and may have required different qualities of voice. The presence of an organ, and hence of an organist, is indicated by the provision (in a passage not summarized above) for a *porteur d'orgues,* who was presumably required to pump the bellows and perhaps to carry a small positive organ for use outside the chapel.

The numbers given above were augmented in subsequent years of Charles's reign. The court secretary Olivier de la Marche reported that there were 40 members of the chapel in 1474, plus twelve battle trumpets, six minstrels of 'loud' instruments (presumably slide trumpets and other wind) and four players of 'soft' instruments.[2] Since 1468 the chamber ensemble of strings had grown from three to four players, perhaps indicating that dance and chamber music was becoming standardized in four parts, as sacred music had been earlier.

A list of chapel members dated 7 June 1477, five months after the death of Charles the Bold and two months before his daughter Mary's marriage to Maximilian (son of the Habsburg emperor Frederick III), contains 27 names, among them that of the distinguished French composer Antoine Busnois (*d* 1492), who had served Charles the Bold before 1467 when he was still Count of Charolais. Having entered the court chapel when his patron became duke, Busnois remained in Maximilian's service. He retired in 1483. Busnois had lent lustre to Charles's chapel and for many years maintained the reputation of Maximilian's.

In 1485 Nicole Mayoul was named First Chaplain in preparation for Maximilian's coronation as King of the Romans at Aachen. Another member of Maximilian's chapel was Jean Cordier (*d* 1501) of Bruges, one of the most distinguished tenors of his time, who appears in the list of chaplains in 1480. Cordier had served at many Italian courts, was admired for his improvised singing by Lorenzo de' Medici and was a close friend of Jacob Obrecht (*d* 1505), one of the most important composers in the Netherlands. Another notable musician who served Maximilian was the composer Jacob Barbireau (*d* 1491) of Antwerp, who was sent by Maximilian as an emissary to Hungary in 1490. His works appear with some frequency in the choirbooks prepared by court scribes under Maximilian's and Mary's son Philip the Fair.

The court accounts give us a glimpse of the musical activities of the chaplains, though rarely of their compositions. In 1480 Pierre Beurse, organist of the chapel since 1473 and also a player of lute and flute, instructed Mary of Burgundy in playing the clavichord. The records show that the chapel musicians frequently entertained Mary and Maximilian at dinner, in their chambers or out of doors. They were sometimes joined by instruments; a striking example is a concert given at The Hague in 1480, when the singers of Maximilian's chapel were joined by his minstrels before his chamber.[3] As usual, there is no way of knowing what they performed, or if singers and instrumentalists performed together or separately, but the effect must have been one of brilliance. The court was entertained not only by its own musicians, but by those of the towns they visited and by itinerant players. The court records give the impression of a lively and varied musical life in which the nobility were both auditors and participants.

The most important figure to enter the court chapel during Maximilian's regency, one who matched Busnois in eminence, was Pierre de La Rue (*d* 1518), engaged by Maximilian in 1492. La Rue was to remain in court service under Philip the Fair, his sister Margaret of Austria and Philip's son and heir, the Archduke Charles. La Rue retired in 1516. His father Jean had been a court trumpeter and he had gained experience in Italy during the years 1482–5 as a singer at Siena Cathedral. He was subsequently a tenor in the chapel of the Confraternity of Our Lady at 's-Hertogenbosch from about 1489 to 1492. He probably came from Tournai, and his name is sometimes given in its Flemish form as 'Peter van Straten', but he seems definitively to have chosen the familiar French form when he entered the service of the court. Nevertheless, of all the composers associated with the Burgundian-Netherlands court, La Rue was the most 'Flemish'. Despite his early experience of Italy and its humanistic orientation, none of his music reflects Italian style – a contrast with the more cosmopolitan and 'Renaissance' tendencies in the work of such colleagues and contemporaries as Agricola, Isaac, Josquin and Obrecht.

After attaining his majority in 1493, Philip the Fair undertook 'to correct the disorders of his minority' (in the words of the court accounts) and to restore his household, which had suffered a decline due to the weak financial condition of the court under Maximilian, who had been frequently absent. The process was necessarily slow, but in 1495 the full complement of 25 members of the chapel received wages, their first since 1492. At that time the First Chaplain was Nicole Mayoul and 'Pierchon de la Rue' was among the singers. Some singers (but not La Rue) are identified by their voice, such as 'tenoriste' or 'haut-contre'. Gouvart Nepotis was organist.[4]

In 1494 Maximilian and his new bride, Bianca Maria Sforza, were received by Philip and the entire court celebrated a reunion at Mechlin. Frederick the Wise, Duke of Saxony, attended and described the ceremonies in his diary: 'On Sunday after St Bartholomew's Day my Lord and other princes rode with the King of the Romans to church. There a delightful mass was sung by the King's foreign [?German] and the French singers'.[5] It is likely that he was referring to a joint performance by the Austrian and Burgundian chapels.

In 1496–7 the name 'Jaspar Dodemere' appears in the chapel lists. This is the composer Gaspar van Weerbeke, who had earned a considerable reputation at Milan and as a member of the papal chapel. He served Philip for less than two years, however. Henry Bredemers, organist from 1500, was a renowned keyboard player who had been organist at Antwerp Cathedral. He was to serve many years at court as performer on a variety of instruments, and as music teacher and instrument buyer.

Philip's chapel was to grow steadily. By 1500 it numbered 28, and in 1506, the year of Philip's death, it had 33 members, among them some of the most distinguished musicians in Europe: besides La Rue and Bredemers, there were Alexander Agricola (1446–1506), who had served in Italy and France and entered Philip's chapel in 1500, Antoine Divitis (entered 1505), and the new First Chaplain, Marbrianus de Orto (*d* 1529).[6] De Orto (Dujardin), who had served in the papal chapel, remained First Chaplain to Margaret and Charles until at least 1517. Along with La Rue and Agricola, he was one of the most important composers of his generation, although his major work, like that of Agricola, appears to have been accomplished in Italy. One work of de Orto that may have been composed for Margaret is his setting of Dido's lament from Virgil's *Aeneid*, 'Dulces exuvie', which in true humanist fashion exploits dissonance and chromatic inflections to evoke Dido's grief. Its composition may have been prompted by Margaret's misfortunes (see p.225).[7]

In 1501 Philip instituted a 'petite chapelle' for private devotions, consisting of a confessor, almoner, two chaplains, two clerics and three *sommeliers*.[8] Its membership drew upon the 'grande chapelle', but it appears to have been limited to the celebration of Low Mass. One of the clerics, however, was Gilles Mureau, a minor composer of chansons. The instrumentalists of the court also increased in number under Philip. In 1506 they included twelve battle trumpeters, eight slide trumpeters and 'pipers' (shawms), two lutenists and four viol players. In that same year the Venetian ambassador reported home from Philip's court as follows: 'Three things [here] are of the highest excellence: silk . . ., tapestry . . ., [and] music, which certainly can be said to be perfect'.[9]

In preparation for his first trip to Spain, in 1501 Philip attempted unsuccessfully to secure the services of the most distinguished living composer, Josquin Desprez, who was then on a mission to Flanders and France to recruit singers for his patron, Ercole I d'Este, Duke of Ferrara. Josquin returned to Ferrara, but again went north in 1504 to take up residence as dean of the chapter at Notre Dame, Condé-sur-Escaut, where he remained until his death in 1521. There is no doubt that Josquin's music was admired at court, and there is evidence that he maintained contact with, and composed music for, Philip the Fair, Margaret of Austria and Charles V (see p.231).

Under Philip, Margaret and Charles manuscripts were increasingly copied for the use of chapel and court and as gifts to other princes and courtiers. Flemish miniature painters were creating the most beautiful illuminated manuscripts in Europe, and the court had its books decorated in the workshops of these artist-craftsmen at Bruges and Ghent.

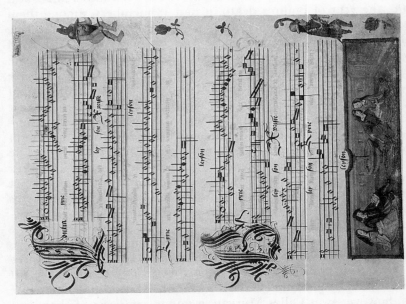

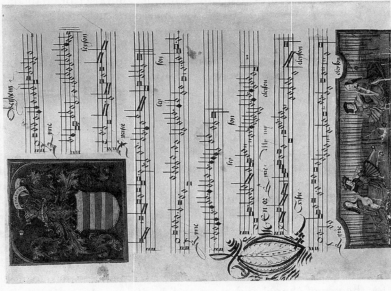

50. Two facing folios (showing the Kyrie from Ockeghem's Missa 'Mi-mi', with courtiers singing and playing the lute, cornett, fiddle and harp) from the 'Chigi Codex', a Netherlands manuscript prepared for a member of the Bouton family and copied by Martin Bourgeois, c1500.

The court itself employed calligraphers and music scribes. The principal music scribe under Philip was the chaplain-priest Martin Bourgeois, who was paid in 1500–02 for making a richly illuminated book of masses, motets 'and other things' for the Emperor Maximilian. Bourgeois continued to work for Charles V until at least 1522, and he or a fellow-scribe produced at least five other major manuscripts of both sacred and secular polyphony during Philip's reign.[10] All the composers represented in them are Netherlanders, some of whom served at Philip's court.

An impression of the role of music in court ceremonies under Philip the Fair can be gained from a letter written in 1501 by the Mantuan ambassador to his government describing the five-day meeting of the chivalric Order of the Golden Fleece, held at Brussels with Philip presiding. The ambassador states that twelve trumpeters welcomed the *chevaliers* to the Palace of Coudenberg, rode on horseback in procession to the church of Notre-Dame-des-Carmes, where the principal ceremonies took place, and announced each course at the banquet. In addition, trumpeters and other instrumentalists attended the induction of Philip's infant son Charles to the Order, while the final meal concluded with 'sounds of trumpets, *piffari* [probably shawms], nakers [kettledrums], tabors and every kind of instrument, in such a manner that it sounded like an earthquake'. Vespers and Mass of St Andrew (patron saint of the Order) were celebrated 'with superb and most exquisite music', and Marian Vespers were also sung 'with music' (undoubtedly polyphony is meant). Most significant is the description of the Office and Mass for the Dead:

> A canon of Cambrai, being the most renowned musician to be found in that area, had composed this Office of the Dead and a mass for three voices, mournful, sad and very exquisite, but he did not let them out during his lifetime, but left in his testament that they should be sung after his death for his soul, but the Order took them for its own use.[11]

The 'canon of Cambrai' can only be Guillaume Dufay (*d* 1474), whose Requiem was copied at Cambrai in 1470–71, with the remark that it was 'newly composed', and whose will directs that it be sung on the day after his death.[12] Dufay's Office and Mass for the Dead unfortunately have not survived, but they evidently were performed for many years at Cambrai and at meetings of the Order. Dufay was the greatest composer of his generation, and the loss of this important late work is lamentable.

Except for Dufay's Office and Mass, the exact music performed at the ceremonies of the Order has not been identified, but many possibilities have been suggested. Marian motets and *Magnificat* settings by court composers are prime candidates, as are masses based on *L'homme armé*; this popular tune about 'the armed man' certainly makes an appropriate emblem for a chivalric order. The first such mass is generally believed to have been that of Busnois, who may have composed it for a meeting of the Order under his patron Charles the Bold.

One of Philip's minstrels was the distinguished German cornettist Augustin, who often performed with the chapel. During the court's visit to Spain in 1501–2, he joined with the chapels of Aragon and Burgundy in a mass at Toledo and also performed with the French and Burgundian chapels at Blois. In 1503 he played with the chapels of Savoy and Burgundy, and later that year with Maximilian's chapel at Innsbruck. (He was to join Maximilian's court, and his portrait appears in the woodcut the *Triumph of Maximilian I*; see p.236.) The Mass at Innsbruck was performed with 'organs and all the instruments'. Instruments were especially favoured by Maximilian; a few days after the Mass just described, another was celebrated by the two chapels. 'The sackbuts of the King [of the Romans] began the Gradual and played the *Deo gratias* and *Ite missa est*, and the singers of *monseigneur* [Philip] sang the Offertory.'[13]

In 1506 Philip undertook his second voyage to Spain. An unpleasant foretaste of the outcome of the voyage was provided by the shipwreck of the entire party on the English coast, with some loss of life, including two of the singers. The survivors were received by Henry VII at Windsor and the instrumentalists of both sovereigns entertained the company at a banquet. Misfortunes continued to afflict Philip's court after they arrived in Spain. Agricola died of fever at Valladolid in August 1506. The tragic dénouement came on 25 September 1506, when Philip the Fair died suddenly at Burgos, plunging the court into confusion. A list of chapel members drawn up in October fails to mention de Orto and other singers. Some may have departed for the Netherlands on their own; de Orto reappears in 1512 in the chapel of the Archduke Charles. The court passed to Philip's widow, Juana of Castile, but the strain these events placed on an already weak mind rendered her incapable of ruling. She refused to sign state papers, and even to pay the salaries of court officers. Yet for a while she made an exception for the musicians:

> Thus the good woman passed her time without wishing to know more than a new-born child of the affairs of the kingdom . . . except that she retained the greater part of the singers of her late husband and treated them very well;. . . she took pleasure in no other thing.[14]

Many chaplains somehow found their way home. Henry Bredemers arranged for the transport of music books to Antwerp. In July 1507 memorial services were held in the church of St Rombaut, Mechlin, for the late King Philip. Margaret of Austria was present, and her court poet Jean Lemaire described the singing of a Requiem Mass by the reassembled Burgundian court chapel: 'The singers of the late King, singing piteous lamentations, begin the Introit of the requiem'.[15] This requiem was undoubtedly that by Pierre de La Rue, who also composed a moving four-voice motet, *Delicta juventutis*, on Philip's death.

THE COURTS OF MARGARET OF AUSTRIA AND CHARLES V

The person chosen by Maximilian to serve as regent in the Netherlands for Philip's six-year-old son Charles was Margaret, who had demonstrated her ability to rule in her five years as Duchess of Savoy and for whom Maximilian had great trust and affection. Margaret's early life, alternating between great promise and bitter disappointment, prepared her for this unexpected responsibility. She had been separated from her family when a mere infant. After her mother's premature death in 1482, Maximilian signed the Treaty of Arras with Louis XI, whereby Margaret (aged two) was betrothed to the dauphin Charles (aged twelve). For the next ten years she lived in France, receiving a French education and developing a taste for French poetry and music that would remain with her for the rest of her life. She never learnt the Flemish language, and although she was devoted to the Habsburg cause, her dedication was filtered through the prism of Burgundian tradition rather than any identification with Flanders.

In 1491, when relations between France and the Empire had reached a low ebb, Charles VIII, Margaret's intended spouse, rejected her in favour of Anne de Bretagne, whom Maximilian had been attempting to marry. This was the first of Margaret's misfortunes and the one that left the deepest emotional scar. She had been treated affectionately at the French court, and on the eve of her departure in 1493 tribute was paid to her in the form of a valedictory poem, *Complainte sur le départ de Marguerite*, by the court poet Octavien de Saint-Gelais. The poem incorporates three rondeaux to be sung: *Tous nobles cuers*, *Le coeur la syeult* and *Tous les regretz*. Settings of these texts are known, the first and last by anonymous composers and also by Pierre de La Rue, and *Le coeur la syeult* by Johannes Ghiselin alias Verbonnet, a Flemish musician active at the French court.[16]

La Rue's settings were undoubtedly composed at the Netherlands court, probably after Margaret's return. The plaintive sentiments of Saint-Gelais's poem and its music would haunt Margaret throughout her life. She would call herself 'l'infortunée', and a great deal of music composed, performed and copied for her would reflect the theme of 'regretz', beloved by poets and musicians of the later fifteenth century but unfashionable in the sixteenth. From 1493 to 1496 Margaret was at the palace of Margaret of York, widow of Charles the Bold, at Mechlin. There she absorbed the nostalgia for old Burgundy that would permeate her own court, which she was to establish in Mechlin in the following decade.

In 1493 the fortunes of the Habsburgs took a fateful turn: Maximilian succeeded his father Frederick III to the Austrian dominions and the imperial throne, and Philip the Fair attained his majority. Maximilian, ever the romantic, foresaw a Habsburg empire extending across Europe; in pursuit of that vision he arranged for the marriage of his children Philip and Margaret to the children of Ferdinand and Isabella of Spain. The treaty was signed in 1495 and the marriages took place in 1496 and 1497. Within months Margaret's husband, Prince Juan, died. In 1499 she returned to the Netherlands a widow, having seen the titles of Queen of France and then Spain snatched from her just as they seemed within her grasp.

Margaret spent the years 1499–1501 cultivating the courtly arts of poetry, music and dance. A memento of this period of her life is a luxurious basse-danse manuscript which contains 58 dance tunes with their choreography, elegantly written in gold and silver on a black background.[17] These melodies served as the basis for improvisation by the typical dance band of 'loud' instruments: slide trumpet playing the 'tenor' and one or two cornetts or shawms, or both, improvising counter-melodies. The repertory of basse-danses was old by the time the manuscript was written. Many of the tunes date back to the early and mid-fifteenth century.

A pictorial representation of dancing at the Burgundian court a few years before this time can be seen in a miniature in the *Freydal*, an account of Maximilian's journey to the Netherlands to wed Mary of Burgundy. Executed between 1502 and 1512, the miniature shows costumes of a generation earlier. Three couples promenade before Mary, while music is provided by flute and drum (fig.52).[18] This music cannot have been polyphonic; the flautist must be playing a dance tune, perhaps with improvised embellishment, while the drummer beats the rhythm. Other illustrations in the *Freydal* and *Weisskunig*, another idealized biography of Maximilian, portray larger ensembles with two or three melody instruments that may be playing polyphony.

In 1501 Margaret married again; this time her husband was Philibert II of Savoy. She thus became Duchess of Savoy, a title she retained until her death. In Savoy she discovered her administrative abilities, ruling its small court in the name of her irresponsible husband. Philibert's death in 1504 caused her less difficulty than her previous misfortunes, but it placed her in a struggle for power with Philibert's half-brother. She remained in Savoy for two more years, planning a memorial chapel for Philibert at Brou, near Bourg-en-Bresse, in which she too would eventually be buried.

A musical document of Margaret's life in Savoy is a small chansonnier containing 24 pieces, some of them incomplete. Decorated with

51. Miniature from the 'Manuscript of Margaret of Austria' (before 1519) showing Emperor Maximilian I, Margaret of Austria, Archduke Charles and his sisters, members of the clergy and nobility and commoners

the arms of Savoy, the manuscript was probably written there at about the time of Margaret's marriage to Philibert. An indication that it was inspired by her is the presence of many works by past and present composers of the Burgundian court: Hayne van Ghizeghem, Pierre de La Rue and Alexander Agricola. The first seven chansons of the album are on the subject of 'regretz'. The manuscript became part of Margaret's rich library after her return to the Netherlands.[19]

The unexpected death of her brother in 1506 caused Margaret to

52. Couple-dance before Mary of Burgundy: miniature from the Freydal Manuscript (1502–12)

return to Flanders in haste to assume the regency for her nephew Charles. She proved to be one of the most judicious and effective of the Habsburg rulers. Although Charles assumed the responsibilities of government when he reached his majority in 1515, the death of Ferdinand of Aragon in 1516 forced him to recall Margaret to the regency so that he might take over the Kingdom of Spain as Charles I. Margaret served as regent of the Netherlands until her death in 1530, living in Mechlin.

Charles maintained the Burgundian court as it had been under his ancestors, restating its traditional ordinances in 1515. In 1525 his 'grande chapelle' numbered 37 members and his 'petite chapelle' seven, many of them chaplains of long standing. The first important addition to the chapel after his assuming the imperial title was Nicolas Gombert, one of the leading composers of his generation, who entered in

1525–6. Gombert was reputed to have been a pupil of Josquin, but his style of dense polyphony and long-breathed, rhythmically intricate melodies is closer to that of La Rue and bespeaks the continuity of Burgundian tradition.

Jean Lemaire de Belges, Margaret's court historiographer and poet in Savoy, and later at Mechlin, referred to her talents in *La couronne Margaritique*, a long poetic biography written in 1504–5:

> Besides feminine work of sewing and embroidery, she is excellently skilled in vocal and instrumental music, in painting and in rhetoric, in the French as well as the Spanish language; moreover, she likes erudite, wise men. She supports good minds, expert in many fields of knowledge; and frequently she reads noble books, of which she has a great number in her rich and ample library, concerning all manner of things worth knowing. Yet not content merely to read, she has taken pen in hand and described elegantly in prose as well as French verse her misfortunes and her admirable life.

And again he wrote, in his *Première epistre de l'amant vert*, which pretends to be a letter written by Margaret's pet parrot pining for his absent mistress:

> I was quite pleased to see you sing and laugh,
> Dance, play, read and write,
> Paint and draw, play the monochords [?clavichord]
> The strings of which you well know how to sound.

The clavichord and similar keyboard instruments were favoured at court. Mary of Burgundy had received instruction on the 'clavicordion' from the organist Pierre Beurse in 1480, and Henry Bredemers had taught the Archduke Charles and his sisters to play the 'manicordium' and other instruments in 1508–10. Margaret had been instructed by the organist Gouvart Nepotis, and among the instruments in her possession in Savoy was an 'espinetta'. Margaret took a special interest in her organist Flerquin Nepotis, presumably a son or nephew of Gouvart. In a letter of 1518 to Charles, she stated that Fleurquin, who had been Bredemers's assistant in 1516, had been 'raised and taught music' under her supervision.

The scriptorium of the Burgundian court chapel during Margaret's regency and the early reign of Charles V was a centre for the production of choirbooks for the princely households of the Habsburgs and their allies. The director of this scriptorium was the many-sided singer, composer, instrument merchant and music scribe Pierre van den Hove (*d* 1536). His professional name 'Alamire' derives from the pitch designations of the note A in medieval music theory: *la, mi* and *re* in the hexachords on C, F and G. The note is often designated 'A-la-mi-re'. The name is appropriate to the many-sided Alamire; in addition to his musical activities, he was a diplomat and double agent who worked as a spy for Henry VIII of England.

Alamire's earliest association with the court is recorded in 1503 when he was commissioned to write a 'great book of music, containing . . . many masses and other things' for Philip's chapel. In 1509 he joined Charles's chapel, and he served in Margaret's private chapel from about 1515 until her death. In 1511 he received an important commission from the Emperor Maximilian for 'two great parchment books of masses', one for the emperor and the other to be given to Margaret. Alamire himself was to make the presentation. The manuscript given to Margaret is described in the inventory of her library taken in 1523 as opening with the mass of St Anne by La Rue. It is tempting to identify this with the magnificent choirbook still preserved in Mechlin, undoubtedly one of Margaret's treasures and containing the arms, portraits and motto of Maximilian. Unfortunately the first mass in the manuscript is Pipelare's *Missa 'Fors seulement'*, and while the remaining six masses are by La Rue, his *Missa de Sancta Anna* is not among them.[20]

The court scriptorium under Alamire produced manuscripts for the chapels and courts of Margaret, Charles, Maximilian and sovereigns allied with the Habsburgs, such as Frederick the Wise of Saxony, Henry VIII of England and Pope Leo X, and even merchants and bankers, such as Raimund Fugger of Augsburg. Most of the choirbooks are devoted to masses by Franco-Flemish composers, the lion's share being by La Rue. Unique among the many choirbooks produced by the scriptorium is a chansonnier written for Margaret between 1516 and 1519 and bearing her arms and portrait, which shows her kneeling in prayer to the Virgin.[21] All but one of the 58 chansons and motets are anonymous, but fifteen of them can be identified as works of La Rue, while Agricola, Compère and Josquin can be credited with four each. The only piece for which a composer is named is Josquin's *Plus nulz regretz*. Setting a poem by Jean Lemaire celebrating the Treaty of Calais between the Empire and England, negotiated by Margaret in 1507, it may have been performed at a public ceremony in Mechlin on 1 January 1508.

Many of the works in Margaret's chanson album are associated with her, or with members of her family and court. Some are settings of her own poetry. One such work is *Pour ung jamais* by La Rue, setting a poem in which Margaret laments the sorrows of her life. Another poem almost certainly by her is *Me fauldra il tousjours languir?*, in which she complains of her loneliness. The musical setting in her manuscript is decorated with daisies ('marguerites'), symbolically identifying her as subject and poet. The chanson that follows it, *Il me fait mal de vous veoir languir*, is a *réponse* of consolation. Both chansons are unique to Margaret's album and may well be the work of Pierre de La Rue.

Some pieces in the songbook appear to have been refashioned to personalize them. La Rue's *A vous non autre* is transformed from a conventional love lyric, as the text appears in other sources, into a personal statement by the composer of hope for reward for faithful service to his lady. The most serious of the works in Margaret's album is the anonymous seven-voice funeral motet, *Proch dolor*, written in black notes, symbolizing mourning, in memory of a German king; the subject can only be the Emperor Maximilian I, who died in 1519. It was added to the album after the rest had been written and in a sense 'completes' her collection of autobiographical chansons and motets.

Josquin's *Plus nulz regretz* strongly suggests that he was in contact with Margaret's court in 1507–8, perhaps through his collaboration with Lemaire. It is known that correspondence passed between Margaret and the Chapter at Condé some time before this, but Margaret did not know of Josquin's presence there before learning of it from the chapter.[22] There is evidence of Josquin's presence at court, however, in the payment by Charles V to a certain 'Joskin', a singer of Condé, for presenting new chansons to him in 1520. One of Josquin's most beautiful chansons, *Mille regretz*, is entitled 'the emperor's song' in a Spanish vihuela tablature of 1538, and may have been among the chansons presented to Charles.

After Margaret's death in 1530, Charles assigned the regency of the Netherlands to his sister Mary of Hungary, who moved Margaret's court, including her private chapel, from Mechlin to Brussels. Charles, on the other hand, giving increasing attention to his Spanish kingdom, made Madrid his principal residence. His court united personnel from the Netherlands and Spain, including his 'Flemish' chapel, which remained intact. Flemish musicians continued to play an important if no longer dominant role throughout the Empire and the rest of Europe in the sixteenth century. Flanders, a remnant of the Burgundian state that rivalled France as the dominant nation in western Europe during the fifteenth and early sixteenth centuries, became merely a province of the Habsburg empire and no longer occupied the seat of political and economic power.

THE COURT OF MAXIMILIAN I

In 1486 the Archduke Maximilian of Austria was crowned King of the Romans, a title that designated him to succeed his father, Frederick III, to the imperial throne. To prepare for his eventual responsibilities, Maximilian turned his attention from the Netherlands to his Austrian dominions. In 1490 he acquired the Tyrol, controlling the route from Austria to Italy, from his uncle Sigmund. Frederick III died in 1493 and Maximilian assumed the imperial office, although he did not acquire the title of emperor until 1508 and never succeeded in being crowned by the pope in Rome, as tradition demanded. His new status forced him to look to Italy to establish and enlarge his power. To gain the support of Milan he took as his second wife Bianca Maria Sforza, daughter of Duke Galeazzo Maria, in 1493. Their marriage took place at Innsbruck, where Bianca Maria was to live until her death in 1510.

Maximilian formed his court, including its chapel, at Innsbruck, taking as its nucleus the existing court of Duke Sigmund. The Tyrolean court included many musicians: trumpeters, trombonists, drummers, pipers, lutenists, harpists and fiddlers, as well as singers and an organist. The emphasis on instruments would remain a feature of Maximilian's court. Among the musicians present when Maximilian assumed control was the most distinguished organist of the time, Paul Hofhaimer (*d* 1537), who had entered Sigmund's service in 1478 and

53. Maximilian I surrounded by musicians of his court, and instruments: woodcut by Hans Burgkmair from the 'Weisskunig' (c1514)

was to remain in Maximilian's until the emperor's death in 1519 and the dissolution of his court in the following year. Comments on the young Maximilian's delight in instrumental music appear in such authorized biographies as the *Weisskunig*, written about 1514. A woodcut illustration by Hans Burgkmair, captioned 'How the young Weisskunig learnt to know music and string playing', shows the young king, dreamily absorbed, surrounded by musicians: a quartet of singers with a cornettist read from a book of music in the background, an organist plays a positive, while other musicians play a harp and a clavichord (fig.53). Music books and instruments are strewn about the chamber, among them a viol, various wind instruments, a tromba marina, lute, drums and trombone.[23] While it is undoubtedly an idealization, the picture embodies at least a grain of truth; these are for the most part instruments used at the Tyrolean court when Maximilian assumed its control. Such instruments continued to give him pleasure in later years, as the woodcuts of the *Triumph of Maximilian I* (1512–19) show (see p.236).

Maximilian, heir to a loose but enormous empire, travelled extensively with his court and was frequently in residence at Augsburg in southern Germany as well as at Innsbruck. In 1496 he travelled with a reduced entourage to Italy, while the chapel, which included twelve boys and men under the Kapellmeister Hans Kerner, remained in Augsburg. At Pisa the internationally famous Flemish composer Heinrich Isaac, who had lost his post in Florence after the expulsion of the Medici, came before Maximilian to apply for a position at his court. Sensing an opportunity to acquire the services of a distinguished composer and to raise the musical reputation of his court to the level enjoyed by Burgundy and Milan, Maximilian readily accepted him as Hofkomponist (court composer) and sent him to Vienna with his wife to join the Hofkapelle there.

Isaac (*d* 1517) had achieved a high reputation in Florence, but even there his relationship to his patron Lorenzo de' Medici had been informal, while his actual appointment was to the cathedral and baptistery choir. The title of Hofkomponist was unheard of, and seems to have been created by Maximilian who instinctively understood that the function of a creative artist was different from that of a cleric or singer. In this, as in other ways, Maximilian showed himself to be an enlightened patron and a man of the Renaissance, even though he liked to see himself portrayed as a knight in tales of chivalric romance such as the *Teuerdank* (1517) and in his many portraits. On his return to Innsbruck in 1497, Maximilian received Isaac's formal acceptance of his appointment. He also endowed a chapel at the nearby town of Hall and directed the performance of the '*Salve* by the organist and singers at the church [of St Nicholas]'.[24] A setting for organ of the *Salve regina* by Paul Hofhaimer, designed to alternate versets with the choir, may be associated with Maximilian's directive.

In 1498 Maximilian assembled his court at the Hofburg in Vienna. The chapel then consisted of a 'Singmeister' and eight singers: six choirboys and two basses (no tenors are indicated). Two of the choirboys were from the Netherlands and the remainder of the singers were from German lands. One of the choirboys was the Swiss, Ludwig Senfl (*d c*1543), who became Isaac's star pupil, then music scribe to the court and an important composer in his own right, succeeding his teacher as Hofkomponist in 1517.

Isaac's privileged position as Hofkomponist allowed him to be absent often. Indeed, he regularly visited Florence, where his wife's family lived and where he still maintained a home, and he spent time at Torgau. He was under no obligation to take clerical orders or to participate in the liturgical functions of the chapel. In addition to composing music for the chapel services he composed a large number of German songs, many of them based on popular tunes placed in the tenor. (Such polyphonic settings are called Tenorlieder.) Not all of Isaac's songs are of the traditional German type, however. The less rigid counterpoint of some betray Flemish and even Italian influences. One of the most charming of the latter is his simple, four-voice setting of *Isbruck, ich muss dich lassen*, in which the tune is placed in the top voice over a relatively homophonic accompaniment, much like an Italian frottola. The song, a sad farewell to the town of Innsbruck, must have been a favourite of the peripatetic emperor. There are, in fact, two settings of it by Isaac; the second, a canonic Tenorlied with the tune in the inner voices, doubles as the Christe of his *Missa carminum*, based on German folktunes throughout.[25] Isaac also composed many *carmina* without text, catering to Maximilian's taste for instrumental chamber music.

In 1503 Philip the Fair visited his father at Innsbruck, and their two chapels joined in singing Mass with instruments (see p.224). The next year the distinguished Netherlands composer Jacob Obrecht visited Innsbruck on his way to assume his new post as *maestro di cappella* at the ducal court in Ferrara and it is recorded that he composed a motet, *Regina caeli*, for the Hofkapelle.

To confirm his title as emperor, Maximilian convened the Reichstag at Constance in 1507. This was one of the most important political assemblies of his reign, and two large-scale motets were composed by Isaac for its ceremonies: *Sancti spiritus assit nobis gratia* for four voices, with its *secunda pars*, 'Imperii proceres'; and the even grander *Virgo prudentissima* for six voices.[26] The text of *Sancti spiritus* contains the following lines:

> May the grace of the Holy Spirit be among us . . .
> God . . . look upon this council, meeting at happy Constance . . .
> Leaders of the Empire, glory of Rome . . .
> Obey pious Maximilian, who is concerned for you . . .

In *Virgo prudentissima*, the choir sings:

> Wisest Virgin . . .
> We appeal to you . . . for the Holy Empire, for the Emperor Maximi-
> lian. May the omnipotent Virgin grant that he overcome his enemies
> and restore peace to the people and safety to the nations. Georgius
> [Slatkonia], singer of the emperor and leader of the chapel . . . ,
> arranges this song for you by means of his devout art . . .

Clearly the first motet was designed to be sung at the opening of the
council. The second, *Virgo prudentissima*, based on the antiphon that also
served Isaac as the basis for his mass of that title, has as its text a
humanistic paraphrase by Joachim Vadian, and may have been performed at the conclusion of the council as a valedictory. The text refers
to its actual performance by the Hofkapelle and its Kapellmeister,
Slatkonia.

After the council Maximilian proceeded to Trent, while Isaac
remained in Constance. In 1508 the cathedral chapter at Constance
honoured Isaac, and through him the emperor, with a commission to
provide them with polyphonic settings of the Proper of the Mass for the
entire liturgical year. Isaac worked intensively on this project during
1508–9, aided by his pupil Senfl, and presented it to the chapter. As
edited by Senfl, it would finally be published under the title *Choralis constantinus* in three volumes in 1550–55, long after both Isaac and Senfl
were dead. Of its three books, the second represents the liturgy of Constance, while the first and last are closer to that of Vienna, indicating
that the final product was a conflation of music for Constance and the
Hofkapelle.[27] The final Proper in the third book includes a sequence for
St Ursula with the comment halfway through the piece, 'Additio
Ludovici Senfls q(ui)a hic Isaac obiit mortem' ('addition by Ludwig
Senfl because here Isaac died'). If the statement is to be taken literally,
Isaac continued to work on the *Choralis constantinus* until his last years.
The completion and editing of the work was undertaken by Senfl, but it
is virtually impossible to distinguish his contribution from that of his
teacher.

Isaac was intermittently present at the Habsburg court until 1514
when he returned to Florence for the last time, dying there in 1517. He
was succeeded as Hofkomponist by Senfl, who acknowledged his debt
to his teacher in his autobiographical lied *Lust hab ich ghabt zur
Musica* and who repaid that debt with interest in his editing of Isaac's
magnum opus.

During Maximilian's later years, Vienna became ever more impor-
tant as the seat of the Austrian court. In 1515 Maximilian convened the
Congress of Vienna to celebrate the future union of Austria and
Hungary through the marriage of his granddaughter Mary to Prince
Louis of Hungary, heir to the kingdom ruled by his father Ladislaus.

The nuptial Mass was celebrated by Slatkonia and the Hofkapelle, as reported by a witness:

> The Bishop of Vienna celebrated the most solemn office with the utmost reverence and accompanied by an amenable selection of music of divers kinds . . . After the nuptials were over . . . all the trumpets were blown, which was wonderful to hear, and at the same time the singers gave out 'Te Deum laudamus'. And Master Paul [Hofhaimer], who has no equal in all of Germany, responded on the organ.[28]

Undoubtedly this was an *alternatim* performance, versets by the choir alternating with those of the organist, a favourite technique in Germany. Hofhaimer's *Salve regina* is a work of this type. Unfortunately no *Te Deum* by Hofhaimer survives; perhaps it was improvised. Maximilian's delight in his organist was shared by King Ladislaus, who knighted him as a sign of his admiration.

The Reichstag at Augsburg in 1518 was Maximilian's swan-song. A woodcut by Hans Weiditz from this time shows the aging emperor hearing Mass at St Anna, Augsburg, with a choir of six boys and four or five men reading their music from a great book resting on a lectern, while opposite them the organist, identifiable as Hofhaimer from portraits by Dürer and Burgkmair, plays a regal (see fig.63 below).[29] Perhaps no court of the Renaissance was depicted by artists so frequently, or in such detail, as Maximilian's. The summit of these representations is the series of 137 woodcuts, about half of them by Hans Burgkmair, that constitute the *Triumph of Maximilian I*. Planned by Maximilian in 1512 as a pseudo-classical triumphal procession, it portrays his court, family, ancestors, events of his life, courtiers and subjects, all meticulously identified. Unfinished at his death in 1519, it was published in its incomplete state in 1526 and has been reprinted many times.[30] Despite the fanciful carts on which many figures ride, drawn not only by horses but by exotic animals such as stags, camels and oxen, the costumes worn and the weapons, banners and musical instruments carried by the figures are shown in scrupulously realistic detail, and many are portraits.

First come the minstrels, 'fifers and drummers' (no.3), and players of soft and loud instruments (nos.18 and 20), led by the lutenist Artus and trombonist Neyschl respectively. The organist (Hofhaimer, no.22), a chamber group entitled 'Musica Suess Meledey' (no.24) and the Hofkapelle (no.26, fig.54) follow. Slatkonia as director shares the limelight with Senfl standing beside him; fifteen boys and men are shown singing, with the cornettist Augustin and trombonist Stewdl accompanying. The following verse accompanies this last woodcut:

> The cornett and trombone we placed
> So that the choral song they graced,

54. Pageant car bearing Maximilian's Hofkapelle, with Georg Slatkonia and Ludwig Senfl standing at the back: woodcut by Hans Burgkmair from the 'Triumph of Maximilian I' (begun 1512; published 1526)

> For His Imperial Majesty
> Has often in such harmony
> Taken great pleasure, and rightly so,
> As we have had good cause to know.

Both woodcut and verse show that Maximilian especially enjoyed the joining of instruments with voices. The number and variety of instrumentalists show that he also enjoyed purely instrumental music. Later in the procession there appear a large number of shawm and trombone players on horseback, the 'Burgundian fifers' (nos.77–9), and further on the 'imperial trumpeters' with kettledrums (nos.115–17).

Maximilian became ill on the return journey from Augsburg, but after a pause at Innsbruck resumed the trip to Vienna only to pause again at Wels, where he died early in 1519. His funeral was held at

St Stephen's in Vienna a few days later. A woodcut by Hans Weiditz shows the emperor's coffin in state, with groups of singers at its head and foot singing from choirbooks.[31] The work being performed may be the funeral motet *Quis dabit oculis nostris*, published in 1538 under Senfl's name and long thought to be by him. Only recently was it discovered that the music is actually by Costanzo Festa and that it was originally composed on the death of Anne de Bretagne (*d* 1514), the Queen of France whom Maximilian once sought for his wife. The name 'Anna' was replaced by 'Maximilianus', with suitable adjustments in rhythm, presumably because Senfl did not have time to compose a new motet.[32]

Charles V's coronation was celebrated at Aachen in 1520, and the blind organ virtuoso Arnolt Schlick performed, as he had at Maximilian's coronation as King of the Romans in 1486. It was evidently for this occasion that Schlick composed a set of eight variations on the Christmas sequence *Gaude Dei genitrix* and a duo and a ten-part setting of *Ascendo ad patrem*, four parts of which are to be played on the pedals.[33] This music is unquestionably among the most impressive organ compositions of the entire century.

In 1520 Charles V ordered the Vienna Hofkapelle to disband. By then it had achieved impressive size: six tenors, six basses, seven altos (one of whom was Senfl) and 21 boys. Senfl eventually found a position at the Bavarian court in Munich, and Hofhaimer entered the service of the Cardinal-Archbishop of Salzburg. As a tribute to the Hofkapelle and the late emperor, and perhaps in an attempt to persuade Charles V to continue the Hofkapelle, Senfl published a collection of motets at Augsburg in 1520 entitled *Liber selectarum cantionum*, representing the repertory of the chapel. Among its 24 motets are five by Isaac, including two of his finest ceremonial pieces, *Optime pastor* for the coronation of Pope Leo X (1513) and *Virgo prudentissima* for the Council of Constance (1508). Six motets are by Senfl himself, including *Sancte pater* to a text by his colleague in the Hofkapelle, the tenor Gregor Valentinian, which contains a reference to its performance by Maximilian's singers. Seven are major works by the most famous composer of the age, Josquin Desprez, including his powerful *Miserere mei, Deus*; and there are single pieces by such internationally prominent composers as La Rue, Obrecht and the French court composer Jean Mouton, as if to demonstrate that the Hofkapelle had reached parity with the finest chapels in Europe.

When Charles V assigned his Austrian dominions to his brother Ferdinand in 1521, the Vienna court was revived, but its personnel and functions were considerably changed. The musical revival, beginning in 1526–7 with the appointment of Arnold von Bruck (*d* 1554) as Kapellmeister, was slow but steady, and both Madrid and Vienna remained for generations the twin centres of Habsburg patronage and power. The choral and instrumental traditions of the Hofkapelle continue to this day in such institutions as the Wiener Chorknaben and the Concentus Musicus Wien, which link eras as remote from one another as Maximilian's and our own and continue to reflect the cultural heritage of the Habsburg Empire.

NOTES

[1] D. Fallows, 'Specific Information on the Ensembles for Composed Polyphony, 1400–1474', in *Performance Practice: New York 1981*, 145–59.

[2] G. van Doorslaer, 'La chapelle musicale de Philippe le Beau', *Revue belge d'archéologie et d'histoire de l'art*, iv (1934), 25f.

[3] P. Higgins, '*In hydraulis* Revisited: New Light on the Career of Antoine Busnois', *JAMS*, xxxix (1986), 69.

[4] Doorslaer, *La chapelle musicale*, 42f.

[5] L. Cuyler, *The Emperor Maximilian I and Music* (New York, 1973), 44f.

[6] Doorslaer, *La chapelle musicale*, 53f.

[7] See M. Picker, *The Chanson Albums of Marguerite of Austria* (Berkeley, 1965), 96.

[8] Doorslaer, *La chapelle musicale*, 48f.

[9] Picker, *Chanson Albums*, 25f.

[10] The five manuscripts are *B-Br* 9126, *D-Ju* 22, *GB-Ob* Ashmole 831, *I-Rvat* Chigi C VIII and *A-Wn* 1783. H. Kellman, 'Josquin and the Courts of the Netherlands and France: the Evidence of the Sources', in *Josquin des Prez: New York 1971*, 209f.

[11] W. F. Prizer, 'Music and Ceremonial in the Low Countries: Philip the Fair and the Order of the Golden Fleece', *EMH*, v (1985), 133. I have revised the translation.

[12] D. Fallows, *Dufay* (London, 1982), 78.

[13] Picker, *Chanson Albums*, 23–5.

[14] ibid, 26.

[15] idem.

[16] M. Picker, 'More "Regret" Chansons for Marguerite d'Autriche', *Le moyen français*, v (1980), 81–101.

[17] *B-Br* 9085; D. Heartz, 'The Basse Dance: its Evolution circa 1450 to 1550', *AnnM*, vi (1958–63), 317–19. A facsimile edition has been published by E. Closson, *Le manuscrit dit des basses dances* (Brussels, 1912). Superb colour reproductions of pages from the manuscript are found in R. Wangermée, *Flemish Music and Society in the Fifteenth and Sixteenth Centuries* (New York, 1968), 162ff.

[18] Heartz, 'The Basse Dance', opposite 294.

[19] *B-Br* 11239; edited with commentary by Picker, *Chanson Albums*. See also M. Picker, 'The Chanson Albums of Marguerite of Austria', *AnnM*, vi (1958–63), 145–285; and Picker 'A New Look at the "Little" Chansonnier of Margaret of Austria', *Musica: Jaarboek van het Vlaamse Centrum voor Oude Muziek*, iii (1987), 27–31. Much of the material in this section is based on the information presented in the above publications. A facsimile edition of the manuscript has been published by Alamire, *Chansonnier of Marguerite of Austria* (Peer, 1984).

[20] See Picker, *Chanson Albums*, 33f.

[21] A facsimile edition of this chansonnier, *B-Br* 228, has been published by Alamire, *Album de Marguerite d'Autriche* (Peer, 1986).

[22] Kellman, 'Josquin and the Courts of the Netherlands', 185f and 207f.

[23] Cuyler, *The Emperor Maximilian I*, plate 2; also *Grove 6*, viii, 12, fig.1.

[24] Cuyler, *The Emperor Maximilian I*, 54.

[25] Both settings are easily available in *Norton Anthology of Western Music*, ed. C.V. Palisca (New York, 1980), no.48; (2/1988), no.52.

[26] See A. Dunning, *Die Staatsmotette, 1480–1555* (Utrecht, 1970), 36–45, where it is proposed that the two parts of *Sancti spiritus* are separate motets, although the evidence that they constitute a single piece is also presented.

[27] See Cuyler, *The Emperor Maximilian I*, 73.

[28] ibid, 95.

[29] ibid, plate 10.

[30] H. Burgkmair and others, *The Triumph of Maximilian I*, translation, introduction and notes by S. Applebaum (New York, 1964).

[31] *Ausstellung Maximilian I. Innsbruck . . . Katalog* (Innsbruck, 1969), Abb.52.

[32] See A. Main, 'Maximilian's Second-Hand Funeral Motet', *MQ*, xlviii (1962), 173–89.

[33] Schlick's autograph manuscript can be seen in *MGG*, ii, cols.1819f. In a note appended to the music, Schlick reports that he participated in the coronation ceremony and that these works are 'new and of rare artifice', implying that they were composed for the event.

BIBLIOGRAPHICAL NOTE

Historical-political background

A good survey of the period is M. P. Gilmore's *The World of Humanism (1453–1517)* in the series The Rise of Modern Europe, ed. W. Langer (New York, 1952). Excellent, but lacking a bibliography, is *The New Cambridge Modern History*, i: *The Renaissance, 1493–1520*, ed. G. R. Potter (Cambridge, 1957).

Kaiser Maximilian I by H. Wiesflecker (Munich, 1971–81) is a monumental, richly documented biography. Brief but good is G. Benecke's *Maximilian I (1459–1519): an Analytical Biography* (London, 1982). A superb catalogue of works of art, books and memorabilia associated with Maximilian, along with pithy essays on aspects of his life and times (including music), was published for the *Ausstellung Maximilian I., Innsbruck . . . 1969)*.

Maximilian's daughter, the regent Margaret, is the subject of an excellent study by G. de Boom, *Marguerite d'Autriche-Savoie et la Pré-Renaissance* (Paris and Brussels, 1935), emphasizing her patronage of arts and letters. Her early life in France, Spain and Savoy is examined in M. Bruchet's *Marguerite d'Autriche, duchesse de Savoie* (Lille, 1927). For English readers, E. E. Tremayne's *The First Governess of the Netherlands: Margaret of Austria* (New York and London, 1908) is recommended. Her personal and political relationship with her father is illuminated in *Correspondance de l'empereur Maximilien I^e et de Marguerite d'Autriche*, ed. A. Le Glay (Paris, 1839). The standard work on her nephew Charles is K. Brandi, *The Emperor Charles V*, trans. C. V. Wedgwood (London, 1939).

Literature and the visual arts

Useful studies of the literature written by and for Maximilian and Margaret include G. Scholz-Williams, *The Literary World of Maximilian I: an Annotated Bibliography* (St Louis, 1982); J. -D. Müller, *Gedechtnus: Literatur und Hofgesellschaft um Maximilian I.* (Munich, 1922); and J. Strelka, *Der burgundische Renaissancehof Margarethes von Österreich und seine literar-historische Bedeutung* (Vienna, 1957). Margaret's poetry and that of her court circle are contained in M. Françon's edition, *Albums poétiques de Marguerite d'Autriche* (Cambridge, Mass., and Paris, 1934). The works of her court poet, Jean Lemaire de Belges, have been edited by J. Stecher (*Oeuvres*, Louvain, 1882–91).

Art in the Habsburg realms of the Netherlands and Germany is surveyed in O. Benesch's, *The Art of the Renaissance in Northern Europe* (Cambridge, Mass., 1945/R1965). The art of the Netherlands is studied by M. J. Friedlaender, *From Van Eyck to Bruegel*, ed. F. Grossmann (London, 3/1969). A fine catalogue by Marguerite Debae of

Margaret's manuscript collection, including music, is *La libraire de Marguerite d'Autriche* (Brussels, 1987). *The Life and Art of Albrecht Dürer* is studied by E. Panofsky (Princeton, 1943, 4/1955). A memento of Dürer's travels is the *Sketchbook of his Journey to the Netherlands 1520–21*, ed. P. Troutman (New York, 1971). One of his works for Maximilian is a book of hours, pages from which are published in *Aus dem Gebetbuch Kaiser Maximilians* (Leipzig, n.d.). A splendid reproduction of the *Triumph of Maximilian I: 137 Woodcuts by Hans Burgkmair and Others*, with an introduction by S. Applebaum, has been published (New York, 1964). A recent comprehensive iconography of the illustrations in Maximilian's literary works, emphasising musical activities, is *Musica Maximiliana* (Neu-Ulm, 1987) by Uta Hennsing.

Music: The Netherlands

The standard survey of the period is G. Reese's *Music in the Renaissance* (New York, 1954, rev. 2/1959), densely packed with information and containing a comprehensive bibliography. Two large, eye-filling books devoted to music in the Low Countries are *La musique en Belgique*, ed. E. Closson and C. van den Borren (Brussels, 1950), and R. Wangermée, *Flemish Music and Society in the Fifteenth and Sixteenth Centuries*, trans. R. E. Wolf (New York, 1968). An overview that attempts to clarify the labels 'Burgundian', 'Netherlandish' and 'Franco-Flemish' is H. L. Clarke, 'Musicians of the Northern Renaissance', in *Aspects of Medieval and Renaissance Music: a Birthday Offering to Gustave Reese* (New York, 1966), 67–81.

A. Dunning's, *Die Staatsmotette, 1480–1555* (Utrecht, 1970) is concerned with ceremonial motets associated with events at various courts, including the Habsburgs'. R. Strohm's, *Music in Late Medieval Bruges* (Oxford, 1985), examines the role of music in one of the great commercial cities of the Netherlands. W. F. Prizer, 'Music and Ceremonial in the Low Countries: Philip the Fair and the Order of the Golden Fleece', *EMH*, v (1985), 113–53, offers a brilliant study of music in the ceremonies of the chivalric order founded by the Dukes of Burgundy and continued by their Habsburg successors. Archival documents pertaining to Philip's chapel are presented in G. van Doorslaer, 'La chapelle musicale de Philippe le Beau', *Revue belge d'archéologie et d'histoire de l'art*, iv (1934), 21–57 and 139–65. Volume iii of *Musica: Jaarboek van het Vlaamse Centrum voor Oude Muziek* (1987) is devoted to 'Music at the Court of Margaret of Austria'. The court of Margaret's successor is the subject of an archival study by G. G. Thompson, 'Music in the Court Records of Mary of Hungary', *TVNM*, xxxiv (1984), 132–73.

On the relationship of Busnois to the Burgundian-Habsburg court see P. Higgins, '*In hydraulis* Revisited: New Light on the Career of Antoine Busnois', *JAMS*, xxxix (1986), 36–86. A monograph on Margaret's court composer is J. Robijn's *Pierre de la Rue (circa 1460–1518): een bio-bibliographische Studie* (Brussels, 1954). Nigel Davison has published a study of 'The Motets of Pierre de la Rue' in *MQ*, xlviii (1962), 19–35, and M. Picker has published 'Three Unidentified Chansons by Pierre de la Rue' in *JAMS*, xlvi (1960), 329–43. There is no comprehensive edition of La Rue's works, but three of his masses are published in Monumenta Musicae Belgicae, viii, ed. R. Lenaerts and J. Robijns (Antwerp, 1960). The series Das Chorwerk includes his Requiem (vol.xi), *Missa 'L'homme armé'* (vol.cxiv) and four motets (vol.ci). *Josquin Desprez* is a comprehensive two-volume study by H. Osthoff (Tutzing, 1962–5); see also M. Picker, 'Josquin and Jean Lemaire: Four Chansons Re-examined', in *Essays Presented to Myron P. Gilmore* (Florence, 1978), ii, 447–56. Josquin's complete works are published by the Vereniging voor Nederlandse Muziekgeschiedenis, and a new edition is in progress. *Nicolas Gombert: Kapellmeister Kaiser Karls V* is a monograph by J. Schmidt-Görg (Bonn, 1938/R1971).

The work of music copyists at the Habsburg-Netherlands court is the subject of studies by H. Kellman, 'The Origins of the Chigi Codex', *JAMS*, xi (1958), 6–19, and

'Josquin and the Courts of the Netherlands and France', in *Josquin des Prez: New York 1971*, 181–216 (the latter volume contains a broad spectrum of Josquin studies and is highly recommended). A facsimile of the Chigi Codex, with a valuable introduction by Kellman, is published in the series Renaissance Music in Facsimile, xxii (1987). An edition of *The Chanson Albums of Marguerite of Austria* has been published by M. Picker (Berkeley, 1965) and a companion article of the same title appears in *AnnM*, vi (1958–63), 145–285. Facsimile editions of Margaret's two chanson albums have been published by Alamire (Peer, 1984 and 1986). Margaret's beautiful basse-danse manuscript is discussed by Daniel Heartz in 'The Basse Dance: its Evolution circa 1450 to 1550', *AnnM*, vi (1958–63), 287–340; it too has been published in facsimile (by E. Closson in 1912, and by Alamire in 1987).

Music: Austria

The musicians of Maximilian's courts at Vienna and Innsbruck have received much attention. An overview is given by L. Cuyler in *The Emperor Maximilian I and Music* (New York, 1973). Chapters on Maximilian's court are contained in J. Mantuani's *Die Musik in Wien* (Vienna, 1907) and W. Senn's *Musik und Theater am Hof zu Innsbruck* (Innsbruck, 1954). Helmuth Osthoff's *Die Niederländer und das deutsche Lied* (Berlin, 1938) examines German song in this period, especially the works of Isaac and Senfl.

The most important study of Isaac is M. Staehelin's *Die Messen Heinrich Isaacs* (Berne, 1977); vol. ii brings together the significant biographical documents. The *Opera omnia* of Isaac, ed. E. Lerner, is in the process of publication; only masses have appeared thus far. Isaac's monumental *Choralis constantinus* is published, the first two books in DTÖ, x and xxxii; book 3 is edited by L. Cuyler (Ann Arbor, 1956), who has also edited *Five Polyphonic Masses* by Isaac (Ann Arbor, 1956). Other Isaac masses, edited by H. Birtner and M. Staehelin, are published in the series Musikalische Denkmäler, vii–viii. Das Chorwerk includes Isaac's *Missa carminum* (vol.vii), a selection of introits (vols.lxxxi and cxix) and four Marian motets (vol.c). Isaac's secular works are published in DTÖ, xxviii and xxxii.

A valuable study of Senfl, emphasizing sources, is M. Bente's *Neue Wege der Quellenkritik und die Biographie Ludwig Senfls* (Wiesbaden, 1968). Senfl's *Sämtliche Werke*, ed. A. Geering and W. Altwegg, is in preparation. The life and works of Maximilian's court organist are examined by H. J. Moser in a monograph that includes his music: *Paul Hofhaimer* (Stuttgart and Berlin, 1929/R1966).

Articles on 'Habsburg' and most of the composers mentioned in this chapter can be found in the major music encyclopedias, *MGG* and *Grove 6*.

Chapter IX

Munich at the Time of Orlande de Lassus

JAMES HAAR

On his journey to Italy in the autumn of 1580 Montaigne passed through southern Germany, spending some time in Augsburg – famed, he said, as the most beautiful city in the country – and then going on to Munich. Of the Bavarian capital he said first, *en bon français*, that it was 'as large as Bordeaux'; then, that it had a 'beau chasteau' and the most beautiful (court) stables he had ever seen. In sum, he concluded, Munich was 'une ville fort catholique, peuplée, belle et marchande'. Had he been shown more, or perhaps been able to hear the ducal chapel perform, he might have said more; but, as he observed, the duke and all his court were out hunting.[1] The dukes of the later sixteenth century, Wilhelm V and his predecessor Albrecht V, were indeed very fond of the chase; but Albrecht in particular had many other interests, including music.

Under Albrecht V, first of the Wittelsbachs to rule alone after a law of primogeniture ending the old medieval custom of dividing the duchy between siblings had been passed in 1506, the programme of building, for which so many of his successors in the following three centuries were to become famous, was begun. Albrecht, who succeeded in 1550, and his Habsburg wife were concerned with increasing the splendour of their various country residences while at the same time embarking on a building programme at the Residenz in Munich. An unpopular but apparently successful series of taxes enabled the duke to commission his architects Wilhelm Egkl and Jacopo Strada to build the Antiquarium, a repository for a collection of classical antiquities and for the Hofbibliothek, the latter rapidly becoming one of the best libraries in Europe. He also built the Münzhof, the first large picture gallery north of the Alps. In addition a Schatzkammer and Münzkabinett were appointed during Albrecht's reign. This multifarious collecting reminds one of the activities of his contemporary, Cosimo I de' Medici.[2]

The splendour of Albrecht's court, culminating in the elaborate festivities celebrating the marriage of his son and heir in 1568, was famed throughout Europe and even impressed the Turkish sultan.[3]

The duke's activities were not confined to building; he was a collector of artists, including the distinguished painter and miniaturist Hans Mielich (1516–73), as well as of books and works of art.[4] And he was determined to have a musical establishment rivalling the best in Europe. For this purpose Albrecht needed to enrich and alter the predominantly German make-up of his chapel, now judged to be unequal to that of rival princes. His first impulse was to acquire Netherlandish musicians, following the pattern established by his Habsburg relatives and becoming common elsewhere in German-speaking lands.[5] Albrecht began modestly, with a certain Matthes Nidlender joining the chapel in 1552.[6] Four years later a group of northern singers were engaged, among them what must be considered the 'catch' of the century: the young Orlande de Lassus.

Under Albrecht V, Munich, in the mid-sixteenth century a city of some 20,000 people and the capital of the united duchy of Upper and Lower Bavaria (with a population of about 900,000),[7] was emerging from a provincial past into a position of rivalry with the greater German cities, in music as in other cultural fields. The city had known earlier moments of musical distinction. The organ installed in the Frauenkirche in 1491 was much admired, and a generation earlier still the ducal court had enjoyed the services of Europe's most famous organist of the time, Conrad Paumann.[8] Both court and town employed instrumentalists for ceremonial occasions, and music was an important part of the city's famed Corpus Christi processions.[9]

The arrival of Ludwig Senfl in Munich, about 1523, marked the beginning of the city's first sustained period of musical greatness. Senfl, apparently engaged as a composer (since another musician acted as Kapellmeister), remained in Munich until his death in 1542–3. He was valued highly by Duke Wilhelm IV (this, as well as the terms of his engagement, suggests a precedent for the relationship between Lassus and the duke's son and grandson). He composed a great deal of music for the ducal chapel, introduced a distinguished repertory of works by Isaac and Josquin, and helped to reorganize the chapel along the lines of the imperial chapel which he had led during the reign of Maximilian I (*d* 1519). Senfl, who was in close touch with the Lutheran Duke Albrecht of Prussia, knew Luther personally; indeed, the Bavarian chapel of Senfl's time was praised by Luther.[10]

Under the directorships of Wolfgang Finck, Andreas Zauner and Senfl's pupil Ludwig Daser, who took over in 1552, the court chapel grew in size to 26 members in 1551 and 33 in 1552.[11] The Kapellmeister was responsible for its musical direction, and in the case of Daser at least, for composing a good deal of new music, for copying manuscripts, training boys and engaging singers and instrumentalists. He received a salary, allowances for food, clothing and other provisions, and gifts at New Year's Day and on other occasions; he was thus a person of some consequence. All of these things were to remain true during Lassus's tenure. Daser was a Lutheran, an awkward fact in this troubled time when the ducal government was trying hard to support Catholicism. And his chapel must have struck the ambitious Duke Albrecht V as old-fashioned, in need of new blood and new artistic direction; in the words of Massimo Troiano, musician and chronicler of the festivities of 1568, the duke saw that the chapel 'conforme al celeste animo suo non era'.[12]

In 1555 Albrecht instigated a search for musicians, entrusting the imperial vice-chancellor Dr Seld to make contact with singers in the Habsburg Netherlands. Seld and his agent, one Egidius Fux, reported that they sang through a good deal of new music and interviewed singers, but pickings seem to have been slim. Many of the singers were old and possessed few skills other than that of *coloriren* (improvising diminutions and ornaments). Some were married; but this did not disturb the duke, who was not thinking like the pope of an all-clerical chapel. Dr Seld, with the agreement of the duke, was looking for singers (or rather, singer-composers) who were expert in the 'new art' and in *musica reservata*, with a good knowledge of languages and a sprightly but refined manner.[13] The ever-mysterious term 'musica reservata' was not defined;[14] it probably referred to music that would appeal to connoisseurs, possessing the subtle contrapuntal textures seen in the music of Cipriano de Rore, some use of chromatic tonal coloration and preoccupation with affective musical rhetoric in the setting of texts.

The breakup of the chapel of Charles V should have provided opportunities for the Bavarians, and Seld wrote that not all of the musicians in Philip II's chapel in Brussels would wish to go with the king to Spain.[15] Philippe de Monte, who had been in Philip II's service but was now in Antwerp, appeared to be such a person and was highly recommended, despite his modestly reticent personality, to Duke Albrecht; but he did not enter the Bavarian chapel.[16] The suggestion that Monte put Lassus forward in his stead is no more than a shrewd guess;[17] but Monte and Lassus, in Naples, then Rome, then Antwerp at the same time, must have known each other, and were on good terms in later life. It was Hans Jacob Fugger, member of the great Augsburg banking family and a trusted adviser of Albrecht V, who seems to have suggested Lassus, writing from Antwerp to the duke about him in the summer of 1556 and sending a Lassus motet, 'new and good', for ducal inspection.[18]

By early 1557 Orlande de Lassus had arrived in Munich, together with half-a-dozen other singers. He was unmarried but not a cleric; and he proved himself to be expert in languages (except perhaps in German) and of the stuff of which good courtiers are made. Furthermore, he was in full command – as his 'op.1' print of 1555, containing madrigals, villanelle, chansons and motets amply showed – of the new style so much in demand. Lassus did not become Kapellmeister until the departure of Daser in 1563, but from his arrival be seems to have been regarded in the way Senfl had been: as a composer whose work and influence could bring the chapel up to date and lend it new distinction.

The young Lassus was certainly kept busy; he supervised the music at the court chapel and also oversaw the *Tafelmusik* for the duke's daily entertainment, involving instrumentalists as well as singers; for a while he was responsible for the education of boys in the chapel, and he undertook an expansion and *aggiornamento* of the musical repertory. Responding to his patron's evident wish for polyphonic music, both sacred and secular, to be performed as often as possible, Lassus wrote a great deal of music – perhaps a third of his total output – during the first decade of his employment at the Bavarian court.[19] This includes masses, *Magnificat* settings, motets, the Job Lamentations (first set) and Penitential Psalms, and a large amount of secular music – chiefly madrigals and chansons but including a set of German lieder.

Much of this music was soon in print: the madrigals were issued by Italian publishers, the chansons by Netherlandish then French printers, the sacred music appeared in Germany as well as in Italy and the Low Countries. Lassus's important association with the Munich printer Adam Berg began with the *Neue teutsche Liedlein* of 1567, three years after Berg set up shop. Berg produced some of the best and most beautifully executed editions of Lassus's sacred music in the *Patrocinium musices* series of the 1570s.

Some compositions by the young Lassus found their way only slowly into print, perhaps because they were prized by the duke as such fine examples of *musica reservata* that he wished literally to reserve them by delaying their publication. This is true of the Job Lamentations and of the Penitential Psalms, the latter printed, says the dedication, more or less 25 years after their composition.[20] An even more extreme case is that of the *Prophetiae Sibyllarum*, settings in the chromatically inflected style fashionable in the 1550s and 1560s of some pagan-Christian humanistic verses on Sibylline themes.[21] A finely illustrated set of manuscript partbooks, with ducal insignia and with the earliest known portrait of Lassus (*aetatis suae* xxviii), datable from the portrait to 1558–60, contains this work, evidently an example of ducal *musica reservata* at its most recherché. It was not printed until after the composer's death.[22]

The ducal chapel bought printed music, forming the basis of the great sixteenth-century collection of the Bayerische Staatsbibliothek of today. With the establishment of Adam Berg's publishing house, Munich gained a music printer who could compete in excellence of product with the best European publishers. But the tradition of manuscript copying went on, for the ducal chapel and, in certain cases (elaborately decorated and illuminated manuscripts), for the dukes themselves. Wilhelm IV supported the preparation of elaborate musical

55. *Folio (showing the section 'Domine labia' from Psalm 60) from the two-volume choirbook (1563–70), illuminated by Hans Mielich, containing Lassus's settings of the Penitential Psalms*

manuscripts, perhaps in imitation of the Habsburg court's practice of commissioning musical codices that were works of art.[23] Under Albrecht V some of the most splendid musical manuscripts of the century were prepared, the work of court copyists such as Jan Pollet and of the painter-miniaturist Hans Mielich. These include a choir-book collection of motets by Cipriano de Rore, a composer evidently much admired by Albrecht V (and, not incidentally, by Lassus as well),[24] and the Sibylline Codex, a set of partbooks also containing the first set of Job Lamentations.[25] Most splendid of all was the two-volume choirbook in which is Lassus's setting of the Penitential Psalms (figs.55, 56 and 58), a magnificently ornamented manuscript containing portraits of Albrecht V, Lassus and Mielich, and group portraits of the court chapel; one shows the singers in the chapel of St George in the Neuvest of the Residenz, and the other depicts the instrumentalists in St George's Hall, scene of many festive court occasions including much of the 1568 wedding celebrations (fig.57).[26]

Even when printed music was available the ducal chapel continued to make use of manuscripts, and Lassus continued this established tradition. His own first book of motets for five and six voices, printed in Antwerp in 1555, was copied in choirbook (single-volume) format by a copyist who had been active at the court chapel since the time of Senfl's tenure. Lassus oversaw this himself and made some autograph corrections and additions to the text underlay.[27] On the whole, Lassus's compositions in the composer's autograph must have served as exemplars for printers; manuscripts for use by the chapel were entrusted to professional copyists supervised by the composer (a possible exception is the Sibylline Codex, which may be in the composer's hand).[28]

In many respects Lassus followed the traditions of the court chapel. He respected its organization, even as its personnel expanded and changed under his leadership; he took part in the Corpus Christi procession, which assumed new splendour and new meaning in Counter-Reformation Munich (a motet by Lassus was even credited with causing a miraculous improvement in the weather at one of these processions),[29] and he participated in the court's secular festivities as well, playing an important role – including the impersonation of a *commedia dell'arte* character, something which must have recalled to him his youthful years in Naples – in the festivities of 1568.[30]

The presence of so extraordinarily gifted a musician as Lassus none the less brought about changes. The chapel membership doubled in size in the first decade of his tenure and the duke spent increasingly large amounts of money – sums he could ill afford – on his musicians, whose fame as a group increased simply because of the presence of Lassus. The young composer's music was heard in Vienna, at the imperial Diet in Augsburg, at the papal court, in Venice, Ferrara, the French court and elsewhere; he was already becoming the 'divin

Orlande' who dominated the musical presses of Europe in the last third of the sixteenth century.[31]

When Lassus entered the Bavarian chapel only its Kapellmeister, Ludwig Daser, was well known as a composer. None of the six Flemish singers who joined the ducal service with Lassus is known to have written music; but gradually a group of composers formed around him. Some idea of the collective skills of ducal musicians in the later 1560s can be gained from a madrigal collection put together by Massimo Troiano and published in 1569 in Venice under the title *Musica de' virtuosi della florida capella dell' illustrissimo et eccellentis. S. Duca di Baviera.*[32] Works by Lassus begin and end this collection, but quite a few other names also appear. Some of the more important ones will be mentioned below. A striking feature of the volume is its concentration (for all but four pieces) on the poetry of Antonio Minturno, a Neapolitan-born prelate, poet and critic whom Troiano may have known personally. Even more striking is the collaborative nature of the volume: the opening poem, Minturno's double sestina *Al dolce suon del mormorar de l'onde*, is set stanza by stanza by eleven composers, beginning with Lassus and ending with Troiano; another sestina, also by Minturno, *A la dolce ombra de la nobil pianta*, has six composers participating, with Troiano included but Lassus absent. Collaborative volumes like this are occasionally to be found in the madrigal literature, though they are never common;[33] but Troiano's anthology may be the first to be devoted to the composers of a single chapel.

If one counts individual stanzas separately in this collection, Lassus is credited with six, Troiano with five. Troiano, a Neapolitan singer and composer, was something of an entrepreneur, perhaps even an adventurer. He arrived at the Bavarian court early in 1568 with little to recommend him other than the composition of some villanelle; having joined the ducal chapel, he took an active part in the wedding festivities for Duke Wilhelm, wrote and published (first in Munich, then in Venice) a detailed account of them, persuaded his colleagues to contribute to this madrigal volume – for which he took credit in the dedication, addressed to Albrecht V – and had the collection published by Girolamo Scotto in Venice. He then joined Wilhelm's chapel at Landshut, but after a year had to flee, pursued by the duke's men, after murdering a colleague (a fellow Italian).[34]

Among the other musicians represented in this volume are singers from the court chapel, including the Netherlanders Anton Gosswin and Leonhard Meldaert; the court organists Ivo de Vento from Antwerp, Gioseffo Guami from Lucca and G. B. Morsselino from Cremona; and several instrumentalists, including the *tromboni* Fileno Cornazzano, Simon Gatto (a Venetian), Francesco Guami from Lucca, and a string player, G. B. Tiburtino, evidently from Rome.[35] Some of these men, particularly Gosswin, de Vento and the Guami brothers, were com-

56. *The Bavarian court chapel in St George's Hall in the Neuvest of the Residenz: miniature by Hans Mielich from the choirbook of Penitential Psalms (Duke Albrecht V stands to the left)*

posers of real stature; others are known only from this print.

The mix of northern and Italian names in this collection is evidence of a trend that was initiated when Lassus became Kapellmeister on Daser's departure in 1563. Italians became increasingly sought after, changing the Netherlandish character of the chapel of the 1550s. It is not surprising that Lassus, whose adolescence and early career were spent in Italy and who spoke and wrote Italian by preference, should have looked to Italy for colleagues in his chapel. None the less it is remarkable that Duke Albrecht, whose predecessor had not only employed German singers but had also chosen as his court composer Ludwig Senfl, a great lied composer and a thoroughly German musician, was willing to have his chapel displayed to the world as singers and composers of Italian madrigals. This may be further indication of the influence of Lassus on the duke. Lassus wrote many chansons and quite a few German songs, but he evidently wished to be particularly recognized as a composer of madrigals. His fourth book of five-voice madrigals of 1567 has a dedication to Alfonso II of Ferrara in which Lassus says that he wants 'the world to know that the Muses in Germany . . . are nourished and protected, with many who cultivate and support them'.[36] In any event one can see here the beginning of a long tradition of Italian musical dominance in Munich, a dominance barely shaken in the time of Mozart's visits there more than 200 years later.

Northern musicians did not disappear from the chapel, of course. The position of assistant Kapellmeister, newly created in 1569, went to the Netherlandish singer and composer Johannes de Fossa, and the German organist Johann Lockenburg was a prominent figure at court in the 1570s.[37] Lassus visited Italy several times during his long tenure in Munich, but he refused all offers to move either there or elsewhere. In 1558 he married a Bavarian gentlewoman; in 1570 he was awarded, through ducal patronage, a patent of nobility from the Emperor Maximilian II. He raised sons with the Germanic – indeed Habsburg – names Ferdinand and Rudolf, and by the end of his life was probably as much a Bavarian in outlook and character as he was an Italian. His surviving sons, both musicians, composed music for Latin and German texts only, and his family (no longer musicians after the third generation) entered the ranks of the Bavarian gentry, still using Lassus's heraldic device with its ♯ – ♮ – ♭ musical motto as late as the mid-eighteenth century.

The most celebrated event in Munich during Lassus's 37-year residence there was the marriage of Duke Albrecht's heir Wilhelm V to Renata of Lorraine. This took place, after a series of difficult negotiations, in February 1568. What sort of music did the 'florida capella' of the duke provide for this occasion? We know more than is usual with such events because of the diligence, the musical expertise and perhaps

57. *Music accompanying the wedding feast for the marriage of Wilhelm V to Renata of Lorraine: engraving, coloured by N. Solis, from Hans Wagner's 'Kurtze doch gegrundete beschreibung des . . . Hochzeitlichen Ehren Fests' (1568)*

the egotism of one of its chroniclers, Massimo Troiano. As a musician and a recently engaged member of the ducal chapel, Troiano was proud of the group and of his association with Lassus. He wrote some music for the occasion and, together with Lassus and some Italian cohorts, devised and put on a *commedia dell'arte* for the last evening of the wedding festivities. The sight and sound of Lassus – at least for those who knew him – playing the role of a Venetian *magnifico* of absurd pretensions must have been one of the highpoints of the entire two weeks' entertainment. As a result of the success of the whole affair Troiano must have received ducal patronage for the publication in Venice of a volume of madrigals composed by members of the chapel (see above, p.249) as well as for his detailed description of the wedding, printed by Berg in 1568 and then, in altered form, in Venice in 1569.[38]

First there is the ceremonial brass music. The town's band and the ducal trumpeters were kept very busy and were joined by groups of brass players from the entourage of important guests, playing on a surprisingly large number of occasions. On 20 February, the day of the bride's arrival in Munich, the town artillery were fired in salute; then 'trumpets, horns, large and small drums from the city's corps and that of the cavalry' were heard, playing joyfully and at length, for the space of half an hour, to welcome Renata and her party.[39] At times they were joined by other groups so that, as Troiano tells us, more than 100 wind instruments were playing at once. Another group of trumpets and cymbals played at the entrance of the bride's party into the Frauen-kirche, before the first festive Mass. After hearing Mass the party moved on to the ducal palace, accompanied by a fife-and-drum band. Throughout the two-week festivities the wind bands were constantly on hand to herald arrivals, departures, beginnings and endings of festivities, as well as to accompany tournaments and hunting parties, to signal good night and, to the bridal pair after their wedding night, good morning. Renaissance princes must have lived with a near-constant sound of ceremonial wind music in their ears.

The duke's *tromboni*, probably players of slide trumpets and perhaps of cornetts and other wind instruments, were also to be heard often. They played at the beginning of every banquet, saluting the arrival of the first course; they often took part in the concerted music offered under Lassus's direction as the meals progressed, and a group of *tromboni* seems to have been a commonly used dance ensemble, playing for the *balli* that ended nearly every day's activity.[40] They apparently had a large repertory, playing *canzoni francesi*, motets and madrigals; and they seem to have had a variety of sizes and types of instrument at their disposal. During a banquet on 22 February these musicians (just how many in all we do not know) played first a *Battaglia a 8* of Annibale Padovano on trombones and curved cornetts; then a seven-voice motet by Lassus, with five curved cornetts and two trombones; next (these pieces accompanied various courses of the meal, so may not have been played in immediate succession) came a madrigal by Alessandro Striggio for six bass trombones, one of which played an octave lower than was normal. This done, trumpets and drums announced the arrival of the next course. Other musicians relieved the wind players for a time on this occasion, but they again took part (five trombones and a cornett) in some twelve-voice works by Annibale Padovano and others, before the meal was over.[41] Finally, the trumpeters provided some of the fun in a mock *giostro alla tedesca* held after dinner on 2 March. During this event, which provoked 'grandissima risa',

[Two warriors] came together with such force that both tumbled headlong from their horses, upon which the trumpets played in highly discordant style a bumbling *aria alla tedesca*, as a joking reference to the

253

two fallen horsemen . . . And two others came on the field, met and rode about with head down and legs in the air, looking like rooted leeks. In jest at this, two trumpeters gave a clumsy rendition of *La bella franceschina*.[42]

String players, particularly of the viola da braccio, were used in concert during the wedding banquets; they usually followed the wind players, who presumably captured the attention of those at table. For instance, after the Striggio madrigal played by six trombones as mentioned above, six viole da braccio played a motet by Cipriano de Rore.[43] Five viol players, dressed as nymphs and riding on a float, took part in a *mascarata*.[44] String players also performed in mixed consorts; one example is an unnamed 24-voice work performed first by eight viole da braccio, eight viole da gamba and eight varied instruments – fagott, cornamuse, mute cornett, curved cornett, bass curved cornett, fife, dolzaina and bass trombone – after which the piece was sung, one would think a trifle anti-climactically, by members of the ducal chapel.[45]

Instruments were thus used in related families and also in mixed consorts, suggesting the usage of the Florentine *intermedi* of the middle and later sixteenth century.[46] They performed motets, madrigals, chansons and dance music, and as part of the *Tafelmusik* they often mixed with voices. Were they used in the chapel as well? Not as a rule, apparently; but Troiano did say that 'wind instruments' played on Sundays and feast-days at Mass and Vespers, in company with the singers.[47] Whether this last phrase indicates doubling of voices by instruments or refers to alternation of voices and instruments within or between pieces of liturgical polyphony is not made clear.

The singers too were busily occupied throughout the festivities. There was a sung mass every morning, many of them identified (though not by title) as the work of Lassus himself but with at least one, said to be for six voices, by Rore, and a 24-voice mass by Annibale Padovano.[48] The choir sang polyphonic responses and doubtless also some motets during these masses. Solemn Vespers were sung several times, once with a twelve-voice setting by Lugwig Daser.[49]

Under Lassus's direction the singers were also present at all the banquets, singing in concert with instrumentalists or alone, the latter usually reserved as a special treat for the dessert course. Troiano spoke with great admiration of the beauty and skill of the singing in what he called 'terzi' and 'quarti', evidently three- and four-voice music for solo singers, heard both in the chapel and at special moments during the banquets.[50] Use of this terminology is evidence that sacred polyphony at any rate was usually sung with many singers to a part.

A surprisingly large number of pieces are mentioned by name. Among them are Lassus's six-voice *Te Deum laudamus* and also his motet *Gratia sola Dei*; a motet by Rore on a text in honour of Duke Albrecht

(*Mirabar solito laetas*); a *Battaglia a 8* by Annibale Padovano; a five-voice motet by Madulana Casulana, *Nil magis iucundum*, and another by Caterina Willaert, said to be the daughter of Adrian, *Vas sacrae adeste tonis* (both of these were commissioned works, with text supplied by Nicolò Stopio, the duke's Venetian agent); Jacobus de Kerle's *Laeta est ista dies*, another motet (*a 6*) specially commissioned for the event; a motet *a 6* by Troiano, *Harmonico cupiens coniunctas*; an unnamed but identifiable 40-voice motet by Alessandro Striggio (*Ecce beatam lucem*); and, during the course of the *commedia dell'arte*, the villotta *Chi passa per questa strada*, one of the great hit tunes of the century, perhaps in the setting by Filippo Azzaiolo, sung and played by Lassus himself.[51] Not all of this music survives, but there is no reason to question the veracity of the accounts which mention them.

In all, both singers and instrumentalists did heroic service during these festivities, more than earning the gifts made to them by departing guests.[52] They certainly worked harder than usual on this and other gala occasions, but they were never idle. Day in and day out there was a sung mass; on Saturdays and vigils of feast-days, Vespers were sung, and not always to the same music. The large number of extant masses by Lassus, not to mention his extraordinary output of *Magnificat* settings for Vespers, testify not only to his creativity but also to the ducal wish for a constant supply of new music. The chapel repertory included works by Ludwig Daser, by singers and organists appointed during Lassus's tenure, and by Josquin, Willaert, Rore, Clemens non Papa, Morales and other great sixteenth-century figures.[53] This music was not simply read through but sung, as Troiano tells us, with the greatest care and skill; under Lassus's expert direction the choir could sing a whole mass cycle with voices perfectly blended and without varying as much as three commas or microtones from the starting pitch.[54]

There was the daily *Tafelmusik* as well; less elaborate, surely, than that of the 1568 festivities, but none the less requiring a large and ever-changing repertory as well as coordination between singers and instrumentalists. The achievement of Lassus in managing all of this, while never ceasing his work as a composer, is little short of miraculous.[55]

After his marriage Wilhelm established his own court at Landshut, in a castle that had long been in Wittelsbach possession. Lassus, who seems to have become more a companion and friend to the ducal family than a servant, remained in Munich – apart from trips inside Germany and to Italy and France; but a series of letters from the composer to Wilhelm, dated for the most part in the 1570s, indicate that he was far closer to the young heir than to the increasingly gloomy Albrecht V. Lassus's letters are famous for their punning and jesting tone; the melancholy of his later years was yet to settle on him, or he hid it well, and at the age of 40 he sounds in these letters as exuberant as the young Mozart. His use of polyglot expression, with one or more changes of language every few lines, was a favourite device, and Wilhelm, who at this time seems more like a Prince Hal than the dour Counter-Reformation zealot he was to become as duke, must have enjoyed such linguistic *spielerei*. Here is an example, containing French, German, Italian, Spanish and Latin:

> Tresillustre prince mons[r] mo*n* gratieux maistre e patro*n* Affin que
> vos*t*re Ex[ce] voie que ie veux acomplir sa bonne volonté, qui est que ie
> donne neü Zeitung a vos*t*re f[ürstlich] g[naden] de omnj buso la dove
> si troviamo, io lasso saber a vuestra Ex[tia] si come per la gratias de dios
> todos las compagnias tambien los Cavallos é la mercedes de los asinos
> se portent mediocrement asses fort bien, et equitamus apud locum
> vocatis clausa, sed pian pianino.[56]

Lassus's creative output remained high, if not at the level of fecundity of his first Munich decade. He appears not to have been especially concerned with changing fashions in composition, all but ignoring, for example, the canzonetta style so popular in Italy in the last quarter of the century; his music developed within his own concepts of the central polyphonic language of the later Renaissance. In all probability Wilhelm V was much less concerned with having his chapel appear up to date than his father had been. In Albrecht's last years the musical establishment was subjected to economies, parings which continued under Wilhelm V. Money was spent on Jesuit enterprises in building and education rather than on secular entertainments.[57] On several occasions it seemed likely that Lassus might leave Munich for a more remunerative post; there were strong rumours of an offer from the French court in 1571, and in 1580 the composer was offered the directorship of the Dresden court chapel.[58]

These offers were declined; the *princeps musicorum* remained in Munich, and his presence alone guaranteed distinction to the chapel. Lassus's sons Rudolf and Ferdinand grew up to become musicians and both obtained positions at minor German courts; both were later to return to Munich where in 1604 they published as an act of filial piety the *Magnum opus musicum*, a collection of 516 motets by their father (including 66 previously unprinted works but omitting many important compositions such as the Penitential Psalms and the Lamentations). The influence of Lassus on German musical establishments was often considerable. For example, the repertory of the chapel at the great Benedictine church of SS Ulric and Afra in Ausgburg was, under its director Johannes Dreer, formed in consultation with Lassus. The Augsburg choirbooks copied by or for Dreer include masses and *Magnificat* settings by Lassus as well as music by Isaac, Kerle and members of Lassus's chapel.[59]

In his later years Lassus became increasingly preoccupied with religion in a melancholy fashion, even making a pilgrimage to Loreto in 1585. This suited his employer well, but it was doubtless inspired by

58. *Orlande de Lassus at the age of 40: miniature by Hans Mielich from the choirbook of Penitential Psalms*

sincere conviction. He was still active as a composer, in particular of motets and *Magnificat* settings. In 1581 a collection of villanelle and *moresche*, some of them probably dating from the time of the 1568 wedding, was published in Paris. In his dedicatory letter to Duke Wilhelm, Lassus said that these works would better have been issued 'in my youth, when I wrote them, than in this "età grave" in which I now find myself'; the valedictory tone of his last years is already present. Two more madrigal collections were to appear. In a 1585 print dedicated to the Veronese musical amateur Count Mario Bevilacqua, Lassus said that the contents were largely written in leisure hours after his chapel duties and 'più gravi studi' were taken care of; the contents are serious and partly religious. This tone is even more marked in a collection of 1587, dedicated to the composer's friend and physician Dr Thomas Mermann.[60] His final composition was, fittingly, a set of spiritual madrigals, the *Lagrime di San Pietro*, on texts by Luigi Tansillo, a repentant and lachrymose poet who had outlived a carefree secular youth. There is no question here, however, of artistic comparison; Tansillo's verse is adequate Counter-Reformation piety, Lassus's music a severely magnificent artistic testament.

The years after 1570 were certainly not all gloomy ones for music at the court. In 1573 the young Florentine lutenist and singer Cosimo Bottegari arrived in Munich and speedily ingratiated himself with the duke, becoming not only a member of the chapel but a gentleman of the ducal chamber.[61] Under Bottegari's direction a second volume of madrigals by the 'floridi virtuosi' of the ducal chapel was published in Venice in 1575. Lassus, though not mentioned in Bottegari's dedicatory letter, which speaks only in general of the 'amorevolissimi servitori' of the duke, is again represented by the opening and closing pieces. Many of the composers in the *Primo libro* of 1569 appear here as well; but Troiano is of course absent, and Bottegari himself is among the new names.

Another fresh name in the 1575 collection is that of 'Giovanni di Andrea Gabrieli'. The great Venetian organist and composer was still young and thus known as his famous uncle's nephew; he was in Munich during the last five years of Albrecht's reign. In 1574 Lassus wrote to Duke Wilhelm about 'le neveu de andreas'.[62] Andrea Gabrieli had himself been in Albrecht's service for a brief period in the early 1560s.[63]

In 1592 the chapel was once more reduced in size, losing six singers and three boys, while all the salaries – save that of Lassus himself – were lowered.[64] On the composer's death in June 1594 his assistant Kapellmeister of 25 years' standing, Johannes de Fossa, succeeded him; there was no question of a search for a young genius to revitalize the ducal chapel. Lassus was mourned not only in Munich but in many other places; in Rome, musicians of the Seminario Romano 'commemorated him with sad lamentations and with compositions written in his memory'.[65] With Lassus's death and that of Palestrina in the same year, the great age of the sixteenth-century polyphonists came to a quiet and fittingly dignified close. New directions were already apparent in court music, chief among them the sung *dramma* or *favola*, written in the new monodic style which interested neither of the greatest of late Renaissance polyphonists.

NOTES

[1] M. de Montaigne, *Journal de voyage en Italie per le Suisse et L'Allemagne en 1580 et 1581*, in *Oeuvres complètes*, ed. A. Thibaudet and M. Rat (Paris, 1962), 1162.

[2] On Albrecht's reign in general see R. Reiser, *Die Wittelsbacher in Bayern* (Munich, 1978), 110–15; D. Albrecht, 'Das Herzogtum Bayern und seine Herzoge zur Zeit Orlando di Lassos', in *Orlando di Lasso: Musik der Renaissance am Münchner Fürstenhof: Ausstellung zum 450. Geburtstag, 27. Mai–31. Juli 1982* (Wiesbaden, 1982), 23–38. In this same volume there is an article on the visual arts in sixteenth-century Munich: H. H. Stierhof, 'Die bildenden Künste am Münchner Hof zur Zeit Orlando di Lassos', 39–49. Both articles include full bibliographical references.

[3] A good account of the background and general character of the 1568 wedding is given by Horst Leuchtmann in the *Nachwort*, 418–64, to his facsimile edition and translation of Troiano's contemporary account: *Die Münchner Fürstenhochzeit von 1568. Massimo Troiano: Dialoge* (Munich, 1980). Of the three chief contemporary accounts of the celebration, only that of Troiano goes into detail about its musical side; those of H. Wagner, *Kurtze doch gegründete beschreibung des . . . Hochzeitlichen Ehren Fests* (Munich, 1568), and H. Wirre, *Ordentliche Beschreybung der Fürstlichen Hochzeyt* (Augsburg, 1568), are much more concerned with the names and lineage of the guests and with the tournaments and jousts held during the two weeks of festivities.

[4] On Mielich see B. H. Röttger, *Der Maler Hans Mielich* (Munich, 1925). The influence of the great Augsburg banking family of the Fuggers was considerable in shaping Duke Albrecht's artistic and cultural ventures. See O. Hartig, *Die Gründung der Münchner Hofbibliothek durch Albrecht V und Johann Jakob Fugger* (Munich, 1917).

[5] A. Sandberger, *Beiträge zur Geschichte der bayerischen Hofkapelle unter Orlando di Lasso* (Leipzig, 1894–5), i, 52.

[6] W. Boetticher, 'Orlando di Lasso: Studien zur Musikgeschichte Münchens im Zeitalter der Spätrenaissance', *Zeitschrift für bayerischen Landesgeschichte*, xix (1956), 467.

[7] Albrecht, 'Das Herzogtum Bayern', 23.

[8] See C. Wolff, 'Paumann, Conrad', *Grove 6*.

[9] H. Leuchtmann, 'Munich', *Grove 6*.

[10] Sandberger, *Beiträge*, i, 23; M. Bente, 'Senfl, Conrad', *Grove 6*.

[11] Boetticher, 'Orlando di Lasso: Studien', 466; cf Sandberger, *Beiträge*, xi, 32–5. These figures are hard to evaluate since one is not sure how many of the members were active singers or how many took part in any particular service.

[12] Troiano, *Dialoge*, 92. The title of the work is *Dialoghi di Massimo Troiano: Ne' quali si narrano le cose piu notabili fatte nelle Nozze dell'Illustriss. & Eccell. Principe GUGLIELMO VI. [sic] Conte Palatino di Reno, e Duca di Baviera; e dell' Illustriss. & Eccell. Madama RENATA di Loreno* (Venice, 1569). The interlocutors, Marinio and Fortunio, are fictitious names; the work is actually a monologue couched in question and answer form.

[13] W. Boetticher, *Aus Orlando di Lassos Wirkungskreis* (Kassel, 1963), 42.

[14] For a survey of the various sixteenth-century uses of the term see B. Meier, 'Musica Reservata', *MGG*.

[15] W. Boetticher, *Orlando di Lasso und seine Zeit, 1532–1594*, i: *Monographie* (Kassel and Basle, 1958), 155. Philip's chapel returned with the king to Spain in 1559.

[16] See M. Steinhardt and R. Lindell, 'Monte, Philippe de', *Grove 6*.

[17] Boetticher, *Orlando di Lasso und seine Zeit*, 154–5.

[18] See *Orlando di Lasso: Ausstellung*, 124–5. A phrase in this letter has been misread by Sandberger and Boetticher as referring to a son of Fugger named David; the correct reading would seem to be not 'daviden' but 'daniden' (danieden), a pun following 'orlando dela sus'.

[19] Boetticher, 'Orlando di Lasso: Studien', 483.

[20] See *Orlando di Lasso: Ausstellung*, 174.

[21] On the texts of which this work is a setting see P. Bergquist, 'The Poems of Orlando di Lasso's Prophetiae Sibyllarum and their Sources', *JAMS*, xxxii (1979), 516–38.

[22] *Orlando di Lasso: Ausstellung*, 160–69. Charles IX of France is said to have been most impressed by this example of Lassus's 'chromatic' art.

[23] *Orlando di Lasso: Ausstellung*, 160. On Habsburg court manuscripts see H. Kellman, 'Alamire' [the name of the chief court copyist in the early sixteenth century], *Grove 6*.

[24] *D-Mbs* Mus. B. See *Census-Catalogue of Manuscript Sources of Polyphonic Music 1400–1550* (1979–84), ii, 232–3. The numerous entries for Munich-copied manuscripts in this volume show something of the extent of the court copyists' work during the reign of Wilhelm IV and the first

part of that of Albrecht V; most of the manuscripts copied during the tenure of Lassus are later than the cut-off date for the *Census-Catalogue*. For a catalogue including these later manuscripts see below, n.26.

25 *A-Wn* Mus. 18744.

26 See J. Meier, *Die musikalischen Handschriften der K. Hof- und Staatsbibliothek* (Munich, 1879), 93–4. There are two volumes of commentary, by the humanist (and first biographer of Lassus) Samuel Quickelberg, that belong with this manuscript.

27 *D-Mbs* Mus. 20, a page of which is illustrated in *Orlando di Lasso: Ausstellung*, 133. For a description of this manuscript see Meier, *Die musikalischen Handschriften*, 92.

28 See Bergquist, 'The Poems of Orlando di Lasso's *Prophetiae*', 516. Bergquist argues convincingly that Lassus found the poems in a print of 1555, presumably in Antwerp, and composed the settings soon after his move to Munich.

29 The motet in question is the five-voice *Gustate et videte*, first published in 1556. See *Orlando de Lassus: Sämtliche Werke*, ed. F. X. Haberl and A. Sandberger (Leipzig, 1894–1926), v, 73.

30 A quite detailed account of this *commedia* is given by Troiano, *Dialoge*, 308–20.

31 There are about 550 extant prints containing music by Lassus that appeared up to the turn of the seventeenth century. See *Orlando di Lasso: Ausstellung*, 61.

32 For a modern edition of this print and its 1575 sequel, see *Musik der bayerischen Hofkapelle zur Zeit Orlando di Lassos, 1. Auswahl: Madrigali a cinque voci de floridi virtuosi del serenissimo Duca di Baviera (Venedig 1569 und 1575)*, ed. H. Leuchtmann, DTB, new ser., iv (1981).

33 An example is the *Corona della morte dell' illustre Signore, il Sig. Commendatore Anibal Caro* (Venice, 1568), settings of sonnets by G. B. Caro in memory of his uncle, edited by Giulio Bonagionta. The composers are chiefly but not exclusively Venetian (Palestrina is among them).

34 See H. Leuchtmann, 'Troiano, Massimo', *Grove 6*. Troiano seems to have disappeared entirely after his flight from Landshut, never being found by the duke's men nor indeed heard from in any connection.

35 See Leuchtmann, *Musik der bayerischen Hofkapelle*, p.ix.

36 For the dedication see E. Vogel, *Bibliothek der gedruckten weltlichen Vocalmusik Italiens aus den Jahren 1500–1700* (Berlin, 1892/R1962), i, 352. Even the title of the volume refers to its contents as 'novamente in Germania composti'.

37 See J. Quitin, 'Fossa, Johannes de', *Grove 6*; W. Boetticher, 'Lockenburg, Johannes', *Grove 6*.

38 For a modern edition of this account see n.3.

39 Troiano, *Dialoge*, 70ff.

40 See for example Troiano, *Dialoge*, 162, where a 'ballo alla tedesca' with twelve *trombette et taballi* (?=*tamburi*) is mentioned. Trombones with shawms formed a common dance band throughout the Renaissance. For an illustration, taken from one of Adam Berg's volumes of Lassus's *Patrocinium musices*, of a mixed consort using trombones, see *Grove 6*, xix, 169.

41 Troiano, *Dialoge*, 136–44. The *Battaglia* (or *Aria della battaglia*) *a 8* of Padovano was quite a well-known work. It was published late, in 1590, with a similar work, also far from new, of Andrea Gabrieli; see Vogel, *Bibliothek*, ii, 734–5.

42 Troiano, *Dialoge*, 298. *La bella franceschina* was a noted dance tune; it is cited in Cesare Bendinelli's *Tutta l'arte della trombetta* (MS of 1614; facs., ed. E. H. Tarr [Kassel, 1975]), f 53*v*, with the tune quoted as trumpets would play it. Whether its appearance here suggests a nose-thumbing at the French (with whom the Bavarian court's relations at this time were so strained that the French were not invited to send a representative to the wedding) is unsure. Bendinelli was chief court trumpeter at Munich from 1580 until his death; see E. H. Tarr, 'Bendinelli, Cesare', *Grove 6*.

43 Troiano, *Dialoge*, 142.

44 ibid, 184.

45 ibid, 238–40. The cornamusa was probably not a bagpipe but rather a shawm-like instrument similar to the dolzaina.

46 On this subject see H. M. Brown, *Sixteenth-Century Instrumentation: the Music for the Florentine Intermedi*, MSD, xxx (1973).

47 Troiano, *Dialoge*, 104.

48 It would be hard to identify individual masses by Lassus from Troiano's descriptions, which may in any event not always be accurate; he mentions a mass *a 7* by Lassus and one *a 6* by Rore, neither known to exist today. The 24-voice mass by Annibale Padovano does survive, in a seventeenth-century manuscript copy. See Troiano, *Dialoge*, n.240, n.287 and n.329.

49 ibid, 120. This work is not known to survive.

[50] ibid, 106 and 200.

[51] ibid, 78, 98, 136, 262–4, 308 and 312. Caterina Willaert here makes her only known appearance in the literature. Willaert was married, but no mention is made in his will or elsewhere of a daughter. I am grateful to Giulio Ongaro for this unfortunately negative information.

[52] On this see Troiano, *Dialoge*, 320.

[53] ibid, 96.

[54] idem.

[55] L. Zacconi, *Prattica di musica, seconda parte* (Venice, 1622/*R*1967), 161, reports a conversation with Lassus (Zacconi was in Munich in the last three years of the composer's life) in which Lassus said 'every day without fail I compose something, if only a fantasia . . . because otherwise when my patron wants me to do something, I should have lost the ability to compose, or would at any rate experience great difficulty – or I might do something unworthy of my well-earned reputation'.

[56] *Orlando di Lasso: Briefe*, ed. H. Leuchtmann (Wiesbaden, 1977), 70.

[57] On Wilhelm V's support of Jesuit activities, see Reiser, *Die Wittelsbacher*, 116–25.

[58] H. Leuchtmann, *Orlando di Lasso: sein Leben* (Wiesbaden, 1976), 54 and 190–91.

[59] For information about Dreer's relationship to Lassus and about the Augsburg choirbooks I am indebted to Phyllis Juszczyk of New York University, who is preparing a dissertation on the sixteenth-century repertory of SS Ulric and Afra.

[60] For the dedications and contents of these works see Vogel, *Bibliothek*, i, 346–53; cf E. Vogel, A. Einstein, F. Lesure and C. Sartori, *Bibliografia della musica italiana vocale profana pubblicata dal 1500 al 1700* (Pomezia, 1977; known as *Il nuovo Vogel*), i, 895 (no.1420) and 911 (no.1462). Both collections make heavy use of the poetry of the devoutly Counter-Reformation poet Gabriele Fiamma; see A. Einstein, *The Italian Madrigal* (Princeton, 1949), ii, 494–5.

[61] Leuchtmann, *Musik der bayerischen Hofkapelle*, p.xii. There is some reason to think that Lassus did not altogether approve of the young Bottegari.

[62] *Lasso: Briefe*, 93

[63] See D. Arnold, 'Gabrieli, Andrea', *Grove 6*.

[64] Leuchtmann, *Orlando di Lasso: sein Leben*, 58 and 210–11.

[65] ibid, 219.

BIBLIOGRAPHICAL NOTE

General history

There is little of substance written in English on sixteenth-century Bavaria. R. Reiser, *Die Wittelsbacher in Bayern* (Munich, 1978), contains a brief and matter-of-fact survey of the ducal regime in the period. Equally concise coverage may be found in *Handbuch der bayerischen Geschichte*, ii: *Das alte Bayern. Der Territorialstaat vom Ausgang des 12. Jahrhunderts bis zum Ausgang des 18. Jahrhunderts*, ed. M. Spinder (Munich, 1969); this work also contains a short section on artistic currents, viewed under the rubric of Mannerism, in sixteenth-century Bavaria. Brief but helpful for its up-to-date bibliographical references, is D. Albrecht, 'Das Herzogtum Bayern und seine Herzoge zur Zeit Orlando di Lassos', in *Orlando di Lasso: Musik der Renaissance am Münchner Fürstenhof Ausstellung zum 450. Geburtstag, 27. Mai–31. Juli 1982* (Wiesbaden, 1982), 23–38.

The arts

On the role of the Fugger family and the early development of the ducal library a helpful work is O. Hartig's *Die Gründung der Münchner Hofbibliothek durch Albrecht V und Johann Jakob Fugger* (Munich, 1917). The Lassus exhibition catalogue (*Orlando di Lasso . . . Ausstellung*) referred to above has a well-organized essay on the visual arts during the period: H. Stierhof, 'Die bildenden Künste am Münchner Hof zur Zeit Orlando di Lassos', 39–49. The elaborate lengths to which ducal patronage of the arts could on occasion extend is well illustrated in Massimo Troiano's *Dialoghi* of 1569 (for its full title, see n.12 above). The only full-length study of Munich's greatest sixteenth-century painter known to me is B. H. Röttger, *Der Maler Hans Mielich* (Munich, 1925).

Music

Studies of central importance for the career of Lassus and the ducal chapel during his tenure are A. Sandberger, *Beiträge zur Geschichte der bayerischen Hofkapelle unter Orlando di Lasso* (Leipzig, 1894–5); W. Boetticher, *Orlando di Lasso und seine Zeit, 1532–1594* (Kassel, 1958); H. Leuchtmann, *Orlando di Lasso*, i: *Sein Leben*; ii: *Briefe* (Wiesbaden, 1976–7). Lassus's music has been edited in the massive but incomplete *Sämtliche Werke*, ed. F. X. Haberl and A. Sandberger (Leipzig, 1894–1926); a new edition, beginning with works not contained in the older one, is the *Sämtliche Werke*, new ser., ed. S. Hermelink and others (Kassel, 1956–). *RBM*, xxxix–xl (1985–6), the report of a Lassus congress held at Mons in 1982, is devoted to special problems in Lassus research. Madrigals by members of the ducal chapel are contained in *Musik der bayerischen Hofkapelle zur Zeit Orlando di Lassos, 1. Auswahl: Madrigali a cinque voci de floridi virtuosi del serenissimo Duca di Baviera (Vendig 1569 und 1575)*, ed. H. Leuchtmann, DTB, new ser., iv (1981).

Chapter X

The Lutheran Reformation

ROBIN A. LEAVER

The religious revolution of the sixteenth century, generally known as the Reformation, took place against the background of wider changes in European society, politics and culture (although some of these changes were brought about by the Reformation itself). Feudalism was coming to an end, capitalism was dawning and patronage of the arts was passing from the church to the courts and the new capitalists. Although the Reformation was inextricably bound up with political ambition and sociological transformation, at root it was a theological revolution. It centred on the question of the nature of the church and its authority. For Catholics the church was regulated from Rome by the authority of the pope, the Vicar of Christ, and beneath him by an authority which was wielded at parish level by the priests of the church. For the new 'Protestants', whether they were Lutheran, Calvinist or Anglican, the church was the creation of the Spirit of God, with a common priesthood of all believers, and grounded in the authority of the written word of Scripture. The Protestant reformers also argued that if Scripture was the final authority for the church it must therefore also be normative for the worship of the church. Thus new patterns of worship were introduced and the role of music was re-evaluated.

The key figure in the Reformation of the sixteenth century was the former Augustinian monk, Martin Luther. It was his stand against the Church of Rome and his voluminous writings which fuelled the religious ferment of Europe. Furthermore, it was Luther who almost single-handedly created the theological and liturgical climate which enabled a new musical tradition to develop within dawning 'Lutheranism', a tradition which was distinctive among the new churches created by the Reformation. This chapter will therefore begin by discussing Luther and his positive approach to music. The practical outcome of his musical leadership will then be traced as it affected certain representative cities throughout Germany. In general one can say that the German Reformation succeeded in those areas where there was either a university protected by a local prince sympathetic to Luther's views, or a free imperial city where the local ruling magistrates had elected to pursue Lutheran reforms. We shall therefore investigate Wittenberg and

59. Woodcut contrasting Lutheran services (left) with the iniquities of Catholic practice (right): woodcut (c1545) by Lucas Cranach the younger

Leipzig as examples of the former and Augsburg as an example of the latter.

Unlike the reformers in Switzerland, Zwingli and Calvin, who either banished music from the sanctuary altogether or drastically restricted its use, Luther enthusiastically accepted the art as an integral part of liturgical worship. The whole of the Reformation movement throughout Europe was marked by a new awareness of the Bible as the Word of God, which was to be heard, believed and obeyed in every aspect of corporate church activity and individual Christian life. The Swiss reformers were suspicious of music because it had a power of its own which, in their view, could undermine the primacy of the Word of God; it was also subject to misuse and abuse, and instead of celebrating the glory of God in worthy hymns it was frequently used to deify the inglorious aspects of human nature in immoral songs. Luther was aware, of course, of the possibility of the misuse of music, but he was concerned to emphasize the positive rather than the negative aspects: instead of undermining Scripture, music, if properly understood, is a bearer of the Word of God. Luther observed that music was an integral part of prophecy in the Old Testament and therefore music and theology must be inextricably bound together.[1] For example, in a letter to the composer Ludwig Senfl, dated 4 October 1530, he wrote: 'the prophets did not make use of any art except music. It was not as geometry, or arithmetic, or astronomy, but as music they delivered their theology. For them theology and music were closely bound together and they proclaimed the truth through psalms and songs'.[2]

Luther sang often, played both flute and lute, was able to compose in four parts and, according to the composer Johann Walter, had some considerable ability in creating – and re-creating – melodies for particular texts of liturgical monody and congregational song. He also had a discriminating musical ear and was able to distinguish between the adequate works of local composers and the really great polyphonic music of the age. He knew the music of the leading contemporary German-speaking composers well and also had a marked preference for the music of Josquin Desprez, whom he regarded as 'the master of the notes' and a preacher of the Gospel through music, since his 'composition flows out joyfully, willingly, tenderly, like the song of the finch, and is neither forced nor constrained by the rules'.[3]

Luther's views on music did not remain in the realms of speculative theory but were worked out in practice, particularly in Wittenberg, the hub of the Lutheran revolution. Here Luther worked under the protection of Duke Frederick the Wise of Saxony and created a new approach to music in worship which exerted a powerful influence on musical composition and practice, first in Wittenberg and later throughout Germany.

60. Martin Luther: portrait (1533) by Lucas Cranach the elder

WITTENBERG

Wittenberg was a small town in Saxony, situated on the banks of the Elbe. The university had been founded by the Elector of Ernestine Saxony, Duke Frederick the Wise, in 1502, in direct competition with the older university of Albertine Saxony at Leipzig. Luther, who had studied law in Erfurt, was called to Wittenberg University in 1508. At first he lectured on Aristotle, but after studying theology and receiving the doctorate he concentrated on theology. Following a visit to Rome on behalf of his order, he became disillusioned with what he had seen and began to test the church of his day by the principles he found in the New Testament. Then there was the great indulgence debate, which he had begun in Wittenberg in 1517 by nailing his 95 theses to the university notice-board (the door of the Schlosskirche). As a result he was summoned in 1520 to the Diet of Worms where he was expected to recant his views. He stood firm and in consequence was banished both by church and state. After almost a year of enforced exile, which his friends had arranged for his own safety, Luther returned to Wittenberg and continued his reforming work under the protection of Frederick the Wise.

As a professor Luther taught in the university; as a priest he celebrated Mass and preached in the Schlosskirche, the university church and also in the Stadtkirche, where he assisted the parish priest Johann Bugenhagen. The Latin Mass was celebrated in both churches, virtually unchanged, with all the attendant plainsong Propers and polyphonic settings of the Ordinary, sung by the Kantorei, or school choir. By the end of 1523 Luther had issued his revised form of the Latin Mass, *Formula missae et communionis pro Ecclesia Wittembergensi*.[4] This Latin order is liturgically conservative but theologically radical. The Mass is no longer seen as a propitiatory sacrifice offered to God by the priest on behalf of the people, but rather as God's offer of forgiveness and grace to the people, in the consecrated bread and wine. The Canon of the Mass is thus truncated by the elimination of all reference to the sacrifice of the Mass; indeed, it now consists of only the Words of Institution. In contrast, practically everything else, especially the music associated with the Mass, was subject to only slight modification. For example, the traditional introit is retained except that Luther directs that a complete psalm, rather than a few verses, should be sung; the use of the Kyrie eleison is to continue 'with the various [plainchant] melodies for different seasons, together with the Angelic Hymn, Gloria in excelsis, which follows it'.[5] Only one Collect for the day is to be used but this should always be intoned; the Epistle and Gospel are to be chanted to lectionary tones; only the shorter graduals and alleluias are to be retained, and in general only shorter sequences are to be sung, such as the Christmas *Grates nunc omnes*; and so on.

The Mass was thus revised rather than eliminated and in the Wittenberg churches polyphonic settings of the Ordinary continued to be sung, together with traditional plainchant. One radical departure was the singing of the Words of Institution by the priest, words which were normally inaudible in the Roman Mass. For Luther these were not words of priestly prayer but of proclamation to be heard by all, and therefore they were to be sung. However, Luther made another radical departure which was to have far-reaching consequences for Protestant church music: to the traditional music of the Mass was to be added a new musical dimension – congregational song.

In the *Formula missae* Luther had stated: 'I also wish that we had as many songs as possible in the vernacular which the people could sing during Mass, immediately after the [Latin] gradual and also after the Sanctus and Agnus Dei'.[6] By the time this liturgy had appeared in print (towards the end of 1523), broadsheets containing German hymns, complete with melodies, were available in Wittenberg. They were written by Luther and his colleagues, such as Agricola, Speratus, Hegenwalt and others. These congregational songs spread like wildfire. The following year, 1524, almost before a collected edition of these hymns could be published in Wittenberg, publishers in such widely separated cities as Nuremberg, Erfurt and Strasbourg issued the Wittenberg hymns.

Luther was a practical pastor and although the concept of congregational singing was regarded as something of an innovation, not everything he gave his congregations was entirely 'new'. Some of the Witten-

61a. The Ambassadors (1533) by Hans Holbein; the painting depicts (left) Jean de Dinteville, French ambassador to England in 1533, and Georges de Selve, surrounded by objects with symbolic connotations, including an open copy of Walter's 'Chorgesangbuch' (2nd edition, 1525; see fig.61b)

berg hymns were translations from the Latin which the people would recognize from the associated melodies they had heard sung over the years. Among such hymns are *Nun komm der Heiden Heiland*, crafted from the Ambrosian *Veni Redemptor gentium*, and *Komm Heiliger Geist*, a translation of *Veni sancte spiritus*. Another familiar source Luther used were the *Leisen* – so named from their common refrain 'Kyrie eleison' – the German folk hymns which had been sung for generations after Mass at the high festivals. Luther usually altered or extended them in some way; among them are *Gelobet seist du, Jesu Christ, Nun bitten wir den Heiligen Geist* and the complete rewriting of *Christ ist erstanden* to form *Christ lag in Todesbanden*. There were, of course, freely-composed hymns which took as their model the Hofweise, the art song of the day. These are notable for their syncopated and rhythmic melodies in a basic *AAB* or bar-form structure, a built-in repetition which would have helped congregations memorize them. Among this type are *Nun freut euch, lieben*

61b. Walter's 'Chorges-
angbuch', with a lute
(detail of fig.61a)

Christen g'mein and *Ein' feste Burg* (see fig.62 below).

In 1524 there was a basic corpus of about 40 Wittenberg hymns, over half of them written by Luther himself. One of the basses in Duke Frederick's Hofkapelle was the 28-year-old Johann Walter, to whom Luther turned when he was ready to edit a hymnal for Wittenberg. This was to be no ordinary congregational hymnal but something rather different. As in other matters, Luther was literally a reformer: he took an old idea and gave it a new and radical expression. He requested Walter to compose choral settings of the hymns. Walter was to take as his model the polyphony associated with the mass; only the cantus firmus settings were to be composed around the melodies of the new Wittenberg hymns rather than around plainsong fragments. Walter accepted Luther's challenge and composed, under his guidance, polyphonic settings of 38 Wittenberg hymns, together with five Latin motets. Thus was created the first great work of Lutheran church music: *Geystliches, gesangk Buchleyn,* the so-called Walter *Chorgesangbuch.* It was issued as a set of five partbooks, clearly intended for choral use in school and church. Luther wrote in the preface:

> These songs were arranged in four parts [some of the compositions are in fact written in three voices, others in five] to give the young – who should at any rate be trained in music and other fine arts – something to wean them away from love ballads and carnal songs and to teach them something of value in their place, thus combining the good with the pleasing, as is proper for youth . . . I would like to see all the arts, especially music, used in the service of him who has given and created them.[7]

Music had therefore educational as well as liturgical functions. These partbooks were to be used in the Wittenberg schools as part of the pupils' musical education, but once the compositions had been learnt they were to be sung within church worship.

Walter's settings of the Wittenberg hymns are in two basic styles. The first follows the older Flemish cantus firmus motet style, echoing the compositions of Josquin Desprez which Walter – like Luther – particularly admired; but it is treated with some freedom (as is also evident in the music of Walter's contemporary, Ludwig Senfl). Imitation and canonic devices derived from the basic chorale melody are common in these settings, which are generally much more concise than the earlier polyphonic masses with plainsong cantus firmi. Unlike many of these earlier examples, in which the cantus firmus is lost within the texture of the music, the chorale melody in Walter's settings is usually more obvious. The second style used by Walter is simpler, more homophonic and similar to the settings of the older composers such as Finck, Hofhaimer and Isaac. Here the chorale melody, usually in the tenor, is supported by three other voices in a basically homophonic structure. In these simple and more concise settings the melody is never hidden but is clearly heard throughout. They represent an embryonic form of the characteristic 'cantional' style of later Lutheran church music.

At this early stage it appears that the Kantorei sang Walter's polyphonic settings of Wittenberg hymns in the church services as the representative of the congregation. Indeed, it seems highly likely that Luther issued this choral hymnbook before a specifically congregational collection so that the choir could teach the congregation how to sing the new hymns. Thus a double educational function was involved: teaching good music to the pupils of the school and teaching the congregation their songs of worship; both aims were achieved with the one important publication. The Wittenberg congregations did not have a hymnal to sing from but they did have the hymns available in broadsheet form. Thus it seems most likely that an *alternatim* practice quickly developed, with the congregation singing alternate stanzas in unison, led by the boys of the choir, in response to the Kantorei singing the other stanzas in Walter's polyphonic setting of the hymn for the day. This practice is known to have occurred in Wittenberg a few years later, especially for the main liturgical hymn, which was sung between the Epistle and Gospel, after the gradual. These seasonal hymns, such as *Nun komm der Heiden Heiland* for Advent and *Christ lag in Todesbanden* for Easter, came to be known appropriately as *Graduallieder*. For most of Walter's polyphonic settings, the chorale melody is in the tenor voice.[8] Therefore, if the tenor partbook is isolated from the others its contents make it look like a unison hymnal, with the texts given with the appropriate melodies. This tenor partbook was clearly the model for a congregational Wittenberg hymnal, 'for the laity' rather than the choir, which was published in 1525 and reissued in 1526. Its texts and melodies are given in exactly the same order as in Walter's *Chorgesangbuch* and the collection is introduced by the same preface Luther had written for the partbooks in 1524.

Thus the Lutheran tradition of combining simple congregational song with complex polyphonic choral music was established. From the beginning it was a partnership of congregation and choir who in unanimity and diversity sang words of praise to God and proclaimed the Word of God to each other. The tradition was also bilingual. Even though Luther published his *Deutsche Messe und Ordnung Gottesdienysts* in 1526,[9] he did not intend that Latin should no longer be used in worship. In the preface to the new liturgical order he wrote:

> It is not now my intention to abrogate or to change this service [the Latin *Formula missae*]. It shall not be affected in the form which we have followed so far; but we shall continue to use it . . . For in no wise would I want to discontinue the service in the Latin language, because the young are my chief concern.

He then went on to explain that the *Deutsche Messe* is 'arranged for the sake of the unlearned lay folk', and concluded, 'These two liturgical orders must be used publicly in the churches and for all the people'.[10]

The German liturgy, therefore, was intended for the churches in small towns and villages, where Latin was virtually unknown. To accommodate the particular needs of such churches Luther introduced the concept of vernacular hymnic paraphrases of the Latin Ordinary, so that instead of listening to the Latin Kyrie and Gloria etc, the worshippers could join in singing such congregational hymns as *Kyrie, Gott Vater in Ewigkeit* and *Allein Gott in der Höhe sei Ehre*. Luther implied that in the larger towns and cities, where there were Latin schools and universities, the language of education would continue to be used in worship. In practice they rarely used Latin alone, but rather a mixture of both Latin and German. Thus many church orders published for use in the various areas of Lutheran Germany conflated Luther's two liturgies and used Latin and German side by side. For example, after the choir had sung polyphonic settings of the Latin Ordinary, the congregation would sing the appropriate German hymnic version. Furthermore in Wittenberg, for example, each verse of the *Te Deum* was sung in Latin by the Kantorei, to which the congregation responded by singing the same verse in Luther's German translation, the whole being punctuated by improvisations on the basic melody by the organist.[11] At Christmas the congregation sang the hymn *Gelobet seist du, Jesu Christ* which was inserted stanza by stanza within the Latin sequence *Grates nunc omnes* sung by the choir with organ accompaniment;[12] and at Easter the same pattern was followed with *Christ ist erstanden* and the sequence *Victimae paschali laudes*.[13]

Johann Walter was only in Wittenberg for a few years. By 1526 he had left to become the Kantor in Torgau and the musical leadership in Wittenberg was assumed by Georg Rhau. Rhau had been a student at

Wittenberg University during the turbulent years of the indulgence debate. During this time he had also worked in printing and publishing with his uncle. In 1518 he left to become the Thomaskantor in Leipzig, returning to take over the publishing business in Wittenberg in 1523. There were many publishers working in Wittenberg – over twenty produced more than 120 musical publications before the end of the century. One of them was Joseph Klug who had published Walter's *Chorgesangbuch* of 1524. In 1529 Klug brought out a new congregational hymnal, *Geistliche Lieder*. Over the next sixteen years he produced at least eight further editions of this Wittenberg hymnal, many of them revisions and expansions of the previous ones. One of the new features developed in the subsequent editions was a section of catechism hymns – that is, hymns written by Luther on the five main parts of his *Small Catechism*: Ten Commandments, *Dies sind die heiligen zehn Gebot*; Creed, *Wir glauben all' an einen Gott*; Lord's Prayer, *Vater unser im Himmelreich*; Baptism, *Christ, unser Herr, zum Jordan kam*; and Communion, *Jesus Christus, unser Heiland*. These chorales were to have immense importance for later Lutheran choral and organ music. The Wittenberg hymnals published by Klug were not exclusively German; they also contained Latin items, and Luther's *Begräbnis Lieder* (burial hymns), which Klug first published in 1542, included Latin *responsoria*. Klug was the principal publisher of hymnals in Wittenberg but Rhau became the most important publisher of liturgical and school music. Rhau did not confine himself to music but also published a variety of theological books

62. *Luther's chorale 'Ein'feste Burg' from Klug's congregational hymnal 'Geistliche Lieder' (1533 edition)*

by Luther, Bugenhagen, Melanchthon and others – Bible commentaries, apologetic and polemic theology, and editions of the Augsburg Confession and Luther's Catechism.

From 1528 Rhau published a succession of books on music theory beginning with Agricola's *Ein kurtz deudsche Musica* and including Spangenburg's *Quaestiones musicae* (1536) and Walter's *Lob und Preis der löblichen Kunst Musica* (1538). Over the next seven years he published a number of major collections of Latin polyphonic settings of the Ordinary and Propers arranged for the church year. The settings were by a variety of composers and ranged from the simple to the finest examples of Franco-Flemish polyphony. These collections demonstrate the conservative style that was favoured by the leaders of the Lutheran reform, who were content to continue to use much of the music written for the Roman rite, providing that the texts did not offend biblical doctrines. Rhau also published collections of music for Vespers by individual composers: Sixt Dietrich's antiphons in *Novum ac insigne opus musicum* (1541) and three volumes of his hymns in *Novum opus musicum* (1545), and two volumes of *responsoria* by Balthasar Resinarius (a pupil of Isaac), *Responsorium . . . de tempore et festis* (1542).

In 1544 Rhau issued two different sets of partbooks with predominantly German texts. The first was the expanded, fourth edition of *Chorgesangbuch* by Johann Walter – who a few years later became Kapellmeister to the Saxon court in Dresden – and the second, a new work, *Newe deudsche geistliche Gesenge*. Unlike Walter's partbooks, which contain the music of one composer, this new work is an anthology of pieces by a variety of people. About two-thirds of the 123 pieces are the settings of five composers: Resinarius, Bruck, Ludwig Senfl, Ducis and Dietrich. The remainder is made up of the compositions of eleven lesser-known composers. Again, as with the volumes of Latin polyphonic music Rhau published, a significant number of the composers in these German partbooks were Catholics and the style is generally conservative. Rhau issued two further editions of Walter's *Chorgesangbuch* (1550 and 1551) and another Wittenberg printer, Johann Schwertel, added to the repertory of masterly polyphony for church and school use by issuing another set of partbooks, *Geistliche und weltliche teutsche Geseng* (1566), composed by Matthaeus Le Maistre, Walter's successor as Kapellmeister in Dresden.

But there was also a concern for liturgical monody, the traditional chant of the church. There was a danger that plainsong might disappear from the new Lutheran churches, even though most of the regional church orders included some of the chants. Therefore Lucas Lossius of Lüneberg compiled a basic anthology of Latin chant suitable for reformed use: *Psalmodia, hoc est cantica sacra veteris ecclesiae selecta* (Nuremberg, 1553). Although compiled in the north of Germany and published in the south, in a sense it carried the Wittenberg imprimatur, since Luther's colleague and successor, Philipp Melanchthon, wrote the preface.[14] Furthermore, Rhau's relatives, who took over the publishing house after his death, reissued the work in Wittenberg in 1561 and at least four more editions followed before the end of the century. Another Wittenberg publisher, Lorentz Schwenck, brought out a further extensive collection of liturgical monody, Johannes Keuchenthal's *Kirchen Gesenge latinisch und deudsch, sampt allen Euangelien Episteln, und Collecten auff die Sontage und Feste nach der Ordnung der Zeit durchs gantze Jahr* (1573).

The liturgical experience that developed in the Wittenberg churches, under the initial leadership of Luther himself, was rich and varied, a combination of Latin and German, traditional monody and contemporary polyphony, the music of Catholic as well as Lutheran composers, choral and organ music, all held together by the common thread of congregational hymnody. It was a liturgical-musical experience shared by other Lutheran towns and cities in which the common tradition was extended. One such city was Leipzig in the other part of Saxony, with its old, established university which had been Duke Frederick the Wise's model when he founded his university in Wittenberg at the beginning of the sixteenth century. Leipzig already had a notable Catholic tradition of liturgical music which was taken over and modified to become the distinctive Lutheran musical tradition that culminated in the Kantorate of Johann Sebastian Bach in the eighteenth century.

LEIPZIG

Leipzig was a medieval walled city situated at the confluence of the Pleisse and Parthe rivers, already famous as much for its annual fairs as its university. There were two principal churches within the city walls, the Nicolaikirche and Thomaskirche. To sustain their liturgical music each church had a school with a Kantorei made up of boys' voices. At the beginning of the sixteenth century the Kantorei of the Thomaskirche already had 300 years of tradition behind it. As with the churches in other centres of trade and commerce at this time, the repertory of polyphonic liturgical music in the Leipzig churches reflected the work of the leading composers the Flemish masters Josquin Desprez, Obrecht and Isaac, and such regional composers as Senfl, Finck, Hofheimer as well as, for example, the local composer Nikolaus Apel, a Leipzig student at the beginning of the sixteenth century and later professor of theology at the university. As elsewhere, the polyphony was a supplement to the traditional liturgical plainchant on which it was based, as is demonstrated by the important fourteenth-century manuscript *Graduale* in the Thomaskirche library.[15]

In the summer of 1518 a new Kantor was appointed to the Thomas-kirche and Thomasschule, Georg Rhau from Wittenberg, who had already distinguished himself by the publication of a treatise on music theory relating to plainchant, *Enchiridion utriusque musicae practicae* (Wittenberg, 1517); while in Leipzig he would issue a second part, *Enchiridion musicae mensuralis* (1520). Within weeks of his arrival in the city, on the strength of his 1517 publication, Rhau was appointed to the faculty of the university to teach music theory. He was obviously recognized as an accomplished musician.

At the end of June the following year, 1519, there was an important theological debate which took place in the Pleissenburg, a fortification built into the walls of the city not far from the Thomaskirche. It concerned the indulgence debate which had been stirred up by Luther – though he was not one of the official participants. The disputation was between Johann Eck of the University of Ingoldstadt, representing traditional Catholicism, and Andreas Carlstadt, Luther's older colleague in Wittenberg. Luther, however, was present and preached in the castle chapel during the proceedings (since he was forbidden to preach openly in parish churches), and inevitably he was drawn into the debate with Eck, since it was principally his views rather than those of Carlstadt which were in dispute. On the day of the opening of the disputation, 27 June 1519, Mass was celebrated in the Thomaskirche with Rhau directing the Thomanerchor in a twelve-voice polyphonic mass he had composed, *Missa de sancto spirito*. Later in the day, in the Pleissenburg, the disputation itself was begun with Rhau directing the Kantorei again, accompanied by the *Stadtpfeifern* (town trumpeters) in the singing of *Veni sancte spiritus*, and concluded with the same ensemble rendering the *Te Deum laudamus*, which made a distinct impression on all present.[16] It seems likely that Rhau sympathized with Luther's position; after all he had been in Wittenberg when the whole matter came to a head towards the end of 1517. Rhau remained in Leipzig for only about a year following the disputation. In 1520 he left the prestigious position in Leipzig – probably because of the hostility shown towards any who sympathized with Luther – and became a teacher in Eisleben, then in Hildburghausen, before returning to Wittenberg in 1523.

The ruler of Albertine Saxony, Duke Georg, present at the Leipzig disputation, was adamantly opposed to everything that Luther stood for. Reformation doctrines and practices were therefore officially banned from his part of Saxony. But this general prohibition did not discourage a Leipzig printer, Michael Blum, from publishing a Lutheran hymnal, *Enchiridion geistlicher gesenge und Psalmen fur die leien* (1530), clearly modelled on the Wittenberg collections. While Duke Georg was still alive, however, there could be no moves in a Lutheran direction. But following his death early in 1536, plans were made for the Reformation to be introduced officially into the churches of the city and area, as well as into the university. It took three years to make the necessary preparations, which had the full support of the new Elector, Duke Heinrich. Luther, who was accompanied by many of his Wittenberg colleagues, preached in the over-full Thomaskirche on the feast of Pentecost, 24 May 1539. The order of service followed the newly drawn-up directory of worship for Albertine Saxony, *Agenda, das ist Kirchenordnung* (Leipzig, 1539), which was republished in an expanded form the following year. The liturgical provisions closely follow the practices of Wittenberg in general and Luther's two liturgies in particular. All the bells of the city churches were rung to announce the first Lutheran Mass, at which the *Graduallied* was *Komm heiliger Geist, Herre Gott*. At the afternoon Vespers service, when Johann Bugenhagen preached, the Pentecost hymn *Nun bitten wir den Heiligen Geist* was sung following the sermon.[17] These hymns were presumably sung from the new hymnal published by Valentin Schumann, following the Wittenberg model, *Geistliche Lieder auffs new gebessert und gemehrt zu Wittenberg* (Leipzig, 1539).

The first Lutheran Kantor of the Thomaskirche and Thomasschule was Johann Brückner, appointed in 1540, but he only stayed for about a year. He was succeeded by Ulrich Lange, a former student in Leipzig who was the Kantor until 1549. During these years it is known that polyphonic masses by Josquin Desprez, Obrecht and Isaac, among others, continued to be sung, together with settings found, for example, in the publications of Vesper music published by Rhau in Wittenberg. Also during Lange's Kantorate the publication of the Wittenberg hymnal was transferred from Klug in Wittenberg to Valentin Bapst in Leipzig: *Geystliche Lieder . . . [und] Psalmen . . .* (Leipzig, 1545), with a new preface written by Luther. Bapst issued a further six editions by 1567 – in addition to numerous hymnals published by a variety of other Leipzig printers.

Lange was followed by Wolfgang Figulus, another graduate of Leipzig University and a noted composer and editor of various collections of church music, the first being his three-volume *Precationes aliquot musicis* (Leipzig, 1553). During the next Kantorate, that of Melchior Heger, 1553–64, a manuscript collection of 243 polyphonic works was compiled. It contains masses, introits, motets and chorale settings, and bears the date 1558. Among the composers are Clemens non Papa, Dietrich, Figulus, Finck, Isaac, Josquin Desprez, Obrecht, Othmayr, Resinarius, Senfl, Stoltzer and Walter.[18] The conservative nature of the Leipzig repertory is confirmed by the inventory of the Thomaskirche music library, drawn up in 1564 by the new Kantor, Valentin Otto.[19] Although some printed works are listed, the library was mostly made up of handwritten partbooks assembled by Otto's two predecessors during the previous quarter of a century.

During Otto's long Kantorate two very important publications appeared, both compiled by colleagues in the Thomaskirche. The organist Elias Nikolaus Ammerbach issued his *Orgel oder Instrument Tabulaturbuch* in 1571, a collection of pieces which generations of organ teachers used with their pupils, including Johann Sebastian Bach who owned at least three different copies. This anthology of keyboard pieces includes a few settings of chorale melodies which are keyboard transcriptions of polyphonic choral models, among them examples from three successive Kapellmeisters to the Dresden court, Johann Walter, Matthaeus Le Maistre and Anthonius Scandellus. Four are chorale settings by Walter and Le Maistre, two from each, which first appeared in the partbooks published by Rhau in Wittenberg in 1551 and 1556 respectively.[20] The pastor of the Thomaskirche and superintendent of the Leipzig churches was Nikolaus Selneccer, one of the theological architects of Lutheran confessionalism and a hymn writer of note. In 1587 he issued his *Christliche Psalmen, Lieder und Kirchengesänge*, an anthology of liturgical monodic chant, similar to the collections of Lossius and Keuchenthal, but arranged according to genre rather than to the church year.

Otto was succeeded in 1594 by Seth Calvisius, a polymath who was expert in history, astronomy and education, as well as in music. He was a composer and one of the most important music theorists of his day. In addition to other works, Calvisius composed 115 four-part settings of Latin and German hymns, with the melodies in the upper voice rather than in the tenor, which had been the usual practice; these were published as *Harmonia cantionum ecclesiasticarum* (Leipzig, 1597) and went through a further four editions before being replaced by Schein's *Cantional oder Gesangbuch Augspurgischer Confession* (Leipzig, 1627). The settings are in a basically homophonic style which has its origin in the simpler settings found in Walter's *Chorgesangbuch* of 1524. With this collection of Calvisius, together with those of Lucas Osiander, Rogier Michael and others, published elsewhere in the last quarter of the sixteenth century, the 'cantional' style of harmonized congregational hymnody was established; and it remained unchanged from the collections of Vulpius, Hassler and Praetorius at the beginning of the seventeenth century, to that of Vopelius, the *Neu Leipziger Gesangbuch* of 1682, which was still in use in Bach's day – and even later. Calvisius established the Thomaskantorate as a position of influence and authority in Lutheran Germany and thereby ensured the impressive sequence of successors throughout the seventeenth and eighteenth centuries: Johann Hermann Schein, Tobias Michael, Sebastian Knüpfer, Johann Schelle, Johann Kuhnau and Johann Sebastian Bach.

In northern Germany the Reformation was fostered particularly in university cities, but in the south it was free imperial cities, such as Nuremberg and Augsburg, that were the centres of reform. Since the music of Nuremberg is discussed later in this book (see p.286) we shall turn our attention to Augsburg.

AUGSBURG

Augsburg is a Roman foundation, its name being derived from the Roman Emperor, Augustus Caesar. Unlike Wittenberg and Leipzig, Augsburg was a Reichstadt, a free imperial city, and was therefore not subject to the rule of one of the many German princes but was governed by its own magistracy. Like other imperial cities, such as Worms and Nuremberg, Augsburg from time to time hosted the Reichstag, or Diet, the parliament of imperial Germany which met under the presidency of the German emperor – Maximilian I at the beginning of the sixteenth century. The combination of freedom and imperial responsibility gave a certain prestige to the city, attracting both commerce and culture. In the arena of commerce Augsburg held a position of leadership because the banking house of Fugger was based in the city. It was the Fuggers who lent a substantial sum to Pope Leo X for the rebuilding of St Peter's in Rome, a transaction which led to the promulgation of a papal indulgence in order to repay the loan, and this in turn led to Luther's protest against what he saw as commercialization of the Gospel. The prosperity which commerce brought to the city enabled the arts in general, and music in particular, to be supported and encouraged. Like Nuremberg, Augsburg attracted such artists as Lucas Cranach and Albrecht Dürer as well as many leading musicians and composers. By the middle of the fifteenth century the Meistersinger had become a significant group in the city and the Augsburg Meistersingerschule predates that of Nuremberg.

Emperor Maximilian I made almost annual visits to Augsburg and when he did so he brought with him the musicians of his Hofkapelle. At the turn of the century the court composer was Heinrich Isaac; he was succeeded in 1514 by Ludwig Senfl, who had sung as a boy under Isaac; and the court organist for many years was Paul Hofhaimer – three leading composers who were to leave their mark not only on Catholic but also on Lutheran church music. The musicians of Maximilian's Hofkapelle performed frequently in the Annakirche, the church of the Carmelite cloister. Jakob and Ulrich Fugger had arranged for the church to be enlarged by the addition of a chapel, with altar and choir stalls, which they intended to use for their burial place. A fine organ was built in 1512 and after the consecration of the chapel in 1518 Hofhaimer became the Fugger organist. The Fuggers also endowed other Augsburg churches, subsidized their musicians and funded valuable collections of music and instruments.

In the same year, 1518, the Diet met in Augsburg and Luther was called to appear before the pope's representative in order to be persuaded to recant his views. Many prominent people in Augsburg received Luther as a hero, and when he refused to deny the doctrine of justification by faith and instead eloquently defended it, the esteem in

63. *Maximilian I attends Mass in his chapel at Augsburg: woodcut (c1518) by Hans Weiditz (the organist is thought to be Paul Hofhaimer)*

which he was held in the city grew even greater. The centre of this support for Luther was located in the Carmelite cloister of St Anna. Johann Frosch, a friend and supporter of Luther, had been appointed prior in 1517. Thus when Luther was called to Augsburg in 1518, Frosch and monks acted as hosts and also secured his safe departure from the city after the Diet. Following years of intense debate, the Annakirche formally adopted Lutheran doctrines and practice in 1525 when most of the brothers of the cloister renounced their vows and Frosch celebrated the Eucharist for the first time following the practice established in Wittenberg. The next year, 1526, an Augsburg imprint of Luther's *Deutsche Messe* was published within weeks of the original Wittenberg publication. Thereafter Augsburg was second only to Wittenberg for the dissemination of Lutheran views. Publishers in the city brought out editions of Luther's writings, including collections of the Wittenberg hymns, which had begun in 1523 with Augsburg imprints of Wittenberg broadsheet hymns.

Luther was again the centre of attention in Augsburg at the Diet of 1530. It was too dangerous for the reformer to appear in person in the city so he stayed nearby in Castle Coburg. During this time Luther wrote his famous letter to Ludwig Senfl (part of which is quoted on p.265). The definitive doctrinal statement of the emerging Lutheran Church, later known as the Augsburg Confession, was presented at the Diet. The Annakirche continued to be the focus of Lutheran reform in the city and in the year following the presentation of the Augsburg Confession, a Gymnasium (Latin school) was established with music being a principal subject in the curriculum. This emphasis on music must have been at the instigation of Frosch, since the very next year he published a music treatise, *Rerum musicarum opusculum rarum ac insigne* (Strasbourg, 1532). In 1540 an important set of partbooks was issued, Johann Kugelmann's *Concentus novi*, which, even though it was commissioned by Duke Albrecht of Prussia, was probably used in the Annaschule, since most of the settings were in three parts, a characteristic of school music at the time. It is a varied collection of 39 settings of Latin and German liturgical prose and German hymns (some of whose melodies appear here for the first time) with an appendix of further settings, in four to eight voices. Most of the compositions are by Kugelmann and Stoltzer, together with some by lesser-known and anonymous composers. The musical leadership of the Annakirche and Annaschule throughout these years was in the hands of a succession of musicians, sufficiently competent to develop a rivalry between the music courses offered in their own Lutheran school and that of the Salvatorschule, a Jesuit institution in Augsburg. The competition continued even after the Peace established by the Diet of Augsburg in 1555, which sought to establish a measure of mutual toleration between Catholics and Protestants of the German states and free imperial cities.

In 1581 a new Kantor was appointed to the church and school of St Anna, Adam Gumpelzhaimer, who remained in the position until his death in 1625. For his pupils in the school Gumpelzhaimer compiled what proved to be a very influential manual of music theory, *Compendium musicae* (1591). During the next 90 years fourteen further editions and reprints were issued. The particular value of this bilingual work, the Latin and German texts being given in parallel columns, is the selection of musical examples which make up two-thirds of the book. Many of the examples were composed by Gumpelzhaimer himself and most of the part-writing allowed for the different parts to be sung by voices of equal range, a significant pedagogical aid. Among his published compositions were volumes of settings of German and Latin texts – *Neue teutsche geistliche Lieder* (1591 and 1594), the first in three voices and the second in four and five voices, and *Sacrorum concentuum* (1601 and 1614), both in eight voices.

Gumpelzhaimer initiated a significant reorganization of the Augsburg Annakantorei in 1596 and assembled a significant music library for practical and theoretical use in the church and school. In 1620 he began to compile a handwritten inventory of all the printed books and manuscripts in the library. It is an impressive listing that demonstrates the richness of musical performance in the liturgy of the Annakirche and in the education offered in the Annaschule. Catholic composers appear side by side with Lutherans, among them Calvisius, Eccard, Ferrabosco, Andreas and Giovanni Gabrieli, Gumpelzhaimer, Lassus, Monteverdi, Palestrina, Victoria and Walter.[21]

The inventory also reveals that Gumpelzhaimer had arranged for virtually all the collections of music composed and compiled by Michael Praetorius to be purchased for the library, the *Musae Sioniae* and other titles of Latin and German masses, motets, litanies, chorale settings and other liturgical pieces – sixteen volumes in all. Praetorius was Kapellmeister to the Duke of Brunswick-Wolfenbüttel who maintained close ties with Wittenberg. Through these important publications Praetorius assumed the mantle of Rhau as the editor, composer and publisher of choral liturgical music for Lutheran Germany. These collections display all the variety of Lutheran church music as it had developed from the roots established by Luther and Walter. For example, the year before Gumpelzhaimer began his inventory of the Annakirche music library Praetorius issued his *Polyhymnia caduceatrix et panegyrica* (Wolfenbüttel, 1619), a collection of compositions based on Lutheran hymns.

Number 30 is *Vater unser im Himmelreich*, scored for six vocal soloists, four-part choir and ripieno chorus of boy sopranos, and accompanied by contrasting groups of four-part strings and four-part trombones, with continuo comprising organ, bass viol and bassoon.[22] The text is the nine-stanza versification of the Lord's Prayer by Luther – third in the sequence of Luther's catechism hymns – which first appeared in the Schumann *Geistliche Lieder* (Leipzig, 1539). By this time the hymn had become the accepted *Graduallied* for Rogate, the Fifth Sunday after Easter, although it was also sung on other Sundays, especially at Vespers when it was customary to teach the catechism. Praetorius called it 'very long, and . . . a half-hour work'.[23] Should the whole composition be thought too long for performance as the *Graduallied* for the day, the composer makes the suggestion that it could be performed in its individual parts and gives the following specific example:[24]

EPISTLE

Vater unser im Himmelreich, part 1
  Sinfonia – instrumental
  stanza 1: duet for two sopranos, accompanied by trombones and continuo
  stanza 2: tenor solo, accompanied by strings and continuo
  Ritornello 1 = stanza 9 for full instrumental, vocal and choral resources

GOSPEL

Vater unser im Himmelreich, parts 2 and 3
  stanza 3: duet for alto accompanied by strings and soprano accompanied by trombones, with continuo
  stanza 4: sextet of solo voices, accompanied by continuo, reinforced by bass trombone and additional bass viol
  stanzas 5 and 6: sextet of solo voices, accompanied by both instrumental groups with continuo
Ritornello 1 repeated

CREED – either chanted in Latin or sung as a congregational hymn in Luther's metrical version: *Wir glauben all' an einen Gott*

PULPIT HYMN – for example, *Herr Jesu Christ, dich zu uns wend*

SERMON

Vater unser im Himmelreich, part 4
  Sinfonia – instrumental
  stanza 7: sextet of solo voices, accompanied by two violins and continuo, reinforced by additional bass viol
  stanza 8: vocal trio, with ripieno chorus of three boy sopranos singing the chorale melody, accompanied by both groups of instruments 'in echo', with continuo
  Ritornello 2 = stanza 9 for full instrumental, vocal and choral resources

Then would follow the remainder of the Lutheran, evangelical Mass, which would have begun with an introit, either plainchant or polyphony, and the Kyrie and Gloria, either sung in Latin plainchant, or polyphony, and/or as German congregational hymns; more congregational hymns, organ playing and choral singing would have concluded.

Such patterns of choral and vocal music, combined with both liturgical monody and congregational hymnody, become the common practice as an ever-widening circle of composers produced and performed liturgical music for the Lutheran liturgy. Thus the distinctive Lutheran tradition of church music was firmly established by the end of the sixteenth century. It was a practical expression of Luther's thinking: a rich and varied combination of the sounds of theology and music within the context of worship.

NOTES

[1] See C. Schalk, *Luther on Music: Paradigms of Praise* (St Louis, 1988)
[2] *Luther's Works*, ed. J. Pelikan and H. T. Lehmann (St Louis and Philadelphia, 1955–86), xlix, 427–9.
[3] *D. Martin Luthers Werke: kritische Gesamtausgabe* (Weimar, 1883–1983), *Tischreden* no.1258.
[4] *Luther's Works*, liii, 19–40.
[5] ibid, 23.
[6] ibid, 36.
[7] ibid, 316.
[8] 'Chorale' from 'choraliter', meaning unison singing, a term used hitherto for the singing of unaccompanied monodic plainchant.
[9] *Luther's Works*, liii, 61–90.
[10] ibid, 62–3.
[11] See A. Boës, 'Die reformatorischen Gottesdienste in der Wittenberg Pfarrkirche von 1523 an. III Teil', *Jb für Liturgik und Hymnologie*, vi (1961), 56–61.
[12] R. F. von Liliencron, *Liturgisch-musikalische Geschichte der evangelischen Gottesdienste von 1523 bis 1700* (Schleswig, 1893), 18.
[13] W. Herbst, *Quellen zur Geschichte des evangelischen Gottesdienstes von der Reformation bis zur Gegenwart* (Göttingen, 1968), 71 and 74.
[14] See W. Merten, 'Die "Psalmodia" des Lucas Lossius', *Jb für Liturgik und Hymnologie*, xix (1975), 4–5.
[15] See P. Wagner, *Das Graduale der St. Thomaskirche zu Leipzig* (Leipzig, 1930).
[16] V. H. Mattfield, 'Rhau, Georg', *Grove 6*.
[17] R. Wustmann, *Musikgeschichte Leipzigs*, i: *Bis zur Mitte des 17. Jahrhunderts* (Leipzig and Berlin, 1909, rev.2/1926), 54.
[18] See *Selected Introits from Leipzig 49/50 (1558)*, ed. L. Youens, RRMR, lix (1984).
[19] Wustmann, *Musikgeschichte Leipzigs*, 111–12.
[20] See R.A. Leaver, 'Bach, Hymns and Hymnbooks', *The Hymn*, xxxvi/4 (1985), 9.
[21] See L. E. Cuyler, 'Musical Activity in Augsburg and its Annakirche, ca. 1470–1630', in *Cantors at the Crossroads: Essays on Church Music in Honor of Walter E. Buszin* (St Louis, 1967), 33–43; and R. Schaal, *Das Inventar der Kantorei St. Anna in Augsburg: ein Beitrag zur protestantischen Musikpflege im 16. un beginnenden 17. Jahrhundert* (Kassel, 1965). The inventory should be compared with the similar contemporary repertory in Nuremberg; see W. H. Rubsamen, 'The International "Catholic" Repertoire of a Lutheran Church in Nürnberg (1574–1597)', *AnnM*, v (1957) 229–327.
[22] See further, H. E. Samuel, 'Michael Praetorius on the Concertato Style', in *Cantors at the Crossroads*, 95–109.
[23] *Gesamtausgabe der musikalischen Werke von Michael Praetorius*, ed. W. Gurlitt, xvii/2 (Wolfenbüttel, 1933), 433.
[24] ibid.

BIBLIOGRAPHICAL NOTE

The Lutheran Reformation

The literature on the Reformation in general, and the Lutheran reform in particular, is enormous and continually growing. Up-to-date literature, in various languages including English, can be discovered in the extensive bibliography which appears each year in the *Luther-Jahrbuch*. Probably the most accessible general account of the Reformation of the sixteenth century is H. J. Grimm, *The Reformation Era* (New York and London, 2/1973), valuable for is conciseness. The equivalent for the German Reformation from the beginnings to the Peace of Augsburg is F. Lau and E. Bizer, *A History of the Reformation in Germany to 1555*, trans. B. A. Hardy (London 1969). For studies more closely related to Luther's life and activities the classic interpretation of R. H. Bainton, *Here I Stand: the Life of Martin Luther* (New York and Evanston, 1963), remains unrivalled. For more extensive accounts of the events surrounding the reformer's life during the formative years until the presentation of the Augsburg Confession, see M. Brecht, *Martin Luther: his Road to Reformation, 1483–1521*, trans. J. L. Schaaf (Philadelphia, 1985), and H. Bornkamm, *Luther in Mid-Career, 1521–1530*, trans. E. T. Bachmann (Philadelphia, 1983).

Luther, music and the arts

As with Reformation and Luther studies in general, up-to-date information on literature dealing with the reformer's attitude towards and influence upon music can be found in the annual bibliography in the *Luther-Jahrbuch*, especially section B.2.k., 'Gottesdienst, Gebet, Kirchenlied', which is not restricted to Luther alone but broadly covers the church music and hymnody of the period. The following studies are basic: W. E. Buszin, 'Luther on Music', *MQ*, xxxii (1946), 80–97, in effect an abbreviated translation of K. Anton, *Luther und die Musik* (Zwickau, 1916, 3/1928); P. Nettle, *Luther and Music* (Philadelphia, 1948); R. M. Stevenson, 'Luther's Musical Achievement', in the author's *Patterns of Protestant Church Music* (Durham, North Carolina, 1953), 3–12; and C. Schalk, *Luther on Music: Paradigms of Praise* (St Louis, 1988). Luther's theology had wider implications than for music alone: see the brief survey by J. W. Cook, 'Picturing Theology: Martin Luther and Lucas Cranach', in *Art and Religion: Faith, Form and Reform: 1984 Paine Lectures in Religion, University of Missouri-Columbia*, ed. J. Brown (Columbia, 1986); the more extensive study by C. C. Christiansen, *Art and the Reformation in Germany* (Athens, Ohio, 1979); and the composite volume, *Luther and Culture*, Martin Luther Lectures, iv (Decorah, 1960).

Lutheran musicians and their music

For information on individual composers and specific cities mentioned in this chapter, standard reference works such as *MGG* and *Grove 6* should be consulted. In the latter the article on Luther and Lutheranism by R. A. Leaver and A. Bond is a suitable starting-point. In connection with Leipzig, the following two titles are useful, though somewhat brief: R. Petzoldt, *The Leipzig Thomaner Chor* (Leipzig, 1962), and P. M. Young, 'The Musical Tradition of the School and Church of St. Thomas', *American Choral Review*, xxiii/3 (1981), 4–50. Collected editions of the works of specific composers should also be investigated, especially the following which have introductory and editorial material translated into English: *Georg Rhau: Musikdrucke aus den Jahren 1538 bis 1545 in praktischer Neuausgabe*, ed. H. Albrecht (Kassel and St Louis, 1955–80), and *Johann Walter Sämtliche Werke*, ed. O. Schröder (Kassel and St Louis, 1953–73).

A brief survey of the Lutheran music of the period can be found in G. Reese, *Music in the Renaissance* (New York, 1954, 2/1959), 673–713, and a more detailed account in F. Blume and others, *Protestant Church Music: a History* (New York, 1974), a translation and expansion of the second edition of the seminal German work, *Geschichte der evangelische Kirchenmusik* (Kassel, 1965). A wider context is explored in J. W. Barker, 'Sociological Influences upon the Emergence of Lutheran Music', *MMA*, iv (1969), 157–98. Specific musical, liturgical and hymnological aspects are investigated in J. Riedel, *The Lutheran Chorale: its Basic Traditions* (Minneapolis, 1967); R. A. Leaver, *The Liturgy and Music: a Study of the Use of the Hymn in Two Liturgical Traditions* (Bramcote, Notts., 1976); and Leaver, 'Lutheran Vespers as a Context for Music', in *Church, Stage, and Studio: Music and its Contexts in Seventeenth-Century Germany*, ed. P. Walker (Ann Arbor, 1989). Specific forms of Lutheran church music are discussed in A. Kirwan-Mott's *The Small-Scale Sacred Concertato in the Early Seventeenth Century* (Ann Arbor, 1981) and H. E. Smither's *A History of the Oratorio*, ii: *The Oratorio in the Baroque Era: Protestant Germany and England* (Chapel Hill, 1977), especially pt.1, 'Protestant Germany: the Seventeenth-Century Antecedents and Origins', which focusses on the emergence of the distinctive Lutheran tradition of extended liturgical choral works for major feasts, such as Christmas and Easter, notably the Passion, for which the classic study is B. Smallman's *The Background of Passion Music: J. S. Bach and his Predecessors* (London, 1957; rev., enlarged 2/1970).

Chapter XI

16th-Century Nuremberg

SUSAN GATTUSO

In spite of having a castle, Nuremberg has never been a princely residence. From the early fifteenth century the city was under the firm control of a Council that continued to amass land, wealth and power. The Council laid down firm regulations on hygiene, trade, craft and behaviour which divided the city into the patricians (those with wealth and property) and the artisans (common working men). By the early sixteenth century the Council was patron of the two parish churches and managed the income and expenditure of all churches and cloisters in the city. Its rule was by then absolute and the city was in a strong economic and political position; it had a large hinterland and had become a trade centre, famous for leather, metal and textile industries, for the publishing of books and music and for the manufacture of astronomical, nautical and musical instruments. By the Reformation Nuremberg was one of the most populous cities in Germany.

The sixteenth century was dominated by the Reformation, and the people of Nuremberg adopted the new religion early and with little dissent. Since church livings were in the hands of the Council, many of whose members had studied at Wittenberg with Luther and Melanchthon, Lutheran preachers had been invited to give sermons in the city since 1516. Protestant doctrine fitted neatly into the philosophy of the Council whose many laws were intended to lead citizens to self-discipline and respect for authority. However, as the century progressed Nuremberg found itself increasingly embroiled in political and religious skirmishes as it attempted to appease the Protestant population while remaining loyal to a Catholic empire to which it had always felt deeply committed. The city amassed considerable debts and no sooner were these settled than it was devastated by plague and religious wars. Prosperity was shattered. By the end of the Thirty Years War Nuremberg had debts of over two million gulden and had lost up to half of its rural population. The city swarmed with refugees. Strict hygiene regulations, on which the city had prided itself for so long, were disregarded and sickness was rife. Demands from the Empire continued, making it impossible for the city to reach the economic self-sufficiency it had previously attained. Nuremberg was never to regain the prestige and stability it had enjoyed during the sixteenth century.

Nuremberg was governed by patricians. Of nine social classes and sub-classes in the city, three (a total of 42 families) were patrician and eligible to hold office in the Small Council. All the power of the Council was invested in this assembly of 34 patricians and eight artisans. The eight artisans represented only the crafts of the cloth makers, tanners, brewers, edging makers, butchers, tailors and metal workers, and were not allowed to vote. A further 300–400 families were eligible for membership in the Great Council of 200 men. They also had no vote but served merely to ratify the decisions made by the Small Council. Below this top stratum of society was the bourgeoisie – the prosperous craft masters and the small merchants. The next level belonged to the workers, to the poorer masters and to journeymen. Still lower down the social scale were those forced to apply to the city for financial assistance. These men were usually wage earners, often with no franchise. Below them were the chronically sick, the unemployed, the homeless and the beggars. The lowest level was made up of prostitutes, grave diggers and the criminal classes. The Council regulated every detail of each citizen's life, from the cost of a bridegroom's wedding gift for his bride to the everyday clothing permitted to each class.

The artisan's day ran from sunrise to sunset. Inns closed at sunset and a curfew was imposed two hours later. Recreation was limited to Sundays, either between or after church services. Civic duties also occupied leisure time. Each district was divided into small sections, the inhabitants of which bore the responsibility for protecting their area from fire, vandalism and attack. The Council encouraged and regulated such activities as crossbow archery as part of civil defence.

The loss of financial control brought about by wars and civil disorders gave rise to crippling inflation and wages varied greatly. In 1623 a labourer working in the construction industry earned about 17 kreuzer a day, a journeyman 25 kreuzer and a master 27 kreuzer. A journeyman stretching cloth earned 22 kreuzer for a thirteen-hour day (about 100 gulden a year), but a fustian weaver's journeyman earned only 2½ kreuzer (10 gulden a year). A teacher and a doctor earned about 60 gulden a year whereas an adviser to the Council could command a yearly income of 500 gulden. Wages increased during the century but prices were always ahead of them.[1] The gulf between artisan and patrician was wide; the former could enjoy a reasonable education and a good craft training but spent most of his life and income maintaining his family. The patrician, however, had surplus wealth for culture and entertainment.

THE PATRICIAN MUSICAL SOCIETIES

In the sixteenth century societies and academies were founded all over Europe to promulgate theories, pursue interests and provide a meeting-place for like-minded enthusiasts. Musical societies became increasingly popular. In Nuremberg music remained largely under the control of the Council, who engaged musicians for all the churches. These men were instrumentalists, composers, choir directors, singers and teachers, and their task was primarily to produce suitable music for church services and schools. Apart from folksongs and work-songs, the only other public outlet for music was the town band which played for festivals, celebrations and processions. All other music was heard at private functions. It was to provide an alternative to such musical occasions that musical societies began to be formed among the patricians and men of high social standing. A good musical education was considered necessary for the sons of these families and a considerable amount of money was paid to secure it. In 1568 a clavichord cost about two gulden and teachers charged one gulden a month for lessons. Diaries show that the men of patrician families came together to play music, some on a regular basis. Such gatherings were known as *Krenzlein*, or 'circles', and were completely amateur and informal. Some were founded as musical

64. *The Nuremberg town band (Stadtpfeiferei) announcing the New Year: pen and ink drawing, with wash, by an unknown sixteenth-century artist*

societies with rules and minutes, others gradually came to assume this form.

The earliest formal *Krenzleinsgesellschaft* for which records still exist was founded in 1568 at the home of Niclas Nützel.[2] The aim of the society was to rehearse instrumental and vocal music of an uplifting nature. Meetings were held every two weeks on a Wednesday, from midday to five o'clock. Instruments and music were paid for by dues of one gulden. A meal of cheese, bread and fruit was served and everyone paid about half a kreuzer for a measure of wine. The members took it in turn to host the meeting and people arriving late or not attending at all were fined. The membership was fixed at thirteen men, and if one resigned or died another took his place. During the seventeen years of its existence there was a total of 22 members. Although only one member, Niclas Nützel, was a patrician, the rest were all from good families; six served on the City Council. It can be seen from table XI.1 that it was primarily a society of educated and professional men. Most of them had studied under Melanchthon at Wittenberg and the society was reputed to be a meeting-place for Calvinists. No mention is made

Table XI.1 PROFESSIONS OF MEMBERS OF THE 1568 MUSICAL SOCIETY

Education (school and university)	5
Preacher	5
Lawyer	3
Doctor	3
Council official	2
Musician (Johann Hayden)	1
Businessman	1
Goldsmith (poet and member of the Small Council)	1
Unknown	1

in the records of the music enjoyed at meetings and it is possible that discussion played as great a part as music. No entries were made after 1585 so it may be assumed that the society did not survive the plague of that year.

In the 1570s two musical societies existed.[3] In 1572 Ivo de Vento, who was either visiting or working in the city at the time, dedicated a book of four-part songs to the members of a society of Council members. Niclas Nützel was one of two men who belonged to both the 1568 society and this group. There were sixteen members altogether; their professions are listed in table XI.2. No rules or records of the society survive, and it probably existed only informally.

Five years later de Vento's pupil Leonhard Lechner, working in Nuremberg from 1575 to 1584, dedicated a book of partsongs to seven young men of high social standing. They were bachelors in their early twenties or thirties who had not yet chosen a profession and three were

Table XI.2 PROFESSIONS OF MEMBERS OF THE 1572 MUSICAL SOCIETY

Council official	7
Businessman	2
Education	1
Lawyer	1
Unknown (Great Council)	3
Unknown (Small Council)	2

patricians (two from the Nützel family). The aim of the society was to stimulate their interest in singing. The group met under Lechner's direction to rehearse and learn so that they could find pleasure in music. No records or rules survive – if indeed any existed.

In 1588 Hans Nützel and two members of the Lechner society joined a society interested predominantly in Italian music.[4] The society was disbanded in 1602 but was revived again in 1626 when it ran for three years. The membership in each case was kept to eleven; in all, 27 men from 21 families were members. Of these families, eleven were patricians and ten belonged to the next social class. Again the members were mostly bachelors or young married men who were highly educated and had travelled widely; details of their professions have not survived. Paul Behaim, a prime mover of the 1588 society, had travelled to Leipzig, Padua and Verona, where he had met a group of the most distinguished people to practise the lute, keyboard instruments, singing and the viol. Erckenbrecht Koler also studied in Verona and had belonged to a musical group there. The Italian influence is also revealed by visitors to the Nuremberg society. In 1594 there were visitors from Venice, and in 1597 Giovanni Gabrieli and Gregorio Aichinger appear to have been present at a meeting.

This society differed from previous ones in that musicians were commissioned, though their works were not the only ones performed. Four musicians were engaged by the 1588 society: Friedrich Lindtner, Caspar Hassler, Jacob von der Hoewe and Martin Paumann, the two last being members of the town band. The 1626 society engaged Johann Staden, one of Nuremberg's most illustrious musicians, his son Sigmund Theo Staden, Hieronymus Lang and Mathias Cuntz. However, none of the works commissioned for the societies has survived. Only on seven occasions is mention made of the music enjoyed (see table XI.3). The society was bound by complicated rules. Meetings were held monthly, in private houses or gardens between 12.30 p.m. and 9 p.m. on a Sunday. A meal formed an important part of the proceedings and wine was passed in the society's engraved goblet. Drunkenness was rife and fines of one gulden were levied as a penalty for being intoxicated. The meetings were hosted by the members in turn. A membership fee of one gulden was charged and members paid

Table XI.3 MUSIC PERFORMED AT THE 1588/1626 SOCIETY

1589	fiddle with two soloists
1590	genteel dancing
1595	voice with instruments
1626	poem in honour of Orpheus
1628	songs of prayer and repentance
1628	lute music
1628	songs of the Passion

six kreuzer at each meeting.

In some respects the 1568 and the 1588/1626 musical societies were similar. Both limited membership, keeping the society exclusive; detailed financial records were kept by allotted members and were inspected regularly; refreshment was included in the proceedings; membership dues of one gulden were charged and fines were levied. The societies differed, however, in the emphasis they placed on behaviour. The 1568 society forbade gaming, arguing and swearing; its members were all intellectuals at odds with mainstream religious doctrines and probably spent much time in heated debate learnt at university. The 1588/1626 society had many young men as members and

65. Frontispiece to the records of the 1588 musical society

66. *Detail of a spinet lid painted in 1619 by Friedrich von Falckenberg (seen to the extreme right, holding a palette); also identifiable are Johann Staden (playing the claviorgan), to his left Lucas Friedrich Behaim (bass viol), and also on the extreme right the organ builder Stephen Cuntz (with an organ pipe) and instrument maker Paul Wissmaier (with a tuning hammer) — the other three players are probably relatives of Behaim, and may have become members of the 1626 society*

the enjoyment of good food was part of their meeting.

The education of artisans was generally good for the period; they mostly attended church schools which were under the guidance of the Council and where music would have been a subject of some importance on the syllabus. Even if artisans were more inclined to watching comedy and listening to ribald (if moralizing) poems and songs as typified in the *Fasnachtspiel* and broadsheet, music was nevertheless a part of their lives and musical societies did exist. In 1551 Michael Baier, himself an artisan, organized a society of goldsmiths, engravers, casters, writers, students, book-keepers and printers.[5] Early on Sunday mornings the group would walk, play the lute and sing, and twice a week it would meet at an inn to sing, play and drink. Presumably most of the members were young men with few family ties. As with guilds and other similar groups, importance was attached to moral character and aspiring members pledged to keep peace and harmony. Unfortunately there is no indication as to what type of music was sung, but the nature of the society suggests that it would have been popular songs and folksongs.

MEISTERGESANG

The most important musical society in Nuremberg during the sixteenth and seventeenth centuries was the artisan cult of Meistergesang, which had grown up in the fifteenth century in south German and mainly Protestant towns. Its origins are obscure but a link can be seen with Minnesang in the style of its music and with the German *Spruchdichtung* in its poetic content. The Meistersinger believed that their music had descended from that of David of the Old Testament and that it was their duty to maintain the traditions of his art. The music was monophonic and performed by a solo voice. The fame of Meistergesang rests on the Singschule, the competitions held monthly at which songs, composed by Meistersinger according to rules written down at the latest by the mid-sixteenth century, were to be reproduced as exactly as possible, the winner being the most accurate singer. A Meistersinger was taught his art as an apprentice and could become a 'master singer', composing his own songs – melody and words – to these same rules.

The songs performed at the monthly meetings, the *Hauptsingen*, were never original. The host for the month assigned the singer a Meisterlied by a Meistersinger on a religious theme. Each song was adjudicated line by line by four *Merker*. Any mistakes in word, rhyme or melody incurred penalties. When everyone had sung, the *Merker* added the scores and the singer with the fewest penalties won. If more than one singer had gained minimum penalties, a second round was held under more exacting conditions until a winner was found. The winner was crowned with the *David* (a chain of gold medallions, the largest of which depicted King David, patron of the 132 Meistersinger) and the runner-up received the *Kranz* (a wreath of silk flowers). Both prizes were returned to the company at the end of the session. The group then held the second part of their competition, the *Zechsingen*, at their local inn. The rules were the same, but the songs no longer had to have a religious content and stories of classical mythology and old German legend were allowed. The winners of both contests were given free refreshment, usually consisting of bread, wine and cheese.

According to legend Meistergesang was brought to Nuremberg by Hans Folz from Worms. He had rebelled against the Singschule in his own town because the early fifteenth-century rules insisted that he could not compose his own Meisterleid but should always reproduce those of earlier masters. He was compelled to leave the school and he settled in Nuremberg about 1460. The first mention of Meistergesang in the town is the reference made in a collection of songs by Folz to a verse written by him and sung at a Singschule in 1496 for a prize of a chain of seals. Mention was first made in the Nuremberg Council records in 1503 when the Meistersinger were told that they had to have permission to hold public meetings.[6] Subsequent entries, between 1520 and 1540, give that permission. From 1555 minutes of each meeting were kept and these survive. Although no minutes survive after 1689 the school did not end until 1778.

The path of the school did not run smoothly. It was frequently enjoined by the Council to refrain from behaving in an unseemly manner, to sing religious songs with modesty and not to embarrass anyone. This warning was not just given to the Meistersinger; other groups in the city were similarly chastized. It was also necessary to apply to the Council for a venue. In 1533 the school was forced to vacate its meeting-place, the Poetenschule, and the Council was not over-zealous in finding it an alternative room. The members were branded as a nuisance and were said to have broken many things in previous quarters, so they were told to go to the recreation fields on the edge of the city. The Meistersinger then wrote a submissive letter to the Council pleading that Meistergesang was a Christian practice for the betterment of young people who would otherwise be engaged in all manner of bad things; they also stated that new moral songs had been written and more people were interested. The Council then allowed them to meet in disused churches: the Spital (1533–1550s), Predigerkloster (1550–1562), St Martha (1562–1620) and St Catharine (1620 – at least 1697) were used by the group.

It is difficult to understand the Council's attitude. It would seem that the Meistersinger were neither decadent nor dissident and that they were trying to enlarge their own horizons, albeit on a small scale. The Council was made up of patricians, men supposedly interested in culture, and yet it was doing nothing to encourage music among the artisans. Georg Harsdörffer, a patrician and prime mover of a later cultural society, described the Meistersinger by inference in 1644; he clearly deplored the society and held that music and literature belonged in more suitable hands. Perhaps this was the widespread conviction of the upper classes. The Council at that time feared any artisan group, especially guilds or religious brotherhoods, and some were broken up by the Council on several occasions, presumably so that rebels could not gain a foothold. Certainly the Meistersinger were not taken seriously until the next century. In 1580 the Council again banned the Singschule for singing frivolous songs too loudly. The ban lasted until 1583 when a new set of rules was devised. It seems that previously the school was responsible for its meetings, the residual money remaining in the coffers, but after 1583 the responsibility for meetings rested with the allotted host rather than with the school.

During the sixteenth century the school stabilized and more rules were made.[7] Its oldest serving member was the leader; he, the next two oldest members and the winner of the previous *Hauptsingen* were *Merker*. One member was treasurer and the money, schoolbooks and Bible were kept in a chest at his home. The income of the school varied. Fines were paid for various misdemeanours, such as singing a song unrehearsed (12 kreuzer), not preparing the adjudication booth (10 kreuzer) and not being present at the annual general meeting (12 kreuzer). A yearly subscription of 12 kreuzer was payable and if a member entered the adjudication booth uninvited the fine was two measures of wine. If a Meisterlied was sung in the city streets the culprit was banned from adjudication for a year. No admission charge was levied on spectators but donations were accepted (the rules state that the two runners-up from the previous meeting must stand at the door to collect the money). The costs of the school were met by the host, but on some occasions the school itself paid for the *zech* and on one occasion paid the preacher at St Catharine's Church a quarter of a bottle of wine if he would make the sermon shorter. Occasionally one of the *Merker* had to step down and sing in order to ensure a contest.

In time prizes were added. There was a *David* winner and a *Kranz* winner and sometimes more than ten prizes were given in one competition. By 1616 money was always part of the prizes but in addition objects such as knives, leggings, candle holders, salt cellars, warming pans, copper and pewter mugs, gloves, spoons and hats were given. On one occasion a piglet was donated. It was presumably the host who chose the prizes: in the schools hosted between 1586 and 1630 Caspar Enderlein, a well-known coppersmith and pewterer, gave prizes in which the predominance of pewter objects suggests that he had donated them.

The host for a school was one of the sixteen longest-serving members. He had to pay for the meeting – including the verger, the prizewinners and the *Merker*. On a feast-day such as Easter, Whitsun and Christmas, the school would cost him over three gulden which could be eight days' work at a rate of 22 kreuzer a day. A monthly meeting would cost about 81 kreuzer or four days' pay. It could be a profitable undertaking, however, for if admission money was donated the host would be allowed to pocket at least some of the surplus. A letter to Council in 1624 speaks of money being taken for private use by some Meistersinger.

To create more interest, and perhaps to attract a larger audience, special schools were inaugurated. A school competing for pewter prizes was held on several occasions and from 1608 the school of All Angels was instituted with a prize of one thaler. This school is interesting in that it reveals the uniformity of some sessions. It was held for eight years, and each year the same eleven songs were performed by a total of eighteen men. One song was sung by Stephan Angerer eight times.

For many years the school ran without problems, but in 1624 there was a major dissension and the Council was called to intervene. A group of mainly young singers believed that they were being badly treated by older members and not being allowed to take their rightful place in the society. When they sang they were heckled, prizes were denied them and they received none of the profits. The older members complained that the younger men held schools in private houses without permission of the Council, that they had caused much unrest in the school and had tried to force new ways into the company so much so that on one occasion there was almost an outbreak of violence. The Council ordered that those in the breakaway group eligible to hold meetings should be allowed to do so and that the younger group should inherit their rightful places on the death or resignation of older members.

The case of the composer Ambrosius Metzger provides more evidence of dissidence among the young. He was the son of a linen weaver who had been given an unusually good education for a member of his social group. He was rejected from the ministry because of poor eyesight and took a poorly-paid teaching post in the city. In 1611/12 he published two volumes of four-part songs of which he had written both words and melodies. Although his collection attracted little attention the songs show that Metzger was interested in recent developments in music, especially Italian ones. His deteriorating eyesight prevented him from continuing to compose partsongs and in 1623 he wrote his first Meisterlied, an easier task. He was taught the art by Hans Winter, a member of the dissident group. Metzger's songs were first sung by Jobst Zolner, also a dissident. During the last ten years of his life Metzger wrote 93 songs which were sung in the school at some time. 43 of these appeared only after his death in 1632. In later years his songs were the most widely sung in the school. When a Meisterlied was composed it had to be accepted by the school and written into the schoolbook. Metzger never became a Meistersinger: the concept of a Meisterlied had therefore apparently changed and it had now become a song written according to the rules of Meistergesang rather than one composed by a Meistersinger, and Metzger's songs were clearly deemed suitable. The young men found the leadership of the school irksome since it adhered to rules laid down nearly a century before, but the older group insisted that the musicianship of the younger men was not up to standard. With the help of a professional musician the younger men could enliven the music created by the school and force through their own brand of song. As these men were allowed to adopt their rightful place in the school's hierarchy, Metzger's songs became more firmly entrenched.

Despite internal troubles in the city, and the upheavals of the Thirty Years War, the school kept to its regular routine until the second half of the seventeenth century. However, meetings had to be cancelled because of war or plague and the school became more interested in the secular competition, *Kranzsingen,* begun by the dissidents in 1624. These schools were frequently held by two people – a member and a patron – in churches or sometimes in private houses. They were nevertheless governed by similar rules to the *Hauptsingen.* It was during this time that the school was visited by Council members who examined the books, inquired about the school and donated half a gulden. In 1643 the school was summoned to sing before Johann Dilherr, who was well known for his artistic interests, and he returned the visit the same year, possibly with Sigmund Theo Staden, the musician commissioned for the 1626 *Krenzleinsgesellschaft.* These two men, with the poet Johann Klaj, were responsible for the first public concert, depicting music throughout the ages, held at Nuremberg in 1644. Despite the apparent acceptance by upper-class Nuremberg, attendance at the schools began to decline from about this time; when the records cease in 1689 only a handful of members were meeting three or four times a year.

Johann Wagenseil left a description of the Nuremberg Singschule.[8] He was not a Meistersinger but he attended meetings regularly and held the singers in high esteem. He relates that a few days before each meeting, posters were placed in the town to advertise it, and the *David, Kranz* and chest were collected from the members responsible for them. Meetings were held on Sundays between church services in St Catharine's church (then disused). In the middle of the chancel a table with a black lectern was erected. This was enclosed by curtains to form the *Gemerk* (adjudicators' booth) where the four *Merker* sat. A small pulpit stood permanently near the church pulpit and the Meistersinger sang from there. He took off his hat and sang his song line by line, pausing between each one to give the *Merker* time to judge the melody, the rhyme, the degree of adherence to the rules of the *Tabulatur* and to ensure that the song followed the Lutheran Bible in teaching and content. Fig.67 shows a Singschule in session, the *David* and *Kranz* hanging from the wall, the *Merker* in their curtained booth and Phillip Hager at the *Singstuhl*.

Not all members of the Singschule were master singers. Although craft guilds were banned in Nuremberg the Singschule followed the guild system in learning the art of Meistergesang. A member first became an apprentice and learnt the rules of writing and singing the texts for Meisterlieder. These forbade such things as feminine rhymes and the use of dialect or foreign words for rhymes. He then composed

67. *Stained glass window showing Phillip Hager taking part in a Singschule, possibly in 1637; on the wall hang the chain of medallions (the David) awarded to the winner and the wreath (Kranz) for the runner-up, and in the curtained booth sit the four Merker who adjudicate the song*

his own words to an existing melody or *Ton*. His next step was to study the melody of Meisterlieder and to compose his own music for existing words. The music of no more than four syllables used consecutively could be identical with an existing melody, and flourishes were encouraged. Obedience to the rules was more important than the musicality of the song, hence the paucity of good Meisterlieder. When a member had composed his own lyrics and melody, could answer questions about Meistergesang in general and certain songs in particular, and could assure the membership that he was of an upright disposition, he was *befreit*; he became a master singer and his masterpiece was written in the schoolbook and named by the company. He could compose as many songs as he wished, but they all had to be accepted and named. Many Meistersinger composed only one song, and some members did not even become master singers.

Only one Meistersinger, Hans Sachs, achieved a considerable reputation as composer and poet, and he owed his fame as much to his *Fasnachtspiele* as to his abilities as a Meistersinger. Sachs was a shoemaker who became interested in Meistergesang when he was a journeyman in Munich. After returning to Nuremberg he joined the infant Singschule and was its leader from at least 1540 until his death in 1576. He composed thirteen Meisterlieder melodies and 86 poems for 244 melodies. His interest in the stage suggests that the Meistersinger also produced *Fasnachtspiele* at that time. It is a remarkable feature of the Nuremberg school that the art did not die with Sachs but found new leaders who developed it from a small society led by one man to a force that influenced schools in other towns.

One of the reasons why Meistersinger are elusive is because as individuals they played a very small part in the life of the town and therefore records pertaining to them are scarce. It is fortunate that the Nuremberg Council held the reins so firmly, for some idea of the life of its members may be gleaned from Council documents.[9] About 200 names appear in the minutes, altogether 22 families being represented by more than one member (usually sharing the same profession). With the notable exception of the Hager family, the second generation was less enthusiastic than the first and some members sang only after persuasion. The Hager family was illustrious in the Nuremberg Singschule. Georg Hager senior, a shoemaker, was followed by his son Georg who was also taught by Hans Sachs, He became leader of the school in 1619 and in turn had several sons and a grandson who, as well as being shoemakers, were also Meistersinger. Two sons, Christoph and Phillip, became respected leaders of the school.

Among the Meistersinger were both rich and poor. Caspar Enderlein, the pewterer, must have been wealthy for he was an examining master in his craft. Benedict von Watt was very poor but nevertheless carried out all the duties of the school, although minutes record that he

68. Poster announcing a Singschule meeting at St Catharine's Church, with a portrait of the Meistersinger Hans Sachs, the competition rules and the poem to be sung by everyone

was supposed to have sold or pawned the schoolbooks. He and Hans Venizer were so poor that the cost of their funerals was met by the school. Hans Griesser was an illuminator. He attempted, unsuccessfully, to become an examining master in the herring industry and was

Table XI.4 CRAFTS OF NUREMBERG MEISTERSINGER

WORKERS IN METAL		WORKERS IN TEXTILES	
cutler	8	line weaver	8
nailer	4	braid maker	6
disc maker	4	weaver	2
arrowsmith	3	dyer	1
coppersmith	3	string maker	1
drillsmith	1	tailor	1
pewterer	1		19
solderer	1	OTHERS	
tap maker	1	woodworker	3
gold-edging maker	1	baker	2
	27	barber-surgeon	1
WORKERS IN ANIMAL PRODUCTS		corn dealer	1
shoemaker	15	whitewasher	1
furrier	4	roofer	1
bag maker	3	potter	1
candle maker	1	clerics	1
skinner	1		11
tanner	1		
	25		

later appointed warder of one of the town-wall towers. Linhart Herdegen was a broom maker and a messenger for the Council, for which services he was paid five gulden a quarter. Jeremias Koller, a fur-edging maker, also became a member of the Great Council in 1645. Some Meistersinger held voluntary posts in their neighbourhood defence schemes. Hans Hager senior and his brother Phillip were sergeants in the defence force for their area. Conrad Amschel was a plumber and a corporal with an armed unit. Balthasar Mayer was also in charge of arms for citizens. Several were *Hochzeitlader*. All but one of the members were craftsmen. These crafts can be organized into groups as shown in table XI.4. The dominance of metal workers and shoemakers has led to the hypothesis that Meistergesang evolved from work-songs. The lack of regular metre in early Meisterlieder tends to refute this, however, and early Meistersinger were neither metal workers nor shoemakers. Hans Sachs was a shoemaker but his teacher was not. It is more probable that the dominance of these two crafts reflects the industry in the town.

★

Two major types of musical society existed in Nuremberg during the sixteenth and seventeenth centuries and in many respects they were similar. All groups were formed to praise God or to thank him for the gift of music – cultured music for the *Krenzleinsgesellschaften* and religious or moral songs for the Meistersinger. Most groups had rules to govern their meetings and personal behaviour; all held annual general meetings. Members took it in turn to act as host for one meeting and all groups allowed time for refreshment. An entry fee of one gulden was charged and fines were levied if rules were broken. The two artisan groups were concerned with the moral character of their members. These societies were open to any who were upright and would keep the rules. The patrician societies limited their membership to twelve or thirteen as befitted their place in a society where only a few families reached the pinnacle.

The nature of the Meistersinger Singschule also reflects the daily life of the artisan. The members competed for a prize. Correct singing according to the rules was the priority, not the enjoyment of the music. Meistersinger improved their ability and status to become master singers and in doing so created a cult that lasted over 200 years whereas the most durable of the *Krenzleinsgesellschaften* lasted about fourteen years. The longevity of the Singschule did not result from the aesthetic merit of its music, nor from its dominant personalities; it could only last as long as members derived benefits from its existence. The ability of the members to rise through the hierarchy gave them a sense of challenge and achievement. They believed that they were maintaining a biblical tradition in which rules were set and innovation was discouraged. In an unsettled epoch traditions have an added attraction. The insular attitude of Nuremberg reflected both in Meistergesang and in music in general, would certainly have hindered musical development among a people whose artistic sensibility was not highly refined. These factors protected the city from the influence of the outside world. It could not, however, long enjoy that protection at a time when Nuremberg was losing its leading position in economic prosperity, craftsmanship and culture.

NOTES

[1] H. Weiss, *Lebenshaltung und Vermögensbildung des 'mittleren' Burgertums* (Munich, 1980), 87ff; R. Endres, 'Zur wirtschaftlichen und sozialen Lage in Franken vor dem dreissigjährigen Krieg', *Jb für fränkische Landesforschung*, xxviii (1968), 5–13; P. Sander, *Die reichsstädtische Haushaltung Nürnbergs* (Leipzig, 1902); E. Scholler, *Das Münzwesen der Reichsstadt Nürnberg im 16 Jahrhundert* (Nuremberg, 1912); G. Strauss, *Nuremberg in the 16th Century* (New York, 1966); and *Nürnberger Meistersinger Protokolle von 1575 bis 1689*, ed. K. Drescher (Stuttgart, 1897/R1963).

[2] *D-Dlb* M185.

[3] Details of these societies are taken from U. Martin, 'Die Nürnberger Musikgesellschaften', *MVGN,* xlix (1959), 185–225.

[4] The minutes and rules for this society are in *GB-Lbm* Add. 25716.

[5] W. Fischer, *Quelle zur Geschichte des deutschen Handwercks Wolfgang Vincentz* (Göttingen, 1957).

[6] The main source for the dealings of the school with the Council is T. Hampe, *Nürnberger Ratsverlässe über Kunst und Künstler (1474–1618)* (Leipzig, 1904).

[7] The most detailed set of rules was that made in 1616 and modified in 1635. This was edited by E. Mummenhoff, 'Die Singschulordnung vom Jahre 1616/1635', *Hans Sachs-Forschungen* (Nuremberg, 1894).

[8] 'Von der meister-Singer holdseligen Kunst', *De civitate Noribergensi* (Altdorf, 1697/R1975).

[9] Irene Stahl has conducted some research into the genealogy of the Meistersinger and much of the information about their lives has been taken from her book, *Die Meistersinger von Nürnberg: archivalische Studien* (Nuremberg, 1982).

BIBLIOGRAPHICAL NOTE

General history

The definitive history of Nuremberg from its beginnings to modern times is *Nürnberg: Geschichte einer europäischen Stadt*, ed. G. Pfeiffer (Munich, 1971). G. Strauss's *Nuremberg in the Sixteenth Century* (New York, 1966) provides a good introduction to the social history of the city. P. Sander's *Die reichsstädtische Haushaltung Nürnbergs* (Leipzig, 1902) examines the economy of Nuremberg and E. Scholler's *Das Münzwesen der Reichsstadt Nürnberg im 16 Jahrhundert* (Nuremberg, 1912) describes the history and workings of the monetary system. For a study of trade in the city, see E. Wiest's *Die Entwicklung des Nürnberger Gewerbes zwischen 1648 und 1806* (Stuttgart, 1968). K. R. Greenfield's *Sumptuary Laws in Nuremberg: a Study in Paternal Government* (Baltimore, 1918) examines some of the laws passed by Nuremberg Council and establishes differences in social rank depending on respective laws and fines. For a study of the population of Nuremberg see R. Endres, 'Zur Einwohnerzahl und Bevölkerungsstrucktur Nürnbergs im 15./16. Jahrhundert', *MVGN,* lvii (1970), 242–71.

Music and the societies

B. R. Butler, *Liturgical Music in Sixteenth-Century Nuremberg* (diss., U. of Illinois, Urbana, 1970), provides a detailed study of liturgical music, customs and the town band. For an illustrated history of music in the city, see H. Zirnbauer's *Musik in der alten Reichsstadt Nürnberg* (Nuremberg, 1966). Other writings which contain some account of the Nuremberg musical societies include T. Hampe, *Nürnberger Ratsverlässe über Kunst und Künstler (1474–1618)* (Leipzig, 1904); U. Martin, 'Die Nürnberger Musikgesellschaften', *MVGN*, xlix (1959), 185–225; W. Nagel, 'Die Nürnberger Musikgesellschaft', *Monatscheft für Musikgeschichte*, i (1895), 1–12; and W. Fischer, *Quelle zur Geschichte des deutschen Handwerks Wolfgang Vincentz* (Göttingen, 1957).

Meistergesang

R. Genée's *Hans Sachs und seine Zeit* (Leipzig, 1894) gives a general description of the city and the cult and provides a good introduction to the subject despite now being superseded by modern research. J. C. Wagenseil's 'Von der Meister-Singer holdselingen Kunst', in *De civitate noribergensi commentatio* (Altdorf, 1697/*R*1975), gives a near-contemporary, although subjective and flattering portrayal of Meistergesang. Two books which cover the general history of Meistergesang are *Der deutsche Meistersang*, ed. B. Nagel (Darmstadt, 1967), and Nagel, *Meistersang* (Stuttgart, 1962, 2/1971). The two sources from which much of the information for this chapter has been drawn are *Das Gemerkbüchlein des Hans Sachs*, ed. K. Drescher (Halle, 1898), and *Nürnberger Meistersinger Protokolle von 1575 bis 1689*, ed. Drescher (Stuttgart, 1897/*R*1963); these contain the minutes, members' rules and diary of the Singschule from 1555 to 1689. H. Kugler, *Handwerk und Meistergesang* (Göttingen, 1977), investigates the social background of the Meistersinger. For a discussion of the 1624 revolt and the role played by Ambrosius Metzger see Kugler, '*Singschulstreit* von 1624', *MVGN*, lxii (1975), and S. Gattuso, 'Der Meistersingerstreit von 1624', *MVGN*, lxxiv (1987), 203–7. An attempt is made to discover the way in which the adjudicators marked the Meisterlied in C. H. Bell, 'A Glance into the Workshop of Meistergesang', *Publications of the Modern Language Society of America*, lxviii (1953). A comparison between the guild system and the Meistersinger Singschule, highlighting the similar hierarchy, regulations and the execution of a masterpiece, is undertaken in H. C. Christiansen, 'Meistersingerschools and the Guild: a Note on their Relationship', *German Life and Letters*, xxvi (1972). *Hans Sachs und Nürnberg*, ed. H. Brunner (Nuremberg, 1976), comprises articles by a number of literary scholars, and *Hans Sachs Dichtungen*, ed. A. von Keller and E. Goetze (Tübingen, 1908), is an edition of Sachs's verse.

Chapter XII

Elizabethan London

CRAIG MONSON

> This city of London is so vast and nobly built, so populous and
> prosperous and so pre-eminent in its crafts and merchant citizens
> that it can fairly be accounted, not only the chief city in the whole
> realm of England, but also one of the most famous in the whole of
> Christendom . . . [It is] so superior to other English cities that it
> is said: London is not in England, but England is in London. For the
> things most worth visiting in England are to be found in or around
> London; so that he who sees London thoroughly together with the
> Royal Palaces in the neighbourhood need not scruple to assert that he
> knows England.[1]

This encomium of London from Thomas Platter's description of
his journey to England in 1599 served as a justification for his neglect
of all the country outside the capital. If it is invoked here some four
centuries later for similarly pragmatic ends it is because it offers an
accurate reflection both of the way things were, and of the way they
were seen to be, as much for music as for most other aspects of culture.
In the sixteenth century London had no rival as the focus of musical
life in Britain. The city afforded the richest opportunities to hear music
in all its varieties. For those who practised the art London offered the
best, the most lucrative and the greatest number of positions. The
city remained the centre of the music business, the site of the music-
printing trade – such as it was – and a home to most foreign musicians,
music teachers and instrument makers. Most important, London
was the seat of the court and the monarch, whose essential role in
the patronage of music can scarcely be overstressed. The sovereign
supported the most and the best musicians, both sacred and secular.
A place in the musical institutions of the royal household remained
the ultimate goal, however remote, of any aspiring musician, while
the musical standards maintained there provided abiding models for all
the realm.

This was especially true in the field of sacred music. Even sixteenth-century Englishmen realized that without Queen Elizabeth

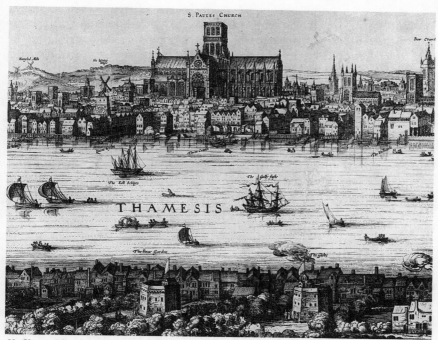

S. PAVLES CHVRCH

Bow Church

THAMESIS

69. View of London: detail of Vischer's 'Panoramic View of London' (1616)

and her royal chapel there would have been no Elizabethan 'golden age of church music'. The English Chapel Royal was entirely a reflection of the royal house it served. Subject neither to an international authority such as Rome, nor to any domestic episcopal body, it answered directly to the reigning monarch, 'the supreme head on earth of all things ecclesiastical and temporal'. It existed completely within the sphere of the court to perform in the chapels at Whitehall and the various 'standing houses' at Greenwich, Richmond and Hampton Court. It might follow the ruler on 'progresses' to the provinces or even farther afield, from the Field of Cloth of Gold in France with Henry VIII in 1520 to Scotland with James I in 1617.

The Chapel Royal was a uniquely national and surprisingly stable institution. By contrast with continental cathedrals or royal chapels, whose choirs were commonly staffed to varying degrees by foreigners, the English Chapel Royal was adamantly English. While the monarch's secular *corps de musique* may have developed a highly international character during the sixteenth century, the chapel choir was determinedly insular, drawing the finest voices from the realm but not from beyond. This is no surprise; the Elizabethan Chapel Royal might remain open to relatively discreet native Catholics of the stature of

William Byrd, but it would hardly have provided a safe or attractive haven for Catholics from abroad. The character of its liturgy, on the other hand, would have held no attraction for many committed continental Protestants.

During the sixteenth century liturgical tradition in the chapel was anything but stable, given the drastic doctrinal swings in the reigns between Henry VIII and Elizabeth I. But although the style of music performed in the Chapel Royal changed radically as monarchs and their religious doctrines came and went, the personnel who performed the music remained surprisingly untouched by these disruptions. Thomas Tallis is only the best known of about half a dozen gentlemen of the Chapel Royal who continued to sing under four monarchs – Henry VIII, Edward VI, Mary Tudor and Elizabeth I – and to endure as many changes in liturgical practice.

From the time of Elizabeth's accession the standard number of gentlemen of the chapel was 32 with twelve singing boys (though the number actually present at services varied). For important occasions the ranks might be swelled by 'gentlemen extraordinary', unpaid, 'honorary' members of the choir. For ferial weekday services, on the other hand, only sixteen men were in attendance. And given the fact that several gentlemen were extraordinarily long-lived (Thomas Tallis served for about 45 years, William Byrd 54, Robert Richemond and Robert Stone no less than 60), at any given time the chapel would have included a number of incumbents who had ceased to serve actively, although they retained their places there.

70. *Gentlemen and children of the Chapel Royal: miniatures from a manuscript depicting the funeral procession for Queen Elizabeth, 1603*

Clearly the Chapel Royal set the standard for the realm in sacred music. With the return of the puritan faction after the demise of Mary Tudor, the Chapel Royal remained the most important bastion of elaborate ritual amid the intense and abiding attack on church music by Genevan reformers. The most common justification for puritan calls to reform was that elaborate music represented just another manifestation of popery, as is clear from John Field's *An Admonition to Parliament* (1572):

> In all their order of service there is no edification, according to the rule of the Apostles, but confusion; they tosse the Psalms in most places like tennise balls ... As for orgaines and curious singing, though they be proper to popish dennes, I mean to Cathedral churches, yet some others also must have them. The queenes chappell, and these churches which should be spectacles of christian reformation, must be patterns and precedents to the people, of all superstitions ... We should be too long to tell your honours of cathedral churches, the dens aforesaid of all loitering lubbers, where master Dean, master Vicedean ... the chief chanter, singingmen ... squeaking queresters, organ players, gospellers, episteolers, pentioners, readers, vergers, etc. live in great idleness .. If you would know whence all these came, we can easily answer you, that they came from the Pope, as out of the Trojan horse's belly, to the destruction of Gods kingdome.[2]

There were limits to what the more extreme reformers could actually accomplish, however shrill their rhetoric, since it was the queen, as head of the church, who had the final say. Nevertheless, the popular image of the 'Elizabethan golden age of church music' becomes somewhat tarnished when one leaves the confines of the queen's own Chapel Royal and other sacred institutions within her sphere, St Paul's, Westminster Abbey and St George's Chapel, Windsor.

Because the Chapel Royal was exempt from episcopal jurisdiction, the puritan clergy could do little about the elaborate music fostered there except to rail against its excesses. The queen's attitude towards church music, as reflected by the differences between the practice in the Chapel Royal and what she permitted in parish churches and provincial cathedrals, accords well with the notion of moderation that characterizes many policies of Elizabeth's reign. Puritan bishops, often quite removed from the capital, were permitted certain reforms, so long as they did not get out of hand or encroach upon the queen's prerogative. Within the circle of the court – which remained the primary, often the sole, attraction for foreign travellers and diplomats, and the most visible manifestation of her policies – the queen fostered an elaborate ritual in which music played a most obvious part.

Elizabeth may have been personally attracted to trappings and ceremonial more akin to papal ritual than to puritan austerity, but she was also well aware of their political usefulness. Religious ceremonial glorified God, but it also exalted the supreme head of his church in Britain. This is particularly clear from a description of the visit to the royal chapel at Greenwich during Whitsun week in 1586 by Henrie Ramelius, ambassador of Frederick II of Denmark:

> The said Ambassador being at the Court, was accompanied with certeine English Lords to hir Highnesse Chapell, and placed not far from hir Excellencie, did heare divine service so melodiously said and sung, both by voice and instruments of consort, as a man halfe dead might thereby have beene quickened. The Gentlemen of the Chapell, with the rest of the quier, bending themselves, both with skile and zeale, that daie to honor their Prince according to their Place. The Bishop of Salisburie and others distinctlie reading part of the divine service, and in presence of all the auditorie dooing such obeisance with knee and countenance as the presence of so gratious a Souvreigne as they had in their eies did require.[3]

By this account, the earthly sovereign was as much the object of veneration as the heavenly one. Indeed, with the clearing away of many Catholic feasts and saints' days by the Reformation and with the growth of popular support and enthusiasm for Elizabeth in the 1570s (particularly after her excommunication), for many people the Virgin Queen of England and her ceremonies supplanted the Catholic saints, even the Virgin Queen of Heaven herself.

Elizabeth must also have realized, on the other hand, that such outwardly 'Catholic' ornaments might serve to reassure powerful neighbours across the Channel that the old order had not been entirely subverted by Calvinist extremes. In 1564, after the visit of the French ambassador, Archbishop Parker recorded:

> I perceive that they thought, before their coming, we had neither state prayers, nor choice of days of abstinence as Lent, &c., nor orders ecclesiastical . . . And so they seemed to be glad, that in ministration of our Common Prayer and Sacraments we use such reverent mediocrity, and that we did not expel music out of our quires, telling them that our music drowned not the principal regard or our prayer.[4]

Foreign travellers frequently remarked, often with some surprise, upon the 'popish' charater of the Protestant services they witnessed in London or at the court. In 1599 the German Thomas Platter commented on the chapel at Windsor: 'Then we heard some glorious music in the church at English vespers, choir with organ, cornet and fife accompaniment, for as stated above, in outward ceremonies they much resemble the papists'.[5] For such foreign observers it was the music and ceremony that presented some of the clearest testimony to the queen's religious moderation; England might be Protestant, but Elizabeth's Protestantism was not Calvin's.

Reports such as the Danish ambassador's suggest that the chapel remained within the arena of international politics and that Elizabeth must have regarded it as a useful instrument of state. Foreign reports throughout her reign suggest that she made a point of displaying the singing of her chapel to foreigners and commonly had them presented to her either en route to services or immediately afterwards. Almost invariably these visitors remarked on the splendour of the music, though usually in less detail than the visual displays. This is perhaps not surprising because then, as now, few observers would have had the musical sophistication to describe chapel singing in anything other than superficial terms. In 1565 the ambassador Adam Zwetkovich reported to the Emperor Maximilian, for example:

> On my arrival I was advised to attend Divine Service with the Queen, as this would please both her and the people and arouse great hopes. And so on the 13th of May I accompanied the Queen from her apartments to the Chapel as is the custom at all courts. They had arranged a special choral service for me as the envoy of Your Imperial Majesty, and the Earl of Sussex interpreted the hymns and anthems. The Queen thanked me, asked me how I liked it and gave me the book [?of common prayer] which I accepted, promising to send it to Your Imperial Majesty.[6]

The scene repeats itself in descriptions by various German and Italian visitors during the 1570s and 1580s, and was played once again at the end of the reign, on Epiphany 1601, on a particularly splendid occasion when the queen was visited at Whitehall by both the Russian ambassador, Grigori Ivanovitch Mikulin, and Don Virginio Orsino, Duke of Bracciano. The Russian ambassador described his encounter as follows:

> And the Queen, rising from her place, bowed . . . and spake: . . . 'Now I go to divine service, and you shall go along, and witness our ceremonies and customs, how in our country the Communion Service is sung.' And she bade Grigori go before her with her greatest lords . . . Then the Queen passed to Chapel; and before the Queen went the courtiers, and after the courtiers the lords, and following the Queen went many ladies and maidens. . . . And at that moment in the Chapel they began to play on the organ, and on wind instruments, with much other music and song. The officer said, 'They are singing the psalms of David.' And in the place where the priests serve is set a dais, and on the dais is placed a table covered with a damask cloth, and on the table lie two books covered with gold, which they call the Apostles and the Gospel; and also on the table are two unlighted candles. The priests were in golden copes, and at the sides stood subdeacons in white surplices. And as they began to

celebrate the Eucharist, the Queen, approaching the place where the priests minister, knelt down, and gave the priest a dish with three things in papers; and the officers said that the Queen in her religion at every [Epiphany] Feast brings as an offering to God gold, frankincense, and myrrh. And having made her offering, she went back to her lodging.[7]

Although Mikulin observed the service from a chamber opposite the queen, Elizabeth apparently achieved a modest diplomatic victory by cajoling Virginio Orsino to accompany her to the 'heretical' service and to observe it from the window of her closet. As Father Antony Rivers reported to Father Robert Parsons:

She invited him to go with her to her closet over the chapel, having before given order that the Communion table should be adorned with basin and ewer of gold and evening tapers and other ornaments (some say also with a crucifix), and that all the ministry should be in rich copes. The Duke, of curiosity, accompanied her, and she was very pleasant thereat, saying she would write to the Pope not to chide him for that fact, with other like discourses; and so, service ended, they returned. But herewithal many Papists are much scandalized.[8]

The reports carried home by all these foreign witnesses, in which the chapel music is frequently singled out, served both to enhance the image of the splendour and good order of the queen's court abroad, and to counteract any tales and vilifications spread by Rome, which had grown particularly intense after Elizabeth's excommunication in 1570.

Because of its high profile great care was taken throughout the century to ensure that the Chapel Royal maintained the highest standards in the realm. To this end writs had been issued as early as 1420 permitting the compulsory recruitment of the most promising choirboys from provincial cathedrals or wherever they might be found. In this the chapel was no different from other instruments of the court, however, for similar means were used to secure the very best services throughout the royal household, from stableboys and bricklayers to choirboys. It is significant that only the choirs of St Paul's, Westminster Abbey and Windsor were immune to such raids. Indeed, these three choirs, which took part in court ceremonies, which remained almost as visible to foreign visitors as the Chapel Royal itself and which might occasionally be visited by the queen, were also sometimes granted writs of impressment.

Although a writ for the compulsory recruitment of singing men as well as boys had been issued in 1448, impressment would scarcely have been necessary to fill the ranks of gentlemen of the Chapel Royal. The pay, working conditions and social status of the singing men stood far above those of other ecclesiastical institutions. The basic pay of £30 per year may have remained unchanged throughout Elizabeth's reign, despite severe inflation, but it was two to three times what might be hoped for in the most remunerative places outside the chapel, such as Windsor (£13. 6s. 8d.) or York (£10), and more than four times what a layman might expect at Norwich (£6. 13s. 4d.).[9] It also compared very favourably with the wage rents in other London trades about 1588, when brewers might expect £10 with meat and drink, dyers £6. 13s. 4d., blacksmiths, butchers and cooks £6, pewterers, draymen and brownbakers £3. 6s. 8d.[10]

Pluralism also offered a means of supplementing Chapel Royal stipends, most conveniently by simply retaining the place held before being called to London. This practice became increasingly common under Elizabeth's successors. If a cathedral chapter attempted to deprive a gentleman of the Chapel Royal of his provincial place it could incur the queen's displeasure, as Exeter discovered from a communication dated 26 May 1601:

> The Queen to the Dean, Chapter and College of Vicars of Exeter. You have dispossessed Wm. Randal, who late had a vicar's place there, of his place, value 10l. a year, and a house pertaining thereto, because he was sent for and entertained to serve in our chapel. We think it unreasonable that those called to our service should lose any benefit thereby, and you can better afford him the profit of his place, because you have long kept vicar's rooms void, and others have enjoyed the benefit. We therefore require the restoration of the said Randal.[11]

The music of the chapel from the early decades of Henry VIII's reign maintained the exuberant, grand-scale polyphonic tradition of the late fifteenth century. The festal masses of Robert Fayrfax, Nicolas Ludford and John Taverner in particular, with their extraordinary diversity of melody and rhythm and seemingly endless, overlapping melismatic phrases, represent the sort of ritual polyphony that prompted the Venetian secretary Sagudino to write in 1515: 'High mass was sung by the King's choristers, whose voices are more divine than human; *non cantavano ma giubilavano*; and as to the counterbass voices, they probably have not their equal in the world'.[12] By comparison the sober music of Edward VI's reign seems decidedly earthbound, much of it limited to four parts declaiming their texts syllabically in plain, chordal style. Even this was too much for many reforming zealots around the boy king. Indeed, it has been suggested that had Edward lived to manhood there would have been no golden age of Tudor church music in the second half of the sixteenth century.

Given the puritan opposition to elaborate music and the new general laxity and inferior musical standards in provincial cathedral choirs in the second half of the century, it must have been primarily Elizabeth's chapel that fostered and performed the extraordinary sacred repertory that has come to be regarded as one of the most brilliant ornaments of Elizabethan culture. Surely none but the queen's own chapel could have managed the intricacies of the most elaborate service music such as Robert Parsons's First Service in up to eight parts, William Mundy's Evening Service 'in medio chori' in nine parts, or William Byrd's Great Service, requiring as many as ten parts. However, even in the Chapel Royal the everyday service music may have been considerably more modest.

A note in Benjamin Cosyn's virginal book, 'These are the six Services for the kings Royal chapel', includes 'Mr Beavins Service, Mr Tallis Service, Mr Strogers Service, Mr Will: Byrde's Service, Mr Or: Gibbons Service, Mr Tho: Weelks Service'. Although the note dates from 1620, half the services go back at least to the earlier years of Elizabeth's reign and suggest a long-standing tradition, while all six belong to the simplest sort of setting, the so-called 'short service', commonly in four parts with some sections in five, basically chordal in style, usually syllabic with very little text repetition, and to modern ears rather plain.

Surviving sources of sacred music give the impression that the early Elizabethan anthem repertory was comparably modest and that in the years shortly after Elizabeth's accession an effort was made to provide a more impressive repertory. William Byrd seems to have been the first composer to accept the challenge of providing large-scale five- and six-part anthems in any quantity, thereby establishing a stylistic norm that remained for decades. Many anthems must have resulted directly from particular needs of the chapel. Apart from those whose texts can be assigned to specific feasts, a few Elizabethan anthems offer direct petitions for Elizabeth's health and welfare: *O Lord make thy servant Elizabeth our Queen to rejoice*, *Thou God that guid'st* and *Behold O God the sad and heavy case*, all by Byrd, and *Bow down thine ear* by William Mundy. Either Mundy's anthem or the first two by Byrd might have served, for example, for 'The Order of receyveing Queen Elizabeth in the Colledge Churche of Westminster, the first Daie of the Parliament, October 13, 1597', which stipulates in addition to much other music, 'After the Sermon a solemne songe with a collecte for the Queene'.[13] Other anthems may also have been intended for royal services. The Cheque Book of the Chapel Royal, a manuscript record of administration of the chapel, lists five anthems for the Maundy Thursday ceremony of Charles I: *Hide not thou thy face from us*, *Prevent us O Lord*, *Call to remembrance*, *O praise the Lord all ye heathen* and *O Lord make thy servant*.[14] The fact that all exist in settings by Chapel Royal composers active in the early decades of Elizabeth's reign – Richard Farrant (nos.1 and 3), William Byrd (nos.2 and 5) and Thomas Tallis (no.4, an arrangement of his motet, *O salutaris hostia*) – suggests that the Caroline order might have been the continuation of an older sixteenth-century practice. Elizabeth made a point of performing the washing of feet on Maundy Thursday,

71. *Opening of the bass part of Byrd's six-part anthem 'O Lord make thy servant Elizabeth our Queen to rejoice'; from a manuscript copied in the late sixteenth century*

like the pope. As she commented to the Spanish ambassador, 'You see, in essentials we monarchs think alike'.[15]

Some anthems may originally have been sung by the choir in extra-liturgical contexts and may then subsequently have found their way into liturgical performances if the musical setting was appropriate. Byrd's verse anthem, *Thou God that guid'st*, which set William Hunnis's 'praier for the good estate of Queene Elizabeth', a text published in 1583 in the flood of prayers, poems and orders of service printed as part of the swelling cult of Elizabeth, was probably first performed in some extra-liturgical ceremony by soloists and viol accompaniment alternating with the full choir. Today it survives only in liturgical manuscripts with the string accompaniment reduced to an organ part for performance in church.

The aesthetic gap separating the queen's chapel and London parish churches in matters of music was a gaping one without parallel in the secular realm. Even London puritans, represented most notably by the lord mayor and aldermen of the city, could find something useful and worth emulating in the activities of the queen's secular musicians. Puritan dogma and anti-Catholic sentiment left no place for the queen's sort of elevated church music, however, and as a result the character of

72. Preaching at Paul's Cross: painting, 'Farley's Dream' (c1616), by John Gipkym

the music in London parish churches changed markedly during the sixteenth century.

Before the Reformation a number of London parishes had maintained musical personnel and choir schools whose music rivalled that of
monastic foundations. By the last decade of Henry VIII's reign 76
London parishes had built at least two organs.[16] But the reforming zeal
of the puritan faction, which waxed particularly strong in the cities and
especially in London in the years after Elizabeth's accession, transformed the role and character of music in worship. By the 1560s money
was increasingly diverted from music to more 'edifying' uses. As one
Jacobean apologist for music put it:

> The first occasion for the decay of musick in Cathedrall Churches and
> other places where musick and singing was used and had in yearely
> allowance began about the nynthe years of Queen Elizabeth, at what
> time the pretence of Reformation for Church discipline having possest
> great persons, it was thought meet by some of them that in the founda-
> tions where such allowance was needless and more fitt to be employed
> better . . . Lectures were more fitt to be erected . . . And it is to be
> remembered that at about the same tyme not so fewe as an 100 paires
> organs were pulled down.[17]

The usual pattern was to allow the organs to fall into neglect, particularly after the demise in 1571 of John Howe, who seems single-handedly
to have maintained many of the organs in the city. Suitable pretexts
could also be found for the removal of singing men, as in the case of one
Beckwith in 1581, who complained to the queen that the governors of
Christ's Hospital had broken Henry VIII's order by expelling him and
the rest of the singing men. In response it was declared 'that Beckwith
had been expelled for his notorious lewdness, and the rest because they
were Laymen, and that the service had been conducted according to the
Book of Common Prayer, and in all points as St Paul's *except the use of
organs and prick song*' (my italics).[18]

In the great majority of London parish churches 'organs and
pricksong' gave way to congregational singing of metrical psalms,
which achieved enormous and abiding popularity. Even as early as
March 1560 Bishop John Jewel could write to Peter Martyr in Zurich:

> As soon as they had commenced singing in public, in only one little
> church in London, immediately not only the churches in the
> neighbourhood, but even the towns far distant, began to vie with each
> other in the same practice. You may now sometimes see at Paul's
> cross, after the service, six thousand persons, old and young, of both
> sexes, all singing together and praising God.[19]

The throngs that gathered for this pious exercise at Paul's Cross
remained large throughout Elizabeth's reign and had no rival within
the realm.

The popularity of metrical psalm singing nourished and was nourished in turn by the printing of musical settings of them, representing the only successful music publishing before the late 1580s. Like the flood of pious, devotional publications in prose or verse, metrical psalms served the increasing number of heads of London households who had learnt to lead devotions in their own homes. The scene described in the diary of the puritan Lady Hoby in 1600 is probably typical: 'I went to supper, then to the lecture: after I sung a psalm with some of the servants and, lastly, read a chapter, prayed, and so went to bed'.[20]

Within St Paul's Cathedral, on the other hand, could be seen and heard some approximation to the queen's royal chapel. The diary of Philip Julius, Duke of Stettin-Pomerania, offers one of many foreign accounts to remark on the popish character of St Paul's. It is unique, however, in specifying that it was the music which drew many to Evensong. Philip Julius is thus a useful witness to the fact that despite the strongly puritan character of the city, church music was not entirely without its advocates:

> Some of our party went to S. Paul's Church to hear the vespers; . . . Gentilhomini assemble in this place, as merchants do at the Exchange, to hear the beautiful music, which is daily performed. The singers as well as the preachers wear white surplices, making use of many Popish ceremonies, all kneeling down on entering the church and otherwise keeping good order.[21]

St Paul's, Westminster Abbey and, slightly farther afield, St George's Chapel, Windsor, all provoked similar comments for their elaborate ritual and music. Their concern for music is partly explained by the fact that all were to some extent satellites of the court, and therefore might be enlisted for court services, ceremonies and, in the case of the choirboys, for dramatic productions.

While the Chapel Royal remained a national institution, largely insular in character and quite consistent in size, whose history as an organized body can be traced back at least to the twelfth century, the secular musical institution at court, which has come to be known as the King's Music or the Queen's Music, was highly international and expanded dramatically in the course of the sixteenth century. Funeral liveries were issued to nineteen court instrumentalists, excluding the trumpeters, for the funeral of Henry VII in 1507; by 1547 Henry VIII had collected perhaps as many as 58 secular musicians around him. Although Elizabeth may have attempted a certain austerity in this area, her secular establishment still averaged about 30 musicians throughout her reign.

Henry VIII was the most significant figure in the remarkable expansion of the King's Music which was accomplished chiefly through foreign recruitment, particularly in the 1540s. By Henry's death the King's Music had assumed the form it would retain for the rest of the century. The full complement of instrumentalists was present, most of them foreigners. The well-known inventory of Henry's musical instruments compiled in 1547 describes a dazzling assortment of 56 keyboard instruments, more than twenty 'horns', nineteen bowed strings, 31 plucked strings and no fewer than 220 wind instruments of various kinds. Under Elizabeth there was little significant change in the make-up of the instrumental ensemble beyond the disappearance of a few of the more archaic instruments. Between half and two-thirds of the Queen's Music consisted of immigrants, chiefly drawn from the Bassano, Lupo, Lanier, Comy and Galliardello families, who had moved to England during the reign of her father.

Recent research has shed light on the character of these immigrant families and may explain both their willingness to emigrate and the court's particular interest in having them.[22] Many of these musical dynasties were not Italians but Jews, who after a sojourn in Italy made more or less permanent homes in England, beginning in the 1520s. By 1540 the majority of foreigners in the King's Music were Jews, including at least nine Ashkenazy Jews among the wind players, while the entire viol consort probably consisted of Sephardim. Post-Reformation England seems to have been viewed by the Jews as a safe haven because it was both anti-Roman and to some degree anti-Lutheran, and was therefore opposed to churchmen at whose hands Ashkenazim and Sephardim had long suffered. Henry and Elizabeth, on the other hand, may have welcomed Jewish musicians whose loyalty to the crown would never waver because of Christian dissension.

On the whole the level of education and the social status of the court instrumentalists may have been somewhat lower than that of the chapel singers. But in terms of basic pay many members of the Queen's Music outstripped most gentlemen of the Chapel Royal. The usual stipend for an instrumentalist amounted to £46. 10s. 10d. a year, including the allowance for livery. Although some were paid less, some might be paid considerably more, particularly the more esteemed foreigners. A place in the chapel already represented an unrivalled attraction to native church musicians, but added inducements were required to tempt some foreign instrumentalists across the Channel. Nicholas Lanier, flautist from 1561 to c1615, received an extra £5 per year, for example. Alfonso Ferrabosco was awarded an annuity of 100 marks (£66. 13s. 4d.) shortly after his arrival in 1562, which was raised to an even £100 in 1567, presumably to tempt him back to Britain after a prolonged absence. It is worth remembering, however, that as impressive and attractive as such salaries may have seemed to musicians outside the court, the earnings of the Master of the King's Music in the early seventeenth century were no higher than those of the king's barber.[23]

All the musicians, whether sacred or secular, might hope for additional largesse because of their proximity to the monarch. A few special rewards were musical in nature, such as the monopoly on the printing and importation of music granted to Thomas Tallis and William Byrd in 1575. But more commonly (and profitably) they involved leases and grants of crown land. In 1588, on the other hand, William Mundy of the chapel was granted a licence to transport 8000 bushels of wheat from the ports of Devon and Cornwall, while in 1598 Arthur, Andrea and Jeronimo Bassano were licensed to export 6000 dickers of calfskins.[24]

As members of the royal household the musicians might also hope for a measure of crown protection. Thus, in November 1573 the Earl of Sussex informed the Lord Mayor of London:

> Her Majesty's musicians had been lately molested with divers new payments and other charges. Being her servants in ordinary they had to attend daily upon her, for which reason they ought not to be chosen to any office, as Churchwarden, Constable, Scavenger, Watchman, nor charged with subsidies nor fifteenths.[25]

William Byrd perhaps offers the best example of crown protection, for although he remained a lifelong and increasingly committed Catholic, he was left alone (though frequently cited for recusancy).

Rarely did a musician establish any sort of special relationship with the monarch. Alfonso Ferrabosco seems to have enjoyed Elizabeth's particular favour, however. On 25 February 1575/6 four Venetian travellers mentioned in their report to the Venetian Senate an unnamed Bolognese, obviously Ferrabosco, who 'is one of the grooms of the Queen's privy chamber, and enjoys extreme favour with her Majesty on account of his being an excellent musician'.[26] Ferrabosco must indeed have enjoyed 'extreme favour', for the queen had been willing to grant him an annuity of £100, had unsuccessfully petitioned the Queen Mother of France, the English ambassador in France and the French ambassador in Rome in 1580 to secure his return to England after he fled the country, was still suing for his return in 1586, and in 1592 granted an annuity of £26. 13s. 4d. to the teenage son he had left behind.

It should be pointed out, however, that in no case would such special relationships have involved friendship or intimacy beyond what might develop between ruler and servant; and no matter how much admired the likes of Alfonso Ferrabosco may have been, in England, his absence left no major artistic gap on the Continent. The Lupos or the Bassanos as Jews, and the Laniers as Huguenots, might have found London an attractive haven from the Inquisition; but they represent the best that could be coaxed to the English royal household. Throughout the century none of the very finest, internationally known continental Europeans was prepared to venture across the Channel for an extended stay.

The instrumental musicians were apparently required to attend daily at court, at least during the winter months, when the queen was in and around London, where they were kept busy with a variety of tasks. A primary – perhaps the primary – duty of the court instrumentalists was to provide music for dancing. As in many courts dance was intimately worked into the fabric of courtly life, serving as a perpetual exercise for the courtesy and decorum underlying the order of the court. Henry VIII had been an enthusiastic dancer who threw himself into the art with the same sense of energy – one might say exhibitionism – that he gave to other forms of noble sport. In September 1513, for example, Paulo de Laude, the Milanese ambassador, wrote from Lille that twice within a week Henry had quite literally danced the night away.

Dancing was a favourite pastime of Elizabeth's. The frequency with which it is mentioned by court observers throughout her reign suggests that this common noble activity must have held particular importance for the queen and the workings of her court. Near the end of her reign she told the French ambassador that 'in her youth she danced very well, and composed measures and music, and had played them herself and danced them'.[27] By her mid-fifties the situation had not changed, to judge by the note from John Stanhope to Lord Talbot dated 22 December 1589: 'My Lo. the Q. is so well as I assure you six or seven gallyards in a mornynge, besydes musycke and synginge, is her ordinary exercise'.[28]

The German traveller, Lupold von Wedel, gives one of the most detailed accounts of the character of the dance at Elizabeth's court on 27 December 1585:

> Men and women linked hands as in Germany. The men donned their hats or bonnets, although otherwise no one, however exalted his rank, may put on his hat in the Queen's chamber, whether she be present or not. The dancers danced behind one another as in Germany, and all the dancers, ladies and gentlemen wore gloves. Though the dance at first sight seemed to be of German nature, it was no German dance, for they made a few steps forward and then back again. Finally they separated. The couples changed among one another, but at the right moment each dancer returned to his or her partner. While dancing they often courtesied to one another and every time the men bowed before their lady partners they doffed their hats. Slender and beautiful were the women who took part in this dance and magnificently robed. This dance was danced only by the most eminent who were no longer very young. But when it was over the young men laid aside their rapiers and cloaks, and clad in doublet and hose invited the ladies to dance. They danced the galliard and the Queen meanwhile conversed with those who had danced. The dancing over, the Queen waved her hand to those present and retired to her chamber . . . But as long as the dancing lasted she summoned young and old and spoke continuously.[29]

Von Wedel not only indicates the decorous distinctions drawn between the participants in the stately paven and the more exuberant galliard, but also that on this occasion the queen was an active observer of the dance rather than a participant, a role she seems increasingly – if reluctantly – to have adopted in old age. The French ambassador de Maisse, who sat beside her at court in January 1598, recorded:

> She takes such pleasure in it that when her maids dance she follows the cadence with her head, hand and foot. She rebukes them if they do not dance to her liking, and without doubt she is mistress of the art, having learnt in the Italian manner to dance high.[30]

Elizabeth's decision to restrain her own dancing in public may owe something to the courtly decorum which dictated that public dancing, as an acting out of the game of courtly love, should be left largely to the young. As Castiglione had put it in *Il cortegiano* (1528), 'these exercises ought to be left of before age constraineth us to leave them whether we will or no'.[31] By assuming the role of observer and critic of the dance Elizabeth followed Castiglione's dictates regarding the proper relationship of the practice of music to the old, who 'much better and sooner discerne, and with much more pleasure judge of it, than other . . . that have not been practised in the variety of pleasant music'.

Such an explanation is not entirely satisfactory, however, because in the rarefied atmosphere of the court in Elizabeth's final years the queen was perpetually young, to be courted as she might have been 35 years earlier. Long after any prospect of marriage had faded, the conceits of the game of love abided as part of the special decorum that surrounded the idea of the Virgin Queen. The dance as an acting out of the loftiest forms of courtesy naturally assumed a special importance. Indeed, dance could become another symbol of the order so frequently noted by foreigners at Elizabeth's court.

To witness the dancing of the court and to see the queen herself dance could become a mark of particular favour, and in the last years of her reign, when the queen could not have been expected to dance publicly, the chance to see her do so became a much coveted honour. Thus Virginio Orsino wrote of his meeting with Elizabeth on 11 January 1601:

> As soon as I came, her Majesty received me with so gracious a countenance that I could not ask more, and led me into a chamber with all the ladies and gentlemen, where a most beautiful ball took place. Her Majesty was pleased to dance, which is the greatest honour that she could do me, according to the word of those informed of this court . . . She had me view all the ladies and gentlemen who danced well in couples; willed me also to stay ever near to entertain her, making me be covered and to be seated, under compulsion of express command.[32]

There may indeed have been something indecorous about the reality of an old lady dancing, as a Spanish secret agent's report of 1599 implies: 'On the day of Epiphany the queen held a great feast, in which the head of the Church of England and Ireland was to be seen in her old age dancing three or four galliards'.[33] But the rarity of what had become largely a private event transformed what might have been a violation of strict decorum into a singular form of courtesy to those who paid court to the ageless queen.

Apart from providing music for dancing the court musicians seem to have been kept busy with many other duties. The grandest involved accompanying processions, removals and ceremonies. Some of these were comparatively intimate, such as the hunt in the park at Cowdray in August 1591, 'where was a delicate bowre prepared, under the which were her Highnesse musicians placed, and a crossbowe by a Nymph, with a sweet song, delivered to her hands, to shoote at the deere'.[34] Many occasions typically sacrificed subtlety for brilliance and bombast, however, such as the diversion on the Thames on St George's Day 1559:

> After supper she took a boat, and was rowed up and down in the River Thames; hundreds of boats and barges rowing about her; and thousands of people thronging at the water-side, to look upon her Majesty; rejoicing to see her, and partaking of the musick and sights on the Thames; for the trumpets blew, drums beat, flutes played, guns

73. *Courtiers of Queen Elizabeth dancing to an ensemble of a lute and three viols: painting attributed to Marcus Gheeraerts the elder, a Flemish artist who spent the years 1568–77 in England*

were discharged, squibs hurled up into the air, as the Queen moved from place to place. And this continued till ten of the clock at night, when the Queen departed home.[35]

It had long been the custom for such progresses by water to be accompanied by 'noise of music'. When Elizabeth made the journey from Whitehall to the Tower by water on her coronation day, the Venetian ambassador commented that it 'reminded me of Ascension Day at Venice, when the Signory go to espouse the sea, with a band of music, as usual when the Queen goes by water'.[36] This telling comparison with the Festa della Sensa, one of the grandest ceremonies of the Venetian Republic, reveals that in even the most discriminating foreign eyes the splendours of Elizabeth's court could rival the most impressive from across the Channel.

Within the palace, waiting upon the monarch generally meant, for musicians, providing music for the royal meal. The Venetian ambassador was less impressed by the music at Elizabeth's coronation banquet than he had been by her progress on the water earlier in the day: 'Much music was performed, but it not being remarkable, and having heard better, I will say nothing about it'.[37] Such indifference to the queen's dinner music is heavily outweighed by others' praise throughout the remainder of her reign. Ceremonial flourishes heightened the solemnity as the various courses were carried in, even though the queen herself was not yet present. According to Paul Hentzner, writing at Greenwich in 1598: 'During the time that this guard . . . were bringing dinner, twelve trumpets and two kettle-drums made the hall ring for half an hour together'.[38] The meal itself presumably involved quieter music of some diversity. The Russian ambassador said of dinner on Twelfth Day 1601: 'While the Queen's dinner was going forward, before her many players performed many pieces'.[39] These would have included vocal as well as instrumental pieces, for the Lord Chamberlain's notes for the festivities required 'The Children of the Chappell to come before the Queen at Dinner with a Caroll'.[40] No specific piece is mentioned, but John Bull's popular verse anthem for Epiphany, *Almighty God who by the leading of a star*, seems a likely candidate for this occasion, even though it is not, strictly speaking, a carol. Lupold von Wedel, describing Elizabeth at dinner at Christmas 1585, seems to confirm the musicians' presence close at hand: 'her musicians were also in the apartment and discoursed excellent music'. But the players may normally have played from the public Presence Chamber while Elizabeth dined alone in the adjacent Privy Chamber.[41]

Between dinner and the start of the dancing the musicians apparently had little rest, at least during festive seasons and on solemn occasions, for music was required to enhance solemnity and to offer diversion. Thus Count Orsini recalled that after dinner on Twelfth Day, back at the residence of Lord Worcester, 'Then there was music,

74. *Four of Queen Elizabeth's trumpeters: miniature from a manuscript depicting her funeral procession, 1603*

of some instruments to my belief never heard in Italy, but miraculous ones; so that with good entertainment we came to the hour of supper'.[42] Orsini subsequently returned to the queen's presence for the evening, once again to the accompaniment of music:

> Hereupon the Queen came in, and commanded me to go along discoursing with her. Her Majesty mounted the stairs, amid such sounding of trumpets that methought I was on the field of war, and entered a public hall, where all round about were rising steps with ladies, and diverse consorts of music. As soon as her Majesty was set at her place, many ladies and knights began a Grand Ball. When this came to an end, there was acted a mingled comedy, with pieces of music and dances.[43]

Orsini's reference to 'a mingled comedy' raises the important relationship between music and courtly drama. Courtly pageants and plays were more than mere entertainment. They might serve, on the one hand, as a mild form of propaganda at the expense of the queen's enemies. The report of the Venetian Il Schifanoya in the month of Elizabeth's coronation, for example, reveals that these entertainments were not without effect:

> As I suppose your Lordship will have heard of the farce performed in the presence of her Majesty on the day of Epiphany, and I not having sufficient intellect to interpret it, nor yet the mummery performed after supper on the same day, of crows in the habits of Cardinals, of asses habited as Bishops, and of wolves representing Abbots, I will consign it to silence.[44]

This is just the sort of anti-papal play that Sir Richard Morison had suggested to Henry VIII as a substitute for traditional mummings in the 1530s.[45] On 20 July 1586, on the other hand, the Venetian ambassador in Spain wrote as follows to the doge and senate:

> What has enraged him [Philip II] more than all else . . . is the account of the masquerades and comedies which the Queen of England orders to be acted at his expense. His Majesty has received a summary of one of these which was recently represented, in which all sorts of evil is spoken of the Pope, the Catholic Religion, and the King, who is accused of spending all his time in the Escurial with the monks of S. Jerome.[46]

Performances seem to have been a significant pawn in the game of courtly courtesy and royal favour. Elaborate measures were taken to accommodate Orsini at the 'mingled comedy' on Twelfth Night 1601, for example: 'The Muscovite Ambassador was not present. I stood ever near her Majesty, who bade me cover, and withal caused a stool to be fetched for me; and although she willed me a thousand times to sit, I would never obey her'.[47] Orsini not only carefully noted the absence of the Russian ambassador, but also his own proximity to the queen – he could see the play and, more important, be seen by the audience as the queen's constant companion. The offering or withholding of an invitation to the masque or play was no small matter among London diplomats, who regarded it as a direct indication of their country's relative importance and as a reflection of royal commitment. As the Venetian ambassador, Marc' Antonio Correr, wrote in February 1609, 'This court gave no other occasion for rivalry for precedence except these entertainments'.[48] By the time Correr wrote this the political complexities had been increased by the introduction of perspective scenery at court. Since the perspective was perfect only from the monarch's seat, the farther an ambassador was from the monarch, the more distorted was his view and the less honour he received.

The international implications of the music in such diversions were insignificant, but the extent of its aesthetic importance for the productions may be gathered from the notes of the Lord Chamberlain in anticipation of Twelfth Night 1601:

> To Confer with my Lo[rd] Admirall and the M[aste]r of the Revells for takeing order generally with the players to make choyse of play that shalbe best furnished with rich apparell, have greate variety and change of Musicke and daunces, and of a Subject that may be most pleasing to her Ma[jes]tie.[49]

Whether or not many Londoners, like the Elizabethan highwayman Ratsey, would have 'often gone to plays more for music' sake than for action',[50] music must frequently have been a significant aspect of the play. This would have been particularly true in many of the plays acted at court by choirboys. The Chapel Royal had been active in dramatic productions since at least the beginning of the sixteenth century, though long before the end of Henry VIII's reign the gentlemen of the Chapel Royal had left such performances to the children. Their dramatic entertainments were often only part of a full evening's diversion, as in the case of the Twelfth Night festivities described earlier. And frequently they were more in the nature of allegorical pageants than spoken dramas, which opened out to focus upon the monarch. During Elizabeth's reign the primary play season from Candlemas to Shrovetide might involve a variety of offerings, not only by the chapel boys, but also by similar companies from St Paul's, various London schools or adult companies. Between 1558 and 1576 court accounts record at least 21 payments to the St Paul's boys, fifteen to the royal chapels, ten to schoolboys and 32 to adult companies.[51]

The great bulk of dances, interludes and songs for such plays is lost, though isolated pieces can be connected with some productions because of their titles, subject matter or references to characters from particular plays. The majority of these play songs were performed by an unaccompanied soloist. Of the surviving polyphonic songs, one of the best-known types involved texts resembling the rhetorical set pieces of spoken dramas. Frequently they lament impending death or the loss of a loved one. Usually the solo soprano's plain and deliberate line stands out above a complex four-part accompaniment, presumably for viols. Such 'death songs' are best known today from Shakespeare's parody of them in the 'tedious brief scene of young Pyramus and his love Thisbe, very tragical mirth' from Act 5 of *A Midsummer Night's Dream*:

> Approach, ye Furies Fell!
> O Fate, come, come!
> Cut Thread and thrum;
> Quail, crush, conclude and quell!
> O wherefore, Nature, didst thou lions frame?
> Since lion vile hath here deflow'r'd my dear;
> Which is – no, no! – which was the dearest dame
> That liv'd, that lov'd, that lik'd, that look'd with cheer.
> Come tears, confound!
> Out, sword, and wound
> The pap of Pyramus!
> Ay, that left pap
> Where heart doth hop.
> Thus die I, thus, thus.
> Now am I dead,
> Now am I fled;
> My soul is in this sky.
> Tongue, lose thy light;
> Moon, take thy flight.
> Now die, die, die, die, die!

Within a decade of Elizabeth's accession the chapel players had begun to move beyond the confines of the court to the city itself. In 1565–6, for example, their master Richard Edwards led them in a few performances at Lincoln's Inn. A more decisive step was taken ten years later when Richard Farrant successfully petitioned to open a 'school' at Blackfriars in which to teach the children of the chapel; but between 1576 and 1584 he employed the choirboys there in dramatic performances that were open to the public. The Blackfriars theatre reopened at the turn of the century and shortly thereafter the company was recalled to court for the first time in seventeen years to perform in Orsini's 'mingled comedy', so frequently mentioned above. The Declared Accounts of the Treasurer of the Chamber record: 'To Nathanyell Giles M[aste]r of the children of the chapple uppon the councills warraunte dated at whitehall iiijto Maij 1601 . . . for a showe wth musycke and speciall songes p[re]pared for that purpose on Twelfth day at nighte C^s – in all xv^lj'.[52]

A few impressions of Blackfriars were jotted down in 1602 in the diary kept for Philip Julius, Duke of Stettin-Pomerania, who singled out one of the most attractive features of the production, introductory concerts of vocal and instrumental music:

> We went to The Children's Comoediam, the argument treated of a *castam viduam*, and was the story of a royal widow of England. The origin of this Children's Comoediam is this: the Queen keeps a number of young boys who have to apply themselves zealously to the art of singing and to learn all the various musical instruments, and to pursue their studies at the same time . . . Those who wish to see one of their performances must give as much as eight shillings of our money, but there are always a good many people present, many respectable women as well, because useful arguments, and many good doctrines, as we were told, are brought forward there. They do all their plays by light, which produces a great effect. For a whole hour before a delightful performance of *musicam instrumentalem* is given on organs, lutes, pandores, mandolines, violins and flutes; and a boy's singing *cum voce tremula* to a double bass so tunefully, that we have not heard the like of it on the whole journey, except perhaps the nuns of Milan did it better.[53]

This inter-act music must have been a primary source of the musical reputation of the child actors, since it was not yet a feature of adult drama.

Apart from the Queen's Music the only other permanent secular musical institution in London was the company of waits, to whom the lord mayor and the aldermen of London turned for the 'official' music of the city. The London waits represented probably the best and the best-paid musicians outside Elizabeth's service. Together with the court instrumentalists they monopolized the bulk of the most desirable and lucrative performing activities in the city, and were the envy of the freemen of the musicians' company who had to subsist on their leavings.

By the sixteenth century the night watches that the six or seven waits and their dozen apprentices maintained (from the Monday after All Saints' Day until the week before Christmas, and from the first Monday in Lent until Lady-day, 25 March) had much to do with musical entertainment and little to do with their old, traditional task of helping to keep the peace. As the importance of their musical responsibilities was increasingly recognized, the city fathers provided them with a variety of instruments. Sackbuts were added to the basic band of shawms or *hautboys* after 1526, viols in 1561, recorders and cornetts in 1568, until by the middle of Elizabeth's reign the full complement of contemporary instruments was available to them.[54]

In addition to their regular watches, the waits served to enhance the splendour of numerous processions and 'marching watches' in the city, chief among them the yearly inauguration of the Mayor of London. Thus, in 1556, Henry Machyn recorded in his diary:

> The furst day of September was sant Gylles day, and ther was a goodly prossessyon abowt the parryche with the whettes, and the canepe borne, and the sacrement, and ther was a godly masse songe as bene hard; and master Thomas Grenelle, waxchandler, mad a grett dener for master Garter and my lade, and master Machylle the shreyffe and ys wyff, and boyth the chamburlayns, and mony worshefull men and women at dener, and the whettes playing and dyver odur mynstrelles, for ther was a grett dener.[55]

The waits' appearance at the St Giles banquet was also typical of their activities, for they were frequently called upon to play privately before the mayor, aldermen and sheriffs, in a role similar to that of the Queen's Music before the sovereign. Complaints by the magistrates that the waits were sometimes unavailable to serve because of prior commitments to the public theatres reveals another field of their activity. They might also be called to court, as for example on Twelfth Day 1601, when the Lord Chamberlain was required 'to send for the Musitians of the Citty to be reddy to attend'.[56]

Perhaps the most interesting obligation of the waits was inaugurated in 1571 when the city fathers ordered them to 'play upon their instruments upon the turret at the Royal Exchange every Sunday and holiday towards the evening'[57] from late March until the end of September. These hour-long performances are not only significant because they form the first regular public concerts in England – one writer has called them a forerunner of the Proms[58] – but they also bear witness to the aldermen's awareness of the waits' usefulness to call attention to the new Exchange, just opened in 1570, and to glorify the city.

The aldermen's interest in the waits is also revealed by the fact that they occasionally required competitive examinations to fill vacancies in the company, and repeatedly raised the waits' salaries – from £6 to £8 in 1568, to £10 in 1571 (the year the Exchange concerts began) and to £11. 13s. 4d. in 1582.[59] This virtual doubling of wages in fifteen years cannot be explained simply by the leading citizens' fondness for good music. It must result at least in part from a particular awareness of the practical value of the waits in the aggrandizement of the city and its officials.

The London waits, together with the Queen's Music, must have been the primary and the ideal performers of the instrumental repertory that began to expand significantly during Elizabeth's reign. Thomas Morley was surely not the only composer who seems to have composed quite specifically with them in mind. His *First Booke of Consort Lessons*, published in 1599 and sufficiently popular to require a second edition in 1611, was dedicated to the mayor and aldermen of the city, while commending the contents to the waits:

> As the ancient custome is of this most honorable and renowned Cittie hath beene ever, to retaine and maintaine excellent and expert Musitians, to adorne your Honors favors, Feasts and solemne meetings; to those your Lordships Waits . . . I recommend the same to your servants careful and skilfull handling . . . proposing hereafter to give them more testimonies of my love towards them.

At the bottom of the social and economic ladder, furthest from the court, stood the largest body of musicians and minstrels in London, who struggled to eke out a living by catering to the remaining musical needs of the city. The difficult task of protecting the interests of this group fell to the 'Wardens and Commonalty of the fellowship of minstrels freemen of the city of London', as the guild was called in the new articles of organization of 1500 that formed the basis of its subsequent history. Throughout the sixteenth century the guild remained one of the smallest and poorest in the city, consistently ranked at the bottom of the lists of city assessments and relieved of all obligations at civic ceremonies beyond their own performing.

The master and wardens seem to have waged an uphill battle to restrain competition, control interlopers and uphold musical standards. They were considerably hampered in this task by the fact that their main competition – the musicians of the monarch and of noble families resident in London – were exempt from their authority. They could do little about the fact that the bulk of the best, most profitable jobs went to these groups or to the city waits. The guild was only partly successful in controlling other non-members. 'Amateur' musicians affiliated to other guilds, for example, might not only steal their trade and then give them a bad reputation by performing badly in public, but might also swell the ranks of practising musicians by accepting an inordinate number of apprentices.

The apprenticeship system, which remained strong in the musicians' company much longer than in other guilds, offered the primary means of controlling competition. In 1518 all freemen except past and present office holders of the company were restricted to a single apprentice. As a further control on the musician population of the city, freemen were also forbidden to teach music to any but their own apprentices. Exceptions might be made, however, in the case of gentlemen or merchants whose music lessons might lead ultimately to additional patronage for members of the company. To control performance standards apprentices were forbidden to perform publicly before their proficiency had been tested by the officers of the company. It was further stipulated that no apprentice might play in public except in the company of two freemen, which not only provided an additional check on musical standards, but also established a minimum number of musicians for any one engagement.

Despite these various restrictions, members of the company faced stiff competition for the most desirable performing opportunities, listed in 1518 as 'triumphs, feasts, dinners, suppers, marriages, guilds or brotherhoods, taverns, hostelries or alehouses'. A few freemen may have garnered some work in the public theatres towards the end of Elizabeth's reign, but here again they were largely supplanted by resident musicians in the acting companies and by their perennial rivals, the city waits and the Queen's Music. Many may have taken to the streets in the hope of casual employment, which included early morning serenades called 'huntsups', described in 1602 in the Duke of Stettin-Pomerania's diary:

> This day early we arrived at Rochester . . . where we heard beautiful music of viols and pandoras, for in all England it is the custom, that even in small villages the musicians wait on you for a small fee; in the morning about wakening time, they stand outside the chamber, playing religious songs.[60]

The nuisance of this activity must occasionally have provoked protest, for shortly after the turn of the century members of the company were specifically forbidden 'to play upon any kind of instrument or instruments, either evening or morning, at or under any nobleman, knight, or gentleman's window or lodging in the street'.[61]

Obviously the great majority of music-making remained in the hands of these professionals. But what of musical amateurs? Evidence suggests that as most other aspects of music grew in the course of the century, so the extent and variety of musical activities by non-professionals also increased. In the realm of amateur music the court again remained the model, and the monarch the prime exponent, not only as patron of professional musicians but also as a practitioner of the art. Henry VIII's prowess as a musician – from what we know of his attitude, 'prowess' seems the most appropriate word – was as frequently the object of comment as his hunting, jousting and dancing. But whereas others at his court might aspire to rival him in these latter 'sports', he seems to have had few courtly competitors in music. Court observers remark upon the king's performing skills on the keyboard, lute, recorder and even the cornett, and on his ability to compose, but they do not mention similar talents among his courtiers. Until the 1540s, at least, very few (if any) courtly amateurs could compose and scarcely any could read and write music. Though some of the nobility may have sung or played, their performances commonly involved improvisation or memorizing, not notation. In addition, few early Tudor households retained professional musicians or employed music teachers. It was only towards the middle of the century that this began to change. In the last years of Henry's reign more evidence survives to suggest an increase in musical literacy, ownership of musical instruments and the employment of musical professionals or teachers, but even then few could hope or perhaps cared to rival the king in music.

Elizabeth would have wished to appear her father's daughter wherever possible or appropriate. Although several of his talents and noble pastimes were reflected in her activities, music seems to have occupied a place of special prominence. Her tutor Roger Ascham – no great enthusiast for music – may have written in 1550, when Elizabeth was seventeen, that 'In music she is very skilful but does not greatly delight',[62] but by her accession to the throne the situation had obviously changed. At the beginning of her reign Paulo Tiepolo, the Venetian ambassador, wrote: 'The Queen's daily arrangements are musical performances and other entertainments, and she takes marvelous pleasure in seeing people dance'.[63] During the next 40 years the image of the musical queen grew. To the French ambassador she herself claimed in 1598 that as a girl she 'composed measures and music and played them herself and danced them', as mentioned earlier. Richard Mulcaster was one of many to express what became the official doctrine of her talents when he wrote in his laudatory verses to Tallis and Byrd's *Cantiones Sacrae*: 'Her Royal Majesty, the glory of our age, is accustomed always to have Music among her pleasures. Not content simply to hear the venerable works of others, she herself sings and plays excellently'. The image was enhanced and carried abroad by foreign visitors such as Thomas Platter who saw several of Elizabeth's instruments while touring her palaces in 1599:

> We saw in addition many more costly virginals, instruments, positive organs, and organs of which Her Royal Majesty is a great lover and connoisseur. And amongst others we were shown an instrument or virginal whose strings were of pure gold and silver, and they said the queen often played this very charmingly.[64]

75. Queen Elizabeth playing the lute:
miniature (c1580) by Nicholas Hilliard

Whereas accounts of Henry's musical activities gave the impression that he was prepared to perform for anyone at court who would listen, Elizabeth seems to have been more careful to abide by the rules of decorum. She would not, for instance, follow her father's example and play the cornett which, in the words of Robert Peterson's translation of della Casa's *Galateo* (1576), was inappropriate for men and women 'if they be not of that base condition and calling, that they must make it a gaine, and an art to live uppon it'.[65] Though she saw to it that everyone knew of her musical talents, few had the honour of witnessing them. An anecdote told by John Melville, the Scottish ambassador who visited Elizabeth's court in 1564, offers the best-known example of how such an occasion might come to pass:

> The same day after dinner my Lord of Hunsdean drew me up to a quiet gallery, that I might hear some music (but he said that he durst not avow it) where I might hear the Queen play upon the virginals. After I had hearkened a while, I took by the tapestry that hung before the door of the chamber, and seeing her back was toward the door, I entered within the chamber, and stood a pretty space hearing her play excellently well. But she left off immediately, so soon as she turned her about and saw me. She appeared to be surprised to see me, and came forward, seeming to strike me with her hand; alleging she used not to play before men, but when she was solitary, to shun melancholy. She asked how I came there. I answered, As I was walking with my Lord of Hunsdean, as we passed by the chamber-door, I heard such melody as ravished me, whereby I was drawn in ere I knew how; excusing my

fault of homeliness, as being brought up in the Court of France, where such freedom was allowed . . . She enquired whether my Queen or she played best. In that I found myself obliged to give her the praise . . . She inquired of me, whether she or my Queen danced best. I answered, the Queen danced not so high, and disposedly as she did.[66]

By this artfully engineered exercise in courtly behaviour – surely everyone knew from the beginning how this scene would play – Elizabeth displayed her mastery of music and of its gentle usages.

To hear her perform became another token of particular favour. Jacob Rathgeb, secretary to Frederick, Duke of Wirtemberg, recorded that during an audience with the French ambassador in 1592 at which Frederick was present, 'Since . . . Her Majesty held Monsieur de Beauvois in especial favour, after he had been conversing with her Majesty very lively and good-humouredly he so far prevailed upon her that she played very sweetly and skilfully on her instrument, the strings of which were of gold and silver'.[67] At the end of the reign, Virginio Orsino would write, 'Before I depart she wishes to enjoy me again, in private; and I hope from the speech I have had with her that she will favour me by playing and singing'.[68]

In such an atmosphere many courtiers must have believed in the special efficacy of music in dealing with the queen. The four Venetians quoted earlier certainly believed that music was the source of Alfonso Ferrabosco's special success at court. Although there was malicious exaggeration in Sir Robert Naunton's claim that 'Sir Christopher Hatton came into court . . . as Perrot used to say, "by the galliard", for he came hither as a private gentleman of the Inns of Court in a masque',[69] such a talent would scarcely have hindered his advancement.

Just as the dance became closely bound up with the mystique of the ageless queen, music found a prominent place in her attendant courtly rituals. It is particularly intriguing that, immediately after his description of the queen's playing for the Duke of Wirtemberg and the French ambassador, Rathgeb should have continued, 'Yet notwithstanding that her Majesty was at this time in her 67th year [*sic*], . . . and has thus borne the heavy burden of ruling a kingdom thirty-four years, she need not indeed – to judge both from her person and appearance – yield much to a young girl of sixteen'.[70] Even a foreigner might be drawn into the cult of the young girl, with music as one of her emblems.

Probably the best-known and most telling illustration of music's power in the immediate circle around the queen is the court gossip passed on to Gilbert Talbot, Earl of Shrewsbury, by his secretary and agent at court, William Brown, on 18 September 1602:

I send your Lordship here inclosed some verses compounded by Mr Secretary [Sir Robert Cecil], who got Hales to frame a ditty to it. The occasion was, as I hear, that the young Lady of Darby wearing about her neck, in her bosom, a picture which was in a dainty tablet;

the Queen espying itt, asked what fyne jewell that was? The Lady Darby was curious to excuse the shewing of it; but the Queen wold have it, and, opening it, and finding it to be Mr. Secretary's, snatcht it away, and tyed itt upon her shoe, and walked long with it there; then took it thence and pinned itt on her elbow, and wore it there sometime also; which Mr Secretary being told of, made these verses, and had Hales to sing them in his chamber. It was told her Ma[jes]ty that Mr Secretary had rare musick, and song; she would needes hear them; and so this ditty was soung which you see first written. More verses there be lykewise, wherof som, or all, were lykewyse soung. I do boldly send these things to your Lo. which I wold not do to any else, for I heare they are very secrett. Some of the verses argue, that he repynes not, thoghe her Ma[jes]ty please to grace others, and contents himself with the favour he hath.[71]

The story has been cited as a useful witness to the fact that a courtier and a professional musician could collaborate in a musical enterprise.[72] What is especially revealing, however, is that this anecdote about the attempted reconciliation of a 69-year-old ruler and her minister indicates the importance of music in a society for whom the aging spinster has become the perpetually young girl. It reveals that to the end of her reign music was both seen – and proved – to be an essential means of treating with Elizabeth.

Because music was important to the queen it had to be important to those around her, as the Robert Cecil affair indicates. Of course, the image of Elizabeth as the supreme noble amateur cannot explain the significant increase in amateur music during her reign, but it must have influenced those who looked to the court as a model of gentle manners and good behaviour. The queen's ultimate control over wards of the court must also have contributed to the musical upbringing of members of noble households. The courtly view of music was reinforced to varying degrees by guides to gentle behaviour such as Hoby's translation of Castiglione's *Il cortegiano* published in 1561. These certainly differed widely in their enthusiasm for the art of music, some advocating nothing more than passive listening and connoisseurship. Thomas Whythorne, at least, seems to have believed in their positive influence by the mid-1570s:

Those that do learn it [music] . . . for the love they have to the science and not to live by . . . are to be accounted among the number of those who the book named the 'Institution of a Gentlemenn' doth allow to learn music, and also which the book named 'The Courtier' doth . . . for they would have the great gentlemen and the courtiers to learn music in that sort . . . Which counsel . . . the nobility and the worshipful do much follow in these days, For many of those estates have schoolmasters in their houses to teach their children both to sing pricksong and also to play on instruments.[73]

The London Inns of Court also provided some encouragement for amateur musicians, particularly among the gentry, both as patrons and practitioners. Professional musicians were paid to perform there on feasts such as All Saints' Day and Candlemas. In 1595 the parliament of the Inner Temple ruled, for example, 'that the gentlemen that keep private commons shall have five marks given them towards their music'.[74] The Inns, too, presented elaborate plays and masques involving music. It might in fact have been the repeat presentation of *Gorboduc* at court in January 1561 by the Inner Temple that first brought Sir Christopher Hatton, then Master of the Game, to the queen's attention.

Records of the Inner Temple attest to the presence of a special 'music room' at least by the second decade of the seventeenth century, though it is unclear how long it had been set aside for such purposes and whether these included the accommodation of members for their own

76. *An Elizabethan masque in performance: detail of the Memorial Portrait of Sir Henry Unton (c1596). Mercury and Diana lead the entry of masquers and torch-bearers who process round a broken consort (a consort of viols can be seen in the upper left-hand room)*

music-making. By the 1570s it seems that increasing numbers of students were dabbling in music and engaging private music teachers. Numerous references to lutes and their common exchange among gentlemen at the Inns may suggest a high level of interest.[75] It is probably no more indicative of considerable expertise or sophistication, however, than the ubiquitous guitars in the hands of students 400 years later.

By the 1570s evidence suggests that a growing number of amateurs could read 'pricksong' and play instruments, particularly the virginals, lute and wire-strung instruments such as the cittern, bandora and orpharion. Less evidence exists for widespread amateur cultivation of the viol before the closing years of the century. How widespread consort playing may have been among amateurs remains open to debate.[76] Much of the repertory of textless polyphony from early in Elizabeth's reign, such as the indigenous genre based on the long-note cantus firmus In Nomine, was in fact probably sung 'to the bare note' rather than played. The repertory from the 1570s and 1580s, which would include the bulk of William Byrd's mature output of fantasias for consort, probably was not originally conceived with amateurs in mind. A significant number of publications directed towards instrumental performance only began to appear in the last years of the century, suggesting that by then, at least, the number of amateurs looking both for books of instrumental music and for printed tutors had increased significantly.

By the same token, the failure of the pioneering *Cantiones sacrae* of Tallis and Byrd, printed in 1575, suggests that at that time amateurs capable of singing anything more complex than metrical psalms were also still comparatively rare. Although there may be disagreement about how to interpret surviving evidence for the next dozen years after the *Cantiones sacrae*, by the late 1580s the situation had changed. When Byrd next ventured into print with his *Psalmes, Sonets and Songs* of 1588, not only did the collection sell well enough to require another two editions in quick succession, but it also signalled the beginning of music printing in England on an unparalleled scale. In the years remaining before the expiration of Byrd's patent in 1596 Thomas East, Byrd's assignee, printed and reprinted about two dozen musical publications. Yet even at its height the English 'industry' appears a modest one by comparison with music printing on the Continent. Musically unpretentious metrical psalm collections promised greater profits than the more 'artificial' and musically interesting music books of madrigals, part-songs, lute songs or motets. In the most active year, 1597, eight of the more elaborate music publications issued from London presses, a number that compares favourably with the output of several continental cities. One need only remember, however, that between 1570 and 1600 only about 40 music prints of all types (except metrical psalms) appeared in England, while Paris produced more than 70 collections of works by multiple composers, not counting publications devoted to single authors. During the same 30-year period Venice saw the publication of 370 multi-author prints alone.

Though it pales in comparison with the Continent, this flurry of publication marks a greater demand for music to sing and play. Family accounts begin to document the purchase of such collections in considerable number. Thus in 1599 the Cavendishes of Chatsworth bought 'Tallis and Bird and Yongs two sets of songs' for 8s., 'Luca Marenzio his 5 pts' for 5s. 4d., 'the same his 6 pts' for 6s. and 'sixe sette of englishe songe bookes viz. 4, 5 and 6 pts of Watsons. Wilkes sett. Est his madrigalls. Rosetters booke, Dowlands 3 bookes. Robinsons schoole of musicke' for 39s. 4d. in 1604.[77] Many collections testify to the vogue for Italian madrigals and their English imitations. Nicholas Yonge, the compiler of *Musica transalpina,* one of the collections bought by the Cavendishes and among the most popular compilations, suggests that his own publication grew out of musical gatherings for madrigal singing in his home near St Paul's:

> Since I first began to keepe house in this Citie, it hath been no small comfort unto me, that a great number of Gentlemen and Merchants of good accompt (as well of this realme as of forreine nations) have taken in good part such entertainment of pleasure, as my poor abilitie was able to afford them, both by the exercise of Musicke daily used in my house, and by furnishing them with Bookes of that kind yeerely sent me out of Italy and other places.

If we take Yonge at his word in this famous and oft-quoted description, there seems little doubt that a demand for foreign, especially Italian, music existed among 'gentlemen and merchants'. The extent to which Yonge's entertainments actually involved the participation of these gentlemen, or attests to their own performance, is less clear. Yonge himself was a lay clerk at St Paul's. His musical gatherings may have included several of his fellow lay clerks, who had a house by St Mary Woolchurch Haw near his own in Cornhill. One suspects that the amateurs' role may have been passive, or at best, secondary to that of these professionals – assuming, of course, that they were prepared to mix with them publicly in consort at all. As for the musicianship of the average gentleman amateur, it may have left much to be desired. Michael East's compliment to Sir Thomas Gerard in the dedication to his *Second Set of Madrigals* (1606) that Gerard's 'perfection in music' was 'rare in a gentleman of your rank'[78] suggests that musically proficient gentlemen were the exception not the rule. Pasarello in Marston's *The Malcontent* put it less politely, 'Yes, I can sing . . . and I can play upon instruments, scurvily, as gentlemen do'.[79]

NOTES

[1] W. D. Robson-Scott, *German Travellers in England 1400–1800* (Oxford, 1953), 71.

[2] P. le Huray, *Music and the Reformation in England 1549–1660* (London, 1967), 38–9.

[3] J. Nichols, *The Progresses and Public Processions of Queen Elizabeth* (London, 1823), ii, 458.

[4] Le Huray, *Music and the Reformation*, 35.

[5] C. Williams, *Thomas Platter's Travels in England, 1599* (London, 1937), 209.

[6] V. von Klarwell, *Queen Elizabeth and Some Foreigners* (New York, 1928), 234.

[7] L. Hotson, *The First Night of Twelfth Night* (London, 1964), 188–9.

[8] ibid, 199–200.

[9] W. Woodfill, *Musicians in English Society from Elizabeth to Charles I* (Princeton, 1953/R1969), 137.

[10] *Elizabethan People*, ed. J. Hurstfield and A. Smith (London, 1972), 57–8.

[11] *Calendar of State Papers, Domestic Series, Elizabeth, 1598–1601*, v, ed. M. A. E. Green (London, 1869), 438.

[12] F. Ll. Harrison, *Music in Medieval Britain* (London, 1967), 171.

[13] Nichols, *Progresses and Public Processions*, iii, 415.

[14] *The Old Cheque-Book of the Chapel Royal*, ed. E. F. Rimbault, Camden Society, new ser., iii (London, 1872/R1966), 178–9.

[15] P. Johnson, *Elizabeth I* (London, 1974), 225.

[16] D. C. Price, *Patrons and Musicians of the English Renaissance* (Cambridge, 1980), 49.

[17] *GB-Lbm* 18.B.xix; cited in Price, *Patron and Musicians*, 51–2.

[18] *Analytical Index to the Series of Records Known as the Remembrancia Preserved Among the Archives of the City of London, A.D. 1579–1664* (London, 1878), 129.

[19] *Zurich Letters*, i, ed. H. Robinson (Cambridge, 1842), 71.

[20] Woodfill, *Musicians in English Society*, 207.

[21] *Diary of the Journey of Philip Julius, Duke of Stettin-Pomerania, Through England in the Year 1602*, ed. G. von Bulow, Transactions of the Royal Historical Society, new ser., vi (London, 1892), 61.

[22] See particularly R. Prior, 'Jewish Musicians at the Tudor Court', *MQ*, lxix (1983), 253–65.

[23] G. A. Philipps, 'Crown Musical Patronage from Elizabeth I to Charles I', *ML*, lviii (1977), 42.

[24] *Calendar of State Papers, Domestic Series*, v, ed. Green, 90.

[25] *Analytical Index to the Series of Records Known as the Remembrancia*, 428.

[26] R. Charteris, *Alfonso Ferrabosco the Elder (1543–1588): a Thematic Catalogue of his Music with a Biographical Calendar* (New York, 1984), 14.

[27] Woodfill, *Musicians in English Society*, 188.

[28] Nichols, *Progresses and Public Processions*, iii, 32.

[29] W. B. Rye, *England as Seen by Foreigners in the Days of Elizabeth and James I* (London, 1865), 338.

[30] Woodfill, *Musicians in English Society*, 189.

[31] O. Strunk, *Source Readings in Music History* (New York, 1950), 285.

[32] Hotson, *The First Night of Twelfth Night*, 210.

[33] Woodfill, *Musicians in English Society*, 189.

[34] Nichols, *Progresses and Public Processions*, iii, 91.

[35] ibid, i, 67.

[36] *Calendar of State Papers and Manuscripts Relating to English Affairs Existing in the Archives and Collections of Venice 1202–1603*, vii, ed. R. Brown and G. C. Bentnick (London, 1890), 12.

[37] ibid, vii, 18.

[38] Nichols, *Progresses and Public Processions*, iii, 426.

[39] Hotson, *The First Night of Twelfth Night*, 194.

[40] ibid, 181.

[41] P. Holman, 'The English Royal Violin Consort in the 16th Century', *PRMA*, cix (1982–3), 49.

[42] Hotson, *The First Night of Twelfth Night*, 201.

[43] ibid, 202.

[44] *Calendar of State Papers and Manuscripts Relating to English Affairs Existing in the Archives and Collections of Venice*, vii, ed. Brown and Bentnick, 11.

[45] R. Strong, *The Cult of Elizabeth: Elizabethan Portraiture and Pageantry* (London, 1977), 118.

[46] *Calendar of State Papers and Manuscripts Relating to English Affairs Existing in the Archives and Collections of Venice 1202–1603*, viii, ed. H. Brown (London, 1894), 182.

[47] Hotson, *The First Night of Twelfth Night*, 202.

[48] *Calendar of State Papers and Manuscripts Relating to English Affairs Existing in the Archives and Collections of Venice*, xi, ed. H. Brown (London, 1904), 232.

[49] Hotson, *The First Night of Twelfth Night*, 180.

[50] ibid, 121.

[51] E. K. Chambers, *The Elizabethan Stage* (London, 1923), ii, 4.

[52] H. N. Hildebrand, *The Child Actors: a Chapter in Elizabethan Stage History* (Urbana, Illinois, 1926), 172.

[53] *Diary of the Journey of Philip Julius*, ed. Bulow, 28–9.

[54] Woodfill, *Musicians in English Society*, 34.

[55] J. Nichols, *The Diary of Henry Machyn*, Camden Society, 1st ser., xlii (London, 1848), 113.

[56] Hotson, *The First Night of Twelfth Night*, 181.

[57] Woodfill, *Musicians in English Society*, 50.

[58] Johnson, *Elizabeth I*, 206.

[59] Woodfill, *Musicians in English Society*, 37.

[60] *Diary of the Journey of Philip Julius*, ed. Bulow, 63.

[61] H. A. F. Crewsdon, *The Worshipful Company of Musicians* (London, 2/1971), 129.

[62] M. C. Boyd, *Elizabethan Music and Musical Criticism* (Philadelphia, 1940), 7.

[63] *Calendar of State Papers and Manuscripts Relating to English Affairs Existing in the Archives and Collections of Venice*, vii, ed. Brown and Bentnick, 101.

[64] Williams, *Thomas Platter's Travels*, 204.

[65] W. Edwards, 'The Performance of Ensemble Music in Elizabethan England', *PRMA*, xcvii (1970–71), 120.

[66] *Memoirs of Sir James Melville*, ed. F. A. Steuart (New York, 1930), 96–7.

[67] Rye, *England as seen by Foreigners*, 12.

[68] Hotson, *The First Night of Twelfth Night*, 208.

[69] Johnson, *Elizabeth I*, 214.

[70] Rye, *England as seen by Foreigners*, 12.

[71] Nichols, *Progresses and Public Processions*, iii, 596–7.

[72] Price, *Patron and Musicians*, 105.

[73] ibid, 15.

[74] *Calendar of the Inner Temple Records*, ed. F. A. Indewick (London, 1896), 410.

[75] Price, *Patrons and Musicians*, 28.

[76] Compare Price, *Patrons and Musicians*, 42, with Edwards, 'The Performance of Ensemble Music'.

[77] Price, *Patrons and Musicians*, 113–16.

[78] Woodfill, *Musicians in English Society*, 227.

[79] Marston, *The Malcontent* (1603), Act 1 scene viii, lines 2–3; quoted in D. G. O'Neil, 'The Influence of Music in the Works of John Marston, I', *ML*, liii (1972), 124–5.

BIBLIOGRAPHICAL NOTE

Historical background

Of the vast literature on London and the court during the reign of Elizabeth only a few works can be singled out here. A useful complement to this chapter is D. M. Palliser's study of various aspects of English social and economic life from c1550 to 1600, *The Age of Elizabeth* (London, 1983), which includes a useful comparison of London and the other important urban centres of the realm. *The Reign of Elizabeth*, ed. C. Haigh (London, 1985), includes among several valuable essays: S. Adams, 'Eliza Enthroned? The Court and its Politics', on the structure and workings of the court; P. Collison, 'The Elizabethan Church and the New Religion', on the problems of the Elizabethan religious settlement; and Haigh, 'The Church of England, the Catholics and the People', on the extent and nature of religious conformity and the survival of forms and features of the Old Religion. For a varied exposition of the political, religious and chivalric aspects of the cult of Elizabeth, see F. A. Yates, *Astraea* (London, 1975). David M. Bergeron's *English Civic Pageantry 1558–1642* (London, 1971) treats the progresses and royal entries of Elizabeth on the one hand, and the London Lord Mayors' shows, on the other. In quite a different vein, G. B. Harrison's *The Elizabethan Journals* (Ann Arbor, 1955) provides a very readable account of day-to-day events, both of the great and the not-so-great, from 1591 to 1603, culled from primary sources, treated with considerable poetic licence.

Art

E. Mercer, *English Art 1555–1625* (Oxford, 1962), vol.vii of the *Oxford History of English Art*, offers a discussion of all aspects of Elizabethan art from painting and sculpture to interior decoration. R. Strong's *The Cult of Elizabeth: Elizabethan Portraiture and Pageantry* (London, 1977) represents a valuable study of the political usages of pageants and portraits, while his *Tudor and Jacobean Portraits* (London, 1969) is a lavishly illustrated and annotated catalogue of the holdings of the National Portrait Gallery, supplemented by significant portraits from other collections.

Music

Most of the Elizabethan musical repertory is accessible in modern edition, though many series from earlier in the century have been revised or supplanted by newer editions. Tudor Church Music, ed. P. C. Buck, A. Ramsbotham, E. H. Fellowes, R. R. Terry and S. Townsend Warner (Oxford, 1922–9), still remains the most accessible and reliable source for Tallis's masses and motets (vol.vi) and Byrd's *Gradualia* (vol.vii). The series Early English Church Music (London, 1963–), currently 32 volumes, includes the sacred works of William Mundy (vol.ii: Latin antiphons and psalms), Tallis (vols.xii–xiii: anthems and Anglican service music), Sheppard (vols.xvii–xviii: responsorial music and masses), Tye (vols.xix and xxxiii: English sacred music, ritual music and motets), Taverner (vols.xx, xxv and xxx: masses, ritual music), Robert White (vols.xxviii–xxxix and xxxii: Latin psalms, votive antiphons, ritual music and Lamentations), plus a wealth of additional material. For a sampling of the determinedly simple sacred style of Edward VI's reign, see *The Tudor Church Music of the Lumley Books*, ed. J. Blezzard, RRMR, lxv (1985). Virtually all of the English madrigal repertory is available in E. H. Fellowes, *The English Madrigalists*, rev. T. Dart and others (London, 1956–), a revision and expansion of Fellowes's earlier *The English Madrigal School*. The lute-song repertory appears in E. H. Fellowes, *The English Lute-Songs*, 1st ser. (17 vols.) and 2nd ser. (21 vols.), rev. T. Dart and others (London, 1959–), a revision and expansion of Fellowes's *The English School of Lutenist Songwriters*. Of the 52 volumes in the national series Musica Britannica (London, 1951–) the following are only the most immediately relevant to the present chapter: vol.vi: Dowland, *Ayres for Four Voyces*; vols.xiv and xix: Bull, *Keyboard Music;* vol.xxii: *Consort Songs*; vol.xxiii: Weelkes, *Collected Anthems*; vols.xxvii–xxviii: Byrd, *Keyboard Music*; vol.xl: *Music for Mixed Consort*; vols.xliv–xlv: *Elizabethan Consort Music*. For the vocal works of Byrd see The Byrd Edition, ed. P. Brett (London, 1976–), which supplants Fellowes's *Collected Vocal Works of William Byrd*. A broad sampling of the Elizabethan musical repertory is also available in various less expensive but frequently less authoritative editions.

For the Elizabethan period there is still no comparable equivalent to John Stevens's much admired *Music and Poetry in the Early Tudor Court* (London, 1961). In addition to the works cited above, however, others may usefully be consulted in connection with specialized aspects of music of the period. The earlier chapters in N. Temperley's *The Music of the English Parish Church* (Cambridge, 1979) complement P. le Huray's *Music and the Reformation in England* (London, 1967). Edward Doughtie's *English Renaissance Song* (Boston, 1986) provides a useful, up-to-date introduction to various aspects of the subject, particularly for non-specialists, and includes an extensive bibliography of primary and secondary sources. Joseph Kerman's *The Elizabethan Madrigal* (New York, 1962) remains the most penetrating study of that genre. On the English music-printing trade see D. Krummel's *English Music Printing 1553–1700* (London, 1975). Several of the important composers of the period have been the subject of monographs. Only the two greatest Elizabethan composers and one minor one will be mentioned here. A very valuable study of the music of William Byrd is provided in the *The Music of William Byrd*: i: J. Kerman, *The Masses and Motets of William Byrd* (London, 1980); iii: O. Neighbour, *The Consort and Keyboard Music of William Byrd* (London, 1978); ii: P. Brett, *The Songs, Services and Anthems of William Byrd* (in preparation). For a much briefer introduction to the life and works of Thomas Tallis, see P. Doe, *Tallis* (Oxford, 2/1976). Thomas Whythorne may be a very minor composer, but his autobiography, *The Autobiography of Thomas Whythorne*, ed. J. M. Osborn (Oxford, 1961), offers a unique opportunity to observe first-hand and in great detail the life and times of an Elizabethan musician.

Chapter XIII

The Spanish Court of Ferdinand and Isabella

TESS KNIGHTON

The importance of the royal court of Ferdinand and Isabella as a centre for musical developments in Spain in the early Renaissance is clearly reflected in the number of composers who served there. Peñalosa, Anchieta, Escobar, Alba, Urede, Tordesillas, La Torre, Ponce, Madrid, Cornago, Rivaflecha, Medina, Diaz, Gijón, Aldomar and many others all sang in the Castilian or Aragonese royal chapels, and their polyphony, both sacred and secular, was composed and performed at court.[1] Service in the royal chapels brought these, the best musicians in all Spain, into direct contact with mainstream musical developments in the rest of Europe, and resulted in constant exchange with the other centres of musical activity in Spain at this time, notably the cathedrals, other ecclesiastical establishments and the households of the nobility.

Prestige, high salaries, clothing allowances, tax exemptions and privileges of all kinds were the attractions which drew musicians into the service of the Catholic Monarchs. The number of musicians employed at court – chapel singers, *ministriles altos* (the players of *haut* wind instruments such as sackbuts and shawms), the corps of trumpets and drums and players of *bas* instruments such as flutes or vihuelas – increased dramatically during their reign. Music was an essential adornment to almost every aspect of court life, and the demand for music can be gauged from the surviving sources of polyphony which can be associated with the royal court. Together with a variety of documentary material, these manuscripts reveal much about the court's musical requirements and the stimulus these gave to the composers serving there. All the evidence affirms that music flourished on an unprecedented scale in Spain during the reign of the Catholic Monarchs. But what was the exact nature of the roles of Ferdinand and Isabella as musical patrons? To what extent were they responsible for the emergence of this new generation of Spanish composers whose music exhibits an awareness of mainstream Franco-Flemish techniques but also adheres local traditions? 500 years after their court was first established and expanded, it is difficult to assess their personal involve-

341

77. *The Catholic Monarchs Ferdinand and Isabella, with Princess Isabella and Prince Juan, kneeling in adoration of the Virgin and Child, accompanied by SS Thomas and Dominic: painting by an unknown artist (possibly the court painter Maestro Bartolomé)*

ment, and even more so to determine whether they had a policy or vision as far as music was concerned. However, their acute awareness of contemporary trends in all matters of court and state make it possible to relate the significant musical developments of this period to the more general aims and policies of their reign.

It is not clear whether either Ferdinand or Isabella received any formal musical training – their education was interrupted by war and unsettled times – nor is there any record that they participated in music-making themselves. Ferdinand, however, would appear to have spent solitary afternoons listening to music in his chambers, if this account by a royal secretary is any guide:

Yesterday his highness rose early and, having prayed, went to church and stayed for the whole service, after which he ate and then rested a little, reading. As usual his highness went hunting and killed two kites. This morning his highness attended Mass in the church, as usual after eating there was vihuela music, after which he went to Vespers.[2]

The king's personal accounts reveal that he signed pay-slips for the purchase of *bas* instruments such as flutes and vihuelas, suitable for performance in the semi-private context of the royal chambers; but they also show that payments for the purchase of hunting birds, such as Milanese falcons, amounted to considerably more. Isabella's accounts, kept by her treasurer Gonzalo de Baeza, reveal that her main expenditure was on the accoutrements of the Castilian royal chapel, including the musical items such as books of chant and polyphony. Indeed, her concern for the celebration of the liturgy in the royal chapels apparently extended to the correction of the singers and chaplains if they mispronounced or misplaced a syllable of the liturgical text while singing:

> If anyone of those who were saying or singing the psalms, or other things of the church, made any slip in diction or in the placing of a syllable, she heard and noted it, and afterwards – as teacher to pupil – she emended and corrected it for them.[3]

Isabella's successor as King of Castile, her grandson Charles V (1517–55), was more musically orientated; he chastized the royal singers if they sang wrong notes. However, if the monarchs themselves had received little musical education, this was certainly not true of their children. From an early age, Isabella, Juan, Juana, Maria and Catalina (better known as Catherine of Aragon) had been taught by singers in the royal chapel, such as Juan de Anchieta, and their households included instrumentalists appointed in the name of the queen. Indeed, the love of music on the part of at least two of the royal children was to have important ramifications for musical developments in Spain in the early sixteenth century: Juan, the heir to the throne, who died shortly after his marriage to Margaret of Austria in 1497, and Juana, known as 'la loca' (or 'the mad one'), who married Philip the Fair the previous year and travelled with him to Flanders.

According to Gonzalo Fernández de Oviedo, a contemporary chronicler, Juan's chambers were full of musical instruments of all kinds, including the first claviorgan seen in Spain, and the prince apparently knew how to play most of them. Fernández de Oviedo's eulogistic tone rings truer in his description of how Prince Juan spent his afternoons singing polyphonic songs with Juan de Anchieta and some of the choirboys in the royal chapel:

> My Lord prince Juan was naturally inclined to music and he understood it well, although his voice was not as good as he was persistent in

singing; but it would pass with other voices. And for this purpose, during siesta time, especially in summer, Juan de Anchieta, his chapel master, and four or five boys, chapel boys with fine voices (among whom was Corral who later became an excellent singer and *tiple*), who went to the palace, and the prince sang with them for two hours, or however long he pleased to, and he took the tenor, and was very skilful in the art.[4]

This description is of great importance for the insight it gives into private music-making at court, and as an example of one way in which polyphonic songs were performed towards the end of the fifteenth century. The prince kept illustrious company; Anchieta, one of the finest composers of his generation, served in the royal chapels from 1489 until Ferdinand's death in 1516, and Antonio de Corral went on to be an adult singer there in 1499, serving alongside his former teacher for the next seventeen years. Perhaps one of the songs they sang together was Juan del Encina's *El que rige y el regido*, dedicated to the prince in the tradition of treatises on the art of governing (such as Rodrigo de Arévalo's *Vergel de los principes*, dedicated to Juan's musical uncle, Enrique IV), in which the virtues of music in the education of an heir to the throne are expounded. It is in this respect that Juan's interest in music, and his personal role as a patron of musicians, was influential.

Juan's historical position was of great significance; the only son of the Catholic Monarchs, he would inherit the thrones of both Castile and Aragon and thereby consolidate the tentative unification of Spain brought about by their marriage. Juan was very much the centre of attention; all eyes in higher society were turned on him, and it is clear that his education and his interests served as a model for all young nobles, especially those in his entourage at court. Humanistically orientated scholars, such as Peter Martyr and Alessandro Geraldini from Sicily, were employed as tutors for the royal children and young nobles. Martyr, although often critical of the nobles' attitude to learning, also commented on their desire to imitate trends at court: 'On the orders of his parents, the heir to the throne, on whom all eyes are fastened, has dedicated himself to the study of letters; consequently all the rest, following the example of their Prince, will apply themselves likewise'.[5]

Tragically for the tradition of royal patronage of music in Spain, Juan was to die young; but perhaps the influence of his passionate interest in music can be detected in the love of polyphonic song which blossomed among the Spanish nobility in the early years of the sixteenth century. The correspondence of the Count of Tendilla reveals the competition and rivalry that this passion engendered in the recruitment of the services of musicians. Writing to Don Iñigo Manrique on 11 April 1513, he discussed the availability of various singers and instrumentalists:

I brought Rodrigo Donaire, as your honour agreed, and now, because of Galiano's refusal I have taken on another instrumentalist who is also a servant of Don Diego Hernández: if he has one *tiple* I have three others exceptional for songs and more. Anything to do with music you might come across over there, let it come here, for this is all the rage now.[6]

Rodrigo Donaire, a vihuelist and singer, had already served Isabella and her children (including Juan), and Galiano may also have been a royal musician at this time. This rivalry among the Castilian nobility for the services of musicians – especially, perhaps, for those who had served at court – illustrates how musical developments, stimulated by the interests and tastes of the royal family themselves, were diffused through the upper echelons of Spanish society.

Another aspect of the patronage of music by members of the royal family resulted in an even more significant stimulus to the cultivation and development of polyphony in Spain at this time. This arose indirectly from the prestigious and highly political marriage alliances that Ferdinand and Isabella sought for their children in the 1490s. The monarchs had gained enormously in stature, both at home and throughout Europe, with the successful reconquest of Granada in 1492; they then sought to consolidate this prestige by marrying their children into the royal and ducal families of their allies, who at this time included the Habsburgs in Burgundy and Austria and the Tudors in England. Thus Juan was betrothed to Margaret of Austria, daughter of Maximilian I, Juana to his son and heir, Philip the Fair, and Catherine to Prince Arthur, eldest son of Henry VII. Margaret came to Spain in 1496, and the same year Juana travelled to Flanders, escorted by a substantial retinue that included several musicians. Juan died shortly after his marriage, Margaret returning forlorn to Flanders, and the series of unforeseen circumstances initiated by his death meant that Juana's marriage was to result in prolonged, direct contact between Spanish and Flemish musicians, including some of the great composers of the day.

Philip, as Juana's husband, became heir to the thrones of Castile and Aragon in 1500, and as such he had to be 'sworn in' by the parliaments of his future kingdoms. Thus in 1501 he set off through France, having gathered an impressive retinue that included an expanded chapel choir. Such illustrious singer-composers as Pierre de La Rue were recruited, although an attempt en route to secure the services of Josquin failed. The Flemish entourage travelled widely through Spain, so that contact between northern and Spanish musicians was not restricted to one place, or necessarily confined to those serving at the royal court, although it was most direct there. A contemporary description of a Mass celebrated in Toledo Cathedral in honour of Philip's visit in 1502 mentions the large number of royal singers taking part in the service: 'On Sunday, 8 May, my Lord and Lady [Philip and Juana] heard Mass with the king and queen [Ferdinand and Isabella] at which the 60 to 80 singers of the king sang'.[7]

The joint choirs of the Aragonese and Castilian chapels amounted to as many as 47 adult singers at this time; perhaps this number, if accurate, also includes the choir of Toledo Cathedral, or other singers drafted for the occasion. As the heirs to the united thrones of Castile and Aragon travelled throughout these kingdoms, the Flemish choir would also have sung at these celebratory services, as was customary on such ceremonial occasions. As a result of Philip's visit in 1502, Spanish musicians, whether serving at court, or in the cathedrals or households of the Spanish nobility, came into contact with the Flemish singers and instrumentalists of his retinue, exchanged repertory, learnt new compositional techniques and heard different performing traditions. When Philip returned to the north, some of his musicians stayed behind in Spain, on the payrolls of the royal courts, so that such contact was further prolonged. The influence of mainstream Franco-Flemish musical developments can be seen in the polyphonic repertory of the royal chapels and in the works of the Spanish composers serving there.

The Flemish choir was to return to Spain in 1506. Following the death of Isabella in 1504, Philip was declared King of Castile, and he duly travelled south once more. After only a few months' reign, however, Philip died and was succeeded by his mentally unbalanced wife, Juana. Juana's love for music appears to have been one of her few sources of solace throughout her unhappy life, and, with the death of her husband, his Flemish choir not only sang the Office of the Dead every day for the best part of a year (since Juana refused to bury Philip's body for about that length of time), but also sang in the privacy of her chambers. She was totally uninterested in affairs of state and the only documents she would sign were the pay-slips for her Flemish singers, who received salaries as high as the most important officials at court. La Rue again led this choir; Alexander Agricola had also travelled to Spain this time but like Philip had met an untimely death there. The only Spanish singer to serve alongside the Flemish choir was Juan de Anchieta, who had apparently first travelled to Flanders after the death of Isabella and served as a spy against Ferdinand, whom, according to the Spanish ambassador to Flanders, he hated at that time as much as if the king had deprived him of the Archbishopric of Toledo. Thus, between 1505 and 1508, when Ferdinand resumed the government of Castile from his unfortunate daughter and Juana's choir was disbanded and returned home, Anchieta sang with a group of some of the best Flemish singer-composers of the period. The unnumbered manuscript in Segovia Cathedral containing many works by Franco-Flemish composers (some unique to that source) and some by Anchieta himself, would almost certainly seem to date from these years. If so, Juana, like her brother Juan, made a direct contribution to musical developments at court and so throughout Spain.

The effect of the Catholic Monarchs' external and internal policies can also be readily discerned in one of the most important facets of their reign: the expansion of their court. Ferdinand's political marriage alliances had reaffirmed a traditional connection between Spain and the Duchy of Burgundy based on established trade routes and, at times, a common enemy in France. The influence of the Burgundian court had long been felt in Spain, not least in cultural matters such as architecture, painting, manuscript illumination, tapestries and music; but it was not until the reign of the Catholic Monarchs that the splendour of the court of the Dukes of Burgundy was deliberately emulated and exploited for its political effects: the enhancement of royal prestige and the establishment of stability. Both the kingdoms of Castile and Aragon had been racked by prolonged internal strife in the years before the marriage of Ferdinand and Isabella in 1469. The prospect of the unification of the kingdoms brought new hope to the people, and Ferdinand's decisive victory over the Portuguese in the war of succession further boosted expectations. But royal propaganda had been seriously undermined by the long years of unrest, and the monarchs turned, as did the Tudors in a similar position in England, to the Burgundian model.[8]

Internal politics led to costly festivities, such as those held in Valladolid soon after Isabella had succeeded to the Castilian throne in 1474, in order (in the words of one royal chronicler), 'to diminish the sadness the people felt from the unfortunate occurrences of the past'.[9] These festivities included jousting (at which the king excelled), disguisings, dancing and music. Several years later, in 1489, with an eye to foreign diplomacy during a visit of the Burgundian ambassadors to Spain, the celebrations were promoted as festivities to rival those of the court of Duke Charles the Bold. Another royal chronicler commented on the Spanish monarchs' political motive behind such occasions:

> The year 1489 opened with the celebration of public spectacles, by the wish of the king as much as of the queen, to display before the ambassadors by demonstration of wealth, magnificence and expense, the great joy for the reason of the visit, which they had already expressed by word.[10]

Such festivities called on the services of painters, illuminators (portraits and beautifully illuminated manuscripts often changed hands on such occasions), embroiderers, jewellers, silversmiths and artisans of all kinds. The services of musicians were indispensable: the chapel singers helped to solemnify any celebratory services with their polyphonic settings of the liturgy; they also sang songs as part of the entertainments, often setting texts with topical allusions or relevance to the occasion; the instrumentalists played dance and background music and accompanied processions; the corps of trumpets and drums, resplendent in their uniforms, heralded the royal presence at every moment in the proceedings. The importance of the musicians' role at court is underlined by the increase in the musical personnel employed, a vast retinue being one of the prerequisites of Burgundian court existence.

At the beginning of their reigns, Ferdinand's chapel included about twelve adult singers and Isabella's only about nine. By the time of the visit of the Burgundian ambassadors in 1487, seventeen singers were employed regularly in the Aragonese chapel and twelve in the Castilian. In 1504, the year of Isabella's death, the singers in her chapel numbered 34 while some 24 were receiving payment in the Aragonese household – sizeable choirs even if all the singers were not present on every occasion. The two choirs undoubtedly performed together on the more important occasions, and it was perhaps because this size of choir had become the norm at court that ten of the queen's singers were immediately appointed after her death to the Aragonese chapel choir, and that this body of singers grew to rival the former size of the joint choir; it numbered well over 40 in the last years of Ferdinand's reign. At least one organist, at times two, were employed in both the royal chapels throughout the period. The same incremental pattern, albeit on a smaller scale, can be observed for the *ministriles altos* and the corps of trumpets and drums.

78. *Ecclesiastical procession: painting (1500) by Miguel Ximénez, once part of a retable depicting the life of S Miguel*

Four trumpeters and one drummer and five or six *ministriles altos* were employed in the Aragonese household at the beginning of Ferdinand's reign; eight trumpeters and four drummers, and at least eight minstrels (though there had been as many as eleven) in 1515. The figures are less complete for the Castilian household, but the trumpeters and drummers increased from six to ten or eleven in the last ten years of Isabella's life, the number of *ministriles altos*, uncharacteristically, remaining more or less the same. The figures fluctuate to some extent over the years, often reflecting the state of the royal coffers, or the needs of a major event, such as the extended campaign which culminated in the reconquest of Granada, when the corps of trumpets and drums expanded considerably while the number of chapel singers was slightly reduced; but the underlying trend was always upwards.

The employment of large numbers of musicians at court had ramifications throughout Spain. This was partly because the court led a peripatetic existence – its main Castilian centres were Valladolid, Seville, Toledo and (after the reconquest) Granada but it also visited the Aragonese kingdom (Barcelona, Saragossa, Valencia) – but more especially because almost all of the musicians at court were of Spanish origin and not, as had been the case in the past (and was still the case at the princely courts of Italy) imported from the north. These last points can perhaps be best explored through a more detailed study of the royal chapels, the home and training-ground of this new generation of Spanish composers.

For well over a century, the royal or ducal chapel had served not only the practical needs of the magnate as regards religious worship, but also the projection of his personal piety, then widely held to be one of the most important attributes of the ruler. Both Ferdinand and Isabella appear to have been very aware of this and consequently to have valued their chapels, a point the Florentine ambassador to Spain in 1513 brought out in his assessment of the king: 'he appears very religious, speaking with great reverence of Godly matters and referring everything to Him; he displays great devotion in divine offices and ceremonies, as is indeed common to the whole nation'.[11]

In 1513 the Aragonese chapel was at its height, with over 40 singers, including the best composers of the generation, Peñalosa and Anchieta; the celebration of liturgical services there, if only on major feasts, must indeed have been impressive. In 1495 another visitor to Spain, the German traveller Ieronimus Münzer, wrote in his log that Isabella was 'pious beyond belief' and that she spent 'vast sums on church ornaments'. The queen's personal accounts confirm this, as well as descriptions of her chapel by other contemporary chroniclers. The music of the chapel was no less important than its appearance. A royal chronicler's apostrophe on her death in 1504 includes a homage to her piety as expressed through the ceremonies and *músicas acordadas* (?polyphony) of her chapel: 'the preachers, the singers, the harmonious music of the ceremony of divine worship, the solemnity of the masses and hours sung continually in her palace . . .'[12]

Among the many payments for the purchase of gold and silver ornaments, tapestries, cushions, carpets, altar cloths and so on, are those for the books of the chapel – missals, breviaries, psalters (some with chant, some without, many highly illuminated and covered in velvet and precious stones) – and the copying of chant and polyphony, mostly by members of the royal chapel. While many of these music manuscripts have since been destroyed or lost, the few that remain bear witness to a rich polyphonic repertory of masses, motets, hymns, settings of the *Magnificat* and the Lamentations and other liturgical texts, mostly composed by singers serving in the royal chapels, but including some works by their Franco-Flemish contemporaries. Unfortunately the extant *Constituciones* for the Castilian chapel do not give a precise indication of when polyphony was sung during the services; they do, however, reinforce the monarchs' reputed concern for the ceremony surrounding divine worship in the royal chapels. The calendar of sung feasts attached to the *Constituciones*, supported by the evidence of the musical sources, confirms that, for the most part, the ritual of the royal chapels followed European traditions as regards the feasts on which polyphony was sung, and Roman – or Italian – practice as to which texts were set. In addition to the Marian feasts, certain saints' days were accorded importance there, and polyphonic Latin motets, or even songs in the vernacular, were composed and sung in celebration: the Archangel Michael and SS John the Baptist and John the Evangelist were particularly favoured in the royal chapels.

Certain other local traditions also become apparent, notably the use of chants not found in Roman usage but which belonged to the Toledan rite; Castilian monarchs had traditionally obtained papal authorization to use this rite in their chapels. Another feature of the calendar of sung feasts, again reflected in the extant polyphony, is the emphasis on the liturgical celebrations during Holy Week and on other related feasts of the Cross. Many of the motets and songs composed for Passiontide set texts which are devotional but not strictly liturgical, and these tend to concentrate on the physical aspects of Christ's suffering on the cross, as in Peñalosa's *Precor te, Domine*. This powerful motet begins:

> Precor te, Domine Jesu Christe, propter illiam inestimabilem charitatem, quam tu rex celestis pendebas in cruce, cum deifica charitate, cum mitissima anima, cum tristissimo dolore, cum turbatis sensibus, cum transfixo corde, cum transverato corpore, cum sanguineis vulneribus, cum expansis manibus, cum extensis venis, cum clamorosa ore, cum ravea voce, cum pallida facie.

> (I pray thee, Lord Jesus Christ, because of that inestimable love, when you, King of Heaven, were hanging on the cross, with Godly

love, with saddened spirit, with deepest sorrow, with shattered senses, with pierced heart, with severed body, with bloody wounds, with out-stretched hands, with extended veins, with groaning mouth, with rasping voice, with pale face.[13]

This penchant for settings of such graphic devotional texts would seem to have been a trend which developed at court, among court composers, and it almost certainly reflects the prevailing vogue there and through-out Spain for the works of Thomas Aquinas and for Ludolf of Saxony's *Vita Christi*, both among the first books to have been printed in the vernacular in the peninsula. Some of these motet texts may indeed have been written by the chapel singers themselves; all the members of the royal chapels received instruction in Latin and the scriptures, a respon-sibility in the heyday of the chapel choirs assigned to the scholar and royal historian Marineus Siculus. His duties can be gauged from a letter written while he was away from the court, working on his historical research: 'What are my colleagues doing (I refer to the royal chap-lains)? And what the singers? Do they spend their time on letters and teachings of the saints? Do they occupy themselves with hymns and the interpretation of the psalms?'[14]

In 1514 Marineus Siculus published a Latin epistolary comprising his correspondence with various dignitaries and pupils, among whom were the royal singers Juan Roman, Juan Ponce and Peñalosa. In the case's of Ponce and Peñalosa, the exchange of letters concerns the composition and setting of a Marian text; Peñalosa had asked Siculus for a troped version of the *Ave Maria*, Ponce for correction of some newly composed Marian verses, he said so that 'chastened by your criticism I may set them to music and sweet polyphony more surely and harmoniously'.[15] Neither Ponce's nor Peñalosa's Marian settings appear to have survived, but among the extant polyphonic motet reper-tory there is a high proportion of Marian texts, whether devotional or liturgical, undoubtedly reflecting the emphasis on the feasts of the Virgin in the royal chapels. A royal tradition had also been established in the fourteenth century for the singing of the *Salve regina* following the celebration of Mass on Saturday mornings, and there is some evidence that it had become customary in the ritual of the royal chapels to replace the *Salve*, on occasion, with other suitable Marian motets.

Thus the polyphonic repertory of the royal chapels was, at least to some extent, composed according to its own needs and traditions. Can its musical style, closely related to the Franco-Flemish mainstream, yet distinct from it, have been born of the particular set of circumstances surrounding the growth of the chapel choirs during the reigns of Ferdinand and Isabella? The reference to Peñalosa's performance of the Passion in the ceremonies of the papal chapel (not long after the death of Ferdinand in 1516, he had left Spain for Rome to serve in the chapel of Leo X), as being according to the 'more hispano', might well be implying only the use of different chants or texts rather than indicating a distinctive style of singing. However, other evidence points in the latter direction. The 'lamenting' quality of the singing of the many Spanish singers who served in the papal chapel at the beginning of the sixteenth century was remarked upon by the papal Master of Ceremonies, Paride de Grassis, in his *Ceremoniale*.[16] A young singer from Milan who entered the service of Isabella d'Este in July 1497 was reputed to sing beautifully 'in the Spanish fashion', whatever this may have been – perhaps something to do with the 'sweetness' of the Castilian style singled out by an Italian correspondent in 1502.[17]

Qualities such as 'lamenting' or 'sweet' are nebulous and evidence for a distinctive style of performance is now harder to assess than that for a particular compositional idiom. The extant polyphonic repertory of the royal chapels shows that while Franco-Flemish techniques of composition were adopted and assimilated by Spanish composers, their music generally remains less contrapuntal and more homophonic – or chordal – in overall effect. This could perhaps be seen as another reflection of the combination of historical circumstances surrounding the expansion of the royal chapels. If the foreign policies of the monarchs brought their chapels into contact with mainstream trends as represented by the Burgundian chapel, they did not, apparently, share in the trend among Italian princes for vying for the services of the best singer-composers from the north. The *maestro de capilla* of the Aragonese chapel early in Ferdinand's reign was Juan de Urede. He is believed to have been of Flemish origin, but he was succeeded by Spaniards, and although some other northern musicians did serve at court (notably one Juan Enrarte from Hainault, who became a naturalized Spaniard in 1492), they did not hold positions of importance and remained in a minority.

Not only does this provide a sharp contrast with the situation at the north Italian courts, but it would also seem to represent a break with tradition. The Aragonese court had, in former times, consistently sent to the north for the best singer-composers that could be lured by promises of high salaries, ecclesiastical benefices, tax exemptions and all the other attractions of court service in the fifteenth century – at least until some time before the departure of Alfonso 'the Magnanimous' to Naples in 1444. The situation during the reign of Ferdinand's father, Juan II, is less clear, partly because his kingdom was torn apart by civil strife during most of the period, and presumably most of the chancery's resources were spent in the war effort, rather than on recruiting expeditions for singers. It is significant, however, that Ferdinand's chapel, first formed for him in 1461 following the death of his elder half-brother, Charles of Viana, included a high proportion of northern singers, among whom the composer Enrique de Paris stands out.

The favours and privileges of royal service were, if anything, increased during the reign of the Catholic Monarchs, as the extant pay documents, and the extensive correspondence concerning the benefices bestowed under royal patronage show. (In this respect Ferdinand and his advisers show themselves well aware of the latest developments at other courts; the king was quick to complain to the pope through his ambassadors in Rome that his cousin Ferrante I of Naples had been granted an indult to bestow benefices on his chapel singers, while this favour had been denied him.) Yet following his marriage to Isabella in 1469, the numbers of northern musicians employed at the Aragonese court declined, and there is no evidence to suggest that recruitment was again directed beyond the Pyrenees. Even Juan de Urede was already in Spain, in the service of the Duke of Alba, when he was appointed *maestro de capilla* of the Aragonese chapel, and this would seem to have been the pattern of events in subsequent appointments of foreign musicians; they were already in Spain (or Naples, as in the case of Ferdinand's sojourn there in 1506–7), not sent for from abroad.

It is hard to establish whether this shift in a long-established tradition was part of a deliberate policy to patronize Spanish musicians – perhaps in the heightened national awareness following the unification of the kingdoms of Aragon and Castile – or whether such reliance on local talent was passive acceptance of a tendency towards provincialism. Artists and illuminators continued to be employed from the north, tapestries and stained glass to be imported from Flanders to adorn royal palaces, and Franco-Flemish music was – at least on occasion – sung in the royal chapels, but by a choir largely consisting of Spanish singers. Whatever the motive, the resulting effect was that singers for the royal chapels were mostly recruited from the cathedrals and other ecclesiastical establishments of Spain, and this undoubtedly stimulated musical activity there, both as regards training and the composition of polyphony.

Ferdinand and Isabella travelled almost constantly throughout their kingdoms – sometimes together, sometimes separately – and with them toured the royal chapels, the portable organs packed on to a cart. They stayed in palaces, castles and monasteries on their journeys, their followers being billeted at nearby inns and houses. At the royal entry into a town, at the service of thanksgiving held in the cathedral and at the fiestas celebrated during the sojourn of the monarchs, the royal musicians took an active role, and also encountered their local cathedral and municipal counterparts. The enrolment documents of the Aragonese and Castilian royal chanceries show that musicians, particularly chapel singers, were often appointed as the court passed through their town. The exact manner in which they applied or were recruited for royal service is not known, but the task of selection was delegated to the deputy head chaplain or other senior members of the chapel, who, according to the *Constituciones*, were to examine the applicant's knowledge of the scriptures and Latin. What standards, musical or otherwise, were required is also not known; musicians of a variety of skills – to sing chant or polyphony, and to compose – were needed. By the second half of the fifteenth century, all the cathedrals and many of the larger parish churches in Castile and Aragon, as well as monasteries such as Montserrat, had choir schools where boys were taught to sing both chant and polyphony, and sometimes to play the organ. Some royal singers, like the young Antonio de Corral, were trained in the royal chapels, but there is little doubt that the cathedral schools were producing the talent required for the chapel choirs. Perhaps it was no longer necessary to look outside Spain for skilled musicians.

Contact between the court and the major ecclesiastical establishments was also maintained through the beneficed members of the royal chapels (although this was very often a source of conflict, with the cathedral chapter opposing the election of an absentee royal chaplain or singer to a canonry or prebend), who visited their post from time to time and often retired there from the pressures of peripatetic court existence, highly paid, but often uncomfortable. The presence, however intermittent, of such singers as Peñalosa or Pedro de Escobar at Seville Cathedral may well have done much to boost musical activity and standards there. Why, for example, in 1510, did the chapter of Seville Cathedral order that a musical manuscript in Peñalosa's possession be valued? Later in the sixteenth century, when the royal chapel was no longer a focal point for the promotion of Spanish music (Charles V brought his Flemish choir with him to Spain in 1518, and no Spaniards were employed in the royal chapel choir throughout his reign), it was the cathedrals which took over its role, and it was there that composers like Morales, Guerrero and Victoria were trained and that their polyphony resounded.

The musical exchange between the royal court and the cathedrals seems even to have extended to the adoption of musico-liturgical practices cultivated in the royal chapels, as in the case of the singing of polyphonic songs in the vernacular on Christmas Eve. This tradition was well established in the Aragonese royal chapel at least by the reign of Ferdinand's father, Juan II. In 1478, shortly before his death, the aged king insisted on attending Matins on Christmas Eve, the service being held in the main hall of the episcopal palace in Barcelona. Beginning at 10 p.m., it was celebrated by the royal chaplains and singers who sang 'some honest songs appropriate to the occasion which told of the joy of the birth of the son of God'.[18] This practice is confirmed by the extant polyphonic repertory of the courts, which includes a number of songs appropriate to this manner of celebrating Matins. A typical example is the simple, anonymous setting of *Nuevas, nuevas de plazer* (in the unnumbered manuscript in Segovia Cathedral):

Nuevas, nuevas de plazer	News, news of joy
y de alegria	and of happiness
que es nacido el mexia.	the Messiah is born.
Quien os lo dixo pastores?	Who told you shepherds?
Un angel, mi fe, señores,	An angel, by my faith, sirs,
que dezia	who said
que parida era Maria.	that Mary had given birth.

This tradition was introduced into the celebration of Christmas Eve at Granada Cathedral by its first archbishop, fray Hernando de Talavera: 'Instead of responsories he had some very devout verses sung, appropriate to the lessons. Thus this holy man attracted as many to Matins as to Mass'.[19]

Granada Cathedral was consecrated following the conclusion of the reconquest early in 1492. Talavera had for some years previously been the royal confessor and he was therefore familiar with the practices of the royal chapels. By the mid-sixteenth century, the singing of polyphonic songs of Christmas Eve was widespread and the composition of them was often listed as one of the duties of the cathedral's *maestro de capilla*. Indeed, the extant polyphonic song repertory of the court of the Catholic Monarchs, largely represented by the *Cancionero musical de Palacio*, a songbook containing well over 400 songs, not only seems to cover almost any occasion, but also reveals a still more pronounced tendency towards a local style, far removed from the intricacies of the Burgundian chanson. Songs with devotional texts were sung not only at Christmas, but also during Holy Week and at Eastertide and on Marian and other feasts. In a more secular context, there were songs of political propaganda, songs of love and war, and songs sung during plays and other court entertainments.

Early in Ferdinand's reign, Fernando de Ribera, *trobador*, was employed in the Aragonese household with the task of chronicling the Granadine campaigns against the Moors in verse. Apparently he wrote his ballads immediately after the event, and they were then read before the king's table at supper, so that those who had participated in the battle or skirmish could approve or correct his tale. Several of the ballad settings in the *Cancionero musical de Palacio* might well have drawn on Ribera's account. Court composers set the verse to music and the songs were sung as part of the celebrations following a victory or successful escapade. The setting of *Pascua d'espiritu santo* by Francisco de La Torre, a singer in the Aragonese chapel, celebrates the surrender of Ronda on 1 June 1485, and was almost undoubtedly sung as part of the festivities held the following day, the feast of Corpus Christi. It begins:

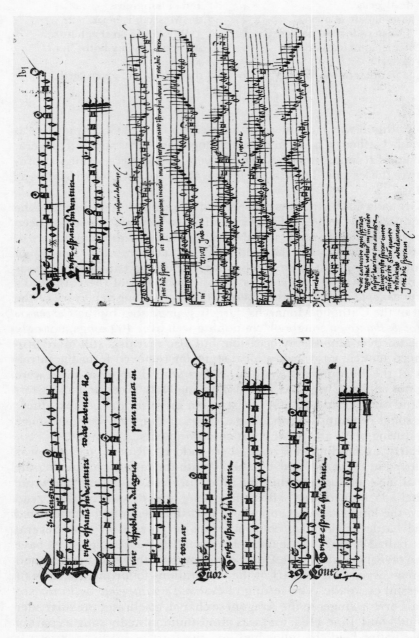

79. *Two facing folios, showing Encina's 'Triste España' (written for the death of Prince Juan in 1497), with Josquin's 'In te, Domine, speravi' added in a sixteenth-century hand, from the 'Cancionero musical de Palacio', copied (c1500) for the court of Ferdinand and Isabella*

Pascua d'espiritu santo,	On the eve of Corpus Christi,
domingo, primero dia,	Sunday, the first of [June],
a la çinco de la tarde	at five in the afternoon,
cavalgo como solia	the good king Ferdinand
ese buen rey don Fernando	he was riding as usual
con su gran cavalleria.	with his great cavalry.
Fue a mirar a Ronda	He went to look at Ronda
como sola conbatia.	which alone was resisting.
A poco pieça de rrato	After a little while
un mensajero venia,	a messenger came, [telling]
como los moros de Ronda	how the Moors of Ronda
se le devan con pleytesia.	had pledged their surrender.

Like all the extant ballads, La Torre's three-voice setting is simple and essentially chordal, with four musical phrases being repeated for each four lines of text, and the end of each being marked by a strong cadence and pause. The words, the narration of the story, were what mattered, and these campaign ballads may have been one reason why the musical idiom of court song developed in the 1480s in the direction of simple, almost folklike settings in contrast to the more complex, contrapuntal textures of the Burgundian chanson.

This genre was well known in Spain, the musical style and the verse and themes of courtly love being adopted in the earlier song repertory of the slightly older generation of court composers, those who like Juan de Cornago, Juan de Urede, Enrique de Paris and, to some extent, La Torre and Madrid, served in the Aragonese chapel in the 1470s and 1480s. Juan de Urede's *Nunca fue pena mayor*, which found fame all over Europe, is a good example of this style. Gradually, however, and even in songs of courtly love in the Burgundian vein, the favoured texture was more homophonic and the phrases carefully balanced in a syllabic setting of the text – as in the ballads, but also as in the prolific output of Juan del Encina.

Encina (1469–1529), poet, composer and playwright, was not, apparently, employed at the royal court, although during his period of service at the court of the Duke of Alba between 1492 and 1498, he would have come into contact with it on many an occasion. During this time he dedicated several of his works to members of the royal family, including his poem *Triunfo de amor*, which was performed with polyphonic songs in celebration of the marriage of Prince Juan to Margaret of Austria. It would also seem that most of his songs were composed in the 1490s; over 50 are copied in the first layer of the *Cancionero musical de Palacio*. Several of them were intended to be sung in the context of simple plays or eclogues, which were performed at the court of the Duke of Alba, usually at Christmas, during these years. Encina took a leading role, and the characters all participated in the singing of the songs interpolated into the plot. These usually took the form of a pastoral dialogue in which the shepherds learn of the news of the birth of Christ and celebrate accordingly. A song was always sung at the end of the play, and sometimes at other strategic points. At least some of these plays were performed before the duke's cousin, Ferdinand; Encina's *Eclogues* certainly established a vogue for this kind of entertainment at court. The pastoral dialogue in which shepherds, not lovesick courtiers, sang of their life and loves in a good-humoured, light-hearted way, sometimes in a rustic, more or less unintelligible, language, also enjoyed great popularity among court composers. The shepherd world of Encina's *Nuevas te traigo, carillo* or *Daca, bailemos, carillo* took on an independent existence, which perhaps represented an idyllic alternative to the rather inflexible code of courtly love. It probably also encouraged the setting of popular tunes by court composers who from the beginning of the sixteenth century adopted the singular, homophonic, clearly phrased style cultivated by Encia.

Thus trends and fashions in Spanish song of the early sixteenth century – when song, according to the Count of Tendilla, was 'all the rage' – had moved rapidly away from the musical style and content of the Burgundian chanson still favoured and cultivated at most European courts for some years to come. It is not clear whether the northern song repertory was performed at court; the French and Flemish songs included in the Segovia manuscript represent the repertory of Juana's Flemish choir and were perhaps not widely sung outside the chambers where she attempted to drown her sorrows in music. Well-known chansons such as *Adieu, mes amours* and *Tous biens plaine*, as well as the ubiquitous *L'homme armé*, were also known by such court composers as Peñalosa and were used as the basis for mass composition. Perhaps it is significant, however, that the one song by the greatest northern composer of the time, Josquin, included in the *Cancionero musical de Palacio* was his Italian frottola *In te, Domine, speravi* (see fig.79). The vogue for polyphonic song at court, therefore, would seem to have centred on Spanish song in its simple, direct musical idiom, much more closely related to the Italian frottola than to the Burgundian chanson.

In the context of courtly expansion and increased wealth and stability, music flourished on an unprecedented scale in Spain during the reign of the Catholic Monarchs. Their reign marked the beginning of a golden age for Spanish polyphony; the momentum of musical activity created by their court was such that, even with the accession of their grandson Charles V to the throne and the exclusion of Spanish singers from musical life at the royal chapel, it continued unabated in the cathedrals and noble households of Spain throughout the sixteenth century. It is hard to gauge whether these developments were the result of deliberate royal promotion, but at least one of the next generation of Spanish composers voiced the disillusion he felt at his exclusion from the royal court of Charles V, nostalgically recalling the halcyon days of the reign of Ferdinand and Isabella. Indeed, in his lament (taken from his *ensalada* entitled *La viuda* of 1539),[20] the composer Mateo Flecha (*d* 1553) places Ferdinand alongside one of the most illustrious music patrons of the early sixteenth century, Pope LeoX:

¿Que fue del papa Leon?	What became of Pope Leo?
los reyes y los señores	The kings and the lords,
¿do se fueron?	where did they go?
¿Que fue de aquel galardon,	What happened to that reward,
las mercedes a cantores	the favours to singers
que se hizieron?	what became of them?
Rey Fernando, mayorazgo	King Ferdinand, first-born
de toda nuestra esperanza	of all our hope,
¿tus favores a do estan?	where are your favours now?

NOTES

[1] After their marriage, Ferdinand and Isabella maintained separate households according to the custom of the period, but, more unusually, the distinction between the Aragonese and Castilian chanceries was also preserved, underlining the tentative nature of the unification of their kingdoms.

[2] *E-Mah*, Colección Salazar y Castro A11, f.301. There is evidence to suggest that 'música de vihuela' might indicate songs with vihuela accompaniment as well as purely instrumental music.

[3] L. Marineus Siculus, *De las cosas memorables de España* (Alcalá de Henares, 1539), f.182*v*.

[4] G. Fernández de Oviedo, *Libro de la cámara real del príncipe don Juan* (Madrid, 1870), 182–3. 'Tiple' would seem to have been a term denoting the upper part, and not specifically a treble or boy singer.

[5] P. Mártir de Anglería, *Epistolario*, trans. J. López de Toro, *Documentos inéditos para la historia de España*, ix–xii.

[6] *Correspondencia del Conde de Tendilla*, ed. E. Meneses García (Madrid, 1973–4), ii, 230.

[7] A. de Lalaing, *Voyage de Philippe le Beau en Espagne en 1501*, in *Collection de voyages des souverains des Pays-Bas*, i, ed. L. P. Gachard (Brussels, 1876), 176.

[8] On the Tudor court, see S. Anglo, *Spectacle, Pageantry, and Early Tudor Policy* (Oxford, 1969).

[9] [A. Flores], *Crónica incompleta de los Reyes Católicos (1469–1476)*, ed. J. Puyol (Madrid, 1934), 165–8.

[10] A. de Palencia, *Crónica de Enrique IV*, ed. A. Paz y Meliá (Madrid, 1973–5), iii, 216.

[11] F. Guicciardini, *Relación de España*, in *Viajes por España*, ed. A. M. Fabié (Madrid, 1879), 201.

[12] A. Bernáldez, *Memorias del reinado de los Reyes Católicos*, ed. M. Gómez-Moreno and J. de M. Carriazo y Arroquia (Madrid, 1962), 489.

[13] *E-TZ* 2 and 3, ff. 261*v*–2.

[14] C. Lynn, *A College Professor of the Renaissance: Lucio Marineo Siculo among the Spanish Humanists* (Chicago, 1937), 113.

[15] L. Marineus Siculus, *Ad illustrissimum principem Alfonsum Aragoneum Ferdinandi regis filium . . . epistolarum familiarum libri decem et espetem* (Valladolid, 1514), f.103*v*.

[16] R. Sherr, *The Papal Chapel ca. 1492–1513 and its Polyphonic Sources* (diss. Princeton U., 1975), 97 and 112.

[17] W. F. Prizer, *Courtly Pastimes: the Frottole of Marchetto Cara* (Ann Arbor, 1980), 9–10.

[18] P. M. Carbonell, *Opúsculos inéditos*, ed. M. de Bofarull y de Sartorio, *Colección de documentos inéditos del Archivo de la Corona de Aragón*, xxvii (Barcelona, 1864), 155.

[19] J. López-Calo, *La música en la catedral de Granada en el siglo XVI* (Granada, 1963), i, 254.

[20] J. Rumeu Figueras, 'Mateo Flecha el Viejo, la corte literariomusical del duque de Calabria y el cancionero llamado de Upsala', *AnM*, xiii (1958), 25–102.

BIBLIOGRAPHICAL NOTE

Historical background

The best guide in English to the historical background to the reign of Ferdinand and Isabella is the second volume of J. N. Hillgarth's *The Spanish Kingdoms, 1250–1516* (Oxford, 1978), while, in Spanish, J. Vicens Vives's *Historia crítica de la vida y reinado de Fernando II de Aragón* (Zaragoza, 1962) and T. de Azcona's *Isabel la Católica: estudio crítico de su vida y su reinado* (Madrid, 1964) provide the most recent and comprehensive studies of the monarchs themselves. Some information on the cultural background will be found in Hillgarth, which also has a useful bibliography, and P. E. Russell's *Spain: a Companion to Spanish Studies* (London, 1973) includes essays on Spanish culture in the fifteenth and sixteenth centuries. F. Fernández-Armesto's *Ferdinand and Isabella* (London, 1975) gives a broader, more readable account of every aspect of their reign.

Music

The most detailed study, to date, of music in Spain in the early Renaissance is Robert Stevenson's *Spanish Music in the Age of Columbus* (The Hague, 1960). Most of the documentary material which formed the basis of this chapter was drawn from my doctoral thesis, *Music and Musicians at the Court of Ferdinand of Aragon 1474–1516* (Cambridge U., 1983). The inspiration for this came from the pioneering work of the Spanish musicologist Anglès; his numerous articles in a variety of languages are gathered in three volumes entitled *Scripta musicologica*, ed. J. López-Calo (Rome, 1975–6). His most detailed studies of music at the court of the Catholic Monarchs, including transcriptions of several polyphonic masses by court composers and a complete edition of the songbook the *Cancionero musical de Palacio*, are to be found in the series Monumentos de la Música Española (MME) with the heading *La música en la corte de los Reyes Católicos*: vols.i (1941, 2/1960), v (1947) and x (1951). In addition, J. Romeu Figueras edited all the poetic texts of the *Cancionero musical de Palacio* and provided the most detailed study of the manuscript to date, in MME, xiv/1–2. Other editions of music from the period include the *Complete Works* of Johannes Cornago, ed. R. L. Gerber, in Recent Researches in the Music of the Middle Ages and Early Renaissance, xv (1984); J. Hardie, *The Motets of Francisco de Peñalosa and their Manuscript Sources* (diss., U. of Michigan, 1983); and *Antxieta: Opera omnia*, ed. S. Rubio (Guipuzcoa, 1980) (although this volume is not readily available in Britain). Peñalosa's *Missa 'El ojo'* is readily available.

Chapter XIV

16th-Century Antwerp

KRISTINE K. FORNEY

The late fifteenth century saw unprecedented social and economic changes in the Low Countries that allowed the rise of Antwerp just as other centres, Bruges in particular, were declining. With access to the sea by way of the Scheldt River, and to the hinterlands of northern Europe through inland waterways, Antwerp was the richest city of Europe and perhaps its largest, boasting a population of more than 100,000 by 1560. Its port was the most active in Europe, surpassing even Venice. Considered the 'Queen City' by the Italian historian Ludovico Guicciardini,[1] Antwerp led the world market not only for cloth and spices, but for books, crafts and the arts trades as well.[2]

Music was an integral part of daily life of this Renaissance city: as a functional enterprise it was central to religious and civic activities; as an economic enterprise, profitable trades included those of music printing and publishing and instrument making; and as a social enterprise, music and music-making permeated Flemish burgher life. Guicciardini, writing when the city's cultural life was at its peak, expressed his great admiration for the musicians of the Low Countries, claiming that 'the Belgians are indeed true masters and restorers of music; they have studied it to perfection, having men and women sing without learning, but with a real instinct for tone and measure; also they use instruments of all sorts which everyone understands and knows'. Of Antwerp in particular, he noted that 'one can see at almost every hour of the day, weddings, dancing and musical groups . . . there is hardly a corner of the streets not filled with the joyous sounds of instrumental music and singing'.[3] The cultural, and especially the musical, ascent of Antwerp in the sixteenth century, its golden age, was due in large part to the strength of the city's confraternities and its bourgeois guilds, which governed all trades, including those of the professional instrumentalist, the music printer and the instrument builder.

In any Renaissance Flemish city the civic purposes for music were the most conspicuous; these were dominated by the wind band, variously called the *stadpijpers*, *menestruels*, *schalmeyers* or *speelleiden*. Traditionally, this ensemble was composed of three or four people playing a sackbut and two or three shawms. Its civic duties included daily outdoor concerts from a central location in the city, participation in religious and occasional processions, triumphal entries and also some church services.[4] *Stadpijpers* are documented in Antwerp as early as 1324, when they were present in a religious procession known as an *ommegang*,[5] and by 1483 the *stadpijpers* were giving a concert, called the *lauweyt*, each evening from the balcony of the town hall.[6]

By about 1500, the strictly loud-wind instrumentation of the group seems to have given way to a broken or mixed ensemble, normally of five players. Documentation pertaining to the Antwerp *stadsspeellieden*, extant from 1530, confirms a five-person band who played a wide variety of instruments, including shawms, flutes, recorders, crumhorns, trumpets and sackbuts.[7] String instruments, particularly viols, are not mentioned in the city inventory until about 1550, at which time the city player Segheren van Pylken was paid for viols and strings purchased for the ensemble;[8] indeed, viols seem to have come late to many Flemish cities. Already popular at northern courts, they are first mentioned in Antwerp in 1545, in the dedication to *Le sixiesme livre des chansons* published by the city band member Tielman Susato. In this book the vocal works are described not only as appropriate for instruments as well as for voices, but more specifically appropriate for viols and other musical instruments ('convenables & propices a jouer sur les Violes. & aultres instrumentz musicales').[9]

Other civic events, especially those of a ceremonial nature such as grand entries of nobility, also featured this band of musicians. For such an occasion triumphal arches and other structures were erected along the procession route by the city and Antwerp's wealthy merchant nations and singers and instrumentalists performed from many of these arches as well as from within the procession. Among the most splendid of these triumphal entries into Antwerp were those of the Emperor Charles V and his son Philip in 1549, the Knights of the Order of the Golden Fleece in January 1556 and the Archduke Albert and Isabella in 1599. The details of the 1549 grand entry were documented by Cornelius Grapheus, greffier of the city. He recorded that the military regiments of halberdiers and other soldiers marched to the accompaniment of many tabours and fifes, and that from every tower of the triumphal arch of Spain, located at rue de l'Hôpital, were heard first the sounds of tabours and trumpets and then sweet harmony of cornetts and flutes, continuing until the prince was at least 100 paces past the arch.[10] The arch of the city, built at the St Catherine bridge, was said to have included twelve figures, among them Music and Harmony who were 'singing sweetly and artfully, in praise of our Prince for his triumphal entry, a chanson of five parts in our mother tongue on diverse instruments, such as harps, rebecs, violins, lutes and the like'.[11] The wealthy Genoese merchant nation constructed a magnificent arch for the grand entry of the Order of the Golden Fleece into Antwerp, where they held their meeting in 1556. On this occasion disaster struck during the procession when this arch collapsed, spilling its musicians to the ground and killing some spectators below.[12]

The city corps of instrumentalists, along with other local singers and players, also participated in religious services and processions, especially those sponsored by the city's lay congregations or confraternities. These religious processions, called *ommegangen*, were held on major feast-days of the city and included representatives of all the civic, trade and religious institutions resident there. Perhaps the most splendid of these processions in Antwerp was the *ommegang* of Our Lady, held since 1399 on the Sunday in the Octave of the Assumption. The artist Albrecht Dürer described this event when he visited the Low Countries in 1520:

> On the Sunday after Our Dear Lady's Assumption I saw the great Procession from the Church of Our Lady at Antwerp, when the whole town of every craft and rank was assembled, each dressed in his best according to his rank. And the ranks and guilds had their signs, by which they might be known. In the intervals great costly pole-candles were borne and their long Frankish trumpets of silver. There were also, in the German fashion, many pipers and drummers. All the instruments were loudly and noisily blown and beaten.[13]

The oldest of the city's processions, dating from the twelfth or thirteenth century, is associated with Antwerp's most sacred relic: the prepuce

80. Stadpijpers playing treble shawm, two tenor shawms, cornett, sackbut and curtal: detail from the painting Procession of the Religious Orders of Antwerp on the Feast Day of the Rosary (1616) by Denis van Alsloot

from Christ's circumcision, reputedly brought to Antwerp from Jerusalem in 1101 by Godefroid de Bouillion and housed in the chapel of the Confraternity of the Circumcision. This occasion also brought the entire ecclesiastical community of the city into the streets, together with the confraternities and guilds, the city officials and the town band, which not only played for the procession but also gave a concert in the town hall's council chamber, after which they were presented with drink money.[14]

The five parish churches of Renaissance Antwerp were also centres of musical performance, and primary among them was the Church of Our Lady, known as the largest parish church in Christendom until its elevation to a cathedral in 1559. The records of this church reveal that instrumentalists played some role, albeit small, in services for the chapter, particularly for Mass on the highest feast-days. On such occasions the members of the town band were brought in to play cornetts and sackbuts with the choir and organ. Antwerp's choir, once reputed to have been the largest in Renaissance Europe, has recently been shown to have been of a standard size, numbering between twelve and eighteen adults and from eight to twelve choirboys.[15] Established early in the fifteenth century with twelve chaplainships reserved for the employment of professional singers, the choir of the Church of Our Lady was renowned throughout northern Europe. Thus it was to Antwerp that many nearby churches and courts turned for recruitment of singers and choirmasters.

The church's singers were required not only to participate in the principal daily services of Matins, High Mass and Vespers, but were employed regularly by the confraternities for the celebration of their daily and weekly devotional services. The largest and wealthiest of Antwerp's lay congregations was the Confraternity of Our Lady, composed of over 100 merchants, bankers and townspeople. Like Marian organizations throughout northern Europe, this confraternity sponsored an evening daily prayer service, called the *lof*, which featured motets sung and played with instruments and organ. This service, which regularly employed four of the adult singers, all the choirboys, the choirmaster and the organist for the performance of discant or polyphony, was but one of a cycle of services held at guild and confraternity altars and chapels, suggesting a very active musical life at the church.[16] It was such activity that surely inspired Dürer to make the following entry in his travel diary in 1520: 'The [Antwerp] Church of Our Lady is so very large that many masses are sung in it at one time without interfering with each other. The altars have wealthy endowments, and the best musicians are employed that can be had'.[17] Guicciardini remarked on the musical services of two confraternities of the Antwerp church; he claimed the Confraternity of Our Lady held Masses, Offices and a daily *Salve regina* sung 'in fine music to the accom-

81. Choir accompanied by cornetts and trombones at Mass: engraving by Philippe Galle after J. Stradamus from 'Encomium musices'

paniment of a perfect organ' and he described Masses and other services, also sung polyphonically with organ, held by the Confraternity of the Holy Sacrament.[18] He further cited six military confraternities, three rhetoricians' chambers and 27 trade guilds, all with altars or chapels in the church at which Mass was celebrated with music and organ on their patron's feast-day.[19]

The *maîtrise* of the Church of Our Lady was under the leadership of a choirmaster, a position held by several well-known musicians of the day. From 1484 until his death in 1491, the composer Jacob Barbireau was head of the musical establishment there; he was succeeded by the master Jacob Obrecht, during whose period of office, from 1492 to 1504, the church first employed the well-known music scribe Pierre Alamire to prepare manuscripts. Perhaps the most stable period for the *maîtrise* was during the employment of Anthonis Barbe, who served as choirmaster from 1528 until 1562. Barbe was the first of three generations of Antwerp musicians: his son Anthonis was first a choirboy and later an instrumentalist at the Antwerp church and was the author of a collection of dances printed in Louvain in 1573; his grandson Anthonis became the organist of the Church of St John in 1596 and wrote a musical treatise in 1599 (now lost).

The duties of the choirmaster included the direction of singers in the principal services of the church, the intoning of certain chants and the supervision and instruction of the boys in the choir school. The choirmaster was responsible for feeding, clothing and housing the boys in a manner conducive to the preservation of their voices. Normally a composer, the choirmaster also oversaw the preparation of music manuscripts, sometimes copied by professional scribes but most often by the church's singers. Copious volumes of chant and especially of polyphonic masses, requiems, hymns and motets were prepared for use by the chapter and the confraternities of the Antwerp church. Of the numerous volumes prepared, motets, especially those with Marian texts, predominated in the repertory for the Confraternity of Our Lady, including settings of such popular texts as *Ave Maria*, *Fit porta* and *Regina caeli* as part of the so-called 'Virgo books'. From about 1550, purchases of printed music (masses and motets) also appear in the church records.[20] Several of these prints can be identified: in 1571 the *Liber primus missarum* of Francisco Guerrero was purchased by the chapter; in 1573 the singer Jaspar purchased a book of five Clemens masses; and in 1588 the chapter bought the deluxe edition of *Octo missae, quinque, sex et septem vocum* of George de la Hèle, issued in Antwerp by Christopher Plantin in 1578. A new genre that was to prosper within the realm of seventeenth-century church music was the *cantiones natalitiae*, polyphonic Christmas carols with basso continuo, composed by local parish musicians of Antwerp, Brussels and Ghent. These simple, strophic, four-part settings were often based on well-known tunes and were used in the devotional services of the confraternities.[21]

Regular payments are also recorded to an organist, a bell ringer and a carillonneur in the Church of Our Lady. By the mid-sixteenth century, the church had no fewer than four organs. The main one, just outside the choir gallery, was in place by 1433 for use on Sundays, high feast-days and for services in nearby chapels. A small positive organ was just inside the choir for use by the chapter, and two large, wealthy confraternities, those of Our Lady and of the Holy Sacrament, had positive organs in their private chapels.[22] The Holy Sacrament chapel replaced the organ destroyed in 1566 by the iconoclasts with one built between 1627 and 1636 to the specifications of the church's noted English organist, John Bull. The organist's duties included playing during the Mass and other services, sometimes with the singers and sometimes in an *alternatim* practice. *Alternatim*, which was clearly preferred for the confraternity *lof* service in Antwerp, was adopted elsewhere as well. In Bergen-op-Zoom, the organist Servaes Vander Muelen was instructed in 1556 to play the verses of the *lof* in the same manner as was done in Antwerp in the Chapel of Our Lady.[23]

The abundance of fine, professional musicians in Antwerp, singers and instrumentalists alike, made the city a major recruitment centre for courts and churches. Among Antwerp's renowned composer-choirmasters who were recruited to courts throughout Europe are the following:[24] Jacob Obrecht, who held the Antwerp position sporadically from 1492 to 1504, when he went to the Ferrarese court of Ercole I d'Este; the choirmaster Nicole Carlir, who served in Antwerp from 1519 to 1522 and abandoned his post to become chapel master at the court of Charles V; Gerard van Turnhout, who left his Antwerp position as choirmaster in 1572 to join the court of Philip II; and Séverin Cornet, Turnhout's successor, who left Antwerp in 1581 to enter the service of Ferdinand at Innsbruck. The Antwerp organist Henry Bredemers, who served the chapter and Marian confraternity from 1493 until 1501, joined the chapel of Philip the Fair, and the organist Benedictus de Opitiis, in service in Antwerp from 1511 until 1516, was recruited to the court of Henry VIII in England. More telling, perhaps, is the fact that when a Low Country ecclesiastical centre, such as the Marian confraternities at 's-Hertogenbosch and Bergen-op-Zoom, or even St Gudule in Brussels, had need of a singer or choirmaster, officials normally turned first to Antwerp.

The large population of musicians resident in Renaissance Antwerp had surely been drawn there by the thriving music trades. By the mid-sixteenth century, the city could provide a composer with an outlet for the publication of his music, and the instrumentalist with the most skilfully crafted instruments of the day, particularly keyboard instruments. The Scheldt city also provided a promising musical education for aspiring instrumentalists through its highly structured musicians' guild of St Job and Mary Magdalene.

Although the art of music printing came relatively late to the Low Countries, the music printing and publishing firm of Tielman Susato, established in 1543, brought the city to the forefront of the music book trade.[25] Other printers soon followed Susato's lead, including Pierre Phalèse, who established his prolific printing house in nearby Louvain, and later Christopher Plantin, archtypographer of the Empire, who issued some of the century's most sumptuous books of chant and polyphony.

The printer's district of the city had been in and around the Kammenstraat, although Susato and at least two other music printers opted to live and do business on the very busy Twaalfmaandenstraat. This short street leads from Antwerp's major thoroughfare, the Meir, directly into the New Bourse, or Exchange, which was the centre for all major financial transactions. Susato, a native of northern Germany, first came to Antwerp as a youth of about fifteen, at which time he was employed by the Church of Our Lady as a music copyist, and soon became a member of the élite corps of *stadsspeellieden*. In 1542 and 1543, he was awarded a subsidy for bringing a new trade to Antwerp, and he stands out as the first musician to prosper in this trade in the Low Countries. In 1552 Susato proved the stability of his business through speculative land purchases in the so-called 'New Town' of Antwerp, a newly developed region outside the old city walls; he moved his business there to a house aptly named 'The Cromhorn'. As a performer and composer himself, he apparently had good contacts with the local and court composers whose music he included in his numerous publications of chansons, motets, masses and Flemish songs. Perhaps the most famous of Susato's publications is his *Danserye* (1551), a collection of simple dance arrangements of popular chansons.[26] These arrangements may well represent the skeletal framework of the improvised dance music of the day.

The motet prints issued by Susato were published in two series: a four-book series of four- and five-voice works, and a large, modally organized series of fourteen books entitled *Ecclesiasticarum cantionum*; these two series include works by numerous Franco-Flemish masters, some little known except through these publications. The motets are mostly built on points of imitation or through-imitation and many works are identified by their biblical text citation or, more often, by their liturgical occasion; presumably these pieces served as music for confraternity devotional services, and perhaps for the Mass and Offices of the church.

The chansons issued in Antwerp prints reflect the interest of the northerners in parody and cantus firmus procedures; many of these works set popular texts of the day and draw on well-known settings using various borrowing techniques. Among the composers involved in these parody procedures were Clemens, Crecquillon, Gombert and Susato himself.[27] Susato's printing competitors were few, but prolific none the less. The team of Waelrant and de Laet, active from 1554 in Antwerp, issued a more international repertory, including a number of madrigal prints by northern masters. These publications were patronized by members of the Italian merchant nations resident in Antwerp, principal among them the Doria family of Genoa. Antwerp music books had been widely disseminated by mid-century, a distribution facilitated by the sales of the Plantin firm and the book fairs of Frankfurt.

The printer Christopher Plantin settled in Antwerp in 1549, and later explained his reasons for doing so in a letter of 9 October 1574 to Pope Gregory XIII:

> I preferred to come to Belgium and to Antwerp above all other towns. The choice was imposed upon me by the fact that for me no other town in the world could offer me more facilities for carrying on the trade I intended to begin. Antwerp can be easily reached; various nations meet on its markets; there too can be found the raw materials indispensable for the practice of one's trade; craftsmen for all trades can easily be found and instructed in a short time; moreover I saw to the satisfaction of my faith, that this town and the whole country shone above all neighbouring peoples by their great love for the Catholic

82. Title-page of George de la Hèle's 'Octo missae' (Antwerp: Plantin, 1578)

religion under the sceptre of a king, Catholic by name and fact; finally, it is in this country that the famous university of Louvain flourishes, where the chairs are taken by professors whose collaboration I hope to obtain to the greater benefit of the public.[28]

Plantin's printing house was the largest of its day, issuing books, pamphlets, maps and works of art of all types. Plantin became interested in the prospect of printing music early on, but spent some years studying the art before starting. To study the technique, he bought up the entire stock of typographic materials from Susato's shop in 1564 and also purchased music type from the competing firm of Waelrant and de Laet.[29] It was not until both these successful firms had closed down that Plantin began issuing music books.

One of his early books of polyphony will long be remembered as one of the most costly of its day: the splendid *Octo missae* published in 1578 by George de la Hèle, dedicated to and probably subsidized by Philip II. In a contractual agreement the composer had promised to purchase 40 copies of his music within the year at the bookseller's price of fifteen florins, taking them six at a time; the composer was unable to afford this bargain and instead took only four of the books himself. However, over 150 copies were distributed between 1578 and 1636 at the Frankfurt book fairs and to booksellers in Paris, Lyons, Königsberg, Mons,

Courtrai and Antwerp; this book of masses also reached southern Europe through exportation by members of the Spanish, Portuguese and Italian merchant communities of Antwerp.[30] Indeed, if it were not for the foreign merchant nations of Antwerp, the music-printing industry might not have flourished at all in the Scheldt city. Among the many music publications patronized by the wealthy Genoese merchants was a print marking the first issue of Italian-texted music in the north: Orlande de Lassus's so-called 'Opus 1'; this collection of madrigals, villanelle, chansons and motets issued by Susato in 1555 was released in a special Italian-titled issue with a dedication to the financier Stefano Gentile.[31]

Notable too among the patrons of this trade were members of the nobility, high-placed ecclesiastics and city officials. The first music book issued by Tielman Susato was dedicated to, and most likely subsidized by, the Regent of the Low Countries, Mary of Hungary, who was well known for her patronage of music and the arts. A woodcut in this 1543 print depicts the presentation of the book by Susato to the regent and is accompanied by a dedicatory poem in which Susato claims, like his earlier rivals in France and Italy, to have discovered, at great expense of time and money, this new and practical method of printing music.[32] An important ecclesiastical patron of music in the Low Countries was the powerful Cardinal Granvelle, Bishop of Arras and counsellor to Charles V and Philip II. Granvelle was clearly an avid music-lover, extolled for his knowledge, appreciation and patronage of the art in numerous book dedications, including one from Tielman Susato in the first book of his motet series *Ecclesiasticarum cantionum* of 1553, one from the imperial composer Pierre Manchicourt in his *Liber quintus cantionum sacrarum* (Leuven, 1554), and a more familiar dedication from Orlande de Lassus in *Il primo libro di motetti* (Antwerp, 1556), in which the composer claims to receive daily many benefices and signal favours from Granvelle, his sole patron and benefactor.[33] Other publications, such as Susato's *Liber primus sacrarum cantionum* of 1546 and the Pevernage collection, *Livre quatriesme des chansons*, issued by Plantin in 1591, were sponsored by Antwerp city officials; the *Liber primus*, which opens with a secular motet in praise of Antwerp,[34] is dedicated to the counsellors and senators of the city[35] and the *Livre quatriesme* was patronized by the magistrate of Antwerp.

The printing trade in Antwerp was regulated both by edicts of the Empire and, to a lesser extent, by the guild of St Luke, to which all booksellers, bookbinders and printers belonged in the late sixteenth century. The artisans' guild, named after the evangelist Luke, the patron saint of painters, was established in 1382 by the gold and silversmiths, sculptors and painters of the city. A regulation of 1557 decreed that all members of the printing trade should join this same guild, together with musical instrument makers.[36]

In the fifteenth century, instrument builders were already active in Antwerp; in 1441 the trumpet maker Pierre Bogaerts became a citizen, and in 1468 a member of the St Luke guild built a zink or cornett.[37] It was, however, during the second half of the sixteenth century and the first half of the seventeenth that the trade reached unparalleled heights. Thus it was to Antwerp that neighbouring cities and musicians turned for wind, string and keyboard instruments; a wind player in Audenarde purchased a case of crumhorns there in 1539, the Antwerp luthier Pietro Lupo sold a case of five viols to Utrecht in 1559 and four shawms and a trumpet to Mechlin in 1561, and Guillaume Emo sold a bombard to the city of Utrecht in 1559. The passing of this trade through one family is illustrated by the Burlon family of Antwerp: Peeter Burlon is recorded at a lute maker in the 1598 guild records, and Peeters, Hans and Frans Burlon were all seventeenth-century viol makers.[38]

The records of the St Luke guild record the membership in the early sixteenth century of two organists: in 1515 Benedictus Ducis (or de Opitiis), organist to the Confraternity of Our Lady, was a guild deacon, and in 1535 Pauwels Bollaert was identified as an organist among the guild membership. Most numerous among instrument builders in Antwerp were keyboard instrument makers; six *claevesimbaelmaekers* and the organ builder Hans Bos all joined the St Luke guild in 1557.[39] It was, however, the Ruckers family, active from 1579 to 1665, that made Antwerp famous for keyboard instrument building; the head of the family, Han Ruckers, was elected dean of the St Luke guild in 1579. Ruckers' virginals and harpsichords were famous in their own day, producing what was considered an ideal sound during the seventeenth and early eighteenth centuries. Numerous instruments survive today to document the fine craftsmanship and unrivalled sound, the result of a

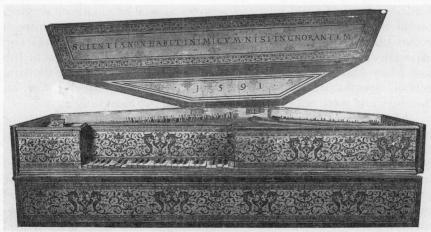

83. *Hexagonal virginal by Hans Ruckers, Antwerp, 1591*

sophisticated design.[40]

Another powerful Antwerp guild was an important force behind music-making, the instrumentalists' guild of St Job and Mary Magdalene, active since at least 1500. A guild document of 1535 specifies that the musicians had sponsored an altar for more than 30 years in St James's Church, Antwerp.[41] Other guild ordinances make it clear that citizenship of Antwerp was a requirement of membership and that the activities of non-citizen musicians were severely limited, except during the time of the annual fairs in the Scheldt city. The cycle of Brabant fairs included two held in Antwerp, the spring Pentecost fair and the autumn St Bavo fair, each lasting six weeks, during which time free musicians could perform in the city. Central to all guild records is a statement of the conditions through which young musicians apprentice to master instrumentalists; there are also several specific contracts extant to document the details of such agreements. Contracts limited masters to a single apprentice and set a minimum time of study at two years, after which the youth had the option to apply for entry as a master in the guild. In 1553 Jaspar Becquet, son of the percussionist Jehan of Lille, was to study with Gregorius de Coninck for five years, during which time the master was to feed, clothe and instruct the boy, in this case not only in how to play diverse instruments but also in how to sing.[42] A late sixteenth-century document suggests that to gain entrance to the guild, an aspirant had to play three motets or other similar pieces; later there is a reference to the stringing and tuning of an instrument on which to play two dances, a galliard and a *perchemagne*.

Instrumentalists were much in demand in Renaissance Antwerp. Indeed the citizenship records list no fewer than 100 from 1530 until the end of the century.[43] Their role in society was multi-faceted. It has already been mentioned that instrumentalists were used frequently in confraternity and guild religious services as well as in church services on the highest feast-days. These musicians functioned at the centre of social life in Antwerp as well, playing for banquets, weddings and especially for dances. A number of ordinances from the Guild of St Job and Mary Magdalene relate to the regulations governing the dancing school. Specifically, dances were not to begin until after 11 a.m. on Sundays and were not to take place at all on the most holy days.[44]

Music for the dance was available in print, first from Paris with the issue of several popular Attaingnant collections beginning in 1530, and later from the local publishers Tielman Susato and Pierre Phalèse. Susato's long-term membership of the Antwerp civic band could well have prompted his famous collection of chansons arranged as dances, published in 1551. Arranged from the most popular of Parisian and northern chansons of the day, this collection features four-part instrumental basse danses, rondes or branles, allemandes, pavans and saltarellos based on the works of Josquin, Sermisy, Janequin and

Passereau among others; these include pavans arranged from Josquin's *Mille regretz* and Janequin's *La bataille*, basse danses arranged from Sermisy's *D'ont vient cela* and *C'est à grant tort*, and rondes or branles arranged from Janequin's *Il estoit une fillette* and Passereau's *Pourquoy donc ne fringuerons nous*. These arrangements present largely chordal versions of their models that probably provided a basis for improvisation. Susato, along with Pierre Phalèse of nearby Louvain, published dances from the Antwerp region. Thus Susato's 1551 collection contains a *Hoboecken dans*, associated with the village of Hoboeken (south of Antwerp on the Scheldt river) and Phalesius published the *Passomezo d'Anvers* in his *Liber primus leviorum carminum* of 1571.

The same publications of instrumental music must surely have found a market among the quickly growing population of amateur musicians in the Low Countries. By the mid-sixteenth century, composed polyphonic music had permeated burgher life to the extent that many middle-class families had collections of music and instruments. Antwerp family portraits confirm the popularity of keyboard instruments and lutes within burgher society. The 1571 wedding feast of the Antwerp painter Joris Hoefnagel, painted by Frans Pourbus, depicts the nuptial couple dancing to the accompaniment of two lutes and a spinet (fig.84), and the painter Cornelis de Zeeuw captures in portrait the austere Antwerp patrician family of Pieter de Moucheron with one of the younger daughters at a spinet. A 1561 painting by either Frans Floris or Adrian Thomaszoon Key is a portrait of the wealthy Van Berchem family of Antwerp, posed with bass lute and spinet. Patrician household inventories and sales records from Christopher Plantin's printing and publishing firm also indicate widespread music-making among the mercantile classes of Antwerp.

One curiosity surrounds the deep interest shown by the Flemish people in playing keyboard instruments: in spite of the importance of Antwerp as a music-printing centre throughout the sixteenth century, no keyboard music prints were issued either there or in surrounding Low Country printing centres until after 1600.[45] Although keyboard music was surely imported to the Low Countries from Paris and Germany, where many prints were issued, it is equally likely that amateurs and professionals used their own intabulations prepared from vocal pieces. Indeed, the popularity in Antwerp of Virdung's *Musica getutscht*, issued in French in 1529 and in Flemish in 1554 and 1568 with directions on how to intabulate the Flemish song *Een vrolijc wesen* in German organ tablature, supports such a premise.[46]

This picture of Renaissance Antwerp as a booming commercial and cultural metropolis begins to fade in the mid-1560s owing to the sociopolitical currents that precipitated the Eighty Years' War. The growing strength of various Protestant cults in the north was met with intolerance by the devoutly Catholic Emperor Philip II and with fear by his

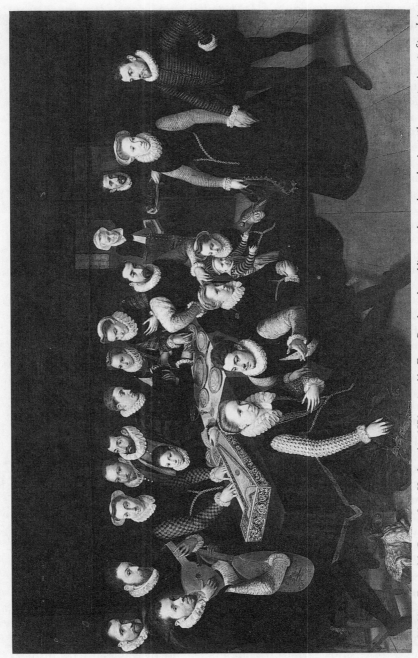

84. *Wedding Feast of the Painter Joris Hoefnagel in 1571, painted by Frans Pourbus; the wedding couple are shown dancing to the accompaniment of two lutes and a spinet*

aunt Margaret of Parma, Regent of the Low Countries from 1559 to 1567. The potential clash between the proud but stubborn Flemish people and their Madrid-based monarch could already have been foreseen in 1549, the year in which Charles V introduced his son Philip to his northern subjects. The entry of Prince Philip into Antwerp was perhaps the most grandiose spectacle of the century in the Netherlands, but it was an occasion marred by torrential rains, the withdrawal of three of the city's largest and wealthiest of merchant nations from the procession, and by an unspecified offence committed by the Antwerp town band at the tournament in the Grote Markt. On 14 September 1549, Segher Pylken, Peeter Bannick, Adriaen vanden Cruyce and Tielman Susato, four of the five members of the band, were summarily dismissed. Although Pylken and Bannick were soon reinstated in the ensemble, vanden Cruyce and Susato were permanently replaced.[47]

A number of musicians of Renaissance Antwerp were associated later with Calvinism, including two of the town band members from the 1549 incident. On 5 May 1568 the Duke of Alba named the instrumentalists Gommaer van Oisterwyck and Segher Pylken as Calvinists and thus banned them from Antwerp; both musicians sought refuge in England, the former with the 'marquis of Norenton' and the latter as a London wait. Susato too can be associated with the Calvinist sect; his daughter Clara and his lawyer son-in-law Arnold Rosenberger were banned from Antwerp as heretics in 1566; Susato had fled the city by 1561, seeking a new life in the polderlands of the north Netherlands.[48]

The fate of many Low Country musicians and artisans at this time seems to have been similar. Even the lives of those devout Catholic musicians who served the parish and collegiate churches were adversely affected by the Calvinists, who rampaged through the churches of many northern centres, destroying the icons, libraries and organs. The iconoclastic destruction of the Antwerp Cathedral of Our Lady on 20 August 1566 left the chapter and the Confraternity of Our Lady without music books or a functioning organ. Pay records for the ensuing years reflect an attempt to rebuild the church library with new manuscripts and prints, but also document a much smaller and less active musical establishment than had existed for the past century.

The years that followed the onset of the war saw increased foreign influence; under the domination of the Spanish, the native musical activity of Antwerp suffered a decline that was, to some extent, compensated for by the influx of foreign music and musicians. The influence of its native polyphonists, such as Séverin Cornet, Cornelius Verdonck and Jean de Castro, was much overshadowed by the international and especially the Italian repertory that was issued in Antwerp, principally through the music-publishing house of Phalèse.

The flight of native musicians to the Netherlands, Germany, England and Scandinavia left prestigious positions open at the Brussels court and at Antwerp Cathedral for several English musicians who emigrated to the Continent. Thus the organist Peter Philips, whose publications appeared in Antwerp between 1591 and 1628, served the royal court of Albert and Isabella, and the celebrated English musician John Bull was employed at Antwerp Cathedral as organist between 1615 and 1628. Best known among the native organists from the Low Countries is Jan Pieterszoon Sweelinck, who was active as a city organist in Amsterdam's Oude Kerk in the early seventeenth century. Organ music remained a favoured genre in the north despite the reform that issued decrees to remove all organs from reform churches. Amsterdam alone refused to adhere to this decree; rather, the city fathers forbade the destruction of church organs and initiated sponsorship of secular organ concerts.

Although Amsterdam gradually replaced Antwerp as the fulcrum of northern commerce and shipping in the seventeenth century, the ensuing blossoming of the arts there did not include music to any great extent. Rather, the northern artistic spirit was manifested in the Dutch school of portrait, landscape and still-life painting, whose best-known exponent was Rembrandt, and in a nationalistic literature, which grew out of the Renaissance chambers of rhetoric. Realism was the common goal of these art forms; Dutch lyric poetry appeared in the form of the *gezelschaplied*, songs of the people set to popular folktunes of the time. Numerous collections were published of this popular poetry with folktunes, among them Adriaen Valerius's posthumous *Nederlandtsh gedenck-clanck* (Haarlem, 1626), an anthology of verse relating the history of the Netherlands through song and including the *geuzenlieden*, songs of the Eighty Years' War.[49] It was, sadly, the preoccupation of the Netherlanders with their religious freedoms that slowed musical development: the Calvinist spirit, which generated a rich output of literature, did not support musical inspiration in the same way that Lutheranism did in the church music of neighbouring Germany.

NOTES

[1] L. Guicciardini, *Descrittione di tutti i Paesi Bassi* (Antwerp, 1567), 61–126.

[2] L. Voet, *Antwerp, the Golden Age: the Rise and Glory of the Metropolis in the Sixteenth Century* (Antwerp, 1973).

[3] L. Guicciardini, *The Description of the Low Countries and of the Provinces thereof, Gathered into an Epitome out of the Historie of Ludovico Guicciardini by T. Dannet* (London, 1593), cited from J. J. Murray, *Antwerp in the Age of Plantin and Brueghel* (Norman, Oklahoma, 1970), 142–3.

[4] On the Flemish wind band, see K. Polk, 'Wind Bands of Medieval Flemish Cities', *BWQ*, i (1968), 93–113; 'Municipal Wind Music in Flanders in the Late Middle Ages', *BWQ*, ii (1969), 1–15; 'Ensemble Instrumental Music in Flanders: 1450–1500', *Journal of Band Music Research*,

xi/2 (1975), 12–27.

5 L. de Burbure, *De Antwerpsche ommegangen in de XIVᵉ en XVᵉ eeuw* (Antwerp, 1878), p.ix.

6 L. de Burbure, 'La musique à Anvers aux XIVᵉ, XVᵉ et XVIᵉ siècles', *Annales de l'Académie d'archéologie de Belgique*, lviii (1906), 243.

7 The Antwerp city players have been thoroughly documented in several studies by G. Spiessens, 'De Antwerpse stadsspeellieden. Eerste deel: 15e en 16e eeuw', *Noordgouw*, x (1970), 1–53; 'Bijdrage tot de Studie de Antwerpse speellieden in de XIVde eeuw', *Antwerpen in de XVIde eeuw* (Antwerp, 1975), 521–31.

8 Spiessens, 'De Antwerpse stadsspeellieden', 48.

9 *Le sixiesme livre contenant trente & une chansons nouvelles a cinq et a six parties* (Antwerp, 1545), Quinta/Sexta, f.lv.

10 C. Grapheus, *Le tres admirable, tres magnifique & triumphante entree, due treshault & trespuissant Prince Philipe, Prince d'Espagnes, fils de l'Empereur Charles V* (Antwerp, 1549).

11 ibid.

12 Citation from *Antwerpsch Chronykje* in G. Persoons, 'Orlandus Lassus in Antwerpen (1554–1556)', *Orlandus Lassus*, ed. I. Bossuyt (Leuven, 1982), 73–4.

13 A. Dürer, *Diary of his Journey to the Netherlands*, introduction by J. -A. Goris and G. Marlies (Greenwich, Connecticut, 1970), 60.

14 De Burbure, *De Antwerpsche ommegangen*, 11.

15 J. Van den Nieuwenhuizen, 'De koralen, de zangers, en de zangmeesters van de Antwerpse O. -L. -Vrouwkerk tijdens de 15e eeuw', *Gouden Jubileum Gedenkboek van de viering van 50 jaar heropgericht Knapenkoor van de Onze-Lieve-Vrouwkatedraal te Antwerpen* (Antwerp, 1978).

16 K. Forney, 'Music, Ritual and Performance Practices: the Laity as Patron in Antwerp's Church of Our Lady', *EMH*, vii (1987), 1–57.

17 Dürer, *Diary*, 50–60.

18 Guicciardini, *Descrittione*, 62–70.

19 ibid, 70.

20 Purchases are abstracted in Forney, 'Music, Ritual and Performance Practices'.

21 On this genre, see R. Rasch, *De cantiones natalitiae en het kerklijke musiekleven in de zuidelijke Nederlanden gedurende de zeventiende eeuw* (Utrecht, 1985).

22 On the organs of the Antwerp church, see G. Persoons, *De orgels en de organisten van de Onze Lieve Vrouwkerk te Antwerpen van 1500 tot 1650* (Brussels, 1981).

23 ibid, 115.

24 On Antwerp's choirmasters, see Forney, 'Music, Ritual and Performance Practices'; and G. Persoons, 'Kapelmeesters van de Onze-Lieve-Vrouwkerk te Antwerpen: Overzicht van 16e to 19e eeuw', *Gouden Jubileum Gedenkboek*, 73–85.

25 On Susato's printing firm, see U. Meissner, *Der Antwerpener Notendrucker Tylman Susato* (Berlin, 1967); and K. Forney, *Tielman Susato, Sixteenth-Century Music Printer: an Archival and Typographical Investigation* (diss., U. of Kentucky, 1978).

26 Modern edn. by F. J. Giesbert, *Danserye zeer lustich . . . om spelen op alle musicale instrumenten (1551)* (Mainz, 1936).

27 *'Responce' and 'Replicque' in the Franco-Flemish Chanson: an Anthology from the Publications of Tielman Susato, 1543–1560*, ed. K. Forney (Madison, forthcoming).

28 Letter of 9 Oct 1574, *Correspondance de Christophe Plantin*, ed. M. Rooses and J. Denuce (Antwerp, 1883–1920), iv, 158; trans. in Murray, *Antwerp in the Age of Plantin and Brueghel*, 3–4.

29 Forney, 'Tielman Susato', 88–92 and 256–64.

30 J. A. Stellfeld, *Bibliographie des éditions musicales plantiniennes* (Brussels, 1949), 26–41.

31 K. Forney, 'Orlando di Lasso's "Opus 1": the Making and Marketing of a Renaissance Music Book', *RBM*, xxxix–xl (1985–6), 33–60.

32 Reproduced in Meissner, *Der Antwerpener Notendrucker*, ii, 16–17.

33 Forney, 'Orlando di Lasso's "Opus 1" ', 39–40 and 58.

34 A. Tirabassi, *Salve Antverpia* (Brussels, 1923).

35 The dedication appears in Meissner, *Der Antwerpener Notendrucker*, ii, 157.

36 P. Rombauts and T. van Lerius, *De Liggeren en andere historische archieven der Antwerpsche Sint Lucasgilde* (Antwerp, 1864–76), i, 205–6.

37 E. Van der Straeten, *La musique aux Pays-Bas avant le XIXᵉ siècle* (Brussels, 1867–88), v, 229.

38 ibid.

39 Robaut and Lerius, *Liggern*, i, 203.

40 See J. Lambrechts-Douillez, 'Documents Dealing with the Ruckers Family and Antwerp Harpsichord-Building', in *Keyboard Instruments: Studies in Keyboard Organology, 1500–1800*, ed.

E. Ripin (New York, 1977); and various articles in *Restauratieproblemen van Antwerpse klavecimbels: Museum Vleeshuis* (Antwerp, 1970).

[41] G. Spiessens, 'Geschiedenis van de gilde van der Antwerpse speellieden', *RBM*, xxii/1–4 (1968), 7.

[42] ibid, 13.

[43] *Antwerpse Poortersboecken, 1533–1608* (Antwerp City Archives, n.d.).

[44] Spiessens, 'Geschiedenis van de gilde van de Antwerpse speellieden', 16–18 and 41.

[45] H. M. Brown, *Instrumental Music Printed Before 1600: a Bibliography* (Cambridge, Mass., 1965).

[46] Issued in 1529 by Guillaume Vorsterman under the title *Livre plaisant et tres utile pour apprendre a faire & ordonner tabulatures hors le discant* and in 1554 and 1567 by Jan van Ghelen under the title *Dit is een zeer schoon boecxken, om te leeren maken alderhande tabulatueren uten discante*.

[47] K. Forney, 'New Documents of the Life of Tielman Susato, Sixteenth-Century Music Printer and Musician', *RBM*, xxxv–xxxviii (1982–4), 37.

[48] ibid, 29–41.

[49] Modern edition with tunes published by K. P. Bernet Kempers and C. M. Lelij, *De liederen uit Valerius' Nederlandtsche gedenck-clanck* (Rotterdam, 1941).

BIBLIOGRAPHICAL NOTE

Historical, political and economic background

The standard general history of Belgium is H. Pirenne's *Histoire de Belgique* (Brussels, 1929–48), and for this period in particular, vol.iii: *De la mort de Charles Le Téméraire à l'arrivée du Duc d'Albe dans les Pays-Bas* (1567). A classic but outdated history of this era is J.L. Motley's *The Rise of the Dutch Republic: a History* (New York, n.d.). Also recommended is the Dutch-language survey in the *Algemene Geschiedenis der Nederlanden*, iv–v (1952). The principal history of Antwerp is F. Prims's *Geschiedenis van Antwerpen* (Antwerp, 1927–48). Other sources on Antwerp in the sixteenth century merit mention: a two-volume general survey by J. Wegg, *Antwerp, 1477–1559: from the Battle of Nancy to the Treaty of Cateau-Cambrésis* (London, 1916) and *The Decline of Antwerp under Philip of Spain* (London, 1924); the very general but readable J. Murray, *Antwerp in the Age of Plantin and Breughel* (Norman, Oklahoma, 1970); and the comprehensive and beautifully illustrated historical study by L. Voet, *Antwerp, the Golden Age: the Rise and Glory of the Metropolis in the Sixteenth Century* (Antwerp, 1973).

The economic history of this era is presented in a highly scholarly account by H. Van der Wee, *The Growth of the Antwerp Market and the European Economy, Fourteenth – Sixteenth Centuries* (Leuven, 1962). The Genootschap voor Antwerpse Geschiedenis has also published a rather comprehensive study of Renaissance Antwerp, with contributions by a number of scholars: *Antwerpen in de XVIde eeuw* (Antwerp, 1975).

Several historical narrative accounts are informative, including one by the German artist A. Dürer, *Diary of his Journey to the Netherlands* (Greenwich, Connecticut, 1970) and another widely published one by the Florentine L. Guicciardini, *Descrittione di tutti i Paesi Bassi* (Antwerp, 1567; Eng. edn., London, 1593).

Artistic, intellectual and cultural life

Several exhibition catalogues provide an excellent picture of the region's artistic activity, including *De eeuw van Bruegel: de schilderkunst in Belgie in de 16e eeuw* (Brussels, 1963) and *Anvers, ville de Plantin et de Rubens* (Paris, 1954). A standard work on the art of engraving is J. J. Delen's *Histoire de la gravure dans les anciens Pays-Bas et dans les provinces belges des origins jusqu'à la fin du XVIIIe siècle* (1934–5). An indispensable reference on Antwerp's printing trade and Christopher Plantin is L. Voet's *The Golden Compasses: a History and Evaluation of the Printing and Publishing Activities of the Officina Plantiniana at Antwerp* (Antwerp, 1969). An important general reference source is A. Gerlo's *Bibliographie de l'humanisme belge, precédée d'une bibliographie générale concernant l'humanisme européen* (1965).

Chronology

MUSIC AND MUSICIANS	POLITICS, WAR AND RULERS
1471 Agricola and Weerbeke in service of the Duke of Milan.	**1471** Murder of Henry VI of England after the entry of Edward IV into London. Borso d'Este created Duke of Ferrara. Death of Pope Paul II; election of Sixtus IV.
1472 Tinctoris in Naples at court of Ferrante I.	
1473 Tinctoris: *Proportionale musices*.	**1473** Muhammed II styles himself Sultan.
1474 Death of Dufay. Josquin Desprez and Compère in Milan in service of Duke.	**1474** Death of Henry of Castile; succeeded by Isabella.
	1476 Murder of Galeazzo Maria Sforza of Milan; succeeded by Gian Galeazzo.
1476 Obrecht in Utrecht. Tinctoris: *Liber de arte*.	**1477** Death of Charles the Bold of Burgundy; succeeded by Mary. Maximilian, son of the Emperor Frederick III, marries Mary of Burgundy.
1477 Busnois in service of Mary of Burgundy.	
1478 Gaffurius joins court of Ferrante I of Naples.	**1478** Sixtus IV excommunicates Lorenzo de' Medici. The papacy allied with Naples against Florence, Venice and Milan.
	1479 Death of John II of Aragon; succeeded by Ferdinand, thereby uniting Aragon and Castile.
	1480 Ludovico Sforza ('il Moro') becomes Regent of Milan.
1482 La Rue at Siena Cathedral (–1485). Bartolomeo Ramos de Pareia: *Musica practica*.	**1481** Death of Sultan Muhammed II; succeeded by Bayezid II. Death of Alfonso V ('the African') of Portugal; succeeded by John II.
1483 Brumel at Notre Dame, Chartres.	**1483** Death of Edward IV of England; succeeded by Edward V, but the throne is usurped by his uncle Richard III; Edward and his brother subsequently murdered. Death of Louis XI of France; succeeded by Charles VIII.
1484 Gaffurius *maestro di cappella* at Milan Cathedral. Juan del Encina at Salamanca Cathedral.	
1485 Isaac in the service of the Medici in Florence (–*c*1493).	**1484** Death of Pope Sixtus IV; election of Innocent VIII.
1486 Josquin in papal choir. Obrecht at St Donatian, Bruges.	**1485** Richard III of England defeated and killed at Bosworth Field. Henry Tudor crowned Henry VII.
	1488 Murder of James III of Scotland; succeeded by James IV.
1489 La Rue a tenor at s'-Hertogenbosch Cathedral (–1492). Pedro de Escobar and Juan de Anchieta singers in Queen Isabella's chapel choir.	**1490** Marriage of Isabella d'Este to Francesco Gonzaga. Maximilian I acquires the Tyrol. Death of Matthias Corvinus of Hungary; election of Vladislav II of Bohemia.
1490 Eton Choirbook compiled (–1502)	

LITERATURE, PHILOSOPHY AND RELIGION	SCIENCE, TECHNOLOGY AND DISCOVERY	FINE AND DECORATIVE ARTS, ARCHITECTURE
1470 Sir Thomas Malory completes (?) *Le morte d'Arthur*. **1471** Death of Thomas à Kempis, probable author of *De imitatio Christi*.	**1470** First French printing press established at the Sorbonne, Paris, and first in the Low Countries at Utrecht.	**1470** S Andrea, Mantua, begun by Alberti. **1471** Michael Pacher paints scenes from *The Life of the Virgin* for the wooden high altar of St Wolfgang, Austria (–1481).
	1473 First Hungarian printing press established in Buda.	**1473** Sistine Chapel built and partially decorated (–1481).
1477 Chaucer's *Canterbury Tales* (written *c*1387) printed by Caxton. **1478** Ferdinand and Isabella, with the authorization of Pope Sixtus IV, establish the Inquisition against heresy.	**1474** First Spanish printing press established in Valencia. **1477** William Caxton produces *The Dictes and Sayings of the Philosophers*, the first book printed in England.	**1474** Leonardo da Vinci paints *The Annunciation*. **1477** Sandro Botticelli paints the *Primavera*. Veit Stoss carves the high altar for St Mary's, Cracow (–1489). **1479** Verrocchio works on his equestrian monument to Calleoni (–1488).
1479 *Hypnerotomacnia Polophili* written by Francesco Colonna. Bartolomeo Platina writes *In vitas summorum pontificum ad Sixtum IV*. **1480** Angelo Poliziano writes *Favola di Orfeo*.	**1480** Leonardo da Vinci designs a parachute.	**1480** Domenico Ghirlandaio completes *The Last Supper*. Hieronymous Bosch paints *The Crucifixion, Christ Mocked* and *The Epiphany*.
1483 Matteo Maria Boiardo writes *Orlando inamorato*. The Spanish Inquisition comes under the joint control of state and church with Tommaso de Torquemada as Inquisitor General.	**1487–8** Bartholomew Diaz sails round the Cape of Storms, renamed Cape of Good Hope by John II of Portugal.	**1481** Filippino Lippi paints *The Vision of St Bernard* (–1486). **1483** Leonardo arrives in Milan and begins his first version of *The Virgin of the Rocks*, completed *c*1495. **1488** Bellini paints the *Madonna with Saints*.
1488 Massacre of the Vaudois (Waldenses) heretics of Dauphiné. **1490** Robert Henryson writes *The Testament of Cresseid*. Aldus Manutius founds the Aldine Press at Venice.	**1490** Leonardo da Vinci records the observation of the capillary action of liquids in small-bore tubes.	**1490** Michelangelo Buonarroti produces the marble reliefs *The Battle of Lapiths and Centaurs* and the *Madonna of the Stairs* (–1492). Vittore Carpaccio begins the *Legend of St Ursula*.

MUSIC AND MUSICIANS	POLITICS, WAR AND RULERS
1492 Death of Busnois. La Rue in Burgundian Hofkapelle. *Theorica musicae*, by Gaffurius, published in Milan.	**1492** Spanish conquest of Granada. Spain united under Ferdinand and Isabella. Albert IV of Bavaria joins the Swabian League. Death of Pope Innocent VIII; election of Alexander VI. Death of Lorenzo de' Medici; succeeded by Piero.
1494 Obrecht at Notre Dame, Antwerp. Cara and Tromboncino in Mantua at the Gonzaga court.	**1493** Death of the Emperor Frederick III; succeeded by Maximilian I. Pope Alexander VI divides the New World between Spain and Portugal.
1495 Tinctoris publishes *Terminorum musicae diffinitorium*.	**1494** Death of Ferrante I of Naples; succeeded by Alfonso II. Charles VIII of France invades Italy. Ludovico Sforza assumes title Duke of Milan.
1496 Gaffurius: *Practica musicae*. Senfl in the Emperor Maximilian I's Hofkapelle (–1519).	**1496** Marriage of Philip of Burgundy to Juana of Castile.
1497 Death of Ockeghem. Isaac becomes court composer to Maximilian I.	**1497** Marriage of Margaret of Austria to Juan, Infanta of Spain.
	1498 Death of Charles VIII of France; succeeded by Louis XII.
1500 Compère provost at St Pierre, Douai. Agricola enters the service of Philip the Handsome, Duke of Burgundy. Weerbeke rejoins the papal choir.	**1499** Ludovico Sforza expelled from Milan by the French. Triumphal entry into Milan of Louis XII. Peace of Basle establishes Swiss independence of the Holy Roman Empire.
1501 Petrucci publishes his first book of music, *Harmonice musices odhecaton A*.	**1500** Great Jubilee Year. Pope Alexander VI imposes a general tithe for a crusade against the Turks.
1502 Tromboncino in the service of Lucrezia Borgia at Ferrara.	**1503** Margaret Tudor, daughter of Henry VII of England, marries James IV of Scotland. Death of Pope Alexander VI; election of Pius III who dies within a month. Election of Julius II which causes the downfall of Cesare Borgia. Henry, Prince of Wales, betrothed to Catherine of Aragon.
1503 Josquin in the service of Ercole d'Este at Ferrara.	
1504 Josquin appointed at Notre Dame, Condé-sur-l'Escaut. Obrecht *maestro di cappella* in Ferrara.	
1505 Death of Obrecht.	**1504** Treaty of Lyons. Louis XII finally cedes Naples to Ferdinand of Aragon. Death of Isabella of Castile; succeeded by Juana, wife of Philip of Burgundy.
1506 Death of Agricola. Brumel becomes *maestro di cappella* to Alfonso I d'Este of Ferrara.	**1506** Death of Philip of Burgundy. Council of Regency.
1507 Escobar becomes *maestro de capilla* of Seville Cathedral.	**1507** Margaret of Austria appointed Regent of the Netherlands.
	1509 Death of Henry VII of England; succeeded by Henry VIII.

LITERATURE, PHILOSOPHY AND RELIGION	SCIENCE, TECHNOLOGY AND DISCOVERY	FINE AND DECORATIVE ARTS, ARCHITECTURE
1492 *Grammatica Castellana* compiled by Elio Antonio Nebrija. Expulsion of Jews from Spain. **1493** Hartmann Schedel completes his *Weltchronik*. **1494** Johannes Trithemius compiles his *Catalogus scriptorum ecclesiasticorum*. **1495** Expulsion of Jews from Portugal. The Aldine Press begins to publish editions of Greek classics. Pieter Dorland van Diest writes Dutch morality play *Elckerlijk*. **1498** Savonarola executed in Florence. **1500** Desiderius Erasmus publishes *Adagia*. First edition of the oldest German *Schwank, Till Eulenspiegel*. Appearance of *Mariken van Nieumeghen*. **1503** William Dunbar writes *The Thrissil and the Rois* in honour of James IV of Scotland's marriage to Margaret Tudor. **1504** Publication of Petrarch's *Rime Sparse* by Pietro Bembo. **1506** Johann Reuchlin completes *Rudimenta linguae hebraicae*. **1507** Polydore Vergil appointed Historiographer Royal to Henry VII of England. **1509** Persecution of Jews in Germany opposed by Reuchlin.	**1492** Christopher Columbus discovers the New World, reaching the Bahamas on 12 October. The first terrestrial globe made by Martin Behaim of Nuremberg. Leonardo da Vinci designs a flying machine. **1493** Columbus returns to Spain to report his discovery. He sets out on a second voyage and discovers more Caribbean islands (–1496). **1497** Vasco da Gama rounds Cape of Good Hope on voyage to India (–1498). **1498** Columbus, on third voyage, discovers Trinidad and the coast of South America near the River Orinoco (–1500). **1499** Amerigo Vespucci and Alonso Hojeda discover the mouth of the River Amazon. **1500** Diego Diaz discovers Madagascar and Pedro Avarez Cabral discovers Brazil. Gaspar de Corte Real explores east coast of Greenland and Labrador. **1501** Second voyage of Amerigo Vespucci to explore the coast of South America (–1502). **1502** João de Nova Castella discovers island of St Helena. Final voyage of Columbus, to Honduras and Panama (–1504). **1503** Explosive mines used for the first time at the siege of Naples. **1509** Peter Henlein of Nuremberg constructs the first watch, the 'Nuremberg Egg'.	**1494** Albrecht Dürer travels to Italy and on his return to Nuremberg sets up his own studio. **1495** Leonardo paints *The Last Supper* (–1497). **1498** Dürer produces woodcuts of the *Apocalypse*. **1499** Michelangelo completes first *Pietà* sculpture. Luca Signorelli completes frescoes in Orvieto Cathedral. **1500** Botticelli paints the *Mystic Nativity*. **1501** Michelangelo carves the *David* (–1504). **1502** Bramante designs the circular Tempietto de S Pietro in Rome. **1503** Leonardo paints the *Mona Lisa*. Henry VII's chapel at Westminster Abbey begun (–1519). **1504** Lucas Cranach paints *Rest on the Flight into Egypt*. **1506** Bramante begins the design and building of the new St Peter's, Rome. **1507** Pope Julius II proclaims an indulgence to fund rebuilding of St Peter's. **1508** Raphael enters the service of Pope Julius II. Michelangelo begins the ceiling of the Sistine Chapel (–1512).

MUSIC AND MUSICIANS	POLITICS, WAR AND RULERS
1511 Cara becomes *maestro di cappella* to Francesco Gonzaga in Mantua.	**1511** Henry VIII joins the Holy League, formed between the papacy, Ferdinand of Aragon and Venice to drive the French out of Italy.
1513 William Cornysh takes Chapel Royal to France.	**1513** James IV of Scotland, allied to France, invades England but is defeated. Succeeded by James V. Death of Pope Julius II; election of Leo X.
1514 La Rue in the service of Archduke Karl's private Kapelle. Costanzo Festa in the service of the French court.	**1515** Death of Louis XII; succeeded by François I. Battle of Marignano. François I defeats Swiss and Venetian armies and enters Milan.
1515 Death of Brumel. Adrian Willaert's presence first recorded in Italy, in the service of Cardinal Ippolito I d'Este.	**1516** Death of Ferdinand of Aragon; succeeded by Archduke Charles (later Charles V).
1517 Death of Isaac. Costanzo Festa enters the papal choir.	**1517** Egypt conquered by the Turks, who now intercept European routes to India.
1518 Death of La Rue. Gaffurius: *De harmonia musicorum*.	**1519** Death of Maximilian I; succeeded by Charles V, King of Spain, despite the candidacy of François I and Henry VIII.
1520 English and French royal chapels meet at the Field of Cloth of Gold. Hans Sachs becomes a master shoemaker.	**1520** Meetings of Charles V with Henry VIII at Dover and Canterbury. Meeting of Henry VIII and François I at the Field of Cloth of Gold. Charles V crowned Holy Roman Emperor at Aachen.
1521 Death of Josquin and Fayrfax. Philippe Verdelot *maestro di cappella* at Florence Cathedral and Baptistry.	**1521** Death of Pope Leo X; election in 1522 of Adrian VI. Death of Manuel I of Portugal; succeeded by John III ('the Pious'). Charles V confers Habsburg possessions in Austria and Carinthia on his brother Ferdinand.
1522 Death of Gaffurius. Willaert at the court of Duke Alfonso I d'Este in Ferrara.	**1523** Death of Pope Adrian VI; election of Clement VII.
1523 Pietro Aaron: *Toscanello de la musica*. Senfl obtains a post in Duke Wilhelm of Bavaria's Hofkapelle.	**1525** Battle of Pavia. The Imperial–Spanish army defeats the French and Swiss, leaving Charles V master of Italy. François I taken prisoner.
1524 Walter: *Geystliche Gesangk Buchleyn*.	**1526** Battle of Mohacs. Hungarian army defeated and Louis II killed by the Turks. Ferdinand of Austria elected King of Bohemia and Hungary.
1525 Attaingnant's earliest surviving book printed in Paris.	**1527** Sack of Rome.
1527 Willaert appointed *maestro di cappella* of St Mark's, Venice.	**1528** England and France declare war on Charles V.
1528 Attaingnant: *Chansons nouvelles*.	**1529** Treaty of Cambrai. France renounces all claim to Italy and Charles V renounces his claim to Burgundy. François I marries Eleanor of Austria. The Turks besiege Vienna.
1529 Agricola: *Musica instrumentalis Deudsch*.	**1530** Charles V crowned Holy Roman Emperor at Bologna by Clement VII. The Medici restored in Florence, under Alessandro. Death of Margaret of Austria.

LITERATURE, PHILOSOPHY AND RELIGION	SCIENCE, TECHNOLOGY AND DISCOVERY	FINE AND DECORATIVE ARTS, ARCHITECTURE
1514 First polyglot bible printed (–1522).	**1513** Portuguese expedition under Jorge Alvarez reaches Canton. Florida discovered by Juan Ponce de Leon. Vasco Nuñez de Balboa sights Pacific Ocean from Darien.	**1511** Completion of frescoes in the Scuola del Santo at Padua by Titian.
1515 Thomas Wolsey appointed Cardinal and Lord Chancellor of England. Lateran Council's decree, *De impressione librorum*, forbids printing of books without permission.	**1514** The Corporation of Trinity House, London, founded.	**1512** Dürer becomes court painter to Maximilian I.
1516 Erasmus publishes New Testament in Greek and Latin. *Utopia* by Sir Thomas More. Ludovico Ariosto publishes *Orlando furioso*.	**1515** Juan Diaz de Solis explores the coast of Argentina.	**1513** Bellini paints *St Jerome*.
	1517 Yucatan discovered by Francisco Fernández de Cordoba.	**1515** Hampton Court Palace begun. François I commissions the Château de Blois (–1524).
1517 Martin Luther nails his 95 theses to the door of Wittenberg Church.	**1519** Gulf of Mexico explored from Florida to Vera Cruz by Alvárez Pineda.	**1516** Titian paints *The Assumption* for Frari Church, Venice (–1518).
1519 In his disputation with Johann Eck at Leipzig, Luther questions the infallibility of papal decisions. Ulrich Zwingli preaches in Zurich.	**1520** Ferdinand Magellan sails through the Magellan Straits into the Pacific Ocean and on to the Philippines.	**1517** Sebastiano del Piombo begins painting the *Raising of Lazarus*.
1520 François I founds the Royal Library of France at Fontainebleau. Papal Bull *Exsurge* excommunicates Luther, who burns it.	**1521** American Atlantic coast explored north to South Carolina by Francisco de Gardillo.	**1519** Diego de Siloe builds the *Escalera Dorada* in Burgos Cathedral (–1523).
1521 Pope Leo X confers the title *Defender of the Faith* on Henry VIII of England. Diet of Worms. Luther banned from Holy Roman Empire. Philip Melanchthon produces *Loci communes*.	**1522** Pascuel de Andagoya leads an expedition from Panama to discover Peru.	**1520** Michelangelo works on the Tomb of Lorenzo de' Medici (–1534).
	1523 The first English manual of agriculture, *The Book of Husbandry*, written by Anthony Fitzherbert. Giovanni de Verrazano discovers New York Bay and Hudson River (–1524).	**1522** Francesco Parmigiano paints frescoes in the cathedral and S Giovanni Evangelista in Parma (–1533).
1526 Luther introduces a German Mass and Order of Service.		**1525** Jean Clouet paints *François I on Horseback*.
1528 Publication of *Il libro del cortegiano* by Baldassare Castiglione.	**1526** Sebastian Cabot explores the Paraná and Paraguay rivers on behalf of Spanish merchants.	**1526** Antonio Correggio paints fresco for the dome of Parma Cathedral. Dürer paints *The Four Apostles*.
1529 *Commentarii linguae graecae* published by Guillaume Budé. Antonio de Guevara writes *El relox de principes*.	**1528** *Die kleine Chirugie* written by Peter Paraclesus.	**1527** Palace of Charles V in the Alhambra, Granada, designed by Pedro Machuca (–1568).
	1529 Bernadios de Sahagún begins his Franciscan mission to Mexico.	**1528** Diego de Silvoe begins Granada Cathedral.
1530 The Confession of Augsburg, prepared by Melanchthon, signed by Protestant princes.	**1530** Posthumous publication of *Decades de Orbe novo* by Peter Martyr.	**1529** Albrecht Altdorfer paints the *Battle of Alexander the Great and Darius at Issus*.

MUSIC AND MUSICIANS	POLITICS, WAR AND RULERS
1532 Moderne begins publishing at Lyons. Claudin de Sermisy *sous-maître* in the French royal chapel.	**1531** Mary of Hungary appointed Regent of the Netherlands.
	1533 Secret marriage of Henry VIII and Anne Boleyn. Henry excommunicated by Pope Clement VII.
	1534 Death of Pope Clement VII; election of Paul III.
1535 Cristóbal de Morales joins the papal choir (–1545).	**1535** Defensive and offensive alliance between François I and the Turks. Death of the last Sforza of Milan. Charles V once more occupies the city.
	1536 Pilgrimage of Grace. A popular rising in the north of England against the dissolution of the monasteries (–1537).
1537 Larnpadius: *Compendium musices.*	**1537** Alessandro de' Medici assassinated. Charles V appointed Cosimo II, Duke of Florence.
1538 Willaert's first collection of madrigals published.	**1538** League of Nuremberg signed by Catholic princes of Germany. Treaty of Nice. François I and Charles V agree to suspend hostilities for ten years. James V of Scotland marries Mary of Guise.
1540 Arcadelt joins papal choir.	**1540** Treaty betwen Venice and Turkey signed at Constantinople.
1542 First edition of the Geneva Psalter published. De Monte in Naples (–1551).	**1542** Battle of Solway Moss. Scotland defeated by the English. Death of James V; succeeded by Mary, Queen of Scots.
1543 Susato establishes printing press at Antwerp. Tallis a Gentleman of the Chapel Royal.	**1544** The English Parliament recognizes the Princesses Mary and Elizabeth as heirs to the throne after Prince Edward.
1544 S Filippo Neri establishes the Oratory in Rome.	**1545** Truce of Adrianople between Charles V, Ferdinand of Austria and the Turks.
1545 Deaths of Costanzo Festa and Taverner. Morales *maestro de capilla* of Toledo Cathedral (–1547).	**1546** The Peace of Ardres ends England's war with Scotland and France.
1547 Cipriano de Rore *maestro di cappella* at Ferrara. Glareanus: *Dodecachordon.*	**1547** Death of Henry VIII of England; succeeded by Edward VI (aged 9). Duke of Somerset appointed Lord Protector. Death of François I of France; succeeded by Henri II. Charles V invades Saxony and defeats the Schmalkaldic League at Mühlberg. Ivan IV ('the Terrible') crowned Tsar of Russia in Moscow.
	1549 Death of Pope Paul III.
1550 Isaac's first volume of *Choralis constantinus* published.	**1550** Election of Pope Julius III. Somerset, Lord Protector of England, deposed; succeeded by Duke of Northumberland.

LITERATURE, PHILOSOPHY AND RELIGION	SCIENCE, TECHNOLOGY AND DISCOVERY	FINE AND DECORATIVE ARTS, ARCHITECTURE
1531 Henry VIII establishes himself as Supreme Head of the Church in England.	**1531** The Great Comet (later known as Halley's Comet) appears over Europe.	**1533** Holbein paints *The Ambassadors*.
1533 Thomas Cranmer consecrated Archbishop of Canterbury. He declares Henry VIII's marriage to Catherine of Aragon invalid, enabling the king to marry Anne Boleyn.		**1535** Michelangelo paints the *Last Judgement* fresco in Sistine Chapel (–1541).
1534 Act of Supremacy. The English church finally breaks with Rome.	**1534** Jaques Cartier sights the coast of Labrador and explores the Gulf of St Lawrence.	**1536** The palace of Landshut is begun.
1535 First complete translation of the Bible, by Miles Coverdale (–1537).	**1535** Jaques Cartier's second voyage to North America, up the St Lawrence River to the sites of Quebec and Montreal (–1536).	**1537** Jacopo Sansovino builds the Library of St Mark's and Venetian Mint.
1536 Sir Thomas More executed. John Calvin publishes *Christianae religionis institutio*. Dissolution of the monasteries in England (–1539).	**1536** Pedro de Mendoza founds Buenos Aires and sends expeditions in search of a route to Peru.	**1538** Titian finishes *Venus of Urbino*.
1540 Jesuit Order confirmed by Pope Paul III.	**1537** Gerardus Mercator produces the first map of Flanders (–1540).	**1545** Benvenuto Cellini works on bronze figure of Perseus (–1554).
1545 Council of Trent convened to discuss Reformation and Counter-Reformation (–1551).	**1542** The first European ships reach Japan under Antonio da Mota (–1543).	**1546** Andrea Palladio designs the basilica at Vicenza (–1550). Pierre Lescot begins work on the Louvre (–1551).
1546 Pietro Aretino publishes an Italian tragedy, *Orazia*; and Hans Sachs a German tragedy, *Lisabetha*.	**1544** *De ortu et causis subterraneis* by Georgius Agricola initiates the study of physical geology.	**1547** Michelangelo is appointed architect of St Peter's, begun by Bramante in 1506. Philibert de l'Orme begins the tomb of François I at St Denis.
1549 Joachim du Bellay publishes *La defense et illustration de la langue française*, the first statement of the *Pléiade*. Publication of the First Prayer Book of Edward VI.	**1545** First European botanical garden founded in Padua.	**1549** Leone Leoni sculpts *Charles V Restraining Fury* (–1564).
1550 Publication of the first four books of *Odes* by Pierre du Ronsard.	**1546** Mercator states that the earth has a magnetic pole.	**1550** Georgio Vasari publishes *Le vite de' più eccellenti architetti, pittori e scultori italiani*. Giacomo Barozzi da Vignola designs S Andrea, Rome.

MUSIC AND MUSICIANS	POLITICS, WAR AND RULERS
1551 Death of Attaingnant. Palestrina appointed *maestro di cappella* of the Cappella Giulia. Ballard and Le Roy established as publishers.	**1553** Death of Edward VI of England; succeeded by Mary I, after the 13-day rule of Lady Jane Grey.
1553 Death of Morales.	**1554** Mary I marries Philip of Spain, son of Charles V. England reconciled to papacy.
1554 First masses by Palestrina published. First published works by de Monte appear in Rome.	**1555** Death of Pope Julius III; election of Marcellus II who dies; election of Paul IV. Philip of Spain renounces imperial claim to Maximilian.
1555 First publications by Orlande de Lassus produced. Palestrina appointed *maestro di cappella* at the church of St John Lateran in Rome; also admitted to the Cappella Sistina. Vicentino: *L'antica musica*.	**1556** Charles V abdicates. Spain, the Netherlands, Milan and Naples resigned to Philip II of Spain, and the Holy Roman Empire to his brother Ferdinand.
1556 Lassus appointed to chapel of Duke Albrecht V at Munich.	**1557** Death of John III of Portugal; succeeded by Sebastian I. England allied to Spain, declares war on France and loses Calais (–1558).
1557 Merulo appointed organist at St Mark's, Venice (–1584).	**1558** Marriage of Mary, Queen of Scots to François, Dauphin of France. Death of Mary I of England; succeeded by Elizabeth I.
1558 Death of Janequin. Zarlino: *Le istitutioni harmoniche*.	**1559** War ends between Spain and France with Treaty of Cateau–Cambrésis. Death of Henri II of France; succeeded by François II. Death of Pope Paul IV; election of Pius IV.
1561 Palestrina appointed *maestro di cappella* of S Maria Maggiore, Rome.	**1560** Treaty of Edinburgh between England and Scotland, breaking the 'Auld Alliance' between France and Scotland. Death of François II of France; succeeded by Charles IX.
1562 Death of Sermisy. Council of Trent begins discussions of music. Alfonso Ferrabosco in the service of Elizabeth I intermittently to 1579.	**1561** Mary, Queen of Scots leaves France for Scotland.
1563 Byrd organist and Master of the Choristers at Lincoln Cathedral. De Rore *maestro di cappella* at St Mark's, Venice.	**1562** First War of Religion in France.
	1563 Peace of Amboise, which grants limited toleration to the Huguenots, ends First War of Religion.
1565 Death of de Rore. Zarlino *maestro di cappella* of St Mark's, Venice. Giaches de Wert *maestro di cappella* at the ducal chapel of S Barbara, Mantua.	**1564** Death of Ferdinand I of Austria; succeeded by Maximilian II as emperor.
	1565 Marriage of Mary, Queen of Scots to Lord Darnley. Death of Pope Pius IV.
1566 Andrea Gabrieli organist at St Mark's, Venice.	**1566** Election of Pope Pius V.
	1567 Second War of Religion in France (–1568).
1568 Death of Arcadelt. De Monte Kapellmeister to Emperor Maximilian II.	**1568** Mary, Queen of Scots flees to England. Revolt of the Moors in Granada. Philip II orders massacre.
1569 Victoria at S Maria di Monserrato, Rome.	**1569** Rebellion of the northern Earls in England. Rising of the Catholic north against Elizabeth I (–1570). Third War of Religion in France (–1570).
1570 Byrd joins Chapel Royal.	

LITERATURE, PHILOSOPHY AND RELIGION	SCIENCE, TECHNOLOGY AND DISCOVERY	FINE AND DECORATIVE ARTS, ARCHITECTURE
1552 Treaty of Passau grants Lutherans freedom of worship.	**1553** Hugh Willoughby and Richard Chancellor sail east attempting to find a north-east passage to China (–1554).	**1553** Titian paints the *Danaë*.
1553 Under Mary Tudor in England, the Act of Uniformity is repealed.		**1554** Antonio Moro paints Queen Mary Tudor to celebrate her marriage with Philip of Spain.
1554 Matteo Bandello produces a collection of 214 tales.		
1555 Peace of Augsburg; Lutheran states free to enjoy equal rights with Catholics.	**1557** The *Whetstone of Wit* by Robert Recorde is the first English treatise on algebra.	**1557** Diogo de Torralva begins the cloister of Cristo monastery, Tomar.
1556 Cranmer burnt at the stake for heresy.		
1558 John Knox writes *The First Blast of the Trumpet Against the Monstrous Regiment of Women*. Publication of the Heptaméron of Marguerite of Navarre.	**1560** The Academia Secretorum Naturae is founded in Naples, the first European scientific society.	**1560** Vasari begins work on the Uffizi, Florence. Giambologna sculpts *Samson and a Philistine*.
1559 Elizabethan Act of Supremacy and Act of Uniformity enforce use of the Prayer Book once more.		**1561** Palladio builds the Villa Barbaro at Maser.
1561 The Calvinist *Confession of Faith*, largely the work of John Knox, adopted by Scottish ministers.	**1562** First English slave-trading expedition from Guinea to the West Indies.	**1562** François Clouet completes *Pierre Quthe*.
1562 *Apologia ecclesiae anglicanae*, drawn up by Bishop John Jewel. Formulation of the Thirty-nine Articles.	**1563** First printing press set up in Russia.	**1564** Death of Michelangelo.
1563 Jesuits gain control of Ingoldstadt University and begin the Counter-Reformation in Bavaria.	**1564** John Hawkins's second voyage to the West Indies (–1565).	**1565** Pieter Brueghel paints the *Months*. Tintoretto begins the *Crucifixion*.
		1566 Palladio commissioned to design S Giorgio Maggiore, Venice.
1564 Pope Pius IV confirms the final Catholic definition of faith, *Professio fidei*.	**1567** Hawkins's third voyage to the West Indies, accompanied by Francis Drake.	**1568** Vignola begins building the church of Il Gesù, Rome.
1568 Publication of the *Bishops' Bible*. Pope Pius V issues the *Brevarium romanum*.	**1569** Mercator produces a map of the world for navigators using 'Mercator's Projection'.	**1569** Juan de Herrera begins palace of Aranjuez. Hans Eworth paints *Queen Elizabeth Confounding Juno, Minerva and Venus*.
1570 Elizabeth I excommunicated.	**1570** The first modern atlas, with 53 maps, published by Abraham Ortelius of Antwerp.	**1570** Nicholas Hilliard paints his first portrait of Elizabeth I.

MUSIC AND MUSICIANS	POLITICS, WAR AND RULERS
1571 Victoria at the Collegio Germanico, Rome. Palestrina choirmaster of the Cappella Giulia. Académie de Poésie et de Musique founded in Paris by Baïf.	**1571** Formation of a Holy League between the papacy, Spain and Venice to fight the Turks.
1572 Death of Goudimel.	**1572** Death of Pope Pius V; election of Gregory XIII. The Massacre of St Bartholomew sparks off the Fourth War of Religion.
	1573 Fourth War of Religion ended by Pacification of Boulogne.
	1574 Death of Charles IX of France; succeeded by Henri III. Start of the Fifth War of Religion. Death of Sultan Selim II; succeeded by Murad III. Death of Cosimo I of Tuscany; succeeded by Francesco I.
1575 Byrd and Tallis: *Cantiones sacrae*. Giovanni Gabrieli at court of Duke Albrecht V in Munich.	
	1576 Peace of Monsieur ends the Fifth War of Religion. Death of Emperor Maximilian II; succeeded by Rudolf II.
1576 Death of Hans Sachs.	
1577 Sweelinck at Oude Kerk, Amsterdam.	**1577** Sixth War of Religion.
1578 Marenzio in household of Cardinal Luigi d'Este, Rome. Victoria at S Girolamo della Carità, Rome.	**1578** Death of Sebastian I of Portugal; succeeded by Cardinal Henry. James VI assumes government of Scotland.
1579 Death of Peñalosa.	**1579** Union of Utrecht: foundation of the Dutch Republic.
1580 First madrigals by Luca Marenzio published in Venice.	**1580** Death of Cardinal Henry of Portugal. Spain invaded under the Duke of Alba. Philip II becomes King of Portugal, thereby doubling Spain's colonial empire. Seventh War of Religion in France.
	1581 Marriage contract between Elizabeth I and the Duke of Anjou.
1582 Monteverdi's first compositions published by Gardane.	
1584 Baïf 's Académie de Poésie et de Musique dissolved.	**1584** Death of the Duke of Anjou. Assassination of William of Orange at the instigation of Philip II; succeeded by Maurice of Nassau.
1585 Death of Tallis.	**1585** Death of Pope Gregory XIII; election of Sixtus V. Elizabeth I takes the Netherlands under her protection. War of the Three Henri's in France (Henri III, Henri de Navarre and Henri de Guise).
1586 Death of Andrea Gabrieli. Merulo organist to the Duke of Parma. Giovanni Gabrieli organist at St Mark's, Venice.	
1587 Victoria in Madrid. Monteverdi's first book of madrigals published.	**1587** Execution of Mary, Queen of Scots after the uncovering of the Babington plot.
1588 Nicholas Yonge: *Musica transalpina*.	**1588** Defeat of the Spanish Armada. Assassination of the Duke and Cardinal of Guise at the instigation of Henri III.
1589 The *intermedi La Pellegrina* performed in Florence.	**1589** Assassination of Henri III. Henri de Navarre claims the French throne as Henri IV.
1590 Death of Zarlino. Monteverdi at Duke Vincenzo I's court in Mantua.	**1590** Death of Pope Sixtus V; election of Urban VII, who dies within the year, then of Gregory XIV.

LITERATURE, PHILOSOPHY AND RELIGION	SCIENCE, TECHNOLOGY AND DISCOVERY	FINE AND DECORATIVE ARTS, ARCHITECTURE
1572 Massacre of St Bartholomew, Paris, which spread to the provinces.	**1572** *Artis auriferae quam chemicum vocant* published at Basle.	**1571** Alonso Sánchez Coello paints portrait of Anne of Austria.
1573 Torquato Tasso writes *Aminta*.	**1575** Tycho Brahe constructs an observatory at Uraniborg.	**1573** Veronese summoned before the Inquisition.
1576 Académie du Palais founded by Henri III in Paris. First theatre opened in Shoreditch, London.	**1576** Martin Frobisher discovers Frobisher Bay, Canada.	**1575** Completion of Longleat House, Wiltshire, England. The first attempt at making porcelain in Europe is commissioned by Francesco de' Medici.
1577 *Chronicles of England, Scotland and Ireland* published by Richard Holinshed.	**1577** Francis Drake circumnavigates the world in the *Golden Hind* (−1580).	**1576** The Gallery at Chenonceaux built (the only work of Jean Bullant for Catherine de' Medici to survive).
1579 St John of the Cross writes *The Dark Night of the Soul* (−1583). Edmund Spenser writes *The Shepheardes Calendar*.	**1578** Discovery of the ancient catacombs of Rome.	**1577** El Greco commissioned for altars in S Domingo el Antiguo (−1579).
1580 Michel de Montaigne writes the *Essais* (−1588).	**1581** *A Discourse on the Variation of the Compass and Magneticall Needle* by William Borough.	**1579** Palazzo della Sapienza, Rome, begun by Giacomo della Porta. Giambologna works on *The Rape of the Sabines* (−1583). Teatro Olimpico, Vicenza, begun by Palladio.
1581 *Gerusalemme liberata* by Torquato Tasso published. Pope Gregory XIII attempts to reconcile Roman Catholic and Orthodox Churches (−1582).	**1582** The Gregorian Calendar (revised by Pope Gregory XIII) adopted in the papal states, Spain, Portugal, France, Spanish Netherlands, Denmark and Norway.	**1580** Smythson builds the revolutionary Wollaton Hall (−1588).
1584 Giordano Bruno writes *La cena de le ceneri* and *De la causa, princepio et uno*.	**1583** English expeditions to Mesopotamia, Persian Gulf, India and China led by Ralph Fitch and John Eldred (−1588).	**1581** Nicholas Hilliard paints portrait of Francis Drake on return from his circumnavigation.
1585 English Parliament passes acts against Jesuits and Seminarists for the security of Elizabeth I.	**1584** Sir Walter Raleigh discovers and annexes Virginia. Gregorian Calendar adopted in the Catholic states of the Empire and Switzerland.	
1587 *Historia von D. Johann Fausten* published in Frankfurt.		**1588** Nicholas Hilliard paints *Man Clasping a Hand* and *A Youth Leaning Against a Tree Among Roses*. Tintoretto paints the *Paradiso*.
1589 Publication of *The Arte of English Poesie* by George Puttenham.	**1585** Thomas Cavendish circumnavigates the world (−1588).	
1590 Spenser publishes first three books of *The Faerie Queene*. *Tamberlaine the Great* by Christopher Marlowe published.	**1589** Richard Hakluyt writes *The Principall Navigations, Traffiques and Discoveries of the English Nation*.	**1590** Fortezza del Belvedere, Florence, built by Bernado Buontalenti (−1595).

MUSIC AND MUSICIANS	POLITICS, WAR AND RULERS
1591 Morley organist of St Paul's Cathedral.	**1591** Death of Pope Gregory XIV; election of Innocent IX, who dies, then of Clement VIII.
1592 Morley sworn in as a Gentleman of the Chapel Royal.	**1592** Death of John Casimir, Elector Palatine; succeeded by Frederick IV.
	1594 Henri IV enters Paris.
1594 Death of Palestrina.	**1596** English sack Cadiz, delaying Philip II's plans for a second Armada.
1596 Death of de Wert. Tomkins *Instructor choristarum* at Worcester Cathedral.	**1597** A Spanish Armada sails from Ferrol against England but is scattered by storms. Abdication of William V, Elector of Bavaria, in favour of Maximilian I.
1597 *First Booke of Songes* by John Dowland, and *A Plaine and Easie Introduction to Practicall Musicke* by Morley published in London. Giovanni Gabrieli's *Sacrae symphoniae* published in Venice.	**1598** Edict of Nantes. Huguenots granted freedom of worship and equal political rights with Catholics. Peace of Vervins, Philip II resigns his claim to the French throne. France united under Henri IV. Death of Philip II; succeeded by Philip III.
1598 Weelkes appointed organist of Winchester College. Wilbye in service of the Kytsons at Hengrave Hall. Performance of Peri's *Dafne* given in Florence.	**1599** Earl of Essex, Lord Lieutenant of Ireland, signs a truce with the rebel Tyrone; he is arrested on his return to London.
1599 Death of Marenzio.	**1600** Henri IV, having divorced Margaret of Valois, marries Marie de' Medici.
1600 Peri's *Euridice* performed in Florence.	**1601** The Earl of Essex leads a rebellion against Queen Elizabeth. He is tried for treason and executed.
1601 Monteverdi *maestro di cappella* at Mantua.	**1603** Death of Queen Elizabeth I. Accession of James VI of Scotland as James I of England. Amnesty in Ireland.
1602 Death of Morley. Weelkes organist and *Informator choristarum* at Chichester Cathedral. Giulio Caccini: *Le nuove musiche.*	**1605** Death of Pope Clement VIII; election of Leo XI who dies, followed by Paul V. Discovery of Gunpowder Plot.
1603 Death of de Monte.	**1608** Protestant Union of German Princes formed under Christian of Anhalt and Frederick IV of the Palatine.
1606 Burmeister: *Musica poetica.*	**1609** Twelve Year Truce between Spain and Holland.
1607 First performance of Monteverdi's *Orfeo* in Mantua.	**1610** Assassination of Henri IV of France; succeeded by Louis XIII (aged 9).
1608 First performance of Monteverdi's *Arianna* in Mantua.	**1611** Death of Charles IX of Sweden; succeeded by Gustavus II.
1610 Monteverdi's *Vespero della Beata Vergine* published in Venice.	**1612** Death of emperor Rudolf II; succeeded by Matthias. Death of Henry, Prince of Wales.
1611 Death of Victoria.	**1613** Marriage of Princess Elizabeth, daughter of James I, to Frederick V, Elector Palatine. Michael Romanov elected Tsar of Russia.
1612 Death of Giovanni Gabrieli.	
1613 Monteverdi appointed *maestro di cappella* of St Mark's, Venice.	

LITERATURE, PHILOSOPHY AND RELIGION	SCIENCE, TECHNOLOGY AND DISCOVERY	FINE AND DECORATIVE ARTS, ARCHITECTURE
1592 First performance of *The Spanish Tragedy* by Thomas Kyd.	**1591** James Lancaster voyages to the East Indies, breaking Portuguese monopoly of trade (–1594).	
1593 Henri IV of France formally declares himself a Catholic.		
1594 William Shakespeare joins the refounded Lord Chamberlain's Men.	**1595** Last voyage to the Spanish Main of Francis Drake and John Hawkins (–1596). Sir Walter Raleigh explores 300 miles up the River Orinoco.	**1595** Annibale Carracci employed to decorate gallery in the Palazzo Farnese, Rome.
1597 The *Demonologie*, a treatise on witchcraft by James VI of Scotland, renews persecution of witches.	**1596** William Barents discovers Spitzbergen and the Barents Sea.	**1597** Michelangelo Merisi Caravaggio paints the *Calling of St Matthew*, the *Conversion of St Paul* and the *Crucifixion of St Peter* (–1601).
1598 Publication of the translation of the first seven books of Homer's *Iliad* by George Chapman. First performance of *Every Man in his Humour* by Ben Jonson.	**1600** Foundation of the English East India Company.	**1599** Adrien de Vries completes *Mercury* fountain in Augsburg.
1599 The Globe Theatre, Southwark, London, built by the actors of the Lord Chamberlain's Men.	**1601** Johannes Kepler becomes court astronomer and astrologer to Emperor Rudolf II.	**1603** Carlo Maderno completes the façade of S Susanna, Rome.
1600 Shakespeare writes *Hamlet* (–1601).		
1605 Miguel de Cervantes Saavedra publishes *El Ingenioso Hidalgo Don Quixote de la Mancha*. Publication of *The Advancement of Learning* by Sir Francis Bacon.	**1603** Beneho de Goes sets out for India in search of Cathay, through eastern Turkestan.	**1608** El Greco paints *View of Toledo*, *Golgotha* and the *Assumption* (–1613).
1608 Publication of *Characters of Virtues and Vices* by Joseph Hall.	**1608** The Dutch Johann Lippershey invents the telescope.	**1609** Francesco Mochi sculpts *The Annunciation* in Orvieto Cathedral.
1609 The English Baptist Church founded in Amsterdam by John Smith and Thomas Helwys.	**1609** Henry Hudson discovers Hudson's Bay (–1610).	**1611** The *Descent from the Cross* painted by Peter Paul Rubens (–1614).
1611 Publication of *The Authorized Version of the Bible*.	**1610** Galileo Galilei produces *Sidereus nuncius*.	**1612** The *Vision of Father Simon* painted by Francisco Ribalta.
1612 Publication of *The White Devil* by John Webster.	**1615** Willibord Snell establishes the technique of trigonometrical triangulation for cartography.	**1615** Salomon de Brosse begins work on the Palais de Luxembourg, Paris. Inigo Jones appointed surveyor of the king's works.

Index

Page numbers in *italics* refer to captions to illustrations.

413

The Renaissance